A Companion to the Symphony

A Companion
to
the Symphony

Edited by

ROBERT LAYTON

SIMON & SCHUSTER

LONDON·SYDNEY·NEW YORK·TOKYO·SINGAPORE·TORONTO

First published in Great Britain by
Simon & Schuster Ltd in 1993
A Paramount Communications Company

Simon & Schuster Ltd
West Garden Place
Kendal Street
London W2 2AQ

Simon & Schuster of Australia Pty Ltd
Sydney

A CIP catalogue record for this book is
available from the British Library
ISBN 0–671–71014–1

Photoset in Ehrhardt 10.5/12 by
Hewer Text Composition Services, Edinburgh
Printed and bound in Great Britain by
Butler & Tanner Ltd, Frome

Contents

Notes on Contributors

David Brown was until his recent retirement Professor of Musicology at the University of Southampton. He has specialized in early Tudor music and Russian music, and is the author of studies of Thomas Weelkes and Thomas Wilbye, as well as Glinka. The fourth and final volume of his authoritative *Tchaikovsky* was published in 1992.

John Canarina teaches at Drake University, Demoine, Iowa. He has conducted symphonies by Bruckner and Sibelius for the BBC as well as American music including symphonies by Roy Harris.

Philip Coad was educated at Christ's Hospital and Queens' College, Cambridge. After a year at the Musikhochschule in Freiburg, he returned to Cambridge where he was awarded a Ph.D for a thesis on Bruckner and Sibelius. He is currently Director of Music at the Edinburgh Academy.

David Cox studied with Herbert Howells and Arthur Benjamin before going to Worcester College, Oxford. After the war he joined the music staff of the BBC where he was External Services Music Organizer (1959–73). He is the author of a BBC Music Guide on Debussy's orchestral music and a survey of the Henry Wood Promenade concerts.

Donald Ellman studied at the Universities of Reading and Cape Town, where he was a pupil of Lamar Crowson. He has made a special study of Clara Schumann and is Principal Lecturer in Music at the Thames Valley University.

David Fanning is Lecturer in Music at the University of Manchester and the author of *The Breath of the Symphonist: Shostakovich's Tenth*. He is a contributor to the *Gramophone* magazine, and *The Independent* newspaper, and broadcasts regularly for the BBC.

Stephen Johnson studied composition with Alexander Goehr at Leeds University, writes music criticism for *The Independent* newspaper and the *Gramophone* magazine, and broadcasts regularly on music for the BBC.

H. C. Robbins Landon is the author of *The Symphonies of Joseph Haydn*, (1955), the five-volume survey *Haydn, Chronicle & Works*, and has edited the Universal Edition of Haydn's Symphonies. He has also written *1791: Mozart's Last Year* and most recently, *Mozart: The Golden Years, 1781–91*.

Brian Newbould is Professor of Music at the University of Hull. His realizations of Schubert's symphonic sketches have been widely performed and recorded, and his publications include *Schubert and the Symphony: A New Perspective*.

Richard Osborne is the author of a study of Rossini in the *Master Musicians* series, and has contributed many articles to *Opera on Record*. He broadcasts regularly for the BBC and is a contributor to the *Gramophone* magazine.

Jan Smaczny is Lecturer in Music at the University of Birmingham. He contributes music criticism to *The Independent* newspaper.

David Wyn Jones is Lecturer in Music at the University of Wales, Cardiff and, together with H. C. Robbins Landon, the author of *Haydn: His Life and Works*.

ACKNOWLEDGEMENTS

Music illustrations are reproduced by kind permission of the following copyright holders. Shostakovich Symphonies Nos 1 and 10, Prokofiev Symphony No. 5, Kancheli Symphony No. 5, Martinu Symphony No. 2 by kind permission of Messrs Bossey & Hawkes; Walton Symphony in B flat minor, Vaughan Williams Symphonies No. 4 by kind permission of Oxford University Press, works by Hindemith, Weill and Tippett by kind permission of Messrs Schott, Rubbra Symphony No. 4 (Messrs Legnick). Every effort has been made to trace copyright holders but regrettably in some cases without success.

Introduction

Robert Layton

The evolution of the symphony must remain one of the greatest achievements of the Western musical mind. In the Renaissance world, music served
spiritual ends (or secular verse) but its polyphony is essentially non-dynamic
in the sense that it never leaves the plane from which it sets out. It was the
gradual emergence of major-minor tonality as a dominant force in musical
thinking in the Baroque era that created an environment in which the
symphony could come into being. By the 1780s and 90s Haydn had not
only laid its foundations but made the symphony and the sonata principle
the foremost vessel for his musical thought, and provided the launching pad
for the greatest symphonist of all. For Beethoven was to the symphony what
Shakespeare was to the English theatre and language. No artist escaped his
shadow.

It was the sheer magnitude of Beethoven's achievement that posed a
central problem to his successors. In his hands the symphony became the
most dynamic and concentrated of all musical genres. The very different
social order that emerged in the wake of the Napoleonic wars opened new
expressive horizons while the development of the orchestra in the nineteenth
and twentieth centuries ensured it the most varied and sophisticated of tonal
palettes. Less than a decade after the Ninth Symphony was first heard, the
Symphonie fantastique burst on to the world, and it was followed before
the end of the century by the mammoth canvases of Bruckner's Eighth
Symphony and Mahler's Second, inconceivable without Beethoven's Ninth
Symphony. So, too, is Wagner, who abandoned the sonata time-scale, to
create his own vast but essentially symphonic structures and proportions.

Any great symphony launches a listener on a mighty voyage; it conveys
its illusion of movement by a complex of factors. Its composer's ability
to generate motivic transformation and growth from a seminal group of
ideas is fundamental. His skill lies in harnessing the tension generated
between related key centres, however nebulous they may have become in
our own times, for it is the rate of tonal change which serves to convey
movement. Its organic cohesion and sense of inevitability must be such
that the listener cannot conceive of the musical journey on which he
is embarked taking any other course. One cannot imagine the Fourth

Symphony of Brahms or the Seventh of Sibelius proceeding in any other way.

In the greatest of symphonies, form and substance are indivisible. Sibelius once spoke of musical ideas themselves determining form, and compared a symphony's development to a river. The movement of the water determines the shape of the river bed, and in his analogy the river-water represents the flow of the musical ideas, and the river-bed that they form is the symphonic structure. Schoenberg put it differently but no less trenchantly: 'form means that a piece of music is organized, that it consists of elements functioning like those of a living organism'. At the same time it must convey the impression, as he puts it, that 'the composer conceives an entire composition as a spontaneous vision'. The two are not incompatible, for conception and realization are different processes, but the impression made on the listener is that the composer has caught a glimpse of something that has been going on all the time in some other world that he has stretched out and captured. A letter Sibelius wrote in the autumn of 1914 puts it perfectly: 'God opens his door for a moment, and his orchestra is playing the Fifth Symphony'.

So vast is the symphonic repertory that no single volume can hope to be remotely comprehensive. There are many symphonists, including such figures as Enescu, Malipiero, Pijper and Pizzetti, whose work is not touched upon in these pages, not because they are wanting in interest or quality but because they have not necessarily advanced the course of the symphony. The present collection of essays by a distinguished team of contributors follows its growth and development up to the age of Beethoven, and then charts its divergent course in the nineteenth and twentieth centuries along largely national lines.

I am much indebted to those who have honoured me by contributing to this Symposium, and to Richard Wigmore, whose brainchild it was and whose patience and forbearance have been much tried during its lengthy birth pangs.

1

The Origins of the Symphony 1730–c. 1785

David Wyn Jones

The symphony as we know it is just over 250 years old. But the term, together with its Italian, French and German equivalents of *sinfonia*, *symphonie* and *Sinfonie* (or *Symphonie*), is much older. From the early decades of the seventeenth century it was most commonly used to denote self-contained passages of instrumental music in vocal compositions, operas, motets, cantatas, oratorios and so on. Thus, works as diverse in genre and date as Monteverdi's *Orfeo*, Schütz's 'Christmas Story', Scarlatti's *La Statira*, Lully's motet 'Misere mei Deus', Bach's Cantata No. 21, *Ich hatte viel Bekümmernis*, and Handel's *Messiah* all contain movements of this type. By the beginning of the eighteenth century writers on music regularly remarked that such music had a subordinate role to vocal music and was usually there to establish an appropriate mood, as a prelude to the main business of music that communicated the meaning of the text.

The history of how the symphony became detached from its vocal surroundings, grew in dimensions, began to challenge the traditional superiority of vocal music and eventually became regarded as one of the most fulfilling genres in music is long and fascinating. It is also complicated, because for the first fifty years or so of its development our knowledge of the repertoire is still imperfect. Jan La Rue, a leading American scholar in this area, has compiled a computer catalogue of eighteenth-century symphonies which has references to over 16,000 works.* The symphonies of Mozart and Haydn account for about one per cent only of this total and even when the names of the better-known composers of the second rank are added –

* Jan LaRue, *A Catalogue of 18th-Century Symphonies. Vol. I. Thematic Identifier*, Bloomington, 1988. A valuable collection of symphonies by minor composers is contained in the following series: Barry S. Brook (general editor), *The Symphony 1720–1840. A comprehensive collection of full scores in sixty volumes*, New York, Garland.

J. C. Bach, C. P. E. Bach, Stamitz, Boccherini and Dittersdorf, for instance – the percentage of this repertoire that is in any way familiar still remains statistically small. Great strides have been made in the understanding of the early development of the symphony but it remains unconquered territory; there are some rudimentary maps so it is possible to find the way, but many details of the terrain are still sketchy.

At the beginning of the eighteenth century one of the most popular forms of instrumental music was the concerto. There were three broad types: the concerto grosso for a group of soloists and orchestra, the concerto for a soloist and orchestra, and the ripieno concerto – that is, a work using the expected formal structures of the concerto but without prominent parts for soloists. While the first two types of concerto are to be found all over Europe, the third is more restricted to Italy, as a letter from Charles de Brosses in Venice in 1739 back home to a friend in France suggests: 'Here there is a kind of music which is not known in France . . . They are large concertos in which there is no solo violin.' Brosses was probably referring to over fifty such concertos by Vivaldi. Other Italian composers who wrote ripieno concertos had included Torelli (1658–1709), Albinoni (1671–1751) and Dall'Abaco (1675–1742). All these works are for strings alone and although they can contain as many as five movements (as in the contemporary concerto grosso), the progressive trend (as in the solo concerto) was towards works in three movements: fast, slow and fast. For the origins of the symphony this repertoire is clearly important: works in three contrasting movements played in private concerts by string orchestras.

If this repertoire established the practice and some of the characteristics of the early symphony, the influence that allowed it to flourish came from the opera house. By the beginning of the eighteenth century the most important symphony in an Italian opera was the one that began the performance, the overture. Designed to create a feeling of expectation, like the more progressive form of concerto, it had crystallized into a normal three-movement structure of fast, slow and fast, but was usually smaller in dimensions. More crucially, the content was lighter, in keeping with the style of the following opera. In 1752 Quantz was to write in his famous treatise *On playing the flute*: 'Sometimes opera composers seem to set about fashioning their sinfonias like portrait-painters who use their left-over colour to fill in the background or the garments.' Part of the atmospheric appeal of the operatic overture was conjured up by its instrumentation, typically using oboes, horns, trumpets and timpani as well as strings. **Niccolò Jommelli's** Overture to *Bajazette*, an opera seria produced in Turin in 1753, is typical of the mid-century overture. In D major, it is scored for oboes, horns, trumpets and strings and has the customary three movements. The first movement has only seventy-nine bars and lasts about two minutes, but its style is recognizably that of the Classical period: very slow rate of harmonic change, themes based on arpeggio movement, immediate repetition of material, and contrast of *forte* and *piano* in a question-and-answer relationship (Ex. 1).

Ex. 1. Jommelli: Sinfonia, *Bajazette*

Ex. 1. cont'd

Later in the movement there are two crescendo passages, an example of music that just rejoices in orchestral sound for its own sake. The movement is an uncomplicated binary form, with little variety or development of thematic material. For the slow movement, an *Andantino* in G major also in binary form, the wind instruments are rested. They return in the concluding *Allegro assai* in 3/8 where their main role is to punctuate the regular phrases; this movement lasts just over a minute. With the exception of scale, all these characteristics are familiar from the mature symphonies of the Classical period and emphasize how close in idiom opera and symphony were in the eighteenth century; indeed many composers, including Haydn and Mozart, regularly converted operatic overtures into concert works.

Jommelli's overture is an effective beginning to his opera but he was not a composer who was interested in developing the symphony as an independent genre. A slightly earlier Italian composer, **Giovanni Battista Sammartini** (1700/01–75), is one of the earliest to devote a substantial part of his output to the symphony, composing seventy-seven works in Milan, where he was *maestro di cappella* in several churches, works that subsequently found their way throughout Europe. Most are for four-part strings alone, reflecting the legacy of the ripieno concerto, and the string writing too shows many features familiar from the Italian Baroque tradition. Unfortunately, not a single title page in Sammartini's hand survives; it would be interesting to know whether he called his works 'concerto' or used the more progressive term 'sinfonia'. None of the symphonies is known to derive from a vocal work, though movements from two did find their way into Sammartini's opera *Memet* (1732). Despite their monochrome scoring, Sammartini's symphonies, as befits works that reflect the independent tradition of the ripieno concerto, are more skilfully argued and longer in duration than the average operatic overture.

Having contributed with great flair to instrumental music in the earlier part of the century, Italy produced very little instrumental music of significance in the second half of the eighteenth century. Opera dominated the musical culture to such an extent that the best composers, such as Cimarosa, Paisiello and Piccinni, concentrated almost exclusively on the genre; none of these composed a single symphony.

Luigi Boccherini (1743–1805), born in Lucca, is a true heir to the tradition established by Corelli, Albinoni, Vivaldi and Sammartini but most of his career was spent in Spain, in the service of Don Luis, the Infante. His output consists mainly of chamber music, including ninety-one quartets and some 130 quintets. Much of this was published in Paris and, later, Vienna and he was a figure who was admired by Haydn. Although his symphonies, about twenty-eight in number, composed at intervals between 1771 and 1799, constitute a much smaller part of his output and did not acquire the same international reputation as his chamber music, they are equal in quality and Boccherini fully deserves his reputation as one of the very best composers of the second division. His melodic invention is always distinctive and memorable, his scoring more imaginative and carefully crafted than that found in the bulk of contemporary symphonies (and, it should be said, in operas by his compatriots) and there is never an awkward corner in the unfolding of the music. His first set of symphonies, Op. 12 (Gérard 503–508), dates from 1771, two years after his move to Spain. Interestingly, in his own catalogue of his music the composer called each work a 'concerto a grande orchestra', a decidedly old-fashioned title by this time. The 'grande orchestra' consists of two oboes or two flutes, two horns and strings. Four of the works are in four movements and two in three movements.

One of the three-movement symphonies, Op. 12, No. 4 (Gérard 506), deserves particular attention. It has a slow introduction in D minor leading to an *Allegro* in D major; the second movement is an *Andantino* in G minor; for the beginning of the following movement Boccherini repeats the *Andante* introduction to the first movement, following it with a section headed 'Chaconne qui représente l'Enfer et qui a été faite à l'imitation de celle de Mr Gluck dans le Festin de pierre'; this turns out to be a modified version of the music that accompanies Don Juan's descent into hell in Gluck's ballet *Don Juan*, first performed in Vienna in 1761. Some contemporary manuscripts of the symphony carry the title *Della Casa del Diavolo* and this nickname is usually used today. Composed four years before Sammartini's death, this symphony shows a range of characteristics not encountered in the symphonies of the earlier composer. The last movement acknowledges a specific debt to Gluck's music which Boccherini would have experienced at first hand in Vienna in the many years he spent in the Austrian capital in the 1750s and early 1760s. Many of the other striking features of the work also show an indebtedness to the Austrian symphony of that time.

Austria

Long before Boccherini visited Austria, several other Italian composers of instrumental music had established a reputation in the country, including Torelli, Vivaldi (who died and was buried in Vienna) and Sammartini. It is natural, therefore, that the early history of the symphony in Austria should exhibit many of the same characteristics.

Most of the symphonies by **Mathias Georg Monn** (1717–50) are scored for strings alone. An exceptional work is a Symphony in D major, dated 24 May 1740 on its surviving autograph score, which is scored for flutes, horns, one bassoon and strings without violas. Three-part strings is a conservative feature which soon gave way to four-part strings in Austrian symphonies, through it remained a feature of much Austrian church music and dance music. The use of wind instruments in a symphony is more progressive, as is the four-movement structure, though neither became the norm in the Austrian symphony until a few years after Monn's death. Monn died at the age of thirty-three, depriving Austria of a composer who might well have contributed with distinction to the later history of the symphony.

Born two years earlier than Monn, **Georg Christoph Wagenseil** lived until 1777, becoming a much more significant figure in the development of the genre. For most of his adult life Wagenseil held various appointments in the Habsburg imperial court and, as well as sixty symphonies, his compositions included some 250 works for solo keyboard, over ninety keyboard concertos, over ninety string trios, seventeen Masses, ten operas and three oratorios. The style of his music is consistently reminiscent of Joseph Haydn's earliest compositions; moreover, the young Mozart held him in high regard.

Ex. 2 quotes the beginning of a symphony in D major by Wagenseil. It originally formed the overture to his opera *La clemenza di Tito*, performed at the Hoftheater on 15 October 1746 to celebrate the name-day of Empress Maria Theresia; it was subsequently distributed as a symphony. In D major and scored for oboes, horns (or trumpets) and timpani, it has the same majestic flamboyance as the Jommelli overture to *Bajazette*; the differences, however, are instructive, revealing a greater mixture of the old and the new. The opening gesture of repeated tonic chords is one that can be traced back to the Baroque period and forwards right through the classical symphonic repertoire to the *Eroica* symphony. Unlike the opening theme of the Jommelli, Wagenseil's theme does not have an in-built contrast of dynamics but continues in a *forte* dynamic to make a phrase of three bars rather than the normal two or four; the dotted figuration emphasized by trills also suggests an earlier era. This mixture of the old and new was to remain

Ex. 2. Wagenseil: Symphony in D major

a crucial feature of Austrian symphonies in the eighteenth century and was the product of two factors: their geographical location half-way between the conservative north and the progressive south and, secondly, the versatility of Austrian symphonists who, like Wagenseil, regularly worked in other genres too, from church music through chamber music to opera. To a greater extent than almost any other area in Europe, Austrian composers of symphonies were able to absorb a variety of stylistic influences as part of a steadily unfolding tradition and this, to a large extent, explains why the country produced the first great composers of symphonies. To return to the particular example, Wagenseil's movement is actually shorter than Jommelli's first movement (seventy-two as opposed to seventy-nine bars), yet it shows greater variety of thematic material and, consequently, a stronger sense of paragraphing. The clear-cut second subject is in the dominant minor, A minor, rather than the normal A major, a temporary switch of mode which is very common in Austrian symphonies of the mid-century. The slow movement is an *Andante* in B minor scored for strings alone (plus two flutes in some sources). The Finale is a *Tempo di Menuetto*, a regularly phrased movement with an ample theme. Wagenseil never departed from this three-movement structure for his symphonies, though he does reveal other alternatives for the Finale, as in the *Vivace* 6/8 conclusion to a symphony in B flat and the simple rondo that ends a symphony in C major (both composed before July 1757).

Most of Wagenseil's symphonies were written by the mid-1760s, by which time a new generation of symphony composers was beginning to make an impact in Austria. They were all born within the period 1729–39: **Florian Leopold Gassmann** (1729–74), **Carlo d'Ordoñez** (1734–86), **Michael Haydn** (1737–1806), **Leopold Hofmann** (1738–93), **Carl Ditters von Dittersdorf** (1739–99) and **Jan Baptist Vanhal** (1739–1813). As contemporaries of Joseph Haydn they popularized the symphony in Austria, experimented with its structure, expanded its resources and provided the *lingua franca* from which Haydn and, later, Mozart were to draw. They all knew each other, but at the same time pursued independent careers: as Kapellmeisters in aristocratic and ecclesiastical courts (Dittersdorf and Michael Haydn), in the imperial court (Gassmann), as a church musician (Hofmann), as a civil servant (Ordoñez) and as an independent artist (Vanhal).

In terms of statistics, the most common pattern for a symphony by these composers is a four-movement one of fast, slow, minuet and fast. This was certainly the most progressive trend, first shown consistently in the symphonies of the 1750s, but it did not become the dominant one until *c.*1780. Many three-movement symphonies continued to be composed and Vanhal, Ordoñez and Michael Haydn, in particular, regarded the scheme as an alternative rather than something that was old-fashioned. Viewed against this background, Mozart's 'Prague' Symphony, K. 504, is not so unusual. Another feature which became increasingly common was the presence of a slow introduction. Hofmann was the earliest to use this resource consistently, immediately giving the symphony a sense of presence, and he was followed by Dittersdorf, Ordoñez and Vanhal. None of these composers strove to create a thematic relationship between introductions and following *Allegro* movements; as with many other aspects relating to compactness of thematic argument, this seems to have been a genuine invention of Joseph Haydn.

More common than three- or four-movement works with slow introductions are symphonies that open with complete slow movements, effectively reversing the order of the first two movements. A symphony in E flat major by Leopold Hofmann composed no later than 1761 anticipates the ground plan of Haydn's Symphony No. 22 in the same key composed three years later: a binary *Adagio* in E flat major; a sonata form *Allegro molto* (*Presto* in Haydn); a Minuet with solo passages for wind instruments in the trio (oboes and horns in the Hofmann, cors anglais and horns in the Haydn); and a concluding animated *Presto* in compound time (3/8 in Hofmann, 6/8 in Haydn) that retains its rhythmic energy right to the end. Ex. 3 shows the beginning of the Finale. Hofmann's symphony did not serve as a model for Haydn's, though the latter may well have known it; it merely shows that Haydn was composing in less of a vacuum that has sometimes been suggested.

The scoring of the Hofmann symphony, pairs of oboes and horns plus strings, is the standard one for the symphony in Austria from about 1760 onwards; other instruments such as flutes, bassoons, trumpets and timpani are used as extra instruments to this basic complement. One instrument conspicuous by its absence is the clarinet; none of the symphonies by the composers listed above requires the instrument and Mozart's 'Haffner' Symphony, K. 385, may have been the first by a composer working in Austria to do so. The key of C major was almost invariably associated with the sound of trumpets and timpani, a tradition that goes back to the Austrian Baroque and that was strongly associated, too, with church music (Masses and settings of the Te Deum are overwhelmingly in C major). Ordoñez is typical in that he composed nine such works but unusual in that one of them, a symphony in C major probably dating from the early 1760s, has two separate trumpet and timpani groups and much antiphonal writing. A church service, perhaps to celebrate the name-day or ennoblement of a particular person, where the instruments would have been located in galleries, was a more likely venue for the first performance of this symphony than an aristocratic salon.

Whereas Wagenseil had not written a single symphony in the minor key, Austrian composers of the succeeding generation all composed several symphonies in the minor, particularly but not exclusively in the period *c.*1762–74, a concentration of usage that is not found elsewhere in Europe in the early history of the symphony. It would not be an exaggeration to state that it amounted to a craze, combining the slow and simple harmonic

Ex. 3. Hofmann: Symphony in E flat

language of the Classical style with the sound of the minor key to create movements and symphonies of great sensibility. Vanhal was a particularly prolific composer of minor-key symphonies: two in C minor, two in D minor, three in E minor, one in F minor, two in G minor and two in A minor. In addition to the tense repeated quavers and the soft dynamic (allowing the later *forte* to make greater impact), the opening of Vanhal's first E minor symphony, composed before 1770 (Ex. 4), shows also an openly melodic quality that was becoming more common in Austrian symphonies in this period. In symphonies in the major key it produced the style later dubbed 'singing *Allegro*' and, as such, it is especially common in symphonies by those composers, like Gassmann and Dittersdorf, who had close contact with opera, but it is found also in symphonies in the minor key as an alternative to motivic or discontinuous writing. Vanhal's E minor symphony ends in the dour sound of minor; only a minority of these Austrian symphonies seek a resolution to the more optimistic sound of the major key, a Beethovenian groundplan which begins to emerge about the year 1780 and which, of course, was to become fundamental to many fervent symphonies in the nineteenth and twentieth centuries.

Ex. 4. Vanhal: Symphony in E minor

As the symphony in Austria began to broaden its expressive horizons, it sometimes embraced a programmatic content, from casual references to folksong (a resonance largely lost to modern listeners) to more pervasive programmes. This, again, is a characteristic largely distinctive to Austria. Vanhal composed a *Sinfonia comista* in C major; that is, a symphony featuring a 'mixture' of contrasting moods: Speranza ('Hope') in the first movement, il Sospirare e Languire ('the Sighing and Languid') for the C minor *Andante*; la Lamentazione ('Lamentation') for the slow introduction to the finale and L'allegrezza ('Gaiety') for the *Allegro* section. In the mid-1760s Dittersdorf wrote a symphony that evoked the national musical styles of five nations, the *Sinfonia nazionale nel gusto di cinque nazioni*. Better known, but, it must be said, not representing the symphonic talents of the composer at their best, are the six symphonies that Dittersdorf wrote twenty years later, based on six incidents in Ovid's *Metamorphoses*. (Six further Ovid symphonies by Dittersdorf are lost.) Each symphony has a title and each movement is preceded by a quotation from Ovid and, as in Beethoven's 'Pastoral' Symphony, the music mixes general evocation of mood with musical depictions of particular incidents, including, as in Beethoven's symphony, a brook, in which Diana (the goddess of the hunt) is bathing. The music is headed with a quotation from Ovid: 'Here the goddess of the wild woods, when weary with the chase, was wont to bathe her maiden limbs in the crystal water' (Ex. 5).

Ex. 5. Dittersdorf: Symphony in D major

As the younger brother of Joseph Haydn and a colleague of Mozart in Salzburg, **Michael Haydn** is of special interest. He arrived in Salzburg in 1763, at the age of twenty-six, and remained there as Kapellmeister until his death in 1806. He was especially noted as a composer of church music and his elder brother, for one, regarded him as pre-eminent in this field. He composed forty-one symphonies and it is an indication of their quality that Mozart took one of them, a three-movement work in G major (MH 330), added a slow introduction and probably performed the work in Vienna in 1784; in the nineteenth century Köchel mistakenly included the work in his catalogue of Mozart's music (K. 444) and it was subsequently published in the Breitkopf and Härtel edition of the collected works as Symphony No. 37. Unlike his brother Joseph, Michael Haydn was an intermittent composer of symphonies, writing very few in the mid-1770s, for instance, when Mozart's symphonies seemed to have figured prominently in the Salzburg repertoire. In the quality of his invention, sure control of structure and, especially, harmonic sophistication, Michael Haydn is superior to all but two composers of the period and only a certain pervasive earnestness prevents him from being a composer of the very first rank. A Symphony in B flat, MH 355, one of three published by Artaria in 1784, illustrates well Michael Haydn's stature; composed shortly before Joseph Haydn's 'Paris' symphonies and in between the 'Haffner' and 'Prague' symphonies of Mozart, it stands up well in any comparison, especially the beautiful slow movement. By this time Michael Haydn had developed a penchant for composing energetic and often lyrical first movements in triple time and finales that use fugal techniques, both features that were to appear with striking individuality in Mozart's last three symphonies. Ex. 6 quotes the peroration of the Finale of a symphony in D major, MH 287, composed in Salzburg c.1778/80. In 1783 Mozart copied out the beginning of this Finale, presumably in order to study it. The four-note figure and its counterpoint are a striking reminder of the Finale of the 'Jupiter' Symphony, though its actual treatment (especially this stretto section) is closer to that found in the Finale of the G major Quartet, K. 387. For modern audiences such

Ex. 6. Michael Haydn: Symphony in D

Ex. 6. cont'd

associations are unavoidable but Michael Haydn's contrapuntal Finales should also remind us of the shared inheritance of Austrian composers of the time, particularly the discipline of species counterpoint and constant fugal practice in church music.

One further Austrian composer of symphonies should be mentioned, Leopold Mozart (1719–87). His well-known Toy Symphony, with parts for toy trumpets, drums, rattle, cuckoo and quail, is not properly a symphony, even allowing for the elastic use of the word in the mid-eighteenth century, rather a seven-movement cassation in the same tradition as the three by his son, K. 63, K. 99 and K. 100; moreover, it is almost certainly an arrangement by Leopold Mozart of pre-existing music. This jocular aspect does not feature in genuine symphonies by the composer. There are some fifty extant symphonies, mostly composed in the 1740s and 1750s and usually scored for strings alone. As to the intriguing question of what the young Wolfgang learned from his father's symphonies, biographers have always recognized that Leopold guided his son's development, and the true extent of the father's involvement in his son's first compositions has become evident in the last twenty years through the sophisticated study of their handwriting. Indeed, some symphonies traditionally ascribed to Wolfgang have been reassigned to Leopold; this is almost certainly true of K. 17 in B flat, and K. 76 in F major is another likely candidate. But the full story of the relationship of father and son in the genre of the symphony has yet to emerge.

Mannheim

In 1902 the German musicologist Hugo Riemann began to publish symphonies by a group of composers who had worked at the court of the Elector Palatine in the eighteenth century. The 'Mannheim School' was immediately hailed as the fountainhead of the symphony and the elusive missing link between the Baroque and Classical periods. Ninety years on this claim is recognized as fraudulent; other places in Europe were developing the symphony and, in particular, the fact that very few of these works found their way into Austria, the home of Haydn and Mozart, weakens the primacy given to the Mannheim School. Nevertheless, the composers did contribute extensively and with character to the genre.

Mannheim rose to prominence as a cultural centre in south Germany early in the eighteenth century, under the active patronage of two successive Electors of the Palatinate, Carl Philipp and, especially, Carl Theodor. A well-endowed opera house was founded, the first theatre in Germany devoted to drama in the German language was established, and academies for the study of economics, natural sciences, literature and the fine arts were set up. The music establishment of the court was mainly directed towards opera, but instrumental music and church music were well supported, too. **Johann Stamitz** (1717–57) entered the service of the court shortly before the accession of Carl Theodor in 1742 and in the following years he was joined by **Franz Xaver Richter** (1709–89) and **Ignaz Holzbauer** (1711–83). Together they established a high reputation for the musical activities of the court and carefully nurtured its continuation through a second generation of composers, of whom the most important were **Christian Cannabich** (1731–98), **Carl Joseph Toeschi** (1731–88), **Anton Filtz** (1733–60) and **Carl Stamitz** (1745–1801). As gifted players and progressive composers, these two generations developed an orchestra

that was widely recognized as the finest of the day. It contained a maximum
of nearly fifty players, more than twice the size of most court and church
orchestras in Austria and including, as Mozart longingly noted, clarinets.
In a celebrated description Daniel Schubart, a German writer on music,
commented:

> No orchestra in the world has ever surpassed that of the Mannheim in
> performance. Its *forte* is like thunder, its crescendo a cataract, its diminuendo
> a crystal stream bubbling into the distance, its *piano* a breath of spring. The
> winds are all used just as they should be: they lift and support, or fill out
> and animate, the storm of the violins.

Clearly, like the very best of twentieth-century symphony orchestras, the
Mannheim orchestra was capable of capturing and holding the attention of
listeners regardless, almost, of what was being said. This is a characteristic
feature of many symphonies by Mannheim composers and though it may
be deemed a potential weakness, it is a feature that many later composers
of symphonies – Berlioz, Tchaikovsky, Nielsen, Shostakovich and others –
have been happy to exploit.

This sense of orchestral display in the symphonies of the Mannheim
composers was encouraged by another critical factor in its development: the
persistent practice in Mannheim of composing the works for performance in
front of a large, public audience. While public performances are by no means
unknown in Italy and Austria (and church services in the larger churches
and cathedrals can be regard as public concerts *manqué*), symphonies in
those two countries were more usually designed to be played in salons in
front of an exclusive and invited audience. In Mannheim, however, concerts
took place twice a week in the *Rittersaal* at the centre of the palace, which
visitors were allowed to attend free of charge; to the accompaniment of
symphonies, concertos and vocal music the audience chatted, played cards
and drank tea. Later in the century, after the musical establishment of the
Mannheim court had merged with that of Munich, the concerts evolved a
more familiar character, though the novelty of the practice is evident from
the following report written in 1783:

> [The concerts] are held in the large Redoutensaal, which is suitably decorated
> and lit, and honoured with the presence of his Serene Electoral Highness
> and the highest and the most distinguished company, and is open to all
> subscribers without distinction of rank or class. The musicians appear on
> a spacious stage, which rises gradually so that everyone is visible. Here
> one can view the most famous living performers and enjoy masterworks
> of art. Furthermore, anyone who has proved his abilities at an audition is
> allowed to appear with these heroes. The works to be included and the
> names of the soloists are announced on the day of the concert by means
> of a printed poster.

One unfortunate result of presenting the Mannheim composers as a
cohesive group is that it ignores the individuality of the best of them and

the development of the symphony in the court over a period of forty years. Richter's symphonies are often very conservative and sometimes, as in the case of a work in G minor that dates from *c*.1745, exhibit an uneasy mixture of the old and the new. Although only eight years younger, **Johann Stamitz** was more forward-looking, moving from three-movement works for strings alone to four-movement works for larger forces, a distinctive move made as early as the 1740s. A crucial factor in Stamitz's development was his willingness to exploit influences from the opera. Ex. 7 is from the beginning of a four-movement symphony, thought to date from the mid-1750s. It bears a striking resemblance to the Jommelli overture discussed earlier. It begins with repeated *forte* chords and a *piano* continuation, followed by a gradual crescendo from *pianissimo* to *fortissimo* over nine bars. Hugo Riemann suggested that Stamitz and his colleagues were the first to notate crescendo and to include it as part of the narrative of the music, but it is clear that it was a resource that was directly taken from contemporary Italian opera. For a significant period in his life Jommelli worked in Stuttgart, only fifty miles from Mannheim, and his operas are known to have been performed at the Mannheim court. Riemann was right, however, to identify the Mannheim crescendo as a cliché in Stamitz's music; in this movement there are three further examples and the *Prestissimo* Finale has two. As is nearly always the case in Stamitz's symphonies, the slow movement is scored for strings alone and, though the Trio of the Minuet has some charming solo work for oboes and horns, extended concertante writing of the type regularly found in Austrian symphonies is absent in Stamitz's symphonies; presenting the orchestra as an instrument in itself was clearly more important than individual virtuosity.

Twenty years later, when Cannabich was in the middle of his career as a symphonist, the Mannheim style had evolved considerably. A symphony in E flat major, from about 1778–79, roughly contemporary with Mozart's visit to the court, has three rather than four movements and is beautifully scored for an orchestra of two clarinets, two bassoons, two horns and strings. There are no mannered Mannheim crescendo passages; nevertheless, the material in each movement has plenty of personality and contrast.

This symphony coincides with the demise of the extravagant musical establishment at Mannheim. In 1778, following the death of the Elector of Bavaria, the courts of Munich and Mannheim were united under Carl Theodor and most of the Mannheim musicians moved to the Bavarian capital. Although Mozart had stayed in Mannheim for four and a half months in 1777–78, dearly hoping that he would be given some position there, he never actually composed a symphony for the celebrated orchestra. Its capabilities, however, can be judged from his opera *Idomeneo*, first performed in Munich in January 1781 and played by former members of the Mannheim orchestra.

If in the past the importance of the Mannheim School in the early development of the symphony has been exaggerated, their output should

Ex. 7. Stamitz: Symphony in D

not be dismissed as attractive works that merely exploited the vaunted orchestral resources of the court. The symphonies became well known in Paris and London long before those of Haydn and other Austrians and they played a critical part in popularizing the genre in those cities.

Paris

French composers played a comparatively insignificant part in the early development of the symphony, up to *c*.1760, but once the form had firmly established itself the French capital played a distinctive part in its increasing popularity. Paris was undoubtedly the commercial capital of music in Europe, possessing more publishers, instrument makers, teachers of music, players and composers than any other city in Europe. In addition to the private concerts held in the salons of the aristocracy, Paris had a thriving public concert life. The Concert Spirituel had been founded in 1725, initially promoting, as its title suggests, sacred music, but by the 1770s a good deal of secular music too, symphonies, operatic arias and concertos; the 1777 season, for instance, contained symphonies by J. C. Bach, Cannabich, Gossec, Joseph Haydn, Toeschi and Wagenseil. The series had a rival, the Concert des Amateurs and later the Concert de la loge Olympique, and Paris can probably claim to have founded the first concerts given by a youth orchestra (if one excludes Vivaldi's concerts at the Ospedale della pietà), the Concert des Associés.

The strength of this concert life was matched by the breadth of its repertoire for, as the symphonies performed in the Concert Spirituel in 1777 demonstrate, symphonies by foreign composers were played alongside works by native or resident composers. In the absence of a strong native school of symphony composers in the middle decades of the century, Paris publishers had built up a market for foreign symphonies. The music of Mannheim composers became known in the 1750s, encouraged by frequent visits by some of the composers, followed by symphonies from Austria and elsewhere. Publishers issued symphonies in two ways: the traditional set of six, sometimes with mixed authorship, and by subscription under the title 'Symphonie périodique', the purchaser receiving one new symphony per month, for instance; the latter scheme had the advantage that it enabled the publisher to bring new names to the attention of the captive purchaser. Haydn was one of dozens of composers whose symphonies were introduced to the Paris public in this way, when Symphony No. 2 was included in 1764 as the fifteenth number in a series offered by the publisher Venier.

One figure dominated musical life in Paris from the mid-1750s right through to Napoleon's Republic, **François–Joseph Gossec** (1734–1829). He was a founder of the Concert des Amateurs, later transferring his entrepreneurial skills to the Concert Spirituel, the Opéra and to the Conservatoire National de Musique. He composed some nineteen operas but his *Messe des morts* (1761), designed to be performed by over 200 musicians, showed an even more striking gift for dramatic music full of grand gestures, a gift ideally suited to the grandiose music demanded of him during the French Revolution and the Republic. Given this background, it would be appropriate to report that his fifty or more symphonies show a synthesis of the symphonic tradition and the dramatic cantata along the lines achieved by Beethoven (in his Ninth Symphony) and Berlioz. Gossec's symphonies, however, are rather conservative, if always very skilfully put together. He began composing symphonies at a time when the four-movement pattern was starting to establish itself as the most forward-looking but, for no apparent reason other than that Paris audiences seemed to prefer shorter works, he came to favour a three-movement pattern. It was such a decided preference in Paris that publishers often omitted minuets from foreign symphonies in four movements and it was a scheme that Mozart was happy to follow in his 'Paris' symphony in 1778.

Although the leading concert organizations in Paris in the last quarter of the century boasted orchestras of over fifty players, Gossec typifies French practice in that only a small minority of his symphonies use instruments other than the basic ensemble of two oboes, two horns, two bassoons and strings. Mozart's scoring for a full complement of woodwind and brass in his 'Paris' symphony must have been a rather rare experience for the concert-goers of the city. By his own testimony Mozart was copying French taste in his symphony. One aspect of this is the slow delivery of events in the music, even when the music is a lively *Allegro*, something that is apparent too in Gossec's symphonies; it may well be deficient creative imagination in Gossec's case, but it seemed to be what the Paris public expected.

Although less prolific than Gossec, **Simon Le Duc** (1742–77) and **Henri-Joseph Rigel** (1741–99) exhibited more individual talents in their symphonies. Simon Le Duc was born in the parish of St Roch, Paris, and began his career in the second violins of the Concert Spirituel before becoming joint director with Gossec. He composed mainly chamber music but the last of his six or so symphonies, a work in E flat major given its first performance a few weeks after the composer's death at the age of thirty-five, suggests that he might well have become the leading French symphonist of the day. It is scored for two flutes, two horns and strings and is in three movements: an *Allegro vivace* preceded by a *Maestoso* introduction, an *Adagio sostenuto* in C minor and a rondo Finale. In the slow music especially, Le Duc reveals a wide harmonic vocabulary carefully complemented by imaginative and liberally annotated expression marks. The *Journal de Paris* reported that at the first rehearsal of the slow movement the director, the violinist and composer Chevalier de Saint-Georges, 'moved by the expressiveness of the piece and recalling that his friend no longer existed, dropped his bow and began to weep; the emotion communicated itself to all the players and the rehearsal had to be suspended'.

Rigel was born in Germany and is thought to have studied with Jommelli and Richter. His most frequently performed work was an oratorio, *La sortie d'Egypte*, but in the proliferating musical institutions of Paris he gained considerable respect as an administrator and teacher. Of his eighteen symphonies a work in D minor, composed before 1786 and published in 1787 as Op. 21 No. 2, is representative of his talents. In the customary three movements the last movement has a unusual demeanour, a hunting movement in a *Presto* tempo and in 6/8, but in the minor key rather than the more normal major. The outer movements are scored for an orchestra of strings, two oboes and two horns but the middle *Adagio*, rather unusually for this late date, is scored for strings only. The main folk-like theme in regular phrases shows why the slow movements of Haydn's contemporary Paris symphonies were so well attuned to the taste of the French capital. However, unlike Haydn, Le Duc is content simply to repeat the opening melody, offering neither a variation nor a dramatic contrast.

Ex. 8. Rigel: Symphony in D minor

Haydn's Paris symphonies were the first that he had written for the public concert hall, a liberating and decisive move in the history of the genre since the concert hall, rather than the church or the aristocratic salon, was going to be its natural home from now on. Ironically, in Paris itself, the city that boasted the most progressive concert life in all Europe, the symphony was being eclipsed in popularity during the 1770s and 1780s by a related genre, the *symphonie concertante*. Scored for between two and six soloists and accompanied by an orchestra, the typical *symphonie concertante* was in two movements only, combining instrumental display and a gentle competitive spirit in an up-to-date musical idiom. Always charming, sometimes frivolous, it did not survive the Revolution.

London

Four years before the end of the eighteenth century John Marsh, an English solicitor and amateur musician, published an essay entitled 'A Comparison between the Ancient and Modern Styles of Music in which the Merits and Demerits of each are respectively pointed out'. He was concerned to pinpoint when the 'Modern Style' had first arrived in England and wrote that 'the first inventor of the style of the modern symphony is said to be Richter'. Franz Xaver Richter had, indeed, visited England in 1754 and in 1760 six of his symphonies were published by the firm of Walsh, Handel's publisher. The symphony was even later reaching England than France and its full impact was not felt until after the death of Handel in 1759. In the same year as the Richter symphonies Walsh published a set of eight symphonies by **William Boyce** (1710–79) which are an interesting indication of changing times. The music of the eight symphonies is nearly all taken from overtures to earlier dramatic works (odes, operas and serenatas) composed as much as twenty years or more before. Walsh had often published Handel's overtures in this way but in the case of Boyce's overtures, the publisher, with the approval of the composer or perhaps at his instigation, used the more modern title 'symphony'. These delightful and energetic works have been recorded several times and fully deserve their popularity but in terms of the development of the symphony in the eighteenth century they were already an anachronism when they first appeared in print in 1760.

England did not become fully acquainted with the new genre of the symphony until the arrival in London of two foreign composers, **Carl Friedrich Abel** (1723–87) and **Johann Christian Bach** (1735–82). Both had been born in north Germany, the one being the youngest son of Johann Sebastian Bach, the other becoming his pupil. Both travelled extensively through Europe before arriving in London as the bearers of the musical avant-garde. Initially they pursued independent careers before joining forces in 1765 to promote a series of public subscription concerts. These remained a permanent feature of musical life in London for nearly twenty years and laid the secure foundation of modern concert life in the capital. The concerts dictated the pattern of their lives; new music was written in the summer and autumn and then performed at the concerts (numbering at their most popular fifteen per season). Over a period of years new works accumulated in a single genre were then published in sets of six. Symphonies by both composers featured prominently in the concerts, Abel composing nearly sixty and Bach over three dozen.

Abel's symphonies were published in six *opera* over a period of nearly a quarter of a century, from *c.*1759 to 1783. Without exception they are in the three-movement format of fast, slow and fast, and none is set in a minor key. In 1759, when Abel's symphonies were first heard in London, the idiom – clearly articulated sonata forms with plenty of contrast between themes, use of crescendo, slow movements for strings alone and *tempo di minuetto* or *presto* finales – was shockingly new. Abel, however, did not expand or develop his interest in the genre and his last symphonies are virtually indistinguishable from his first. During his visit to London in 1764–65 the young Mozart wished to become acquainted with Abel's music and copied out a symphony in E flat by the composer, his Op. 7, No. 6 (published in 1767). In the nineteenth century this Mozart manuscript was rediscovered, assumed to be the work of the *Wunderkind* and was published as his Symphony No. 3 (K. 18). Mozart's copy is scored for two clarinets rather than the two oboes, horns and strings of the version published in 1767, suggesting that London publishers standardized instrumentation in order to maximize sales.

Even in eighteenth-century London, J. C. Bach was recognized as superior to Abel. He had arrived in the city in 1762 to supervise the production of two new Italian operas, *Orione, o sia Diana vendicata* and *Zanaida*, at the King's Theatre, Haymarket. Although several other operas by him were performed in London over the next twenty years, most of his energies were devoted to instrumental music. Many of his symphonies were published in Europe too and three further operas were written for performance abroad: *Temistocle* (1772) and *Lucio Silla* (1774) for the Mannheim court, and *Amadis des Gaules* (1779) for Paris. Mozart first became acquainted with Bach's music in London in 1764–65 and often expressed his admiration for the composer.

At his death Bach was supervising the publication by the London firm of Forster of six symphonies, Op. 18. The symphonies had been composed over a nine-year period and show the full range of Bach's style. Op. 18, No. 3, in D major is the oldest work, composed in 1772 as the overture to the serenata *Endimione*. It has the customary three-movement format, but the instrumentation is highly novel. It is scored for two orchestras, the first consisting of oboes, horns, bassoon and strings, the second of flutes and strings. Sometimes the orchestras play together, sometimes they alternate paragraphs, and at other times they engage in more rapid dialogue. The symphony was performed several times in the 1770s and its success encouraged Bach to compose further works for 'double orchestra', a work in E flat published as Op. 18, No. 1, and another in E major published as Op. 18, No. 4. In the last volume of *A General History of Music* (1789) Dr Charles Burney commented:

> Bach seems to have been the first composer who observed the law of *contrast*, as a *principle*. Before his time, contrast there frequently was, in the works of others; but it seems to have been accidental. Bach in his symphonies and other instrumental pieces, as well as his songs, seldom failed, after a rapid and noisy passage to introduce one that was slow and soothing. His symphonies are infinitely more original than either his songs or harpsichord pieces, of which the harmony, mixture of wind-instruments, and general richness and variety of accompaniment, are certainly the most prominent features.

The qualities identified by Burney are at their most apparent in the symphonies for double orchestra, helped by the changes in scoring, but the works remain in the memory, too, for their many finely cut melodies, as at the beginning of the final movement of Op. 18, No. 4 (see Ex. 9). The remaining three symphonies in the collection are for 'single orchestra'. Op. 18, No. 2 was originally the overture to *Lucio Silla* and shows Bach writing in full acknowledgement of the gifted wind players of the Mannheim orchestra, with grateful parts in solo and ensemble for a wind section that includes flutes and clarinets as well as the usual oboes, horns and bassoons. The slow movement of Op. 18, No. 4 was taken from the overture to *Temistocle* but the two surrounding movements, a bustling *Allegro con spirito* and a rondo marked *Presto*, were newly composed. The final symphony in the collection, also in D major, draws heavily on *Amadis des Gaules* to make a work in four linked movements; the first two movements are taken from the overture and the last two from the body of the opera.

Ex. 9. J. C. Bach: Symphony in E, Op. 18, No. 4

By the time of Bach's death, London was beginning to vie with Paris as the commercial capital of musical Europe. The success of Bach and Abel had encouraged other subscription concert series, and several publishers issued symphonies and other music from abroad. London, however, did not rival Paris in the number of resident, particularly native composers of symphonies. There were some publications of well-crafted works by John Collet, Thomas Erskine (the sixth Earl of Kelly) and William Herschel (the famous astronomer), but they are insignificant in the wider history of the genre.

North Germany

In many respects the prosperous cities and courts of north Germany – Berlin, Dresden, Hamburg and Schwerin – possessed a variety of musical life that seemed ideally suited to nurturing the symphony: a strong instrumental tradition, active and well-regarded opera houses, private patronage and a developing tradition of public and semi-public concerts. But the symphony never made much headway in this area of Europe in the eighteenth century and certainly never reached the popular status it easily achieved in contemporary Austria, south Germany, France and England. North German writers on music, reflecting a long tradition of serious-minded writing on music, regarded the new genre (and indeed, the new Classical style in general) with some contempt, as frivolous, indulgent and potentially demeaning. These attitudes ensured that the Baroque tradition in music lasted much longer in this area of Europe than any other.

In **Carl Philipp Emanuel Bach** (1714–88), however, second son of

J. S. Bach, north Germany produced one of the most original musical minds of the century, albeit one that reflected local attitudes. In an output that contained nearly 900 compositions there are over seventy concertos but only eighteen symphonies, and the new genre is eclipsed by the twenty-one settings of the Passion by the composer. As the keyboard player at the court of Frederick the Great in Berlin, Bach's principal duty was to accompany the king in his flute recitals, and in Hamburg, from 1768 until his death, he was the musical director of the city's five principal churches, neither position encouraging to a composer of symphonies. His eighteen symphonies were composed intermittently between 1741 and 1776. The first twelve are scored for strings alone but this conservative feature is soon forgotten when the listener is confronted with the boldness of the invention, which has tremendous energy coupled with an almost perverse propensity to surprise. Melody, harmony, rhythm, dynamic, phrase patterns and structure are never what the listener feels they ought to be, yet the audacity hardly ever raises a smile, more a feeling of unease. Certainly more than one contemporary referred to C. P. E. Bach's style as bizarre. Bach himself recognized an almost Beethovenian distinction between music that was composed out of a duty to please and music that was composed for self-fulfilment, advising the young Kuhnau: 'In works that are to be printed, in other words, intended for general consumption, be less abstruse and put in more sugar.'

Gottfried van Swieten, friend and patron of Haydn and Mozart, recognized the power of Bach's sugar-free music and in a set of symphonies he commissioned in the early 1770s (Helm 657–62) he requested that the composer 'give himself free rein, without regard to the difficulties of execution' which were bound to arise. In the slow movement of the third symphony in the set Bach pays tribute to van Swieten, the connoisseur of old music as well as the supporter of new, in a typically arresting manner: cellos and basses begin the movement by declaiming the motif B [= B flat] – A – C – H [= B natural] with strongly contrasting dynamics and unsettled harmonies (see Ex. 10). The symphony, like all eighteen by Bach, is in three movements, fast, slow and fast.

In always omitting a minuet, Bach was perhaps reflecting the view expressed by his fellow composer and theorist Johann Adam Hiller (1728–1804):

> Minuets in symphonies always seem to us like beauty patches on the face of a man; they give the music an effeminate appearance, and weaken the virile impression made by the uninterrupted sequence of three well-matched serious movements, wherein lies one of the greatest beauties of execution.

Bach's last six symphonies were composed in 1776, twelve years before his death, and are scored for an orchestra of two flutes, two oboes, one bassoon, two horns and strings. They were published posthumously in Leipzig but, significantly, they never became available in Paris or London. The first of the

Ex. 10. C. P. E. Bach: Sinfonia in C, Wq 182, No. 3.

set, in D major (Helm 663), opens with a firm testing of musical continuity. A seven-bar passage gradually gains in rhythmic momentum but as there is little or no sense of harmonic progression, it is very difficult to gain a sure feeling of pulse and there is no obvious melody. This opening gesture is followed by a silence of two beats before being repeated a third lower on a B minor chord, and then, after a second silence, down another third on a G major chord. Pulse, melody, theme, harmony and tonality are all attenuated: more bluntly, Bach is writing music without some of its basic ingredients. Not until bar twenty-seven, some forty seconds into the movement, does the music begin to gain a conventional sense of momentum. As was Bach's habit, the opening movement in sonata form runs directly into the slow movement which, in turn, leads without a pause into the Finale. The *Largo* takes the form of a duet for two flutes with the melodic line doubled two octaves lower by a solo viola. The choice of key too is highly unorthodox, E flat major, creating a bold contrast with the surrounding D major. Haydn's last piano sonata uses the same relationship, following an E flat major first movement with a slow movement in E major, and it is one that fascinated Beethoven too. The telling difference between Bach on the one hand, and Haydn and Beethoven on the other, is that the relationship remains a gesture in Bach's symphony and is not part and parcel of the wider argument of the work. The last movement is the most conventional, a 3/8 *Presto* with only one brief passage (sudden silence followed by a couple of unsure phrases in the minor key) showing that it is from the pen of C. P. E. Bach.

C. P. E. Bach was admired in his day, not so much by the public but by fellow composers (including Haydn, Mozart and later, Beethoven) and writers on music who recognized that here was someone who was prepared to try consequences with the evolving language of the Classical style; if in the process of avoiding the routine Bach sometimes also perplexed his audience, he nevertheless demonstrated that the symphony could challenge as well as entertain.

2

The Symphonies of Joseph Haydn

David Wyn Jones

Haydn had a clear memory of when he composed his first symphony. He told his biographer Griesinger that it had been written while he was music director to Count Morzin, identifying the work as a symphony in D major (No.1). Haydn had entered the service of Franz Morzin in 1759 and remained there for two years until he became Vice-Kapellmeister at the Esterházy court. Morzin was a minor aristocrat who, when he was in Vienna, usually stayed at the palace of the Batthyány family; he had a summer residence at Lukavec in Bohemia and his own palace in Prague. Nothing is known about the orchestral forces available to Haydn and, despite the composer's confident association of Symphony No.1 with the Morzin court, it is possible that it was actually composed a little earlier. Indeed, the number of symphonies composed for the Morzin court cannot be determined with any certainty; a conservative estimate would be six, a generous one nineteen.

Although posterity was to label Haydn 'the father of the symphony', he was in reality a late beginner. He had been composing church music, keyboard music, divertimentos and German opera for the best part of a decade before he turned to the symphony, a genre already well established in Austria. The composer to whom Haydn's early symphonies, such as No. 1, seem most indebted is Wagenseil. The orchestra consists of the typical two oboes, two horns and strings with the middle slow movement being scored for strings alone; the three-movement structure culminates in a *Presto* in 3/8 time; the thematic material, even in the *Andante*, is dry and rhythmic rather than melodic and ornate; and there is little or no contrast of mood within movements; even the switch to the sound of the dominant minor key in the second subject in the first movement is a resource frequently found in the symphonies of Wagenseil and other Austrian composers of the time.

It was as a result of hearing a Haydn symphony performed by Morzin's Kapelle that Prince Paul Anton Esterházy engaged Haydn as Vice-Kapellmeister to the Esterházy court, the richest in the Austrian monarchy. The head of the music establishment was Gregor Werner (1693–1766), a conscientious and faithful servant, but now decidedly behind the times in musical taste. The Prince, who was an educated musician and well acquainted with musical fashion throughout Europe, employed Haydn to assist the ageing Werner and to inject a new dynamism into the musical life of the court. It was, as Haydn often pointed out, a lucky moment in his career, but in terms of the development of the symphony it was momentous. Encouraged by the richly supportive resources of the Esterházy court Vice-Kapellmeister (from 1766 Kapellmeister) Haydn composed over sixty symphonies that established him as the leading composer in Europe and the genre itself as the most popular, challenging and rewarding in instrumental music. He may not have been the 'father of the symphony' but he was certainly recognized as its guardian and mentor for much of the eighteenth century.

As well as the arrival of Haydn, a virtually new orchestra was established at the Esterházy court in 1761, many of the players being known to the composer from his freelance days in Vienna. Haydn's first symphonies for the new orchestra were the trilogy, Nos. 6, 7 and 8, which the composer entitled *Le matin*, *Le midi*, *Le soir*. It is unlikely that a detailed programme was applied to the music in the manner of Vivaldi's *Seasons*, since only one movement carries a descriptive title, the Finale of No. 8 (*La tempesta*), though the slow introduction to the *Le matin* is clearly meant to represent a sunrise (a rather brisk one compared to the celebrated passage in *The Creation*). The use of French rather than Italian or German titles, reveals the Francophile taste of Austrian culture at the time. In 1734 and 1752 Paul Anton himself had visited France, returning with a large collection of music by Boismortier, Campra, Mondonville, Rameau and others. The music was catalogued and several of the keyboard pieces with descriptive titles such as *L'automne*, *L'hiver* and *Le printemps* were transcribed by an unknown court musician for mixed ensembles of instruments without keyboard, thus becoming part of the Austrian divertimento tradition. The resulting colourful concertante scoring as well as the use of descriptive titles is reflected in Haydn's three symphonies. They are scored for one flute, two oboes, one bassoon, two horns and strings and there are solo passages for all the instruments of the orchestra with the exception of the viola. The concertante scoring has often encouraged the observation that Haydn was uniting the tradition of the Baroque concerto grosso with that of the symphony, but this is a rather artificial interpretation since Haydn himself probably did not know any music of the older type; certainly the division of forces into concertino and ripieno and the use of ritornello structures are entirely absent from his symphonies. Haydn's concertante writing is instead superimposed on a four-movement structure of fast, slow, minuet and fast and is much more spontaneous, imparting a carefree atmosphere of ensemble virtuosity that must have delighted the players and the Esterházy court. Haydn's orchestra at this time numbered no more than seventeen players so that the continual interweaving of full ensemble, reduced ensemble, single soloist and multiple soloists had the character that modern audiences more readily associate with chamber music than with the symphony. Compared with other early symphonies by Haydn (whether for Morzin or Esterházy) the thematic writing, too, is more diverse. Integrating these various elements into coherent four-movement structures is a remarkable achievement in the early history of the symphony and one that must have cost the eager young Vice-Kapellmeister a good deal of effort.

It would be a mistake, however, to state that these works lay the foundation of Haydn's future development of the symphony. They are unique to the first few months of his service at the Esterházy court, since they were not followed by any further sets of symphonies with titles or by works that feature soloistic writing in all movements; even the groundplan of four movements in the order fast, slow, minuet and fast (preceded by a slow introduction in *Le matin* and *Le midi*) was not to be the composer's norm for many years. They were highly experimental works, typical only in the sense that they demonstrate Haydn's concern that a symphony should be a reasoned and balanced whole.

Symphonies Nos. 6, 7 and 8 had been Haydn's first symphonies for the Esterházy court, composed and performed in 1761. The following year, 1762, seems to have produced at most one symphony, No. 9, which may have started life as an overture to an unknown vocal work. But the year after that, 1763, marked the beginning of the most concentrated period of symphonic composition in Haydn's life. Over the next decade the composer produced some forty symphonies, over a third of his total output. The period was one of intense productivity in other genres too, including opera, church music, quartet and sonata. Such a prolific output might suggest that the composer had settled into a routine as the Kapellmeister, producing works of similar character on demand. But quantity in this period is matched by diversity as well as quality, as Haydn experiments with a wide range of techniques and idioms. Altogether, it was a period of intense creative ferment. Anyone surveying the symphonies would be struck immediately by the variety of movement patterns used by the composer. The conventional three-movement pattern of fast, slow and fast is still used in several works such as Nos. 12, 16, 17 and 19. In No. 18 the balance is different with the first two movements reversed so that the three-movement cycle opens with a slow movement and the last movement is a Minuet and Trio rather than a fast tempo. Haydn's last three-movement symphony, No. 26, was written before 1770, the composer relishing the greater opportunities for experimenting with the different movement-types and balances that a four-movement scheme offered. The prevailing trend was towards a four-movement structure in the order fast, slow, Minuet and fast but a handful of symphonies from *c*.1760 shows Haydn experimenting with a pattern that displays exaggerated contrast from one movement to the next. In Nos. 21 and 22, for instance, an opening slow movement is followed by a *Presto* rather than an *Allegro* sonata-form movement, then the Minuet is followed by an another *Presto* movement (*Allegro molto* in No. 21). Beginning a symphony with a complete slow movement offers a more difficult challenge to the listener than the conventional fast movement (even with a slow introduction), a response which in the case of No. 22 prompted the nickname 'Philosopher' for the work, even though the remaining movements are anything but philosophical. The *Presto* movements that follow these opening slow movements are correspondingly less weighty than opening sonata-form movements. Though this structure had some attractions, it also limited Haydn's enthusiasm for argued sonata forms in *Allegro* tempo and this is perhaps why there are no further examples after No. 49 of 1768. What was to become the standard arrangement for a four-movement cycle – sonata-form first movement, slow tuneful second movement, Minuet and lighthearted Finale – presented a less formidable challenge to the listener and allowed Haydn greater scope. Haydn was not alone in making this discovery, though the process is most vividly seen in his symphonies of this period, and its fundamental nature is shown by the fact that no major composer of symphonies between Haydn and Mahler (in his Ninth Symphony) began a work with a complete slow movement. Several composers, Tchaikovsky and Mahler for instance, have ended the cycle with a slow movement and this, too, is found in Haydn's symphonies, in the celebrated 'Farewell' Symphony (No. 45). The *Presto* Finale suddenly comes to a halt and the music ends with a lengthy section of slow music. The unusual conclusion was prompted by Haydn's wish to remind Prince Nicolaus Esterházy that the musicians wanted to return to their families after an unusually long period in the summer residence at Eszterháza. In the course of the concluding *Adagio*, the texture gets progressively thinner as each player comes to the end of his line until, eventually, only two violins are left. The story relates that the ploy was a successful one, yet this charming incident has too often obscured the impeccable resolution of accumulated musical tension that this ending achieves.

The orchestra of the 'Farewell' Symphony is the standard one of two oboes, two horns, one bassoon and strings. Often during this period Haydn was able to augment his orchestra with other instruments. A flute player was available from 1761 to 1765 and from 1767 to 1771 and a handful of symphonies include the intrument; two additional horn players were employed for most of the period and Symphonies Nos. 31 and 72 (a misleadingly high number) make sensational use of the full complement of four. Trumpets were only very occasionally available to Haydn, usually hired from the town of Oedenburg, and Symphony No. 56 in C is one of the few symphonies from this period to require them. Haydn, however, developed a very satisfactory substitute for trumpets, that is requiring the horns to play in C alto, an octave higher than was normal for the instrument and in the register normally occupied by trumpets. The 'Maria Theresia' Symphony (No. 48), performed in 1773 when the Empress made her only visit to the Esterházy court, is one of several C major symphonies to use this exciting sonority. When composing church music and operatic music in E flat major

Haydn often substituted cors anglais for oboes in this period; No. 22 in E flat is the only symphony to use the instrument, producing the doleful sound that partly encouraged the nickname 'Philosopher'. Many slow movements and trios or minuets have extensive concertante passages for solo instruments, especially flute, violin and cello, but in slow movements the progressive trend is away from such movements in favour of music that relies less on gentle ostentation and more on individuality of melodic and harmonic invention.

Orchestral sonority and colour fascinated Haydn throughout his life, whether exciting, unnerving, idiosyncratic or comic, and they are an indivisible part of the argument of the music. With the eager and skilful orchestra of the Esterházy court at his disposal Haydn made some exciting discoveries in the 1760s and 1770s. Glittering C major music and poignant E flat music with cors anglais are evidence of this sensitivity but the most telling is Haydn's exploitation of the minor key. His first symphony in a minor key was probably written in 1765, No. 39 in G minor, and over the next few years it was followed by symphonies in C minor (No. 52), D minor (No. 26 and No. 34), E minor (No. 44), F minor (No. 49) and F sharp minor (No. 45), a total of seven works that explored the dark sonorities of the minor. Emotionally they are often very highly-charged works with only two of the symphonies turning to the major key to resolve or ease the drama. Single works such as the 'Trauer' Symphony (No. 44) and the 'Farewell' Symphony (No. 45) are as powerful as any symphony that Haydn was to produce in later years and this spate of minor-key symphonies has always captured the attention of commentators, who quite legitimately find an expressive intensity in them that contrasts with the sometimes more inscrutable character of earlier symphonies. Clearly the challenge of writing symphonies in hitherto unused keys was one that fascinated Haydn and of the most common minor keys only A minor was not used, yet it is unlikely that the composer, the players, the Prince and his guests would have focused attention on these works to the extent that later generations have. They would have been more aware than modern audiences of the sources of the idiom, minor key arias from contemporary opera dealing with heightened emotions such as anger, or visual images such as a storm. For instance in Haydn's opera *Lo speziale*, Volpino has been rejected by Grilletta and sings an aria in G minor, *Amore nel mio petto si è convertito in isdegno* ('Love in my heart has turned to rage'); the music is similar to a passage from near the beginning of Symphony No. 44 (see Exs.1 and 2).

Haydn's players, too, might well have pointed out that this greater degree of emotional commitment is shared by the symphonies in the major key from the period. Symphony No. 46 in B major was written in 1772, the same year as the 'Farewell', and is an equally impressive and individual work, sharing many characteristics with the contemporary minor-key works but, because it has not acquired a nickname and is in the major key, it is now much less frequently played. Even more so than in the minor-key works the choice of key, B major, is startlingly novel. Apart from a keyboard sonata that is

Ex. 1. Haydn: Lo Speziale

Ex. 2: Symphony No. 44

now lost, Haydn had never composed any music in this key and from the immediate Austrian musical heritage there is only one known precedent, a symphony by Monn probably composed in the 1740s. For the horn players it was as unprecedented as playing in F sharp minor in the 'Farewell' symphony; for both works Haydn had to sanction the purchase of specially made crooks from Vienna. The symphony opens with two balancing phrases, in a question-and-answer relationship common in the Classical style, unison and *forte* for the question, *piano* and harmonized for the answer (Ex. 3). More individual to Haydn is that the opening four-note motif is to figure throughout the movement, sometimes shortened to three notes and played quietly, but always drawing the music together and providing the source for many of its most concentrated passages. The technique is not peculiar to this symphony – the 'Trauer' symphony (No. 44) is very similar though with different emotional results – and probably had its origins in Haydn's studies of traditional counterpoint. Many contrapuntal tags, such as the

Ex. 3. Haydn: Symphony No. 46

well-known 'Jupiter' motif which Haydn himself had used in Symphony No. 13, have four notes, but always in a restricted compass; here and elsewhere in Haydn's music the four notes are spread across a wider compass. To contrast with passages that are generated by this four-note figure Haydn has more extrovert music, first presented as in Ex. 4 but later in a highly charged passage in F sharp minor:

Ex. 4. Haydn: Symphony No. 46

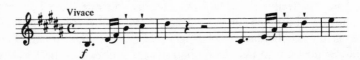

The entire first movement can be heard in terms of alternating discussion of these two ideas, but the layout of that discussion shows how hopelessly inappropriate the principles of sonata form as formulated by nineteenth-century theorists are to Haydn's symphonies, especially in this period. The contrast between the two ideas are not the textbook ones between first and second subject and the recapitulation shows a typically resolute tendency to tighten the argument through further development rather than relaxing it through a carbon copy restatement of the exposition.

Rather than changing key for the slow movement and for the Trio section of the Minuet, several symphonies in the minor key from this period have all four movements in the same tonic, changing only the mode for the slow movement. A similar attitude is present in Symphony No. 46. Rather than being placed in E major or (less likely) F sharp major, the *Poco Adagio* is in B minor. In demeanour it is quite different from the preceding *Vivace* and following Minuet, possessing a circumspect lyricism which typically wavers between the comforting and the uneasy. The 6/8 *siciliano* rhythms are played *con sordini* by the violins and there is the added written instruction that semiquavers are to be played 'staccato assai'.

The *Menuet* is more generous in its appeal, the main theme rising confidently through an octave and scored sonorously for the full orchestra. The Trio is in complete contrast, stranger even than the slow movement. It has the expected regular flow of phrases but the dynamics lunge to a *forte* at the end of each phrase, there is no melody to speak of and only the off-beat crotchets of the bass give the music any momentum; Haydn was rather fond of this type of trio in which there is just enough invention to keep the music going with the result that the surrounding minuet sounds positively bountiful.

The Finale is a highly rhetorical movement moving at great speed (*Presto e Scherzando*) and culminating in a dramatic gesture as original as that in the Finale of the 'Farewell' symphony. All the thematic material of the movement is derived from the opening (Ex. 5), first heard in two parts and in a *piano* dynamic:

Ex. 5. Haydn: Symphony No. 46

Once again there is a passage in the dominant minor before the dominant major, and the exposition ends quizzically with two bars of silence. Like the most accomplished of actors Haydn is a complete master of silence, its placing and its duration, one of the facets of his technique that distinguishes him from Mozart. There is a short development, comparatively uneventful it might be thought, before the recapitulation is heard. It almost reaches its appointed close when it is deflected on to a dominant chord followed by an expectant silence. The listener might now reasonably expect one last look at the main idea but what follows is shockingly unorthodox: a repetition of material from the previous movement, the *Menuet*. After the initial surprise it turns out to be a process of integration rather than dislocation since the quotation begins at the point in the *Menuet* when the thematic line most closely resembles that of Ex. 5, a correspondence clinched by the subsequent quotation of a passage built on a descending stepwise sequence (with suspensions) that also had figured in the main section of the movement. In due course, the quotation of the *Menuet* reaches an anticipatory pause followed by silence. The main theme of the *Presto* returns but Haydn at this stage of his symphonic development is as likely to undermine a would-be bravura conclusion as he is to fulfil it, and the initial self-confidence is soon tempered by a reduction to a single *pianissimo* line, silences and quiet cadential phrases over a held pedal point; finally, two *fortissimo* chords end this most inventive and absorbing work.

Symphony No. 46 is one of three symphonies known to have been composed in 1772, when Haydn was forty years old, and a further two or three symphonies can be assigned to the same year. From 1772 on to the end of the decade he produced fewer symphonies, some twenty works, half the number produced between 1763 and 1772. This reduction in the number is complemented by their content; there is less creative variety and intensity than in previous years and, though there are many charming and entertaining works, there are none as compelling as No. 46 or the 'Farewell'. If it was a period of reduced intellectual involvement in the genre it should not be thought that Haydn was less busy as Kapellmeister from day to day or that it was a period of no consequence in his development. On the contrary, it was during this period that opera played an increasing and eventually dominating role in his duties and began to influence the style of his instrumental music too. A purpose-built opera house had been opened at Eszterháza in 1768, joined by a second theatre for marionette performances in 1773. From 1776 onwards a full-time opera company was based at Eszterháza performing works by all the leading contemporary composers of Italian opera, Anfossi, Cimarosa, Gluck, Guglielmi, Paisiello, Piccinni, Sarti and others. Between 1768 and 1783 Haydn composed ten Italian operas of his own, works which he regarded at the time as more significant than his symphonies; in addition there were operas in the German language and also some incidental music for the plays that were performed in Eszterháza. In idiom, works such as Symphony No. 46, the 'Farewell' and virtually all of Haydn's symphonies up to that time are quite different from that of Italian opera, prone to argument rather than simple presentation, compressed rather than expansive, and, in many works, predominantly serious and impressive rather than extrovert and uncomplicated. Taking the broadest possible view of the development of the symphony in the eighteenth century Haydn's works from around 1770 marked not only a period of accelerated development but also one that was going off at a tangent from the evolution of the genre throughout Europe. During the 1770s Haydn comes closer once again to the mainstream of development, as his symphonies began to absorb the influence of the opera house to project a more popular and for a while, certainly a less characterful image. Several symphonies were adapted with minimum alteration from his operatic music and other theatre music: Symphony No. 50 was probably the overture to *Der Götterrath*, No. 60 uses incidental music originally written for the play *Der Zerstreute*, the first movement of No. 63 was originally the overture to his opera *Il mondo della luna* and the last movement of No. 73 was originally the overture to *La fedeltà premiata*; it is likely that other symphonies had their origins in incidental music composed by Haydn and now lost. Apart from No. 60, which is a unique five-movement work, these works are not markedly different from original symphonies of the time.

The increasing influence of the theatre takes many forms. There is the appearance of the burlesque, as in the Trio of the Minuet of Symphony No. 67 which is scored for two solo violins, the second with its lowest string tuned down to F so that it can play a drone accompaniment, or the increasingly common use of *pizzicato* to create an almost flippant atmosphere (e.g. the Trio of Symphony No. 69). Unexpected harmonic gestures occur, of the type that on stage would signal a new direction in the drama, as when the exposition of the finale of Symphony No. 71 ends in F major and the development is plunged into D flat major. There is the comparative absence of contrapuntal passages, which had featured in earlier symphonies, whether they be canonic minuets or fugal episodes. Most important, the pace of delivery in *Allegro* music is now much slower. Ex. 6 quotes the first subject of the first movement of Symphony No. 53 which is clearly less eventful than opening passages quoted earlier: a long held pedal point, only one change of chord in eight bars and a melody that moves through the constituent notes of the chord. This simplicity is set up by a fully scored slow introduction and it encourages Haydn to project a movement that is longer (246 bars as opposed to the 151 of the first movement of No. 46) and more varied in content. The second subject shows this contrast, a highly singable tune that is repeated as a unit rather than developed immediately (Ex. 7):

Ex. 6. Haydn: Symphony No. 53

Ex. 6. cont'd

Ex. 7.

The second movement of No. 53 is a set of variations on two alternating themes, one in the major, the other in the minor, a form invented by Haydn which, in its patterned regularity and use of a folk-like melody, communicates in an entirely uncomplicated way. Variation movements (on a single theme or on alternating themes) become increasingly common towards the end of the decade as does another highly appealing form, the rondo Finale. However, the two are hardly ever found in the same work, a principle that was to remain constant in Haydn's symphonic output.

Under the influence of opera, therefore, Haydn diffused the intensity of his musical language, discovering the value of increased contrast, comic incident and, in particular, the appeal of simple sectional structures of variations and rondo. In the remaining couple of decades of symphonic composition he was to combine this broader approach with ever-increasing imagination, flamboyance and intellectual control. In creating this unrivalled mix of the appealing and the sophisticated he was responding to one other factor: a public rather than a private audience.

Haydn's symphonies were first performed in the various palaces owned by the Esterházy family, in the Wallnerstrasse in Vienna, at Kittsee (across the Danube to the then Hungarian capital of Pressburg), in the hall of the main residence in Eisenstadt and in the smaller rooms of the summer palace at Eszterháza. Of these the largest venue was at Eisenstadt, capable of holding some 400 people and with a resonant acoustic. Apart from ceremonial occasions such as the visit of Maria Theresia or the wedding of a member of the Esterházy family Haydn's symphonies were performed in front of a small audience of the Prince and his guests; frequently, the small orchestra must have outnumbered the listeners. Outside the Esterházy court Haydn's symphonies quickly spread around other aristocratic courts in the Austrian monarchy and empire where the performing circumstances were similar. In addition the many Austrian monasteries in the region that had rich and varied musical practices, such as Göttweig, Melk, St Florian, Zwettl and Klosterneuburg, were regular collectors of Haydn symphonies. In these institutions they were played as accompaniments to meals (*Tafelmusik*), concerts for special occasions and during Mass services. Some symphonies by Haydn may well have been composed with church performance in mind; the 'Alleluja' Symphony (No. 30 in C) quotes the Gregorian Alleluja chant associated with Easter and the 'Lamentation' Symphony (No. 26 in D minor) quotes two church melodies associated with Holy Week. Finally, symphonies by Haydn were occasionally played as entr'actes in theatres.

However, public concert life in Vienna was very underdeveloped in comparison with that found in other European capitals, especially Paris and London; the first known public performance in Vienna of a symphony by Haydn occurred in March 1780, at one of the bi-annual charity concerts of the Tonkünstler Societät. In Paris and London by that date there were two regular subscription series, the Concert Spirituel and the Concert des Amateurs in Paris, and the Bach-Abel concerts and the Pantheon concerts in London. Although symphonies were still occasionally disseminated in France and Britain by means of manuscript copies, by 1780 printed copies of symphonies had become more common. In Paris Haydn's symphonies had been available in this form from 1764; in London from 1773. These new commercial forces in the two largest cities in Europe promoted the popularity of Haydn's music in general; more specifically they were to determine the wonderful expansion of style that occurred in the composer's symphonies in the last two decades of the century.

That Haydn was able to take advantage of these new opportunities is due to a wholesale revision of his contract with the Esterházy family which took place on the first of January 1779. The fourteen clauses of the original contract signed in 1761, which had specified restrictions as well as obligations, were reduced to six, the most significant change being the freedom to accept commissions for new music from outside the Esterházy court and to arrange for its publication. Haydn was still the Esterházy Kapellmeister with the same responsibilities, but he was now free to exploit the international reputation he had already earned. This change is clearly reflected in his output of symphonies during the 1780s, for of the nineteen composed during the decade only five were written for the Esterházy court.

London was the first city to make direct contact with the composer.

An instrument maker named William Forster was anxious to expand his business to include the publication of music. In 1781 after only a few years experience as a publisher he took the bold and, in terms of English publishing practice, hitherto unprecedented decision to negotiate an agreement with a foreign composer direct, rather than relying on the traditional sources of unauthorized copies and taking material from other publishers. Forster's bold gamble paid off, significantly helped by the death on New Year's Day 1782 of J. C. Bach. Haydn's symphonies had already made a limited impact in the city but he was now poised to take over Bach's position as London's leading composer. In the period 1780–90 concert promoters regularly attempted to persuade Haydn to visit London to be the resident composer in the subscription concerts, the tradition that Bach and Abel had established. With direct access to the composer Forster was well placed to take advantage of and promote this sudden upsurge in interest in Haydn's music and he duly published several first editions of symphonies. The first symphonies to be published were Nos. 70 and 74, followed by three more, Nos. 76–78, which Haydn had intended to present during a projected visit to London in 1783, an invitation that had been extended by the organizers of the Hanover Square Grand Concert.

The new symphonies build on the achievement of the previous decade without straining to make a particular impact. Undoubtedly, to the English musician weaned on a diet of Bach and Abel, the richness of Haydn's harmonic vocabulary and its audacious deployment would have been striking. A case in point is the Finale of No. 76 where, at the beginning of the development, the composer plays cat and mouse with the listener as to its harmonic direction, suggesting successively E flat, C minor, A flat, F minor, E flat and C minor before moving off into a more routine sequential pattern. The slow movement of the same symphony is a ternary *Adagio ma non troppo* in B flat major in which the middle section in B flat minor generates a good deal of anguish to contrast with the charm of the principal section. During the repetition of the principal section the music reaches a climactic 6/4 chord followed by a written-out cadenza for the violins, later joined by the full orchestra; Haydn had already used this attractive idea in the *Adagio cantabile* of No. 71, and was to do so again in the slow movement of No. 84.

As well as selling these would-be London symphonies to Forster (published in March 1784), Haydn sold them to Torricella in Vienna (published in July 1784) and to Boyer of Paris (published some time in 1785) – three publication fees for works which could also be used at the Esterházy court! Paris also commissioned new symphonies from him. The commission came not from the long established Concert Spirituel but from a much younger rival, the Concert de la loge Olympique, set up in 1780 following the demise of the Concert des Amateurs. As its title suggests this public concert series was supported by a masonic lodge. They approached Haydn by letter in 1785 with the request that he compose six new symphonies; Haydn agreed and the six 'Paris' symphonies were first performed in the 1787 season.

The correspondence between the Concert de la loge Olympique and Haydn is unfortunately lost and certain fascinating questions will never be answered. Did they invite Haydn to Paris? Did they give him an indication of Parisian taste in symphonies? Did they stipulate the scoring or the length of a work? Haydn would certainly have known something of musical life in Paris from the accounts of travelling musicians, including Mozart, and he seems to have reacted positively to its distinguishing features. The orchestras in French concerts were the largest in Europe at the time, that of the Concert de la loge Olympique having sixty-five members with a string section of fourteen first violins, fourteen second violins, seven violas, ten cellos and four double basses. Though Haydn had had some experience of writing for large forces in his oratorio *Il ritorno di Tobia*, performed in Vienna in 1775 and 1784, he had never heard his symphonies performed by such forces. He did not take the opportunity of writing for clarinets, using the familiar instruments of one flute, two oboes, two bassoons, two horns and strings, joined in No. 82 in C and No. 86 in D by trumpets and timpani. In a great feat of aural imagination Haydn responded to the challenge of writing for such a large orchestra playing in front of an audience, all the symphonies revelling in a thrilling tutti sound and an ever-changing palette of colour. Though sound for sound's sake is a feature of Haydn's style in the Paris symphonies, it is always supported by a strongly argued content. For instance the first movement of No. 83 ('La poule') uses Haydn's favourite technique, now revitalized, of permeating the texture with the opening four-note motif, usually presented against an energetic accompaniment and with a variety of dissonant harmonies on the third note (a distant tritone from the tonic); in the opening presentation it is followed by a bar's rest and energetic fanfares. The physical energy of this opening is followed by a deliberately lightweight second subject, repeated with the clucking accompaniment that gave rise to the symphony's nickname. The movement has whimsy as well as power.

Other strongly projected qualities in these symphonies include great delicacy, as in the second movement of No. 85 ('La reine') which is a series of different orchestral settings of the French folksong 'La gentille et jeune Lisette', and the caricatural, as in the bear-dance in the Finale of No. 82 that gave that symphony its nickname of 'L'ours'. That three of the six symphonies acquired nicknames in France testifies to their popularity but it has led to the unfortunate neglect of one of the finest, No. 86 in D major. The richly scored introduction is followed by an *Allegro spiritoso* that begins at a tangent to the main key, a technique Haydn first exploited in his quartets and for the first time in his symphonies in the Finale of No. 62. Lightly scored, it is followed by the full and energetic splendour of a tutti in D major. This contrast between intricacy and simplicity is maintained throughout the movement. The slow movement is undoubtedly the most profound in the 'Paris' symphonies. In G major, its tonal range encompasses F sharp major and the chromatic harmonies show an enquiring resourcefulness that is usually thought the prerogative of Mozart in this period; the result, however, is quite unlike Mozart, showing a reserve of power with little or no melancholy. The Minuet is the most questing in the 'Paris' symphonies, set off by a Trio featuring Haydn's increasingly favoured doubling of a string melody by the bassoon. The symphony ends with a Finale that skilfully gathers more energy as it proceeds, culminating in a grandiose deflection from the main D major to B flat major, a broad gesture calculated to thrill any audience.

After writing such flamboyant symphonies for a public concert it is difficult to imagine Haydn returning to composing symphonies suitable only for the Esterházy court; the symphony had made a decisive and liberating move from the salon or church to the concert hall, from now on its permanent home. If Haydn himself recognized this process he would have been encouraged by social developments in his own country. During the penultimate decade of the century the traditional venues for performance of symphonies in Austria were becoming less numerous as the aristocracy and monasteries declined in wealth and consequently, powers of patronage. Whereas Mozart was trapped by these circumstances Haydn was able to survive because he had the richest patron in the monarchy and he was in demand by the new commercial forces in music making, centred in Paris and London. Nos. 88–92, too, are written with these new circumstances in mind.

Symphonies Nos. 88–92 were all associated to a greater or lesser extent with Paris. No. 88 and No. 89 were composed in 1787 and, along with the quartets Opp. 54 and 55 and some piano sonatas, were entrusted to Johann Tost, a violinist in the Esterházy orchestra, who agreed to secure their publication in Paris. When Tost reached Paris he did indeed sell the symphonies but failed to forward the money to the composer! Meanwhile, the works had been published in London by Forster, forming the last two in a series identified by letters of the alphabet rather than numbers. To this day 'Letter V' has remained in use in English-speaking countries as a nickname for Symphony No. 88. It is a work that builds on the achievement of No. 86 in particular, with a searching slow movement surrounded by movements of tremendous energy; the melodic material is even more inspired, whether it be the catchy tunefulness of the outer movements, the swagger of the Minuet, or the broad cantabile of the *Largo*. The last-mentioned occasioned Brahms's well-known comment, 'I want my Ninth Symphony to be like this', presumably inspired by a much slower and more romantic performance of the movement than any Haydn would have heard.

One of the founder members of the Concert de la loge Olympique was Comte Claude-François-Marie Rigoley d'Ogny (1757–1790), who played the cello in the orchestra as well a leading part in its administration. Following the success of the six 'Paris' symphonies he personally commissioned three further symphonies from Haydn, Nos. 90–92, composed in 1788–89 and duly played at the concerts of the society. Haydn sold them also to Prince Kraft of Oettingen-Wallerstein for his celebrated orchestra to play, but again it is the public concert hall rather than the private salon that inspires these works. Symphony No. 90 in C pokes fun at a prime convention of the concert hall: enthusiastic applause. The Finale reaches an apparent conclusion with fourteen bars of martial rhythms in C major. Four silent bars later the movement continues, *pianissimo* in D flat major, moving to an even more resolute conclusion in C. Haydn then tests the memory of his audience by requiring that the development and recapitulation be repeated and thus the outrageous joke too. This easy rapport with his audience was to be enhanced in the London symphonies.

When Haydn was given his honorary doctorate at Oxford University in July 1791, the celebratory concert included his Symphony No. 92, since when it has been known as the 'Oxford'. It is another masterpiece to rival No. 88 and, indeed, any of the later symphonies that were first composed for English audiences. Even though it shares the same key as No. 88, G major, it is quite different in temperament, less aggressive and with more *concertante* writing for the woodwind than in the earlier work; the melody of the slow movement is at least as impressive as that which attracted Brahms in No. 88, yet with an added, wistful quality.

When Haydn was composing Symphonies Nos. 90–92 in 1788–89 he had no reason to believe that there were going to be fundamental changes in his day to day life. The administrative duties of the Esterházy Kapellmeister were as demanding as ever, the opera house at Eszterháza maintained a full programme of premières and revivals, and Haydn was in active correspondence with publishers all over Europe. In September 1790 the situation changed fundamentally. After a short illness Prince Nicolaus died. His successor, Prince Anton, promptly disbanded most of the large musical retinue, retaining Haydn, the leader Tomasini and the wind band (*Feldharmonie*). Freed at a stroke from his daily responsibilities the composer was now able to accept invitations to travel. A few years earlier he might well have gone to Paris, but the political and social tensions that had activated the storming of the Bastille in July 1789 were now affecting the well-being of musical life in the capital; as a dutiful member of the *ancien régime* Haydn may well have decided that Paris was uncongenial as well as dangerous. In December 1790 Salomon, the violinist and impresario from London, travelled to Vienna and signed an agreement with him, so that after nearly a decade of persistent rumour Haydn finally arrived in London in January 1791. He was to be the central attraction in a series of concerts – 'Mr Salomon's Concert' – held every Friday in Hanover Square. Haydn's contract ran for two seasons, 1791 and 1792. The concerts were so successful that he returned for a further two years in 1794–95; in 1794 the concerts were once again organized by Salomon but in 1795 Haydn joined a consortium of people known as the 'Opera Concert' and the concerts were held in the Concert Room (not the main auditorium) of the King's Theatre, Haymarket.

It was for these concerts that Haydn wrote his last twelve symphonies, works of irrepressible invention and commitment. They are written very much with the public in mind, an experienced concert-going public with whom Haydn was in direct contact, pleasing them, teasing them, shocking them and, invariably, uplifting them; they make resourceful use of the orchestra, some forty players in the first three seasons, about sixty in 1795; and they appealed to the connoisseur and layman alike. Just over a century later Mahler made the famous observation that a 'symphony must be like the world; it must be all-embracing'. Haydn's 'London' symphonies certainly were that at the end of the eighteenth century.

The twelve symphonies were given their first performances on the following dates:

No. 96	March or April 1791	No. 99	10 February 1794
No. 95	April 1791	No. 101	3 March 1794
No. 93	17 February 1792	No. 100	31 March 1794
No. 98	2 March 1792	No. 102	2 February 1795
No. 94	23 March 1792	No. 103	2 March 1795
No. 97	3 May 1792	No. 104	4 May 1795

With the possible exception of No. 95 they were received with great enthusiasm, encouraging the composer to enhance and broaden his style further. Although the symphonies have many features in common, which no doubt gave the audience a broad framework of understanding to help them appreciate the special qualities of each work, every symphony is strongly characterized. Thirty years of service as a Kapellmeister had taught Haydn how to be diplomatic and adventurous at the same time; these same qualities are found in the 'London' symphonies with the composer, orchestra and public now forming one creative community.

Symphony No. 101 ('Clock') opens with a slow introduction, a standard feature in the 'London' symphonies. As well as that of tempo (*Adagio* followed by *Presto*) it allows many other contrasts to be set up: between D minor with attendant chromatic harmony and a more diatonic D major, legato phrases versus staccato phrasing, 3/4 versus 6/8, and carefully considered orchestral colouring (provided by oboes and bassoons) as opposed to more stable instrumentation. The opening phrase of the symphony has a polite formality provided by the crescendo and decrescendo leading to a cadence, but there is raw force too, supplied by the creeping rising scale and the unexpectedly early intrusion of a chromatic chord (Ex 8). It is wholly typical of Haydn in the 'London' symphonies that he should make a connection between the slow introduction and the *Presto*, to draw the opposites together; the first subject of the *Presto* is built on the same rising scale (Ex. 9). Stravinsky, the neo-classicist, was fascinated by this theme, pointing out that its anacrusis is a whole bar and a beat, not a single beat, with the result that the theme has two balancing five-bar phrases rather

Ex. 8. Haydn: Symphony No. 101

Ex. 9.

than the more pat four-bar phrases. Mozart had never begun a symphony in 6/8, a metre usually associated with finales, but the 'Clock' and the 'Drumroll' symphonies are two examples by Haydn in which the easy onward momentum of the metre is joined by a forceful thematic and harmonic argument. Another distinction between the two composers is revealed in the following orchestral tutti where the rhythmic energy of the music is emphasized by several *sforzando* markings; exaggerated accentuation and forceful sonorities are two features of Haydn's style which the young Beethoven was to make his own. In its review of the first performance, the London newspaper *The Morning Chronicle* drew attention to another feature of Haydn's craft. Having first commented upon the attractiveness of the material – 'Nothing can be more original than the subject of the first movement' – it continues 'and having found a happy subject, no man knows like HAYDN how to produce incessant variety, without departing from it'.

Modern commentators have coined the term monothematicism to describe such sonata forms by Haydn but if this implies a relentless sameness then it is inadequate; as *The Morning Chronicle* clearly states there is plenty of contrast but it is all drawn from the same primary source. Ex. 10 is the second subject; its relationship to Ex. 9 is obvious, though an interesting difference is that the phrasing is now a series of two-bar units. Initially, the development section is dominated by this later version of the material, played by upper strings before the tutti enters grandly in C major with an inverted form of Ex. 9. Thereafter, it becomes impossible to distinguish between the two subjects as the development moves with relentless energy through D minor, E minor, G major and B minor, before coming to a rest on the dominant of D in preparation for the recapitulation. In terms of numbers of bars, the recapitulation is thirty bars longer than the exposition so that the tonic is securely established and there is a general balance between the two sections. But, as was the case in the Symphony No. 46, Haydn retains the interest of the listener by mixing restatement with further development. Ex. 9 is stated exactly but the following tutti is compressed and the second subject (Ex. 10) is completely recast to form a newly-composed paragraph. Finally, the music returns to Ex. 9 to lead the movement to a close. The fluency, wit and brilliance of the music are captivating and it requires a conscious effort to acknowledge the considerable intellect that is also there.

Ex. 10.

There is some evidence to suggest that some of the 'London' symphonies were conceived around their slow movements rather than being composed in movement order, so that their total character grew out of finding a suitable context for slow music. Perhaps as many as four symphonies were composed in this fashion: certainly No. 100 ('Military'), possibly No. 101, and less likely, No. 102 and No. 103. The easy tunefulness of the slow movement of No. 101 provides a complete contrast to the rhythmic bustle of the first movement; at first, however, it is the uncomplicated regularity of the accompaniment, played by bassoons and pizzicato strings, that captures the attention, if only because it seems so pedestrian after the first movement. *The Morning Chronicle* remarked, 'The management of the accompaniments of the andante, though perfectly simple, was masterly . . .'. Within four years the symphony had acquired the nickname 'The Clock' and, like 'La poule', 'Surprise', 'Drumroll' and others, it shows how a small colourful detail etched itself on the memories of listeners and, in the absence of a standard numbering system, allowed a particular work to be readily identified. Typically, this simplicity is followed by a passage of impassioned sensibility, as the music turns to an agitated G minor; *forte* interludes, featuring trumpets and timpani, are to be found in Haydn's symphonies from No. 88 onwards and are a particular feature of slow movements in the 'London' symphonies. In some movements it sounds like a rhetorical gesture; here, as in the slow movement of No. 104, it is more integrated in that the thematic material is drawn from the main theme of the movement. The third section of the movement is a repeat of the opening material now delightfully rescored, the tune in the first violins and the ticking accompaniment in flute and bassoon. Up to now the music has been firmly rooted in G major and G minor, with only the most transient of modulations to D major in the second half of the theme. In the fourth stage of the movement Haydn capitalizes on this exaggerated stability, switching the direction of the music after a bar's rest to a rich E flat major. The music returns to G major for a final decorated statement of the theme, including a characteristically brash passage in which horns and trumpets are briefly entrusted with the ticking accompaniment figure. The movement ends quietly over a long sustained tonic pedal.

The brisk activity of the *Menuet* offers immediate contrast, the natural

Ex. 11. Haydn: Symphony No. 101

accentuation of 3/4 at first being emphasized so that the later cross-rhythms can make the maximum effect. The Minuet itself was first written for one of the mechanical organs built by the Esterházy librarian Niemecz. The endemic and comic fallibility of such instruments may well have suggested the content of the Trio. Repeated D major chords in the strings underpin a solo flute melody but the chords 'forget' to change to the dominant when the melody suggests that they should (bar six of Ex. 11).

The nineteenth century thought that Haydn had erred and with Victorian (or Franz Josephine) rectitude proceeded to correct the score. That it was another of Haydn's jokes is proved by the fact that the accompaniment bars are numbered in the autograph and, crucially, the conventional repeat is written out fully so that Haydn can make one alteration – changing the chord under the top E of the flute to a dominant. The distinctive character of static harmonic movement with the occasional *forte* outburst is maintained in the rest of the Trio, supplemented by some delightfully polite dialogue between solo flute and bassoon. The Trio too caught the attention of the critic of *The Morning Chronicle*: '. . . and we never heard a more charming effect than was produced by the trio to the minuet'.

Most of the 'London' symphonies conclude with a rondo Finale, the sectional structure and the regular repeat of the opening melody producing the easy listening that made the form so popular in the last twenty years of the eighteenth century. In the symphonies composed for the second London visit, the form becomes ever more unified in its content and serious in its purpose; as a result the Finales emerge as appropriate conclusions to the intellectual imagination of the previous movements, rather than mere lightweight appendages. It was an achievement that remained unique to Haydn. Rondo form in Mozart is found in many of the piano concertos (where it has its own special qualities), but in none of his mature symphonies does he use the form. Beethoven, however, took up the challenge in the Finale of his Second Symphony, a very brusque enhancement of a typical Haydn symphonic rondo. The Finale of No. 101 has an uncomplicated five-part structure, ABACA. There is plenty of contrast in mood but these contrasts are always drawn from the same source, 'A'; in addition, there is very little wholesale repetition. To adapt a cliché, the process is one of diversity from unity in order to demonstrate the essential unity. 'A' is twenty-eight bars long (effectively fifty-six with the repeats) and, as is Haydn's wont, is played at a soft dynamic throughout, making the listener wait for the first tutti. Ex. 12 shows the opening bars of A, the omission of the lower octave (double bass) in bars five and six being a typically subtle use of orchestral colour. The following tutti concludes on the dominant of A major for section B but, instead of a completely new theme, a variant of the main theme is given, more restricted in its compass. The three ascending notes that are the most obvious link between the two themes are given prominence in the next *forte* passage. Haydn now shows his complete mastery of timing in music as the energy of the music is allowed to dissipate

Ex. 12. Haydn: Symphony No. 101

gradually over a dominant pedal, only to pick up equally gradually with a varied repetition of A. Section C arrives without preparation, a *fortissimo* passage in D minor for full orchestra, held together by a simple rhythmic pattern of three minims derived once more, and quite without artifice, from the main theme. The final return of A is marvellously resourceful; it is part of a fugal texture that continues for twenty bars, carefully marked *pianissimo*, as if Haydn was apologizing for displaying contrapuntal skill in the concert hall. The contrapuntal fabric is gradually loosened in readiness for the final tutti, containing one last look at the source of the argument before the movement and the symphony reach a jubilant close.

The Morning Chronicle concluded its review of the first performance of the 'Clock' Symphony with the wondrous sentence, 'It was HAYDN; what can we, what need we say more?' More than any other composer in the eighteenth century Haydn had brought the symphony to a central place in musical tradition, where it has remained. When Haydn was beginning to compose the 'Clock' Symphony in Vienna in 1793 he was teaching a sensationally talented, if wilful pupil named Ludwig van Beethoven, who was ideally placed to become acquainted with the symphonic thought processes of the master. It was to take the best part of ten years for Beethoven to first absorb, then enhance Haydn's style and so perpetuate its intellectual mastery.

3

The Symphonies of Mozart

H.C. Robbins Landon

In 1764, when Mozart wrote his first symphony in London, the form flourished all over Europe. In those days, Paris was the centre of European music publishing, and it was there that many German and Austrian, as well as local French and Italian, symphonies were distributed throughout the continent. In Austria and Germany, it was cheaper to copy a symphony and sell it in manuscript form, usually as a set of parts (scores were very rarely copied). In Vienna, there was a whole series of *scriptoria* which did a flourishing trade in manuscript parts of the latest symphonies, selling their copies all over the Austrian monarchy. Many symphonies by the Austrian school survive only in copies prepared by those Viennese music firms. This situation continued to obtain until about 1780, when in Vienna several publishers such as Torricella, Artaria and Huberty began to print parts of symphonies. But for the next twenty years the copyists continued to sell manuscripts of symphonies alongside the published editions, which were still considerably more expensive.

From its origins as a three-movement overture to an Italian opera, the form had moved north and become a concert piece (though one Italian, G. B. Sammartini, specialized in non-operatic symphonies, largely composed in Milan). By the 1750s composers like Wagenseil and Georg Reutter Jr were composing concert symphonies in Vienna. The standard number of movements remained three: fast, slow, very fast – or (something of a Viennese speciality) fast, slow, *Tempo di Minuetto*. By about 1760, Viennese composers like Leopold Hofmann, the cathedral chapel master at St Stephen's in Vienna, and Joseph Haydn, then Kapellmeister at the court of Count Morzin in Bohemia, were composing four-movement symphonies with a Minuet in second or, more usually, third place. This too had been an Austrian speciality since 1740, when a composer named Mathias Georg Monn had composed a symphony with a very Austrian-sounding Minuet. At this crucial date of 1760, yet another kind of four-movement symphony had entered the Austrian vocabulary, one that had its origins in the old Italian church sonata (*sonata da chiesa*) where there was an entire opening slow movement. Joseph Haydn took over this idea and adapted it to the Austrian symphony. Sometimes he composed such a work in three movements, ending with a *Tempo di Minuetto* (as in Symphony No. 18); sometimes there are four movements: slow, fast, Minuet and Trio, very fast. Three such symphonies of the late 1750s (Nos. 5, 11, 17) were written for Haydn's Bohemian court, and one of the curious specialities of this church sonata symphony was that all its movements were in one and the same key.

Thus in his formative years in Salzburg, Mozart had many models upon which to base a symphony. But as matters turned out, his first symphonies were actually composed when he was on the Grand Tour. The Mozarts had journeyed through Germany to France, where Wolfgang had published his first music (violin sonatas). After five months in Paris, the Mozart family moved to London, arriving there at the end of April 1764. Leopold Mozart contracted a throat ailment which made him dangerously ill, and to recover, the family rented a house (which still exists) in Ebury Street, Chelsea. Many years later Wolfgang's sister Nannerl recalled that 'in order to occupy himself, Mozart composed his first symphony with all the instruments of the orchestra, especially trumpets and kettle drums'. He also told his sister, 'Remind me to give the horn something worthwhile to do!' It appears that this symphony is lost, but fortunately there is at least one work preserved in autograph and dated 'Sinfonia di Sig. Wolfgang Mozart a london 1764'. This is K. 16 in E flat, composed when Wolfgang was eight, and first played, together with other symphonies, at a concert first announced for 15 February 1765 and then postponed until the 21st.

HAYMARKET, Little Theatre.

THE CONCERT for the Benefit of Miss and Master MOZART will be certainly performed on Thursday the 21st instant, which will begin exactly at six, which will not hinder the Nobility and Gentry from meeting in other Assemblies on the same Evening.

Tickets to be had of Mr Mozart, at Mr Williamson's in Thrift-street, Soho, and at the said Theatre.

Tickets delivered for the 15th will be admitted.

A Box Ticket admits two into the Gallery.

To prevent Mistakes, the Ladies and Gentlemen are desired to send their Servants to keep Places for the Boxes, and give their Names to the Boxkeepers on Thursday the 21st in the Afternoon.

In a letter to his friend and landlord, Lorenz Hagenauer, Leopold writes: 'All the symphonies at the concert will be by Wolfgang Mozart. I have to copy them myself, unless I want to pay one shilling for each sheet.' Later in the season, there was a benefit concert for the two Mozart children:

For the Benefit of Miss MOZART of Thirteen, and Master MOZART of Eight year of Age, Prodigies of Nature.

HICKFORD'S Great Room in Brewer Street, this Day, May 13, will be A CONCERT OF VOCAL and INSTRUMENTAL MUSIC.

With all the OVERTURES of the little Boy's own Composition.

The Vocal Part by Sig. Cremonini; Concerto on the Violin Mr

Barthelemon; Solo on the Violoncello, Sig. Cirii; Concerto on the Harpsichord by the little Composer and his Sister, each single and both together, &c.

Tickets at 5s each, to be had of Mr Mozart, at Mr Williamson's, in Thrift-street, Soho.

There is also a recently discovered symphony, in F major, K. Anh. 223 (19a), which is now part of the music collection of the Bavarian National Library: the source is a set of manuscript parts largely copied on French paper by Leopold Mozart. There are two possibilities: either this was paper taken with them from France in April 1764, or it was composed (or revised?) after the Mozarts left London. On the title page of the work, Leopold Mozart writes: 'di Wolfgango Mozart / compositore de 9 Anj'. Wolfgang had turned nine on 27 January 1765, so there is the distinct possibility that this was one of the symphonies given at the two public concerts listed above.

When the Mozart family arrived in London, they found a flourishing symphonic life, the principal protagonists of which were the German émigrés Johann Christian Bach, youngest son of Johann Sebastian, and Carl Friedrich Abel. These two prodigiously talented musicians had banded together to form a subscription concert series called the Bach-Abel Concerts. Their symphonies were supple, sophisticated and immaculately orchestrated; together, they created an intoxicatingly attractive new orchestral style, and it was natural that the young Wolfgang should fall under their spell. He sat on Christian Bach's knee and they improvised music together, Bach playing a phrase on the harpsichord and Mozart continuing it. Wolfgang was equally impressed by Abel and copied a whole E flat symphony on British paper (such as he also used for his own Symphony K. 16), using clarinets, which was at first thought to be a genuine Mozart work, K. 18 (Anh. 109).

The Mozarts left hospitable Britain for Holland, where they stayed as guests of the Princess of Weilburg, sister of the Prince of Orange. They gave concerts in Ghent, Antwerp, The Hague and Leyden. At The Hague, on 30 September 1765, there was an orchestral concert, announced in *'s-Gravenhaegse Vrijdagse Courant*:

By permission, Mr MOZART, Kapellmeister to the Prince-Archbishop of Salzburg, will have the honour of giving, on Monday, 30 September 1765, a GRAND CONCERT in the hall of the Oude Doelen at the Hague, at which his son, only 8 [sic] years and 8 months old, and his daughter, 14 years of age, will play concertos on the harpsichord. All the overtures will be from the hand of this young composer, who, never having found his like, has had the approbation of the Courts of Vienna, Versailles, and London. Music-lovers may confront him with any music at will, and he will play everything at sight. Tickets cost 3 florins per person, for a gentleman with a lady 5.50 fl. Admission cards will be issued at Mr Mozart's present lodgings, at the corner of Burgwal, just by [the inn called] the City of Paris, as well as at the Oude Doelen.

And there was soon another, to be given on 22 January 1766:

> By permission, the children of Mr Mozart, Kapellmeister of the orchestra of
> the Prince-Archbishop of Salzburg, will have the honour of giving a grand
> concert on Wednesday, 22 January 1766, at the Oude Doelen at the Hague,
> at which his little son, 8 years and 11 months of age, and his daughter, aged
> 14, will play concertos on the harpsichord. All the overtures will be from
> the hand of this young composer, who, never having found his like, has
> had the approbation of the Courts of Vienna, Versailles, and London. The
> price of admission is 3 gulden per person, for a gentleman with a lady 1
> ducat. Tickets are issued at Mr Mozart's lodgings at the house of Monsr.
> Eskes, master watchmaker, on the Hof-Spuy, the Hague, where the Court
> of Utrecht is situated, and also at the Oude Doelen.

Again, there is a symphony which has survived only in a copy written in
Leopold Mozart's hand, K. 19 in D, the cover of which shows that there
were at least three works in the genre apart from K. 16 in E flat in circulation
by 1765–66: the above-mentioned F major (now K. 19a), the lost one in C
(with the trumpets and drums? an incipit of a symphony in C, K. Anh. 222
= 19b, with a very Christian Bach beginning) and K. 19 in D. As for the
second concert in The Hague, we have yet another symphony, this time in
B flat (K. 22), again copied, this time in score, by Leopold and dated by
him 'Synfonia / di Wolfg. Mozart à la Haye nel mese December 1765'. A
final work composed in Holland for the installation of the eighteen-year-old
William V, Prince of Orange, as Regent of the Netherlands, was entitled
'Galimathias musicum', K. 32, a kind of burlesque miniature symphony with
popular folk melodies, including a Christmas carol set as a kind of *pastorella*,
or pastoral substitution for the Minuet and Trio. There is a kind of draft
version, partly in Leopold's hand and partly in Wolfgang's, which is housed
in two libraries: the Gemeentemuseum, The Hague; and the Bibliothèque
Nationale, Paris. But there is a more complete, 'authorized' manuscript,
made by a professional scribe, for a performance at the Fürstenberg Castle
in Donaueschingen Castle, which is the version used in the authoritative
Neue Mozart-Ausgabe.

Both Wolfgang and his sister were seriously ill in Holland, and that
may have lengthened the family stay there. They gave a whole series of
concerts, many with orchestra, from January to April 1766 at Amsterdam
and other places, where Wolfgang produced his new symphonies, which
were much liked. One of the new works he wrote for performance in The
Hague is a G major symphony known (because it was discovered in that
Benedictine monastery's abbey) as the 'Old Lambach' Symphony, K. Anh.
221 = 45a, possibly also composed for the investiture of William V along
with 'Galimathias musicum'. The Bavarian State Library owns a set of parts
of K. 45a which appear to represent the original performance material. The
first and second violins are in the hand of an unknown scribe, the *Basso* part
is in Nannerl's hand and the rest are in Leopold Mozart's highly professional

hand, as is the title page: 'Sinfonia / à 2 Violini / 2 Hautbois / 2 Corni / Viola / et / Basso / di Wolfgango / Mozart di Salisburgo / à la Haye 1766.' By the time the Mozarts gave this and another by Leopold to Lambach Abbey in Upper Austria – the parts are marked 'Dono Authoris 4ta Jan. 769' – Wolfgang, possibly with his father's assistance, had revised the work, mainly in the inner parts.

The Mozarts travelled homewards via Paris and Versailles (from about 10 May to 9 July), where the family friend and writer Baron von Grimm included news of the Salzburgians in one of his famous newsletters:

> This marvellous child is now nine years old. He has hardly grown at all, but he has made prodigious progress in music . . . [Now] he has composed symphonies for full orchestra, which have been performed and generally applauded here.*

Later the young Mozarts played in Dijon, Lyon and Switzerland, ending their tour at the Bavarian court in Munich. In many of these places, Wolfgang's symphonies were performed.

On balance, Mozart's earliest symphonies are charming, with the occasional structural flaw, but deftly fashioned. If Mozart's name were not attached to them, they would hardly be so frequently played and recorded. When he returned to Salzburg, he seems to have had the occasional request for a symphony – not surprising at a court where Johann Michael Haydn was producing a constant stream of interesting and occasionally brilliant symphonic serenades as well as actual symphonies.

On 11 September 1767, the Mozarts set out for what was to be their second trip to Vienna (they had been there in 1762 and had been received at court). But on 15 October Archduchess Maria Josepha died of the smallpox which was raging in the city; a week later Leopold and his family fled to Olmütz, where Wolfgang contracted the disease but recovered, as did Nannerl. During this long stay in Vienna, to which the Mozarts returned in January 1768, Wolfgang expected to produce a new opera, La finta semplice, which was, however, abandoned because of massive intrigues. While at Olmütz, he completed a serenely cheerful symphony in F, K. 43, and when he returned to Vienna another, in D, K. 51 (46a), with trumpets and kettledrums, which he later used as the overture to the doomed opera La finta semplice (which he brought back to Salzburg, where it was subsequently performed); when he revised the symphony as an overture he made several changes, omitting the Minuet and Trio and reorchestrating the whole score. Just before he left Vienna to return to Salzburg, Wolfgang composed another D major Symphony, K. 48 (the autograph is dated 13 December 1768,

---

* Melchior Grimm: *Paris zündet die Lichter an*, Munich, 1977, pp. 257–59. English translation of this and the previous quotations from Otto Erich Deutsch: *Mozart, A Documentary Biography*, London, 1965 (new edition 1990), pp. 41 (London), 44f. (London), 49f. (The Hague), 50 (The Hague, 22 January 1766).

Vienna), perhaps for some private concert. (Prince Galitzin was one of Mozart's patrons: as Russian ambassador he kept an elegant palace and gave concerts to which the nobility was invited.)

Like Michael Haydn, Mozart composed large-scale orchestral serenades for various occasions in Salzburg – weddings, the end of the university year, the elevation of a family to the nobility would all provide the cue for a bright, multi-movement serenade. Many of these works had miniature concertos or concertante movements built into them (for solo trombone in one of Michael's, for trumpet in another of his, for wind band in Mozart's 'Posthorn' Serenade, K. 320, and for solo violin in his 'Haffner' Serenade, K. 250). After the event for which the serenade was written, composers often turned these long works into shorter symphonies by removing some of the more boisterous solo movements and a Minuet and/or Trio. The first such serenade that Wolfgang wrote was one in D, K. 100 (62a), performed some time during the year 1769. Its original form of nine movements was shortened to four to make a symphony. Although these compressed 'symphonic' versions are very effective as concert pieces, and were enjoyed as such in the eighteenth and nineteenth centuries, in the twentieth it was usually the long, 'serenade' versions that were performed. Recently, however, since publication of the 'symphonic' versions in the *Neue Mozart-Ausgabe*, these shortened versions of the Serenades K. 185 (167a), 203 (189b), 204 (213a), 250 ('Haffner', K. 248b) and 320 ('Posthorn'), are beginning to enter the symphonic repertoire again – and rightly so. In one case (K. 250) Leopold Mozart added a kettledrum part for the revised version. Of these attractive serenade-symphonies, which are, incidentally, all in the bright, trumpet-related key of D, the 'Haffner' and 'Posthorn' symphonies are outstanding and we shall be meeting them again in more detail.

Mozart went to Italy three times in the period 1769–73. For his first journey, which began on 13 December 1769, Leopold Mozart was not only granted leave of absence but Archbishop Schrattenbach gave him 120 ducats (600 gulden). In a second document, dated 27 November 1769, Wolfgang was given official permission to travel to Italy but was also granted the unpaid but prestigious position of *Konzertmeister*, promising him, when he returned from Italy, 'the remuneration due to that office.'* The main reason for these three visits was, in each case, an opera commission from the court theatre at Milan, then under Austrian sovereignty under Archduke Ferdinand, governor and captain-general of Lombardy (one of Maria Theresia's many sons, brother of Emperor Joseph II and Leopold, Grand Duke of Tuscany). But apart from these operas, Wolfgang was called upon to give, or participate in, many orchestral concerts for which he urgently needed symphonies in the Italian style to open and close the long programmes fashionable at the time.

* A Latin document. Deutsch, op. cit., pp. 94f.

It is thought that the Symphony in C, K. 73 (75a), was possibly composed between 1769 and 1772, in other words for one of the Italian journeys (scholars are still arguing the exact date). Other symphonies pose more problems (K. 73 exists in autograph): K. 97 (73m), very Italian in spirit and in D with trumpets and kettledrums, has no proper sources at all, whereas another D major work, K. 84 (73q), survives in a contemporary manuscript (Gesellschaft der Musikfreunde, Vienna) with the contradictory inscription 'In Milano, il Carnovale 1770/Overtura', followed by 'Del Sig[re] Cavaliere Wolfgango Amadeo Mozart a Bologna, nel mese di Luglio, 1770', which means possibly that Mozart began the work in Milan and finished it in Bologna. It, too, is very Italian in spirit. The G major Symphony, K. 74, is on paper used by Mozart in Rome in April 1770,[*] and is one of those works where the first movement effortlessly merges into the second. When Wolfgang finally got round to composing the overture to his new Milan opera, *Mitridate, rè di Ponto*, he began it with a customary three-movement Italian *sinfonia*, i.e. without Minuet or Trio. This was soon circulated as a concert symphony, and trumpets and drums, missing in the opera sources, appear in a contemporary manuscript in Donaueschingen.

On his return journey, with Leopold acting as mentor and agent, Wolfgang received a commission in Padua to compose Metastasio's *azione sacra* entitled *La Betulia liberata*, which he accordingly did in the summer of 1771. Listeners fortunate enough to have heard this extraordinary work at the Winter Festival in Salzburg in 1989 were astonished at its modernity and profundity. This music is in signal contrast to the prettily conventional Italianate symphonies Wolfgang was composing; and for the first time in our story we are given an introduction to the stern, and sometimes tortured, world of the *Sturm und Drang* symphonies in the minor key composed principally by Joseph Haydn but also by his brother in Salzburg: can it be a coincidence that Michael wrote in this very year 1771 a darkly impassioned *Introduzione* to a drama called *Der büßende Sünder* which includes not two but four horns, an unusual feature also of the overture to Mozart's *azione sacra*? The same ferocious repeated notes (quavers in Mozart, semiquavers in Haydn), the same relentlessly forward-moving music, inform both works. *La Betulia liberata* is Wolfgang's first bid to greatness.

The remaining symphonies composed, or probably composed, in Italy need not detain us except in a very general way. One, in C with trumpets and drums, existed (the source was destroyed in World War II) in one east German manuscript but may be an authentic work all the same (K. 96 = 111b). The overture to *Ascanio in Alba* (K. 111 + 120, 111a) was first performed at Milan on 17 October 1771 as part of the nuptial celebrations for Archduke Ferdinand and Princess Maria Ricciarda Beatrice of Modena. When he turned it into a concert symphony, Mozart had to replace the original choral Finale with a new instrumental movement in 3/8 time:

* Alan Tyson in Neal Zaslaw, *Mozart's Symphonies*, Oxford, 1989, p. 178.

the scoring includes trumpets and drums. About a fortnight later he had occasion to write the Symphony in F, K. 112, for a private concert held in Milan by the keeper of the privy purse to Archduke Ferdinand: the autograph is dated Milan, 2 November 1771, and the work's layout shows it to be a real concert symphony, with the flanking movements and the *Andante* marked with repeats (this was dispensed with in opera overtures, partly to save time). The series of Italian overtures that were turned into concert symphonies concludes with Mozart's final Milanese operatic commission, the grand and impressive *Lucio Silla* of 1772: its festive and somewhat cold three movements again contain parts in the flanking movements for trumpets and timpani. After its successful première on Boxing Day 1772, the work ran for twenty-six performances. Meanwhile a new archbishop, Hieronymus Colloredo, sat on the throne in Salzburg and was impatiently awaiting the kiss-of-the-hand which *Konzertmeister* Mozart was expected to give upon his return.

When the old Archbishop Sigismund von Schrattenbach died, in December 1771, the Mozarts lost a faithful and understanding prince, who had supported them and allowed them an extraordinary amount of freedom to travel. The way the new wind was blowing can be seen in the answer to Leopold Mozart's petition as Vice-Kapellmeister to the new Archbishop Colloredo for payment of some of his salary (the confusion arose over the fact that when Leopold was away in Italy with Wolfgang, the father's salary was withheld). The new archbishop granted the payment but added 'without precedent for the future, nor for other court musicians absenting themselves'.* It was not going to be as easy as it had been hitherto. Yet there was the good news that Wolfgang now received a salary of 150 gulden per annum as *Konzertmeister*: it was a position that had carried no salary up to then.

In our discussion of these symphonies, we have included only those works for which there is ample evidence of their authenticity. Even in the old Collection Edition by Breitkopf and Härtel, there were some symphonies which scholars now believe were composed by Leopold. And although the *Neue Mozart-Ausgabe* includes without any apparent doubts a work like the Symphony in F, K. 75, its only source was a set of parts in the archive of Breitkopf and Härtel, Leipzig, which are now lost; while there are many features that suggest Leopold was its composer.

During the reign of Archbishop Schrattenbach, Wolfgang does not appear to have considered it necessary to supply the Salzburg court with many symphonies, and in the summer of 1771, when he was busy writing *La Betulia liberata*, he found time for one symphony only, that in G, K. 110 (75b). It is a merry little piece that reveals the influence of both Joseph and Michael Haydn, especially in the canonic Minuet which is based on two symphonies in the same key, Joseph's No. 23 of 1764 and Michael's

* Deutsch, op. cit., p. 139. Mozart's salary, see p. 142.

overture to *Die Hochzeit auf der Alm* of 1768. (The autograph is dated Salzburg, July 1771.) The beguiling slow movement replaces the oboes with flutes and gives independent parts to two bassoons, which in the other movements merely double the string bass.

Between the second and third Italian journeys Wolfgang's position had changed. He was now on an official (if rather meagre) salary to the new archbishop, but this position was not granted until August 1772. Two weeks after Wolfgang arrived (16 December 1771; Schrattenbach had died the day after), he composed the first in a series of eight symphonies written before he left for Italy to compose *Lucio Silla*. This sudden and quite unexpected burst of symphonic ardour was obviously designed to illustrate his powers to the new prince-archbishop. The works are:

1) A major K. 114, 30 December 1771 (this and all other dates from the autograph manuscripts)
2) G major, K. 124, 21 February 1772
3) C major, K. 128, May 1772
4) G major, K. 129, May 1772
5) F major, K. 130, May 1772 with the unusual scoring of flutes, two horns in C *alto*, two horns in F and strings
6) E flat, K. 132, July 1772, again with four horns, two in E flat *alto* (the only known case on record of this pitch) and two in E flat *basso*, i.e. the normal pitch)
7) D major, K. 133, July 1772 (with trumpets)
8) A major, K. 134, August 1772 (with flutes and horns)

And in August, Wolfgang received notice of his official salary – hardly a coincidence? The musical and sensitive Colloredo must have been impressed not just by the sheer weight of numbers but by the quality of the material and the elegance and sophistication with which it is presented. Many of the new features appear in Haydn symphonies of the period, especially Joseph's, including the experimentation with four horns (symphonies 13, 39 and – wildly out of place chronologically – 72) and the quick-metred slow movements in triple time (3/8) in K. 130 (Nos. 38, 39 – both from the late 1760s). Yet there is a very specially Mozartian quality about these works: as usual, Mozart has received the influence, assimilated it and turned it into his own special musical language. This is most clearly seen in the rightly celebrated A major, K. 114, which begins softly and with that peculiar delicacy which Mozart was soon to make his own. There is a wiry self-sufficiency in this music which bodes well for the future. Another work of the highest calibre is the large-scale K. 130 in F, with its bizarre Trio (modal harmonies and Haydnesquely high horn writing for Joseph Leutgeb, for whom Mozart later wrote magnificent horn concertos and a quintet) and unusually taut, weighty Finale.

Some time after the performance of *Il sogno di Scipione*, a *serenata* for the installation of Archbishop Colloredo in May 1772, Mozart decided to turn its two-movement overture into a symphony. In point of fact the whole serenade had been composed for the previous archbishop in 1771, and was brought out in 1772 when it was, perhaps very suddenly, required. Originally the overture had led into the opera after the slow movement, but some time between 1772 and 1774 Mozart composed a Finale (K. 163) and this was added to the work, which confusingly has another Köchel number, 161. It is one of Wolfgang's formal Italian *sinfonie*, coolly magnificent with trumpets and timpani and rather lacking in personality.

That last description can hardly fit the next bout of symphonic activity – the orchestral music that Mozart wrote when he returned from Italy in 1773. The works used to be bound in three volumes, as follows:

Vol. I: Serenade in D, K. 185 (167a) (probably August 1773)
          March for the Serenade, K. 189 (167b)

Vol. II: Concertone in C, K. 190 (186E) (31 May 1774)
          Serenade in D, K. 203 (189b) (probably August 1774)
          Serenade in D, K. 204 (213a) (5 August 1775)
          Serenade in D, K. 250 (284b) (probably July 1776) ('Haffner')

The third volume was sold by auction at Sotheby's in London in 1987 and fetched the highest price ever for any collection of music: £2,350,000. A curious feature of this volume, which includes only symphonies, is that the dates have been tampered with, probably when Wolfgang had them sent to Vienna in the 1780s and wanted to palm them off as 'modern' works. Most of the dates have been restored, though some questions remain.

Vol. III: Symphonies
           C major, K. 162 (19 or 29 April 1773)
           D major, K. 181 (162b) (19 May 1773)
           B flat, K. 182 (173dA) (3 October 1773)
           G minor, K. 183 (173dB) (5 October 1773)
           E flat, K. 184 (161a) (30 March 1773)
           G major, K. 199 (161b) (10 or 16 April 1773)
           C major, K. 200 (189k) (12 or 17 November 1774)
           A major, K. 201 (186a) (6 April 1774)
           D major, K. 202 (186b) (5 May 1774)

With this group of works, we arrive at a new level of inspiration. Mozart's technique has become flawless, and some of these works are great masterpieces. The first is the 'Haffner' Serenade, which he turned into a shorter symphony, adding a kettledrum part. This is glorious *al fresco* music: of the slow movements, one has a meltingly beautiful violin solo (there are three movements with violin solo, all of which were omitted in the symphony version), which is music for love under the starry Salzburg night; the slow introduction to the Finale has a moving dignity and depth, surprising in the context of a serenade; while the majestic first movement turns surprisingly dark in the development section – here is the 'Great Precursor'. This, in my opinion, is Mozart's first great orchestral work. It was composed for a wedding in the Haffner family, long-standing friends of the Mozarts.

Among the actual symphonies, and taking them in chronological order, the D major, K. 181 (with trumpets), is a three-movement overture with no break between the movements. There is a special D major brilliance in the first movement which is in the best operatic *sinfonia* tradition – racing chords, repeated semiquavers, dashing alternations of *piano* and *forte*; in short, all the tricks of the orchestral trade. All of which in no way prepares us for the *Andantino grazioso*, which starts out as if it were an ordinary 3/8 movement in serenade style; but suddenly the music turns into a miniature oboe concerto, with magical effect. Another interconnected three-movement symphony (also with trumpets) is in E flat (K. 184 = 166a = 161a), this time of sterner stuff than the charming D major, K. 181. In fact it may have begun life (as did K. 181) as a real operatic overture, for some serious drama. The first movement generates a real sense of passion, and is followed by a sombre, restless *Andante* in C minor – a portent of the great minor-keyed slow movements of Mozart's maturity. When Johann Böhm's theatrical troupe put on a play called *Lanassa*, in the 1780s, he used K. 184 as the overture, followed by much of the magnificent and stirring incidental music which Mozart wrote for *Thamos, König in Ägypten* (in 1773, with revisions and additions in 1776 and 1779–80, K. 345).

The so-called 'little' G minor Symphony, K. 183, has been much discussed. It forms part of the *Sturm und Drang* legacy of Austrian symphonists, foremost among them Haydn, of the late 1760s and early 1770s, with works in keys like F sharp minor, C minor, E minor, F minor, G minor and D minor (symphonies, piano sonatas, string quartets, church music). Haydn and other Austrian composers, especially J. B. Vanhal and Carlos Ordoñez, between them developed a special 'passion' language – melodies with wide leaps and agitated syncopations, repeated quavers or semiquavers, crashing chords, dramatic use of silence, and often four rather than two horns (Haydn, Vanhal, Ordoñez). The direct model for Mozart's K. 183 were Haydn's Symphony No. 39 in G minor and a Vanhal symphony in the same key – both with four horns and the other characteristics of this 'storm and stress' school – which incidentally took its name from a German play by Klinger of 1776, whereas the Austrian music preceded the German literary movement by a decade. Although Mozart wrote only one exercise in this manner in the mid-1770s, later, when he moved to Vienna, he would return to it with a vengeance.*

The spirited C major Symphony, K. 200 (with trumpets), was one for

* For a discussion of this movement, see H. C. Robbins Landon: *Haydn, Chronicle & Works, Haydn at Eszterháza 1766–1790*, London, 1978, pp. 266–393, also *Mozart's Vienna*, London, 1991.

which Mozart added a kettledrum part in autograph; it was sold by auction in 1929, but contemporary copies have been located and it is printed in the critical notes to the *Neue Mozart-Ausgabe* (from sources in Graz and Prague).* It has always been a popular work and was one of the few early Mozart symphonies available on records before World War II (Berlin College of Instrumentalists, conducted by Fritz Stein, the man who found the 'Jena' Symphony, then attributed to Beethoven). Two enchanting features of K. 200 are the solo horn 'echoes' in the Minuet and the trill-laden Finale, with its witty dovetailing of development and recapitulation.

Always the most popular of this group of eight symphonies has been the A major, K. 201, for its lyrical grace, refined craftsmanship and sheer inspiration. The haunting beginning (Ex.1), with its dipping octaves and subtle rhythmic sequence in the violins and the slow-moving minims with long legato slurs in the lower strings, immediately announces the symphony's originality. An equally astounding moment comes towards the end of the stately, rather Baroque, *Andante*, which sounds like a priests' march: the music stops, and the oboes and horns intone a fanfare; the strings have been playing hitherto with mutes, which during the fanfare they lift off, entering upon the fanfare's conclusion and repeating it as a stirring close. The Finale is an exhilarating but densely organized *Allegro con spirito* with a magical second subject (string textures of quartet-like finesse here) and searingly high horn fanfares towards the end which slice through the repeated semiquavers of the strings in a tightrope walk which spells alarm to any but first-rate players.

In December 1774 Mozart went to Munich to supervise the production of his new opera, *La finta giardiniera*, which was first performed there on 13 January 1775. Later, Mozart took the two feathery movements of the overture and added a third to make a concert symphony; but the curious thing is that this third movement (K. 121 = 207a) is written on Italian paper of a type used by Mozart in Milan principally between November 1772 and early 1773. Either he took the paper with him to Salzburg or the little movement was originally for another work.†

Similarly, Mozart created another three-movement symphony out of his new opera, *Il rè pastore* (called 'serenata', K. 208) by adding a Finale to the original two movements which, according to the paper used,‡ was written in 1776 (K. 102 = 213c). At any rate Wolfgang took it with him on his trip to Germany and Paris two years later, performing it at the house of his friend and composer colleague, Christian Cannabich, in Mannheim on 13 February 1778. In this light-textured work (which includes trumpets) Mozart reverts to his previous Italian *sinfonia* language, but the music as always with Mozart displays great charm, especially in the *Andantino* slow

---

* Mozart, *Kritische Berichte*, Serie IV, Orchesterwerke, Werkgruppe 11, Band 4 (Hermann Beck), Kassel, 1963, pp. d/44f.
† Zaslaw, op. cit., p. 293 (with information from Alan Tyson).
‡ Zaslaw, op. cit., p. 298.

Ex. 1. Mozart: Symphony in A major, K. 201

movement, which in the opera was the music of the first aria (Arminta, the shepherd king); Mozart is able to do this by assigning much of the castrato soloist's role to an oboe.

With this symphony-overture and the bustling, festive symphony in D, K. 202, Mozart came to the end of his first Salzburg period. He was increasingly frustrated and unhappy in the pretty provincial town of Salzburg, and it was decided that he should seek his fame and fortune in Germany and Paris. Since Archbishop Colloredo would not let Leopold Mozart leave for such an extended trip, and since it was rightly thought that Wolfgang was in many respects a naïve and immature young man in need of a chaperone, they decided to send his mother along, too. The trip was a financial failure and culminated in the tragic death of Mozart's mother in Paris. Moreover, Mozart fell in love with a young singer, Aloysia Weber, in Mannheim, but when he found her again in Munich she spurned his love, leaving him broken-hearted. It is to the one symphony created during this unhappy trip that we must turn our attention – the 'Paris' Symphony in D, K. 297.

Mozart composed K. 297 for the Concert Spirituel in Paris, where it was performed on Corpus Christi Day, 18 June 1778: it had been given a trial run on the 12th at Count Sickingen's, envoy of the Palatine Electorate. Mozart wrote to his father on that day about the new work, saying he had been careful not to neglect *le premier coup d'archet*, the grand orchestral opening of the Parisian orchestras which was so famous. After the performance he wrote that there was a passage in the first movement

> which I felt sure must please. The audience were quite carried away – and there was a tremendous burst of applause. But as I knew, when I wrote it, what effect it would surely produce, I had introduced the passage again at the close – when there were shouts of 'Da Capo'. The Andante also found favour, but particularly the last Allegro, because, having observed that all last as well as first Allegros begin here with all the instruments playing together and generally unisono, I began mine with two violins only, *piano* for the first eight bars – followed instantly by a *forte*; the audience, as I expected, said 'hush' at the soft beginning, and when they heard the *forte*, began at once to clap their hands. I was so happy that as soon as the symphony was over, I went off to the Palais Royal, where I had a large ice, said the Rosary as I had vowed to do – and went home . . .*

Mozart's patron Le Gros (Joseph Legros), who was responsible for the symphony's commission, disliked the original slow movement and requested another, which Wolfgang dutifully wrote. There has been a long series of discussions as to which was the first and which the second; but I believe the lesser-known one (in 3/4 rather than 6/8) to be the final version, because

---

* *The Letters of Mozart and his Family* . . . (trans. Emily Anderson), 2nd ed. prepared by A. Hyatt King and Monica Carolan, London, 1966, 2 vols., II, pp. 557f. I believe the successful passage in the first movement, repeated in the recapitulation, was bars 105–118 and 251–275.

when Legros – to whom Mozart had ceded the rights when he left Paris – published the work with Sieber in 1789, not only did he publish the 3/4 movement but also extensive revisions in the other movements, including different trumpet and drum parts, etc. – all of which patently reflect Mozart's second thoughts. As a composition, K. 297 is in some ways a conventional, 'public' work, but not without real flashes of genius. Written for the largest orchestra Mozart had ever used, its textures have a new, sonorous grandeur; but unlike the other, later masterpieces, the 'Paris' Symphony requires a great conductor to make the long stretches of virtually athematic D major orchestral writing come to life. Mozart wrote to his father:*

> But in order to satisfy him [Legros] (and, as he maintains, several others) I have composed another Andante. Each is good in its own way – for each has a different character. But the new one pleases me even more . . . On August 15th, the Feast of the Assumption, my symphony is to be performed for the second time – with the new Andante . . .

I cannot believe that Legros would have printed the first, rejected version, and since he obviously had both to choose from, I think the revised one must be the *Andante* in 3/4, only recently available complete (the missing bassoon parts for all three movements of the Sieber edition were printed in modern times as an appendix to Zaslaw's book, pp. 564ff.). Mozart carried a copy of K. 297 with him when he returned to Austria and there is evidence – *vide infra* – that he performed it on several occasions in Vienna and intended to revise it for Prague at the end of 1786.

Mozart had been dismissed from the archiepiscopal service when he went on his long journey to Paris. Leopold managed to secure for his son the position of court organist upon the death of Anton Kajetan Adlgasser (who had died in 1777, but was not immediately replaced). Wolfgang arrived in Salzburg on 15 January 1779, and at once submitted a petition to Archbishop Hieronymus, Count Colloredo, begging submissively for the position; this was granted by a decree of 17 January 1779, giving Mozart the annual salary of his predecessor, 450 gulden (much more than he had received as second *Konzertmeister*). Although Mozart detested Salzburg, he set to work on all sorts of tasks, using the large orchestra which consisted, in the years 1779 and 1780 when he remained in Salzburg, of twenty violins (they included a kettledrummer and two trumpeters), two violas, two cellists, four double-bass players, five oboists (who doubled as flautists), three bassoon players and two horn players.

Mozart had returned from Paris a changed and saddened man. His style now became richer, more involved, more profound, with many dark undertones. C major, always the key of ceremonious music and high Masses

* Anderson, op. cit., p. 565.

with trumpets and kettledrums in Austria, becomes especially ambivalent. In the C major church music of this amazingly productive final period in Salzburg, there are two large-scale Masses (including the celebrated 'Coronation' Mass, K. 317) and two Vespers settings. In all this music, we find not only the peculiarly heavy accent on brass instruments – the church music included three trombones which doubled the alto, tenor and bass voices in the choir) – but Mozart began increasingly to cultivate a more sombre side to this music of pomp and circumstance. The same increase in variety and richness is also immediately noticeable in the three symphonies and serenade of this period. The first, K. 318, is a powerful work in G with three interconnected movements, scored for four horns and two trumpets (in the autograph, no timpani part is found) and dated 26 April 1779. The trumpets were added to the autograph on separate sheets, and since they are on paper used mostly in Vienna in 1782 and 1783, it is presumed that the enlarged orchestration was created there.* The traditional kettledrum part (reproduced in small notes in the *Neue Mozart-Ausgabe*) derives from several early manuscripts, and it is likely that the work was performed with an improvised drum part, as was often the case in the eighteenth century. For its small size – many scholars have wondered if the work was not intended as an operatic overture or the prologue to a spoken drama with incidental music – this is a richly integrated and brilliantly orchestrated piece with the exceptionally large wind band of flutes, oboes, bassoons and four rather than two horns. In it we find powerful Mannheim crescendos, and extraordinary shades of scoring, made possible by the large orchestration; towards the end of the Finale which is, in effect, the recapitulation of the opening section delayed by the intervening *Andante* there is an explosion in the orchestra when the bassoons, brass instruments and timpani (with a roll) – all marked *ff* – reach out to seize us in this unexpected switch into E minor (bar 259). It suddenly opens a vista into the kind of scoring that we find in late Haydn symphonies and early Beethoven.

The second Salzburg Symphony, in B flat, K. 319 (9 July 1779), is quite another sort of work. It uses a delicate orchestration (oboes, bassoons and high B flat horns) and is in the long Austrian tradition of chamber symphonies, wherein there is a great deal of legato string work which, in order even further to underline the unaggressive language, is set off by a principal theme with staccato quavers. There is no double bar in the first movement and great is our surprise to find Mozart beginning a whole new section in the development based on the ancient Gregorian 'Credo' theme which, in Mozart's most sinewy legato fashion, glides subtly from key to key with bewitching inner voices to accompany its beautiful metamorphosis. And the E flat slow movement, in sonata form with a recapitulation that reverses the order of themes, is all of the same general pattern – quiet, restrained, with a thoughtful juxtaposition of legato and staccato. The Minuet and

* Zaslaw, op. cit., p. 345.

Trio were added in Vienna on paper mostly used in the latter part of 1785 but sometimes in scores of 1784.* In fact the Minuet has very Joseph Haydnesque features, a little like the Minuet in his Symphony No. 43 ('Mercury'). The racy and racing Finale alternates triplets with series of dotted figures, and whole blocks of music where there are no triplets at all. This gives, in some curious way, a very light, airy texture, so that this beautiful and sophisticated symphony is all of one piece: considering that the Minuet was added some five years later, this is no mean feat.

K. 319 was published by Artaria in Vienna together with K. 385 ('Haffner'), part of an unrealized project whereby Mozart wanted to dedicate three symphonies to the Prince von Fürstenberg. They were the only ones of Mozart's last nine symphonies to be published in his lifetime – we exclude the symphonic version of the 'Posthorn' Serenade, K. 320, from this list – a curious and not easily explicable phenomenon, when it is considered that Artaria's edition was very widely circulated, also in England (where copies were imported by Longman and Broderip – one is in the Bavarian State Library in Munich) and Paris, as well as Germany.

The third of this great Salzburg trilogy, in C, K. 338, is the most dramatic and grandly symphonic of the three. Here it is time to speak of one of the most widespread of Mozartian 'fingerprints' (to borrow the term from the world of art and particularly the great American art historian Bernard Berenson): the dotted rhythm ♩ ♪♩♩ ♩ the same in larger note values ♩ ♩. ♪ | ♩ ♩ |). In that *fortissimo* E minor outburst noted in the last pages of Symphony K. 318, it is characteristic that the bar is in this dotted rhythm, which pervades long sections of the opening movement in K. 338. This is a marching rhythm which is as all-embracing and all-pervading as the much-commented march 'complex' in the music of Gustav Mahler. We find it in marked profusion in the opening movement of the 'Haffner' Symphony, K. 385 and in countless piano concertos (the beginnings of K. 451, K. 456 and K. 459, for example) and in all manner of other music, especially the operas (*La clemenza di Tito*'s overture, its last chorus, and elsewhere).

Another aspect of K. 338's expansive opening is the way in which, at the end of the exposition, the music begins to darken, as if huge black clouds were piling up in its brilliantly sunny sky – and what a touch are those 'toy' trumpets, underlining the final lead-back into the recapitulation! Note also that *opera buffa* – brought into the concert symphony by Haydn in the 1770s and 1780s – has now become a part of Mozart's questing spirit. The great slashing chords and dotted rhythm of the opening are suddenly echoed, softly, by the strings and bassoons (those old comic figures) – it is like a scene with Colombine and Harlequin in a Watteau tableau. The slow movement, scored only

* Zaslaw, op. cit., p. 348.

for strings and bassoons, is a study in refinement and delicacy: when sending a set of parts to Prince Fürstenberg's castle in Donaueschingen (Germany), Mozart changed his original marking *Andante di molto* to *Andante di molto più tosto Allegretto*, and the additional instruction to all parts, *sotto voce*, tells us that the expressive, finely spun lines must be played with the greatest restraint. There was, between the first and second movements, originally a marvellously symphonic Minuet which Mozart seems to have torn out of the autograph: only a page survives.*

The Finale is again a kind of perpetuum mobile in 6/8 time, marked *Allegro vivace* and a virtuoso showpiece for any orchestra. It will be noted that the texture is like an insert into one of the great Salzburg serenades, with prominent parts for the two oboes. And this brings us to the last of the large orchestral serenades of this period, that in D, K. 320 ('Posthorn'), completed at 'Salisburgo li 3 d'Augusto 1779'. This is the most profound, the grandest and most densely symphonic of all the serenades, which far transcends its immediate purpose: the celebration of the end of term at Salzburg University's faculty of philosophy. The serenade version consisted of nine movements (the beginning and end a march), with two Minuets or Trios and an insert for wind band and strings with horns (*Concertante* and *Rondeau*), which Mozart later performed in Vienna as an entity in March 1783. When he came to compress the serenade into a symphony, Wolfgang selected only the massive opening (with a slow introduction which is later introduced after the development without returning to the original time signature: the note values are simply doubled, which means that there is a very precise mathematical relationship between the introduction and the *Allegro con spirito*). This is followed by an extremely sombre D minor *Andantino* and the original and brilliant Finale. Again, the tremendous energy of K. 338 is to be found here, with an added nervous tension. The forward drive of this opening movement is something palpable: never have Mannheim crescendos sounded so electrifying, never has that famous dotted rhythm been used with such a powerful sweep.

Mozart was ready for Vienna, in more than one sense.

When he was hastily summoned to proceed to Vienna from Munich, where he had performed his new opera *Idomeneo*, Mozart had enjoyed a particularly happy period with congenial colleagues. He was insulted

---

* This Minuet was completed and a Trio from another work by Mozart added in a reconstruction by the present writer. It was first played by the Mozart Orchestra of Philadelphia, conducted by Davis Jerome, in 1981. The proposal that Mozart's very symphonic Minuet in C, K. 409, was added in Vienna to this symphony is not tenable simply because K. 409 includes parts for two flutes, which do not figure in the authentic sources for K. 338.

at having to occupy a place below the salt at the archbishop's table for servants in the vast building of the Order of Teutonic Knights. Colloredo and his retinue were paying a state visit to Vienna and his orchestra had accompanied him. Mozart arrived there on 16 March 1781. He was soon involved in a whirl of activity, playing at the house of the Russian ambassador (Prince Galitzin) and then appearing for the first time in a large public concert, the Lenten pair which was an annual event of the Society of Musicians (Tonkünstler-Societät). This famous organization, which boasted a volunteer orchestra of some 180 players, gave two more or less identical concerts at Christmas and another pair in Lent. With the archbishop's grudging permission, Wolfgang gave his 'Paris' Symphony and played a piano concerto. The Emperor was present. Mozart's Viennese career had begun. And his Salzburg career ended.

The history of the ignominious row between the archbishop and Mozart is too well known to repeat here. In the end Mozart was booted out of the audience chamber by Count Arco, the archbishop's master of the kitchen. Mozart moved into the quarters of the Weber family – they had meanwhile moved to Vienna and Aloysia, his first love, had married the actor Joseph Lange – where he proceeded, much to Leopold Mozart's horror, to court and finally marry a younger daughter, Constanze. But all that is peripheral to our symphonic history, which must now move forward to July 1782, when Leopold Mozart commissioned a new symphony as part of the celebrations for the ennoblement of Sigmund Haffner Jr. Actually what Wolfgang wrote was another large-scale serenade, with an opening march and a second Minuet (the latter is lost). He sent it off with instructions as to how it must be performed ('The first *Allegro* must be played with great fire, the last – as fast as possible'), on 7 August 1782. Mozart needed the score for his concerts in the 1783 season and when his father sent it to Vienna, he wrote, on 15 February 1783, 'My new Haffner Symphony has positively amazed me, for I had forgotten every single note of it. It must surely produce a good effect.' This good effect was enhanced by Wolfgang adding two flutes and two clarinets for the first and last movements.

This was Mozart's farewell to the grand orchestral serenade in D major, of which he had composed so many fine examples. But there is a change: Mozart's symphonic style, under the influence of music being played by Vienna orchestras (and not just Joseph Haydn's), has become tauter and more concentrated. Haydn had meanwhile perfected a kind of monothematic way in which to treat these broad-scale opening movements, and Mozart shows that he has once again assimilated to perfection a 'foreign' concept. This imposing, closely argued movement is largely based on the opening octave jump plus our old friend, the dotted figure, worked with astonishing imagination and resource (Ex.2):

Ex. 2. Mozart: Symphony in D major, K. 385

The second movement is still in the warm-hearted manner of the previous Salzburg serenades, but there is one touchingly beautiful moment at the end of the first section – a wash of colour as Mozart provides a short but extremely poignant lead-back to the home key and the recapitulation. The remaining Minuet and Trio are concise but again the lyrical Trio has that youthful and warm-hearted innocence which Wolfgang will soon find it hard to recapture. And as for the Finale, to go 'as quickly as possible', it is a magnificent *tour de force*, with elements of the *opera buffa* alternating with vividly orchestrated tuttis (note the dashing off-beat timpani rolls).

Wolfgang took his new bride Constanze to Salzburg to meet Leopold and Nannerl, at the end of which visit Constanze sang solo soprano in the new Mass in C minor by her husband, performed in St Peter's Abbey. After that, the couple left for Linz, where Wolfgang put on a hastily organized concert in the theatre. He writes back to Salzburg; 'On Tuesday, November 4th, I am giving a concert in the theatre here and, as I have not a single symphony with me, I am writing a new one at break-neck speed . . .' Between 30 October and 4 November, then, a space of five or six days for composing and causing to be copied, and rehearsing this new work, the 'Linz' Symphony was born. It is in its composer's clear, radiant C major, solidly symphonic in the outer movements and with a tremendous innovation in the F major slow movement: here, for the first time in the Viennese Classical symphony, the trumpets and kettledrums are retained in a slow movement. Their presence lends a solemnly ceremonious atmosphere to this majestic and often rather sombre *Adagio* which suggests Haydn's slow movements in 6/8 time (like, for example, that for the 'Maria Theresia' Symphony No. 48 of 1769). But if Haydn's influence is also felt in the presence of a slow introduction, very rare in Mozart's symphonic music, once again Mozart has taken the idea and turned it into his own. The last two movements return to the symphonic gaiety of the first movement, while the Finale is another brilliant conclusion which is different in texture from the first only because it is in quick metre (2/4) and therefore lighter. Throughout the development section, Mozart uses the theme in the new Viennese way, tossing it from instrument to instrument, which is both audibly and visually witty. In this dashing Finale there are also serious moments, such as the beautiful *fugato* continuation of the second subject. This 'Linz' Symphony is definitely a milestone in Mozart's symphonic career, the portal, as it were, to the last four works in the genre, where their composer elevates the whole form to a new level of inspiration and complexity.

During most of the nineteenth and twentieth centuries, the last three Mozart symphonies were treated as an entity, the *ne plus ultra* of his symphonic output; but in recent years, scholars and indeed the general public have come to broaden that trilogy into a tetralogy by including the 'Prague' Symphony in D, K. 504, completed in Vienna on 6 December 1786. It may be that the work came into being by a very peculiar circumstance. Recently Alan Tyson has identified the paper used by Mozart for an autograph trumpet part to the 'Paris' Symphony. It is on paper used largely in December 1786 and 'contains bizarre variants, suggesting either that it was written from memory or that Mozart undertook revisions to K. 297'.* The Finale of K. 504 was composed on paper that Mozart used in Acts III and IV of *Le nozze di Figaro* and was presumably composed at that time, i.e in the first few months of 1786. Tyson therefore proposes that the Finale of K. 504 was originally intended to replace the more conventional ending of K. 297 in a revised version. There are also rejected sketches for a slow movement of K. 504 (in the Mozarteum) and an 'Ultimo allegro per una sinfonia' (reproduced in Zaslaw, p. 418) that suggest Mozart was very much preoccupied both with revising K. 297 and with writing the rest of a new D major Symphony to go with his new Finale to K. 297.

The sketches for the first movement of the 'Prague' show, like those for the string quartets dedicated to Haydn, that not every kind of music came easily to Mozart. The towering intellectual structure of the first movement of K. 504 has suggested to some critics that it might be considered the greatest opening symphonic movement of any in the Mozartian canon. The first thing that surprises us is the very opening, with its grand unison flourishes; for it is not until the second beat of bar 3 that we know whether the music is in D minor or D major (a similar ambiguity occurs at the outset of Haydn's Symphony No. 97, also with a remarkable slow introduction). And this ambiguity is played out on a large scale when in bar 16 of this massive introduction, the music shifts – using our omnipresent dotted 'fingerprint' – into D minor, where it remains *until the end of the introduction* (bar 36). The following *Allegro* is one of Mozart's supreme contrapuntal achievements, worked out in staggering detail, and when it is not enmeshed in counterpoint, other intellectual factors are brought to play: there are two distinct second subjects, the first with a characteristic melody – which is then turned into minor. When that happens a variant

* A. Tyson: *Mozart – Studies of the Autograph Scores*, (Cambridge, MA and London, 1987, p. 140; also Zaslaw, op. cit., p. 418).

of the theme is given to the bassoons as an accompaniment and in order
to bind the second of the two themes to the first, Mozart continues this
bassoon accompaniment but assigns to it the beginning of the music it
accompanied. It is no mean feat and the point is to lead the listener through
variety by retaining continuity, an old Mozartian principle. We might note
the extraordinary turbulence and contrapuntal virtuosity of the development,
wherein, characteristically, the music darkens and at the same time speeds
up rhythmically, with the semiquaver groups gradually taking over. What
follows is one of Mozart's supremely poignant lead-backs to the tonic and
the recapitulation, as anguished and troubled – and beautiful – a sequence
as you can find in Gesualdo or other Mannerists.

Ex. 3. Mozart: Symphony in D, K. 504

The G major *Andante*, in 6/8 time, continues this painfully intense
chromaticism, beginning in bar 3 with the first violin line; and altogether
the movement is remarkable for its veiled emotion and indeed ambiguous
message: who is to say if this music is happy or sad? The obvious statement
that it is both does not entirely answer the questions posed by this quiet,
unsettling movement.

Nor does the Finale, with its flamboyant unconventionality, solve the
dilemma. The fact that Mozart omits the Minuet must mean something,
for it is the only one of the last six to do so. Among the many novelties
in this *Presto*, one notices the long wind band solo at bars 31–46 and
altogether the great freedom with which the wind instruments are treated
– a clear reflection of the excellence of the Viennese *Harmonie* (wind band)
established by Emperor Joseph II a few years before. (We should remember
that the symphony was not written for Prague but for Vienna; Mozart
brought it with him when he visited the Bohemian capital early in 1787 and
played it there.) After the double bar, with its curiously disquieting timpani
part, we arrive, via an increasingly complex instrumental palette, at one of the
most startling passages in Mozart. It is a series of searing dissonances (bars

186ff.) which offer a syncopated top line with a stable bottom and then, in the manner of double counterpoint, the same with top and bottom reversed. This persists until bar 204. It is no wonder that many listeners considered Mozart's music on the edge of the lunatic fringe. It is very similar in spirit to the upward-moving dissonant progression in syncopations just before the coda of Beethoven's overture *Leonore III*. The 'Prague' Symphony belongs, with Haydn's 'Paris' and 'Salomon' symphonies, Mozart's final Trio and Beethoven's Symphony No. 1 (composed in the eighteenth century), to the greatest symphonic legacy of the outgoing *settecento*.

Mozart's last three symphonies have become so celebrated and so surrounded with myth that it is very difficult to approach them with that objectivity which must be any critic's primary goal. The first myth is that they were composed in isolation, out of an overwhelming desire to crown the eighteenth century with three representative masterpieces, and that they were never performed in Mozart's lifetime. Otto Biba and, some years later, the present author have attempted to show that Mozart put on a series of subscription concerts at the Casino in Vienna in 1788, at which these three works were first performed. And there is evidence that the revised version of K. 550, with clarinets, was first performed at a 1791 concert of the Tonkünstler-Societät in Vienna. There is also a textual tradition of orchestral parts which derives, presumably, from these performances and not from the autograph manuscripts. Mozart also must have taken them – his latest orchestral works – on tour in Germany in 1789 and 1790. Why would he have left them at home?* There can be little doubt that Mozart not only wrote but revised these three works with very specific concerts in mind.

The E flat Symphony, K. 543, has the highly individual scoring of one flute, two clarinets, two bassoons, two horns, two trumpets and kettledrums – in other words without oboes. This was the same orchestration that the composer had used with such beautiful and original effect in the great E flat Piano Concerto, K. 482 (completed 16 December 1785 in Vienna); and that brings us to the curiously autumnal sound of this E flat Symphony – which is surely not inflicting upon it any posthumous Romantic ideas, but is quite simply a deliberate calculation on Mozart's part. E flat is a peculiarly suitable key for the wind instruments (this has purely technical reasons which are not necessary to relate here) and has always occupied a very special position in the Vienna Classical school – consider not only these works in the Mozartian corpus but also the Serenade for wind band, K. 375, or the big E flat concerted Finales in his operas (end of Act II in *Figaro*). And in Haydn we could mention two of the greatest London

* Otto Biba: 'Grundzüge des Konzertwesens in Wien zu Mozarts Zeit', *Mozart-Jahrbuch 1978–9*, pp. 132ff. H. C. Robbins Landon: edition of *Neue Mozart-Ausgabe* – Symphonies, vol. 9, Kassel, 1957, and *Kritische Berichte*, Serie IV, Orchesterwerke, Lieferung 4, Werkgruppe 11, Sinfonien, Band 9, Kassel, 1963. *1791, Mozart's Last Year*, London, 1988, pp. 31–3. Zaslaw, op. cit., pp. 421ff.

symphonies, No. 99 (very autumnal, too) and the extraordinary No. 103 ('Drum Roll'), with the most sinister beginning in all eighteenth-century symphonic music. In Beethoven, one thinks of the 'Eroica' Symphony, but also the 'Emperor' Concerto. There is something wistful and at the same time generous, like a great October wine harvest, in their use of E flat.

Mozart realized by this time that symphonies of this physical size and spiritual magnitude need to be more than four individual movements: the music must hang together, even if by means that reach only the listener's unconscious. German critics have long ago demonstrated that there is a kind of *Ur-cantus firmus* that underlines all four movements of the 'Jupiter' Symphony. And in the E flat, the long legato downward scales of the violins, which occur as soon as the opening *forte* of the majestic and dramatic slow introduction settles into *piano*, reappear in the ensuing *Allegro*, almost note for note. Notice, too, how the dotted chains in the introduction reappear in the *Allegro*, most spectacularly in the trumpets at the end of the movement. The curiously unsettling timpani rhythm at the beginning may have Masonic overtones: we must remember that E flat is the principal Masonic key in eighteenth-century Vienna and that it is the golden thread in *Die Zauber-flöte*. The legato theme of the *Allegro* has also a spirituality and a haunting quality which may derive from the fact that, like many of Mozart's (and *not* many of Haydn's) melodies, this one could be sung by a lyric soprano. Schubert remembered the explosive and profoundly disturbing character of those violent forays into the minor in the A flat slow movement of this symphony, which is otherwise as inscrutably beautiful as the smile of *La Gioconda*. These tremendous emotional outbursts occur in F minor (bars 30ff.) and, with heightened intensity, in an ominously remote B minor (bars 96ff.). This kind of compositional procedure is, of course, exactly what happens in the second movement of Schubert's 'Unfinished' Symphony, where similar mountains of energy displace the quiet processional music of the main theme.

In the Minuet and Trio, we find Mozart setting up a kind of Austrian *Ländler*: you can almost hear the country folk stamping their feet. But some of the feet have the pretty feminine ankles for which Austrians have always been famous – so that Mozart's accents are often delicate hints (*mfp* is one – a sign never encountered in the whole of Haydn). In the Trio we have evidence of the profound influence of the clarinet-playing Stadler brothers in Mozart's music. The first clarinet has the melody, framed with huge, loving legato slurs, while clarinet II has the gurgling Alberti-bass accompaniment which is peculiarly suited to the instrument and would soon become a standard device: here it is used almost for the first time in a symphony (though astute listeners could already have heard the device in Mozart's concertos and operas).

The Finale is the most complicated and multi-layered of any thus far in Mozart's oeuvre. It sounds at the beginning like Haydn, but its construction and continuation are profoundly Mozartian. It is intently monothematic –

even little fragments derive from the opening material; and its tonal structure is completely original. As soon as the second section begins (both parts are to be repeated), we find ourselves in the remote key (in relation to E flat) of E major; and in the next few bars Mozart displays another technical device he had learned from his friend Joseph Leutgeb, the horn player, who was a specialist in so-called 'stopped' notes. These were produced by inserting the right hand into the bell of the horn, and thus lowering the pitch by a semitone, a whole tone or even one and a half tones. Here, in swift succession, we have six stopped notes in both horns. It is doubtful if anyone in the usual orchestras of London, Rome or Paris could even *play* these notes on their horns – or indeed the clarinet parts either (clarinet playing of this kind being largely limited to Vienna and central Europe) – which meant a limited circulation of this bold, innovative and profoundly personal work.

The G minor has always been regarded as one of Mozart's most personal revelations. It gave rise to a whole school of thought in the Romantic era. Nowadays, its violently neurotic and compulsive language is linked to a theory that Mozart was a prey to depressions of a nearly maniacal sort. There is, after all, a whole series of works, some of which easily approach, if they do not outdistance, this anguished music of K. 550 – the Piano Concertos in D minor (K. 466) and C minor (K. 491), the String Quartet in D minor (K. 421), the String Quintet in G minor (K. 516); and the list could easily be continued. But neurotic though this great and seminal symphony may be, it is brilliantly organized and contains as rigorous and intellectual a self-discipline as any music of the period. There is not a ounce of musical fat on its lean structure. Originally Mozart intended to use four horns, as he had done in the 'little' G minor Symphony, K. 183 – two in G and two in B flat *alto*. But the second pair was cancelled after a few bars, probably from motives of economy – these were after all intended for concerts which he was organizing and for which he would have to pay the orchestra; and what would the two horns otherwise do the rest of the evening?

The first version of K. 550 is scored for a flute, pairs of oboes, bassoons and horns, with the usual strings. Because of the nature of valveless horns, Mozart had to use one horn in G and one in B flat. In the nineteenth century the piercing slashes of colour from these horns, intruding rudely into the polished framework of, say, the Finale, used to be toned down to the extent that they were almost inaudible. Played as they are nowadays, especially with period instruments, they underline the violence of the score. This is music stretched to breaking point.

When Mozart came to revise the score, possibly for the aforementioned Tonkünstler-Societät concert in April 1791 in Vienna, he not only added clarinets but rewrote the oboe parts.* Some prefer the leaner, original

---

* The watermarks of these added clarinet and revised oboe parts are, however, partly the same as that of the original score, which suggests less of a gap than summer 1788 and April 1791.

version, some the more opulent revision. There is one passage in the slow movement, repeated later, which contains music that is very difficult for the exposed woodwind (bars 29–32 and 100–103). At some time and for some performance, probably in Germany, where the woodwind were not so adroit as in Vienna, Mozart rewrote this passage, giving the difficult downward-moving music to the more agile strings and giving the woodwind long held notes.*

There is one passage in K. 550 which might sum up the whole message of innovation, *Angst* and compositional self-discipline. That is immediately after the double bar in the Finale (*Allegro assai*), where Mozart peers ahead a century and a half by flirting with the Grim Reaper: he introduced, obviously to illustrate the point of tonal (and personal?) disintegration, all twelve notes of the scale, presented in a series of diminished sevenths. The way in which they are set forth, with abrupt jumps, a whirling triplet gesture and accented crotchets, is profoundly disturbing, like the message of the symphony altogether.

It was the great impresario Johann Peter Salomon who christened the final part of this trilogy the 'Jupiter'. Salomon had come in 1790 to engage, if possible, both Mozart and Haydn; in the event, he persuaded Haydn to come with him to England, and it was agreed that Mozart should follow another year. So it is fitting to preserve the connection between the eighteenth century's greatest impresario and music's greatest genius by means of the work which many people consider the eighteenth century's greatest symphony: K. 551 in C.

It is rooted in tradition – Mozart's music always is: the use of C major as the key of princes, archbishops, of coronations (*La clemenza di Tito* is in C), of abbeys and *Applausus* cantatas for prelates (Haydn's *Applausus* Cantata of 1768), of great solemn Masses for festive occasions. Trumpets and drums in this key have a rich and sonorous character, less brilliant than D and not as mellow as (say) B flat. Haydn had composed countless C major symphonies for festive occasions, and the very sound evoked all those things to the audiences. So although the fugal Finale, with its resplendent coda that combines all five of the movement's themes is one of the great *tours de force* of its kind in the history of music, its arrival on the C major scene was not perhaps, entirely unexpected. The audience would have been immediately reminded of the Credo theme in the Sunday Mass he or she had just attended, because the first four notes of the *cantus firmus* are literally 'Credo in unum Deum' – and that in itself is significant, since Mozart was a much more deeply religious man than secular twentieth-century critics give him credit for. Everyone would have thought also of the splendid fugues that were traditionally used for the close of the Gloria ('In gloria Dei patris,

---

* *Neue Mozart-Ausgabe*, ibid., pp. 267f. The Bärenreiter miniature score (Landon) also contains this revision, pp. 63f. This revision, which is obviously the result of external pressure, is not usually performed. It can be heard on the Oiseau Lyre version of the complete symphonies conducted by Christopher Hogwood.

Amen'): for the close of the Credo ('Et vitam venturi saeculi, Amen' – another hint at what motivated this incredible music, 'world without end' and 'life everlasting, resounding down the centuries', like the trumpets and drums that hurl the 'Jupiter' bolts into the twenty-first century); and most of all, the end of the Ordinary, 'Dona nobis pacem', the wish of every civilized human being, under threat when Mozart wrote this symphony in the midst of a cruel, unprofitable and inflation-creating war between Austria and the Ottoman Empire. So perhaps the conclusion of the Mass, 'Ite Missa est', is also the unwritten conclusion to Mozart's symphonic life: the blessing that the priest confers on the faithful after Mass, and Mozart's blessing too, with the 'Jupiter' symphony, on a deeply threatened and fragile world.

4

Beethoven

Richard Osborne

Writing about the Beethoven symphonies in a letter to Elgar in January 1919, the critic Ernest Newman remarked: 'The music unfolds itself with perfect freedom; but it is so heart-searching because we *know* all the time it runs along the quickest nerves of our life, our struggles & aspirations & sufferings & exaltations'. Years later, in a series of background notes prepared for the BBC's Third Programme, Hans Keller suggested that 'in the entire history of the symphony, no composer traversed as much *spiritual space* [my italics] as did Beethoven between his First and Ninth symphonies'. Such judgments are, I think, worth quoting at the outset of any latter-day survey of the Beethoven symphonies because they reassert – in a sceptical and at times needlessly analytical age – the source of the music's wide and long-standing appeal. There will always be those, of course, who will be happy to echo the turn-of-the-century critic who claimed that 'the Fifth Symphony is not what it was'; and after Belsen and Buchenwald we might have even greater cause to question Beethoven's transcendent optimism at the end of that particular work. And yet it endures, not least because of the originality, the craggy individuality, of Beethoven's Finale during which the Scherzo's eerie theme reappears, very much the spectre at the feast. E. M. Forster put it well in a famous description of the Fifth Symphony in his novel *Howards End*: 'But the goblins were there. They could return. He had said so bravely, and that is why one can trust Beethoven when he says other things'.

By and large, Beethoven was trusted more or less from the outset of a career that made him what we can now recognize to be the most powerful and innovative of all great symphonists. In a famous essay, 'Beethoven's Instrumental Music', first published in 1813, E. T. A. Hoffmann acknowledged that 'the musical rabble is oppressed by Beethoven's powerful genius'; but in the next breath he added: 'it seeks in vain to oppose it'. From the time of the *Eroica* onwards, Beethoven was Europe's best-known and most revered living composer. He was also unique – and was to remain unique for some time afterwards – in having his *complete* symphonic output in print in full score during his lifetime. Nor did his reputation go into rapid decline in the years immediately following his death (a common occurrence with even the greatest artists). In subsequent decades, the symphonies inevitably suffered private censure – Debussy once grumpily observed that it is more profitable to watch the sun rise than to hear Beethoven's 'Pastoral' Symphony – but the musical and historical pre-eminence of the Nine has never been seriously questioned. Such questions as can be intelligently raised are of a more speculative and philosophical nature: what is music for, and to what extent does it engage the society on whose behalf it claims to speak? Because a composer like Sir Michael Tippett has asked these questions of himself, he can perhaps ask them of Beethoven, too, quietly and with none of Debussy's flippancy or rancour. In his essay 'Poets in a Barren Age', Tippett writes: 'Europe was being riven by the French Revolution and society turned upside down by the Industrial Revolution. It was indeed possible to feel that these artistic affirmations could be illusions and that the artist could be right outside the realities of the social life of his period. And he was impotent – he neither conversed with God nor spoke realistically to his fellows.' Perhaps so, but that is certainly not how Beethoven saw it. His mission as a symphonist dictated otherwise.

The symphony is not an intimate medium, nor did Beethoven consider it as such. We come closest to him personally, perhaps, in the great body of solo piano music and in movements from the later string quartets. But when Beethoven eventually and decisively placed himself before the Viennese public on 2 April 1800 he knew what he was about. The concert was a typically gargantuan affair; and it ended – after two concertos, arias, improvisations, and Beethoven's Septet – with the newly written First Symphony. Both Haydn and Mozart had given public symphony concerts. Both craved grand orchestras and substantial audiences. But it was not until the turn of the century that the idea of a genuinely large, semi-democratic public began to emerge and with it the kind of halls and state-of-the-art instrumentation that could meet the heady aspirations of the new public. This was to be Beethoven's own special demesne, the new forum in which issues of politics and humanity – or Beethoven's own private transmutation of them – could be powerfully confronted.

A new agenda also implied new procedures. Had his deafness not intervened, Beethoven would almost certainly have become the very model of the modern orchestral conductor. Not only does his music invite control, technically, from some powerful central authority; it also invites interpretation. In his own day it rarely received it, though it is significant that it is Beethoven's music that threw up the first substantial body of written analysis of contemporary music. When the *Eroica* Symphony was performed in Leipzig in 1807, explanatory notes were provided for the audience. Charles Rosen dates the rise of written analyses from 1811. (Hoffmann's essay on Beethoven was begun, in fact, in 1810, though not finally assembled and published until 1813.) Yet there were other respects in which Beethoven was a conservative, even circumspect figure. Despite new halls and new audiences, Beethoven spent most of his career as a symphonist using an orchestra – strings, two flutes, oboes, clarinets, bassoons, trumpets, horns and timpani – that is more or less identical with Haydn's. What additions there are come slowly and discreetly: a third horn in the *Eroica*, three trombones, piccolo, and double bassoon in the Finale of the Fifth Symphony and then – and only then – some considerable expansion and augmentation many years later for the second and fourth movements of the Ninth Symphony.

By the 1820s there is evidence of expanding numbers of orchestral players and of strategic reinforcement of the sound in some tutti passages, but throughout his career as a symphonist Beethoven is a man for whom force of argument is always preferable to force of numbers. The sense of huge and unalloyed power we often take from his music is a result, not of brute force, but of Beethoven's astonishing command of time and symphonic space. The harmonic reach of his music is phenomenal yet it is never won at the expense of a symphony's essential rootedness; it is simply that Beethoven roams on a longer and stronger lead than other men. Nor was this merely a phenomenon of his mature years. By 1824 we are probably not surprised when the second subject of the first movement of the Ninth Symphony, originally in B flat, returns in F sharp minor. But the recapitulation of the second subject of the Finale of the First Symphony in F major rather than C almost certainly caused a few eyebrows to be raised in the Hofburgtheater on 2 April 1800. From the first with Beethoven, the dramatic elements are coterminous with the epic.

Nowadays, perhaps, we are less consistently aware than his contemporaries must have been of the sheer reach of Beethoven's music, though even in the post-Wagner and post-Bruckner age it is difficult not to be awestruck by the sheer scale of something like the first movement of the *Eroica* Symphony. What is undiminished, though, is the feeling any newcomer to Beethoven must have of the protean power of the music, of the sense it gives of an inexhaustible ability to develop, change, and transform. As the century progressed, so composers schooled in textbook theories of 'sonata form' (an idea uncodified in 1800) learned how to fake this sense of inner organic growth. With Beethoven, by contrast, the processes are central to the creative act itself. To see how this works it is necessary to examine Beethoven's famous sketchbooks where it is often possible to see not only the evolution of themes and longer-term arguments but also the emergence of motifs that will infiltrate whole areas of a given symphony (most famously the celebrated four-note motto that begins the Fifth Symphony). To study the notebooks is to enter the blacksmith's forge. In one respect the effort evidenced there is torrential. One is reminded of Yeats's lines in his poem *An Acre of Grass*:

> Grant me an old man's frenzy,
> Myself must I remake
> Till I am Timon and Lear

Or that William Blake
Who beat upon the wall
Till Truth obeyed his call.

Part of Beethoven's art, however, lies in his ability to strive but not to over-revise. Paradoxically, his symphonies are superbly ordered creations which none the less leave the sense of struggle palpable. In this respect, one of the most revealing remarks he ever made was to his friend Ferdinand Ries: 'Between ourselves, the best thing of all is a combination of the surprising and the beautiful'.

In the event, Beethoven chose to begin his career as a symphonist with a surprise as rude as it is representative. Though advertised as being in C major, the First Symphony begins with a wind and pizzicato string chord (nightmarish to co-ordinate) on the dominant seventh of the key of F major. By the fourth bar of the symphony G major has been reached, though whether this is a further act of usurpation or merely the dominant of the advertised key of C is something different ears hear differently. Such niceties apart, the overall effect is startling from almost every point of view. Certainly, it is difficult to imagine a shrewder start to a great symphonic career. As the Chorus says in *Henry V*: 'For now sits Expectation in the air'. For some contemporary critics, the sonorities of this symphony were bizarre. One writer, who relished Beethoven's 'considerable art, novelty, and wealth of ideas', complained that the wind instruments were too much used 'so that there was more *harmony* [in German 'Harmonie' indicates 'Wind Band'] than orchestral music as a whole'. Yet without the peculiar colouring of wind chords against bare pizzicato strings even this harmonically audacious opening would seem less novel than it really is.

With the arrival of the *Allegro* (Beethoven's *con brio* marking perhaps an act of supererogation in the circumstances) we meet the composer in characteristic guise, purposeful and alert. We also meet the man who sees further and notices more than most of those around him. After four bars of thrustful C major, two whole bars of sustained harmony intervene, the music stayed for seven whole beats until the propulsive little downward semiquaver (a rich source of ideas later on in the symphony) relaunches the principal theme, this time screwed up a tone, from C to D. There is nothing genteel or static about such music; its centre of gravity appears to be rising all the time. (There is a similar effect at the start of the slow movement where within eight beats a rising fourth has been compressed to a third and, finally, a minor second.) The first movement of this First Symphony by Beethoven is indeed surprising and beautiful in almost equal measure, its beauty residing not so much in the second subject, exquisitely songful on oboe and flute, as in the music's glorious sense of proportion and the sense it conveys of power beneficently used.

The slow movement is less remarkable, though the hushed use of trumpets and drums at one point is a strikingly poetic effect. By contrast, the third movement is a *tour de force*. Beethoven marks it *Menuetto*, a term that has no more validity than the genuflexion of a seditious valet. The initial tempo is searing – *Allegro molto e vivace* – and the mood uproarious: C major gamely astride a bucking bronco of a movement that is a Scherzo in both pace and comic intent. What is more, the surprising and the beautiful are once more imaginatively twinned, with the Trio section opening out huge vistas. Harmonically, this Trio is as spacious as it is stable. Rhythmically, it creates a sense of massive calm that is reinforced rather than diminished by the strings' scurrying altercations with the implacably serene wind choir. In spirit, it is the kind of idyll that Aaron Copland might have envied. Nor is it any surprise to learn that the young Elgar copied out the music, note for note, for his further contemplation and study.

At the start of the Finale, we return to the seditious valet and to Beethoven's monomaniac desire to fashion a lot out of next to nothing. The *Adagio* preface to the movement could outmanoeuvre Uriah Heep himself in protestations about its humble origins. What is it, after all, but a repeated G 'ever so 'umbly' co-opting all the notes of the diatonic scale? And who, in an upwardly mobile age, could reasonably object if from this single note and its attendant scale an entire uproarious movement was to be fashioned? The delights of this Finale are endless largely because most of the jokes bear frequent retelling. Who has not smiled, and smiled again, as the woodwinds graciously usher in the recapitulation only to find that the bounder has already made his entrance? And what larks there are at the start of the coda where the upwardly mobile scale is given a terrible ribbing by the entire orchestra. Thus, the First Symphony ends as an essay in undiluted comedy. By contrast, the allegedly comic Eighth Symphony is funny, as we shall see, only up to a point.

If the First Symphony is a comically subversive work, the Second Symphony, no less fiery if properly conducted, is on an altogether grander scale. It is by no means lacking in wit and humour. (The last two movements are uproarious in their rough-hewn way.) What is different here is the long-range planning of this extraordinary *dramma giocoso*. In particular, the flat sixth (B flat) of the home key of D major stalks through the symphony like Till Eulenspiegel, turning over apple-carts wherever he can find them. It first appears in bar 12 of the symphony's slow introduction, it strikes again in the Scherzo shortly after the double bar, and finally frightens the wits out of everyone at bar 372 during the Finale's enormously extended coda. Paralleling this new preoccupation with long-term thinking is a complementary preoccupation with sonata form and internal musical developments (even the Scherzo and its Trio have vestigial development sections). Though we expect the first movement to be in sonata form, and, possibly, the Finale as well, it is more surprising to find the slow movement also in fully worked-out sonata form – and worked out with a prodigality of theme, sub-theme, and variant scoring that must have made even Schubert gaze.

At the time of its first performance in April 1803, this was the longest symphony yet to be written. Curiously, the *Adagio* preface to Mozart's great D major Symphony, K. 504, the 'Prague', is longer than Beethoven's, but even here Beethoven compensates by moving through an altogether wider range of keys, abandoning the tonic after the opening summons and only returning to it, this time in the minor, for a devastating unison descent that inevitably carries for us indelible associations with the mood of the yet-to-be-written Ninth Symphony. Beethoven's introduction also has more dramatic momentum than Mozart's. Where Mozart's *Allegro* emerges like Blake's sunflower seeking its sweet golden clime, Beethoven's is like a spontaneous outflow from the introduction itself. It is also interesting how, in the *Allegro* itself, Beethoven's thematic material is plainer than Mozart's tends to be whilst at the same time being more distinctive than much of Haydn's. One of the hallmarks of Beethoven's way with sonata form is his love of well-contrasted first and second subjects. In the first movement of the Second Symphony the contrast is less acute than usual, both themes rising and falling through a simple triad. But one wonders whether Haydn would have thought it necessary, as Beethoven did, to smooth out the descent in the first theme so as to reserve the superbly impulsive (and now rising) dotted rhythm for the march-like second subject. If we examine Beethoven's sketchbook we see (Ex.1) what Beethoven originally had in mind.

Ex. 1. Beethoven: Symphony No. 2

By substituting plain crotchets in bar 3 and using the (dramatically important) written-out turn in bar 1 as the basis for a flurrying transition in bar 4 (Ex.2), Beethoven both tautens the idea and leaves himself energy in reserve for the second subject.

Beethoven's superb ear for orchestral texture is also evident here. With the second subject destined for an initial statement on clarinets, bassoons and horns, the first subject is given, initially and unexpectedly, to the violas and cellos: a complementary texture but also a contrasted one. Armed with just two principal themes, and that propulsive little written-out turn, Beethoven proceeds to build a movement that combines *élan* with a surprising amount of full-throated songfulness. Sir Donald Tovey refers to the 'choral grandeur' of the coda's climax, shrewdly identifying the source of the inspiration as 'The Heavens are Telling' from Haydn's *The Creation* (Vienna, 1798).

The symphony's full-throatedness continues in the superbly spacious

Larghetto after which the third and fourth movements appear to set a slightly different agenda, one that appears to want to question and put into perspective the almost Panglossian – 'All is for the best in the best of possible worlds' – scenario of the work so far. The Scherzo is full of surprises, its Trio even more so. This begins with an *al fresco* song on oboes, bassoons, and (eventually) horns. At which point a unison F sharp breaks in on the strings: a blustering intruder equipped – F sharp being the dominant of D major's relative key, B minor – with a perfectly valid search warrant. The winds, though, will have none of this intrusive bluster and the lower strings are dispatched to provide a pizzicato accompaniment to the Trio's closing bars. In the Finale there are tougher battles to be fought. For one contemporary critic, the coda – where both the B flat and the F sharp make fearsome chordal intrusions – was 'a pierced dragon which will not die, dealing vain but furious blows with its tail'. And it must be said that this lengthy movement (442 bars, *cf.* the Fifth Symphony's 444 bars) is astonishing in the explosiveness of its opening gesture, the thematic

Ex. 2.

Ex. 2. cont'd

complexity of the first subject group, and the sheer breadth and generosity (gloriously scored) of the second subject itself.

It is interesting that this A major second subject soon drifts into the minor: interesting, because beneath this symphony's exuberance there is often an undertow of tragedy. It has often been noted that the Second Symphony is more or less contemporary with the famous 'Heiligenstadt Testament', the great confessional statement drafted by Beethoven in the early days of October 1802 where he confronts the trauma of his growing deafness, contemplates suicide, and eventually stoically rejects it. The coincidence of the Heiligenstadt Testament and the D major Symphony has often been used as an earnest of Beethoven's courage, of his ability to separate out personal vision and private suffering. In practice, the matter is not quite as simple as this, not least because, as some scholars have pointed out, the symphony was probably finished a good six months before the drafting of the Testament. That said, Beethoven's otosclerosis was a progressive condition and as such must have been a fact of his life throughout the period of the gestation and completion of the D major Symphony. In the end, all that one can safely say is that the symphony anticipates the emotional crisis of the Testament itself, and its life-affirming outcome, as surely as it anticipates the enormously enlarged architectural scale of the *Eroica* Symphony that was shortly to follow.

In the course of the Heiligenstadt Testament, Beethoven observes: '*Patience*, they say is what I must now choose for my guide, and I have done so – I hope my determination will remain firm to endure until it pleases the inexorable Parcae [Greek goddesses of Fate] to break the thread. Perhaps I shall get better, perhaps not, I am ready'. In such a mood, he began to labour over one of the crucial works – perhaps *the* crucial work – of his career, the *Eroica* Symphony, No.3 in E flat major. The key, the nickname, and some of Beethoven's own comments and written subscriptions suggest that the concept of heroism was one of the work's informing ideas. It is typical of Beethoven, though, that his thinking on such a subject took place at several levels. In formulating the *Eroica* Symphony, Beethoven contemplated the heroism of the young Napoleon and the heroism of the fire-stealing and god-defying Prometheus; and to these contemporary and Classical precedents he added his own heroic defiance of deafness and incipient despair. Of these, the last two are probably a good deal more important than Napoleon ever was to the scheme of the *Eroica*. In his *Beethoven and the Voice of God*, Wilfrid Mellers goes so far as to see them as a composite: 'So Beethoven–Prometheus is an intermediary between man and the gods; the gift of fire he steals may include material power, but it is also the divine spark which can be lit in man only through suffering'.

Certainly, if we are looking for programmes within the symphony, Prometheus or Beethoven–Prometheus must be our man, particularly in the Finale where Beethoven's use of the theme from his ballet *The Creatures of Prometheus* is open to possible programmatic interpretation. Dr Barry Cooper has observed: 'The ballet begins with a storm and so does the symphony finale; Prometheus then encounters his two clay statues, and what could be more statuesque than the stiff, unharmonized bass-line that begins the main part of the symphony finale?' Thereafter, he concedes, the programme is more difficult to pursue as musical developments – fugue, variations, and unfettered dance – take over before the theme's oboe-led transformation, *Poco Andante*, at bar 348. In an earlier age, this was seen as the hero's 'flight to the skies' (Sir George Grove); and even the sober-suited Tovey likened the oboe's entry to the 'opening of the gates of Paradise'. In fact, the *Andante*'s continuation is far too *angst*-ridden for the electrifying *Presto* that ends the symphony to be anything other than an ebullient celebration of a sense of well-being provisionally restored. As Beethoven wrote in a postscript to the Heiligenstadt Testament: 'Oh Providence – Grant me at last but one day *of pure joy*'.

The dangers of crediting the symphony with the exploration of the fate of a particular hero are all too evident when it comes to explaining the work's continuing life after the funeral rites of the second movement, the *Marcia funèbre.* 'Funeral games around the grave of the warrior, such as those in the *Iliad*', was Berlioz's somewhat lame explanation of the Scherzo's presence and mood. As this clearly will not do, it is better to approach the *Marcia funèbre* as the exequies not of one hero but of any hero, and as an earnest of Beethoven's fascination with public ceremony and the rituals of power. Musically, it is a colossal rondo that becomes ever more colossal as the initiating ideas fragment and develop within the music's intensely slow-moving progress. Using some of the same key centres – C minor and E flat major – that Mozart deploys in his Masonic Funeral Music, K.477, Beethoven sublimates grief and at the same time creates a superb essay in the musical picturesque. This is a solemn cortège set against louring temples and crumbling classical pediments such as David or Delacroix might have painted. Later, such ideas will be distilled, abstracted almost, in the yet more impersonal grieving of the Seventh Symphony's A minor *Allegretto*. The *Eroica* Symphony, though, requires more guile on Beethoven's part in getting from Funeral March to Scherzo. And how superbly he brings it off, the music making its dancing entry *sempre pianissimo e staccato*, hushed and furtive in B flat: an opening as imaginative as the drum-troubled end is awesome.

It is not, however, the last two movements, or even the great Funeral March, that makes the *Eroica* Symphony the towering and innovatory thing it is. It is the monumental first movement, and the huge shadows it casts, that gives the work its formidable importance and force of character. What's more, in approaching this movement it is worth bearing in mind some words addressed to the BBC Symphony Orchestra in the Queen's Hall, London in 1937 by the great Arturo Toscanini: 'No! No! Is-a not Napoleon! Is-a not 'Itler! Is-a not Mussolini! Is-a *Allegro con brio*!' In other words, this is music, pure, albeit not so simple, whose dramatic power and epic reach require of conductors nothing more than the kind of singleness of purpose and clarity of vision which Beethoven brought to the composition of the music in the first place. Certainly, no single symphonic movement seems to have been worked on by Beethoven as assiduously as this. Examine the sketches and you will see the sweep of Beethoven's imaginative vision – how, at quite an early stage, the melody's dissonant C sharp in bar 7 of the symphony (Ex.3) is already linked to the C sharp [= D flat] in the visionary bridge from development to recapitulation at what will eventually be bar 418. At the time, Beethoven had no more idea of how to cross the space between than a mountaineer contemplating a distant col from the valley beneath; and, indeed, he wrote out the skeletal development of the movement on a single stave many times before the whole enormous structure fell finally into place.

The idea of the symphony as a voyage of discovery was crucial to Beethoven. By taking the plainest of musical materials – in this case an E flat major triad stated vertically as a pair of commanding introductory chords and horizontally as a principal melodic subject – he makes the

Ex. 3. Beethoven: Symphony No. 3

equivalent of an axiomatic statement. But it is an axiom that must now be rigorously tested in a world of living sensation where an alien C sharp may turn up, not arbitrarily, but as a proponent of ideas yet to be encountered. Hans Keller once observed that even nowadays, when we hear the opening notes of this work, we realize instinctively that nothing remotely like this had been heard before. We also realize instinctively that we are dealing with music on a huge scale. The first movement of the *Eroica* is the longest opening movement in the cycle of the Nine and the longest of all Beethoven's symphonic movements apart from the Ninth's choral Finale. Initially, its sheer length (691 bars) caused Beethoven to have second thoughts about the inclusion of the exposition repeat that runs the grand total up to 846

bars, making the movement half as long again as the first movement of the
mighty Ninth. But whatever contemporary faint-hearts might have preferred,
Beethoven ultimately had no choice but to recognize that the movement's
vast development, and the unprecented length and sweep of its coda, balance
out a structure that had the idea of an exposition repeat built into it from the
outset. In fact, structural balances apart, it does none of us any harm to hear
the symphony with the repeat in place simply because the exposition itself is
so packed with detail and incident. Never before was Beethoven so obviously
fired up at the start of a work, so determined to have his say. Equally, it is
astonishing how almost every utterance serves the twin aim of advancing the
argument whilst at the same time sustaining the structure. This applies to
the two opening chords which act not only gesturally but also (assuming the
conductor plays them in strict time) as rhythmic markers, allowing the E flat
major theme in bar 3 (Ex. 3) an ease and impulsion it could not possibly have
had without those prefacing chords. It is also interesting to note how well
the contemplative second subject (bar 87) is protected from the *espressivo*
elements in the first subject group, Beethoven separating the two with a
mass of highly energized rhythmic ideas. The exposition is also notable
for its ferocity – for the mass of misplaced accents and for the barbaric
dissonance of the tonic-plus-dominant chords near the end. No wonder
one listener at the first public performance in April 1805 cried out from the
recesses of the gallery: 'I'll give another Kreutzer if this thing will stop!'

But there is worse to come. As the development whips itself into a huge
storm, the screaming dissonances on the brass cry out for at least fifty
Kreutzers-worth of relief. What we are in fact given, as the storm abates,
is generally thought to be an entirely new idea (Ex. 4), though, as Charles
Rosen has pointed out, the subsidiary cello voicing bears a striking outline
resemblance to the movement's opening idea.

Ex. 4. Beethoven: Symphony No. 3

Be that as it may, it enters with all the emotional force of a new idea.
Leonard Bernstein once likened it to 'a song of pain after the holocaust'.
The partial assuaging of that pain, and Beethoven's astonishing search for a
bridge back to the recapitulation in a passage of unsurpassed originality and
visionary beauty, has been much written about. The harmonic processes are
better understood by us now than they were by baffled contemporaries; but it
is not so much how Beethoven goes about his business (lucidly described by

Rosen in *Sonata Forms*, pp. 290 ff.) as the astonishing effect on the listener of this transition, beginning with the second horn's abortive attempt (bar 394) finally to claim the motivating E flat theme for itself. Fifteen bars later, the first horn does acquire it, *dolce* and in F major on a fresh instrument tuned to the supertonic F, before the flute's seraphic D flat major repetition, gloriously poised (such scoring!) over rising and falling pizzicato violins, cellos and basses. We are 400 bars on, and that hawkish C sharp has finally turned itself into a dove-like D flat, symbolically serene.

In the coda of the movement, Beethoven makes even grander strides. The passage after bar 555 is famous for the space it covers: E flat, D flat, and C with sharply etched dynamic shifts. The great coda is not, however, a Victory Symphony. Just as Beethoven denied the second horn his moment of glory at bar 394, so he aborts the trumpets' blazing statement of the theme in bar 658, at the same time reserving the real *fortissimo* climax point for the arrival on the B flat chord in bar 671 before the movement's somewhat querulous end. The fact that for several generations (and still occasionally today) conductors have granted the trumpets the full run of the theme at bar 658, allowing it to blaze out as an unchallengeable climax, only goes to show how we have come to like our heroes: Hollywood-style and inconceivable as creatures with feet of clay. Beethoven knew otherwise.

After the *Eroica*, Beethoven began work on what we now know as the Fifth Symphony, a fact that rather undermines the idea that he consciously commuted between the powerfully dramatic odd-numbered symphonies and the more lyrical even-numbered ones. That said, the Nine were assembled with a good deal of care (they are, for instance, rooted in eight different key centres) with Beethoven showing characteristic genius in differentiating between works which he worked on more or less simultaneously: the Fourth and Fifth symphonies and, later on, the Seventh and Eighth. The contrast between the gamesome and lyrical Fourth and the fearsomely dramatic Fifth, which Goethe thought subversive and a threat to civilization as he knew it, is particularly interesting since the two works have a certain amount in common. In the Fourth Symphony, for example, we first meet the idea of Beethoven bringing the third movement Trio round twice, an effect he was also inclined to use in the Fifth. (The whole question of whether Beethoven intended the Trio repeat in the Fifth Symphony to stand – and the knock-on effect such a decision has on whether or not to repeat the Finale's exposition – has been much debated by scholars, most notably by the composer, Robert Simpson, who favours the restitution of the Trio's repeat.) Still more interesting is the pivotal role of the timpani in the two works. The drum-led transition to the Finale of the Fifth Symphony is one of music's most celebrated instrumental inspirations; but no less remarkable is the preparation for the recapitulation of the first movement of the Fourth Symphony where the drum single-handedly reasserts the tonic B flat. After being held in reserve by Beethoven, it suddenly becomes both the rock and the lighthouse in a sea of uncertainty; and, again, it achieves its effect by stealth. Drums are generally for beating but here the drum effects its miracle of stabilisation and control with three *pianissimo* rolls.

There is, though, an even more profound connection between the two works; and that is their mutual concern with ascent towards the light. The overwhelming problem facing Beethoven during the composition of the Fifth Symphony was that of realizing his transcendentalist vision within the context of the Classical forms he had inherited and as yet only partly transformed. As we now know, he eventually came up with the unprecedented solution of linking the Scherzo with the Finale. But that solution appears to have come only after the writing of the Fourth Symphony; a symphony which actually *begins* by addressing the comparable problem of effecting an ascent from a Stygian underworld to the bright light of day.

The sense we have at the start of the Fourth Symphony of a soul lost in outer darkness was not, however, the real seat of contemporary disaffection with this astonishing *Adagio* preface. (The start of Haydn's *The Creation* had won no such notoriety.) Rather, it was the extreme slowness of the music harmonically. Carl Maria von Weber made the point, in a purely negative way, when he exclaimed: 'Every quarter of an hour we hear three or four notes. It is exciting!' Nowadays, we have drugs to treat Weber's condition in the form of sugar-coated academic disquisitions on the nature of the up-beat. (Bars 1 to 14 – well over a minute's music – are explained away as a gigantically slow upbeat.) Strange as this opening is, the ascent to the light is gradual and the transition to the *Allegro vivace* almost staid, with no gradual increase of tempo and only a handful of unvarnished dominant sevenths to announce that B flat major will, after all, be the tonic key. It is often said that the Fourth Symphony breaks no new ground, that it is a tribute to Haydn by a composer who now wears his own nose and who has absolutely nothing to fear from being thought old-fashioned. That is one, perhaps rather unimaginative way, of looking at it. Another would be to rejoice in the Apollonian loveliness of the piece, in its fiery lines, and astonishing equanimity. But these, in turn, are part and parcel of the wonderful self-confidence of Beethoven who, around the year 1806, was in the full leaf and flower of his art. The symphony's outer movements are richly various, expansive and abrupt, playful yet controlled, exuberant yet given to moments of hypnotic quiet. 'Very tragical mirth', Peter Quince's oxymoronic phrase, might adequately sum it all up.

Everywhere in this symphony the craft is consummate, not least in areas we perhaps too often take for granted with Beethoven – the use of dynamics (often there in the originating sketches) and orchestration. The wonderfully terse coda to the first movement would be nothing without the simple allure of the *subito piano* in bar 483 prefacing the *fortissimo* roar eight bars later. And how wonderfully the wind choir is used in this symphony, with Beethoven lavishing special craft and affection on the writing for flute, clarinet and bassoon. This is especially to the fore in what is the loveliest

Ex. 5. Beethoven: Symphony No. 4

of Beethoven's symphonic *adagios*. Among other things, the *Adagio* is an essay in the interplay of stillness and motion – the serene opening melody, that still unravished bride of musical quietness, made the more calm by the persistence of a rocking accompanying figure which we also meet (slightly modified) in the sublime Adagio of the second Razumovsky String Quartet, Op. 59, No. 2. It is said that Beethoven was in love with the Countess Therese von Brunsvik whilst he was at work on this symphony, and one can well believe it. A man who can dream up and then so idly forget the kind of melody that flits by at the start of the first movement development (Ex. 5) is clearly walking on air.

After the completion of the Fourth Symphony, Beethoven returned with changed perspectives to work on the unfinished symphony in C minor. Gone now is the idea of building an independent Finale on a wimpish theme in 6/8 time (Ex. 6) which Beethoven clearly recognized as a near-plagiarization from the Finale of Mozart's C minor Piano Concerto, K. 491. The miracle of the drum-based transition is now in place and, after that, a terrific march in which Beethoven promised his patron Count Franz von Oppersdorff not only three trombones but also 'more noise than 6 kettledrums and better noise at that'. The new transition to the Finale is in every respect a momentous event, whether we see it as the acting out of a revolutionary age's will to transform; or as Beethoven's own spiritual ascent from within, the moment when the composer, increasingly deaf and isolated, moves from the gloom of the mind's inner landscapes to greet with joy a daylit world of heroic action; or, more mundanely, as an exercise in the dramatic power of minor and major tonality. Certainly, it is difficult to ignore the political and philosophical implications of the passage, whatever warnings purists may give us against imposing programmes on abstract music. It is no coincidence that Classical sonata form, with its use of theme, counter-theme, crisis and synthesis is to some extent a mirror of the Hegelian dialect: an enactment in music of the transforming vision of a revolutionary age.

Ex. 6. Beethoven: Symphony No. 5

The dramatic process starts with the Scherzo's mysterious birth (Ex. 7). Berlioz described this as being like 'the gaze of a mesmerizer', but how Beethoven laboured over it, experimenting with a prolonged up-beat (Ex. 7a) and no up-beat at all (Ex. 7b) until, as Nottebohm points out, he had the right pulse and impetus with which to give the apex of the melody its most telling placement. Later, the pizzicato link to the passage on the drum takes us into a spectral, twilit world from which there seems to be no escape. Against this background, the drum sounds its repeated low C, a note so laden at this point with the feeling of C *minor* that at each new hearing all ideas of resolution are, to normal sense, more or less unthinkable (and there are some harmonically ambiguous asides on the cellos and basses to reckon with, too). Yet after a single short crescendo a proud march is launched. The C of C minor, we realise with hindsight, was also the C of C major. In the midst of sorrow there is joy, and out of despair victory springs. In a troubled world in which pain necessarily coexists with happiness, Beethoven's music rings true in ways which the great mass of people intuitively understand.

Ex. 7.

EX. 7(a)

EX. 7(b)

Beethoven's sketchbooks also reveal how manfully he laboured over the celebrated first movement, how persistently he worked on the fermatas – the held notes of the opening – until they became like tidal barriers holding back the great onrush of sound. (Wagner writes of Beethoven 'arresting the waves and laying bare the very ground of the ocean', and all this, we might add, with a very un-Wagnerian, classically-sized orchestra.) How boldly Beethoven eventually lopped off a projected array of concluding chords, leaving the coda after the final statement of the four-note motto wonderfully terse, the oboe crying out plaintively. As a movement it is both grand and economical – 'compressed like some high-temperature star' is Basil Lam's memorable phrase. Even the lyrical second subject retains a tautness; and when the music slows midway and a sublime oboe cadenza sings through the texture, the mood is heightened, not diminished. Passion and pathos become one until, with a lovely outflow of feeling, the music moves off once more on a short, singing crescendo, only to find itself transformed in the recapitulation as Beethoven subtly revises the orchestration. Drums now cast a shadow beneath the second subject before the level crotchets of that same subject release an idea that adds formidable new motor-power to the coda of the movement. Though the tension is to some extent lowered in the slow movement (inimitably direct and eloquent), this is a symphony that raises musical *concentration* to a level that no symphonist will match until we encounter Sibelius's five mature symphonies.

Meanwhile, the miraculous Sixth Symphony, the 'Pastoral', continued to ripen in Beethoven's mind. It was first performed in December 1808 in a concert that also included the première of the Fifth Symphony; but its origins went back many years. In 1803, for instance, we find a notebook entry (Ex. 8) with the kind of written annotation Leonardo da Vinci might have approved:

Ex. 8. Beethoven: Symphony No. 6

The larger the stream the deeper the note

This anticipation of accompanying figures in the 'Scene by the Brook' is complemented in the 1803 notebook by another sketch headed 'murmur of the streams'. Throughout his life, Beethoven's dedication to the countryside was absolute. Walter Savage Landor's affirmation: 'Nature I loved and, next to Nature, Art' would almost certainly have found its way into Beethoven's notebooks had he lived to encounter it. 'He loved to be alone with Nature, to make her his only confidante', wrote Therese von Brunsvik. In Vienna he once refused to take lodgings (he was an inveterate mover) because there were no trees nearby: 'I love a tree more than a man' he is said to have retorted. On his many walks round the villages of Nussdorf and Heiligenstadt where the 'Pastoral' Symphony was finally gestated and written in the summer months of 1807 and 1808 he took endless succour from the broad meadows, rocky clefts, elm-girt woodland paths, and murmuring, rushing brooks. It was a beauty that often moved him to religious fervour. The autograph manuscript of the Finale of the 'Pastoral' Symphony has on it the words (in German): 'We give Thee thanks for Thy great glory'. And, indeed, the symphony ends with a song of thanksgiving that reaches its apotheosis in an awed *sotto voce* statement of the theme – the musical equivalent of his diary entry of 1815, 'O God, what majesty there is in woods like these. In the height there is peace, peace to serve Him'.

Yet, for all these religious and potentially programmatic elements, the

'Pastoral' is never really in danger of forsaking its status as a Classical Symphony. True, there are five movements, and some imitative bird song towards the end of the slow movement; but the latter is little more than an inventive cadenza and the former is self-evidently part of – or a powerful preface to – the Finale. Moreover, the craftsmanship is unwavering. There is perhaps no finer storm in all music, yet Beethoven achieves this with a startling economy of means, restraining potential belligerents like the trombones and drum whilst at the same time exploiting to the full the sonic potential of the bass and cello sections. Conductors weaned on Strauss and Puccini often beef up the timpani part with comic maladroitness, overlooking the fact that the storm's terrific impact owes a good deal to what Beethoven has consciously omitted to do earlier. For instance, the storm's first *fortissimo* chord (bar 21) is this F major Symphony's first (and only) chord of F *minor*: an astonishing piece of strategic planning by the composer. Similarly, in the 'Scene by the Brook', the remarkable sense of leisure and the superb scoring, luminous and deep, are underpinned by Beethoven's shrewdness in first delaying and then to some extent masking the music's F major orientation. Thus the 'Scene by the Brook' forms a contrast with the first movement yet is also a continuation of it.

The reliance in the first three movements on diatonic writing and endless thematic repetition has often been remarked on. The result is a combination of unaffected loveliness, breadth, and ease of utterance. Tovey writes of a symphony that has 'the enormous strength of someone who knows how to relax'; and Sir George Grove countered any possible criticisms of Beethoven's radical approach to the subject by asserting that 'only when the sameness of fields, woods, and streams become distasteful will the "Pastoral" Symphony weary its hearers'. One of the joys of the symphony is the naïf, almost primitive, feel there is to its opening movements. The Scherzo, with its rustic jaunts and drowsing bassoonist, is a scene Bruegel might have painted, yet again what craft and musical daring there is here: the drunken lurch into the sub-mediant key of D major after a mere eight bars, the wonderful fashioning (much laboured over in the sketches) of the oboe melody that lies above that somnolent bassoon, or the electric effect of withholding the trumpets completely until the cadence of the earthy *Allegro* in 2/4 time.

Beethoven summed up the impact he intended the symphony to have when he wrote: 'The whole work can be perceived without description – it is feeling rather than tone-painting'. In other words, it is the spontaneous activity of the mind and the imagination in which Beethoven is interested; and in this he was at one with his contemporary, William Wordsworth. When Wordsworth revised his long autobiographical poem *The Prelude*, he saw more vividly than ever what Beethoven, writing his 'Pastoral' Symphony, was immediately aware of: that his art was not charting landscape or seasons or country happenings, but the interrelationship between landscape and the conscious mind. This is what Beethoven intends when he writes over the opening movement, 'Awakening of cheerful feelings on arrival in the country'. Later, in the Finale, he becomes the shepherd sharing his sense of thanksgiving and even, perhaps, feeling a slight autumnal chill, the chill of dying life, as the muted horn winds into the distance on the symphony's final page.

It was to be five years before Beethoven presented the Viennese with another symphony, the Seventh in A major; and according to his amanuensis Anton Schindler it proved to be a momentous event 'at which all the hitherto divergent voices united in proclaiming him worthy of the laurel'. ('Ripe for the madhouse', was Weber's verdict after hearing the astonishing first movement coda, but that was perhaps a minority verdict.) In some respects, the Seventh is the most remarkable symphony ever written, an elemental outpouring that, to use Tovey's phrase, is 'untranslatable'. Other symphonies exist as art-works; the Seventh simply *is*.

The key to the symphony is its unflagging rhythmic life. For Wagner it was 'the apotheosis of the dance', a description which brilliantly encapsulates the obsessive rhythmic drive which permeates the work: dactylic in the second and fourth movements, part cretic, part dactylic in the first movement, and trochaic, with dazzling inversions and variants, in the famous Scherzo. So all-powerful are the rhythms in the Seventh Symphony, they effectively dominate thematic formulation. Contrasts between first and second subjects become imperceptible, and barely matter when themes function as explosive molecules of energy. In the end, rhythm becomes an intoxicant, reminding one of Beethoven's famous boast: 'Music is the wine which inspires us to new acts of generation, and I am the Bacchus who presses out this glorious wine to make mankind spiritually drunk.'

Rhythm is not, however, the only remarkable feature of the symphony. Harmonically it is built on a massive scale with two key centres, C major and F major – both strategically remote from the tonic A major – playing a crucial role in the unfolding drama. Robert Simpson, in a memorable perception, has called them 'more like dimensions than keys' – 'dimensions' that are unambiguously laid out for us in the symphony's huge slow introduction. Simpson also points to the kind of 'progressive tonality' we don't otherwise encounter until the symphonies of Nielsen (or Mahler, one might add). The Seventh Symphony's famous *Allegretto* is in A minor, a key closer to C or F than to A major itself. After that the Scherzo is in F, with a D major Trio where A major becomes a dominant pedal as the first and second violins (antiphonally spread) drape an octave A before us like a beautiful theatrical gauze. Re-establishing A major as the home key after all this is a formidable task, formidably met by the tremendous summoning fanfares at the start of the Finale and the incredible rhythmic surge that follows them. One is reminded here of Walt Whitman's famous line, 'I sound my barbaric yawp over the roofs of the world'.

For contemporary audiences, though, it was not so much Beethoven's barbaric yawp that set them by the ears as the other-worldly pathos of the

Allegretto. In form it is not unlike the Funeral March of the *Eroica* Symphony. There is a similar march pulse, a central fugato, and a disintegrating end. That said, the *Allegretto*, as well as being quicker, is more concentrated, a *distillation* of the idea of heroic pathos. It also shares with the symphony as a whole an astonishing spareness of sound whilst at the same time seeming less stable, something Beethoven imprints in our imagination by both beginning and ending the movement with a specially poignant treatment of the chord of A minor. It is a movement that haunted Schubert for most of his working career, as, indeed, did the symphony as a whole. Schubert's 'Great' C major Symphony is the Seventh's country cousin.

Not that Beethoven required anyone else to provide a sequel to the Seventh. He did it himself: not in the unashamedly programmatic 'Wellington's Victory' Symphony – orchestral war-games, premièred alongside the Seventh – but in the ebullient F major symphony which he completed, five months after the Seventh Symphony, in October 1812. Beethoven is said to have called this his 'Little' Symphony, a plausible sobriquet until we reach the Finale which at 503 bars is the longest he had yet written. In fact, the appeal of the Eighth Symphony rests to some extent on its ability to change character depending on whose company it is currently keeping. Under the direction of an urbane *boulevardier* like Sir Thomas Beecham it can seem vital and agreeable. The *Allegretto scherzando* with its good-humoured mocking of Johann Mälzel's chronometer (forerunner of his more famous metronome) always gives pleasure, not least because of the watchmaker-like craft with which it is assembled. And the third movement *Tempo di Menuetto* can take on the air of the eighteenth century revisited. There is also a good deal of high comedy in the piece. Though the end of the first movement was originally a blunt *fortissimo*, Beethoven later added to it so that it now concludes with a wittily inconsequential statement of the symphony's opening phrase (Ex.9). It is as though a particularly garrulous conversationalist has given up in mid-sentence – Jane Austen's Miss Bates, perhaps – except that garrulity is the last thing Beethoven is guilty of in this movement.

Ex. 9. Beethoven: Symphony No. 8

That said, a rather different view of the work is taken by scholars, and by firebrand conductors like Toscanini. Hans Keller expressed this view with waspish good humour when he wrote: 'Stylistically, the Eighth Symphony is easy on the ear, especially if you don't listen to it; once you do, your mind is fully occupied with the sheer pace of structural events, of violent contrasts chasing each other'. Looked at from this perspective, the Eighth Symphony is a large-scale, albeit astonishingly concise work, that throws down a number of gauntlets (the opening idea among them) with pardonable frankness.

Such plainness, and such seeming spontaneity, was the result of much labour on Beethoven's part, as the sketchbooks reveal. In the earliest sketches the initial six-note figure – which will dominate much of the first movement – is nowhere to be seen. But its eventual emergence, quarried out of a simple downward arpeggio, is typical of Beethoven's skill in formulating an idea that is thematically cogent and rhythmically alive – so alive that it can bear the burden of launching the work without resort to the pulsing ostinato (shades of Mendelssohn's 'Italian' Symphony) which Beethoven originally had in mind. The terseness of this opening, like the swift arrow-flight of the movement's development section, is remarkable; but Beethoven the obsessive is complemented in this symphony by Beethoven the 'lunatic, the lover, and the poet'. After its abrupt beginning, the exposition makes huge strides harmonically and generates a mass of unexpected ideas – chords in cross-rhythm (bars 59 ff.), for example, that promptly yield up a delectably flowing idea in level minims and crotchets.

Beethoven's decision to replace the slow movement with a kind of scherzo and the scherzo with a kind of Minuet is itself an unprecedented act and can make a particularly powerful effect if the *Tempo di Minuetto* is given a proper weight and breadth of utterance. In his essay *On Conducting*, Wagner expresses horror at the contemporary habit of playing this movement as a quick Ländler. After hearing one Kapellmeister's attempt (approved by Mendelssohn) Wagner found himself 'staring into a veritable abyss of superficiality, a complete emptiness'. Certainly, we need something to prepare us for the symphony's consummating Finale. The idea of a symphony's weight being thrown forward to a huge Finale was not unknown pre-Beethoven. Mozart's 'Jupiter' Symphony is an example. But in the case of Beethoven's Eighth Symphony the tail is demonstrably wagging the dog, as for instance, the movement's initial motivating figure (Ex.10).

As Beethoven's sketches reveal, the little three-note figure in bar 2 is first cousin to a comparable idea in the symphony's *Allegretto scherzando*. The sketches also reveal how self-contained the initial ideas are, characteristically forceful and abrupt. But where Beethoven was happy to let this be in the first movement, in the Finale he endlessly harasses his material, expanding the first-subject group and even going so far as to throw an alien C sharp into the F major argument at bar 17 (shades of the *Eroica* first movement). And it is this C sharp that will cause havoc on all subsequent appearances. How

Ex. 10.

one identifies these appearances is something upon which commentators are divided. This 503-bar Finale has elements of both sonata form and rondo, of which the former is by far the most prominent. It also has an exceptionally powerful coda, though whether we see this as starting at bar 267 or bar 438 is a matter for debate. In practice, it is far easier to trace the course of Beethoven's argument if we follow the outline of exposition, two developments and recapitulations (91/161 and 267/355), and coda (438). In this scheme the greatest comic uproar occurs during the second recapitulation. After a shameless act of appeasement in which the wolfish C sharp is accepted as a sheep-like D flat, the wolf violently protests its true identity, at which point all hell breaks loose in a F sharp minor uproar which is eventually settled *force majeure* by the superior force of the drum and heavy brass. It is savage music serving a boisterous comic vision: a vision that confirms Susanne Langer's idea of comedy as 'an image of human vitality holding its own in the world amid the surprises of unplanned coincidence'.

Had Beethoven ended his career as a symphonist in 1814 with the Eighth Symphony his influence would have been enormous; but it was the publication of the Ninth Symphony in 1824 that changed him in the eyes of the world from a musical genius into a cultural colossus. Gustav Mahler acknowledged as much during a famous meeting with Sibelius in Helsinki in 1907 when he is said to have remarked: 'The symphony must be like the world. It must be all-embracing'. The words may have been Mahler's but, as he knew all too well, the concept was Beethoven's. (As a young man, Mahler had been seriously concerned that his own First Symphony with choral Finale, the 'Resurrection', might be taken 'as a superficial imitation of Beethoven'.) In some ways, Mahler's formula could be said to underestimate the scope of the Ninth Symphony. 'Like the world . . . all-embracing' suggests the contemplation of a single state of existence, where the Ninth Symphony appears to address several worlds: not only this one, but worlds above and below and beyond it.

How, then, did this final masterpiece come about? It was, quite simply a lifetime's endeavour, a concept glimpsed by a visionary apprentice-musician and brought to fruition after Herculean labours by a raddled master spared by his Maker just long enough to realize in music this mighty song of innocence and experience. Schiller's poem *An die Freude*, his 'Ode to Joy', which forms the basis of the Finale of the Ninth Symphony, had preoccupied Beethoven since the 1790s. On 26 January 1793 the poet's sister Charlotte Schiller received a letter about 'a young man [Beethoven] whose talents are universally praised, and whom the Elector has sent to Haydn in Vienna, who proposes to compose Schiller's *Freude*. I expect something perfect, for as far as I know the young man is wholly devoted to the great and the sublime'. Later, in 1798–9, sketches for such a setting appear in Beethoven's Notebooks. After that there is a thirteen-year interlude, though even this is not without its interest. The variations-based Finale of the *Eroica* Symphony anticipates aspects of Beethoven's method in the Finale of the Ninth, and there are even clearer hints of things to come in the wayward and provocative Choral Fantasy for piano, chorus, and orchestra, first performed in 1808. The first indication we have of a projected symphony in D minor – ominous key – comes in the wake of the completion of the Seventh and Eighth symphonies in 1812, though it is not until 1815 that the first ideas begin to be seriously explored on paper. Significantly, in the wake of the Eighth Symphony, it is the Scherzo that emerges as the new starting-point. Fugue was greatly preoccupying Beethoven at the time and we can observe the composer shaping momentous fragments: first a pair of fugue subjects, then a grander amalgamation (Ex.11a) and much later the thing itself (Ex.11b).

At one point in the sketches, Beethoven writes 'gleich', in the sense of 'immediately'; but the five-part fugal exposition does not begin immediately. In the completed work, the initial gesture (bar 1 of Ex.11a) is dispersed through eight bars down the chord of D minor, with the drum, tuned to the minor third of the chord, making its own spectacular intrusion in bar 5. Later on, in the middle of the Scherzo's development section, the drum will single-handedly drive the music into F major. No wonder the timpanist's

Ex. 11. Beethoven: Symphony No. 9

entries were greeted with cries of 'Bravo!' at the first performance in Vienna in 1824.

In 1815–17, the idea of what the English like misleadingly to call a 'Choral' symphony was nowhere in evidence. For just as Beethoven had spent time and mental effort contemplating possible routes from darkness to light during the composition of the Fourth and Fifth Symphonies, so now – though on a vastly extended time-scale – he was locked into the tragic phase of the work's creative evolution, a phase that culminated around 1818 in work on the first movement of the new symphony. 'What is now proved', wrote William Blake, 'was once only imagin'd'. How easy it is now to analyse this opening movement whose appearance in the sketchbooks resembles its effect in performance: a pre-ordained statement of ineluctable tragic power. The very opening, in Robert Simpson's phrase, is 'like the genesis of music itself'. No composer in post-Renaissance Europe would have dared contemplate such an opening before Beethoven; and none later – not even Brahms or Bruckner – quite equalled the literally terrific sense of alienation we feel at the point of recapitulation where the plunge into D *major* has us, like Milton's Satan:

> Hurled headlong flaming from th'ethereal sky
> With hideous ruin and combustion down
> To bottomless perdition.

In other respects, Beethoven owes a great deal to his predecessors in a first movement of extraordinary polyphonic complexity. Tovey, whose précis of the Ninth Symphony (*Essays in Musical Analysis*, Volume 1) is still the best blow-by-blow account of what happens in it, talks of 'the broadest and most spacious processes set side by side with the tersest and most sharply contrasted statements'.

In 1822 Beethoven set first movement and Scherzo side by side, with the Scherzo's Trio – wonderfully spacious, muddled tempo markings notwithstanding – hinting at pastoral felicity in what is now wholly uncontaminated D major. And how typical of Beethoven to bring the trombones into the texture here. In the first movement they were not needed; now they appear, serene and majestic, to add colour and sustain sonority. The sense of spiritual ascent, temporarily suspended in the Scherzo's reprise, is taken a stage further in the slow movement. The mood at the outset is one of grieving, of limitless pathos, but the spirits are lifted with the entry of the sublime alternative theme in D major, an inspiration that began life as a slow minuet as lofty as anything you will find in the works of Gluck. The sense of spiritual flowering is underpinned in this movement by the extended use of variations; and there is even room for the first time in the symphony for a touch of humour as the fourth horn (Beethoven's player, it is thought, equipped with a primitive type of valved instrument) suddenly takes off on a strange virtuoso excursion of his own.

By now Beethoven had begun to think the unthinkable: a symphony with a choral Finale. After a 30-year wait, Schiller's *An die Freude* had found a fitting context. As a poem, it does not rank as one of the masterpieces of German Romantic literature, though it was sufficiently well known for Schubert to have made a setting of it in 1815. Its appeal to Beethoven lay, not in the language or the versification, but in the ideas: 'Joy! Joy! Oh, joy thou lovely spark of God – All men shall be brothers – He who has won a tender wife – All creatures drink joy at Nature's breast – His suns speed through the glorious plain of Heaven – Brothers, above the starry heavens a loving Father must surely dwell'. It is not, then, a hymn to freedom, as some would have us believe, but a song of the cosmos driven by the human emotion of joy. (Remember the postscript to the Heiligenstadt Testament of 1803: 'Grant me at last but one day *of pure joy*'.) In order to make the transition to this unprecedented choral Finale, Beethoven re-lives with us part of the creative process. First, terror and emptiness, then the survey of movements past, their rejection, and the forging of a new idea, the famous joy theme – part hymn, part folk-tune, part symphonic subject – over which, like most things in this symphony, Beethoven laboured long and hard. When the baritone enters, he declares on Beethoven's behalf: 'Oh friends, not these sounds! Let us strike up something more pleasing and more joyful!' Beethoven wrote the words himself, freeing the symphony into song, as solo baritone and chorus, *using* the new theme, launch into Schiller's Ode.

Beethoven once said: 'I carry my ideas with me for a long time, rejecting and re-writing until I am satisfied. Since I am conscious of what I want, I never lose sight of the fundamental idea. It rises higher and higher, until I see the image of it, rounded and complete, standing there before my mental vision'. In the Ninth Symphony we have the consummation of that vision as Beethoven was capable of expressing it in a public and secular context. That it found lofty expression in other contexts – in the *Missa Solemnis* and in the private world of the late sonatas and quartets – only serves to confirm the scope of his genius. Our concern, though, is the symphonies, the traversal of that 'spiritual space' mentioned at the outset, and here the achievement is a unique one, worthy, certainly, of the accolade Beethoven unblushingly conferred on himself when he announced: 'I was Hercules at the crossroads.'

5

Schubert

Brian Newbould

Schubert's commitment to the symphony was remarkable, though it hardly impinged on the awareness of contemporary society. True, some of his symphonies were played by his school orchestra or in private 'music salons', but evidently few. Yet not only did he begin a new symphony thirteen times in eighteen years; by the crude measure of bars-per-year-of-productive-life, he was a more prolific symphonist than any other composer in the nineteenth century, including Beethoven, Dvořák and Bruckner. (This calculation excludes the fifteen movements which were left incomplete or have survived only in part.) Despite the fact that problems of one sort or another prevented him from finishing nearly half of the symphonies he began, he cherished symphonic ambitions to the last. In the early 1820s, just when he had abandoned four symphonic torsos in a row, he bounced back with the eager desire to write a 'grosse Symphonie', expressed in a letter to Leopold Kupelwieser dated 31 March 1824 and fulfilled in the years ahead as the 'Great' C major came to fruition. And although such works remained unknown to all but himself, he clearly saw them as major products of his art. Writing to the publisher Schott in February 1828, he included a list of songs he could offer for publication, but added: 'I have also written three operas, a Mass, and a symphony. I mention these only to acquaint you with my efforts in the highest forms of musical art.' Neither publication nor performance followed, yet Schubert was back at the drawing-board a few months later, in the last weeks up to his death in November, working on another symphony (D. 936A).

This attachment to the symphony dated from the boy composer's early teens. The first surviving fragment (D. 2B) probably belongs to 1811, when he was fourteen. Once the First Symphony in D had appeared in 1813, more followed in quick succession, the Sixth coming just six years later. He was not writing to meet a public demand; nor were his teachers the sort to press the claims of the symphony or to guide his symphonic thinking. Salieri, who taught Schubert at the City Seminary, where he was a pupil from 1808, was a seasoned composer in the vocal media of opera and oratorio. Michael Holzer, choirmaster at Liechtental Parish Church where Schubert was a choirboy, provided encouragement for him to produce church music, including the Mass in F of 1814. Neither was the obvious person to instruct a young composer with a flair and appetite for symphonic composition at a time when Beethoven had already produced eight of his nine works in the medium.

Where, then, did the aspiring symphonist learn his trade? He learned it directly from its leading practitioners. The works of Haydn, Mozart and Beethoven were more than enough to fire and sustain his youthful enthusiasm. He came to know these works as a violinist in his school orchestra. It was customary at the City Seminary, or *Stadtkonvikt*, to rehearse orchestral music every evening. On each occasion, according to Josef von Spaun, who was leader of the second violins, in the year after Schubert's death, a complete symphony and several overtures would be played. The youthful forces, he says, were equal to the demands of Haydn's, Mozart's and Beethoven's masterpieces. Listening to the early symphonies today, it is possible to hear Schubert learning on the job. It was an apprenticeship by assimilation, and if sometimes a theme or passage from the work of one of the three mentors figures with a touching degree of exactitude in a Schubert score, this can be accepted as a by-product of the self-help (or help yourself!) method. It should be remembered that Beethoven went through no such teenage self-education on the production-line: he was thirty before he issued a symphony, by which age Schubert had completed his Ninth. Moreover, it is doubtful whether either of Mozart's two teenage symphonies which could be said to hold their place in the repertory (No. 25 in G minor and No. 29 in A) do so more securely than Schubert's Third and Fifth.

Schubert's early confidence is astonishing, even to the reader of his fragmentary D. 2B manuscript. It is true that the nineteen bars of *Allegro* that follow the eleven-bar *Adagio* introduction owe a self-effacing debt to Beethoven's Second Symphony, which Spaun recalled as being one of the boy Schubert's favourites. But the orchestration is assured and telling, and it is evident that Schubert is composing directly into orchestral score without the use of a preliminary piano sketch. This way of composing in score, without prior work on two staves, probably served Schubert for all the first six symphonies, helping to promote both continuity of invention and a better visual perception of longer-term structure.

Evidence of creative confidence is signposted on the very first page of the First Symphony. Schubert does the Haydnesque thing of prefacing his *Allegro vivace* with an *Adagio* introduction, although as it proceeds it shows more allegiance to Mozart, and in particular to the opening of the 'Linz' Symphony. It is only when this opening returns later in the movement that the daring of its conception is revealed. Halfway through the main *Allegro* the path is being cleared for a recapitulation of its opening. When the return comes, it is not a return to the opening of the *Allegro*, but to that of the *Adagio*. Yet there is not a return to its slower tempo. Instead, Schubert writes this recapitulated introduction in notes of twice their original length, assuming that the *Allegro* will be about twice as fast as the *Adagio*. Thus the returning introduction is heard at about its original tempo, so that the listener may imagine the *Adagio* has returned. Yet one may hear it simultaneously at *Allegro* tempo, for there is nothing to contradict that interpretation. Schubert has thus engineered a reprise of a slow introduction without abandoning, as Beethoven did and Haydn before him, the faster current tempo. This new perspective on first-movement form was to have consequences in Schubert's last completed symphony, the Ninth.

The first theme of the *Allegro* combines youthful vitality with Haydnesque formality. The second subject is more overtly Beethovenian, echoing the 'Prometheus' theme used by Beethoven in the Finale of the *Eroica* Symphony as well as the 'Prometheus' ballet. Thereafter Schubert perhaps displays more fluency, even garrulity, than judgment, his boyish exuberance being reflected also in the altitude of the trumpet parts, not maintained in the later symphonies. The inner movements are more conservative. The simple, affecting *Andante* skilfully conceals its debt to the slow movement of Mozart's 'Prague' Symphony until the last seven-note phrase of the oboe, heard just before in first violins, betrays it. Of all the movement-types Schubert inherited, the Minuet is the most circumscribed by generic traditions. He is content for the time being to add a dash of Beethovenian resolve to the hearty good humour of the Haydnesque strain, without in any way disturbing the structural conventions.

The Finale offers nothing so imaginative as the re-cycling of introduction in the first-movement *Allegro*, but it trips along with carefree gait, sporting its own little idiosyncrasies. At the end of the exposition, when first and second subjects have run their course, the ear is led to believe that the whole exposition will be repeated. But Schubert has laid a false scent: he makes no such repeat. Did he at first have a repeat in mind? The autograph score yields no clue. But he could well have changed his mind at the last moment, when reflecting that his first subject-group had comprised two themes both of which had been immediately repeated, while the ensuing second subject had brought a sense of *déjà entendu* in that it is only a slightly more distant relative of Beethoven's 'Prometheus' theme than is the second subject of the first movement.

Schubert spent longer on his Second Symphony (1814) than on his First, to produce a work of shorter duration. The voluble schoolboy was already beginning to add substance to fluency. One can go some way towards explaining how his ideas acquire more character in this work by pointing to the use of well-placed accents and an increasing use of dissonance with both short- and long-term effect. At the same time, Schubert did not simply do more positively here what he had already done tentatively in the First Symphony. For a start, he abandoned the concept of a slow introduction being subtly integrated within the flow of its following *Allegro*. The introduction of the Second Symphony neither returns nor has any thematic bearing on the rest of the work. That was not necessarily a retrograde step, nor would it have seemed so to a youngster still reeling under the impact of Beethoven's Second Symphony.

Moreover, Schubert ventured a new approach to key-structure in sonata form. Specifically, this first movement brings us the first example in the symphonies of the three-key exposition, and of the subdominant recapitulation. In a three-key exposition, Schubert reaches an unorthodox key for his second subject-group and moves thence to the orthodox key (the dominant) for a third and final stage of the exposition. That is a perfectly acceptable diversification of the usual tonal structure.

In this particular movement, Schubert begins his recapitulation in the unorthodox key of the subdominant, in this case E flat major. Some critics have observed that this strategy allows him to repeat the whole exposition a fourth up without having to modify the modulation of the transition between first and second subjects. Mosco Carner went further, claiming* that in this Second Symphony the recapitulation is a literal repetition of the exposition, all transposed. In fact, it is no such thing; nor could it be, since in the exposition the second subject was not in the dominant but in the subdominant. To save labour, which is the motive Carner suggests, Schubert would have had to begin his recapitulation in the dominant. Schubert's only symphonic movement in variation form follows. Haydnesque in spirit but Schubertian in parlance, it has some felicitous touches of scoring and some affectionate flute writing. More prophetic is the Minuet, which anticipates the 'Tragic' Symphony (No. 4) in more than key. Its solid, massed wind rhythms pitted against choppy short notes in the strings, with jabbing accents here and there, bespeak a decidedly *Sturm und Drang* unease. The Second is not only the first of his symphonies in which Schubert set the minuet in a key other than the title-key of the work, after the model of Beethoven's Seventh. Schubert, unlike Beethoven, thereby produces a three-key symphony (movements I and IV in B flat major; II in F major; III in C minor), establishing a genus which – with its progeny in the Fourth, Fifth and Seventh Symphonies – is almost certainly without precedent.

The Finale is possibly the first sonata-form movement in which a composer working within a major home key sets his major-key second subject in a minor key when recapitulating it. But rhythmically the movement is no less enterprising, for it is a riot of galloping dactyls. The long-short-short pattern which launches the first theme (Ex.1) is seldom absent for long, and not absent for one bar in the marvellous development section. If a *joie de vivre* inherited from the typical Haydn finale lies behind Schubert's, what sustains it is an inexhaustible exhilaration and quality of invention personal to its composer.

---

* In Abraham, G. (ed.), *Schubert – a Symposium*, 1946.

Ex. 1. Schubert: Symphony No. 2

Hard on the heels of a symphony in which the spirit of adventure led to diversification and expansion, especially in its outer movements, came one which invokes the scale and ethos of the late eighteenth-century genre. The Third (1815) is Schubert's shortest symphony up to this point, and evidently cost him little time and effort: once the slow introduction and first few bars of *Allegro* were on paper, the rest occupied him for eight days. A Classical restraint prevails, the emphasis on elegance, suavity and polish suggesting a renewed reverence for Mozartian ideals. This is no pale carbon copy, however, of a generalized bygone model. Schubert, an admittedly impressionable eighteen-year-old (the symphony was finished in the middle of 1815), stamps his character on it from the outset by interrelating the introduction and *Allegro con brio* in a novel way. Early in the *Adagio maestoso* the violins extend their scale-ascent with repeated notes (Ex.2); the resultant idea is taken up by the *Allegro*, not as its first theme, but as a second idea in the first group – that is, as an immediate sequel to the first theme, before the modulation away to a second subject (Ex. 3). As though to acknowledge the unifying force entrusted to this passage, Schubert marks it up dynamically and precedes it with a rather bland first theme. Indeed, the appearance of the autograph score suggests that the clarinet line which we think of as the first theme was an afterthought, and that the supporting string accompaniment was once the 'theme'.

Ex. 2. Schubert: Symphony No. 3

Ex. 3.

After the delicately-scored slow movement in a transparent ternary form, the sonorous accented upbeats of the Minuet adumbrate the more disruptive cross-currents in the Minuet of the following symphony. The Trio, as relaxed as any in the pre-Beethoven age, is sung by the oboe and bassoon in string-accompanied duet throughout, such soloistic largesse being alien to the Finale, which sustains its tarantella-like energy by means of corporate zest. Homogeneity is the keynote, as Schubert develops a brand of ensemble scoring peculiar to his purpose. This racy finale needs no long development, but Schubert crowns its coda with a thrilling excursion (from and back to the home key) which was no doubt sparked off by the excursion in the first movement coda of Beethoven's Second Symphony. What Schubert learned here – that amid the long final bedding-down of the tonic key traditional and necessary to sonata form, a sudden stepping aside from and fresh clamorous return to that key can contribute to a rousing peroration – was to serve him well in the outer movements of the 'Great' C major Symphony.

Schubert should be readily forgiven the juvenile hyperbole of the epithet *Tragische* that he attached, as an afterthought, to his Fourth Symphony (1816). He was deeply affected by certain late eighteenth-century symphonies he heard and played, including those relatively rare instances in minor keys. Of all these minor-key *Sturm und Drang* works none impressed him more than Mozart's G minor Symphony. *Sturm und Drang* symphonies were concerned with the darker issues, and Schubert's choice of title was perhaps a way of drawing attention to the fact that, unlike the Third Symphony which focuses on shades of light, the Fourth peers into life's shadows: it is his *Sturm und Drang* symphony.

It is not relentlessly minor-inflected, as Haydn's *Trauersymphonie* was; nor, in its incorporation of much major-key music (two-thirds of the whole, in fact), does it embody the idea of triumph over Fate in the manner of Beethoven's Fifth. Rather, it celebrates the interplay of darkness and light, without any orderly 'programme'. But 'major = light' and 'minor = darkness' are over-simplistic equations, and in any case heavy chromatic inflections in the major can stimulate a similar emotional response to that prompted by the use of the minor, and there is an abundance of them here.

The only hint of programme manifests itself if one detects as a remote model behind the slow introduction Haydn's 'Representation of Chaos' prelude in *The Creation*, in which case Schubert's starting-point is a world without illumination. Various Beethoven sources have been identified as background to Schubert's tense little *Allegro* theme. Eventually it spawns continuous short notes, in the strings, which persist as accompaniment to the second subject, a characteristic shared by the Finale.

Schubert chooses the rare orchestral key of A flat major for his slow movement, a songful impromptu, at its best anticipating the poetic eloquence of the 'Unfinished' Symphony, but enclosing minor-key episodes which pulsate with *Sturm und Drang* tensions. Less conventional in origin are the tensions of the ensuing minuet (as Schubert calls it), for it is in the major key of E flat, oddly enough, and conveys its *Sturm und Drang* turbulence not by minor inflection but by tortuous articulation and accentuation.

Ex. 4. Schubert: Symphony No. 4

In fact Schubert would have raised no critical eyebrows by calling it a scherzo, as that is its true genre. The Trio is tuneful and regular in build, though with some poignantly expressive moments at its heart.

Schubert has thus inverted the pattern of his Second Symphony, where a minor-key minuet is contained within a major-key symphony, by including a major–key minuet in a minor-key symphony.

Schubert begins his Finale with a four-bar 'curtain', anticipating that which begins the Fifth Symphony. The first theme is a long paragraph, linked by an energetic transition to a second subject which is characterised by a heart-warming succession of fragmentary exchanges between violins and woodwind. The development is full of drama and colour, and the three Cs which are all Schubert adds by way of coda seem a rather peremptory substitute for the climactic 'excursion' which crowned the Third Symphony.

The Fifth (1816) and most popular of Schubert's early symphonies is on the face of it the most retrogressive. Having required the standard Beethovenian symphony orchestra, without trombones, for his first four symphonies, he now dismisses the trumpets and drums, as well as the clarinets and second flute, and for the remaining trim classical ensemble writes a work so eighteenth-century in scale and form that one could believe Beethoven had not written eight of his symphonies meanwhile. If one seeks proof that great music need not be innovative, here it is. The tell-tale signs of its eighteenth-century inspiration are the formal cadences marking off sections and themes, the triadic basis of many of the themes, the athletic leanness of invention as of design. But although the language is an adopted one, it is spoken with such freshness, sincerity and vitality that there is no incongruity. Aspiring to Mozartian economy and purity seems to have liberated rather than stifled the creative flow at this stage (a few months after the Fourth Symphony), and Schubert's personality shines through.

For the first time, he dispenses with a slow introduction, but the four-bar 'curtain' which opens on to the sunniest of his symphonic themes is not thematically anonymous or without consequence, for it returns later to provide material for development. Several writers, including the august Tovey, have wrongfully accused Schubert of beginning his recapitulation in the subdominant in order that the second subject may come automatically into the tonic without needing an altered transition-passage. Schubert *does* alter the transition, replacing the twelve original bars with sixteen brand-new bars. And near the close he again inserts a passage, not heard in the exposition, to provide the movement with its soaring climax:

Ex. 5. Schubert: Symphony No. 5

The first theme of the slow movement seems to derive its rich eloquence from a combination of factors; the expressive leaps of the melodic line, the warm colouring of the orchestration, the pitch placement in the lower middle range. The contrasting episode, which comes twice, offers – with the transition that leads into it – a glimpse of the modulatory magic to come in corresponding parts of the slow movements of the Seventh and Eighth symphonies. As in the Second Symphony, Schubert sets his minuet in a neighbouring minor key. This time the key is G minor, and reminiscences of the Minuet of Mozart's Symphony in that key are not hard to find, although more tangible are references to Schubert's own *singspiel* of 1813–14, *Des Teufels Lustschloss* (Nos. 2 and 5). Similarly, the Finale theme has its germ in an 1815 Schubert opera, *Die Vierjährige Posten* (Duet, No. 2). But in technique and spirit this Finale owes more to late eighteenth-century exploits in the string quartet medium, and could indeed be transcribed for string quartet without the need for too many adjustments. Yet it is a *tour de force* orchestrally – another example of superfine ensemble scoring, like the Finale of the Third Symphony. What could be more appropriate than such exquisitely-scaled exuberance to close Schubert's 'chamber symphony', written for Otto Hatwig's music salon, where the orchestra had as its nucleus the Schubert family string quartet?

The Sixth Symphony, written when Schubert was twenty-one in 1818, neither builds securely on the foundations laid in the first five nor points unequivocally to the fully mature symphonies – finished and unfinished – still to come. Broadly speaking, the Third and Fifth had achieved a superfine polish within a fairly circumscribed framework of style and scale, while the Second and Fourth had shown more imaginative daring and idiosyncratic self-indulgence. The Sixth lacks both the certainty of touch and the self-revealing rumination. On the other hand, it offers no glimpses of a brave new symphonic world waiting to be discovered, except for some tantalising, prophetic flashes of the greatness of another C major symphony towards its close. Instead it glances sideways, beyond Austria and beyond the symphony, but fails to find the conviction, the sureness of purpose that would distinguish the Eighth and Ninth as it had, within different parameters, the Fifth.

Rossini's operas had already travelled to Vienna and met with huge public success. The bold, direct, extrovert musical style of the Italian appealed to Schubert, and the Sixth Symphony is the first to reflect this. At the same time, its first movement has something of the flavour of an overture about it; if Schubert had used its slow introduction and its *Allegro* themes in an overture, posterity would not have found the ingredients miscast. This is charming music, giving delightful prominence to the wind choir, though tending to squareness of gesture. The second subject is more Schubert than Rossini, and the development could not have been conceived by the Italian. The lead into the recapitulation is done with a bold harmonic move worth recycling in the second subject of the great String Quintet of Schubert's last year. And the coda recalls Beethoven's *Leonora No.3* rather than any Rossini overture.

Prettiness is perhaps the Rossinian quality that invades the slow movement, until the all-pervasive triplets of the middle section rise to throbbing dissonances that belong north of the Alps. The Scherzo owes nothing to Rossini. Adopting the title 'Scherzo' for the first time in a symphony, Schubert seems to remember the inventor of the symphonic scherzo. In theme and harmonic disposition this movement pays homage to Beethoven's First Symphony, but in dimensions (with its fully worked sonata form and its extensive and wonderful development section) it anticipates that composer's Ninth. It is particularly disappointing that such an impressive first Scherzo should lead to a Trio – marked to be played at a slower tempo – doomed by its meagreness of material and process. The gently-paced Finale sounds more like a series of episodes than a repository of true symphonic thrust, until, about 400 bars into it, Schubert suddenly works to build up a head of steam and generate a conclusion worthy of a symphony. It is in these last minutes that he discovers something of the rhythmic drive and harmonic impetus that was later to energize the 'Great' C major Symphony.

Within a few months of the Sixth, Schubert began another symphony (D. 615), sketching it tentatively in piano score. Two movements were begun, and neither finished. For all the tuneful grace of the second fragment, which is evidently a finale, the first, after a venturesome slow introduction, fails to take wing, and one can understand Schubert preferring to begin again. This he did not do until the winter of 1820/21, when he made a start on all four movements of a further Symphony in D, D. 708A. Again writing in piano score, he began an initially impressive Allegro, left a fragment of a slow movement containing some lyrical counterpoint of real beauty, took the Scherzo and Trio to an advanced stage of composition, and had two attempts at a finale. This symphony has been orchestrated, though only the scherzo can be completed with much hope of divining Schubert's ultimate intentions. Schubert's modulatory enterprise took him to key areas beyond the reach of certain of the instruments available to him, which is presumably one reason why the work was abandoned.

Later in 1821, forestalling such problems of realizing his ideas in orchestral dress, he began a further symphony, this time working in score from the start, with no sketches. The Symphony No. 7 in E was, in one sense, finished. For every bar of a four-movement structure of some 1350 bars, at least one instrumental line was written. But only the first 110 bars were fully worked out and scored; thereafter the maximum number of staves filled is seven, but for two-thirds of the symphony there is a single line only.

The addition of trombones to the orchestra is a surface sign of a new symphonic outlook. From the start Schubert enjoys a depth of sonority far removed from the sound-world of the first six symphonies, and clearly relishes too the juxtaposition of this new richness with passages of poetic delicacy. Thus the range of expression expands, and in consequence an enlarged structural scope is required. The first movement, though it lacks the conventional exposition-repeat, outlasts any of Schubert's previous first movements, even if their repeats are taken. The Finale too is substantial, and Schubert did build in an exposition-repeat here. In both these outer movements he tried a new bonding of development to recapitulation by omitting the first theme at the point of recapitulation and giving the illusion of telescoping the two sections together.

Schubert is clearly moving towards a new conception of what a symphony should be, even if both outer movements sport Rossinian tunes. It is in aspects other than 'tunes' that this symphony charts new territory; in transitions, developments, codas – all core components of a symphonic edifice. Schubert would have needed only time and ink, but no more paper, to finish his score. But he had promised Franz Schober to join him at a country retreat to work on a new opera, and indeed *Alfonso und Estrella* occupied him for the remaining four months of the year. By then, in this period of fast stylistic development, his aspirations had probably already changed, and he was perhaps considering what sort of symphony might follow. Before the next year was out, that next symphony was begun, and itself abandoned. Although it was the fourth symphony to be left unfinished in a row, it represents the first goal towards which, if hindsight may be permitted, he had been striving during this difficult four-year period since the Sixth.

Schubert's symphonic writing declares its coming of age on the very first page of the 'Unfinished' Symphony (1822). This is not the first symphony to begin with a movement having three beats to the bar, but in earlier instances the triple time provides a framework for rhythmic vitality (Mozart 39, Beethoven 3 and 8), whereas Schubert aspires to breadth, with an *Allegro moderato* marking. At the same time he presents an unaccompanied theme deep in the bass, which, despite its initial upward striving, falls back steeply to the low point of an inverted arch. If Haydn's 'Drumroll' Symphony (No. 103) was in some way a precedent, its slow introduction beginning (after the drum roll) with an unaccompanied theme in the bass, it is a remote ancestor; for one thing, Schubert's theme inhabits the world of B minor, a key beyond the symphonic horizons of Haydn, Mozart or Beethoven, except for the B minor slow movement of Haydn's Symphony No. 46 in B major (see page 36–37).

Clearly a strong motivation took Schubert to B minor for this symphony. After all, he had to accept the special problems it created for the composition of effective brass parts – a probable reason for others avoiding the key as a basis for orchestral music. He did write a good number of songs in B minor, and as Mosco Carner pointed out they share with the symphony a broadly 'depressive' character. If we accept the correlations between musical shape and emotional purport which Deryck Cooke proposed in *The Language of Music*, we may well hear the falling fifth which initiates the woodwind theme which soon enters over the string accompaniment as being true to its depressive context. This is no dynamic opening for a symphony; at least, its dynamism is latent. As the string-accompanied woodwind theme unfolds, the dynamic potential of the supporting string texture begins to surface, and a first climax cadences *fortissimo* in the home key. This lyricism-to-drama cycle, in which the drama grows out of the lyricism, could be seen as a template for the inventive processes underlying the movement as a whole. It operates again after the famous second subject, begun in the cellos after a minimal transition, most of which consists of a long held note in the horns, gives way to complete silence for a few moments. And it initiates the powerful development section, where the opening bass theme sinks to mysterious new depths, inviting what is perhaps the most original, imaginative, and compelling span of climax-building in all Schubert.

In all of this, the mastery of orchestral resource is supreme. Indeed, one may speak of creative orchestration in two senses: Schubert exposes and exploits the timbres of instruments as never before, devising textures which seldom remind one of anything in the first six symphonies; secondly one has the impression of the orchestral sound being born simultaneously with the musical idea, an observation not in conflict with the fact that Schubert first sketched this symphony on two staves only. The first movement ends with a coda in which the opening bass theme is reduced until nothing is left of it except its minor-key ambience. There is no facile resolution in the tonic major, as in the first movement of the Fourth Symphony, but only what we have to call a tragic ending. Thus the weight of anticipated resolution (one way or another, in the major or – by way of positive non-resolution – in the minor) is thrown forwards to the later movements; not to the slow movement, which never resolves such tonal issues but traditionally shelves them by opting for a key away from the title key, but in the fourth, which always closes the tonal circle. Since the symphony is usually heard as a two-movement work, only its first movement and slow movement having come down to us, we have to suppress this expectation of a tonal resolution. Some find it harder than others to do so.

Like the first movement, the slow movement is in triple time. The tempi of the two movements (*Allegro moderato* and *Andante con moto*) are also similar – so similar as to be virtually identical in some performances. But the E major key of the *Andante* sets it apart, and the movement begins and ends in serene tranquillity. The contrasts between times are not sharp, but are appreciable. Schubert uses trombones, for the first time in a symphonic slow movement, but uses them for sonorous enrichment rather than brilliance. The first theme is preceded by a short 'refrain' (wind supported by plucked double basses) similar in shape to the theme itself but differently scored: it is as though a sepal draws away from a flower-bud before the first petal opens out:

Ex. 6. Schubert: Symphony No. 8

But when the refrain returns a few moments later to follow the theme's first phrase, it is then heard also as a varied echo of that phrase-end. If one fancies that such natural processes underlie this music, one is then tempted to hear the second subject, with its long sinuous woodwind solos unfurling above some magical shifts of key-colour in the strings, as a complete bloom opening for the sun to reveal its tints. And in the coda the tiny refrain itself finally blossoms into a complete and satisfying phrase.

For his third movement Schubert returned to B minor. He sketched a complete Scherzo on two staves, and wrote a melody line for the first section of a Trio. He also completed two pages of the orchestral score of this movement. Of the Finale there is no direct trace, yet there are several reasons for supposing that a movement used a year later as part of the incidental music to *Rosamunde* had been conceived as the Finale to the symphony, and all the reasons so far advanced for this not being possible have been discredited. The Entr'acte in question, in B minor and in sonata form, is more suited to a symphonic function than for its ultimate purpose within *Rosamunde*, which is not to say that it is an ideal finale for the 'Unfinished'. Indeed, Schubert may have discarded it on musical grounds, or it may simply have ceased to have a use when he failed to bring the

Scherzo of the symphony to a satisfactory conclusion. The whole range of speculation as to why the symphony was not finished has also been reviewed and evaluated elsewhere.*

Schubert's Ninth Symphony shares the third decade of the nineteenth century with Beethoven's Ninth and the *Symphonie fantastique* of Berlioz. The three stand as unassailable and unlike pinnacles of symphonic endeavour. Schubert's is the most 'Classical' of them all, observing the traditions which were sidestepped by Berlioz and Beethoven in different ways, one admitting a programme, the other a verbal text. Indeed the 'Great' can lay claim to being the last great Classical symphony, for all that it was conceived in the atmosphere of burgeoning Romanticism. It is the only symphony Schubert completed in the last ten years of his life, after a steady flow of almost annual boyhood productions. Seven years and four aborted symphonies after the Sixth, he had amassed a new confidence through the composition of expansive chamber works, among which he himself saw the Octet as a preparation, although the *Grand Duo* for piano duet was obviously an important building-block too.

The 'Great' owes as little to Beethoven as the 'Unfinished' does, yet Schubert's two mature masterpieces have little in common with each other either. The only echo of Beethoven, and it may well have been a conscious one, is the allusion (in the development section of Schubert's finale) to the 'joy' theme in the finale of the 'Choral' Symphony. It may be significant that Beethoven's only vocal movement is the one cited, for the 'joy' theme is one of a long line of unsung 'joy' themes in Schubert's score. No wonder these 'heavenly lengths' uplifted Schumann's spirit, for on almost every page a pure *joie de vivre* finds song-like expression. At the same time the symphony is sublimely instrumental in conception, even if it is true that the relentless patterns in parts of the Finale found the stamina rather than musical understanding of the string players wanting when the symphony was rehearsed at the Gesellschaft der Musikfreunde in 1827. (The work was not performed in Schubert's lifetime.) It is also notable for its rhythmic drive, in which respect Beethoven's Seventh – much admired by Schubert – may be a remote model. This onward rhythmic impetus is one feature that distinguishes the 'Great' from the 'Unfinished'. The 'Unfinished' adopts a leisurely gait, with three beats to the bar throughout. The 'Great' presses forward in duple time throughout, except in the Scherzo, where, however, the grouping of the bars in twos and fours becomes itself a potent shaping force; and the 'slow' movement is an undallying *Andante con moto*, full of pointed, articulated rhythms.

The term 'introduction', as defined by the practice of symphonists up to

* In the author's *Schubert and the Symphony: A New Perspective*, London, 1992, which also contains fuller discussion of all Schubert's symphonies, finished and unfinished. The author's 'realizations' of the Symphonies Nos. 7 and 10, his completion of the Scherzo of the 'Unfinished', and his orchestrations of the sketches, D.615 and D.708A, have been broadcast and recorded.

early Schubert, implies an opening section characterised by its own tempo and material, and outside the sonata form scheme of the *Allegro* to which it leads. It has to be re-defined for the 'Great'. It is true that the *Andante* opening is not part of the sonata form which begins at the *Allegro ma non troppo*, but some proportional tempo relationship between the two has to be considered, as the *Andante* theme returns to crown the coda of the *Allegro*. Moreover, this theme infiltrates all phases of the design of the sonata-allegro. Soon after the second subject has appeared, there comes a passage regarded as a *locus classicus* of the use of the trombones for hushed, theme-bearing purpose. Its topic is the second bar of the *Andante* theme (see Ex.7), recast in several arresting ways to build an end-of-exposition climax. The same motif dominates the second half of the development, with further new transformations. And the famous trombone treatment of the motif returns in the recapitulation, before the coda, at a faster tempo, goes through an extended process of climax-building in readiness for the *Andante* theme, almost complete, to bring the movement full circle in triumphant fashion. Is the *Andante* theme, then, more important than the first subject proper (that which begins the *Allegro*)? It is worth noting that Schubert changed the shape of his *Allegro* theme after he had completed the movement. It would have been inconceivable to change the *Andante* theme at that stage, so fundamental were its features to the subsequent course of the movement. Indeed there is a new balance of thematic roles in this movement, a striking innovation that develops a trend noted in the Third Symphony, which is no less germane a precedent than the First Symphony, where the introduction returned to usher in the recapitulation but invaded the *Allegro* in no other way.

Ex. 7. Schubert: Symphony No. 9

The second movement is in A minor, and begins with a little preface in the cellos and basses which is a very free pre-paraphrase of the ensuing oboe theme. A steady tread is a persistent background feature of this movement, sometimes holding the foreground. In fact, from beginning to end there is no bar in which notes are not struck on both the two main beats, but for one exception which is therefore all the more cataclysmic. A one-and-a-half-bar silence interrupts the principal climax of the movement, stilling it as with a flash of strobe lighting. A hushed pizzicato ensues, changing the harmony by one note that gives it a quite new direction. It is a moment of tense drama that Tchaikovsky could not have bettered. Yet the intimacies are hardly less eloquent – the smooth, subdued second subject in three-part texture with its freely-moving, expressive middle part, or the reprise of the first theme with delicate adornments which cast the trumpet in the role of a woodwind instrument, as it were.

For his third movement Schubert takes the germ of the unfinished Scherzo of an earlier symphony (D. 708A) and forges a vibrant, weighty new Scherzo on a scale commensurate with the rest of the hour-long symphony. Arguably Schubert leaves tradition nowhere further behind than in his Trio section. No rustic tune or courtly dance will do for him here, nor the contrapuntal wit of Beethoven's Ninth; instead, the woodwind sing in full-throated chorus, with the brass adding harmonic strength and rhythmic kick to the accompaniment of the strings. Never had such sonorous fervour filled this particular corner of a symphony.

The Finale resumes, in its own terms, the pulsating energy of the first movement. Naturally enough, the strings are chief protagonists in the rhythmic hyper-activity, and in that respect one could regard the orchestral texture typical of the outer movements of the Fourth Symphony as a distant ancestor of Schubert's scoring here. When the woodwind present their second subject (Ex. 8), the continuing triplet arpeggio patterns in the strings below – however demeaning they may seem to the players – are Schubert's vital and exhilarating means of maintaining bar-for-bar vitality while the woodwind focus on larger spans (willing one almost to hear four bars as one). Indeed, the four repeated notes that end Ex. 8 become full-orchestral hammer-blows in the coda, capping a huge build-up from nothing, in four blocks of twenty bars and more, that sets the seal on Schubert's inspirational skill in sculpting climaxes within a time-scale twice as long as that he set out with at the other end of his symphonic career.

Ex. 8. Schubert: Symphony No. 9

Until the last quarter of the twentieth century, the 'Great' was taken to be Schubert's last symphony, written in his last year. It is now known that it was substantially composed three years earlier, in 1825, with some revisions in 1826 and perhaps even in 1827, and that a further symphony was begun a few weeks before Schubert died in November 1828. Just as the 'Unfinished' gave no clue as to what kind of symphony would follow it, so the 'Tenth' moved in new directions not suggested by the Ninth, which would have remained an extraordinary achievement for a twenty-eight-year-old composer even if Schubert had completed his 'Tenth'. Schubert moved into his brother Ferdinand's apartment in Kettenbrückengasse early in September of his last year. He probably began his last symphony in October at about the same time that he began a course of counterpoint lessons with Simon Sechter, and his death on November 19 prevented him from finishing either. He had one lesson from Sechter, and sketched out three movements of the symphony score. The peculiarities of the third movement suggest that it was ultimately destined to act as a finale too, and that the symphony is therefore a three-movement one.

The work has been dated by the type of paper it was written on, but corroborative evidence is provided by the fact that the second movement was sketched on a sheet already bearing counterpoint exercises, possibly worked for Sechter, while the third movement is the most far-reaching exploration of contrapuntal technique ever undertaken in a symphonic movement, by Schubert or anyone else. Although the sparse instrumental indications include a mention of trombones, the texture clearly implies that this was not to have been a 'tutti-symphony' to the degree that the Ninth was, but would demand a more restrained hand in orchestration.

All three movements break new ground in different ways. The first movement lacks a slow introduction, but adopts a slower tempo for its development section. The slow movement combines the bleakness of 'Der Leiermann' in *Die Winterreise* (1827) with the poetry of the 'Unfinished' Symphony, whose key of B minor it shares, and has been heard as prophetic of the slenderer scores of Mahler. In shaping its desolate first theme, the oboe seems to rise with difficulty to its second note (Ex. 9), and the reduction of this step to a half-step in the coda (Ex. 9 again) is the ultimate symbol of world-weariness. The second subject, added as an afterthought when Schubert expanded the movement slightly after completing the sketch of the third movement, is one of its composer's most haunting melodic thoughts.

Ex. 9. Schubert: Symphony 'No. 10'

The contrapuntal techniques exploited in the third movement include canon, invertible counterpoint, augmentation and fugato. The final *tour de force* is the simultaneous combining of its two themes. Initially conceived as a Scherzo, although in duple time, this movement came to resemble more and more a Finale as it progressed: it is in duple time, and replaces the conventional Scherzo form (Scherzo in binary form with two sections each repeated, Trio likewise, reprise of Scherzo) with a rondo-like structure. There are vestiges of the Scherzo form, however, and more particularly of a Scherzo character, as is to be expected in a movement which was initially intended to be a scherzo. The two themes, one angular and contrapuntally supported (Ex.10), the other smooth and chorale-like over a plucked bass (Ex.11), appear to have been conceived as the themes of the Scherzo and Trio respectively, and both begin with two short repeated sections, reminiscent of the old binary modules.

Ex. 10.

Ex. 11.

Did Schubert really intend to end his symphony with this movement – a scherzo-finale? The suggestion is not as outrageous as it may seem. He did, after all, return to do further considerable work on his slow movement, as though it was worth going back because he had finished all that was to follow. And there is a precedent for a Scherzo-Finale in rondo form, though not in a symphony. Schubert would surely have known Beethoven's Piano Sonata in G, Op. 14, No. 2. There is no reason why he should not later transfer an idea discovered in the solo keyboard medium to a symphonic context. If so, a three-movement scheme would be the logical result, for Schubert as for Beethoven.

Schubert was thirty-one when he died, the amendment to the slow movement of this symphony being probably his last creative act. Blessed with Beethoven's relative longevity, he would have lived to 1854. By then Mendelssohn and Schumann had finished their life's work, Berlioz had finished writing symphonies, and Schubert could have heard Liszt's Piano Sonata and Wagner's *Lohengrin*. One can only guess what sort of symphonies he might have written had he survived to enjoy that scenario. What is not a matter for conjecture, though, is the fact that none of the symphonic endeavours of others in the second quarter of the nineteenth century ventured down the avenues Schubert had explored, unbeknown to them, in his last symphony of 1828.

6

The Symphony in Nineteenth-century Germany

Donald Ellman

The background of political unrest and discontent in nineteenth-century Germany and the changing and unstable position of the composer within society, led to musicians asserting their own individuality and originality in a quest for identity through their own work, rather than with their contemporary cultural environment. This brought about a period of great change in music and the arts, with the result that the symphony developed according to personal motivations and beliefs rather than through conformity to an evolving standard, though the great traditions of the Viennese Classical symphony were seldom out of their thoughts. There are few nineteenth-century symphonies that do not relate in some way to the symphonies of either Mozart, Haydn or Beethoven. The range and variety of this legacy, however, made it impossible to construct an ideal conception of the symphony, and allowed composers to find various starting points from which they could develop and further extend and diversify the nature of the form.

It was the Beethoven symphonies that had the greatest attention from his successors. These works had transformed the genre into a form of monumental proportions and hence, to compose a symphony became a compositional ambition of the highest order. The Romantic generation regarded them as works of inspired individual genius embracing earthly and spiritual values of a personal yet universal significance. Composers saw them as prophetic landmarks at the beginning of a new age that set a peerless example of individual self-expression. Their view of these works was not all broad-based however, but was combined with a thorough understanding of musical processes at work, some of the more obviously influential of these being the introduction of the programmatic in the *Eroica* and 'Pastoral', the hints at cyclical development in the Fifth and the thematic recalling and choral elements in the last movement of the Ninth.

In addition to fulfilling his musical ambitions, the symphony was the form through which the composer could gain public recognition and social prestige. The emergence of the symphony concert as one of the main forums for public music making reflected the popularity of and demand for these large-scale works. It was also an exciting time to be writing for the orchestra, with the development of instruments and the emergence of more disciplined ensembles. A survey of the music played at the Lower Rhine Festivals from the 1820s throws up an abundance of symphonists trying to make their mark in the genre, whose work is forgotten today; Ferdinand Hiller, Franz Lachner, Norbert Burgmüller, Julius Rietz, Carl Reinecke, Carl Czerny and Ferdinand Ries.

The legacy of the Viennese Classical symphony has led to some harsh judgement of the nineteenth-century German symphony, with the notable exception of Brahms. The disregard of such symphonists mentioned above, who were often too keen to merely copy the models of their predecessors, may well have justification. However, for those symphonists who were also immersed in the freer formal and imaginative values of the Romantic age, such as Schumann, Mendelssohn and Spohr, the earlier criteria are not altogether appropriate and it is only comparatively recently that these Romantic symphonists have received their due.

Carl Maria von Weber (1786–1826) has gained recognition in the opera house, but his two symphonies, which interestingly reflect much of his operatic expertise, are seldom heard in concert today. They were both written in the space of two months in December–January 1806/07 for Duke Eugen Friedrich Heinrich von Württemberg-Ols. The Duke, who had modelled his household on that of Versailles, had built up a small cultural utopia in the forests of Karlsruhe, complete with grottos, temples and Romantic landscapes. In patronizing the arts the Duke saw himself as the creator of a new Weimar. He was keen, therefore, to invite Weber, one of the leading musicians of the day, to Karlsruhe, to stay for a few months in the the the purely honorary rôle of Intendant. Weber was pleased to have respite from his irksome duties at the Opera in Breslau and later described his stay as a 'golden dream' creating a congenial environment for composition.

In his operas, Weber's imaginative use of instruments and instrumental colour to depict dramatic effects and evocative scenarios, created a romantic style of orchestration that was to influence composers for the remainder of the century. Naturally this style of orchestration in which, as Debussy observed, he 'scrutinized the soul of each instrument' is reflected in his instrumental works, where he also freely displays his penchant for the virtuosic and brilliant, particularly in the concertos for the clarinet and for the piano.

The two symphonies are Weber's most extended works in the purely orchestral medium. They are both in C major and follow a similar four-movement pattern. The Duke's orchestra had no clarinets, so Weber was unable to use one of his favourite instruments. This gives the orchestra the look of an earlier period, but he treats it in a very different manner, with much expressive use of woodwind and brass and a frequent emphasis on the darker orchestral colours. The *Adagio* of No. 2 is particularly striking in this respect with solos for viola, oboe, bassoon and French horn, each accompanied by different combinations of instruments, and in its final pages one encounters some of Weber's most evocative sounds with unusual scoring for horns, bassoons and trumpets.

The rich heritage of the Classical symphony, being so close in time, is inevitably reflected in these works. In the bold opening statement of No.1 Weber clearly has Mozart's 'Paris' Symphony at the back of his mind and in the Finale of No. 2 there is humour of a Haydnesque quality with continual quirky pauses and a joking final cadence bringing the work to a bright conclusion. However, these features never override the elegant, poetic character or the moments of rhythmic verve and ebullience that give Weber's music such individuality.

The qualities of Weber's orchestral writing were greatly admired by **Felix Mendelssohn** (1809–47) on whom they were undoubtedly influential. Mendelssohn's own contribution to the development of the symphony as composer and performer was prodigious. In addition to writing seventeen symphonies (including the twelve early string symphonies), he was tirelessly energetic as a conductor, for the most part of the Leipzig Gewandhaus Orchestra, reviving the music of the past and bringing the works of his contemporaries to public notice. He not only raised the playing of the Gewandhaus Orchestra to a level of virtuosity that it had not attained since its formation in 1781, but he also helped to establish the tradition of the public symphony concert in Germany, a tradition that had been slow to emerge, owing to the continuing influence of the courts and their predominant wish to maintain a flourishing, especially Italian, operatic tradition, in addition to the dearth of suitable public concert halls for the performance of symphonic music.

Mendelssohn's proficiency in writing for the orchestra was developed from his early years. In his youth his parents had been able to give him a privileged musical education, even providing him with a small chamber orchestra formed from members of the Berlin State Orchestra, that tried out his early compositions and included them in private concerts in the large Mendelssohn home in Berlin. With his thorough musical training from Karl Friedrich Zelter, a precocious talent and an insatiable appetite for study, he was able to make full creative use of these opportunities and by the age of twelve he had produced as many symphonies for strings! These lay unpublished amongst other autograph scores of Mendelssohn juvenilia in the Berlin State Library up to the 1950s when they were published and in 1971 they received their first complete recording. They are an important chronicle of Mendelssohn's early symphonic development, enabling us to observe him learning his craft and finding his own style through the absorption of and experimentation with earlier musical techniques, especially those of Bach and the Viennese Classical masters. At the same time, however, they are delightful works in their own right, filled with youthful exuberance and displaying an astonishing technical versatility and confidence in the handling of the string orchestra.

It is particularly in the last six symphonies that one can hear the young Mendelssohn gaining confidence in his handling of material and introducing individual structural devices. The first six symphonies all have three short movements where the development of themes is concise and very dependent upon fugato techniques learnt from his zealous study of Bach. The later symphonies have varying numbers of movements from one (No. 10), four (Nos. 7, 8 and 9), to five (No. 11), only No. 12 retaining the three-movement format. Mendelssohn provided two versions of No. 8, one for strings, the other for full orchestra, his earliest large scale venture into that medium. The sonata-form movements of these later symphonies are generally more extended and show a greater variety of thematic development than hitherto. The influence of Haydn and Beethoven is apparent in the motivic nature of the themes which provide great cogency and tautness of musical argument. The musical effects, covering a wide range of mood, are communicated with a youthful enthusiasm that can often be exhilarating, as for instance in the first movement of No. 7 or in the well-proportioned No. 9, one of the most successful of the set.

Mendelssohn considered the twelve string symphonies as study pieces and withheld them from publication. Though he numbered his next symphony in the autograph score No. 13, it was published in 1828 as No. 1, and it was with this work that he ventured into the public arena for the first time. The numbering of Mendelssohn's five symphonies follows their order of publication and since his self-critical attitude led him to delay publication of his 'Italian' and 'Reformation', the numbering gives a misleading chronology. The completion dates of the five symphonies are as follows:

Symphony No. 1 in C minor Op. 11 (1824)
Symphony No. 2 in B flat Op. 52 'Hymn of Praise', Symphony–Cantata
   (1840)
Symphony No. 3 in A minor Op. 56 'Scottish' (1830–42)
Symphony No. 4 in A major Op. 90 'Italian' (1833)
Symphony No. 5 in D major Op. 107 'Reformation' (1830–32)

The first performance of the Symphony No. 1 on 1 February, 1827 in the Leipzig Gewandhaus under J. Ph. Ch. Schulz, though well received, was not entirely praised by the critics; 'palpably uncertain in what is known as style', wrote Gottfried Fink in the *Allgemeine Musikalische Zeitung*. Two years later Mendelssohn set out on his first journey to England, where he presented the symphony at a concert of the Philharmonic Society in the Argyll Rooms and this time it was a triumph. On 26 May 1829 he wrote home: 'They demanded the *Adagio* da capo: I preferred to acknowledge my thanks and proceed, for fear of tediousness. The Scherzo, however, was so firmly demanded, that I had to repeat it, and after the Finale, they applauded without pause while I thanked the orchestra and shook hands, and continued until I was out of the hall.' The Scherzo on this occasion was an arrangement of the Scherzo from the string octet, substituted for the original Minuet. It was this work more than any other that paved the way for his glorious career in England, involving nine further visits. It was thus the English who gave him his first recognition. Later in his life he talked of this reception as 'having lifted a stone from my heart'.

The sonata-form first movement opens with a taut theme based upon a descending five-note motif, which is characterized by a rhythmical élan reminiscent of Weber. This motif is the focus of attention throughout the greater part of the movement and also provides the basis of the second subject, showing the young composer striving for unity of thematic effect, a musical aim he most probably learnt from his knowledge of Haydn. There are also similarities with Beethoven's First Symphony, most noticeably in the imitative presentation of the second subject between strings and wind instruments. Mendelssohn's fondness for extended codas, so frequently used to good effect in the string symphonies, is not a resounding success here and though its beginning with an extended B flat on the horns promises an interesting conclusion, the further reiteration of the opening motif creates a loss of impact.

The *Andante*, with its smoothly melodious main theme and decorative variation, shows a fluency of invention that later becomes so typical of his slow-movement style. This is well contrasted by the 6/4 Minuet, its strong emphatic rhythm characterized by notes tied over the barlines. The Trio of this movement is most engaging with an arching cantilena on the woodwind airily accompanied by broken chords shared by all the strings, followed by a mysteriously evocative passage of divisi strings, static harmonies and ominous timpani strokes, one of the highlights of the work. The Finale, with its C minor gusto and nod in the direction of Mozart's great G minor Symphony, has an energy typical of the young composer, exemplifying once more his love of fugato as a developmental device.

Mendelssohn's next symphony, the so-called 'Reformation', was written for the tercentenary celebrations of the Augsburg Confession in 1830. However, owing to the revolutionary disturbances of that year the celebrations were cancelled and so delayed the first performance until 1832 when it was given under the title 'Symphony to celebrate the Church Revolution'. It marks an advance in Mendelssohn's handling of the expressive range of orchestral sonority and also shows the composer exploring the possibilities within symphonic structure. Though the composer's judgement of orchestral effects does not always come off, especially in the last movement, with its rather bland second theme and a final peroration that tries too hard and ends up sounding merely noisy, there is, nevertheless, much to admire in this work, especially the characterful woodwind writing and the inner unity of the thematic invention that makes it an early example of a cyclic structure.

A masterly introductory *Andante* sets an appropriately ecclesiastical tone with an opening psalmodic *incipit* (the same four-note theme used in the last movement of Mozart's 'Jupiter' Symphony) spread through the orchestra contrapuntally. This soon leads to an incantatory theme on the wind in octaves, which forms the basis of the two important themes that follow almost immediately; first the famous Dresden Amen, magically stated by the strings, and secondly the opening theme of the *Allegro con fuoco*, strongly recalling the opening of Haydn's 'London' Symphony. All this material, though varied in effect, has a melodic outline that spans a fifth, a characteristic carried through to the other movements and thereby forming the basis of the cyclical integration referred to above. Once the main *Allegro con fuoco* gets going it is only the lyrical second subject that provides any respite from its strong forward momentum. The development section is particularly successful and unusually treats all the important material, including that of the introduction, in varying combinations. The Dresden Amen returns at the end of this section with awesome presence, which leads to an unexpectedly quiet recapitulation, though by the end of the movement a dramatic climax is reached.

The first movement is clearly intended to portray the Lutheran struggles with the Catholic church and it is not until the last movement, after a light-hearted Scherzo and a tuneful slow movement, that the ecclesiastical tone returns with an effective statement of the Lutheran chorale *Ein' Feste Burg* on solo flute, which emerges without a break from the slow movement. This full sonata-form movement built upon new material conveys the magisterial glories of the Lutheran church and acts as a counter-balance to the struggles and aggression depicted in the first movement. After the first performances, Mendelssohn withdrew the symphony, writing to Julius Rietz on 20 June 1838, 'I cannot stand it any longer, I would rather burn it than any of my other pieces; it should never come out'. In fact it was not published until 1868 after its revival by Rietz and Reinecke.

Mendelssohn spent the years 1829 to 1832 travelling, first to England, Scotland and Wales, and then to Italy. After his experience of the wet, wild northern landscapes, the contrast of the sunlit south inspired him to write the 'Italian' Symphony. Such was this stimulation, that he wrote the symphony at great speed, completing it in Berlin in 1832 (in comparison, the 'Scottish' Symphony took thirteen years to complete). The apparent creative spontaneity spills over into the mood of the work, which is one of his brightest, filled with a warmth and energy that recall the exhilarating style of the Octet. It was this spontaneity, perhaps associated in his mind with his dislike of the improvisatory bravura of his contemporaries, that lay at the heart of his dissatisfaction with this work and which led him, once more, to delay publication. It is a portrayal of the inner feelings roused by the sights and sounds of Italy. According to the composer a variety of impressions are depicted, from art and nature as well as from the energies and vitality of the Italian people. The work is laid out in four movements with an expressive 'Song without Words' intermezzo, written against a Minuet background, replacing the more usual Scherzo in the third movement. Thematic interrelationships between movements are not apparent, yet there is a compelling unity of mood and effect provided by the composer's understanding of the Italian temperament. Tovey describes the 'Italian' Symphony as 'the work of a young man with an energy matched only by his technical facility'.

The first movement opens in a bright 6/8 manner with an extrovert, uplifting theme promoting an energy that Mendelssohn maintains throughout the movement, the chattering momentum of which is characterized by deft imaginative orchestration. The development section introduces a new theme, which receives his favoured fugal treatment. The contrast that this theme provides is especially effective if the exposition is repeated, a feature that is all too often ignored in performance despite the addition of a lengthy twenty-three-bar first-time repeat section. As in the 'Reformation' Symphony, Mendelssohn makes a significant expressive gesture in the passage that leads back to the recapitulation; here there is an effective easing of the 6/8 thrust through the augmentation of the first subject creating a wonderful moment of seemingly non-gravitational suspension.

An *Andante con moto* in D minor introduces a darker mood. The short intoned phrase that opens the movement and the regular 4/4 tread give the impression of a religious procession, a picture that recurs in Berlioz's *Harold en Italie* and perhaps has its origin in the *Allegretto* of Beethoven's 7th Symphony. This somewhat disguised ternary form movement has some most effective scoring, particularly in the use of wind instruments, which not only adds colour, but also highlights the movement's formal structure. Eventually the movement fades away, as the procession disappears into the distance.

After the lyrical third movement, again in ternary form, the symphony closes with a vivacious Saltarello, somewhat surprisingly in the tonic minor key. Throughout his career Mendelssohn was always keen to explore the wide expressive possibilities of the minor mode. Once more this last movement displays the composer's mastery of the orchestration, an outstanding example being the manner in which he controls the extended crescendo that forms the development section.

The mood of the 'Scottish' Symphony, like the landscape that inspired it, is in sharp contrast to the 'Italian'. The initial inspiration for the work came from a visit to Holyrood palace in July 1829 and he worked on it over the next two years, but, after the exhilaration of his Italian journey, he wrote to his family in March 1831: 'Who can wonder that I find it impossible to return to my misty Scottish mood? I have therefore laid aside the symphony for the present'. The Scottish misty mood did not return until 1841. The work was completed the following spring and dedicated to Queen Victoria.

At the head of the score Mendelssohn instructs the performer to allow the movements to follow on from one another without a break. In this way the composer felt that the contrasting moods of the four movements would be shown to best advantage, and that a greater sense of overall structure would be communicated. Schumann commented upon the unity of the score in his review of the work: 'Mendelssohn's symphony is distinguished by the intimate connection of all four movements ... more than any other symphony it forms a closely interwoven whole'.* This feeling of unity is helped by thematic relationships primarily brought about by the recurrent use of the rising fourth first heard in the introductory theme. This introductory theme appears again in modified form in the coda to the Finale. Overall, this is a more ambitious work than the 'Italian' symphony, composed on a grander scale and containing some of Mendelssohn's finest orchestral writing.

The work opens with an elegiac introduction, where an outstanding feature is the poignant sense of isolation created by expressive unaccompanied lines for unison first and second violins. The *Allegro* that follows is orchestrated with great skill providing a heavy sombre atmosphere which is further emphasized by the squareness of rhythmic gesture. It is a consistent and unified mood picture with evocative pedal points and expressive modulations. Especially memorable are the counter-melody played by the cellos against the main theme in the recapitulation and the inspired return of the introduction at the end of the movement.

The following Scherzo, unusually in full sonata form, brings a lightening of mood and colour. The opening theme is based upon the pentatonic characteristics of Scottish folk-music which is treated in a delightfully discursive manner against the background of bubbly semiquavers. The following *Adagio* is a noble, sustained movement, rich in Mendelssohnian sentiment, which, as many commentators have pointed out, bears resemblances to the *Adagio* of Beethoven's 'Harp' Quartet, Op. 74. Mendelssohn describes the Finale as an *Allegro guerriero* on the title-page of the score and later indicated that he wanted the final coda to sound like a 'male choir'. This suggests that the composer had programmatic intent, which the listener today can assume as being some form of battle which culminates in a triumphant song. This is one of Mendelssohn's strongest finales, with a turbulent main theme, some wonderfully light fugato development leading to a powerful reprise and some subtle suggestions of bagpipe drones in the beautifully quiet sustained moments before the hymn-like coda turns to A major with a genial transformation of the symphony's opening idea.

Mendelssohn's Second Symphony, 'Lobgesang', is a symphony-cantata which was his contribution to the quatercentenary celebrations of the

---

* H. Pleasants, *The World of Robert Schumann*, London, 1965, pp. 180–182.

invention of printing in 1840. It has an superficial similarity to Beethoven's
Ninth, with three instrumental movements followed by a nine-part cantata
for chorus and solo voice, though in effect the extended nature of the cantata
reduces the three orchestral movements to the role of a prologue. This
work represents his most concerted effort at cyclical structure, the opening
motto, intoned by trombones, recurring like a leitmotif throughout all four
movements.

Robert Schumann (1810–1856), unlike his friend and contemporary
Mendelssohn, did not complete his First Symphony until later in his career
in 1841. In 1839, Clara Schumann wrote in her diary, 'I believe it were best
if he composed for the orchestra: his imagination cannot expand sufficiently
on the keyboard. . . . His compositions are all orchestrally conceived, and I
believe incomprehensible to the public for this reason, for the melodies and
figuration are so intermingled that it is very difficult to hear the beauties of
the work. . . . My highest wish is that he should compose for orchestra –
that is his field! May I persuade him to enter it'.

For the first twelve years of his composing life from 1828, he had devoted
his energies to writing almost solely for his own instrument, the piano, with
only the occasional foray into other media, one of the most notable being
the early Symphony in G minor of 1832, of which we only have three
movements. He devoted 1840 entirely to the composition of songs, but
in the following year, in a spate of feverish compositional excitement, he
produced the greater part of his orchestral output: two symphonies (No.
1 in B flat major, the 'Spring' and the first version of No. 4 in D minor,
revised in 1851), the *Overture, Scherzo and Finale* in E major and the first
movement of the Piano Concerto in A minor. Over the next ten years he
produced two further symphonies, No. 2 in C major (1845–46) and No.
3 in E flat major, the 'Rhenish' (1850).

Robert Schumann had spent the greater part of his youth enthusing over
the literature of his Romantic contemporaries, especially the writings of Jean
Paul Richter and E. T. A. Hoffmann, whose work he alluded to in many of
his piano works such as the *Abegg Variations*, Op. 1, *Papillons*, Op. 2 and
Kreisleriana, Op. 16. The richly-textured sonorities of his piano writing
strongly suggest the dark, mysterious world of North German Romanticism
with which he was so involved and, as Eric Sams demonstrated in a
fascinating series of articles in the *Musical Times*, Schumann was able
to transfer his interest in the literary to music through the cunning use
of musical ciphers, thereby suffusing his textures with cryptic literary
suggestion.

Whilst the richness of texture is generally accepted as an essential
ingredient of the Schumann sound world in his piano works and indeed
provides an constant source of interpretative delight to pianists and listeners
alike, Schumann has come in for a considerable amount of criticism for the
transference of this sound world to the orchestral medium, in particular for
the thick textures brought about by unnecessary doublings of instruments

and a generally insecure handling of the orchestral palette. The apparent deficiencies in orchestral technique led Gustav Mahler, who greatly admired Schumann's music, to re-orchestrate all four symphonies. Mahler cleaned up the orchestral sound but in doing so he also changed the music's essential character, removing it from the mysterious, half-lit world of North German Romanticism to a much sunnier world that too often seems incompatible with the musical content. The ineffectiveness of Mahler's re-orchestrations shows that the materials of these works and their means of expression have a vital interdependence that should not be tampered with. Moreover recent performances on period instruments has shown that there is really very little wrong with Schumann's sound world.

The First Symphony was sketched with great fervour and speed in four days; 23 to 26 January, 1841. The full score appeared on 20 February and the first performance took place on 31 March in the Leipzig Gewandhaus, conducted by Mendelssohn. This great burst of Schumann's creative energy was most probably brought about by the excitement of his recent marriage to Clara together with her urging him to write for the orchestra. The symphony was inspired by a poem about spring by Adolf Böttger. Schumann comments in a slightly enigmatic manner upon the writing of this symphony in a letter to Spohr dated 23 November, 1842: 'Description and painting were not part of my intention; but I believe that the time at which it came into existence may have influenced its shape and made it what it is.' His desire not to be purely descriptive perhaps influenced him to withdraw the titles he originally gave the four movements: 1: 'Spring's Coming', 2: 'Evening', 3: 'Merry Playmates', 4: 'Full Spring'.

Schumann wished the opening brass fanfare of the introduction to sound 'as if from on high, like a call to awaken'. The importance of this figure to the symphony is fundamental, generating the main material of the following *Allegro molto vivace* as well integrating the rest of the work, the rising three-note figure *a* recurring in most of the thematic material of the other movements. Schumann used the motivic unifying device more thoroughly in his Fourth Symphony.

Ex. 1. Schumann: Symphony No.1

The introduction leads into the *Allegro molto vivace* by means of an *accelerando* – a favourite device of Schumann's for whipping up energy.

This sonata-form movement becomes one of his most infectiously ebullient creations, where the dotted rhythm of the main theme is tirelessly developed through repetition and sequences. A gently urging second subject contrasts the main rhythmical thrust of the movement delightfully, but this does not delay for too long the vigours and energies of the movement as a whole reaching a glorious climax, where the opening fanfare resounds in its original tempo through augmentation of the *Allegro* note values. Schumann closes this movement unexpectedly with a new melody of great lyrical warmth. The closing of a structure with new material was a technique that he frequently used in his songs and its use at the end of this movement suggests his thoughts were not far from the genre he had found so rewarding the previous year, and introduces a significantly romantic gesture into the development of symphonic structure.

The noble, twenty-four bar *cantabile* tune played by the violins which opens the slow movement, once more shows that Schumann's thoughts were not far from his songs. This melody is restated first by cellos and then by a solo oboe, each statement displaying the variety of Schumann's orchestral imagination. This movement leads directly into the Scherzo by means of one of the many imaginative transitions to be found in the symphonies, with the trombones, which have been silent throughout the movement, solemnly forecasting the main theme of the Scherzo. This is another Romantic gesture, that blurs the edges and formalities of inherited classical structures.

The D minor Scherzo bursts forth with sturdy syncopated rhythmic character. Schumann introduces into this movement two contrasting Trios, the first in D major in 2/4 time and the second in B flat major where he makes much use of canonic devices. The ABACA structure of this Scherzo is a derivation of rondo form and it appears here for the first time at this point in a symphony. Schumann may have been influenced by Beethoven's repetition of the Trios in the Scherzos of his Fourth and Seventh symphonies. The last movement reflects the triumph of spring, which like the first is characterized by great rhythmic ebullience and creates a dancelike grace in the lightly tripping quaver motion of the main subject. An unusual feature of this movement is the flute cadenza that appears shortly before the recapitulation, boldly introduced by a rising horn figure.

Despite a few alarms in rehearsal about the appropriateness of the orchestration, especially with regards to the opening fanfare, the First Symphony was an instant success, no mean achievement for his first major work for the orchestra. Two months later in May, he was at work on a second symphony in D minor, which he presented to Clara on her birthday, September 13. It did not, however, receive the same accolades as the 'Spring' Symphony at its first performance in December, maybe because in Mendelssohn's absence it was conducted by Ferdinand David, whom Schumann found less than adequate. This unsatisfactory experience led Schumann to lay the score aside until December 1851 when he decided to revise and rescore the work for one of his Düsseldorf concerts. In his revisions Schumann was primarily concerned with the orchestration, thickening textures and underpinning important lines by what many consider to be unnecessary doublings. The revised score, which became his Symphony No. 4 in D minor, received its first performance in December 1852, and it is this version that is generally played. Brahms, who preferred the less congested scoring of the original, persuaded Breitkopf and Härtel to publish the score and parts of the earlier version in 1886, which has enabled it to receive an occasional performance today.

In the Fourth Symphony Schumann created one of his most unified and satisfying structures. His original intention was to compose a 'Symphonic Fantasy', the single movement concept of which was carried through to the symphony, where the four movements are to be performed *attacca*, and whose material is unified by the recurrence in each movement of a thematic idea first stated in the noble introduction.

Ex. 2. Schumann: Symphony No. 4

The derivations from this material may be traced as follows:
The first movement:

Ex. 3.

The second movement:

Ex. 4.

The third movement (inverted form):

Ex. 5.

The fourth movement:

Ex. 6.

The wide range of moods in this symphony – the passionate nature of the opening movement, the wistful reflectiveness of the slow movement (where some of Schumann's most delicate orchestration can be heard), the vigorous striving of the Scherzo and the exuberant energy of the Finale – are not only brought together through organic unity of the melodic material, but also through Schumann's subtle control of musical momentum especially during the connecting transitional passages. The transition from the Scherzo to the Finale, for instance, produces some of Schumann's most inspired writing with an almost religious intensity created by hushed tremolo strings, solemn chorale-like brass, the gradual emergence of Ex. 6 and the excited fanfares on the wind. The Finale is exhilaratingly concluded by a fugato *Presto* that is reached by a well-gauged *accelerando*, a favourite device used at the conclusion of all the symphonies and perhaps most effectively in this instance.

Schumann started the Symphony No. 2 in C major in December 1845 shortly after his first serious nervous breakdown. He considered his work on the symphony therapeutic, helping him to return to health and a period of emotional stability. Despite his recent ailments, this symphony, like the 'Spring' Symphony, was sketched at great speed between 12 and 18 December. What must have been extremely intensive work took its toll, however, and he was only able to complete the score in October of the following year and in November it received its first performance in Leipzig with Mendelssohn conducting.

Schumann commented that the first movement was full of the fight against his illness and indeed it has a strong sense of Beethovenian struggle. The style, especially in terms of the presentation and development of material, is more obviously classical in outline than his previous symphonic work. In addition, Schumann's recent studies of J. S. Bach are evident in his abundant use of contrapuntal textures throughout. This is clearly in evidence in the first movement's introduction, a beautifully sustained passage of sombre mood. This introduction opens with a 'motto' theme of rising and falling fourths and fifths, which reappears at the ends of movements one, two and four.

In the following *Allegro ma non troppo* Schumann again shows his fondness for dotted rhythms, but in comparison to the exuberant fervour that builds up in the first movement of the 'Spring' Symphony, his development of this dotted figure lacks an overall sense of musical direction and is inclined to run a little dry. The second subject, based upon a subsidiary theme from the introduction, has a restless energy and contains some characteristic chromaticism and it serves to bind the development section together effectively.

Schumann, perhaps once more following Beethovenian models, places the Scherzo second. Here, the dark moods of the first movement are largely forgotten and the violins play a virtuosic perpetuum mobile in a somewhat Mendelssohnian manner. Again Schumann delights in using two contrasting Trios, each providing apposite relief from the incessant semiquaver motion. In this movement Schumann regains some of the verve that seemed lacking in the first movement and it whirls effectively to an exuberant ending. The yearning melancholy of the wonderful slow movement probably reflects a mood he experienced all too frequently in his illness of 1845. The scoring of this movement is impeccably transparent, and displays some novel effects such as high climactic string trills that accompany the final statement of the tune in each of the movement's two main sections.

The Finale is the most extended movement of the four and the longest of all his symphonies. In a letter to D. G. Otten who was preparing a performance of the work in Hamburg, Schumann stated that it was while composing this movement that he started to feel more fully himself and this is borne out by its general energetic character. The music seems to suggest that he has come through tough times, the restatements of the opening 'motto' and the main theme from the slow movement seemingly jogging the listener's memory of the less happy days of the previous movements, all of which enables the composer to provide a dénouement of the drama and a psychologically satisfactory conclusion to the work.

In 1850 Schumann moved with his family to Düsseldorf to take up the conductorship of the Düsseldorf orchestra, a position that Ferdinand Hiller had vacated the year before. This move inspired him to further orchestral composition and by the end of the year he had produced a cello concerto and the Symphony No. 3 in E flat, which received its first performance under the composer's baton in February the following year. The move to Düsseldorf had brought Robert and Clara great contentment and they spent much time exploring the environment, including a memorable trip down the Rhine, where the Gothic majesty of Cologne Cathedral made a profound impression on him. The new symphony, spread on a grand scale over five movements, was written in buoyant mood and expresses his excitement over his Rhenish experiences with vivid intensity.

For the first time in his symphonic work Schumann dispenses with an introduction and opens the first movement with a long soaring theme, which bursts in seemingly as if he could no longer contain his pent-up energies. The first six bars of the first subject, with their hemiola effect of twos against threes, provide a restless, surging momentum that dominates the greater part of the movement. It takes some ninety bars for the initial thrust to die down, relieved by a neatly turned, lyrical second subject, whose stay is relatively shortlived. Both subjects are tightly interwoven in the development section leading to a glorious climax at the recapitulation where the first subject is stated on four unison horns over a tonic six-four chord. Overall, the movement has an irresistible symphonic sweep which, with its masterly understanding of the nature of the material, make it one of Schumann's most outstanding sonata structures.

The exuberance of the first movement gives way to a folksong-like simplicity in the next two movements. The second movement, though marked Scherzo, shows none of the customary characteristics of that form and is much closer to a *Ländler*, and the third movement is a graceful, song-like intermezzo where Schumann seems to be turning back to the homely world of *Kinderscenen*.

At the heart of this symphony is the fourth movement in E flat minor, one of Schumann's most outstanding miniature tone poems. The movement originally bore the inscription 'In the manner of an accompaniment to a solemn ceremony', the ceremony being the elevation to the Cardinalate of Archbishop Geissel of Cologne in 1850, at which the composer was present. Schumann's study of Bach is reflected in beautifully controlled polyphonic writing which Tovey went so far as to describe as 'one of the finest examples of ecclesiastical polyphony since Bach'.* The effectively layered scoring of this movement, especially for the brass instruments, creates an awe-inspiring religiosity and conjures up the Gothic grandeur of Cologne Cathedral. To turn from this movement to the last one is like stepping from the sombre atmosphere of a religious ceremony to the busy sunlit world outside. Though often considered to be the weakest movement of the five this is nevertheless one of the most rewarding and thematically inventive movements of the

* D. Tovey, *Essays in Musical Analysis*, Vol 2, Symphonies, London, 1935, pp. 53–56.

four symphonies. In a subtle and at times witty manner Schumann makes reference to material from previous movements. The whole symphony demonstrates a thematic continuity, deriving in particular from the figure of a rising fourth and falling second which saturates the 'cathedral' movement but makes its presence felt throughout the work.

None of the ten symphonies of **Louis Spohr** (1784–1859) find a regular place in concert programmes today. This neglect belies the esteem in which he was held during his lifetime and for the remainder of the nineteenth century. During the 1830s and 40s he was considered to be one of the dominant forces in German music, admired and respected by Mendelssohn, Chopin, Schumann, Brahms and Wagner among many others. Critics compared him favourably to his great Viennese forerunners, and his operas were compared to Weber's and show undoubted influence on Wagner. Posterity has indeed been hard on him, yet a study of his work as a composer, performer and writer are essential to an assessment of early nineteenth-century music. Keenly responsive to the spirit of his time, Spohr's music reflects many of the features that were important to the Romantics: a leaning to the literary and pictorial, a quest for the innovative and original, a delight in the virtuosic, a strong lyrical sense and an emotive use of the harmonic language through expressive use of the chromatic scale.

The demise of Spohr's popularity may well be due to the nature of his musical personality, which, next to his more extrovert contemporaries, is more conservative and subdued. In addition, much of his music has an eclecticism that is not always synthesized into a stylistic unity. However, an extended acquaintance with his music, a chance that is so little given to us today, shows a musical voice of some individuality and distinction.

Spohr's symphonic output ranges over the best part of half-a-century:

Symphony No. 1 in E flat, Op. 20, 1811
Symphony No. 2 in D minor, Op. 49 1820
Symphony No. 3 in C minor, Op. 78 1828
Symphony No. 4 in F major, Op. 86, 'The Consecration of Sound', 1832
Symphony No. 5 in C minor, Op. 102, 1837
Symphony No. 6 in G major, Op. 116, 'Historical', 1840
Symphony No. 7 in C major, Op. 121, 'The earthly and spiritual in mankind' 1841
Symphony No. 8 in G, 1847
Symphony No. 9 in B minor, Op. 143, 'The Seasons', 1853
Symphony No. 10 in E flat, Op. 156, 1857, unpublished

Unusually, there is no recognizable development in his handling of the form. In fact Symphonies 6, 8 and 9 display a distinct decline in freshness and inspiration, perhaps, as many commentators have suggested, due to their overreliance on programmatic elements. Each symphony shows Spohr experimenting with and stretching the boundaries of symphonic form. When this adventurous nature is harnessed to purely musical development the results are often most rewarding and effective and only in Symphonies 4 and 7 does he manage to direct the stimulus provided by a programme to really pertinent musical effect. Significantly both these symphonies work well with or without a knowledge of the programme.

Though there is an innovative spirit in Spohr's writing, he never loses sight of his Classical predecessors, especially Mozart. This is most noticeable in his melodic style that is frequently characterized by a flowing lyricism that has at times a Mozartean eloquence. His melodies often give an impression of length, but on closer inspection are usually made up from small motivic units, as in the first subject of No. 3:

Ex. 7. Spohr: Symphony No. 3

The nature of Spohr's melodic writing inspires extended forms of development rather than taut dramatic argument based on short contrasting ideas. His concern throughout the symphonies is for thematic homogeneity especially within his sonata-form structures. This is exemplified in the first movement of the Third Symphony where Ex. 7 appears again as the second subject with a varied continuation. A further study of Ex. 7 reveals other notable stylistic features such as a delight in chromatic embellishment both harmonic and melodic, a contrapuntal fluency that is always interesting and beautifully balanced and a love of flowing compound time.

The Third is one of the most successful of his non-programmatic symphonies. After the chamber-like sonorities of his Second Symphony, the Third shows a greater richness of orchestral sonority, which, combined with an urgency of melodic and rhythmic style, imbues the work with a Romantic spirit. Spohr seldom creates a sonata-form structure without introducing a novel feature and in the first movement of this work he reuses the sustained introduction as his development in a rearranged 6/8 format, which has the effect of throwing greater emphasis on the recapitulation and coda, where, with additional chromatic restlessness the movement reaches an effective conclusion. The *Larghetto*, thematically linked to the opening of Ex. 7, is characterized by a typically long-drawn melody that was greatly appreciated by his contemporaries, though perhaps to modern ears it is of a rather meandering nature. The second subject of this movement displays some interesting orchestration, with unison violin, violas and cellos, accompanied by the rest of the orchestra. After an engaging Scherzo and Trio, the work concludes with a full sonata movement, which like the first movement derives from a minimum of material, and in the development section he introduces fugue, displaying his love of the contrapuntal; like Mendelssohn, Spohr had great admiration for Bach, and conducted several performances of the *St Matthew Passion* in the 1830s.

Throughout these symphonies one marvels at Spohr's controlled, imaginative use of his orchestral forces. His experience as a conductor gave him an extensive knowledge of instrumental capabilities and the nature of orchestral sonority, which, together with his delight in unusual, innovatory effects, makes him one of the most interesting orchestrators of the nineteenth century. Nowhere is this better seen than in the Fourth Symphony. This work, entitled 'The Consecration of Sound', is based upon a poem by Carl Pfeifer. The poem describes the effects of sound in nature and its power to transform the condition of man. Spohr retains the four-movement pattern, but he modifies the internal structures as required by the dictates of the poem. In the first movement, after a typically long, expressive first subject, delicate semiquavers on the strings, depicting breezes, lead to evocative, bird-like phrases on brass and wind of almost Messiaenic realism. This passage forms the second subject, unusually distinguished by its sound rather than by melodic contour. This pastoral scene gives way to a dramatic storm, forming the development section, and using entirely new material; the storm effectively subsides in the coda. The slow movement demonstrates the role of music as lullaby, dance and serenade, each having their own theme (the lullaby in 3/8, the dance in 2/8 and Serenade in 9/16), orchestrated with a chamber-like simplicity and with telling solos for the clarinet (lullaby) and solo cello (serenade). These three themes eventually become ingeniously combined, creating some intriguing polymetric effects. The third movement is a march and the Finale, in a somewhat Mendelssohnian manner, is a Chorale Prelude, based upon an *Ambrosianischer Lobgesang*, again displaying the composer's fondness for contrapuntal forms.

During the 1850s and 60s the ideals, stemming from the Beethovenian models, of the symphony as the 'grand form' in which composers tried to reach the utmost limits of their art became subsumed in the pursuit of the programmatic through the symphonic poem, inspired by the progressive ideals of the 'New German School'. It was not until the 1870s with the symphonies of Bruckner, Brahms, Tchaikovsky and Dvořák amongst others that the form could be said to have continued its development. To the upholders of the Classical ideals this fallow period was considered critical in the development of symphonic form, though ironically it was Beethoven's introduction of programmatic elements, continued by Spohr and Berlioz, that had led to its apparent demise. Meanwhile two composers who continued to produce symphonies almost entirely of a programmatic nature were **Joachim Raff** (1822–1882) and **Franz Liszt** (1811–1886).

Raff spent the years 1850–56 in Weimar and for the first four years of that period was one of Liszt's closest colleagues. Liszt had invited him to help in the preparation of his orchestral scores, the techniques of which the master had little experience. It was Raff together with the experience of conducting the court orchestra that helped Liszt find his orchestral feet. Raff soon fell in with a number of other young musicians, including Bülow, Cornelius, Reubke and Draeseke (a composer of four symphonies seldom heard today), who felt that it was with Liszt that the future of music lay. This group under the master's leadership became known as the the the 'New German School', who were intent on looking to the future of German music. The musical consequences were far-reaching, bringing about the extension of harmonic language through increased chromaticism, the development of new forms, the exploration of new orchestral sounds and a renewed interest in bringing the art-forms together.

Raff wrote eleven symphonies between 1864 and 1883, all of which, with the exception of Nos. 2 and 4 have titles. Apart from No. 5, based on Bürger's 'Lenore', and No. 6, which has the extravagant motto 'Gelebt, gestrebt, gelitten, gestritten, gestorben, unworben' on its title-page, the others celebrate nature, such as No. 3, *Im Walde* and No. 7, *In den Alpen*. The Symphony No. 1, 'To the Fatherland', was awarded the prize of the *Gesellschaft der Muscarine* in Vienna and success followed him through his productive life, and he became highly esteemed throughout Germany. In 1875 Ebenezer Prout wrote, 'Among living German composers there are three, who, by common consent, are admitted to stand in the front rank. ... Many of my readers will anticipate me when I name as these musical chiefs – Wagner, Brahms and Raff'. However, time has not justified such a claim and his music faded abruptly from popularity after his death. What fame he has today rests on his collaboration with Liszt at Weimar and a few salon piano pieces. Raff's symphonies are written on a grand scale – the First Symphony, for instance, lasts some seventy minutes in performance. Although there is much delightful orchestration and a homely, fluent melodic style, the nature of the material does not always warrant such extravagant treatment, and though the programmes help to focus attention, interest in the extended structures can often flag. The Symphony No 5 in E major, which has received a few performances since his death, and a recording, is one of his most successful symphonies, containing many passages of great strength, where his breadth of gesture is effectively matched by a mature control of the harmonic pulse in a late Romantic style. It is a symphony that does not deserve its neglect, and in the history of the genre stands as a most important pivotal work between early and late-romantic styles.

The 'Lenore' Symphony is based upon an eighteenth-century ballad by Gottfried August Bürger. Lenore's lover, Wilhelm, has gone to war, but he does not return after battle, which leads her to despair and to blaspheme, proclaiming to her mother, 'What is salvation, mother? What is Hell? Salvation is with Wilhelm; without him is but hell'. That night a mysterious rider on a charger appears who carries her away and after a furious ride comes to a graveyard at cockcrow, when the rider reveals himself as a skeleton, the charger vanishes in flames and phantom spirits dance around her, intoning 'Forbear! forbear! though hearts should break, Blaspheme not, lest God's wrath thou wake, Thy body's knell we toll, may God preserve thy soul!'. The symphony falls into three parts entitled 'Happiness in Love', 'Parting' and 'Reunion in Death'.

The opening two movements, an extended sonata-form *Allegro* and an *Andante quasi larghetto*, make up the first part. The jubilant *Allegro* is based upon a typically extended first subject where sequence, a device that Raff loved, plays an important part – it is found again in the gently yearning second subject. The frequent repetition of material in this movement is effectively brought to life by much variety of instrumentation and imaginative interchanging of instrumental roles between the main part and accompaniment.

The highlight of this work is the sublime *Andante*, an impassioned love scene. It is in this movement that one is fully able to understand the contemporary admiration of Raff's work and his identification with the 'New German School'. Here there are strong portents of what is to come later in the century, with writing that combines a Brucknerian breadth and dignity with an almost Mahlerian stringency. Raff controls the pacing of the movement with consummate mastery and with particularly lovely writing for the strings. The expressive contour of this movement is in a arch form, with the climax reached in a passionate central section in A flat minor.

The content of Bürger's poem is more explicitly portrayed in Parts 2 and 3 of the symphony. Part 2, representing Wilhelm's departure for battle, is a march containing a neatly turned, dotted tune, and Part 3 is entitled 'Reunion in Death', an extended movement which unlike the previous movements takes its form more from the programme than from a purely musical development. The early part of the movement is a picture of Lenore's anxiety for her absent lover and abounds in reminiscences of material from previous movements invested with anguished expression. This process is clearly derived from Beethoven's Choral symphony, a technique Raff also used in his Fourth Symphony. The greater part of the movement depicts the horrible midnight ride which eventually collapses after further reminders of the second movement and closes with a hymn of the spirits. The composer-conductor Bernard Herrmann went so far as to say, 'The *Lenore* Symphony is one of the finest examples of the Romantic Programme School – it deserves a place alongside the *Symphonie fantastique* of Berlioz, the *Faust* Symphony of Liszt and the *Manfred* Symphony of Tchaikovsky.'*

Liszt's *Faust* and *Dante* symphonies, together with twelve of his thirteen symphonic poems (*From the Cradle to the Grave* was written in 1881–2) were all written during his Weimar period (1848–1860) and sum up the avant-garde spirit of the times. The two symphonies cannot be considered as symphonies in the ordinary sense, but are better described as extended symphonic poems. Though the earlier nineteenth-century symphonists previously discussed, such as Spohr, Mendelssohn and Schumann, incorporated some cyclical transformation of themes in their works, it was Liszt who allowed thematic transformation sufficient freedom to generate new formal structures, the techniques of which he had usefully developed through his long experience of improvisation at the keyboard.

The Faust legend haunted Liszt for most of his career from 1830, the year in which Berlioz introduced him to Goethe's *Faust*. He started sketching the symphony in the 1840s, but it was not until the 1850s after further inspiration from Berlioz with a performance in Weimar of his *Damnation of Faust* that Liszt found the stimulus to finish it. Eventually the symphony was completed at great speed between August and December 1854 and first performed in December 1857; it was, not surprisingly, dedicated to Berlioz. However, Liszt continued to revise it, producing a new score in 1861, and adding a further ten bars to the second movement as late as 1880.

* In Edward Johnson's sleeve notes to Herrmann's recording of the symphony, UNS 209, 1970.

The full title of the work is *A Faust Symphony in three character studies (after Goethe): 1. Faust; 2. Gretchen; 3. Mephistopheles.* In a previous character study, his symphonic poem *Hamlet,* Liszt showed acute sensitivity to the portrayal of human nature, through his imaginative use of chromatic harmony and evocative orchestral textures. In the *Faust* Symphony, by representing different character traits thematically and by elaborate development and transformation of these themes, he probes even deeper, providing searching and dramatic portrayals of his three characters and evoking psychological depths that would be worthy of a *fin de siècle* artist.

The first movement characterizes Faust through depicting the opposing sides of his personality. His brooding unease, represented by the two opening ideas (Exx. 8a and b) contrast a restless, passionate nature, striving for higher ideals, represented by a surging idea usually played on the strings (Ex. 9):

Ex. 8. Liszt: *A Faust Symphony*

Ex. 9.

The movement contains two other important themes, Ex. 10, idea descriptive of Faust's longing and Ex. 11, a more martial theme, which commentators have suggested derive from Faust's words, 'Im Anfang war die Tat' (In the beginning was the deed):

Ex. 10.

Ex. 11.

The intense, intricate nature of the musical development in this movement, roughly based around a sonata form structure, parallels Liszt's deeply
involved, complex view of Faust, whose striving, exploratory nature Liszt
found much with which to identify.

The second movement, *Gretchen*, with its pellucid orchestration and
chamber-like textures, offers a profound contrast to the storm and stress
of the first. Gretchen is portrayed as a fresh, innocent youth, by a delicate
theme played, after an introduction, on the oboe, tenderly accompanied by
a solo viola. The appearance of Ex. 10 shows that Faust is not far from
her thoughts, and it is during the discussion of this theme that Liszt
makes a direct reference to the 'He loves me, he loves me not' episode
of Goethe's drama, with alternation of a short rising phrase between wind
and strings. The lovers come together in a passionate central section, with
the appearance of more themes from the first movement. This is followed
by a re-orchestrated reprise of the opening section and movement subsides
into a contented lethargy.

In the final movement, *Mephistopheles*, Liszt introduces no new themes,
but parodies the Faust themes, thereby representing Mephistopheles as
the corrupter and distorter. Gretchen's is the only theme that remains
unpolluted by the Devil's influence, a symbol of beauty and innocence
that forms a significant contrast to the demonic flavour of the rest
of the movement. Liszt fills this movement with much spiky, virtuosic

orchestration, showing an obvious debt to the soundworld of Berlioz's 'Witches Sabbath' in the *Symphonie fantastique*. The original version ended in exhaustion with nostalgic references to Gretchen; however, Liszt later added a reflective final 'Chorus mysticus' sung by a solo tenor and male choir, the words of which are taken from Part 2 of Goethe's drama: 'Alles Vergängliche ist nur ein Gleichnis . . .' (All that is transitory is but reflected . . .).

Another composer who experienced considerable success during his life-time, but who is largely forgotten today was **Hermann Goetz** (1840–1876). He wrote two symphonies of which only one exists today, the Second, in F, Op. 9, written in 1873. Bernard Shaw greatly admired this work and wrote, 'Goetz alone among modern symphonists is easily and unaffectedly successful from beginning to end . . . You have to go to Mozart's finest quartets and quintets on the one hand and to *Die Meistersinger* on the other, for a work of the quality we find . . . in the Symphony in F'. This four-movement work is indeed a beautifully crafted work, showing an individuality of style that looks forward at times to the world of Richard Strauss and Mahler and in the most extended and interesting of the movements, the slow third movement, he reaches an almost Tchaikovskian breadth and intensity in his development of the noble opening cello theme. Goetz's is a confident and imaginative symphonic voice that deserves to be heard far more often.

In his four symphonies, **Johannes Brahms** (1833–1897) stands apart from the ideals of the 'New German School' by re-affirming the musical values of the past. Brahms's understanding of musical techniques right back to Palestrina was the most thorough of any major composer of the nineteenth century. His grasp of early contrapuntal techniques and the structural and developmental principles of the Viennese Classicists, together with his astute awareness of late-nineteenth-century developments, enabled him to forge an individual style which was no less modern than that of his contemporaries, but which nevertheless affirmed a continuity with his musical forebears.

On the surface, Brahms symphonies show many similarities. They all retain the four-movement structure, each movement being formally closed and with all first movements following a sonata form plan. In each work the slow movement is placed second, followed by a movement in which Brahms shows an innovatory spirit, introducing a lyrical *Allegretto* intermezzo, with the exception of the Fourth where he has an *Allegro giocoso*, the closest he comes to a Scherzo. Throughout these works he is concerned for thematic continuity and the integration of material through all four movements. Yet, despite the similarities and without recourse to programmatic devices, each of these works is inherently different, brought about primarily through the nature of the material and thorough exploration of its musical possibilities.

The gestation of the First Symphony was long and painful. In 1862 Brahms showed a draft of the first movement to Albert Dietrich and

Clara Schumann, but it was not until 1876 that the work was completed and released to the world. Paramount in his thoughts was the figure of Beethoven, confirmed in a letter to the conductor Hermann Levi: 'You don't know what it is like always to hear that giant marching along behind me.' Brahms was fully aware that the composition of a symphony was the summit of a composer's art, and as such he would be judged by the very highest standards, and in particular those of Beethoven. The time he spent on the composition of the symphony was a period during which he not only came to terms with the form but also with the orchestra. Like Schumann, Brahms's natural medium was the piano. All his orchestral works sound well on the piano, especially in the keyboard arrangements that the composer himself produced and it is perhaps significant that his first attempted orchestral work, a Symphony in D minor, was eventually re-worked into the First Piano Concerto. It was, however, with the First Symphony that Brahms found his true orchestral voice. Here the orchestration takes on a new authority and character where the material is effectively enriched by his innate sense of textural proportion and the strength and clarity of his draughtsmanship. The sound of this symphony is of a mature romanticism, which, though perhaps lacking in the brilliance and technical wizardry of some of his contemporaries, is, like Schumann, indelibly associated with the nature of the material.

The symphony has two large outer movements, both preceded by suspenseful introductions, flanking two shorter, intermezzo-like movements. The tonal relationships between the movements follow a pattern of major thirds, C minor, E major, A flat major, C minor, a relationship to which both Schubert and Beethoven were frequently disposed.

The first movement opens with a sostenuto introduction in 6/8 time:

Ex. 12. Brahms: Symphony No. 1

These two chromatic, contrapuntally diverging lines, the upwardly striving top part firmly tethered by a tonic pedal, and a texture of breadth and weight, suggest the aspiration, conflict, and dramatic unease that are the underlying characteristics of this movement. The material itself forms the main focus of discussion of the following *Allegro* which, with Ex. 13, also from the introduction, creates a powerful momentum that carries the movement forward in a combative manner:

Ex. 13.

The intensity of this music is heightened greatly by Brahms's inexhaustible contrapuntal skills and the relentless drive of the 6/8 rhythm. Only occasionally does this relax, producing moments of a darker, more despairing character, which is eventually the mood in which the movement closes with sustained treatment of the rising chromatic phrase from Ex. 12 over a quiet pulsating tonic pedal.

In contrast to the tensions of the first movement, the E major slow movement introduces a calmer, more serene mood. It is in ternary form, the first section characterized by two lyrical themes, first on the strings and the second on the oboe. The string theme makes direct reference to the rising chromatic theme from Ex. 12. The middle section, in the relative minor, introduces a more unsettled, meandering theme on the oboe and clarinet in turn. The orchestration throughout the movement shows great subtlety and imagination and his writing for the strings shows a wide expressive range, from a soft brooding lower register to an unusually high, soaring lyricism.

The third movement, also in ternary form, opens with an folksong-like tune on the clarinet that bears a resemblance to the oboe and clarinet tune in the middle of the slow movement. There are many contrapuntal felicities in this relatively lightweight movement, in which Brahms subdues the usual energetic exuberance of a Scherzo that has the effect of throwing greater expressive weight on to the Finale. This is further emphasized by the last movement introduction, an unusual feature that reflects the transitional introductions to the last movements of Beethoven's Fifth and Schumann's Fourth symphonies. This is not transitional, however, and its independence from the previous movement creates an altogether more portentous effect. In addition it re-establishes the home key of C minor, it provides a lighter mood through a shift to the major with a sublime horn solo, and it solemnly introduces the chorale theme on the trombone that eventually forms the resplendent climax to the symphony.

The well-known tune that opens the following *Allegro non troppo* reflects Brahms in his most noble mood, bearing similarities to the opening tune of the B major Trio, Op. 8. The composer was somewhat sensitive to those who likened this theme to the 'Ode to Joy' theme, remarking that 'any jackass could see that'. The similarities are nevertheless there not only in its shape but also in its placement after a dramatic introduction. A full sonata-form movement follows and is concluded by the triumphant statement of the chorale.

Once Brahms had completed his first symphony the others followed in comparatively quick succession, No. 2 in 1877, No. 3 in 1883 and No. 4 in 1885. Symphony No. 2 in D major, Op. 73, was written during one of his happiest creative periods on holiday at Pörtschach in Carinthia. Two other important major key works come from this period – the Violin Concerto and the G major Violin Sonata. In comparison with the tensile First, the mood of the Second Symphony is warmer and more genial and has occasionally been called his 'Pastoral' symphony. Nevertheless the sunnier colours of this symphony are still tinged with an introspective darkness that allows its broad design to be filled with constant interplay between light and shade. These moods are suggested from the outset by the statement of the complex of themes in the first nine bars:

Ex. 14. Brahms: Symphony No. 2

This opening material, as in the First Symphony, forms the thematic basis for the first movement. The semitonal oscillation in the basses generates material in all four movements. The warmly lyrical melodic idiom is strikingly different from that of the First, and throughout the symphony there is a more relaxed unwinding of thematic material that has more in common with Schubert than Beethoven. This broadening of outlines however, does not mean that his handling of his material is less concentrated; in fact this score is the most thematically economical of any of the symphonies.

Orchestrally, the Second Symphony is a most colourful score. The richness of texture provided in the opening statement by bassoons and horns, contrasted by the lighter wind colours of the answering phrase is the first of many instances in this symphony of the composer's delight in juxtaposing different orchestral colours and registers. Another example is heard in the second subject of the first movement, where the warm glow of the theme on violas and cellos is immediately answered by high woodwind. Brahms's use of a wide range of pitch is an important expressive device, which adds greatly to the work's breadth and inner tension, a feature which is also found more obviously in the solo violin writing of the Violin Concerto. Brahms's use of brass is particularly effective throughout, trombones snarl or softly sustain, trumpets bring zest to the rhythmic momentum in the last movement, and an extended passage for the French horn in the coda of the first movement is one of the glories of the work.

As in the First Symphony, Brahms puts the structural weight on the outer movements. Some of the darkest moments of the symphony, however, are to be found in the slow, ternary-form second movement in B major, characterized by long sustained lines, neo-Baroque fugal developments and a central, impassioned climax in B minor. The mood lightens for the final two movements, a delightful Intermezzo followed by one of the composers most extrovert and resplendent Finales.

The Third Symphony opens with a rising motif, based on the notes F-A flat-F, a minor version of the musical cypher F-A-F which Brahms's biographer, Kalbeck, suggested was the composer's personal motto, 'Free but happy'. In the *passionato* descending string theme that follows, the A flat is immediately countered by an A natural, giving the first hint of the important part major and minor contrast is to play throughout the work. The opening motif, which bursts in on wind and brass, forms the foundation for the opening section up to the second subject. It also generates a strong forward momentum, the effects of which Brahms exploits to great expressive effect. This characteristic is further emphasized by the brief *Un poco sostenuto* section, prior to the return of the opening material in the recapitulation. Throughout the symphony Brahms is constantly concerned with the pacing of his material, whether it be a restless forward surge with defiant weak-beat accents, a flowing lyricism or moments of a quiet stasis. It is significant that for the first time in his symphonies he ends all four movements quietly, not so much to reflect as to bring the musical momentum created to a gradual halt.

The one moment of calm in the first movement exposition is found in the lyrical second subject in A major. This is first stated on the clarinet, continued after four bars by the oboe and violas in octaves and concluded by the flute. The balance and weighting of this scoring shows great subtlety, and is one of many examples that could be cited that make up one of the composer's most felicitous orchestral scores. The care he took over this score is evident in the manuscript with many fine adjustments of detail.

The flowing folksong-like simplicity of the opening of the second movement makes a striking contrast to the drama of the first. Variants of the opening material constitute the main substance of this movement and once more Brahms enlivens the textures with some delightfully imaginative scoring. A chant-like theme accompanied by repeated chords on the strings adds a hint of apprehension which leads to a passage of haunting suspense in which the repeated chords are iterated with mysterious harmonies in each register of the orchestra. This movement is the first of two of intermezzo-like character, the second being of a more melancholic nature, where again the spirit of Schubert is evident, most notably in the major mode continuation of the opening C minor theme.

The Finale brings together many of the themes and musical features of the preceding movements. Much of its character derives from the tension generated between the major and minor modalities, already implicit in the opening bar of the whole work. The F minor opening theme, reminiscent of the opening of the Finale to the Second Symphony, is soon interrupted by a more static theme, clearly derived from the chant-like theme of the second movement. This is not the second subject and its place, seemingly outside the sonata-form structure, creates a formidable presence, a feature that becomes more apparent as the movement progresses. After each of its first two appearances, a passage of great rhythmic vehemence bursts in, which leads to the second subject, a more cheerful, less brooding theme in the major, all this activity reiterating the composer's delight in the dramatic juxtapositions and major/minor conflicts evident from the start. The remarkable coda to this movement displays a beautifully controlled easing down of the musical pace, with varied representations of the movement's main theme in gradually slower tempi. Eventually, references to the work's opening motif, F-A-F, appear and the curtain comes down slowly in F major with a hushed statement of the descending string theme from the very opening.

The Fourth Symphony followed only two years after the Third, but unlike that work it displays different developmental processes. It is a work of cumulative power, in which variation plays an integral part, most particularly in the final Passacaglia. This was Brahms's last extended composition to use variation technique and it is a fitting climax to his other works in this form, of which the Haydn variations were the only previous orchestral example. Indeed in many respects this symphony may be considered a summing-up of most of what Brahms had worked for, especially the marriage of past techniques with the idioms of the late nineteenth century and the close-knit integration of material. It is a *tour de force* of formal and developmental construction where the application of technique never overrides the imaginative creation, producing a work of immense musical power and range, one of the supreme masterpieces of the nineteenth century.

Like his previous symphonies, the opening has a fundamental significance for the work as a whole, but here there are no motifs or motto themes but a series of gestures that hint at some of the important tonal relationships and suggest a basis for melodic material to follow. It is, at the same time, a beautiful tune in its own right (Ex. 15):

Ex. 15. Brahms: Symphony No. 4

The first four notes of this theme with the significant move to C (notably emphasized in its augmentation in the recapitulation), presages the important rôle the key of C is to play throughout the work, as, for example, in the deceptive C major opening of the E major slow movement, and the bold C major of the Scherzo. The interval of a third, in the move from the tonic E minor to C major, is further emphasized melodically by the opening eight notes of the tune, which produce a chain of seven descending thirds. It is this interval that pervades almost every bar of the first movement and a great deal of the others, as, for instance, in the successive use of thirds at the end of the Finale, a feature that Schoenberg* suggested 'unveils the relationship' between the opening theme and the Passacaglia theme of the Finale.

Furthermore, the Neapolitan relationship of C to the dominant B gives the first flavour of the Phrygian mode that is to colour a great deal of the work. This mode, whose character has long been considered one of the darkest and yet most consoling of the church modes, gives this work a strong elegiac character. This is never morose; the strong flowing impulse sustained throughout the work counters any tendency to dwell gloomily and frequently suggests a nobly heroic inevitability.

Unlike the previous symphonies the Fourth gets into its stride from the very outset with Ex. 15 in alla breve pulse, creating a searching lyrical momentum from which there is seldom a pause for breath. This opening movement is in sonata form, though with no exposition repeat, a wide-ranging development section and the subtle use of variation technique, the usual landmarks of sonata form are disguised and the composer's desire to continually throw new light on his material is effectively realized.

The modal inflections are most apparent in the beautiful *Andante* with the opening horn melody, ostensibly in C major, deceptively preluding a movement in E major. This opening leads to a movement of wide expressive gesture, with characterful variations of the main theme and a contrasting second subject, first stated on the cellos, that is one of his most richly glowing and noble melodies.

Scherzos abound in Brahms's other instrumental work, but it was not until this work that he introduced one to the realms of the symphony. The form, however, is unusual, with a concise, boisterous sonata-form structure (in C major, recalling the *Andante's* conflict between C and E) sweeping away any hint of a Trio. Brahms chose to write this movement last, enabling him to

* A. Schoenberg, 'Brahms the Progressive' (1947), in *Style and Idea*, ed. E. Stein, London, 1975.

calculate its effect astutely. A piccolo, contra-bassoon and triangle add to the atmosphere of a movement that gives an exultant lift to the whole work and throws into relief the sombre, dramatic and heroic events of the Finale.

The Passacaglia Finale is the crowning glory of this work – and of all his work in variation form. There are many features of the symphonies that reflect the composer's admiration for Beethoven and Schubert, but in this movement it was Bach that was his starting point. Brahms had some time before shown an interest in the Chaconne bass of the finale of Bach's Cantata No. 150, *Nach dir Gott verlanget mich*, which here (with the addition of a chromatic step, A sharp, highlighting the dominant note) forms the Passacaglia theme stated at the very opening in harmonized form by brass and wind. There follow thirty variations encompassing an astonishing range of colours and emotional contrasts and culminating in a long, elaborate coda, all of which creates a mighty climactic structure worthy to stand next to Bach's great organ Passacaglia in C minor.

Brahms's contemporary, **Max Bruch** (1838–1920), had a long and prolific career, but his fame today rests on just a few works, notably his first Violin Concerto in G minor, *Kol Nidrei* for cello and orchestra and the 'Scottish' Fantasy. Over the years, his three symphonies have all but vanished from concert programmes, but they are, nevertheless, solid, well-crafted works that show a propensity for strong, lyrical lines and an ease in handling the orchestra and symphonic form.

The most successful is the Third in E major, Op. 51. It was written in Liverpool, receiving its first performance in New York, in 1882, under Leopold Damrosch, the work's dedicatee. In a letter to Philipp Spitta, he wrote, 'This symphony is a work of life, of joy . . . and it should have the title *On the Rhine*, since it is a real expression of feelings for the Rhineland'. It has four movements, the first an extended sonata-form movement with an expressive introduction, characterized by impressively broad themes and a pleasantly outdoor ambience. The writing for the horns in this movement, as it is throughout the symphony, is particularly noteworthy. Both the middle movements are successful, a capricious Scherzo, which later achieved fame as a separate piece in its own right, contrasts a lovely slow movement containing some most expressive contrapuntal writing and a feeling of religious awe that is reminiscent of the Cologne Cathedral movement of Schumann's 'Rhenish' Symphony. The Finale has a charming melodiousness, which, with the frequent use of pedal points, creates the mood of a rustic celebration. This is an unexpectedly fresh piece compared to the darker, more openly serious nature of contemporary symphonic works.

7

Bruckner

Philip Coad

There seem to be two contradictions concerning Bruckner's creative output. First: if he was such a celebrated organist, why did he write no organ music of significance? If his powers of improvisation were as great as his tours to France in 1869 and London in 1871 indicate, why did he not fashion his improvisations into written works for organ? The lack of organ music is still more surprising when we realize that Bruckner had been a composer, mainly of church music, from an early age. Among his earliest models were the mass settings of Haydn and Mozart. Mendelssohn's *St Paul* struck him deeply in 1847, while his knowledge of earlier music, from Palestrina onwards, would have been consolidated during six years of intensive study of harmony and counterpoint – which took place, quite remarkably, when Bruckner was in his thirties, during a creative abstinence upon which his teacher insisted.

The first major discovery of the 1860s was Wagner. It was, as Robert Simpson puts it, 'the majestic deliberation of Wagner's invention and its growth into vast forms'* which appealed to Bruckner – who ignored the subject matter of the music dramas completely. The second discovery, in 1866, was Beethoven's Ninth Symphony; by this time his own First Symphony and two other symphonic essays had already been written. In 1868 Bruckner left his position as organist of Linz Cathedral and became Professor of Harmony and Counterpoint and of Organ at the Vienna Conservatory, later lecturing at the university as well. Vienna wore two distinct faces for Bruckner. Trained as a schoolteacher at sixteen in rural Lower Austria, he had a flair for communicating to students without any kind of pretentiousness. His pupils often became close allies and friends; and although they never studied directly with him, Mahler and later Wolf were deeply supportive members of his student coterie. But Bruckner's undisguised, childlike adulation of Wagner won him many opponents in faction-crazy Vienna, headed by Hanslick, who failed to appreciate how different Bruckner's music really was from that of his idol. Bruckner even met critical and public acclaim in New York, with

* *The Essence of Bruckner*, London, 1967, p. 23.

the performance of his Seventh Symphony in 1885, before it was genuinely his in Vienna.

Although Bruckner continued to compose church music throughout his life, the symphonies, from the Second onwards, were the main achievements of the Vienna years. And here we meet the second contradiction. As Derek Watson* has pointed out, Bruckner's self-confidence can be measured by the fact that, with the exception of the Second, each symphony was written before he had heard a performance of the previous one; and yet no other composer revised his work so obsessively. A conductor friend, Johann Herbeck, suggested cuts to the Second Symphony in 1876, and from then on Bruckner listened to and even sought the advice of mere pupils. The second-hand report of conductor Hermann Levi's qualified reaction to his Eighth Symphony in 1887 threw him into deep despair. Admittedly he had revered Levi as his 'artistic father'; but the conductor's verdict led to four years of revision-mania which only Mahler attempted to curb, and which with hindsight probably prevented him from completing his Ninth.

The performing versions of the symphonies made in the years immediately before and after Bruckner's death by well-meaning though presumptuous pupils – with their wholesale cuts, rescoring in the style of Wagner and even reharmonizations – have long been ignored. But Bruckner's own revisions still leave lesser questions to resolve. Only that of the Eighth is a real improvement – it was an immediate revision. The Fifth, Sixth and Seventh were left largely unscathed. Late revisions of the first four symphonies in those unhappy years are generally ignored; but an earlier revision (in 1878) of the Third, expunging large tracts of Wagnerian quotation, is usually respected, as is Bruckner's replacement of the final two movements of the Fourth at around the same time. We owe much to the International Bruckner Society, responsible for publishing the original versions from 1930 – but the issue remains complex, for two editors have successively put two points of view. The instinctive Robert Haas, for instance, incorporates elements of the first version of the Eighth into the second; the scientific Leopold Nowak publishes them both separately. Haas's inspired daring is much admired.

Such ambiguities had not surfaced when Bruckner in 1874 began his Fourth Symphony, just two days after completing his Third. This feat, not unique in his creative life, suggests a continuity of purpose towards a single symphonic goal. Indeed, to say that there is a grain of truth in the *bon mot* that Bruckner composed the same symphony over and over again is now almost as wellworn an observation as the original *bon mot* itself. But the grain of truth is substantial enough to permit the examination of one work, movement by movement, for the light it can shed on all the others. With the Fourth Symphony in E flat major we

* *Bruckner*, London, 1975.

stand at the threshold of Bruckner's maturity – a good place from which to look forward and back.

The opening of the Fourth is no doubt Bruckner's most famous opening; and to isolate typical elements which can be found in other works is not to deny its quite distinctive sound. A *pianissimo* string tremolo on the tonic chord introduces a theme for solo horn, built almost entirely on the interval of a perfect fifth:

Ex. 1. Bruckner: Symphony No. 4

Bruckner characteristically plants a theme of strong rhythmic profile against a rhythmically neutral background. The rhythmic element of his principal ideas is always vitally important (Ex. 1, incidentally, is nothing other than a 'tightening-up' of the opening trumpet idea in the Third Symphony). Parallels have often been drawn with the opening of Beethoven's Ninth Symphony, and there is no doubt that Bruckner was profoundly affected by it. But the essential difference between the typical Bruckner opening and that of Beethoven's Ninth highlights a much more wide-ranging contrast between the two composers. Beethoven is building a theme out of increasingly agitated gestures as he moves from dominant to tonic; Bruckner, based calmly on his tonic chord from the outset, already has his theme ready made. The generalization that Bruckner's music, despite all its local modulations, is too static tonally and thematically to fall into line with Beethoven's type of sonata procedure contains far more than a grain of truth, as we shall see.

Bruckner's setting off on a tonic chord tremolo is therefore indicative of an essential part of his musical personality. So is the single note which prevents Ex. 1 from being made up entirely of perfect fifths. It is astonishing how consistently Bruckner's more motivic ideas use the immediate neighbours of the important tonic and dominant notes at the expense of the third of the tonic triad (see also Exx. 2, 4 and 7) – a significant departure from the triadic announcements of much of the classical repertoire. So Ex. 1 contains no G, but instead a C flat which forces the first change to the background tremolo. This tendency is illustrated more forcefully in the first main theme of the Finale (Ex. 2):

Ex. 2.

and in many other works. It inevitably colours the harmony, especially introducing chords built on the flattened second and flattened sixth degrees of the scale – and, by extension, the tonal frameworks of whole movements and even whole symphonies are affected.

Ex. 1 is taken up by the woodwind, in a dialogue with the horn, and moves briefly through various keys, including E major, as the musical texture appears to extend itself chromatically in both directions. A scalic figure then comes to prominence, introducing a further important idea which demonstrates Bruckner's penchant for a combination of duplet and triplet groups:

Ex. 3.

This type of grouping has been coined the 'Bruckner rhythm', but is in fact only really common in the Third, Fourth and Eighth Symphonies, developing out of the quintuplet groupings of the First and Second.

Ex. 3 is not only characteristic rhythmically: it is also typical of Bruckner that it should appear in descending and ascending form – and here even simultaneously. Bruckner clearly found inversion an invaluable device for extending the possibilities of his thematic material. The music is led to the threshold of the dominant key via C flat major, and we expect the Fs sustained by two horns to usher in a second thematic group in B flat major. The held horn note may well remind the listener of Schubert's tendency to offer a pivot note at this point between sections, instead of a genuine bridge-passage – most notably in the Unfinished Symphony. The difference is that here Bruckner has prepared us for the 'right' new key, and so it is a genuine surprise when the strings begin new material in D flat major.

The second thematic complex of the movement offers quite a contrast in atmosphere. Its initial idea is typical: although polyphonically rich enough to be considered a double theme, it is at the same time reminiscent of a gentle Austrian folk dance. Bruckner referred to the second sections of his outer symphonic movements as *Gesangsperiode* (song periods), and they are characterized by their relaxed, tonally ruminative treatment of material. Again it is Schubert's second groups which provide the closest parallel. Bruckner's bass line moves very slowly from one pedal point to another, but there are more signs of E major before the music settles once again, after forty bars, on the dominant of B flat.

We might assume now that a second chance to establish the 'right' key will be taken in a final round-up of the exposition. But no, the exposition still has more than seventy bars to run; indeed, within eight bars there is even a brief return to E flat major. At this point Bruckner habitually introduces a fully-fledged third group of material, with its own thematic and tonal contribution to make. His third groups may sometimes, as here, make use of first group material; they may or may not begin in the key in which the exposition is to end; but alongside the typical tonal diversity are qualities which invariably set them apart from the rest of the exposition. These qualities include a certain rough-hewn simplicity of texture, and the use of abrupt contrasts. Rich harmony often disappears as more or less elaborated unison textures take over. In this movement, the strings set up a rushing unison figure made up of oscillations between tonic and dominant and scale passages, while wind and brass contribute another unison fragment based on Ex. 3. The music moves quickly away from B flat major down to a quiet landing on G, then rising in chromatic steps to a climactic emphasis of D flat major again. Another hush, and a further chromatic ascent for strings and wind, totally in unison, leads to a mighty affirmation of D flat major for full brass alone. Their *fortissimo* is succeeded immediately by strings *pianissimo*, who recall a fragment of the *Gesangsperiode* in their slightly contrived, though long-awaited establishment of the 'right' dominant key. If the arrival of B flat major does sound rather perfunctory here, we should remember that first and second groups both ended with an expectation of that key. There is long-range planning even in such a roomy tonal scheme.

The end of the Bruckner exposition is always a point of quiet repose, with a liberal use of silence or, as here, a *pianissimo* roll on the timpani. He writes a double bar, but after three leisurely groups of material does not invite a repeat. The development begins as the exposition left off; the timpani roll on B flat continues for a total of thirty-six bars beneath a few hints of Ex. 1. Then a more continuous texture evolves, with a string tremolo and Ex. 1. The next thirty-six bars are engaged in a most characteristic building of a climax. Ex. 1 is given out in original form, in inversion, and in combination with itself and Ex. 3. In due course its first four bars are forced into two bars, and then – overlapping with itself in ostinato manner – into even less space. An increased rhythmic excitement complements a dogged insistence over eight bars of dominant chord reiterations, before E flat minor finds

Ex. 3 coming into its own. Ex. 3 is treated similarly to Ex. 1: inversions and combinations are used to propel the music through a richly chromatic sequential journey, with sudden ebbs and flows of dynamic. Eventually it all seems to start again, with a new *pianissimo* string tremolo and further permutations of Ex. 1.

Bruckner's developmental methods appear to depend a great deal on the use of certain devices which do not require the motives themselves to change or be internally developed. Because of this it has been said that he does not so much develop his ideas as put them through certain contrapuntal elaborations. However, the way in which his ideas are, in practice, altered demonstrate where his priorities lie. He is quite content to sacrifice the entire melodic shape of an idea and keep merely to its rhythmic profile in order to suit his harmonic plans. This is how, for instance, he sustains interest during a long chordal reiteration such as the eight-bar dominant preparation of E flat minor here. There are plenty of instances throughout his symphonic output of themes being 'heard' on a monotone.

It may seem negative to sacrifice the melodic character of an idea, but Bruckner is about to show what he can do with the remains of Ex. 1. Using its rhythmic properties only, he now builds three majestic chordal phrases for a choir of trumpets, trombones and tuba. They are striking, first because they are by far the longest phrases of the movement so far; secondly because Bruckner has waited until now to reveal his brass section in this manner; and thirdly because his sense of harmonic progression in a modulatory context is so strong. Bruckner himself called the climactic brass passage at the end of his Fifth Symphony a chorale, and the association with a triumphant hymn is glimpsed here too.

The brass subsides into echoes of Ex. 1 in its original form, and the music comes to a halt on G major harmony. After such a culmination, we are left with no expectations; and there is certainly no sense of urgent anticipation in the music which leads into the recapitulation – this would indeed be inappropriate if the recapitulation is to begin as the exposition did. Bruckner's strings quietly reflect on the opening double theme of the *Gesangsperiode*, moving back towards E flat major in music devoid of all tension. What was often a moment, even *the* moment, of high excitement in the classical symphony is here total calm.

Nor is the tonal scheme of the recapitulation quite as we might expect. The first group in the exposition ended by preparing the way for the dominant key before the surprise of D flat major; but in the recapitulation it ends on the brink not of the tonic key, but of the subdominant – and the same kind of surprise therefore lands us in B major. Bruckner's scale is not classical: he still has a long way to go, and his use of tonality emphasizes that. The third group does begin in the tonic key, but only to plunge into C minor by way of descending chromatic phrases for unison strings. It is interesting that Bruckner's tonally varied scheme has not permitted the relative minor until now.

Bruckner's codas invariably begin quietly, and are often built in two sections, each growing to a climax. Reminders of his development techniques occur in inverted forms of Ex. 1 and reiterations on a monotone for brass, these over another typical tonic-dominant ostinato for strings. After twelve bars the harmony hauls itself up a semitone; then a sudden unprepared *fortissimo* demonstrates the rude power of Bruckner's *tutti unisono* textures. Back equally suddenly to *pianissimo*, a chromatic climb brings us over the tonic chord to E major once again.

This may seem to be yet another forestalling of the final outcome; but it is in fact the beginning of the end, in a subtle demonstration of the unity between motive and tonal movement noted earlier. For the second phrase of Ex. 1 – C flat – E flat – B flat – is now answered exactly in a bass movement of E (F flat) – A flat – E flat which is spread over forty-one bars. The importance of notes, chords and keys directly above tonic and dominant is clear. The huge chordal blocks which result from this bass movement are enlivened typically by ostinati; and the rhythm of Ex. 1 appears in ever-increasing diminution as the tonic chord looms. The final tonic emphasis of sixteen bars and a beat exhibits the power and pre-eminence of Bruckner's brass section: the horns and third trumpet will not be swayed from Ex. 1's first phrase, while the other two trumpets and three trombones give out antiphonal reiterations of a faster dotted rhythm.

Ex. 1 reappears in the symphony's Finale; indeed its rhythmic profile will round off the whole work. Bruckner used the word *Hauptthema* (main theme) for such themes of supreme importance, and they are employed with some consistency in all his subsequent symphonies. But, drawing away from the Fourth in order to look at the other first movements, it is clear that the technique took time to evolve, and that Bruckner achieved variety within self-imposed limits.

The opening theme of the First Symphony (1865–6; revised 1890–91) neither revolves around tonic and dominant notes, nor reappears in the Finale. Its steady dotted rhythm against a march-like accompaniment seems to look forward more closely to Mahler's Sixth than to any later Bruckner opening. The fact that Bruckner had not yet heard the start of Beethoven's Ninth may be significant. The opening theme of the Second Symphony (1871–2; revised 1875–6) does revolve around the dominant and is set against a background tremolo, but lacks the assertive character needed for participation in the final climactic bars of a movement. On the other hand, the so-called Symphony No. 0 in D minor (1863–4), written before the first but not considered worthy of a real number, may have been withdrawn because the Court Kapellmeister in Vienna asked where the principal subject was. Certainly Bruckner never underplayed the thematic element of a first group again.

With the Third (1873–7; revised 1888–9) a solution is found. Bruckner uses the trumpet thematically for the first time in a *Hauptthema* much admired by Wagner, the symphony's dedicatee. Like Ex. 1, it is a theme clearly conceived for a brass instrument, and is therefore suitable for brass peroration at the end of both outer movements. The Fifth Symphony (1875–6) begins with a slow introduction of vast contrasts, suggesting a new scale. The full brass section is heard on its own in a totally convincing manner for the first time. The *Hauptthema* which follows is instrumentally more flexible; and instead of dominating both outer movements on its own, it combines with other important ideas (see Ex. 7). The Sixth (1879–81) contributes a harmonically elusive quality from its very opening bars. A tremolo background is replaced by a rhythmic ostinato high in the violins. This is perched firmly on the third of the A major tonic chord, as the *Hauptthema* below explores around tonic and dominant; but the effect is unsettling, partly due to the bare, widely spaced texture:

Ex. 4. Bruckner: Symphony No. 6

Like the Second, the Seventh Symphony (1881–83) begins with a *Hauptthema* of a more lyrical quality for cellos. But there are extended possibilities with this theme: the opening rising arpeggio lends itself readily to subsequent brass treatment, and its long-breathed sequel is capable of detaching itself from this opening – it has a life of its own at the end of the development and in the coda. There are further surprises in the Eighth

(1884–7; revised 1889–90). The *Hauptthema* is introduced by a tremolo on the subdominant, and the tonic key of C minor is only suggested. Rhythmically the theme is identical to the first theme of Beethoven's Ninth. Such a strong profile is made much of; but it is also smoothed out in two different ways during the course of the exposition, contradicting Bruckner's normal habit of preserving rhythm at all costs.

Ex. 5. Bruckner: Symphony No. 8

In the opening of his unfinished Ninth (1891–6), Bruckner moves still further from what might incautiously be called his 'norm'. The idea which follows the initial tremolo is not of sufficient character to be the *Hauptthema*, although it begins with the semiquaver upbeat familiar from the *Hauptthemen* of the Sixth and the Eighth. Movement away from the tonic is caused by an arresting horn phrase, but when we reach the enormous *tutti unisono* in bar 63, we realize that everything up to now has been introductory. The further increase in scale might be thought to lead to incoherence, but Bruckner's mastery of gradual climax-building is by now consummate. A look back at the short-winded double statement of the Third, in the same key, confirms this progress. Certainly Bruckner has no need in the Ninth to repeat his opening paragraph, as he had often done in earlier works; and a fragmentary aftermath leads straight into the second group.

The main advance in Bruckner's development sections is his growing ability to handle a central climax. In the Third, the *Hauptthema* is presented rather plainly and statically, destroying momentum and leaving nothing more to be said; the Finale of the Fourth has better concealed but similar problems. The Fifth succeeds through an increase in contrapuntal energy and a subtle re-ordering of material within its huge contrasts; the Seventh uses a remote key and only part of the *Hauptthema*. In the Eighth, the *Hauptthema* appears augmented in the bass so that we are scarcely aware of it, and is combined with an augmented derivation from the second group and some enlivening brass fanfares: an example of genuine developmental subtlety in Bruckner's own terms, and a wonderful passage.

The Sixth Symphony's methods are simpler: the developmental climax simply becomes the recapitulation as the music reaches the tonic key of A major from the improbable starting-point of E flat. In his late works Bruckner acquired the ability to disguise the moment of recapitulation – and then to go further still. The first-movement recapitulations of the Seventh and Eighth Symphonies begin more quietly, at low tension. But there is no sense of preparation, even by the dominant chord, in the Seventh; while the *Hauptthema* of the revised Eighth manages to insinuate itself beneath a flute ostinato in the wrong key, and the shortened first group is virtually over before we realize it has begun.

In the Ninth Symphony Bruckner reaches a central climax built on the main theme, which starts in the tonic key. This is what he had arrived at in the corresponding point of the Third Symphony; but his increased assurance in handling a large scale and in his own kind of developmental procedure leads him to a new outcome. The climax expands itself so vastly that any kind of reprise of the *Hauptthema* afterwards is impossible – especially with its original introduction. The argument as to what is first group development and what first group recapitulation is futile; it is all one.

Four of Bruckner's first six symphonies (including No. 0) gesture once again to Beethoven's Ninth in their use of an ostinato at the start of the first movement coda. Other works use different methods to build a climax from a state of quietness. But the brass instruments – except in the Eighth – and the *Hauptthemen* dominate all the first movement endings from the Third onwards. It is not all automatic, however. The first movement of the Sixth Symphony conclusively reaches the tonic chord only at the last possible moment, after a kaleidoscopic series of chord changes; while the Seventh's first movement ends with 53 bars of tonic pedal, 31 of which are tonic chord reiterations. In the Ninth, the coda makes an important new thematic point, resolving a harmonic question posed in the *Hauptthema*, and then allows the rising horn figure from the introductory build-up to have the last word. Most notable of all, though, is the coda in the revised version of the Eighth. *Pianissimo* throughout, it is the only movement in the symphonies, slow movements apart, which ends quietly; the effect was well worth Bruckner's second thoughts. Even so, Bruckner does not deny the *Hauptthema* its pre-eminence here; this coda provides a good example of the diversity in unity found in his opening movements.

In his slow movements, Bruckner reveals the full expressive weight of his rich harmonic language, in sustained structures usually of extreme slowness and breadth. This is especially true of the last three symphonies. In the Seventh's *Adagio*, Bruckner uses a quartet of 'Wagner tubas' for the first time, in addition to four horns, three trumpets, three trombones and contrabass tuba; appropriately, since Bruckner heard of Wagner's death as he was writing the movement, and particularly associated the coda with his memory. The *Adagios* of the Eighth and Ninth Symphonies each last about half an hour, and are placed after the Scherzo presumably for reasons of balance.

For these and some of his earlier slow movements, Bruckner seems to have used the slow movement of Beethoven's Ninth as his formal starting-point. Two contrasted groups of material alternate; the second group is presented twice between increasingly elaborate and climactic statements of a first group ($A\ B\ A^1\ B^1\ A^2$). Variations on this basic structure occur in earlier works. The First, not surprisingly, does not take Beethoven's lead but is in ternary form; the Third develops subsidiary material at the expense of A^1; the beautiful *Adagio* of the Sixth is closer to sonata form. Although Bruckner was happy to settle with the Beethoven model in the end, the slow movement of the Ninth gives climax-building elaborations of unparalleled – even tortuous – intensity to the return of the second group (B^1) instead of the first.

The slow second movement of the Fourth is untypical in various ways. First, it has a faster *Andante* marking with the atmosphere of a slow march; secondly, the two groups both rely to some extent on a trudging pizzicato accompaniment and are therefore not particularly contrasted; and thirdly, A^1 (bars 83–154) at first disguises the main thematic ideas by presenting them in the bass or with prominent countermelodies, before allowing a rather plain shortened restatement.

In the first movement of the Fourth Bruckner was at least prepared to pay lip service to the dominant key as principal tonal rival to the tonic. But here, despite a great deal of local modulation, there is really no tonal polarity of this kind. The opening statement of the two groups of material ($A\ B$) is all firmly based in C minor, despite chorale-like excursions into other keys. Although C flat major makes fleeting appearances in all three A sections (climactically in A^2) to suggest an unusual tonal rivalry, it is easily pushed aside before it has a chance to establish itself as a new point of reference. It is certainly not 'classical' to find Bruckner using the same key for both groups of material; nor is it conventional then to bring back the second group in the supertonic (D) minor. Bruckner's treatment of key is quite individual and apparently instinctive; in such a context the most conventional moves often sound the most contrived.

Bruckner gets away with quite wide-ranging local modulations within both groups because his part-writing is so perfect in balance and direction. He was once dubbed the 'Palestrina of the nineteenth century', no doubt partly for this reason, although of course his chromatic harmony is quite of its own time. The second movement contains elements familiar from the first, despite its difference in character. Not the least significant of these elements is the falling and rising dominant-tonic-dominant contour of the opening of the first idea. There is much writing for strings alone – both B sections add only an occasional horn – and the brass are left to bear the main thematic burden in the final climax. Sections are clearly delineated by silence; but here sometimes Bruckner goes further than this. Even the individual phrases of *B* material are separated from each other; many of these phrases begin on the second beat of the 4/4 bar.

As *A* material becomes more elaborate, imitations and inversions play an important part, followed by increasingly rapid figuration for upper strings. We never lose sight of the basically slow tempo, although Bruckner's scale, and the degree of slowness, was to increase still further in later works. Descending sequential phrases at the ends of *A* and *B* hint at the patient unwindings in the slow movements of the Fifth and Sixth Symphonies, before Bruckner's subtlety grew beyond such obvious use of the device.

Bruckner's style is perhaps most easily recognized in the Scherzo movements; and the Scherzo of the Fourth may well be the most archetypal of all. After an introductory *pianissimo* tremolo on an open fifth for strings, the horns gradually assemble in a hunting figure which uses only the notes of the B flat major tonic triad. Note also the return of the 'Bruckner rhythm' and the typical upbeat stutter:

Ex. 6. Bruckner: Symphony No. 4

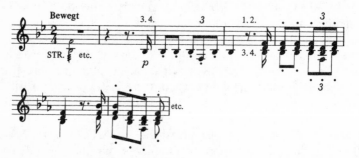

After eight bars of horns, the background harmony changes and a trumpet enters, imitating the horns. Another eight bars, and the trombones force another harmonic change with their version of Ex. 6, each reiterating a single note. Meanwhile the other two trumpets have entered, and the rhythmic imitation is in three parts. Such hectic brass activity dominates the strings' tremolo and the woodwind support, and generates a climax which reaches its peak after a further eight bars.

The predominance of the brass and the rhythmic dimension, the introductory string tremolo and the use of imitation to generate excitement – these are all elements which were found in the first movement. In the Scherzos – and particularly in those of the Fourth, Sixth and Eighth – Bruckner adds to those elements a massively deliberate harmonic background which gains strength from its totally regular and fundamentally slow motion. Over twenty-four bars Bruckner has used only three chords – and all over a tonic pedal. The procedure is extended at the end of both sections of the traditional binary-form structure which Bruckner uses. The final perfect cadence takes up forty bars: twenty on a dominant pedal, twenty reiterating the tonic chord. This sounds dull; but Bruckner's use of a rising chromatic sequence over the dominant pedal, his total exploitation of the rhythm of Ex. 6 and the powerful certainty of the outcome can be quite exhilarating. But an important part of the overall effect is the eventual sudden halt which, despite so much reiteration, manages to sound abrupt and unexpected. A constant chordal battering followed by silence is perhaps the single most unmistakable Brucknerian event.

More subtle, yet just as characteristic, is Bruckner's preoccupation here with the flattened submediant (the note or key directly above the dominant), as in the first movement. The first climax is reached with an unexpected G flat major chord for full brass alone; and although the music proceeds from there to the dominant key, the second part of the movement begins with a low G flat from cellos and basses, a horn call in G flat and then the subsidiary idea in G flat major. The preoccupation reaches its fulfilment in the pastoral Trio section. Bruckner's Trio sections are unusual in that they are always slower than the outer Scherzo sections, the Ninth Symphony apart. Here in the Fourth, Austrian folk music is again suggested, especially the *Ländler*. The first part of the Trio even returns for a moment to B flat major; the longer second part takes in some enharmonic modulations which might be called daring if they were not managed with such subtle smoothness of voice-leading. At moments like these, Bruckner shows a fine assimilation of his debts to sixteenth-century polyphony and to Schubert. Then the Scherzo itself returns, and both are forgotten.

Bruckner's other Scherzo movements, entirely regular in form, do nevertheless manage to enhance the individuality of the symphonies to which they belong. For instance, the use of unequal phrase-lengths in its main Scherzo idea is one of the various unorthodoxies of the First Symphony overall. Reaching perfection of a kind in the Fourth, the next two works experiment. The Scherzo of the massive Fifth Symphony recasts the *Adagio*'s opening idea at a new hectic speed, and then slows right down into *Ländler* tempo after only twenty-two bars. The fluctuations of speed and material help to give the movement a grander scale, as does some more heroic writing than usual in the Trio section. The Scherzo of the unpredictable Sixth Symphony adopts an untypically moderate speed, but is also notable for the blunt and unexpected arrival of the concluding cadential bars, cutting its final phase very short.

The Seventh and Eighth Symphonies exhibit striking thematic economy. The Eighth's Scherzo has stated virtually all its material by the end of the third bar, and its thematic single-mindedness is emphasized by its motoric regularity and cumulative power. The Scherzo of the Ninth is quite different from all its predecessors, and far more disturbing in character. As in the first movement, the element of suspense is built up through introductory material. Upper woodwind and pizzicato strings show how far Bruckner could stretch harmonically the concept of dominant preparation, without preparing us at all for the brutality of the main subject. Later an accelerando away from the opening speed adds to the unease; and the faster Trio, although beautifully delicate in texture, adds further elements of rhythmic and harmonic disquiet.

Bruckner never completed the Finale of the Ninth: at his death he left 184 sheets of manuscript, including six different orchestral drafts. The struggle he had always had in his Finales seems to show itself in two ways. First, his revision work focused mainly on them: there are far more questionable cuts in the Finales than in the other movements put together. Secondly, his last four Finales are very different in length (while the first movements of the same works are more uniform in this respect): the Finales of the (Nowak) Fifth and Eighth are 635 and 709 bars long respectively, those of the Sixth and Seventh 415 and 339 bars (all these movements are in a similarly paced time). Bruckner's decision to cast his Finale in the same basic form as his opening movement must have intensified his problem of achieving a distinctive finality at the end of his symphony.

The problem is scarcely encountered in the First Symphony, in which the prevailing atmosphere is classical. What is so remarkable about the Symphony No. 0 is the attempt made to fuse development and recapitulation together: something not attempted in the first movements until much later, as we have seen. The Second's Finale opts for an unhurried approach; in terms of bars it is very nearly Bruckner's longest. One quotation from the Benedictus of his F minor Mass at the end of the exposition prompts Robert Simpson to say: 'This is the kind of slowness on which all else is superimposed, and we begin to understand Bruckner when we realize that it is the movement of the earth itself that is constant, not the flurries of activity on its surface'.* There are no short cuts made in the recapitulation, but it is interesting that Bruckner proposed to cut it entirely when he revised the work in 1892.

Returning to earlier works in his last years, Bruckner clearly felt that his Finale recapitulations were inclined to sound redundant. The problem was at its most severe as he revised the Finales of the Third and Fourth symphonies. The Finale of the Fourth begins with a characteristic pile-up of thirds over a dominant pedal: minor ninth (C flat), eleventh and minor thirteenth are gradually added to dominant seventh harmony, amid rhythmic references back to the Scherzo, to build a fitting platform for the *tutti unisono* power of Ex. 2. But the tonic key is far from established by Ex. 2; it is left to a majestic return of Ex. 1 at the very end of the first group to assert E flat major harmony. Three quiet E flats from the timpani and the *Gesangsperiode* begins in C minor. How far from classical procedure Bruckner is here, to save his first tonic chord emphasis for the passage immediately prior to the second group – and yet, at the same time, how close to Schubert!

* op. cit., p. 59.

A memorable example of Brucknerian 'terracing' occurs as the somewhat inconsequential *Gesangsperiode* is abruptly interrupted by a powerful third group full of open fifth figuration elaborating a unison texture. Its return in the development is still more terraced. A rather listless passage settles into reiterations for strings on E major – a key of significance, as we shall see, but now abruptly hurled aside by a *fff* combination of Ex. 2 for brass and third group figuration. It is a magnificent climactic passage, sustained through adventurous modulations, but, just as it was totally unprepared, it is totally unfollowable. As Simpson has pointed out, the final fragmentary part of the development feels like an aftermath, not a preparation for the recapitulation. The development climax has dwarfed its context, and has left little more for the first group (and Ex. 2 in particular) to do. Bruckner's late revisions of the Third and Fourth cut the return of the first group; but the resulting imbalance is generally thought to make matters worse, and these revised versions are rarely performed. But the coda, beginning quietly and built typically in two waves, provides not only a marvellously paced final climax but also a tonal resolution to the whole work. A string figuration oscillating between E flat and F for thirty-eight bars reflects the much slower alternation of E flat and C flat brought on by the presence of the first three notes of Ex. 2 in inverted form. They are eventually reconciled into A flat minor harmony by the brass, before the second wave begins like the first. But now, movement up a semitone (on to E major again) begins a rich modulatory sequence. Strings, wind and brass begin a long ascent. The final peak has three important unifying messages. First and secondly, the notes F flat (or E) and C flat and all that they have implied throughout the symphony are reconciled into E flat major. The closing tonic reiteration is preceded not by the dominant chord, but by a four-bar emphasis of F flat major; while C flats appear in the continuing violin figuration right up until the penultimate bar. Thirdly, the very opening idea of the whole work, whose second phrase opened the tonal issue at stake, revives its memorable rhythmic profile in full E flat major brass harmony. The effect of the coda is so consummate that, in Simpson's words, 'one is briefly convinced that, after all, the Finale must have been a masterpiece'.*

So it was the presence of big, self-completing development climaxes which made Bruckner's Finale problem greater in the Third and Fourth Symphonies than it had been in the Second, in which the development section is modest in proportions. Bruckner's late anxiety about these movements was probably more acute because he knew that, in different ways, he had in the meantime written more successful Finales.

The Finale of the Fifth is both successful and subtly different in method from its predecessors. Bruckner gives his contrapuntal skill a higher profile than ever before, combining fugal methods with his own kind of sonata procedure, taking a lead perhaps from the Finale of Mozart's 'Jupiter'. From

* op. cit., p. 101.

Beethoven's last Finale he borrows a method of introduction: elements from the first two movements alternate with new fragments which then become the first subject proper in due course (Ex. 7a). A fugal first group is followed by a normal, but exceptionally diverse and roomy *Gesangsperiode*; and the third group augments the opening of the first. Remnants of the *Gesangsperiode* appear to be winding up the exposition, but suddenly a new idea (Ex. 7b) bursts in *fortissimo* on the brass, alternating with *pianissimo* string phrases: the enormous contrasts of the whole symphony's opening are recalled. The development treats the new theme fugally and is eventually joined by the first subject as the fugal texture continues. A long dominant pedal heralds the recapitulation. Bruckner marks the structural point by dismissing fugal writing altogether, so that the return of the first group can contribute something new in its quite plain combination of the two themes. Their welcome in a new guise is not outstayed; Bruckner quickly moves on, and the *Gesangsperiode* puts discussion in limbo. The third group too has something new to contribute, recalling the *Hauptthema* from the first movement (Ex. 7c). It is combined in various ways with the first subject; these combinations are all made possible by the leanings of all three subjects towards flattened second (C flat) and sixth (G flat). Augmentation of Ex. 7a provides a convincing recapitulatory culmination. Finally the coda brings back Ex. 7b in augmentation for a triumphant brass Choral punctuated by elements of Ex. 7a – and a few last hints of the *Hauptthema*.

Ex. 7. Bruckner: Symphony No. 5

The Finales of the Sixth and Seventh Symphonies are in comparison terse and brief. Although they are very different to the Fifth's Finale, they too both succeed in avoiding anything redundant or tautologous. In the Sixth, musical statements are raw and matter-of-fact; their concision prevents the development from becoming too climactic in its own right, and the recapitulation arrives abruptly. A major only establishes itself conclusively over F and B flat rivals at the very end with the return of the *Hauptthema*.

The Seventh Symphony chooses the option of making development and recapitulation all one. With hindsight it might be argued that he recapitulates the groups in reverse order; but if the listener is used to Bruckner's sectional developments, he will not hear anything as 'recapitulatory' until the opening of the expanded first group returns at the very end of the process.

Having at last made something of his discoveries in No. 0, Bruckner seems to return again to the challenge of the large-scale movement which makes no formal short-cuts. The Finale of the Eighth lasts half an hour, but it is a triumph of balance and proportion in Brucknerian terms. Nothing in the lengthy development recalls the glorious but concisely stated opening subject in its entirety; only the second half of the theme returns climactically during the central section, so that there is no question of its recapitulation sounding redundant. To reinforce its climactic reprise, Bruckner expands the first group to nearly double its original length, then tightens up the ruminations of the *Gesangsperiode* by the same degree. The understated third group prepares the way for a suitably lengthy dominant pedal before the coda, over which the first movement's *Hauptthema* appears in augmentation. As the coda builds up, elements from the middle movements also reappear in the brass to make way for the final C major reiteration, in which Bruckner manages to combine the rhythmic profiles of themes from all four movements. A unison blaze in *Hauptthema* rhythm concludes the work. After such a Finale, it is no wonder that Bruckner returned to earlier Finales to try desperately to repair them. The sketches for the Ninth's Finale (complete up to the beginning of the coda) show a return to the Fifth's combination of fugue and chorale, and some melodic resemblances to the Eighth's Finale, as if Bruckner was trying to draw on his two most successful large-scale Finales to help him meet a last challenge.

It is a feature of Bruckner's progress throughout his symphonic career that he draws on methods used in earlier works, and refines them. There is a sense of a journey towards a single goal – but the balance between unity and diversity is fine. In Bruckner's orchestral methods, for instance, there is certainly unity. He tends to contrast blocks of instrumental colour, with little doubling across the main orchestral groups of brass, woodwind and strings, and few transitions between one sonority and another. Even in orchestral tuttis the three main groups often have quite separate roles. For this reason the analogy of separate organ manuals, with their different stop characters, is often employed. How different this is to the smoothly blended Wagnerian orchestration which Bruckner's pupils tried to impose upon his music! And yet those who only know the late symphonies, with their fifteen-strong brass sections, will be surprised to find the brass so limited in the Second; those who love the woodwind writing in the Sixth and Eighth will find that the wind are very poor relations in the Fifth. Nearly all the symphonies have something compellingly individual: from the magnificent trombone theme in the opening movement of the First, with its hints of Bruckner's first Wagner discovery, *Tannhäuser*, to the delicious ambiguity of the polka/chorale combination in the Finale of the Third; from the rhythmic complexity and tonal abruptness of the Sixth (which Bruckner described as 'die keckste' – his cheekiest) to the monumental slowness of the last two movements of the Eighth, and the disturbing, prophetic harmonic departures of the Ninth, with its battering, nightmarish Scherzo.

But aspects of Bruckner's music which we find everywhere – the kaleidoscopic local modulations and the huge chordal reiterations which 'earth' them, the construction in blocks of material, deliberately discontinuous and often separated by silence, the apparently inconsistent use of keys at structural points, the three group expositions and the rather statuesque approach to development – these aspects emphasise how consistently Bruckner was striving for a kind of momentum quite different from classical sonata style. Criticized ruthlessly by the Viennese for this nonconformity, he is reported to have said:

> They want me to write differently. Certainly I could do, but I must not. God has chosen me from thousands and given me, of all people, this talent. It is to Him that I must give account. How then would I stand there before Almighty God, if I followed the others and not Him?*

Bruckner's faith in a God-given symphonic mission was of course a vital ingredient in his inner self-confidence; his diffidence sprang no doubt from a fear that he was falling short of fulfilling it. Despite his apparent willingness to allow alterations by others to his scores, he always kept the original versions, saying that these were 'for later times'. How right he has been proved. The impetus of Bruckner's faith is perhaps the most central unifying factor of all – not just in his symphonies, but in his whole output; for five of his symphonies, from No. 0 to the Ninth, and the String Quintet quote from his church music. It is clear that as Bruckner turned to concentrate almost exclusively on the symphony after his three large Mass settings of the 1860s, he was moving not further away, but closer to his own kind of spiritual fulfilment. The Ninth Symphony's dedication, *dem lieben Gott*, demonstrates this best of all. And no doubt the inspiration found in organ improvisation, not reaching consummation in organ works, also contributed to the achievement of that unifying goal.

* Quoted in A. Göllerich (edited by M. Auer), *Anton Bruckner: Ein Lebens- und Schaffensbild*, Regensburg, 1922–37, Vol. 4, Part 3, p. 115.

8
Mahler

Stephen Johnson

It is just possible that one day somebody will write a book about the Mahler boom – that extraordinary surge of interest in both the music and the man in recent years. If the subject does appeal, there are several important questions to be addressed: for instance, why did it take so long for Mahler's significance to be widely recognized? One has only to compare the entries under his name in the ninth edition of the old *Oxford Companion to Music* (1955) and in the *New Oxford Companion* (1983) to realize the enormous change in Mahler's official status in this country over the last three decades. Such a study would also have to devote a fair amount of space to the effects of the rise of Mahler on composers, performers, concert and record audiences, and on ideas about music in general. As a footnote, it might also observe the birth and ascendance of a new adjective: 'Mahlerian' – as popular and, apparently, as open to indiscriminate use as those other critical stand-bys, 'Existentialist' and 'Kafka-esque'.

As so often when a term is over-used, one begins to wonder if it has – or ever had any concrete meaning. Judging from the way 'Mahlerian' has figured in reviews, record sleeve-notes and other widely disseminated writings, it can mean nothing more than 'very intense'. But there are cases where something rather more complicated is implied: a distinct attitude, reflected in a wide but somehow related group of musical practices, and apparent throughout Mahler's output, but especially so in the ten symphonies and the 'symphonic' song cycle *Das Lied von der Erde*. To explore this thoroughly would require rather more space than this book allows, but the fact that more than thirty years after the rise of Mahler began in earnest, his name can still be used in vague incantatory ways suggests that even a brief survey such as this could be of some value.

So where does one look for a definition of 'Mahlerian'? We could do a great deal worse than to start with the remark Mahler is reported to have made to Sibelius in 1907 when the two composers met in Helsinki and, according to Sibelius, 'discussed all the great questions of music thoroughly.' Inevitably the conversation turned towards the symphony, with Sibelius stating that what he admired about the form was 'its severity of style and the profound logic that created an inner connection between all the motifs.' 'No,' said Mahler, 'the symphony must be like the world. It must embrace everything.' This ringing declaration has been quoted often enough in this volume for it to come to be seen as self-explanatory, but for our purposes it needs pinning down. Fortunately Mahler was more specific elsewhere. Footnotes in the scores confirm over and again his desire that the music should evoke images of the natural world, either in sweeping vistas or in intimate detail. 'Everywhere and always,' he wrote on completing his Third Symphony in 1896, 'it is always the voice of nature.' A little later, when Bruno Walter admired the mountain scenery of the Salzkammergut where the Third Symphony had been composed, Mahler told him, 'No need to look up there – I've already composed all that.'

Elsewhere Mahler's remarks can seem contradictory: first he gives elaborate, hugely ambitious programmes for his Second and Third symphonies – talk of suffering, death and resurrection in the Second, Pan-Dionysus and God the Father in the Third – and then he roundly rejects them.* And yet, as he admitted in a letter to Arthur Seidl after the publication of the Second Symphony in 1897, whether the work has an explicit programme or not there are elements that cry out for extra-musical interpretation – the essence, he says, is still the communication of 'feelings and ideas'. The source of these feelings and ideas can only be himself, but to condemn Mahler as self-obsessive is to do him less than justice. What he seeks is not merely to express the personal – which he does with exceptional force – but to find in it the universal: the type of humanity as a whole. Music, for Mahler, is also the voice of human experience.

That these two great themes – nature and human experience – remained at the heart of Mahler's musical vision throughout his life is generally accepted. But one obvious question follows: how does music 'embrace' the extra-musical? That it can express human feelings is a long-established belief, though problems often arise when one tries to say exactly *what* is being expressed. And if a composer denies him- or herself the assistance of words (as Mahler did completely in six of his symphonies and for the greater part of three others) how can his music refer outside itself in such a way that audiences will be able to grasp what is being depicted?

A simple answer might be, by imitation – musical onomatopoeia for instance, or the use of widely understood musical symbols. Examples of this kind of *Malerei* are easy to find in Mahler. First there are the sounds of nature: woodwind birdsong, the harp imitating the lapping of the brook in the Finale of *Das Lied von der Erde*, shimmering high strings suggesting mountain heights – perhaps with cowbells for added realism, and a host of sounds which, though less obviously specific, seem to have remarkable power to evoke landscapes and the life teeming amongst them –

---

* 'And with that Mahler seized his glass and emptied it, crying "Perish all programmes!"' Ludwig Schneidermair: *Gustav Mahler* (1901).

that mysterious musical archetype, the horn-call, for instance.* Then there are sounds that seem to stand for human beings and their pursuits: trumpet fanfares, folk or folk-like melodies, bells – in one case with the instruction to be played 'in the distance, struck softly and irregularly', suggesting a faraway church peal – or the human voice itself, alone or in chorus. In addition there are those characteristic rhythmic and melodic patterns which inevitably suggest human movement: dancing – civilized waltz or rustic *Ländler* – and walking or marching tunes.

Characteristic as such tone-painting is, it could hardly be described as peculiarly Mahlerian. This kind of musical mimesis has many precedents: Vivaldi's *Four Seasons* for instance, or Beethoven's 'Pastoral' Symphony; even the use of distance effects is strikingly anticipated in Berlioz's *Symphonie fantastique*, a work for which Mahler the conductor appears to have had a particular *penchant*, and of course he would have had plenty of experience of musical 'staging' in the opera house. And as we have already seen, Mahler had more in mind than simple pictorialism: he is not content simply to conjure up images – he also wants to convey feelings and ideas about them. It hardly needs stating that his use of funeral marches in the first movements of the Second and Fifth symphonies are much more than simple depictions of *cortèges*. What stands before us is death itself, highlighted in the Fifth Symphony by a rich display of Mahlerian *grotesquerie*, and with the composer-spectator's emotional reactions set out in both movements in Mahler's intensely expressive melodic lines. Even if you had not read the programmes for the Second Symphony (and, as we have seen, the older Mahler would probably have preferred that you didn't) it would be difficult to miss the broad intention.

Other cases provide equally rich food for thought. In the third movement of the Third Symphony comes one of Mahler's most famous uses of spatial effect (fig. 14): a posthorn, marked 'as if in the far distance' (and traditionally placed off-stage), sings out a long, sentimental tune to an ethereal accompaniment of sustained high violins, marked *ppp*. The distance doesn't merely 'lend enchantment'; it conveys the idea of *remoteness*. In other words the calm sweetness it conveys is a quality immeasurably far away – a voice from a lost past perhaps, in contrast to the obviously 'present' music of the Scherzo.

Still more fascinating is the rôle played by the woodwind birdsong motif in the first movement of the First Symphony. The clarinet first imitates the call of the cuckoo just before fig. 2 (the score is quite specific at this point) to the interval of a falling perfect fourth. We have heard this falling fourth before: it is almost the first sound in the work, though in longer note-values

---

* Another good example is the long succession of string trills and flowing semiquavers beneath the flutes' march in the Fourth Symphony's opening movement (fig. 10 *et seq*). What might they represent – the breeze? The buzzing of insects? Nothing so specific, surely – and yet one senses that something along those lines, however indistinct, must be intended.

and *legato*, and the 'cuckoo' form of it is neatly prepared by woodwind a few bars later. Gradually it falls lower (too low for most normal cuckoos) until it is taken up by the cellos as the first two notes of the vocal line of *Ging heut' Morgen über's Feld* ('I went this morning through the fields') from the song cycle *Lieder eines fahrenden Gesellen* which Mahler uses as the movement's principal theme. So Mahler's Wayfaring Lad takes his prompting from the bird, while both can be felt to have grown from the seminal opening fourth – a true Mahlerian *Urthema*. Later on in the movement (fig. 15), horns recall irresistibly the style of the German folk chorus, the repeated descending fourths at the close suggesting that this is the kind of song with a refrain to the words 'Cuckoo! Cuckoo!' The wandering individual, the communal singers and the sound of nature are linked motivically, and the listener may well hear in this bonding of images the suggestion of a kind of ideal pastoral unity – constrasted with, but not yet seriously challenged by darker, more introspective music. The alienation and pain of the third and fourth movements are still some way off.

Mahler's use of dance music similarly carries tone-poetry way beyond the merely picturesque. As implied above, the contrast between the sophisticated urban form of the Viennese waltz and its ruder rustic ancestor the *Ländler* lends itself to a rich array of interpretative possibilities. But perhaps the most arresting aspect of the Mahlerian use of dance elements – or of popular music styles in general – is the way they often seem to acquire quite startling new meanings in context. Take the begining of the Scherzo of the Fifth Symphony: heard by itself it resembles a slightly over-ebullient *Ländler*, but coming as it does after the final dark disintegration of the *Allegro* second movement, its sudden, unannounced brightness is not a little disturbing – particularly so since it literally waltzes in to the key of D major, in which the previous movement made such determined – but ultimately fruitless – efforts to exult.

This brings us neatly to one of the most celebrated Mahlerian devices: the use of naïve, or even downright banal material in a way which, far from bringing a sense of bathos, can convey intense feeling. It is one facet (but only one) of the so-called Mahlerian irony. Again context is everything: the clarinet's *Ländler* tune 13 bars before fig. 30 in the Scherzo of the Second Symphony is innocuous in itself, but after the haunted opening one can read all manner of sinister possibilities into it; the childlike oboe tune of the Sixth Symphony's second movement Trio has an intrinsic oddity in its alternation of 3/8 and 4/8 bars, but coming as it does at the heart of what is perhaps the classic Mahler 'horror' Scherzo, it can be deeply unsettling. A rather different effect, much more difficult to describe, is achieved in the first movement of the Ninth Symphony, 26 bars after fig. 13, where two solo violins sing out a sweetly sentimental phrase (marked 'very tender, but expressively prominent') with just a hint of a yodel in its upward-swooping sixth. After the eerie *pianissimo* passage that precedes it (Mahler marks it 'shadowy'), this really should be bathetic – and yet, even with critical defences raised, it can come as a wave of reassuring warmth.

There is a popular explanation for this. In 1910, Mahler met Sigmund Freud and submitted himself to psychoanalysis. According to Freud's biographer Ernest Jones, Mahler found his conversations with Freud revelatory, claiming at the end that he now understood why so often his music was 'spoilt by the intrusion of some commonplace melody'. Apparently he remembered witnessing, as young boy, a particularly painful scene between his father and his adored mother. Deeply upset, he had run out of the house, only to be confronted with a hurdy-gurdy merrily churning out the popular tune *Ach, du lieber Augustin.* 'In Mahler's opinion the conjunction of high tragedy and light amusement was from then on inextricably fixed in his mind.'

As Michael Kennedy says in his *Master Musicians* study, it is all too pat. And even if one accepts every detail, it actually explains very little. If the association between intense feeling and banal music was rooted solely in one person's traumatic experience, why then should it strike sympathetic chords in so many listeners? And why should so many composers since Mahler have tried to imitate it? No, what is significant here is surely that Mahler has touched upon a common human experience: the personal has indeed proved the type of the universal. 'Extraordinary how potent cheap music is', wrote Noël Coward; and three centuries earlier, Sir Thomas Browne made this very Mahlerian observation: 'Even that vulgar and tavern music, which makes one man merry, another mad, strikes in me a deep fit of devotion.' Other composers had sensed this: the 6/8 March section in the choral Finale of Beethoven's Ninth Symphony is a fine example of a composer bringing music off the street into a great art work, and one that must have left its mark on Mahler (think of the 'Resurrection March' in the Finale of his own Second Symphony) – but no-one else had made such varied, or indeed such extensive use of it.

So far, the musical devices we have been considering are the kind which, either because of some intrinsic quality or by long-established association, seem able to provoke remarkably similar responses in large numbers of listeners. But there are ideas in Mahler which – perhaps from the way they are made to stand out from their context – appear to carry some symbolic significance, but whose meaning it is difficult to define. The use of the tenor horn (a very distinctive sonority, and one very rarely found in orchestral music) at only certain key moments in the first movement of the Seventh Symphony is arresting enough to demand explanation. Mahler's remark that it represents 'a voice of nature' comes for many as a kind of confirmation – we had already sensed that it must be *something* like that. And yet even with such help from the composer, it retains its dream-like inscrutability.

Just as interesting, but in a rather different way, is Mahler's invocation of other composers or styles – not this time the popular styles of the waltz or the hurdy-gurdy tune, but those of musical high art. I stress *invocation*, in contrast to imitation, conscious or otherwise. It is easy to pick out things in Mahler which resemble passages in the works of other composers; in fact there was a time when detractors used to make quite a game of it. The conductor Zubin Mehta recalls that as late as the 1950s a Mahler joke was still current amongst members of the Vienna Philharmonic Orchestra. A messenger boy is seen carrying a pile of scores – Beethoven, Berlioz, Wagner – to Mahler's rooms. 'Aha', says one of the players, 'He's composing again.' Certainly Mahler had a very retentive musical memory, and he may often have unwittingly duplicated musical ideas that had once made a strong impression – Freud has some interesting things to say about this sort of thing in *The Psychopathology of Everyday Life*. But again this would be understandable only when one had found the cause in Mahler's personal experience. What concerns us here are references or allusions to composers or musical styles which carry a more widely comprehensible significance.

A good example of stylistic allusion can be found in the first movement of the Fourth Symphony. The exclusion from the score of trombones and tuba has been seen as a move towards a classical orchestral sound – though the wide range of woodwind and percussion colour tends to contradict this. But stylistically the whole first group, right up to the cultivatedly naïve modulation to the second subject, is a remarkable example of what Deryck Cooke calls 'neo-rococo' – a style popular since Tchaikovsky's *Variations on a Rococo Theme* of 1876, but to this writer's knowledge, never before used in a serious symphonic work. The implication is of a long-vanished and (especially for audiences of Mahler's own time) innocent past, highly appropriate for the beginning of a work that is to culminate in a vision of heaven as portrayed by a child – touching, but clearly unattainable. As with the spatial effects in the Third and Sixth Symphonies, a psychological distance is created between the listener and the music, in this case setting the scene right from the start in the dimension of the not-quite-real.

But what of invocations of specific composers? There is a particularly striking example in the Fifth Symphony. This work is often cited as an example of Mahlerian 'progressive tonality'. It begins in C sharp minor, but ends in D major, and there are signs quite early on that D is envisaged as the ultimate goal: it is the key – as we saw above – in which the second movement makes its premature attempt to rejoice. D major is a key with strong associations: much of Bach's Mass in B minor – especially the triumphant or laudatory movements – is in D, as are the 'Hallelujah' and 'Amen' choruses from Handel's *Messiah*; and then there is the Finale of Beethoven's Ninth and the *Missa solemnis*. Of course there are plenty of cases in Mahler where the use of D major plainly carries no such connotations, but here the potential association is strongly underlined at the first and last arrivals of the key by the use of a splendid brass chorale. There is more than one possible reference here. The Lutheran chorale is recalled – one phrase (II, one bar before fig. 29, and more strongly V, five bars after fig. 33) resembles the old German hymn *Wie schön leuchtet der Morgenstern* ('How brightly shines the morning star') – but the massive brass sound, plus pealing string unisons in the Finale, suggests one name in particular: Bruckner – Mahler's teacher and artistic father-figure, and regarded by many as the embodiment of simple Catholic piety even in his own lifetime. For the musically well-travelled listener, these allusions may well back up what he or she has deduced already, that Mahler is making a statement of – or about – faith: whether in God, Christian or otherwise, or in Life addressed in archetypal religious terms is a matter for debate; but the collaboration of expressive and referential elements make it difficult to resist the conclusion that the burden of the song is joyous affirmation of belief – or at the very least the image of it.

Another figure invoked by Mahler, and in a rich diversity of ways, is Beethoven. We have already observed the resemblance of the 'Resurrection March' in the Second Symphony to the March episode in the Finale of Beethoven's Ninth – and it seems that the effect of the 'Choral' Symphony on Mahler is still widely underestimated. Other echoes of Beethoven are more perplexing: for instance the remarkable similarity of scoring and harmony between the opening of the third movement of Mahler's Fourth Symphony and the introduction to the Quartet from Act 1 of *Fidelio* (both are in G major) – or is it possible that in anticipating his own impossible *Himmlisches Leben* Mahler was momentarily reminded of poor Marzelline's childlike 'Mir ist so wunderbar' ('It is so wonderful to me')? In other places the allusions – conscious or not – may be easier to understand. To these ears, the opening of the *Adagio* Finale of Mahler's Third Symphony invariably brings strong suggestions of two great Beethoven slow movements: the *Lento assai* from the String Quartet Op. 135, and the second part of the main theme of the *Eroica* Symphony's *Marcia funèbre* (Ex. 1).

A passing resemblance? Or could we be justified in calling this a reference, conscious or unconscious? Perhaps Mahler has summoned up the ghosts of two of Beethoven's finest slow movements because he wants so very deeply to create something on a similarly exalted level: 'I could almost call this movement "What God tells me" ', he informed the soprano Anna von Mildenburg; it is the culmination of a work which 'begins with inanimate nature and ascends to the love of God.' Whether or not one feels that he succeeded in the final stages of his ascent (this writer is among those who have yet to be convinced) makes little difference: the Beethoven allusions could be interpreted as a musical declaration of intent, or as a sign of one composer drawing on another for strength and inspiration. Whatever the case, one senses that Beethoven, like Bruckner, has taken on a special symbolic significance for Mahler, just as figures like Milton, Michelangelo or Klopstock did for William Blake.

Ex. 1. Mahler: Symphony No. 3

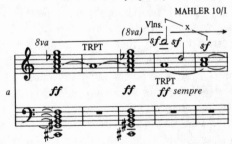

At other times more than one figure seems to be invoked. Take the astonishing nine-note dissonance that Mahler piles up in blocks at the climax of the *Adagio* first movement of his Tenth Symphony. 'Prophetic' elements in Mahler, and particularly in this symphony, have often been pointed out, but at the same time the listener may catch echoes of the past (Ex. 2):

Ex. 2. Mahler: Symphony No. 10

Ex. 2 cont'd

At the time Mahler began his Tenth Symphony, the Bruckner was available only in a bowdlerised version by Ferdinand Löwe in which that culminating discord was cleaned up, but given Mahler's involvement with Bruckner it is likely that he had seen the original and, if so, that the appearance of such grinding, convulsive sounds at the high point of Bruckner's last completed movement (another *Adagio*) would have left a strong imprint on him. The Schubert too comes at the climax of a slow movement, and in another final symphony.* In the Schubert and the Bruckner the discord is left to shudder into silence; Mahler, as it were, writes in a reverberation in the form of the high sustained trumpet *a''*, but the effect is strikingly similar. Thus, at a crucial moment, Mahler invokes the past – proclaims at this most intensely personal moment that even here he is aware of his lineage. Such self-consciousness is very characteristic – and, one might add, very modern.

In one interesting respect, however, what Mahler does is different from what Schubert and Bruckner do – not at the climax itself, but in what follows. Just before the end of the movement, he presents what one could call a 'diatonicized' version of the discord, similarly built-up in thirds above a C sharp – G sharp bass, and then gently resolves it (in the treble only) into the home key of F sharp major (Ex. 3):

---

* Mahler would almost certainly have shared the general belief that Schubert wrote the 'Great' C major Symphony in 1828 – the last year of his life. He could not have known that Schubert was also working on a Tenth Symphony just before he died.

Ex. 3. Mahler: Symphony No. 10

While this certainly isn't a resolution of the discord of Ex. 2a in the textbook sense, the listener may well sense an analogous relationship between it and the expanded dominant chord in Ex. 3 (subtly underlined by the motivic cross-reference of *x*), and perhaps interpret its tentative, treble-only resolution as an expression of provisional hope – a suggestion (as yet not fully realized) that the painful tensions of Ex. 2a can eventually find release.

These are just some of the ways in which Mahler's music gives the impression of drawing images, feelings and ideas into its embrace. Any of the lines of enquiry begun above could be followed much further, and we could open up many more, quite apart from adding a long list of sound-symbols invested with specific meaning by Mahler himself: the hammer blows in the Finale of the Sixth Symphony for instance, the xylophone's 'Devil's laughter' or the major-minor 'Fate' motif that pervade the same work, or the 'cry of disgust' that breaks up the Scherzo of the Second and later on sets the Finale in motion. But space is limited, and however enjoyable this kind of sign-hunting may be, it begs a further question – and one can't help feeling that if Sibelius did put it to Mahler, it's a shame he didn't record the answer. Given that music can embrace the extra-musical, and in such a variety of ways, what is it that makes the resulting work *symphonic?*

For an answer one could point to the original meaning of the word symphony – 'sounding together' – and claim that the simple fact that such diverse elements do indeed sound together is in itself justification of the term. Carl Dahlhaus, for instance, has written of Mahler's 'forcing heterogeneous material to coexist, without glossing over the inconsistencies, [creating] a panorama which truly fulfils the claim he made for the symphony.' Thus Mahler sets his face against 'the law of symphonic 'motion' which since Beethoven 'has been incessant goal-directedness.' Certainly Donald Mitchell's description of 'an almost Ivesian collage' in parts of the first movement of the Third Symphony rings true, and however extravagant it may seem, Luciano Berio's collage-expansion of the Scherzo of the 'Resurrection' Symphony in his own *Sinfonia* seems to grow at almost every level from its Mahlerian model.

But the suggestion that Mahler's symphonies act in constant defiance of 'the law of symphonic motion' does not hold up. 'Goal-directedness' may be rather too loaded a term to describe his symphonic thinking in general, yet there is a characteristic type of long-term movement in Mahler: a process that is entirely in keeping with his view of the symphony. And the term that comes nearest to describing it is one put forward by Mahlerians as diverse as Donald Mitchell and Pierre Boulez – 'narrative'. Neither Mitchell nor Boulez is suggesting that a Mahler symphony tells its story with the unambiguous directness of Enid Blyton or the Brothers Grimm, but those who respond to Mahler often feel that something like story-telling is at work, no matter how hard they may find it to be categorical about events or *dramatis personae*.

The essence of narrative, as one of the characters in Robertson Davies's *What's Bred in the Bone* observes, is change; and examples of change – or to use a more musicological term, transformation – are easy to find in Mahler, most obviously in the way certain leading motifs are treated. A striking example can be found in the D major–minor episode (18 bars after fig. 36 *et seq*) from the *Rondo Burleske* third movement of the Ninth Symphony.

Ex. 4. Mahler: Symphony No. 9

The trumpet's version, Ex. 4a, has something of the fey sweetness of the posthorn solo in the third movement of the Third Symphony, though coming as it does after a long stretch of hectic *Allegro assai* (also marked *Sehr trotzig* – 'very defiant', 'obstinate' or even 'sulky'), the effect is rather different – a touch ironic perhaps. In Ex. 4b, however, the first phrase of the trumpet's tune becomes a high clarinet shriek, a brutal parody of its former self.

Again it is possible to find precedents. Something very similar happens to the *idée fixe* – the theme of 'the beloved' – in the Finale of the Berlioz *Symphonie fantastique*, and Berlioz's use of the E flat clarinet to represent the transformation from 'nobility and shyness' to the 'mean, trivial and grotesque' was an obvious gift to Mahler. Nevertheless, despite the important entrances of the *idée fixe* in all five movements of the *Symphonie fantastique*, its role in terms of the thematic argument of each movement – except for the initial 'Rêveries, Passions' – is relatively slight. It now seems highly likely, for instance, that the single statement of the *idée fixe* at the end of the 'Marche au supplice' was actually grafted on to music already composed for the unfinished opera *Les Francs-juges*. In the Mahler example, however, the theme brutalized in Ex. 4 emerges from the fabric of the main movement, and further mutations are to form an important part of the following *Adagio*. Mahler makes motivic transformation a unifying principle of whole movements, or even whole works, to a degree never even attempted by Berlioz.

Other models could be suggested: Liszt's *Faust* Symphony, for instance, or his B minor Piano Sonata; but Liszt's manipulation of his leading motifs can be wooden – pantomimic even – compared with Mahler. What makes Mahler's transformations generally subtler than Liszt's is not just their greater ingenuity, but the way they seem to be involved inextricably with every facet of the musical argument, from passing evocation of images and feelings to long-term harmonic movement. We have already seen how a hint of motivic cross-reference between Exx. 2 and 3 emphasizes what may already be felt as an important harmonic analogy in the first movement of the Tenth Symphony, and how the 'cuckoo' falling fourth heard in the slow introduction of the First Symphony establishes a bond between musical images. Now it is time to look at some examples in greater detail.

Certain important elements in the 'story' of the Fifth Symphony have been pointed out in the earlier part of this chapter. The first movement, called by Mahler *Trauermarsch*, assembles a variety of moods – sombre, maudlin, sardonic, protesting – around the central image of death. The basic tonality is C sharp minor, but this is not the key in which the Symphony is to end, and there are indications as early as the second movement that the music is aspiring towards D major, identified at its first and last appearances with the majestic sound of a brass chorale. But already this is beginning to sound perilously subjective: even granted the symbolic significance of funeral march and chorale in this work, what grounds have we to talk of the music 'aspiring' from one to the other?

The adventures of a particular leading motif provide an answer. The A minor second movement of the Fifth Symphony (marked 'Stormy, lively. With the greatest vehemence') quickly introduces a three-note figure (*x*) which is to play a vital part in the argument (Ex. 5):

Ex. 5. Mahler: Symphony No. 5

The third phrase already suggests that *x* is capable of mutation without losing its identity: in other words, so long as it maintains its characteristic shape – a straining upward leap (Mahler marks the rising diminished tenth of *y* 'as vehement as possible') followed by a step downwards – we sense that it is essentially the same figure, modified for expressive purposes. This motif goes through many transformations, begetting longer ideas as diverse as the violins' figure *y*, the cellos' slow plaint eleven bars after fig. 11, or the woodwind's hearty quick-march at the end of Ex. 6c. Most importantly, *x* becomes the basis of a series of what are plainly upward-striving crescendos. Ex. 6 gives four examples – plus a striking anticipation (Ex. 6a) from towards the end of the Funeral March:

Ex. 6. Mahler: Symphony No. 5

Ex. 6. cont'd

Ex. 6a culminates in grinding dissonances, harshly scored, and marked *Klagend* ('Lamenting'): it seems that Mahler's first attempt to raise the music out of its morbid brooding has failed. But in the much more energetic conditions of the second movement, the crescendos themselves become increasingly charged, and the culminating points grow steadily brighter in harmony and in orchestration (Ex. 6b–e). At last (Ex. 6e), the music reaches a solid-sounding D major; trumpet fanfares introduce the Brucknerian-Lutheran chorale on full brass ... but the splendour fades, and D major turns to D minor in what sounds very much like a pre-echo of the major-minor 'Fate' motif from the Sixth Symphony. Then D minor turns to the original A minor, and the movement dies away (Mahler's marking is *morendo*) with muted versions of *x* and *y*. It seems that the striving of Ex. 6 has culminated in a momentary revelation of exultant faith, but has failed to consolidate it – the possibility but not the actuality. At the end of the second movement we are back where we started. The Scherzo's blithely dancing D major opening can be oddly disconcerting after this, even if Mahler's 'long pause' between the movements is observed; and yet, is there a suggestion of *x* in its opening horn phrase (Ex. 7)?

Ex. 7. Mahler: Symphony No. 5

One more point about the narrative of the Fifth Symphony must be made. We have noted above that the chorale appears again, this time in an unequivocal D major, at the end of the work. Here the theme that brings about the triumphant final turn to D is not the 'vehement' Ex. 5 *x*, but a folkish tune (Ex. 8a), like something from *Des Knaben Wunderhorn*, now presented in grand augmentation by trumpets (Ex. 8b) – though with perhaps another echo of the *x* shape in its first three notes.

Ex. 8. Mahler: Symphony No. 5

Surely it isn't imposing too much on the music to read a message in all this. What takes the Fifth Symphony beyond the vision of faith to its actuality is not the heroic striving of Ex. 6 but the effortless transfiguration of the folk-like tune in Ex. 8 – ''tis the gift to be simple'? Many more threads could be drawn into this – the quotation of the *Wunderhorn* song 'Lob des hohen Verstandes' (a highly ironic 'praise of lofty intellect') at the opening of the Finale, for instance, and nothing has been said about the possible rôle of the *Adagietto*, with its closing recollection of another song, 'Ich bin der Welt abhanden gekommen'; but already we have seen something of how the narrative element in this Symphony works: motivic transformation combines with orchestration, expression, musical symbolism and especially long-term harmonic movement to create what feels like a story-line – and one that contains a possible statement about mortality and faith.

Of course the listener is still allowed considerable freedom in how he or she interprets this 'statement'. What exactly are we to have faith in? Does the Finale's answer to the second movement convince (some listeners think not)? If not, was it *intended* to convince? Or does Mahler's invocation of Bruckner contain just a hint of what Hardy heard in the singing of the Darkling Thrush – 'Some blessed Hope, whereof he knew/And I was unaware'? Granted this is a piece of music, not a novel; and yet, as we have seen, it can point the way – give us as it were the bones of the story, which we can then flesh out from our own experience and beliefs.

One can anticipate an objection here – that the Fifth Symphony is a special case. It is arguably his most humanist – his most goal-directed work. But even in a very different case like the Ninth Symphony, one senses that a kind of story-line runs through the work – most powerfully and consistently in the outer movements, but also drawing in elements from the second movement and the *Rondo Burleske*.

Ex. 9. Mahler: Symphony No. 9

As in the second movement of the Fifth Symphony, a tiny motif plays a vital part in the unfolding of the Ninth's opening *Andante comodo* – in this case a simple falling second, either major or minor.

Once again what Mahler does with Ex. 9a/b is inseparable from the other strands of the musical argument. The flattening of the F sharp (Ex. 9a) to F natural (Ex. 9b) by the horn signals the first turn from D major calm to turbulent, impassioned D minor. (A later motif, Ex. 9c, is a clear derivation from the falling seconds of Ex. 9a and b.) Major-minor alternations occur frequently in this movement, often with powerful expressive or dramatic effect, and again one may be reminded of 'Fate' from the Sixth Symphony. There is another important feature of the motif Ex. 9a/b: no matter how often one hears it, one never quite loses the expectation that it will do the conventional thing and fall to the tonic – but even in the coda of the movement the final fall is from the second of the scale to the fifth (Ex. 9d).

A kind of resolution does appear in the second movement's *Ländler* theme (Ex. 9e), but this is in a different key, and the banality of the figure further denies it the expressive force of a long-delayed release – here the intention can only be ironic. This movement comes much closer to the Dahlhaus-Mitchell category of 'collage' than the other three, but towards the end, at the height of a particularly *Angst*-laden passage, there is a reminiscence of Ex. 9a on the trumpet, continuing in a kind of written-out accelerando on the violins, marked *klagend* (27 bars before fig. 26) – a reminder of tensions still unresolved, and a momentary re-engagement with the first movement's motivic-harmonic storyline. Something more like the expected resolution of Ex. 9a/b happens in the first theme of the Finale, only not in the first movement's D, but in D flat (Ex. 9f) – where it now yields a figure very much like the *Lebewohl* ('Farewell') motif from Beethoven's *Les Adieux* Sonata, Op. 81, the harmonic surprise on the third beat strongly underlining the similarity.

This overall move from D to D flat looks almost like a reversal of the broad tonal plan of the Fifth Symphony, and when one compares the keys of the individual movements, other resemblances become apparent:

No. 5: c # (i) a – D/d – a (ii) D (iii) F (iv) D (v)
No. 9: D/d (i) C (ii) a – D/d – a (iii) Db/c # (iv)

So the Ninth's final involvement with D major is in the third movement, the *Rondo Burleske*. It begins with the trumpet tune Ex. 4a, and gradually builds towards a climax. For a moment it looks as though this section is going to clinch D major with what is fundamentally a perfect cadence (Ex. 10):

Ex. 10. Mahler: Symphony No. 9

But the culminating D is unsupported – a particularly hollow sound after the harmonic richness of the preceding crescendo. Quietly the music turns to D minor – and it is then that we hear the clarinets' mockery of Ex. 4b. Again it looks as though a particular point is intended: the Symphony has tried to re-establish D major, and failed. Perhaps the whole episode already had a mirage-like quality: it is difficult to believe whole-heartedly in Ex. 4a's sentimental song after the turmoil of the main movement (what a masterstroke it was to give it to the trumpet!), and high shimmering strings plus occasional quiet glissandi add to the general impression of unreality. And now perhaps we can understand why the clarinets are so derisive – 'Did you really think that with a tune like *that* . . .?'

After the *Rondo* comes the *Adagio* Finale. It is now tempting to look on D flat as a kind of 'depressed' D. Could it be that the broad reversal of the key-scheme of the Fifth Symphony implies a reversal in meaning too: that instead of moving away from Death, the Ninth moves *towards* it? That may sound highly tenuous, but then what about *Lebewohl* (Ex. 9f), or the reference to a passage from the *Kindertotenlieder* cycle where the poet thinks of joining his dead children 'in bright sunshine . . . up on the heights'? And then there is the coda itself – a protracted dying away that outdoes the end of Tchaikovsky's *Pathétique*. One small detail deserves to be picked out here (Ex. 11): just before the music finally settles in D flat major/minor, and the strings put on their mutes for the last time, a solo cello sings a little plaint *on the dominant of D major*, followed by a reminiscence of the turn from Ex. 4 – a final fleeting memory?

So here are two examples of how motifs interact with other elements, and particularly with long-range harmonic movement, to create the effect of narrative – a narrative which may be shadowy compared with that of a novel or epic poem, but one which can indicate particular lines of interpretation with surprising force. We could spend much more time probing into these examples, or begin looking at others: the motivic-tonal arguments in the Finales of the First and Tenth Symphonies show what different worlds of experience this kind of symphonic thinking can encompass. But even in these short analyses, something fundamental to Mahler's symphonism is revealed.

Ex. 11. Mahler: Symphony No. 9

Perhaps this can also help us to understand why certain works – or at least parts of them – can fail to convince. As we have seen, the Fifth Symphony has left one or two listeners in doubt: the sudden change in style and tonality between the second and third movements is too much for some (Deryck Cooke spoke of 'dangerous' disparity), just as the lurch to G major *buffo* after the death of Don Giovanni in Mozart's great opera strains credibility. But on the whole audiences and critics seem to regard the Fifth as a success. There is much more disagreement about the second part of the Eighth Symphony – the setting of the final scene of Goethe's *Faust*. 'Episodic' is one complaint – Robert Simpson finds it for the most part 'a string of arias' – while others feel that in this case sentimentality has gone too far: not the image of *kitsch*, viewed with that characteristic mixture of affection and sharp criticism, but the thing itself. For these ears, however, the fundamental problem is what happens – or rather what *doesn't* happen to two of the leading motifs:

Ex. 12. Mahler: Symphony No. 8

We hear Ex. 12a and b fairly frequently during the Finale section of Part Two* – not in itself a problem: what is striking, and thoroughly

---

* Ex. 12a is actually an offshoot of a figure heard in the opening *poco adagio* of Part Two, but it is established firmly as a motif in its own right near the beginning of the Finale section.

uncharacteristic, is how little they are varied. Both lend themselves to a little sequential modification (Ex. 12b less so), but in general variation is no more than decorative: the vital interaction between these motifs and the other strands in the argument – the source of so much of the dramatic and expressive energy of the Fifth and Ninth Symphonies – is largely absent. This helps explain a strange phenomenon: that the final climax can be less convincing in context than when one simply listens (thanks to the compact disc) to the last ten minutes or so. It is not simply that there has been too much of Ex. 12a and b, but that their effect has grown stale through the lack of meaningful transformation.

Nevertheless, the point of bringing in this example of Mahler on less than top form has not been to cut him down to size – quite the opposite: the aim is to emphasize the originality, ingenuity and power of his finest structures – works like the Fourth, Fifth, Sixth and Ninth Symphonies, or even the incomplete Tenth. In these great works Mahler not only succeeds in his aim to draw worlds into his embrace; he also manages to fuse images, feelings and ideas into a significant order – a kind of musical story in which we may recognize both his and our own experiences, and even find the beginnings of philosophical conclusions. It may be that the gap between Mahler and Sibelius revealed in that brief recorded exchange of 1907 is not so vast after all. Just as Sibelius's symphonies can be said to throw their embrace more widely than he would sometimes have cared to admit, so Mahler's attempt to 'embrace everything' shows itself to be fully compatible with the demands of the form he inherited – to have its own 'profound logic'.

9

The Symphony in France

David Cox

To generalize – always a hazard – the French temperament is animated, voluble, demonstrative, preferring to live *au jour le jour*, with an uncomplicated love of pleasure, and without the Germanic sense of guilt, *Angst*, introspection, stern conscientiousness and thoroughness. At the same time, there is with the French a liking for order, precision, logic, colour and variety – which in music finds expression most readily through the smaller forms, clear in thought and feeling, precise in craftsmanship, loving the sensual enjoyment of sound. The preference therefore is for episodic expression. The effect is more immediate: you don't listen 'with your head in your hands'.

Combining the arts has always appealed to the French: music with some literary or pictorial connection; ballet and opera at their most picturesque. If Debussy had not called *La Mer* 'Three Symphonic Sketches' (a very modest and quite inadequate description) but instead had labelled it a symphony, nobody would have queried its right to that description, for each of these so-called 'sketches' is like a finely-constructed symphonic movement; and together (with the second one as Scherzo) they form a unified whole in purely musical terms. On the other hand, Berlioz could call a work a symphony when it was in many aspects closely related to music-drama. The question 'When is a work a symphony?' is not a straightforward one, particularly when discussing the diversity of the symphony in France. As a basic criterion, we must look for strong formal elements in a work, development in purely musical terms, a wide range of contrasts, and at the same time an overall feeling of unity in style and purpose.

By the eighteenth century, Paris had become a great cosmopolitan music centre, where French composers and executants were constantly vying with those of other countries, and where music publishing flourished. Opera dominated French music at the time; but from 1725 André Danican Philidor, instrumentalist and composer, established the 'Concerts spirituels' in the Salle des Cent Suisses in the Tuileries – at first, with special reference to religious music, but gradually an important place was given to instrumental works by French composers and by those of other nationalities, including in particular Haydn. Also, the musical patron Alexandre de la Pouplinière had a private theatre where concerts were regularly given, conducted for a time by Rameau and later by Stamitz, whose symphonies were often performed there. In 1740 Louis-Gabriel Guillemain (1705–1770), composer and violinist, published six symphonies described as *dans le goût italien* – which is to say, influenced by the school of Corelli and Vivaldi. With the strong influence of the Mannheim school of composers, and later that of Vienna, the national identity of the French symphony in the eighteenth century is not easy to distinguish; but a number of composers developed recognisably personal styles – notably **François-Joseph Gossec** (1734–1829), Netherlands-born, but active in Parisian musical life for three-quarters of a century. His many four-movement symphonies show strong German influence in structure and orchestration; they are often enterprising in their scope, melodic invention, and orchestral textures (a symphony in F major of 1809 has 17 separate instrumental parts; another is a *Symphonie militaire*). The following is an example of Gossec's writing for strings, from the middle movement of his symphony in D (for two oboes and strings) dating from 1756.

Ex. 1. Gossec: Symphony in D

After Gossec, one of the most striking eighteenth-century composers in the genre was **Simon Le Duc** *l'aîné* (1742–1777), much admired during his short life for exceptional melodic gifts, and his works show considerable rhythmic subtlety. But probably the most important figure between Gossec and Berlioz was **Étienne-Nicolas Méhul** (1763–1817). Most famous in his time for his operas, he turned to the symphony after the declining success of his stage works; his four mature symphonies, all recorded, were written between 1808 and 1810. He was an intelligent and self-critical composer, and each of these works is truly symphonic in construction and purpose – influenced by the Viennese classics, but always decidedly individual in style and orchestration. These attractive and often brilliant works contain some highly original features for their time, such as the use of extended pizzicato in the Menuet movement of the Symphony No. 1; and the Finale of No. 3 is an exciting *tour de force*, exploring in virtuoso style the capabilities of the various instruments. Remarkable, too, is the use of solo cellos in the *Andante* of No. 4; and in the same work the Menuet, marked *Allegro*, is both lively and serious – not a Scherzo in spirit. The scores of Symphonies No. 3 and No. 4 were lost; but the orchestral parts of these were discovered by David Charlton as recently as 1979, and from them the full scores have been reconstructed.

Beethoven described **Luigi Cherubini** (1760–1842) as his greatest contemporary. Born in Florence, he made France his home from 1786, becoming an important figure in the musical life of Paris for half a century – particularly in the fields of opera and musical education. His one symphony, in D, and in four movements, was written during a visit to London in 1815 to a commission from London's Philharmonic Society. Although this is a well-constructed and attractive work, it was largely forgotten until 1935, when, on the occasion of the 175th anniversary of the composer's birth, it received a new lease of life. The basic inspiration is Mozart and Haydn, but the symphony has many of Cherubini's Italianate characteristics – spontaneous and colourful melodic forms, a harmonic richness, and often a dramatic force, including some sudden and violent dynamic contrasts and some touches of humour. The symphony was re-worked in 1829 as a string quartet (No. 2 in C) with the outer movements largely unmodified, but with a new slow movement. (The Minuet of the symphony has the indication *Allegro non tanto*, and in the quartet the same music is called Scherzo and is marked *Allegro assai*.)

With **Hector Berlioz** (1803–1869) an overwhelming change occurs in the French symphony. In the early nineteenth century, Parisian taste continued to favour opera and ballet. Berlioz, in his late twenties, was discouraged by not being given the opportunities he longed for with the leading opera houses of Paris. He therefore turned his musico-dramatic instincts towards concert music, hoping in that way indirectly to impress opera managers. The results are not easily classified. At once the form of the symphony is stretched to its limits and beyond, to admit an enormous range of dramatic material in musical terms. For Berlioz – the Romantic, self-expressive composer *par excellence* – art and life were inseparable, and in every work it feels as though the arts were combining, but with music predominating. Berlioz was a great admirer of the Beethoven symphonies, and it's possible that, in form, the initial idea for his *Symphonie fantastique* (1830) came from Beethoven's five-movement 'Pastoral' symphony, with its imaginative freedom and evocation of scenes and events – though the musical content owes little, if anything, to Beethoven. The avowedly autobiographical character of the work stemmed from his violent passion for the young Irish actress Harriet Smithson. Much of the musical material, however, is directly borrowed, or transformed, from earlier compositions.

Berlioz's intense love of Shakespeare – hero-worshipped by the whole Romantic movement – took him in September 1827 to the Odéon Theatre in Paris. There, a season of Shakespeare was being given, starting with *Hamlet*, in which Ophelia was played by Harriet Smithson, with whom Berlioz immediately fell desperately in love. The tantalizing way in which Harriet subsequently treated him nearly drove him mad – though he pretended to despise her as a vile creature incapable of appreciating his great love. (Later, she did become his wife for eight far-from-happy years; then they separated.) Berlioz described the *Symphonie fantastique* as a *drame instrumental*. When the image of the beloved comes to mind, it is always accompanied by a musical thought, or *idée fixe*, in which can be discovered 'qualities of grace and nobility similar to those bestowed on the loved one'. This *idée fixe*, passionate and aspiring, first appears on flute and first violins in unison, and then is heard in different guises at various times throughout the work (Ex. 2).

Despite the extremes of expression and the violence of some of the musical images, everything in the work is kept under the most rigorous intellectual control – the whole having a consistency and clear sense of form. In each movement we find an organic growth very different from sonata form, but equally consistent and dramatically contrasting, achieved by wide-spanning melody which develops through continual variation and extension, underlined by originality of harmony and instrumentation.

Ex. 2. Berlioz: *Symphonie fantastique*

'Rêveries, Passions'; 'A Ball'; 'Scene in the Country'; 'March to the Scaffold'; 'Nightmare of a Witches' Sabbath' – by giving only the titles of each movement, as Berlioz eventually required, the literary ideas behind the work become generalized: the music is not the expression of feeling about one person; it is a universal statement about love and idealism, through the medium of art. One can listen as one chooses. The essential is to put the musical structure first – which has meaning in itself – and then the other backgrounds can be added, or not, according to what one's own nature may require in finding a satisfying artistic experience.

In his *Mémoires* Berlioz wrote much about his travels in Italy. And the

Italian scene (but not Italian music, which he disliked) certainly affected his next two symphonies – *Harold en Italie* and *Roméo et Juliette*. The genesis of *Harold en Italie* was a lucrative commission from Paganini for a composition to display a fine Stradivari viola which he had acquired. But he never actually played the work himself – presumably because when he saw an early draft, he thought the viola part was not sufficiently important: he wanted to be playing all the time and more spectacularly. Berlioz, however, continued as he wished it to be, and it became the work as we now know it – a four-movement symphony, or perhaps more accurately a sinfonia concertante, for solo viola and orchestra. The 'hero' was from Byron (another Romantic key-figure) – his *Childe Harold*, impersonated by the viola, with his personal theme recurring in all four movements – not integrated and transformed, as was the *idée fixe* of the *Symphonie fantastique*, but unchanged, suggesting an objective observer of the scenes represented (a feeling which perhaps gives a unity to the diversity of material in the work). The four movements represent Harold in the mountains; a march of pilgrims (with some monastery bells and intonations); an Abruzzi mountaineer's serenade; and a frenetic orgy of brigands.

The way in which the unchanging motto theme is combined with other thematic material, which develops in its own way, is an interesting feature of the second and third movements. For example, the motto theme in long notes combines with the pilgrims' 'canto' (Ex. 2a):

Ex. 2a. Berlioz: *Harold en Italie*

*With Clarinet I and Horn I

The third movement goes further – not only combining the 'serenade' theme with the motto, but also devising a combination of 'serenade', motto, and the other principal thematic idea of the movement (a lively peasant dance).

But the most fascinating movement is the last – the brigands' orgy.

Berlioz, in his *Mémoires*, wrote: '. . . wine, blood, joy and rage mingle in mutual intoxication and make music together, and the rhythm seems now to stumble, now to rush furiously forward, and the mouths of the brass to spew forth curses, answering prayer with blasphemy, and they laugh and swill and strike, smash, kill, rape, and generally enjoy themselves . . . while from the viola, the pensive Harold fleeing in dismay, a few faint echoes of his evening hymn still hover on the vibrant air.'

The movement begins, like the Finale of Beethoven's Ninth, by recalling themes from previous movements; the viola is involved but takes no part in the orgy. Towards the end, however, it reappears in a brief reminiscence of the pilgrims' theme. The movement as a whole is a remarkable *tour de force* of exciting rhythms and expressive contrasts, with much that is highly original and telling in its orchestral textures . . . Berlioz – 'Wild Spirit, which art moving everywhere', like Shelley's West Wind. But there was one side of his nature which could keep everything in strict control.

The four movements of *Harold en Italie* can be said to suggest roughly those of the usual symphony. Not so the 'dramatic symphony' *Roméo et Juliette*, based on Garrick's acting version of Shakespeare's play, which Berlioz saw in Paris in 1837. Here, the operatic and symphonic come together in a tremendous synthesis which contains some of his most inspired music. Within the overall structure, four of the seven movements are symphonic in character and purely orchestral, but not related in key. They represent Romeo alone, and the Capulets' ball; a love scene; the Queen Mab Scherzo; and the scene at the tomb. The other, surrounding movements are realisations in dramatic style of various aspects of the play, using choruses, soloists, and choral recitative, and with an elaborate operatic Finale, ending with a double-choral reconciliation. At the first performance, in Paris, conducted by Berlioz, 101 voices and 100 instrumentalists took part.

The *Grande Symphonie funèbre et triomphale* (1840) was a *pièce d'occasion* which Berlioz wrote for the official commemoration of the tenth anniversary of the July Revolution. Scored originally for outdoor performance by a very large wind-band, it opens with an impressive funeral march, followed by a 'funeral oration' with trombone solo (using material from his early opera *Les Francs-juges*), and finally, 'Apothéose', a triumphal march. (Berlioz later added optional string parts, and a part for chorus near the end.) Despite all the literary associations, and despite frequent impressions of Romantic imagination run riot, and remarkable experiments in orchestral effects, the *musical* structure of Berlioz's symphonies is always of primary importance, its detail always carefully and scrupulously worked out. Much is unconventional, but nothing is undisciplined or haphazard in its realization.

The symphonies of Berlioz, however, were isolated phenomena, exerting no significant influence on the succeeding symphonic composers in the mid-nineteenth century. In 1854 when **Charles Gounod** (1818–93) wrote two altogether delightful symphonies, in D and E flat, he was already well established as a religious composer. With his other main interest, the theatre, he had been having far less success (*Faust* was still five years away) and the prospect of writing some 'pure' music came as a relief. The first movement is thought to have been composed a decade earlier in 1843 at the Villa Medici: design and style are neo-Classical with some debt to Haydn and Beethoven, and some 'advanced' Schumannesque touches. But despite these influences, the sheer elegance and lightness of touch in both scores are unmistakeably Gallic. The textures are clear; the scoring skilful and always effective, the invention is full of spirit. Yet this exhilarating music rarely penetrates the concert hall and inhabits the peripheries of the record catalogue.

The now-famous Symphony in C of **Georges Bizet** (1838–75) was also a youthful work, written when he was seventeen and showing brilliant promise. His model was the D major Symphony of Gounod which he had transcribed for piano duet in 1855, not only in matters of scoring but even in such details as a fugal development of the material in the slow movement. Indeed he wrote to Gounod: 'You were the beginning of my life as an artist. I can now admit that I was afraid of being absorbed'. Bizet, however, goes beyond Gounod in scope and imagination. Scored for the usual classical orchestra (without trombones), Bizet's four-movement Symphony shows remarkable understanding and skill in orchestration; and the vitality, charm, and personal flavour of the work – with many suggestions of things to come – have established it far more firmly in the orchestral repertoire than either of Gounod's symphonies. But it was not heard until 1935, 80 years after its composition. In 1933 some manuscripts of Bizet were presented to the Paris Conservatoire by the composer Reynaldo Hahn. Hahn considered that there was little of any interest, and failed to recognize any merit in the Symphony, which was included among the manuscripts given him by Bizet's widow. Recognition came when the English musicologist D. C. Parker, who had published a biography of Bizet in 1926, was doing research in Paris, where he was shown the Bizet manuscripts. He was struck by the Symphony and drew it to the attention of the conductor Felix Weingartner, who in 1935 gave the première in Basle – which was the start of its popularity.

At nineteen, Bizet won the important Prix de Rome, and the three years that he spent in Italy, free from financial concern, were probably the happiest of his generally troubled life. His memories of Italy are enshrined in his 'Roma' Symphony, also in C, composed between 1860 and 1868 – and revised in 1871, after Jules-Étienne Pasdeloup* had given its première in Paris two years before. The 'Roma' Symphony was originally described as *Fantaisie symphonique – Souvenirs de Rome*, and titles were given to three of the movements – reminiscent of Berlioz's *Harold en Italie*. The first movement, with its prominent role for the horns, represented 'A Hunt in the Forest of Ostia'. The second is a Scherzo, with some interesting fugal

---

* The French conductor Pasdeloup had founded in 1861 his Concerts Populaires, an important platform for works by French composers of the time (and for much else). After his death these concerts continued for a time, renamed Concerts Pasdeloup.

writing. The third was called 'A Procession', the broad religious-sounding theme, with its variations, suggesting a pilgrims' march. Finally, 'Carnival' (as it is still called) with its wild merriment; and here a second subject (*con franchezza*), introducing a love episode, has already been heard in a different form in the previous movement. In its overall effect, 'Roma' is as attractive a work as the early Symphony and deserves to be heard more often.

Gounod hailed his younger colleague **Camille Saint-Saëns** (1835–1921) in no uncertain terms: 'He is a musician armed with every weapon. He is master of his art as no other composer is; he knows the classics by heart; he plays with and makes light of the orchestra as of the piano. He is neither finicky, violent, or emphatic. He has no system, belongs to no party or clique; he does not pose as a reformer of anything; he writes as he feels and makes use of what he knows.'

The range and variety in his vast output is enormous. While Bizet's far more special output was cut short by early death, Saint-Saëns was to go on composing prolifically for over 70 years. His very facility worked against him: everything came so easily and rapidly that there seemed little time for self-criticism. He believed that a composer produces music 'as naturally as an apple-tree produces apples'. The important things were clarity of style (of many different styles), purity of line, fine craftsmanship, satisfying form. Like Stravinsky, he set little store by inspiration and the expression of emotion. Saint-Saëns was steeped in the Viennese models of sonatas, symphonies and concertos, and was strongly influenced by Mozart, Bach, Mendelssohn and Schumann. The result was a generally conservative style in which Germanic influences are combined with certain French traditions, and with at times Spanish and oriental colouring. There is also a sense of humour.

We listen to Saint-Saëns against this indiscriminate background. Facility of invention is already apparent in the Symphony No. 1 in E flat, Op. 2, written when he was eighteen. Two earlier ones have remained unpublished, but have been recorded. The sprightly A minor symphony, known as No. 2, was written in 1859, and in contrast to No. 3 (which followed much later) it is scored for a small orchestra without trombones. In four movements, it shows a firm grasp of Classical form, and the Scherzo is particularly effective. But it is the Symphony No. 3, in C minor, Op. 78, known as the 'Organ' symphony (because of its important organ part), which has become most famous and is most often heard. The dedication is 'à la mémoire de Franz Liszt', an important friend and patron of Saint-Saëns. Liszt's impressive style of organ-writing was certainly an influence. The work was the result of a commission from the London (now Royal) Philharmonic Society. Saint-Saëns enjoyed popularity in England (and still does); and the English have a special liking for the organ. Saint-Saëns appeared as pianist and conductor at the Society's concert in St James's Hall, London, on 19 May 1886, when he was soloist in his Fourth Piano Concerto and, in the second half, conducted the première of his C minor Symphony – which naturally received an ovation. The four movements are arranged in two parts – the first, interlocking *Allegro* and *Adagio*; the second, Scherzo and Finale. The use of a very large orchestra was in tune with the composer's wish to write (for this occasion) a powerful and grandiose work; and it remains a show-piece of some interest.

The symphony in D minor of **César Franck** (1822–1890) was completed in 1888, two years before the composer's death at the age of 68. At first it was not well received; but subsequently it was to become the most often performed of French symphonies throughout the world, and this is still the case – with (more recently) only Berlioz's *Symphonie fantastique* as rival. Franck's one symphony came nearly at the end of a decidedly routine life of teaching (in which field his influence was enormous) and as organist of Ste Clotilde in Paris, having begun his career as a pianist prodigy, touring his native Belgium when he was only eleven. Franck was a great organist and a brilliant improviser, and both these aspects are reflected in his compositions, including those for orchestra. His orchestration in the Symphony is direct, but unsubtle and rather unimaginative. Musically, the work has a strong character, a sense of serious purpose, a harmonic richness stemming from Wagner, and a melodic invention which, though often four-square in construction, is memorable and entirely characteristic. In form, Franck adhered to a principle of cyclic composition, as found in Beethoven's Op. 13 piano sonata and widely exploited by Liszt – a method of composition in which a theme recurs, often transformed, in the different sections or movements of a work.

The opening of the symphony is related to the *Grande Pièce symphonique* for organ and to certain other compositions of Franck. Also, the first phrase is a variant of the famous *Muss es sein?* (Must it be?) of Beethoven's F major Quartet, Op. 135. The idea of questing and of positive response symbolized by this and the other principal theme of the first movement reflect the concept of spiritual conflict underlying much of Franck's music.

The use of the cor anglais in the second movement was considered very startling at the time. But this is a very satisfactory middle movement to the symphony, combining slow movement and restless Scherzo, and with characteristic Franckian modulations. The main key there has been B flat minor. The final movement, *Allegro non troppo*, re-establishes D as the tonal centre, and it is now in the major – 'festive, effective, leisurely' (as Donald Tovey described it). But a distinctly foreboding atmosphere returns with a contrasting idea in the brass. Previous themes are recalled as part of the unifying cyclic process, before the final peroration – which can be interpreted as an affirmation of faith after doubt and perplexity, or a message of triumph over adversity, or indeed the triumph of good over evil.

Ex. 3. Franck: Symphony

The permeating influence of Wagner had its effect in France as elsewhere. Musicians, writers, poets, artists would make summer pilgrimages to Bayreuth: Saint-Saëns, Delibes, Dukas, Chabrier, Fauré, d'Indy, Chausson and Debussy all visited the shrine. Some reacted (often with difficulty) against the Wagnerian influence. For Franck, however, and for many of his followers – *la Bande à Franck* – it was an important and positive ingredient. This was true particularly of **Vincent d'Indy** (1851–1931), Franck's most ardent follower – a founder of the Schola Cantorum in Paris (which became the École César Franck). Though his opera *Fervaal* was known as 'the French *Parsifal*' and there were many Germanic elements in his compositions, d'Indy consciously adopted a lighter, Gallic style in his most famous work, the *Symphonie sur un chant montagnard français* (1886), also known as the *Symphonie cévenole*. D'Indy was a descendant of an aristocratic family of the Ardèche region of the Cevennes, and the folk-tune on which the work is based was collected in that area. Franck's *Variations symphoniques* for piano and orchestra, with its lightness of texture and simple, 'popular' thematic material, could well have been the model which led d'Indy to a fusion of symphony and concerto, which this symphony is – but using the piano as an instrument of the orchestra (as Falla later did in *Nights in the Gardens of Spain*, and as Berlioz had used the viola in *Harold en Italie*) rather than as a display instrument with orchestral accompaniment. The folk-tune could hardly be simpler – one short line, repeated with altered ending, plus another similar (Ex. 4).

From this unpretentious beginning, d'Indy, with fine imagination and craftsmanship, varies, transforms, and creates related material from the theme. The three movements, beautifully scored, consist of variations and developments, each with a definite symphonic shape, according to the cyclic and germinal processes which d'Indy inherited from Franck, and further back, from Beethoven. The Finale – a combination of rondo and a set of variations – displays exceptional rhythmic variety.

D'Indy's Second Symphony in B flat, completed seventeen years later, is a masterly work – and also a strong personal testament. It represented a conflict in more than one sense: symbolically, the forces of good and evil – with the final victory of the good; also, in musical terms, the aesthetic conflict of the traditional values, for which d'Indy stood, and those of the so-called

Ex. 4. D'Indy: *Symphonie cévenole*

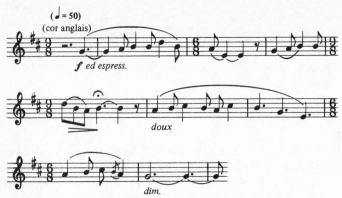

'advanced' Debussyists. Such considerations are only of significance in that they can stimulate what is a normal symphonic conflict in purely musical terms – in the appreciation of which, extra-musical ideas need not enter. That side is fully realised here. In the Scherzo, a folkloric melody is used as the basis for development (recalling the *Symphonie cévenole*); and the Finale is a *tour de force* of complex construction and brilliant orchestration.

Composed between the war years of 1916 and 1918, the Third Symphony of d'Indy was a *pièce d'occasion*, and of less importance than the other two. As a young man, d'Indy had served as a soldier in the Franco-Prussian War. Now he wanted to express his feelings about the First World War, in which a son of his and some other relatives were involved. Thus, the subtitle of the work is *Sinfonia brevis (de bello gallico)*. To his friend, the composer Guy Ropartz, he confided a summary of the character of the movements: (1) Mobilization, la Marne; (2) *Andante* – Latin art and Germanic art; (3) Finale – victory, with the (plainsong) hymn of St Michael as peroration. To another friend, however, he wrote about the work: 'There is *something of war* in it, but I don't want that to put people off, and it shall be called simply *Third Symphony*'. But he changed his mind.

If d'Indy could come to terms with Wagner and assimilate his influence in a positive way as an essential part of his personal style, **Ernest Chausson** (1855–1899) – another member of *la Bande à Franck* – was constantly trying to free himself from it, as his correspondence shows. In 1888, the year before he began writing his Symphony in B flat, Op. 20, we find him writing to a close friend: 'There is above all that frightful Wagner who is blocking all my paths.' In a wide-ranging output, his one completed symphony is his most important orchestral work. In three movements, and employing the cyclic principle, this symphony has sometimes been compared to Franck's – even described as Franck No. 2. But the differences are greater than the similarities, and it is a fine, serious, personal expression in its own right. An interesting aspect of the work is the accomplished and varied scoring – superior to Franck's; it was a technique of combining orchestral colours in much the same way that Elgar was to do in his two symphonies. A detailed comparison between the Franck Symphony and that of Chausson can be found in Ralph Scott Grover's study, *Ernest Chausson* (London, 1980). Sketches for a second symphony were left by Chausson at his untimely death.

The one symphony of **Paul Dukas** (1865–1935) is, like that of Chausson, notable for masterly orchestration. In style very different from his ever-popular *L'Apprenti Sorcier* and his 'impressionistic' Maeterlinck opera *Ariane et Barbe-Bleue*, this Symphony in C (1896), in its outer movements, follows the extrovert Classical style of Gounod and Saint-Saëns, but with more prolixity of development. Although vigorous and positive, the thematic material is perhaps not memorable enough to carry the work into the general repertoire, and it is only rarely heard. The slow movement (in E minor) is, however, beautifully constructed and deeply expressive, and could stand as a substantial piece in its own right.

Joseph Guy Ropartz (1864–1955) was another composer who began as a follower of César Franck, attending his improvisation classes at the Paris Conservatoire in his early twenties – classes which were more like composition seminars. Ropartz's mature style, however, is very different from that of Franck or d'Indy (both of whom he admired greatly). He was also strongly drawn to literature, and in his early years published three volumes of poetry in Paris. Much of Ropartz's career was away from Paris – in Nancy and Strasbourg. And something of the folk-music and landscape of his native Brittany is reflected in his works. Ropartz's five symphonies form a significant part of his large and wide-ranging output. Of these, No. 3 in E major (1905), for soloists, chorus, and orchestra, gives an overall impression of his musical personality and characteristic style – a style harmonically varied and rich (without being cloying), melodically clear and warmly expressive. It is an extended work lasting almost an hour; the text is by the composer, and the form is unusual in that the orchestra comments at length on the sentiments which are expressed in the sections for voices at the beginning of each of the movements and elsewhere. In the last movement, all the forces are employed in an impressive reflection and summing-up. The text presents Nature in its various aspects of beauty and power – the sea, the plain, the forest, the sun. But Nature is indifferent to the suffering and the fate of mankind. Only in the love of humanity can mankind find peace and hope.

The famous *Symphonie espagnole* by **Édouard Lalo** (1823–1892) is in all but name a violin concerto. His later four-movement Symphony in G minor (1886) has many similar attractive qualities, and strong Germanic elements. The work is, however, something of a hotchpotch, because much of the music is a re-working of material from Lalo's unperformed opera *Fiesque* of twenty years earlier. For example, the Scherzo is taken directly from a vocal and instrumental Scherzo in the scene at the ball. Nevertheless, the composer has made a skilful attempt to unify the diverse material.

There has been in recent years a revival of interest in a very individual French symphonist, **Albéric Magnard** (1865–1914), and all four of his symphonies have been recorded. Magnard turned to musical composition after first taking a degree in law. With a wide interest in the arts, he entered the Paris Conservatoire in 1886, studying composition under Massenet, but soon switching to become a private pupil of Vincent d'Indy for four years. During this time he was much influenced by Franck's ideals and methods, and became particularly drawn to orchestral writing. His affluent family circumstances enabled him to devote his time fully to creative work. Ruthlessly and single-mindedly, with little thought for success or applause, he sought perfection of form and content in his work – his commitment summed up in one of his sayings: 'The artist who does not draw his strength from abnegation is either close to death or to dishonour.' Purity of form, direct statement, the formal devices of canon, fugue and variation, cyclic structure – all this became an obsession, and he applied strict and somewhat inflexible principles to his symphonic writing, as he did also to his stage works.

His best compositions belong to the period after his father's death in 1894. These include the Symphony No. 3 in B flat minor (1895–96), and, much later, the Symphony No. 4 in C sharp minor (1913). In 1896, also, he became a teacher of counterpoint at d'Indy's Schola Cantorum (he was a natural contrapuntist), and in the same year he married. The Fourth Symphony was his last important work, written shortly before his tragic and untimely death near the beginning of the First World War, when, after he had sent his wife and children away to safety, he was killed resisting the German invasion of his country house at Baron (Oise).

With the first two symphonies Magnard had not yet found his mature and personal style. The Third was first heard at Nancy – a performance organized by his close friend and fellow symphonist Guy Ropartz. Later it was well received in Paris, where Paul Dukas wrote of it: 'It is one of those all too rare creations which do not strive mainly after special sensations of harmony and texture, but aim at something higher than the egotistical expression of a particular viewpoint.' This symphony is more relaxed, more immediately attractive, less austere than much of Magnard's writing. After a slow introduction, and an elaborate and substantial opening movement (*modéré*), distinctly romantic in feeling, there follows a Scherzo-like movement entitled *Danses*, in which vigorous, rhythmically exciting ideas are offset with a stately processional contrasting middle section. The slow movement, entitled *Pastorales*, is developed at some length in an individual song-like manner (not related to folk-music). This is followed by an animated Finale, which near the end broadens briefly into something like an optimistic Franckian chorale melody, before the final flourish.

The Fourth, written seventeen years later, is perhaps the most important of his symphonies – a highly personal testimony, in the realization of which Magnard experienced great difficulty. Often during its composition there were crises, lack of self-confidence, feverish creativity beset by doubts, even at times sinking to 'un marasme des plus complets' ('the very depths of mental depression'), as the composer admitted. The scoring is for a large orchestra (including piccolo, cor anglais, bass clarinet and harp). In the opening section (*modéré*), the main elements of the work are presented, to be treated cyclically. The *Allegro* has two main themes, harshness contrasting with more lyrical expression, developing along traditional lines. The lively but somewhat sombre Scherzo becomes cyclically linked (through reference to thematic material of the opening movement) with an extended movement marked *sans lenteur et nuancé*, in which the thematic material is elaborately varied and contrasted in striking and original ways. The animated Finale is a serious movement, overshadowed by doubt and perplexity; and the impression of the work as a whole is one of searching without fulfilment – a sincere expression of this composer's complex and uncompromising personality. That personality was summed up by his friend Pierre Lalo: 'By nature he was upright, proud, and unsociable, with something of asperity in his accent and his abrupt, direct manner of speech.'

With the work of **Albert Roussel** (1869–1937) the symphony in France reaches something of a climax. In the opinion of one author, Martin Cooper: 'In Roussel the deepest-rooted and sanest traditions of French art are to be found.' Roussel was twenty-five when he abandoned a naval career and decided to devote himself to music. He had already shown promise, and after being introduced to d'Indy, enrolled as a student at the Schola Cantorum, where later he was appointed a professor of counterpoint. As a composer, he managed before long largely to separate himself from d'Indy's powerful influence, to have 'the freedom of personal vision'. But in the so-called First Symphony (1904–6) the precepts of the Schola loom important – including the emphasis on cyclic practices. This work, however, hardly warrants the title 'symphony'. The middle two movements came first, written as unrelated orchestral pieces in 1904 and 1905. Then, in 1906, Roussel composed another two movements, bringing the diversity all together under the title *Le Poème de la Forêt* (Symphony No. 1). The final result was a sequence of attractive nature poems, colourfully orchestrated, each representing a different season of the year – starting with winter, *Forêt d'hiver*; then, *Renouveau* (spring's awakening and renewal); *Soir d'été* (the languor of a summer evening); and a rondo representing the autumn sports of *Faunes et Dryades*. The poetic thread, however, is quite not enough to unify the work as a symphony.

The Symphony No. 2 in B flat major was composed much later – 1919–21. In the meantime, Roussel's style had become personal and independent, developing on the one hand the French symphonic traditions as represented by Franck and his followers, and on the other, cultivating the imaginative fusion of the visual, literary and musical arts, which is also a strong French tradition going back to the seventeenth century. Another powerful influence in Roussel's eclectic personal style was an extensive tour of India and south-east Asia which he and his wife undertook in 1909. An important result was the opera-ballet *Padmâvatî*, based on a Hindu legend and written just before the Second Symphony. Certain elements of *Padmâvatî* were developed in purely musical terms in this symphony. Closely related to it, also, is the symphonic poem *Pour une Fête de Printemps* (one of the composer's most elaborate and fascinating works) which belongs to the same period in Roussel's development. It was to have been the second part of the Second Symphony, as a Scherzo, with a strongly contrasted middle section; but it grew into a complex work in its own musical right and free of any programmatic intentions. In this connection, Roussel himself has written: 'Impressionism had exercised its charm upon me. My music was perhaps too attached to exterior factors and picturesque processes which, as I have come to think, robbed it of part of its specific veracity. I resolved, during the years 1914–18, to broaden the harmonic sense of my writing, and tried to move towards a conception of music as willed and realised for its own sake.'

And yet – in contradiction to this – in 1922, for the première of his Second Symphony, Roussel provided a 'programme' relating the three movements to different stages of human life. It was intended to help the audience to appreciate a work which the composer knew was difficult and, as he said, 'rather hermetic'. He withdrew the 'programme', however – and it's best for the work to be considered purely as music. The first movement consists of slow introduction, which contains the main thematic material of the work, followed by an *allegro* in sonata form – with a difference that in the recapitulation the first and second subjects are inverted. The second movement is in the form of a Scherzo, but with a slow movement replacing the trio section (harking back to Schola Cantorum training). The very personal final movement is turbulent and striving, but leading to no triumphant affirmation or heroic outcome: rather it suggests a reconciliation in which discord is resolved into a vision of serenity. In its individual view of traditional forms and practices, its development of a personal, astringent harmonic language, chromatically rich but always tonal-based, and in its contrapuntal ingenuity and its highly developed rhythmic structures – in all this, the Second Symphony is important in the evolution of this composer's style – a style in which musical instinct is always intellectually controlled, however imaginatively expanded.

It was with the Symphony No. 3 in G minor – and at the age of sixty – that the late-developing composer found a personal symphonic expression that was both more condensed and more liberated. The work was commissioned by the Koussevitzky Music Foundation for performance (under Koussevitzky) at the fiftieth-anniversary celebrations of the Boston Symphony Orchestra in 1930. Perhaps anticipation of the spectacular occasion may have influenced the character of the work – which is the most immediately attractive and striking of Roussel's symphonies. The opening movement, which is basically ternary, brings into strong contrast and reconciles a wide range of textures, from the emphatically rhythmic patterns of the opening to the spatially flowing contrapuntal lines of the second subject matter. A motto theme of five notes:

is used for linking material and in the climax of the first movement and the coda of the Finale; also, in modified form, it shapes the main theme of the second movement (including, in the second bar, an inversion of the first three notes):

Ex. 5.

This movement is an extended ternary structure, powerful and deeply expressive, with a contrasting middle section in fugal style. (But, as a whole, the symphony is not contrapuntal in style.)

The Scherzo has about it an uninhibited gaiety, temporarily free from intellect and scholarship – an expression of unsophisticated enjoyment which all can share. Nevertheless, there is a serious core to the music, as is also found in the equally approachable and positive last movement.

Four years later, the Symphony No. 4 in A major is very different from its predecessor. This one is contrapuntal, emancipated, and one of the composer's most personal utterances, comparable perhaps to Sibelius's Fourth. It was composed in a remarkably short time – between 10 August and 31 December 1934. The cyclic principle has here been all but abandoned. The material of the lively first movement is diverse – far less co-ordinated than in the corresponding movement of the previous symphony. The beautiful and richly developed lyrical slow movement is undoubtedly the finest part of the symphony. In places it also exemplifies Roussel's use of bitonality, a characteristic form of harmonic enrichment – but always firmly related to an established key, and never falling into atonality. The *Allegro scherzando* movement has an urgency and a rhythmic sophistication; and the final *Allegro molto* is a short but richly constructed movement, purposeful and imaginative, basically in a freely-adapted rondo form. In the history of French symphony, Roussel's distinctive contribution stands rather apart, representing self-contained personal expressions and having little influence on later symphonic writing, which favoured less traditional, freer forms.

So far a French tradition has emerged, based on a chain of teacher-pupil relationships: Franck teaching d'Indy, Chausson, Ropartz, and many others; d'Indy teaching Magnard, Roussel, Honegger (of whom more later). Within this tradition the individual character of each of these composers could establish itself. And alongside those of the Franck-Schola Cantorum group there were others such as Bizet, Gounod and Saint-Saëns, who were trained in the very different atmosphere – more liberal (under Massenet and Fauré) and more opera-oriented – of the Paris Conservatoire. The Schola Cantorum, with its emphasis that 'only from the art of the past can the art of the future grow', and its revival and study of French music of the seventeenth and eighteenth centuries, was undoubtedly an atmosphere more conducive to purely symphonic composition.

Born in France of Swiss parents, **Arthur Honegger** (1892–1955) had his musical training in Zürich and in Paris. His general culture and outlook were predominantly French, but there was a hereditary Germanic streak in his make-up: French sensitivity, clarity and order were combined with a seriousness, depth and discipline, so that even when he was at his most adventurous and daring as a representative of the music of his time and as a member of *Les Six* in Paris, his work always had an independence and a basis in tradition. His five symphonies were spread over twenty years, the first in 1930 when he was thirty-eight and had so far achieved fame mainly through the large-scale 'dramatic psalm' *Le Roi David* and the so-called 'symphonic movements' *Pacific 231* and *Rugby*. Like Roussel, Honegger was commissioned to write a symphony for the fiftieth anniversary celebrations of the Boston Symphony Orchestra in 1931, and it was first performed in that year, conducted by Koussevitzky.

From the start, Honegger has always been clear in his intentions. He attached great importance to the architecture of a work: the frame of a large-scale composition had first to be decided. 'A symphonic work', he said, 'must be built logically, without the possibility of injecting the slightest anecdotal element between its different parts . . . One must give the impression of a composition in which all is linked, the image of a predetermined structure.' The structure favoured in his five three-movement symphonies was a highly-developed kind of sonata form – and that is the pattern for all but three movements. Honegger developed a new and personal attitude towards traditional form – basically, exposition (usually with several main themes, not just two); development of the material, freely and adventurously; then recapitulation, which really amounted to further development, and often (for architectural symmetry) the main themes treated in reverse order. All the elements – melodic, rhythmic, harmonic, contrapuntal – were highly developed and purposefully co-ordinated. 'I am neither polytonalist, nor atonalist, nor dodecaphonist,' said Honegger. 'Our contemporary musical material is based on a ladder of twelve chromatic sounds, but used with freedom.' The freedom was a predominantly polyphonic style in which tonality could be obscured or treated flexibly in more traditional fashion.

Melodic and rhythmic equilibrium was sought, as distinct from traditional tonal contrasts. So much, in broad outline, for the style. Each movement of the Symphony No. 1 is in an enlarged and personal version of sonata form. The material of the last movement is more diatonic than the rest, and is treated in various contrapuntal ways.

During the second world war Honegger taught at the École Normale de Musique in Paris, and wrote music criticism. His Second Symphony, for strings, belongs to this period. Inspired by the late string quartets of Beethoven, it was written in 1941, and its moods reflect the frustration, anger and despair felt in Paris during the German Occupation. In the first movement, a sorrowful motto-like figure, around three notes and much repeated, dominates everything with haunting and tragically beautiful effect.

A final chorale theme played by the first violins (with an optional trumpet to reinforce the melody) brings a message of hope. This is a sombre work, but the intensity of feeling, the personal directness, and the accomplished, imaginative writing for strings – all this has led to it being the most admired (and recorded) of Honegger's symphonies. It was written for the conductor Paul Sacher and his Basle Chamber Orchestra, who gave the first performance in Zürich in May 1942. (Throughout his life, Honegger maintained a close connection with his Swiss heritage.)

Although the symphonies can all be justified in purely musical terms, the different circumstances in which they were written had a direct effect on the character of the music in each case. The *Symphonie liturgique* (No. 3) came at the end of the war (in 1945–6), and again the first performance was in Zürich, this time conducted by Charles Münch. Here the composer has said that he wanted to symbolise the reaction of modern man against the tide of barbarity, stupidity, suffering, mechanization and bureaucracy which had assailed him for several years. The symphony became a drama, an inner conflict between the blind forces of evil and the instinctive striving for happiness, peace, and divine refuge. The title 'liturgique' underlines the religious inspiration of the work; the titles of the movements can be linked with the Requiem Mass: *Dies Irae*, the tumult of destruction (but still including a faint glimmer of hope). *De profundis clamavi* (Psalm 129), a cry from the depths of despair, with 'the dead, smoking city; the new day breaking; an innocent bird warbling above the rubble'. And *Dona nobis pacem*, in which a heavy march, brutal, idiotic, leads to a utopian vision of what life could be like in mutual brotherhood and love.

In contrast to the tormented nature of the Third, the Symphony No. 4 (1945–6), subtitled *Deliciae Basiliensis* ('the pleasures of Basle'), is a respite, reflecting a temporary escape, a summer spent in Switzerland surrounded by happiness and friendship. The slow movement quotes a popular song, *Z'Basel a mi'm Ryn*, and the third draws on a traditional carnival song from the *Basler Morgenstreich*. The relaxed, joyful atmosphere of this symphony, however, was not to last. In 1947 Honegger was commissioned by the

Ex. 6. Honegger: Symphony No. 2

Koussevitzky Music Foundation to write a work in memory of Nathalie Koussevitzky, the conductor's wife. But while on tour in America Honegger suffered a heart attack and was obliged to spend several months in a clinic there. He was left an invalid. The Symphony No. 5 ('di tre re') was composed in Paris in 1950, and a feeling of mental anguish and tragedy pervades the work. There are temporary glimpses of light and hope, and the middle movement is a combination of scherzo and brooding *adagio*, displaying great contrapuntal skill; but the final struggle seems to end in catastrophe and emptiness. The subtitle of the work, 'di tre re', may be a pun, but it is not intended as an allusion to the Three Kings who came to Bethlehem; it simply refers to the three notes of D (re) which conclude each movement. (Banteringly, the composer said he had given it a subtitle to prevent it being confused with Beethoven's Fifth!)

With their intensity of expression, vitality, and commitment, the five symphonies of Honegger must have an important place in French music. No. 3 and No. 5 are not easy to appreciate fully without repeated hearings. Those who are coming new to Honegger's symphonies should perhaps start with No. 4 and No. 2, in that order.

Earlier, we quoted Saint-Saëns saying that he believed a composer produces music 'as naturally as an apple-tree produces apples'. If ever the dictum was fulfilled by a composer it was surely by **Darius Milhaud** (1892–1974) who, over a period of more than 60 years, was probably the twentieth century's most prolific composer, his output covering the widest possible spectrum, much of it displaying originality in form and content, much of it experimental and forward-looking, cosmopolitan in the extreme, with an outlook widened by much travel to many parts of the world – and all this despite a crippling rheumatic condition for the larger part of his life, necessitating the use of a wheelchair during his last two decades. The enormous output is extremely variable in quality – one might almost say promiscuous in style – with fine and memorable works appearing from time to time.

Two early influences on Milhaud's style were Debussy and, in particular, Charles Koechlin, another prolific composer, whose style was in some ways similar to what Milhaud's became. (Koechlin's output included several symphonies, mostly put together and orchestrated from existing material composed for various other purposes – from chamber music to film music.) Milhaud himself described his style:

> If one accepts the system of twelve definite tonalities, each based on a different degree of the scale, and the possibility of passing from one tonality to another by means of modulation, then it is quite logical to go further and explore the ways in which these tonalities can be superimposed and heard simultaneously. Contrapuntal writing should also lead to this conclusion. The day that canons, other than those at the octave, were conceived of, the principle of polytonality was proclaimed.

The result was a general stylistic freedom, with polytonality and free counterpoint as important ingredients. Melodically, a diatonic link with tradition is usually to be found, but on an untraditional harmonic and contrapuntal background. In fact, he made use of many kinds of techniques, old and new, adapting them to his own purposes, to express a very wide range of feelings and ideas. He also adapted folksong to his use, and for a period jazz was important.

Milhaud's first large-scale symphony – the first of twelve – was not composed until 1939, when he was nearly fifty. Before that – between 1917 and 1923 – he had written 'Six Little Symphonies', each for a different small ensemble. Each is between three and six minutes in duration and is in three contrasting sections. The first three little symphonies are called *Le Printemps*, *Pastorale*, and *Sérénade* respectively, titles popular with this composer. No. 4 is for ten stringed instruments; No. 5 is for ten wind instruments, and the composer was particularly pleased with this predominantly aggressive five-minute work. The last of the six, for vocal quartet, oboe and cello, is mostly calm and expressive.

The first two were written during the two years that Milhaud spent in Brazil at the end of the First World War; the other four when he was back in Paris and a member of *Les Six* – coming, to some extent, at least, under the iconoclastic influence of Satie and Cocteau. Well before 1939, however, Milhaud was independent, following no aesthetic but his own. Like his life-long friend Honegger, Milhaud was to start writing symphonies in the usual present meaning of the word – namely, large-scale, integrated, purely musical works, usually in three or four movements. (Eight of Milhaud's twelve are in four movements.) The symphonies of Milhaud do not, generally speaking, have the consistency, concentration and purpose that we find in those of Roussel and Honegger. First movements are generally in a personal version of sonata form: several thematic ideas in the exposition, developed according to the composer's contrapuntal methods, with a freely-adapted recapitulation. And the final movements tend to be freely fugal in character. Between, there can be movements that are expressive, fantastic, pastoral, meditative, and so on.

The menace of war overshadowed the First Symphony (1939). Thanks to a commission from the Chicago Symphony Orchestra for a work for its fiftieth-anniversary celebrations in 1940, Milhaud, a Jew, was enabled to flee his country with his family, and arrived in the United States nearly penniless. Milhaud himself conducted the première in October 1940. It begins, in very French style, with a 'Pastoral' – but one in which peaceful textures are dramatically juxtaposed with menacing, warlike suggestions and gloomy forebodings. The tension erupts into a Scherzo of astonishing power and brilliance, very original in its striking orchestration. The slow movement is akin in atmosphere to that of Honegger's Second Symphony, with its deeply-felt lament, and including a clarinet solo of great tragic beauty. Then, in contrast, the Finale is optimistic, with a strong chorale-like element alternating with exhilarating dance-like ideas. In all, a work rich in invention and dramatic contrast.

The Second Symphony (1944) was commissioned by the Koussevitzky Music Foundation and dedicated to the memory of Nathalie Koussevitzky. The American composer Virgil Thomson found the work 'neo-Romantic': 'In this work we have Milhaud in three characteristic moods – the pastoral, the serene, and the jubilant. The second and third movements are, in addition, devoted to mystery and pain. The latter achieves an intensity of expression in the vein of dolor that is unusual to this composer and rare in all music. The jubilant Finale, "Alleluja", is also a striking piece of discordant writing and in every way invigorating.'

The French Radio commissioned the Third Symphony – first, as a *Te Deum* to celebrate the end of the war; but it grew into a four-movement choral symphony. In the impressive second movement, a wordless chorus is used antiphonally with the orchestra, and the final *Te Deum* movement is a very individual treatment of the liturgical text. Shortly after, in 1947, Milhaud wrote the Fourth Symphony on the ship taking the Milhaud family back to France. It was a work to commemorate the 1848 Revolution, the movements having a definite programmatic purpose. But the Fifth, commissioned by the Italian Radio, and written in 1953 at Mills College, Oakland, California (where Milhaud had a teaching post), was purely musical in conception. Its attractive features include a light and delicate third movement in the time-signature 5/4 – but also highly syncopated; and this is followed by a brilliantly colourful Finale.

The Sixth (1955) was another Koussevitzky memorial work, commissioned by the Boston Symphony Orchestra. While working on it in the USA, Milhaud received another commission, this time from the Belgian Radio, and started simultaneously working on his Seventh. Typical of the composer, both symphonies were finished within a few months of each other. No two works could be more different – the Seventh being the shortest of the twelve (fifteen minutes, and in three movements) and relatively simple in style and mood; while the Sixth is a complex four-movement work, rather similar to the First in its shape, dramatic contrasts, and the character of its movements (slow, tumultuous, slow, joyous), but with sixteen years of musical development between.

The Eighth (1957) is the most frequently heard, and generally considered to be the one most immediately attractive. As Smetana portrayed the progress of the river Moldau, so Milhaud similarly represented the Rhône in its varying aspects, generalized in the four movements by the respective indications: 'Avec mystère et violence', 'Avec sérénité et nonchalance', 'Avec emportement', and 'Rapide et majestueux'. Ex. 7 is a typical Milhaud polytonal passage from the last movement.

By his Eleventh Symphony Milhaud had reached Op. 384. Its subtitle is 'Romantic', and the designation 'in D' emphasizes that Milhaud had not abandoned a definite feeling for tonality, however flexible. The Twelfth (1961), commissioned by the University of California at Davis has the subtitle 'Rurale' – a musical reflection of the campus's activities in the development of agriculture.

Ex. 7. Milhaud: Symphony No. 8

In all, Milhaud's contribution in the field of French symphony was astonishingly extensive, colourful, and varied. When music is written at such speed, quality can fluctuate; but at least the First, Fifth, Sixth and Eighth should continue to be of importance.

The *Symphonie marine* of **Jacques Ibert** (1890–1962) has all the attractive qualities of the composer's style – diversity, clarity of textures, beautiful scoring, rhythmic exuberance. Ibert was forty when he wrote it – a romantic 'chant de l'amour et de la mer' – concise and purposeful (fourteen minutes in length), a one-movement work, continuous, but in several sections. A striking feature of it is some very expressive saxophone writing. There are also (perhaps inevitably) some echoes of Debussy's *La Mer*. 'This will be my last departure', wrote Ibert. He then hid the work away so that it would not be heard until after his death.

At various times, the symphony in France has been indebted to the Koussevitzky Music Foundation, set up by the American conductor Serge Koussevitzky as a permanent memorial to his wife, the funds being used to commission works from composers of all nationalities. These, as we have noted, included symphonies from Roussel, Honegger, and Milhaud. And what turned out to be one of the Foundation's most spectacular commissions was the *Turangalîla-Symphonie* by **Olivier Messiaen** (1908–92).

Messiaen belonged to no school, and accepted a wide range of influences in the formation of an individual and highly complex musical language: 'An abundance of technical means allows the heart to expand', the composer once said. For Messiaen, a committed Roman Catholic, the main purpose of his music has been 'to shed light on the theological truths of the Catholic faith'. *Turangalîla* (1946–48) is, however, part of a trilogy (with his other works of the same period, *Harawi* and *Cinq Rechants*) based on the legend of Tristan and Isolde, the subject being love and death in a universal (not specifically Catholic) setting.

When Messiaen was ten, he was given the score of Debussy's *Pelléas et Mélisande* – and that, he said, was 'probably the most decisive influence in my life'. It was Debussy's wider vision of tonality and a freeing of rhythm from its conventional framework of pulse that were important and led Messiaen to the development of far greater freedoms and rhythmic elaborations in his works.

The title *Turangalîla* is derived from two Sanskrit words: *Turanga*, 'time', extended to movement and rhythm; and *Lîla*, which is 'play', extended to divine influence on the world. Messiaen described the work as a love-song. It represents a climax in the composer's early style, and is a very complete and inventive display of his technique and individuality. For a comprehensive and detailed account of Messiaen's style it is necessary to turn to the composer's book, *Technique de mon langage musical* – available also in an English translation. It involves the study of Hindu rhythms, Greek modes, plainsong, a personal attitude to tonality and serialism, rhythmic counterpoints and tonal and non-tonal harmonic textures – textures often superimposed in ways that provide new orchestral sonorities. The orchestra employed is a very large one, including a vast array of percussion instruments, with glockenspiel, celesta and vibraphone having prominent parts often gamelan-like in effect, and the electronic instrument ondes Martenot providing a strange glutinously-expressive colour. Also, the piano has a very difficult and important part. With all this, however, thematicism and an overall feeling for tonality are never abandoned.

There are ten substantial movements, and some aspects of traditional symphonic form are still discernible. For example, the fourth movement is a Scherzo with two trios; the ninth is a series of variations; the final movement is in something resembling sonata form. Also, the composer has described the eighth movement, which has the subtitle 'Developpement de l'amour', as being a development section for the symphony as a whole. The work, which lasts nearly an hour and a half, divides into two halves. In the first half, two strongly contrasted aspects of love are represented – passionate, carnal love and tender, idealistic love – leading to the 'Joie du sang des étoiles', a long, frenzied dance of joy. Two important contrasting cyclic themes occur in the Introduction – one (Ex. 8a) in heavy thirds on the trombones and tuba; the other (b) tender, slow, and graceful, on the clarinets:

Ex. 8. Messiaen: *Turangalîla – Symphonie*

The opening movement of the second half, 'Jardin du sommeil d'amour', has another cyclic theme, representing idealistic love – a long slow melody for ondes Martenot, backed by the strings, and decorated by piano and other percussion instruments (Ex. 8c).

Throughout the three 'Turangalîla' movements, love is brought into contact with a brooding on death, leading to a *Tristan*-like Love – Death reconciliation.

Since its first appearance, *Turangalîla* has always been a subject of controversy. After its first New York performance the critic of *Musical America* (January 1950) was of the opinion that 'Messiaen has produced

Ex. 8 cont'd

a work of a vulgarity scarcely paralleled in the entire history of serious music'. Nevertheless, despite its length and complexity, *Turangalîla* has proved that it can be popular with audiences. Perhaps its programme content has something to do with this.

One of the most original and rewarding of the more recent French symphonists is undoubtedly **Henri Dutilleux** (b.1916), whose early influences have included Debussy and Ravel. Debussy expressed the view that the symphony was an extinct form. This was contradicted by Dutilleux when he said that by returning to polyphony, by renouncing the usual orchestral structure (*le magma orchestral*), and by dividing to the extreme the various parts of each orchestral unit (the strings in particular), he was convinced that symphonic works could be composed which would be unified like those of the past and open (or free in form) like those of the present. In his two symphonies of 1950 and 1958–59 this concept is wonderfully realized.

Dutilleux has held important posts with the Paris Opera and French Radio and has been a professor of composition in Paris at the École Normale and at the Conservatoire. He has also been connected with the International Society for Contemporary Music and the International Music Council of UNESCO. He is a man of wide culture and is interested in all new developments in art. As a composer, however, he is an isolated and independent figure, with a highly personal style which he has sought to define very clearly. His output is not large, and only the works written since the Second World War are representative. Unlike Honegger, he avoids any prefabricated structure, choosing a freely developing and meticulously-crafted variation technique, and certain kinds of sonority, with a preference for what he calls 'the sound of joy'. Any feeling of 'programme' or 'message' is sedulously avoided – 'though naturally I do not deny a meaning of a spiritual order to our art'. The music takes on a fluid and improvisatory character, a constant metamorphosis. The ideas are developed gradually, rather than being suddenly presented, undergoing constant modifications and unforeseeable transformations, subtle and extremely detailed.

The First Symphony of Dutilleux is scored for a large orchestra, with a percussion section almost as varied as Messiaen's in *Turangalîla*. Particularly in the first and last of the four movements, the composer separates small instrumental groups from the orchestra, and each of these instruments can be treated as a soloist. Thus, the soloist or small group can be set in opposition to the general orchestral sound, creating a new and subtle play of sonorities, space, and colours.

In similar vein, the Second Symphony, subtitled 'Le Double'* becomes an unexpected development of the traditional concerto grosso, but still without any feeling of prefabricated form. In this case, the orchestra is in two groups: the normal orchestral body and a small ensemble of twelve players placed in a semicircle around the conductor. The ways in which these two bodies are treated – in opposition, in combination, in projection one on the other – create an original world of sonority and rhythm, the spirit of variation in new and exciting guises. Over all there is a consistency, a unity in diversity – and that, of course, is the hallmark of a symphony, in France or any other country.

Other symphonists deserve mention: **Paul Le Flem** (1881–1984), a pupil of d'Indy and later Roussel (and remarkable not only for his longevity), he composed his First Symphony in 1910 and his Fourth as recently as 1978 when he was ninety-six! It is a work of considerable quality too! **Georges Migot** (1891–1976), who has thirteen symphonies to his credit though no scores or recordings of them are readily accessible; the conductor **Jean Martinon** (1910–76), another Roussel pupil with four symphonies to his credit, the Second of which, *Hymn à la vie*, was recorded on LP, as was his Second Violin Concerto. Nor should the four symphonies of **Marcel Landowski** (b. 1915) be overlooked. They cover no fewer than four decades: the First ('Jean de la Peur') comes from the 1940s while the Fourth and most recent was composed in 1988. They are imaginative, rewarding and resourceful scores though they are much indebted to Honegger. Nonetheless they affirm the vitality of the French symphony and belie the widely-held belief that the form is alien to the French genius. France's contribution to it in the twentieth century is both valuable and important.

* The French word 'double' means, among other things, 'variation'.

10

The Czech Symphony

Jan Smaczny

Any consideration of the music of the Czech national revival inevitably focuses on opera. The clearest manifestation of a national identity presented itself in the works written first for the Provisional Theatre (Prozatímní divadlo), opening in Prague in 1862 and later for the National Theatre (Národní divadlo), an institution which still remains the nation's 'one artistic hearth and home'.* Looking beyond the operatic repertoire in Bohemia and Moravia, the orchestral genre most frequently employed as a celebration of nationhood among the Czechs in the generation of Smetana (1824–1884) and after is the symphonic poem. Such celebrations of locality as Mendelssohn's 'Scottish' and 'Italian' symphonies have no obvious parallel among the Czechs whose nearest equivalent to Schumann's 'Rhenish' symphony is Smetana's cycle of symphonic poems, 'My Country' (*Má vlast*).

But a prevailing tendency to favour the Lisztian symphonic poem in the second half of the nineteenth century did not exclude the more abstract virtues of the symphony from the national revival. The foundations of a symphonic tradition had been laid in the first few decades of the nineteenth century by an appreciable array of composers. Some, like Václav Jan Tomásek (1774–1850) and Jan Václav Kalivoda (1801–1866) are relatively well known, others, like Jan Kaňka (1772–1863) and Václav Jindřich Veit (1806–1864), remain virtually unknown, even to Czechs, today.

By comparison with the rampant symphonic productivity of Czech émigrés, such as Johann Stamitz (1717–1757) and Johann Vanhal (1739–1813), whose fertility in this area rivalled Haydn,† the efforts of nineteenth-century Czech composers appear drastically curtailed. During a century of sturdy endeavour not a single composer of significance resident in Bohemia and Moravia

---

* Karel Hoffmeister's assessment of the National Theatre in Prague in the 1880s, see K. Hoffmeister, *Antonín Dvořák*, Prague, 1924, p. 74. In English translation by R. Newmarch, London, 1928, p. 92.
† See H.C. Robbins Landon, *Haydn, Chronicle and Works, 1766–1790*, London, 1978, p. 389. Paul Bryan puts the number of authentic symphonies at rather less, at present *c*. 76. See P. Bryan, *The Symphonies of Johann Vanhal*, diss. U. of Michigan, 1955 and introduction to *Johann Vaňhal: Six Symphonies*, 1985, Madison, Wisconsin.

reached double figures when it came to writing symphonies and very few wrote more than five, though the greatest of all Czech symphonists, **Antonín Dvořák** (1841–1904), was also the most prolific. Apart from Dvořák, the most extensive contributions to the genre in the late nineteenth and early twentieth centuries came from Zdeněk Fibich (1850–1900) and Josef Bohuslav Foerster (1859–1951). For most other Czech symphonists in this later period the symphony was something of a rarity, with only two from Josef Suk (1874–1935), a symphony and *sinfonia* from Otakar Ostrčil (1879–1935), a sinfonietta and the unfinished 'Danube' (*Dunaj*) symphony from Leoš Janáček (1854–1928) and nothing at all from Vítězslav Novák (1870–1949).

Looking back to before the heyday of nationalism and its roots in the early nineteenth century leads the reader into an area which challenges the very notion of Czechness in music, a far from easily defined term.* While the Czech crown lands in the eighteenth century were well known as an area of extraordinary musical activity, the benefits were rarely felt to full effect within the bounds of Bohemia and Moravia. The admiration felt by the historian Charles Burney (1726–1814) for Czech musicians derived from his encounters with them on his travels throughout Europe as much as from his trip to Bohemia.† In the eighteenth century the end of the road which began for many a Czech musician in the village schoolroom was, more often than not, in a foreign court far beyond the confines of the Czech crown lands. The most frequent destinations were to the courts of Germany in the north and to Vienna and Italy in the south. But Czech composers and performers were to be found in the eighteenth century as far east as Moscow and as far west as Dublin. Apart from a general excellence of achievement and in some cases‡ their native language, there is very little in the work of the composers of this diaspora which may be identified as specifically Czech in origin. In an age where a true musical *lingua franca* existed for the whole of Europe, local accents were soon ironed out. To examine the role of Czech composers in the growth of the symphony in the second half of the eighteenth century would involve, for instance, a thorough-going study of the Mannheim school given the signal contributions of Franz Xaver Richter (1709–1789) and of course Johann Stamitz (see pages 17–21). Such an approach would need to be brought to bear on Antonín Rejcha's (1770–1836) sturdily Haydnesque, though sporadically innovative output – the final movement of his last symphony in C, replete with four canons, is a

---

* All major Czech composers have offered accounts or explanations of their Czechness. The gamest attempt to unravel the question of Czechness in music is to be found in M. *Beckerman*, 'In Search of Czechness in Music', *19th-Century Music*, x/1, 1986–7, pp. 61–73.

† See C. Burney, *The Present State of Music in Germany, the Netherlands, and United Provinces*, London, 1771, ed. P. A. Scholes as *Dr Burney's Musical Tours in Europe*, London, 1959.

‡ Franz Benda (1709–1786) recalled speaking Czech to other native speakers on his arrival as a child in Dresden in 1720.

funeral march* – and the work of more than one Benda.† To see the work of these composers, many of whom left their native land in childhood, from a purely Czech point of view would be to deny them their full role in a history which belongs more properly to a broader consideration of the European symphony. Similarly, works which might be felt to have honorary Czech credentials, like the nineteen symphonies Haydn wrote for Count Morzin's orchestra at his Bohemian estate of Lukavec, are more usefully seen in a wider context than as part of a burgeoning native tradition. Conversely, an approach which excludes the work of Czechs who lived abroad would eliminate from consideration the most renowned Czech symphony of all, Dvořák's Ninth, 'From the New World' ('Z nového světa'), and every one of Martinů's six symphonies. Thus any consideration of the Czech symphony has to be something of a compromise hedged around by questions of style as much as geography. The present chapter is offered as a guide to the means of defining such works as may be called Czech and aims to provide a context for and a commentary on the finest examples of the genre.

Classical and Early Romantic

The use of national elements, usually in the shape of a folksong, was, of course, widespread in the eighteenth century. Haydn himself made frequent use of folk melody, sometimes Bohemian,‡ and a broad range of émigré Czechs adopted similar practices. A major figure among these, owing in large part to his enormous facility with the symphony was Vaňhal. Burney described his symphonies as '. . . spirited, natural, and unaffected', noting that they '. . . seem to have preceded those of Haydn, at least in England'.§ A tendency to favour passages harmonized in thirds, especially in Trios, anticipates a characteristically Czech texture cultivated in the later nineteenth century.

A more thorough embracing of the folk style is to be found in **Johann Stamitz**'s fascinating *Sinfonia pastorale*, published as Op. IV, No. 2 in Paris in 1758. All four movements of this engaging work are redolent of that favourite of Central European popular musical culture, the *pastorella*. Composed for Christmas, the *pastorella* was most usually written for voices and orchestra to a vernacular text involving chiefly the awakening of the shepherds by angels

---

* Composed c. 1808 in Vienna and probably completed in Paris, the Beethovenian resonance in the symphony is further advanced by the subtitle of the piece: 'Musique pour célébrer la mémoire des grands hommes et des grands événements'. Owing to the nature of the orchestra, with its field pieces and large percussion section the audience was advised to stand some fifty paces from the performers! See O. Šotolová, *Antonín Rejcha*, Prague, 1977, pp. 30–31 and 145–146.

† See Franz [František] Benda, Georg [Jiří Antonín] Benda (1722–1795), Friedrich Benda (1745–1814) and Friedrich Ludwig Benda (1752–1792).

‡ See E.K. Wolf, *The Symphonies of Johann Stamitz*, Boston, 1981, p. 303.

§ C. Burney, *A General History of Music from the Earliest Ages to the Present Period*, vol. 4, London, 1789, p. 599.

to tell them of the birth of the Christ child. In addition to simple folk texts, folk instruments would be used or imitated, such as the bagpipes – presented as a drone with melodies above harmonized in thirds or sixths – and the *tuba pastoralis* with characteristic fanfare-like melodies. Two instrumental *pastorellas* by Stamitz survive and there are clear correspondences between the first, in G major, and the symphony. Eugene K. Wolf suggests a link between the main theme of the first movement of the *Sinfonia pastorale* and the Czech folksong *Nesem vám noviny*, but the cited fragment (Ex. 1) is typical of many Czech and Central European lullabies associated with Christmas. The connections with the *pastorella* in this symphony are much more extensive. Throughout, the work owes much to the genre, from the tolling bell figure of the opening set against a 'shivering' tremolando, through the 'lullaby' fragments in the *Larghetto*, to the Finale whose main theme could belong to almost any mid-eighteenth-century Czech pastorella:

Ex. 1. Stamitz: *Sinfonia pastorale* Op. 4, No. 2

An undated, though presumably contemporary or very slightly later, *Sinfonia pastoralis* by **Jiří Ignác Linek** (1725–1791 or 1792), a Czech who stayed at home, exhibits certain similarities to Stamitz in the use of solid orchestration and long pedal bases, but thematically seems, if anything, to make rather less use of familiar clichés.

While undoubtedly appealing, these early pastoral symphonies comprise an episode rather than the foundation of an identifiably Czech tradition. Such works add to a strong existing tradition whose most characteristic manifestations are to be found in the Christmas Masses prevalent in Bohemia, Moravia and Slovakia, the most famous example of which remains Jakub Jan Ryba's (1765–1815) *Hej, mistře* of 1796.

Outside the Czech-speaking lands the work of Bohemian and Moravian émigrés tends to the urbane, generalised style of the late-eighteenth-century Classical symphony found throughout Europe. The elegance and imagination of the symphonies of **Leopold Kozeluh** (1747–1818), based on a sound musical education in Prague from his cousin Jan Antonín Kozeluh (1738–1814) and Mozart's friend **František Xaver Dušek** (1731–1799), are certainly impressive. Kozeluh's three-movement G minor Symphony (published in 1787) is notable for its tight construction, vigour and emotional depth, and should certainly be heard from time to time as an alternative to Mozart's K. 183. But this work apart, the symphonies of Kozeluh, for all their virtue and sophistication, do not represent an especially individual strand. Though it is pleasant to dwell on such entertaining oddities as the programmatic 'Aphrodite' Symphony of 1792 by Anton (Antonín) Wranitzky (Vranický, 1761–1820), brother of the more famous Paul (Pavel, 1756–1808), whose slow movement leads straight into a tarantella-like Scherzo section, his symphonic output as a whole is unlikely to find a place in the modern repertoire. Until a taste for 'lesser contemporaries' develops in the listening public, the same harsh justice remains for the honest endeavour of composers like Vaňhal, F. X. Dušek and Adalbert Gyrowetz (Jírovec, 1763–1850), to name but the most prominent, whose work continues to provide an underexplored background for the Viennese classics, Haydn, Mozart and Beethoven.

The most substantial musical figure in Prague in the first half of the nineteenth century was **Václav Jan Křtitel Tomášek** (Tomaschek, 1774–1850). Although Tomášek travelled widely he made his home in Prague and came to dominate its musical life, exerting influence on a series of distinguished pupils. Although Tomášek's piano works, such as the 42 Eclogues and 15 Rhapsodies (published before 1820), and some exquisite Goethe settings, look forward to the style and outline of early romantic music, his three symphonies, C major, Op. 17, Grande Sinfonia, 1801; E flat major, Op. 19, published 1805; D major, Op. 30, 1807, are more conventional. Far from adumbrating the practices of a later age, these three accomplished symphonies seem to epitomize the admiration for Mozart which seized native Czech composers for nearly three decades after the Austrian composer's death. An approach to form and content which marks little if any advance on the externals of late Haydn and Mozart does not, however, exclude an occasional original touch, for instance an unexpected excursion into E minor shortly after the recapitulation in the final movement of the C major symphony, or the almost furiant-like cross-rhythms in the same work's Menuetto:

Ex. 2. Tomášek: Symphony in C, Op. 17

Far more adventurous than Tomášek was his pupil **Jan Václav Voříšek** (1791–1825) whose dissatisfaction with the rather hidebound attitude towards musical innovation prevalent in Prague led to his departure for Vienna. In the Austrian capital Voříšek won the admiration of Beethoven and made friends with Schubert. His piano Impromptus, Op. 7, were important in the history of the Romantic piano piece and his single Symphony in D major, Op. 24, composed in 1821, is the first major contribution to the genre by a Czech in the nineteenth century. Unlike his teacher, Tomášek, Voříšek builds on rather than repeats the gestures of the Classical symphony. The work has no obvious models but the vigorous dotted motif:

which pervades all the important punctuation points of the exposition of the first movement suggests that Beethovenian methods may have been at the back of Voříšek's mind when crafting this movement. On the other hand, the way in which the development (*Allegro con brio*) falls into clear, closed periods, occasionally a little four-square, is more reminiscent of the later Schubert. The *Andante* begins solemnly with four descending chords, the first two of which take up the dotted rhythm of the first movement. Voříšek does not maintain the elevated tone, but successfully sets the scene for an anguished central section which in turn resolves into a serene conclusion for the movement in B major. The Scherzo (*Allegro ma non troppo*) has a Beethovenian determination replete with rhythmic surprise, but succeeds entirely on its own terms. A particularly effective touch is the way in which the driving 9/8 quaver rhythm of the Scherzo relaxes into a background accompaniment, emerging as a reminder of more turbulent activity from time to time (Ex. 3 – see notes in squares).

After an effective call to attention the ebullient Finale, in simple sonata form, provides an attractive conclusion. There are few formal surprises

Ex. 3. Voříšek: Symphony in D

Ex. 3. cont'd

in this excellent work although the B major conclusion to the *Andante*, which begins conclusively in B minor, is something of a novelty. Beyond an extraordinary command of the externals of symphonic convention, Voříšek's musical personality manifests itself in the energy of his motivic writing, moments of rich internal counterpoint and piquant chromatic inflection, all of which are linked to a persuasive logic at climaxes. Owing to his tragically early death, Voříšek left only one symphony. To interpret its contents solely in terms of the compositional giants of his age exposes an inadequate understanding of the contemporary musical lingua franca. Voříšek's first symphony shows every sign of enormous promise and certainly stands comparison with any of Schubert's first four works in the genre.

Returning to Prague, the familiar Mozartean stereotype rears its head in Jan Kaňka's single symphony, in E flat major, of 1808. Against this background the first of **Jan Václav Kalivoda**'s (Kalliwoda) seven symphonies, in F minor, cuts a perceptible dash with strong early romantic credentials. Premièred in Prague in 1826, slightly more than three years after Kalivoda had abandoned the Czech capital for an appointment as music director in Donaueschingen for Prince Fürstenberg, the work is classically proportioned. The *Adagio non troppo* certainly looks back to Mozart, but the outer movements have an originality which foreshadows Mendelssohn and Schumann. The *Menuetto* (*Allegro assai*) is not only notable for its canonic characteristics, but for a clear anticipation of the Scherzo of Schumann's Fourth Symphony:

Ex. 4. Kalivoda: Symphony No. 1 in F minor

Kalivoda was too young to be influenced by Mendelssohn, so any similarities in style between the two composers evident in this work derive from a common source and development.

The next few decades in Czech music, however, show that the influence of Mendelssohn and Schumann and Weber was gaining ground. The extent of the influence is clear in the work of two more of Tomášek's pupils, **Leopold Eugen Měchura** (1804–1870) and **Jan Bedřich Kittl** (1806–1868). Měchura, a gifted and wealthy amateur, produced six symphonies, all of which remain in manuscript. The melodic material of the works composed as late as the 1860s (Symphony No. 4 in F major, Op. 86, 1862; Symphony 5 in D major, Op. 87, 1864; and Symphony No. 6 in C minor, Op. 90, 1865) still betray Mendelssohnian features in the melodic writing, not least in the chorale-like second theme of the Finale of Symphony No. 4. Contrasting with the conventionalized thematic writing are occasional pentatonic flurries and in the D minor Scherzo of Symphony No. 5, an exciting irregularity of rhythm.

Jan Kittl had considerably more influence on his contemporaries than Měchura, taking up the directorship of the Prague Conservatory in 1843, a post he held until 1865. His friendly relations with a range of important composers whose work he was prepared to foster, among them Spohr, Mendelssohn, Liszt, Berlioz and Wagner, did much to enliven the musical life of the Czech capital. His four symphonies, No. 1, in D minor, Op. 19 (1836); No. 2, in E flat major (*Jagdsymphonie*), Op. 9, 1837; No. 3, in D major, Op. 42, 1842 and No. 4, in C major, 1858, the last of which was premièred at a concert on 7 July 1858 commemorating the fiftieth anniversary of the founding of the Prague Conservatory, at which the young Dvořák played the viola, had considerable public success during his lifetime. Kittl's Second Symphony resembles Voříšek's D major in being entirely successful on its own terms even if it does not quite match the quality of the earlier work. Entitled 'Hunting Symphony' (*Jagdsymphonie*), each movement has a programmatic title: *Adagio – Allegro agitato*, 'The start of the hunt' (*Beginn der Jagd*); *Andante*, 'Rest from the hunt' (*Jagdruhe*); *Scherzo*: *Vivace*, 'Revel' (*Gelage*) and *Allegro con fuoco*, 'The conclusion of the hunt' (*Schluss der Jagd*). In pursuit of the hunting motif the work opens, after a brief trumpet call, with a frantic introduction in 6/8 for four horns before the main part of the *Allegro agitato* gets under way. The horns remain prominent in this movement and return to take a leading role in the rather four-square, march-like Finale. As with Voříšek's symphony, the value of Kittl's Hunting Symphony lies more in the details than an innovatory, challenging outline. Kittl attempts nothing he cannot fulfil and he brings his considerable skills to a work which is both brisk, melodious and at certain stages attractively evocative, as in the ear-catching moment from the end of the exposition of the first movement (Ex. 5).

Bedřich Smetana's (1824–84) one contribution to the genre* is a considerable advance on those of his more recent Czech predecessors. The 'Triumphal Symphony' (*Triumph-Sinfonie* or *Slavnostní symfonie*) was composed as a celebration of the wedding of the Emperor Franz Josef to Princess Elizabeth of Bavaria on 24 April 1854. Smetana's composition catalogue provides evidence that he had begun work on the piece in advance of the announcement of the engagement on 1 August 1853, but the event provided the spur for the completion of the work as a commemorative symphony. To see a contradiction in a Czech composer writing a work in celebration of an Austrian crown event at a time of growing nationalist fervour is to misunderstand the nature of events in Bohemia and Moravia in

* Four pages of sketches from 1883 exist for another symphony for large orchestra with violins divided into four parts. Written hardly less than a year before Smetana died, the composer's final illness prevented him from concentrating on the work.

Ex. 5. Kittl: Symphony No. 2

the 1850s. The fiscal and commercial reforms of Franz Josef's early years as Emperor had encouraged the Czechs to hope for greater liberalization within the confines of the Austrian Empire. Their hopes were disappointed, but in the early 1850s there would have been nothing inappropriate in Smetana offering his symphony as an expression of loyalty. In the event nothing was heard from the Imperial Court and it was left to Smetana to arrange a première himself on 26 February 1855. Apart from the Scherzo the work was not a great success and Smetana developed something of a horror of the piece. The next two and half decades saw him pouring his energies into opera and the symphonic poem but he became reconciled to the score in 1881 when, recognising its excessive length, he made some useful cuts in the first and last movements.

Smetana himself referred to the work's 'old form' in 1881 and by comparison with his later symphonic poems the 'Triumphal Symphony' must have seemed old-fashioned. Even so, the handling of symphonic form has an originality not found in the Czech symphony up to that time. Mendelssohn and Schumann are occasionally called to mind in turns of phrase, but Smetana's work in the outer movements lacks the formal neatness of either composer. The initial *Allegro vivace* develops considerable impetus although Smetana is inclined to overwork the rather insistent rhythm which concludes the first theme. Nevertheless, the same rhythm is also used with great skill when it retreats into the background as an accompaniment for an attractive melodic excursion for the solo clarinet in the development section. Further on in the development Smetana permits some rather aimless sequences, although the preparation for the recapitulation is splendidly dramatic. An impressive introduction hinting at Haydn's 'Emperor's Hymn', which had already made a brief appearance towards the end of the development section of the first movement, lifts the curtain on the stately *Largo maestoso*. At times in this splendidly sustained movement the orchestration and aspiring melodic lines look forward some twenty years to the more elegiac moments of the symphonic poem cycle, 'My Country' (*Má vlast*).

The delightful Scherzo (*Allegro vivo*) balances dynamic rhythmic impetus with delicacy both of orchestration and thematic development. The Trio (*Allegro moderato*) maintains the high level, possessing an almost operatic character which anticipates the comic elements in *The Bartered Bride* (*Prodaná nevěsta*). As a whole this Scherzo was Smetana's most successful orchestral work up to that point and is by far the most satisfactory movement in the symphony, prompting Dvořák, who attended a rehearsal of the whole piece, to state: 'Man, that was a Scherzo! As long as I live I will never write one like it.'

Dvořák and the Czech Symphony

At a time when the appearance of a symphony anywhere in Europe was becoming something of a rarity, the debut of two Czech symphonies in 1859 has to be seen as something of an event. The C minor Symphony of **Alois Hnilička** (1826–1909), excepting the sturdy, chorale-like opening of the finale, is disappointing with uninspired, predictably symmetrical melody and a retrospective approach to form. The E minor Symphony, Op. 49, of **Václav Jindřich Veit** (1806–1864) is a quite different matter. If Veit is remembered at all today, it is for his wicked parody of Berlioz's *Symphonie fantastique*, entitled 'An episode in the life of a tailor' (*Episoda ze života krejčovského*) of 1846. His Symphony in E minor also bears witness to a fundamental mistrust of musical progressives such as Berlioz and Wagner, although it also shows an extraordinary command of the more conventional musical vernacular. For all his conservatism, Veit's melodies have a freshness and plasticity which sustain the symphonic argument with conviction. The E major Finale (*Allegro assai*) in particular has a splendid, free-wheeling energy generated by its broad-ranging first theme. The third movement (*Allegro*), however, a 2/4 time Scherzo (Ex. 6a) can lay greatest claim to being the

significant novelty of the work. Not only is the time-signature unusual;
both this and the phrasing of the theme along with its instrumentation and
polka-like rhythm anticipate by six years the third movement of Dvořák's
First Symphony (Ex. 6b):

Ex. 6a. Veit: Symphony in E minor

Ex. 6b. Dvořák: Symphony No. 1

Dvořák did not come to Prague until 1857, two years after the first and
only performance of Smetana's 'Triumphal Symphony' in its original form.
Although he did not know Smetana's single symphony at this time, he might
well have played in the first performance of Veit's under František Škroup
on 27 November 1859. Quite why Dvořák turned to the symphony in 1865
is likely to remain a mystery.

The motivation for writing his first opera, *Alfred*, (B 16) albeit to a
German text, is easy to explain at a time when the genre was a natural
means of expression for any Czech composer with national sympathies. But
Dvořák's muse in the 1860s was unpredictable. When very few composers
in Prague appeared to be writing chamber music, Dvořák produced four
string quartets and a string quintet. Much the same is true of the song-cycle
'Cypresses' (*Cypřiše*, B 11), the A major cello concerto (B 10) and, of course,
the two symphonies of 1865, No. 1 in C minor ('The Bells of Zlonice', B 9)

and No. 2 in B flat major (B 12).* What would have been clear about the C minor symphony, had anyone heard it at the time of its composition or during the composer's lifetime, was that it was the product of a new and powerful voice. The period from 1865 to 1873 was a time of rich musical experiment in Dvořák's career when his compositional horizons were in no way limited by the requirements of publisher, public or helpful friends and colleagues. The results can at times be awkward, not least in the First Symphony, but they can also be visionary.

Dvořák wrote the score of his First Symphony in less than six weeks, between 14 February and 24 March 1865, though it seems likely that he had made sketches before setting to work on what is a very neat manuscript. The symphony's subtitle, 'The Bells of Zlonice' (*Zlonické zvony*), appears nowhere on the manuscript, but occurs instead in a list of compositions Dvořák made in 1888. Dvořák's affection for the small market town of Zlonice was well founded since the two years he spent there as a teenager (1854–1856) were rich in musical experiences and were probably decisive in setting him on the road to a lifetime of composition. Nevertheless, the appearance of a picturesque title for the symphony – one which seems to have no programmatic counterpart in the score – so many years after its composition and at a time when Dvořák undoubtedly considered the score lost,† suggests that the composer may have been indulging in nostalgic reminiscence rather than indicating the true background of the work.

Whatever Dvořák was thinking when he penned the opening of the C minor Symphony, no-one could accuse him of a lack of confidence. The introductory gesture is a bold unison theme on four horns and bassoon, punctuated by firm string and wind chords, which comes to rest on the dominant. What follows is a marvellously arresting opening for the main *Allegro*. Under a vigorous, pulsating ostinato:

$$\left(\begin{smallmatrix} 3 \\ 4 \end{smallmatrix} \quad \bullet \; \bullet \; \bullet \; \bullet \quad \bullet \quad | \right)$$

one which the composer made good use of twenty-five years later in the *Dies irae* of his Requiem – Dvořák introduces a brooding, modally-inflected theme. The tension is sustained by maintaining a pedal C against a change to an E flat major chord before a repetition of the first theme. So far, the motivic material and long pedals have suggested a broad, almost Brucknerian scale and on this basis the build towards the first tutti is no disappointment. Sadly, the tutti, when it comes, is simply a breathless reinforcement of C minor with no clear link to the opening material; a strange and inappropriate

---

* The numbering of Dvořák's symphonies in chronological sequence is now universally accepted. Dvořák himself, though often vague about his early compositions, had a clear idea of the sequence which he noted in manuscript on the title page of the 9th Symphony ('From the New World') (see J. Burghauser: *Antonín Dvořák, Thematický Katalog*, Prague, 1960, p. 617). The list begins with the B flat symphony, Dvořák having been reconciled to losing the manuscript of the first symphony in C minor. Thus, in Dvořák's numbering, his last symphony appears as the 8th.

† Dvořák had, in fact, included the symphony in a list of 'compositions which I have torn up and burnt'. Burghauser, op. cit., p. 617.

outcome, perhaps based on late-eighteenth-century models, to a promisingly original start.

The move to the second theme, while purposeful, is unduly protracted with a repetition of the first subject which would do very nicely by way of a recapitulation but does little to help proceedings in the exposition. The development, after an exposition repeat which might be thought rather too much of a good thing, is handicapped by an unwillingness to let go of C minor. Once this has been achieved, after a quotation of the introductory theme, Dvořák proceeds to an exploration of material drawn mainly from this same introduction and first-subject group. The real formal novelty in this movement is the lack a remotely conventional recapitulation. Dvořák gives every appearance of approaching the tonic via the Neapolitan chord and the dominant, but the expected C minor is clouded by a diminished chord and the composer veers off towards remoter key areas including E major and A minor. There is no full quotation of the first-subject group and no secure arrival at the home tonality until the second subject, exquisitely arranged for solo cello and soft trombones, is presented in C major. After this, Dvořák continues in heroic mood with some ringing transformations of the introductory theme in the horns set against a fairly unimportant subsidiary in strings and woodwind, before calling a halt to proceedings at bar 658. For all the unorthodoxy of its second half this movement is, for the most part, bold and confident. Dvořák seems to understand the implications of his opening theme and the implications of breadth in its tonal plan, yet at times he handles his material in an almost improvisatory manner. The result is usually engaging and occasionally commanding, but not always entirely purposeful.

The remaining three movements of the symphony do not possess the vigour or audacity of the first. Even so, the central *Adagio di molto* and *Allegretto* have distinct charms of their own. Those belonging to the A flat major slow movement are present largely in the ravishing melody for oboe – a favourite solo instrument in the orchestral music that Dvořák wrote in 1865 – which appears after a brief introduction, and the instrumentation. As a whole, the movement does not seem organized to best effect. The near-vocal first theme frames developments of itself and two additional melodies, the first of a decidedly military cut and a second, quietly noble in the Beethoven manner. While it is possible to admire the subtle derivation of the march-like military theme, which first appears at bar 83, from an earlier subsidiary figure (bar 29), its triumphalistic quality sits uneasily in an *Adagio* which should provide a relaxed alternative to the movements before and after. The real achievement of this movement is Dvořák's frequently sensitive orchestration and his ability to invest chordal accompaniments with a sense of movement.

The pagination of Dvořák's manuscript of his First Symphony reveals that the work was originally conceived in three movements. The *Allegretto* third movement was added after the completion of the other three. This attractive and original alternative to the traditional Scherzo was a happy afterthought. A tendency toward developmental activity not entirely appropriate to a Scherzo movement should alert the listener to the possibility that this movement may have started life as a Finale. The 2/4 time signature is unorthodox, though there is a precedent in Schumann's Second Symphony and more locally in Veit's E minor; and the scale is large, though somewhat smaller than the two outer movements. The complexity of development in this *Allegretto* and the way in which the main melody of the central section emerges from subsidiary material from the first suggests that if Dvořák were not thinking of a possible Finale he was looking to some very broadly-developed scherzos by way of precursors. After a short introduction, Dvořák presents his catchy first theme canonically and works up to a tutti statement (bar 57) before working towards a more motivic second idea (bar 78) which provides the rhythmic basis for the main melody of the central section. Replete with two melodies and strong developmental tendencies, including references to the opening section, this central section is a Trio in all but name.

In common with the three other movements in the symphony, the Finale begins with a brief introduction. As in the first movement, the implications of scale suggested by the tonic underpinning of the first theme are large. Dvořák deals with this unpromising, fanfare-like melody with energy and imagination, extending possibilities by shifting its dotted quaver second beat to the first. Schumann's Second Symphony is called to mind in some of the more congested tuttis (bar 113f) and also in a transitional subsidiary theme which first appears at bar 89. An indulgently lyrical second subject provides the necessary contrast with the motivic vigour of the first theme. The development of this material is where the problems arise. Thrilled by the potential of all this motivic richness, Dvořák lets it go to his head, allowing counter-melodies and thematic transformation to highjack the direction of the movement. Two appearances of the ostinato theme from the first movement hardly qualify the work for motto-symphony status; indeed, they reinforce the feeling that Dvořák was slightly carried away by the material at hand rather than attempting thorough-going thematic integration. Šourek's suggestion that Beethoven's Fifth Symphony may have been a model for the work can hardly be sustained: the ostinato hardly 'thunders forth' in the peroration of the Finale; the appearance on the drums, if indeed it is intentional, is lost beneath a full orchestral tutti. If there were a model for this work, its identity is lost in the flood of Dvořák's own invention. There are passing hints of Beethoven, though more usually his Third rather than his Fifth Symphony, and Schumann, a frequent exemplar for Czechs in this period.

Had Dvořák not lost the score of the symphony he may well have revised it in the manner of his second. With so much clear compositional virtue – rather more than in the nearly contemporary A major cello concerto – it is hard to believe he would, as he stated in 1882, have destroyed the piece. At its worst the First Symphony is overblown and inclined to pomposity. But in all its enormous length – one of the longest Czech symphonies before Suk's

Asrael – the energy and quality of invention is such as to hold the listener throughout. In the context of the more conventional Czech symphony of the 1850s and 1860s Dvořák's debut with the form is doubly impressive. Work on the C minor Symphony seems in no way to have sapped Dvořák's energy or sated a taste for large-scale composition. By the beginning of August that year he was already at work on the Second Symphony, in B flat major. Scoring followed rapidly with the first movement finished by 18 August and the entire work completed on 9 October. Unlike the lost First Symphony, Dvořák had the opportunity to revise the B flat major Symphony. The first and most major assault on the score took place in 1887 when Dvořák was preparing to offer it to Simrock for publication. Although the publisher turned the work down, Dvořák made further revisions in advance of its première on 11 March 1888. Both sets of changes involved cutting, some quite extensive, and a general tidying-up of details of orchestration and occasional motivic treatment. The work was first performed by the orchestra of the National Theatre under Dvořák's old friend Adolf Čech and the composer was pleased to report that '. . . everybody liked it very much'.

There are inevitable benefits to be felt in the later revision of the work; the form in which the symphony is invariably heard today. Dvořák's changes to the orchestration mean a lighter texture than that found in the C minor symphony and in general the structure is more clearly apprehended by the listener, though not always necessarily more purposeful. One feature all the movements of the Second Symphony have in common with the first is that each begins with some introductory gesture. Where the opening of the First Symphony was assertive, the start of the Second is gentle though no less effective: a luminous affirmation of B flat major which, in the revised version, concludes with a quotation of the opening of the main theme. The same passage played a third higher in D major generates an introduction to the exposition proper (bar 63). This imaginative and unusual 'a tempo' introduction looks forward directly to similar devices in the Finale of the Seventh Symphony and the beginning of the Eighth. The main theme itself has a superbly aspiring, almost Straussian quality (Ex. 7). The secondary material is far less well defined and a tendency to extend by overly-literal sequence between bars 176 and 198 is taken to extremes. The conclusion of the exposition, however, makes a powerful climax to this first part. More than one commentator has noted the similarity between this *Allegro con moto* and the first movement of Beethoven's 'Pastoral' symphony. Dvořák does not appear to have set out to write an equivalent of Beethoven's work, despite pastoral elements such as drone bases, but the repetitions at the start of his development in order to build broader paragraphs have strong affinities with the work of the earlier composer. Dvořák goes much further than Beethoven in a development which lasts 181 bars but, notwithstanding some daring harmonic moves, to considerably less effect. The recapitulation, exquisitely prepared, is

Ex. 7. Dvořák: Symphony No. 2

more regular than that of the First Symphony and provides a satisfying conclusion.

Dvořák may also have had the slow movement of Beethoven's 'Pastoral' symphony in mind when he set his own *Poco adagio* in 12/8 time. This apart, there are few similarities. The advances over the First Symphony are much more striking in this movement. As a whole it moves with fluent assurance with Dvořák eschewing the military contrasts present in the *Adagio molto* of the First Symphony. Dvořák might with advantage have curtailed the recapitulation to a slightly greater extent than his *vide* markings indicate, but all told there is very little in this movement that smacks of an uncertain hand. Sadly, the same cannot be said of the Scherzo (*Allegro con brio*). As in the First Symphony, this movement has something of the scope and manner of a Finale. The tendency to overdevelop ideas and on occasion to lose a sense of direction is a pity in a movement which has a great many attractive features. The thematic material is effective and the instrumentation delightful. Dvořák fails, however, to produce a consistency of tone. This is most damaging in the Trio section where the exalted nature of the opening is swept away by busy subsidiary figures.

Apparently unaware that the Scherzo has stolen something of the Finale's (*Allegro con fuoco*) thunder, Dvořák begins in confident mood. All the thematic material, from the self-generating first theme through the second subject to a magnificently free-wheeling concluding melody (bar 141) – again prophetic of Strauss – is enormously bracing. Dvořák himself recognized the value of one particular thematic idea, occurring first at bar 133, some thirty-five years later by making it the climax of the last act of his penultimate opera, *Rusalka* (1900). Dvořák rarely allows the impetus to flag in this movement and, in general, it leaves a more coherent impression than the Finale of his first symphony. Viewed together, warts and all, these two symphonies have quite enough of value to justify an occasional concert performance. Perhaps they will come into their own when the battle to find a stage for the Third and Fourth symphonies has been won.

Dvořák did not return to the symphony until 1873. In the intervening eight years he was far from idle, producing two complex opera scores (*Alfred*, B 16 and the first version of 'The King and the Charcoal-burner' (*Král a uhlíř*, B 21), three string quartets (B 17, 18 and 19), a piano quintet (B 28), several songs and the choral *Patriotic Hymn* (B 27). This was a time of acute compositional experiment which saw Dvořák pushing form and tonality far beyond conventional bounds in the E minor string quartet (B 19). The culmination of this period was Dvořák's decision to apply to the charitable society Svatobor in 1873 for funds to free him from giving music lessons and to enable him to visit Liszt, presumably with a view to studying composition. The change towards a more palpably national style and a simpler, more classically orientated approach to form succeeded this neo-Romantic phase. However one views this major change of direction it is a mistake to see it simply as a move from immaturity of style to maturity. In the two opera scores and at least two of the quartets, Dvořák showed himself to possess far greater technical facility than any of his Czech contemporaries other than Smetana. The Third Symphony comes at the climax of this impressive early development and for a number of reasons may be considered a masterpiece. The history of the work is complicated. Dvořák himself gave three quite different years of composition, but it now seems likely that a full sketch was ready in 1872, possibly arising from work begun two years earlier, and that the full score was completed in July 1873. The manuscript of the symphony indicates two major layers of revision: the first was carried out shortly after the première under Smetana on 29 March 1874 and the second between 1887 and 1889 when Dvořák was revising a number of his earlier compositions with a view to performance and publication. The manuscript as it comes down to us certainly does not represent the first form of the symphony, and until the parts used in the original performance come to light the work will only be known in its later version. There is no evidence that Dvořák conceived or originally wrote the work in four movements and its three-movement structure certainly requires no apology or explanation.

The first movement *Allegro moderato* amply demonstrates Dvořák's new-found confidence as a symphonist. The powerful, surging rhythm of the first two bars underpins many later developments, and with unchallengeable effect *and* logic crowns the concluding bars. A lengthy and magnificent first melody provides Dvořák with nearly all he needs for a substantial symphonic movement:

Ex. 8. Dvořák: Symphony No. 3

The rolling figure *a* reinforces the upbeat quality of the accompanying rhythm providing throughout this opening theme a strong sense of self-generating development. Everywhere in this first movement figure *a* has an almost leitmotivic role, being present at all important junctures. After an assured and occasionally stormy transition we find that the second subject, in G flat major, derived from figure *b* in the first subject, also incorporates figure *a*. Dvořák is skilful in preventing the monothematic nature of the movement from allowing the musical material to pall. A certain amount of development is reserved for the recapitulation where it takes the place of the repeat of the second subject and leads to a thrilling coda. Dvořák's grip on the momentum never falters. His approach to form already foreshadows the lucidity of his later the works: the triumph here is that Dvořák produces such a convincing symphonic structure with such unconventional, quasi-operatic material.

The *Adagio molto, tempo di marcia* with its measured, sombre tread has something of the funeral march about it. Dvořák borrows the swirling figure *a* and another rhythmic pattern $\begin{array}{c}2\\4\end{array}$ ♪ ♩. ♪ ♫ from the first movement in the cause of what turns out to be an impressively sustained first section. The trick of making a slow movement 'move', which Dvořák had learned in his first two symphonies, pays dividends in flowing orchestral lines. Some may find the climax of the central section a touch hectoring, but once again it is filled with a powerful sense of purpose. With a nod in the direction of *Tannhäuser* and *Lohengrin*, Dvořák's orchestration of this central section, complete with harp, is particularly gorgeous. If any further proof were needed of Dvořák's symphonic maturity, then the superbly-crafted return to the opening material provides it. A misty farewell to the heroic central section concludes this marvellously evocative movement.

As a whole the Finale remains on the same exalted level as the rest of the symphony. Dvořák had the sense to direct the focus of attention away from the rather insistent rhythm of the first subject, including a bold layering of 2/4 and 3/4 time simultaneously. While not as consciously monothematic as the first movement, much of the melodic material in the Finale finds its origins in the rhythm and energy of the buoyant first subject. The first performance under Smetana on 29 March 1874 was a major early success for the composer and the virtues of the work were further rewarded when Dvořák, having submitted it with the Fourth Symphony and another work to a commission appointed to award funds to struggling artists, won 400 gulden – more than three times the salary he was paid as a church organist.

Less than three months after completing the third symphony, Dvořák was at work on his fourth. He sketched the new symphony towards the end of 1873 and completed the full score on 26 March 1874. By comparison with the magnificent flexibility of the first movement of the Third Symphony the Fourth, at times, seems stiff and awkward. Written at a time when his style was showing signs of fundamental change, the composer relies rather too much on repetition. Both the introductory theme and the second subject of the frequently gripping initial *Allegro* rely on threefold repetition of their first phrases. The form of the movement also seems a touch self-conscious: Dvořák has abandoned the instinctive organic growth of the Third Symphony for an almost textbook presentation of a sonata exposition. He does little to conceal the transition passages and as a whole the movement emerges as one of his most artificial.

Formally, the slow movement (*Andante sostenuto e molto cantabile*) is also straightforward. A series of variations on a theme, which takes more than a little from the pilgrims of *Tannhäuser*, allows Dvořák to exploit his genius for orchestration and the devising of attractive counter-melodies. Dvořák's manuscript indicates that the Scherzo, *Allegro feroce*, probably started life as a separate movement, raising the possibility that Dvořák originally had in mind another three-movement symphony. The composer drew this bracing and original movement into the ambit of the whole work by incorporating a reference to the opening of the first movement in its coda. After this successful and unpretentious movement the Finale (*Allegro con brio*) returns to the repetitious style of the first movement. The main lyrical relief is an attractive (*Poco meno mosso*) second subject, hermetically-sealed from the battering of the first subject. For all its intrinsic beauty, this lovely episode cannot really compensate for the dead-pan dullness of the surrounding material, built on a very unpromising first subject.

The Fourth Symphony shows the advantages and disadvantages of Dvořák's changing style. Formal clarity has been achieved at the cost of adopting an artificially motivic melodic style heavily dependent on the repetition of minute rhythmic cells. Within hardly more than a year, Dvořák had abandoned its stilted symphonism. The Fifth Symphony, composed between 15 June and 23 July 1875, inhabits a world untroubled by pointless repetition, almost as if Dvořák had recovered all his previous symphonic instinct after a period of gradual refinement. A greater certainty in his personal circumstances may also account for new stylistic assurance. The Fifth Symphony was composed in the year when Dvořák had first won the Austrian state prize and the event seems to have released enormous creativity in the composer. The year 1875 was one of the most prolific of Dvořák's composing career. Apart from the symphony he composed the marvellous E major string serenade, three major chamber works, four Moravian duets and the absurdly underrated five-act grand opera *Vanda*.

Despite a rapid pace of creativity there is barely a hint of haste in the planning of the symphony. As with his previous symphonies Dvořák made revisions to the Fifth, but there is no sign of a lack of confidence in the original form of the work. Indeed, from the start of the symphony Dvořák exudes a sureness of hand. The very opening is the quintessence of the Czech style as the composer would have understood it. The initial gesture of the work is an orchestral sublimation of one of the most characteristic Czech sounds, the bagpipe. The horns and lower strings provide a drone above which two clarinets provide the first theme, harmonized in thirds and sixths, in a distant but credible facsimile of the Czech musette bagpipe. The national tone is further enhanced by a pentatonic swirl at the conclusion of the first subject:

Ex. 9. Dvořák: Symphony No. 5

Though apparently undynamic as an idea, Dvořák seizes on the dotted element *a* to produce a dynamic lead up to the first tutti which introduces another nationally-inflected theme with polka underpinning. The structure of the movement is lucid without banality. The development is long and Dvořák limits further development in the recapitulation to the provision of new counter-melodies to the second subject. Although the movement ends quietly, Dvořák places a strong tonic tutti shortly before it, anticipating the blazing conclusion of the first movement of his Sixth Symphony five years later.

The modestly proportioned slow movement (*Andante con moto*) is built on a graceful A minor theme with a central A major alternativo (*Un pochettino più mosso*). The resemblance is less to the Dvořákian Dumka, as John Clapham suggests,* where the alternations of tempo are usually more extreme, than to the slow movement of Beethoven's Seventh where the opening section relaxes into the major key contrasting passage. The real novelty of Dvořák's movement is the link between slow movement and Scherzo: not merely an *attacca* but a fully worked bridge based on the first theme of the slow movement. The balanced melodic phrases of the *Allegro scherzando* have distinct affinities with the dance styles Dvořák was to exploit so successfully in the Slavonic Dances some three years later. No specific national model springs to mind, but the accent is unmistakably Czech. Both Scherzo and Trio are broadly developed though neither outstays its welcome.

The opening of the Finale (*Allegro molto*) in A minor confirms Dvořák's interest, not at all unusual by the 1870s, in key relationships of a third. Not only does he begin his F major Finale in A minor, but he maintains the foreign key for over fifty bars. He attempted something similar, though with markedly less success, in the E major string serenade. In the symphony the initial absence of the tonic lends enormous impact to its appearance with a solid tutti – rather more definite than in the serenade – at bar 55. Dvořák provides another fairly lengthy development but severely curtails the recapitulation in order to prepare the major *coup* of the symphony: an exquisitely gentle return to the opening material of the first movement. Clearing all tonal activity away from his recapitulation Dvořák introduces bars 9 and 10 of Ex. 9, *pianissimo*, but unmistakeable. The violins and violas play a languid reminiscence of the pentatonic swirl which followed the first theme of the symphony before the momentum increases in a long celebration of F major.

Dvořák did not return to symphonic composition for five years and did so as a result of the success of the third Slavonic Rhapsody under Hans Richter in Vienna in 1879. Dvořák promised Richter and the orchestra a new symphony which he began sketching on 27 August 1880. The full score was completed less than two months later on 15 October. This was a time when Dvořák was making important links with Viennese musical society and his friendship with Brahms was beginning to burgeon. With this in mind the Czech composer might well have felt that more discriminating eyes would be brought to bear on his new symphony. The Sixth Symphony has always been a focus of comparison between Dvořák and Brahms. Given the overwhelming presence of the German composer it is easy to forget that influence can be a two-way traffic. Brahms knew three, if not four, of Dvořák's symphonies before he completed his first in 1876 and doubtless he was much heartened to see so much rampant symphonic creativity from a younger contemporary.†

The fact that Dvořák was a master of symphonic form well before he embarked on his Sixth Symphony is worth remembering when comparison is

---

* See J. Clapham: *Antonín Dvořák: Musician and Craftsman*, London, 1966, p. 69.
† I am indebted to Jarmil Burghauser for drawing this fact to my attention.

made, as it frequently is, between this work and Brahms's Second Symphony. Even cursory analysis reveals only superficial resemblances and anything more penetrating reveals only fundamental differences between the two works. The clearest point of contact between the two symphonies is at the start of the finales. Beyond this specific affinity, the comparisons are reduced to the common key and time-signature of the first movements. Some parallel sixth harmonies in the first movement of Dvořák's Sixth may have been inspired by Brahms as might the striding development at bars 34–36 etc., but from most points of view the listener hears and the analyst observes two quite different masterpieces. If antecedents are necessary to justify the worth of this marvellous piece, then Beethoven springs more readily to mind than Brahms and the dactylic rhythm which shadows the secondary material of the first movement owes more to Smetana than Brahms. A simple formal difference between Brahms's first movement and Dvořák's is also fundamental. Where Brahms leaves his ravishing second subject, in B minor, as a separate lyrical incident, Dvořák draws his secondary material into the developmental process. Dvořák's orchestral sound is also richer and more luminous than Brahms and where the older composer rarely lets listeners forget the initial idea of the first movement, Dvořák leads them without any loss of purpose away from the iron hand of his opening idea.

The care with which Dvořák organizes the growth of his movement may be felt from the very start of the first theme which grows from a simple rising fourth into a lyrical span full of developmental potential. The development is one of Dvořák's most successful and most carefully planned to date. The opening retreats into misty distances with slow harmonic rhythm and only a gradual increase in pace. The sketches of this section show that Dvořák, at one stage, considered an F minor fugato; all that remains of this idea is a powerful rising scale which leads back into the recapitulation. The main thrust of this last section is the magnificent climax Dvořák engineers from his first subject shortly before the final bars: after a scale passage, similar to the one which introduced the recapitulation, the bass drops out of the orchestra and the brass ring out with fanfares against a held A in the upper strings – a moment which looks forward to Janáček.

A reference to the slow movement of Beethoven's Ninth Symphony at the start of Dvořák's introduces one of the composer's now familiar 'moving' *Adagios*. Unlike earlier examples, the orchestral resources are more economically used. Dvořák's seriousness of purpose is clear in the developmental rhetoric at the end of the first section leading to a broad dramatic statement at bar 104 which stands in marked contrast to the surrounding calm. More complex and less obviously lyrical than the *Andante con moto* of the previous symphony, this *Adagio* fulfils its more serious role with complete success. The Scherzo is Dvořák's only explicitly national symphonic movement. The subtitle 'Furiant' refers to the cross-rhythms (2/4 against a basic 3/4) which gives the Scherzo its extraordinary energy. The rhythmic and melodic thrills apparent in the first set of Slavonic Dances are here placed at the service of a strong developmental impulse: the impact is at times almost overwhelming and the delicate, almost *Ländler*-like Trio provides an appropriate contrast.

The long theme which opens the Finale has an almost Mahlerian *Knaben Wunderhorn* quality about it for all the affinities with Brahms. Dvořák extends its potential through cheerful variants which carry a deal of the developmental burden. The movement is full of creative variation and leads to a huge climax which gives way to a brilliant *Presto* conclusion rivalling the overture to *The Bartered Bride* in high spirits. The success of this symphony in its day was well deserved as is its comeback to concert platforms in the last fifteen years. The chief strength in a work with so many virtues is that none predominate; each movement is as strong as another in a profoundly impressive whole.

The D major Symphony did much to guarantee Dvořák's success in England. A performance of the work under the composer in March 1884 led to a commission for a new symphony from the Philharmonic Society. While Dvořák was concerned to do his best for the Philharmonic Society and a new, admiring public, it would be wrong to see this work entirely separately from the composer's very real national aspirations. The first theme of the D minor Symphony was inspired by the arrival of a festival train in Prague from Budapest. This was far from being the idle musing of an avid train-spotter, since the train was full of anti-Habsburg patriots. The national associations of this stirring theme and the work as a whole are further advanced by Dvořák's comments to his friend Alois Göbl on the completion of the slow movement of the symphony: 'Today I have just finished the second movement, Andante [*sic*], of my new symphony, and am again so happy and contented in my work as I have always been and, God grant, may always be, for my slogan is and shall be: God, Love and Country! And that alone can lead to a happy goal'. Along with this upsurge of national sentiment, Dvořák was keen to write a symphony of major significance. Perhaps with a view to the Brahmsian exemplar Dvořák associated value with concision. The work is considerably shorter than the D major Symphony and after the first performance, under the composer in London on 22 April 1885, Dvořák cut forty bars from the slow movement and wrote to his publisher Simrock: 'Now I am convinced that there is not a single superfluous note in the work'.

Dvořák began sketching the D minor Symphony on 13 December 1884 and completed the full score on 17 March 1885. The design of the material of the first movement is superb. While there are no obvious links between themes, nothing happens as an isolated incident. The first idea offers the most immediate evidence of Dvořák's constructive genius: this tense, modally inflected melody is given symphonic impetus by an upbeat jump on to a diminished chord. Dvořák takes the heat out of this powerful start with an attractive descending scalic theme, but allows a tutti statement of the opening theme before the lyrical relief of the second subject. There is no exposition repeat and the brief development slams headlong into a tutti *fortissimo* recapitulation. As with the Fifth and Sixth symphonies Dvořák saves the real climax of the first movement for the end, where off-beat accents create an overwhelming effect. Dvořák may have benefited from the example of Brahms in this work but in reality he looks back beyond his exemplar to the world of Beethoven.

The *Poco Adagio* is richer in sentiment than any previous slow movement by Dvořák. The melody is ripe for development, and keeps a vocal quality. He also manages to hold open-hearted lyricism and more darkly expressive elements in fruitful balance; for instance, the following eloquent line:

Ex. 10a. Dvořák: Symphony No. 7

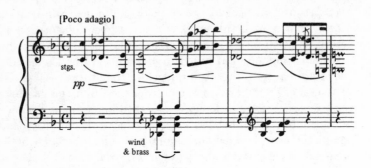

eventually results in this glorious horn melody:

Ex. 10b.

There is very little structural repetition in this movement. Ex. 10a acquires a new highly expressive counter-melody on its reappearance at bar 79 and even the first theme does not enter again until the very closing bars (bar 95). The whole is a continuous, rapturous development: the true measure of Dvořák's genius in this work is that he succeeds in doing this without any loss of formal integrity.

The Scherzo has the cross-rhythms of the 'Furiant' but does not develop them, as in the Sixth Symphony, to such aggressive effect. Indeed, the tone of the movement has an elegance matched by its structure, something which Dvořák, as the sketches reveal, found by no means easy to achieve. The ravishing Trio begins as a pastoral fantasy before developing more serious intentions providing a perfect foil for the vitality of the Scherzo. The intensity of the movement is much enhanced by shortening the *da capo* and the insertion of a moment of profound reflection, followed by a powerful close.

Some commentators have found the Finale does not quite measure up to previous movements, but its design seems every bit as inspired as that in other movements. There can be no doubt that the first theme is precisely what it sets out to be: heading the recapitulation and furnishing much of the developmental material. Yet with its measured tread and perceptible pull up, just before the entry of the second tonic theme, this first subject has all the effect of an in tempo introduction. The impact of this aspect of design is to shift the developmental emphasis towards the climax of the movement. Lyrical contrast is provided by the glorious A major second subject, but very little holds up the inevitability of a conclusion where the second tonic idea blossoms fully in a *stretto* plunge towards the final cadence – an inspired *tierce de picardie*.

Dvořák's Eighth Symphony inhabits a completely different world from its predecessor. Sketched between 26 August and 23 September 1889, the score was completed by 8 November. Dvořák did much of the composing at his country home at Vysoká in south Bohemia and the symphony is redolent of the happiness the composer felt in these surroundings. But the differences from the Seventh Symphony are more than ones of mood. The Eighth dispenses with the inspired classicism of the two previous symphonies. In structural terms the new symphony must rank as one of Dvořák's most experimental works since the early 1870s.

Even the mode of the first movement is ambiguous. The *Allegro con brio* ends in an uproarious G major and yet the first theme to be heard is in G minor. This same theme gives every indication of heading the recapitulation and is also the only melody to be presented in closed musical phrases:

Ex. 11. Dvořák: Symphony No. 8

The remainder of the thematic material of the movement, even down to what is usually regarded as the second subject (bar 77), gives the impression of being transitory. The G minor opening theme, with its slow, expressive qualities, might be a suitable candidate for viewing as another in tempo introduction, but it heads the recapitulation and provides much of the developmental impetus, derived mainly from *a* (Ex. 11). A dogmatic interpretation of sonata form in this movement simply will not do. Dvořák rewrites the rules by providing a profusion of melodic material in the exposition* and yet never loses a clear sense of symphonic purpose.

The *Adagio* is equally inspired and equally original. The movement begins in sombre guise and yet barely a quarter of the way in the mood is one of gentle merrymaking. It is tempting to speculate that the source for this kind of alternation is to be found in Haydn, the slow movement of the Symphony No. 103, for example, although Dvořák's handling of the contrasts is entirely his own. There is some impressive rhetoric at bar 77 and a section of great tension succeeding it at bar 101. But by the Tempo 1 at bar 133 all is smiles again. This wealth of incident is based on a single theme, but one with extraordinary developmental potential and contrast.

The *Allegretto grazioso* is Dvořák's gentlest third movement. It is neither called a Scherzo nor does it shelter that genre's more vigorous characteristics anywhere in its modest length. The first theme with a falling scalic characteristic and bubbling woodwind accompaniment is irresistibly evocative of a woodland stream flowing downhill. The main theme of the Trio is taken from the opera *The Pig-headed Peasants*. Its affectingly wistful character derives from the lament of Toník in scene 9 who imagines that his love, Lenka, will be married off to his father.

After the fluent originality of the first three movements the Finale, in an unsympathetic performance, can seem halting. It begins with a brisk trumpet call and a theme followed by a slightly faster variant.† The fast variant is interspersed with what are effectively two Trios. The development which follows is highly effective and leads to a terrific climactic return of the trumpet fanfare. While no-one could argue that this movement was a hotch-potch of ideas, Dvořák does not manage quite so successfully the blend of weight and spontaneity achieved in previous movements. This is not for want of trying: the main theme of the Finale went through some ten variants in sketch before reaching its final form. Perhaps the problem was one generic to many composers in the late nineteenth century where

---

* Although there is no exposition repeat, Dvořák indicates the start of the development with a double bar.

† Conductors invariably play the theme too slowly and its variant in relation too fast. Dvořák marks the first *Un poco meno mosso* against a basic tempo of *Allegro ma non troppo* with the metronome mark ♩ = 108; the fast variant is marked *Un poco più mosso* with the metronome mark ♩ = 116. Ignoring these indications usually results in the opening sounding too slow and the variant a scramble.

Finales were concerned: how to create sufficient weight in a conclusion without inflating the structure unduly.

Dvořák's Ninth Symphony, his greetings 'From the New World', was the first work the composer conceived, sketched and scored completely in America, and is the work by which Dvořák is best known. What is perhaps less obvious, though it may account for its extraordinary success, are the profound stylistic differences beween this and previous symphonies. Both form and content are new, a fact which Dvořák recognized when he wrote to his friend Emil Kozánek that '. . . it will be very different from my earlier works'. As in the F major String Quartet, 'The American', and the E flat major String Quintet, Dvořák relies on repetition. This is not the occasionally directionless repetition of ideas encountered in the early symphonies, but a dynamic building of musical paragraphs from short, developmentally derived fragments. When piled up sequentially to intensify the harmonic effect, these repetitions can be overwhelming.

Along with this heady sense of power derived from repetition in the fast movements, there is a new simplicity of design. There is a textbook quality to the presentation of sonata form in the first movement, with each stage following rapidly on another: the conclusion of the second subject, for instance, comes only fourteen bars before the end of the exposition. This almost analytical clarity may derive in part from Dvořák's experiences as a teacher in Prague and New York, but also from a desire to provide his American pupils with a model for inspiration.* In an interview with the *New York Herald* published a day before the première of the symphony, Dvořák stated the following: 'I have simply written original themes embodying the peculiarities of the Indian music, and, using these themes as subjects, have developed them with all the resources of modern rhythms, harmony, counterpoint and orchestral colour.'

The composer could easily have been talking to his composition class at the National Conservatory. The catch-all, 'Indian music', refers to a broad range of spiritual and plantation melodies, which along with the original compositions of Stephen Foster comprised an American equivalent to the Czech sources of national as opposed to folk, music which comprised Dvořák's experience of native art in the new world. The effect on his melodic style in this work was an intensification of the pentatonic element in his musical language, apparent since the 1860s, and a greater symmetry of phrase length in the main themes. Many of the melodies of the 'New World' symphony have a vocal quality which combined with repetition makes them catchily memorable and hummable.

Another feature of the work is the fact that every movement has some sort of introductory gesture. Certainly this does not indicate any loss of symphonic nerve in the first movement nor in the masterly transition from E major to D

---

* Dvořák shared his box with some of his composition pupils at the first performance of the symphony in Carnegie Hall on 16 December 1893.

flat major effected by that in the slow movement. The introduction to the Scherzo, with its reminiscence of Beethoven's Ninth, is effective enough, but the flailing of the strings at the start of the Finale is little more than a dreary vamp. Such strictures apart, there is a great deal to admire in this work, especially in the first three movements. The development and melodic material may well be simple in the first movement, but the climax just before the close manages to be both harmonically straightforward and magnificently exciting.

None of Dvořák' slow movements are as vocal as the *Largo* of this symphony. Subtitled 'Legend' in the sketches, Dvořák himself stated that the *Largo* was inspired by the 'Funeral in the Forest' from Longfellow's *Song of Hiawatha*, with which he had toyed as a possible operatic subject during his stay in America. Both the magical opening chords and the famous melody on cor anglais deserve all the accolades they have received in nearly a hundred years of performance. Just before the return of the main theme, Dvořák articulates a huge climax with the first and second subjects of the opening movement. Since neither has a motto function the purpose of their return at such a prominent point is far from clear. Much the same is true of the return of the opening theme of the first movement as part of the link between the Scherzo and waltz-like Trio and later with a reminiscence of the second theme in the Scherzo's coda. The stimulus for this bracing movement, according to the composer, was a 'celebration in the forest, where the Indians dance'. The melodic content is slightly more generous than in previous Dvořák Scherzos, with an attractive excursion into E major in addition to the Trio.

Pounding, march-like rhythms and infectious melody get Dvořák quite a long way into the Finale. But the ideas, while fluent enough in themselves, do not really flow one from another and when the development falters into a rather naïve *pot pourri* on themes from earlier movements, the listener is right to question Dvořák's judgement. The impetus is recovered in the recapitulation and the almost leitmotivic juggling with the themes towards the end of the work is far from objectionable, though for all Dvořák's ingenuity this section has none of the impact of the inspired return of the opening and slow movement themes at the end of the B minor Cello Concerto.

Fibich and the later Romantic Czech symphony

As Dvořák was putting pen to paper on his First Symphony in 1865, the fifteen-year-old **Zdeněk Fibich** conducted his own first attempt at the genre in Chrudim. Sadly, neither this work nor a G minor symphony written the following year survive, though doubtless they both reflected the influence of Mendelssohn, reinforced in the young composer by two years of study (1865-1867) with Moscheles and E.F. Richter.

While he was admired in his own day, Fibich never achieved the popularity of Smetana or Dvořák; this is a pity, since at his best Fibich shows an enormous skill, rising at times to genius. He was at once more romantic and intellectual than Smetana and Dvořák, composing a notorious piano diary for his mistress, Anežka Schulzová and experimenting with music drama and melodrama. Because the music of Dvořák and Smetana tends to dominate our understanding of Czech style, Fibich's sounds less inherently national. Both rhythmically and melodically, Fibich seems less drawn to national models, although he could assay attractive pentatonics, as in the slow movement of his piano quintet, or a credibly Czech orchestral sound, as at the start of his First Symphony in F major:

Ex. 12. Fibich: Symphony No. 1

This evocative opening to his first symphony has obvious affinities with that of Dvořák's Fifth, although since Fibich completed the first movement on 10 February 1877 he cannot have known the work. As is often the case with Fibich, a first idea is ear-catching and extremely lyrical, but he rarely shows anything like Dvořák's resource in developing themes.

Such is the case here, with the unexceptional triplet idea from the end of the theme taking an unjustifiably large role in the second subject and development. As a whole both the Scherzo, *Allegro assai*, and the slow movement, *Adagio non troppo*, succeed better for being less ambitious in scope. Both resort to national colouring in the Trio and in the central section of the slow movement where woodwind writing in thirds abounds.

The Finale, *Allegro con fuoco*, is the least satisfactory movement. Fibich wrote the work over a long period and did not add the present Finale until 1883. Much of the material for it seems to have come from one of his earlier symphonies which perhaps accounts for some uncertainty of purpose. The romantic second subject area and the reference to the first movement just before the coda must have been later additions. By comparison with Dvořák in the 1870s and later, Fibich seems almost a sleep-walker where broad symphonic spans are concerned, but there is more than enough in his first symphony for ear and mind to justify the occasional performance.

The Second Symphony in E flat major, Op. 38, composed in 1892 and early 1893, is a vast improvement on the First. From the very opening there is a strong sense of purpose which sees Fibich pursuing the first idea of this predominantly monothematic movement to a satisfyingly logical conclusion. This movement (*Allegro moderato*) shows Fibich at his best, being both lyrical and economical, perhaps having taken note of Dvořák's successful treatment of material in the Sixth and Seventh symphonies. The only failing is an old one: a tendency to over-emphasis in the latter parts of the movement. The noble *Adagio* maintains the high level of inspiration present in the magnificent first movement. The first theme has a Beethovenian breadth and the march-like second subject area provides contrast without destroying the atmosphere of the movement. The opening rhythm of the first movement heard at the end of the *Adagio* reappears more pervasively in the Scherzo (*Presto*). Despite the slightly archaic pose struck by the Trio, this movement makes a fine companion to the previous two. The suspicion that this symphony is cyclic in the manner of its exact contemporary, Dvořák's Ninth, is confirmed by the Finale (*Allegro energico*). Sadly, judging from this overwritten conclusion, Fibich found finales to be even more of a problem than did Dvořák at this stage. Not only does he lean back on Schumann for his opening material, but the introduction of material from earlier movements is surprisingly crude. While this Finale is certainly never dull, it is a disappointment after the excellence and enterprise of the three earlier movements.

Fibich's Third Symphony in E minor, Op. 53, explores cyclic devices still further. Composed during 1898 as the composer was getting over a bout of scarlet fever, the work seems less clearly focused than the previous symphony. The first movement (*Allegro inquieto*) resembles that of the Second in being economical with its subject matter: a semiquaver catch which provides fuel for ostinati and a memorable rising and falling main theme. The main novelty of the second movement (*Adagio*) is a fast introduction (*Allegro con fuoco*) which shares the rising scale characteristic of the main theme of the first movement. In fact, both this introduction, the main theme of the *Adagio* and the Trio section of the Scherzo were derived, as were many works after 1893, from Fibich's piano diary of pieces for Anežka. The Finale shows the best and worst of Fibich's symphonism. It begins with a promising introduction (*Allegro maestoso*) based on the main theme of the first movement and through a development of the rising scale element indicates that much of the thematic material of the main part of the movement will be similarly derived. But when Fibich reaches the main *Allegro vivace* he retreats towards the well-padded Schumannesque manner of his other finales.

Although the Ninth Symphony was Dvořák's last work in the form, it was not quite his last word on the subject of symphonism. In a fascinating article on Schubert published in New York in 1894, Dvořák spoke about the modern symphony, in particular Bruckner's Eighth, being too long. As a general exhortation to his fellow composers Dvořák suggested that 'We should return to the symphonic dimensions approved by Haydn and Mozart'. It would have been interesting to know how Dvořák would have viewed the Second Symphony of his favourite pupil and son-in-law **Josef Suk** (1874–1935). Not only is the *Asrael* Symphony one of the longest Czech symphonies ever composed, it is now coming to be recognized as one of the greatest.

Suk's First Symphony in E major, Op. 14, was written between May 1897 and July 1899. There are clear debts to Dvořák, but also a hint of Bruckner in the opening horn melody. There is also an interesting parallel with Fibich's Third Symphony in the use of a pervasive semiquaver figure in the Scherzo. As in the marvellous string serenade of 1892, many of the characteristics of the mature Suk are present: a tendency to veer towards the melancholy and an ability to sustain the musical interest across broad, slowish spans. But for all the qualities of this engaging work, it is completely eclipsed by the *Asrael* Symphony. The events which refined Suk's talent into genius were the twin tragedies of losing, quite unexpectedly, his father-in-law and mentor Antonín Dvořák in 1904 followed by the death of his wife Otylka a year later. The death of Dvořák had stimulated Suk to compose a five-movement symphony taking its name, *Asrael*, from the biblical angel of death. Three movements and much of a fourth had been completed when the loss of Otylka caused Suk to scrap the existing fourth movement and plans for a variation Finale in favour of two *adagios*. The whole was finished in 1906 and dedicated 'to the noble memory of Dvořák and Otylka'.

Asrael is not a comfortable work and even though it is gaining greater acceptance, performances are likely to remain relatively rare. Suk's ability to evoke grief and a sense of desolation, at times anticipating Shostakovich, is achieved through extraordinary melodic eloquence and structural control.

The musical language is entirely original, owing little or nothing to Suk's teacher Dvořák. A personal note is struck by the use of the Death motif, a rising and falling pair of augmented fourths from the suite from *Radúz and Mahulena* (1899–1900) whose love Suk associated with his relationship with Otylka.

In the following *Andante* Suk makes use of a theme reminiscent of the expressive main motif of Dvořák's Requiem Mass, developing it into an intense and terrifying funeral march. This in turn is succeeded by a fantastic Scherzo (*Vivace*) extending and enhancing the sinister tone of the previous movement. The central section of this movement, rich in nostalgia, offers a respite in gentler vein, a mood taken up in the fourth movement (*Adagio*). With the return of the Death motif on the drums, the fragile consolation of the fourth movement is shattered by apparently relentless tragedy. The Finale does eventually offer a moving, understated comfort, hard-won after a terrifyingly energetic and occasionally grotesque central section. The impact of the whole is astonishing and provides one of the most disturbing and rewarding experiences of the late-Romantic repertoire.

Suk did not compose another symphony, preferring to cultivate the symphonic poem. His older contemporary **Josef Bohuslav Foerster** (1859–1951) produced the finest of his five symphonies at more or less the same time as Suk's *Asrael*. Foerster's First Symphony in D minor had been composed in 1888 and shows more than a student's competence in handling form. His Second (1892) moves still further from local stylistic models with the main theme of the slow movement owing a perceptible debt to César Franck's D minor Symphony. The Third Symphony (1896) was written when the composer was living in Hamburg where his friendship with Mahler had a perceptible effect on his style. But the climax of these early developments came in the Fourth Symphony in C minor, Op. 54, composed in Vienna in 1905 and entitled 'Easter' (*Veliká noc*). There are parallels with both Suk and Mahler in the first movement (*Molto sostenuto*): a superbly sustained, quasi-funeral march representing 'The Road to Calvary'. Like Suk, Foerster's genius lay in maintaining effective, slowish symphonic spans while conveying a sense of continuous evolution. The Scherzo, complete with Furiant cross-rhythms, evokes 'A child's Good Friday', enhanced by some Mahlerian writing for the horns.* The eloquent slow movement is a representation of solitude and contemplation before the last movement's 'Victory of Holy Saturday'. Beginning *Lento lugubre*, there are further reminiscences of Mahler before the main part of the movement. A flowing section (*Un poco animato*) unfolds eloquently before the main *Allegro moderato*. Drawing on the *Un poco animato* introduction this section, in turn, leads purposefully to a climax at which point Foerster introduces an old Czech Easter hymn on the organ, played as it would be in a village church.

---

* To my mind this is one of the most exhilarating Scherzos in *all* Czech music, second only to Dvořák 6 and Martinů 4. (Ed.)

Around this dignified melody the orchestra erupts in celebration, taking the work to an inspiring conclusion. Foerster did not return to the symphony until 1924 when he began to compose his Fifth in D minor as a reaction to the tragic death of his only son Alfréd. The work was not completed until 1929 and lacks the originality, single-mindedness and sheer exultation of the Fourth.

While opera continued to be the main measure of changing style amongst the Czechs, the two symphonic works of **Otakar Ostrčil** afford an interesting glimpse of developments in Bohemia in the first two decades of the twentieth century. His early symphony in A major (1904–1905) reflects both a respect for his Czech roots, in the shape of Fibich and to a lesser extent Dvořák, an interest in Strauss at the start of the first movement and a passion for Mahler in the introduction (*Quasi maestoso*) to the second movement. As a whole the symphony is exquisitely orchestrated and offers a much more sensuous image of late romanticism than the more austere Foerster. Ostrčil's five-movement *Sinfonietta* of 1921 is very different in atmosphere. Mahler still appears to be an influence, but the composer has greatly extended his tonal language. As well as pushing tonality towards the limits, the use of polyrhythms and complex counterpoint also enriches the texture, features found in Suk's works in this period. The sound is rarely describable as post-romantic, although certain turns of phrase, including the *Più largamente* melody in the first movement and parts of the Scherzando third movement look forward to Prokofiev in the 1930s.

Stanislav Suda's (1865–1931) autobiographical symphony, 'A Life at dusk' (*Život ve tmách*, 1921–1923) is only sporadically interesting, despite a 5/4 representation of youth. Inevitably, it yields to the most remarkable Czech programme symphony of the 1920s, the *Sinfonietta of* **Leoš Janáček** (1854–1928). With his fascination with language and clear identity with national music, Janáček seems to us the quintessence of Czechness in the early twentieth century. And yet his musical style is remote from that of his Czech contemporaries: it stands *sui generis* as one of the truly original voices of the twentieth century. To point out the characteristics of his style in terms of ostinati, the juxtaposition of material and speech-melody both lyrical and angular, does little to appraise the listener of the exhilarating, almost frightening life which informs Janáček's music.

Owing to its well-deserved popularity, the *Sinfonietta* epitomizes the Janáček style for many listeners. While it is possible to discern a tradition, if rather a quirky one, linking Janáček's programmatic string quartets to those of Smetana, the *Sinfonietta* stands on its own with no obvious predecessors. The work was born out of Janáček's enthusiasm for life and his native land, although the immediate musical stimulus was no more remarkable than a military band concert. The first movement of the *Sinfonietta* started life as a series of fanfares for a gymnastic festival. These fanfares grew into a five-movement work by the end of March 1926 which was dedicated as a 'Military Sinfonietta' *(Vojenská symfonietta)* to the Czechoslovak Armed Forces. Although Janáček's aim was to express 'the contemporary free man, his spiritual beauty and joy, his strength, courage and determination to fight for victory', he also added that the work drew much inspiration from the growing fortunes of the Moravian capital Brno, providing appropriate titles to each movement.

While the work is excellent to hear in any circumstances, it is best when *seen* in concert. A vast array of brass instruments, no less than fourteen trumpets, surrounds the normal symphony orchestra. Nothing in the *Sinfonietta* is conventional and attempting an orthodox consideration of the work soon founders. The build-up from the swaying opening parallel fifths to the frantic fanfares of the conclusion is one of the glories of the Czech repertoire. Each movement relies on the repetition of short ideas, but each has a distinct character. The climax of the second movement is a breezy *Maestoso* which presents yet another ringing theme, albeit one with distant links to the fanfares of the opening. The third movement starts as an idyll, but threatening gestures from the trombones cause a rise in temperature leading, through a passage which stretches the horns to their limit, to a wild *Prestissimo*. A chattering trumpet figure opens the fourth movement providing a scherzo-like foil to the quiet beginning of the Finale *(Andante con moto)*. Once again the movement proves to be a gradual crescendo assisted by some wild woodwind figures towards the climactic return of the opening fanfares.

Nowadays the *Sinfonietta* cannot be regarded as Janáček's sole symphonic contribution. A splendidly idiomatic realization and instrumentation of the 'Danube' Symphony *(Dunaj)* has given new life to this torso. In a sense the work is outside the scope of this chapter since it was intended as a symphonic poem, but its surviving four-movement structure, of what might have been a five-movement work, draws it towards the ambit of the *Sinfonietta*.

For all its inimitable originality, Janáček's *Sinfonietta* did have a successor in the shape of the 'Military Sinfonietta' (also *Vojenská symfonietta*) by the talented woman composer **Vítězslava Kaprálová** (1915–1940). Composed in 1937, the work owes something to Janáček, but also to her teacher at the time, Vítězslav Novák. Kaprálová's early death may well have denied the Czechs a composer of importance since her effective, post-impressionist works of the mid-thirties show considerable gifts. But the symphonies of her teacher **Bohuslav Martinů** (1890–1959) form the cornerstone of our appreciation of the mid-twentieth-century Czech symphony.

It is an irony rising to tragedy that none of Martinů's symphonies were written in his native Czechoslovakia. The first five were composed in America during the enforced separation of the years of the Second World War and the last in self-imposed exile after the Communist takeover of his nation in 1948. In many ways it is surprising that a self-confessed 'Concerto Grosso type' should turn at all to the symphony. After an unsuccessful attempt at a symphony in 1912 Martinů had filled the years up to 1942 with every genre but the symphony. His musical instincts, which tended towards Debussy, the English madrigal and the Baroque concerto grosso, were not particularly conducive to symphonic composition. Although there is more than a hint of symphonic integration in the three-movement orchestral *Inventions* of 1934, no formal symphony appeared until Martinů was commissioned by Serge Koussevitzky to compose an orchestral work in memory of his wife Nathalie.

Martinů's First Symphony was composed between May and August 1942. Negotiating the 'problem of a symphony' for the first time proved difficult; not only did Martinů find it uncongenial to work at his home in New York, but his first idea, a minor chord followed by a major one, did not seem to offer much potential. In the event, linked by a chromatic scale, it made an ear-catching opening to the work. The sound world of the symphony is perceptibly different from his more angular works of the 1930s, possessing a warm glow often resulting from the polyphonic use of four horns. While the instrumentation can look thick on the page, it is always delicate to the ear. The main themes on the first movement have a gentle, syncopated spring in contrast to the more driving rhythms of the exhilarating Scherzo. The *Largo*, one of Martinů's most profound movements up to that time, is an object lesson in the creation of seamless melodic lines from tiny cells. The Finale grows from a shadowy march through some distinctly catchy thematic ideas to a rollicking conclusion. Martinů's achievement in this symphony was one of sustaining a long non-programmatic composition using primarily tonal material and without resorting to any banal expedients.

Having, as it were, worked up a certain pressure of symphonic steam, Martinů composed his Second Symphony in less than two months in 1943. Dvořák would doubtless have approved of the sentiments expressed in Martinů's programme note for the work. After speaking about the growth in size of the symphony after Beethoven, Martinů went on to note: 'In contemporary hands, the symphony has returned to older, more reasonable proportions' without the loss of '. . . the expression of something grandiose, tragic or pathetic'. But despite the fluency of his work Martinů had a false start with the piece and replaced his original idea of a march-like beginning with a much more delicate opening. The main theme is insufficient for the development appropriate to a symphonic first movement and this role is taken by some accompanimental figures. The work was commissioned by the citizens of Cleveland, Ohio, of Czech origin – Martinů dedicated the work to 'My Fellow Countrymen in Cleveland' and in the slow movement he was pleased to note parallels to Moravian folksong and even Janáček. Here Martinů made use of the familiar Czech device of floating a melody in thirds and sixths over a drone (Ex. 13):

Ex. 13. Martinů: Symphony No. 2

The slightly military cast of the Scherzo points to its origins in the march which Martinů abandoned for the first movement.* The Finale is lighter in tone, though ultimately exultant, driven by infectious motor rhythms alternating with swaying lyrical elements.

The fertility suggested by the completion of a symphony a year from 1942 can be misleading. Homesickness and a dissatisfaction with his surroundings, compounded by the news in June 1942 of the destruction of the Bohemian village of Lidiče in retaliation for the assassination of the Nazi military governor, Heydrich, led to a rare period of creative inactivity. When Martinů began to work again, in April and May 1944, the product was a new symphony, of far greater urgency and intensity than hitherto. Martinů stated that Beethoven's *Eroica* lay behind the musical language of the work, but his own Double Concerto, written in the dark days of the Munich crisis, seems a more likely candidate for the power generated in the first movement. Here the melodic vocabulary eschews the engaging warmth heard at the start of the first two symphonies: dissonance is more prevalent and linked to forceful rhythms dedicated to creating a powerful climax on the final page of the movement. The *Largo* preserves the tension generated by the first movement and increases, rather than dissipates, the feeling of disquiet with a curiously blithe flute solo. The consolation achieved at the end is swept away by the aggressive opening of the Finale. Here, Martinů anticipates some of the more fraught passages in the Sixth Symphony and some of the more militaristic sonorities look back to the marvellous pre-war *Field Mass*. The conclusion – E major chords clouded by chromatic lines – gave the composer some doubts until he heard the work under Koussevitzky and the Boston Symphony Orchestra on 12 October 1945.

---

* The supposed quotation of the *Marseillaise* towards the end of the Scherzo noted by Šafránek and other commentators does not seem to have any strong basis in fact. The fragment in question – a descending figure on the trumpet – is clearly derived from existing material.

The Fourth Symphony, again composed in less than two months and completed on 14 June 1945, seems the antithesis of the Third. Martinů returns to the radiant diatonicism of the earlier symphonies, but with a new warmth that anticipates his works of the 1950s. He may have been consciously provocative when he stated that the whole symphony emerges from a single motif. If this is so then the minor third, prominent at the start, seems the most likely candidate for such a seminal role. Many of the themes in the four movements of the symphony use it either as a springboard or fill it out in order to make theme and accompaniment. The best example of this organicism is to be found in the Scherzo where both the ostinato accompaniment and the main theme start life in this way, the former filling out a rising minor third, the latter a falling one. The opening of the first movement fulfils the dual role of a motivic quarry for the rest of the symphony and an in tempo introduction, almost in the Dvořák manner. While predominantly open-hearted, this symphony has more variety than its predecessors and makes an ideal introduction to the composer's music. Along with all the luminosity in the first movement there is a compensating darkness, just as in the predominantly good-humoured Scherzo there are moments of serenity. The *Largo*, beginning with the almost leitmotivic rising scale – in these works – is one of Martinů's most successfully sustained slow movements. Under an extended, seamless melody a richly layered accompaniment is illuminated by wind and piano playing shorter rhythmic subdivisions. At times Martinů reveals a rapt, mystical quality resembling, though not deriving from, Vaughan Williams. The magnificent stillness of this movement gives way to a return of the mood and manner of earlier movements in a Finale which proves to be the composer's most extrovert to date.

Composed in 1946, the Fifth Symphony was written at a time when Martinů had every reason to believe that he could return to his native land. The successful conclusion of the war and the prospect of homecoming brought forth new resources in him. The symphony was composed between March and 13 May 1946 and eventually dedicated to the Czech Philharmonic. Martinů was unable to attend the première under Rafael Kubelik at the first Prague Spring Festival in 1947 owing to a fractured skull resulting from a near-fatal fall on 25 July 1946. While no less rounded or remarkable than the Fourth Symphony Martinů's Fifth is perhaps less immediately appealing. While the composer had every reason to hope for a happy change in circumstances early in 1946, he also experienced considerable depression which led to difficulties with the composition of the work. The overall shaping is less conventional than in the three previous symphonies. The lack of a slow movement is compensated for by substantial passages of slow music in the first movement and Finale. In the opening *Adagio-Allegro* the slow music acts as both an introduction, interlude and conclusion. Martinů avoids a lack of integration by providing skilful transitions and keeping a strict tempo relationship between the sections. The central *Larghetto* is a new, slightly muted image of the Martinů Scherzo and harbours a more introspective element introduced by an angular flute theme which in turn results in an extraordinary passage of ringing trumpet sonority. As in the first movement the slow music, *Lento*, takes on the role of a kind of ritornello, framing and setting off the thrillingly energetic *Allegro*. The contrast between the soulful, highly expressive *Lento* and the *Allegro*, built on a dotted rhythm akin to that in the first movement of Beethoven's Seventh, is acute. Their combination at the crisis of the movement results in one of Martinů's most forceful symphonic conclusions.

The five years which separate the completion of the Fifth Symphony from the point at which Martinů began to work on the Sixth in 1951 were among the most painful for the composer. His head injury required lengthy convalescence and was compounded by marital difficulties. This was followed by the Communist putsch in Czechoslovakia which effectively left him without a native land. The artistic fruits of this personal exile are to be found in his nostalgic and richly lyrical works of the 1950s. Elements of this lyricism are to be found in the Sixth, Martinů's most novel solution to the 'problem' of symphony. The work was composed for an old friend from Martinů's days in Paris, the conductor Charles Münch and was intended to suit his '. . . spontaneous approach to the music, where music takes shape in a free way'. A draft of the first movement was complete by 21 April 1951, but the work was not finally finished until 26 May 1953. On the way to completion Martinů abandoned the three pianos he had originally intended for the score, having taken fright at the prospect of so many large instruments on stage, and also changed his original title, *New Fantastic Symphony*, to the less obviously Berliozian *Fantaisies Symphoniques*. There are many referential elements in the work: passages which look forward to the opera *The Greek Passion* and a quote from *Julietta* which the composer claimed he included just in case he should never hear the work again. Whether Martinů intended the chromatic main motif of the first movement – which also plays an important part in the Scherzo and Finale – as a reference to that of Dvořák's Requiem or not cannot be ascertained. The shape of the cell is, however, so close to a characteristic Martinů thematic element that a passing resemblance to Dvořák's theme hardly matters.

A feeling of exploration is clear from the start of the work which grows out of murmuring shadows into the clarity of a pure major chord. Martinů may well have been inspired by Münch's conducting technique in a movement which has something of an improvisatory feel to it. But this is only a superficial impression: the real developmental power which results from the alternation of lyrical and driving elements is derived from a clear sense of cohesion in the thematic material. The extent to which Martinů had become a natural symphonic thinker, possessed of an almost unconscious command of integration, is clear in this first movement and the dramatic, broad-ranging Scherzo. The Finale, while still modest in scale, manages to suggest great breadth by drawing in apparently disparate elements against a background of tight thematic control. The process resembles the conclusion of the Fifth Symphony, but is much more complex with Martinů juggling with far more ideas. The conclusion has something of the pain present at the opening of the movement, but now ameliorated by gentler harmonies. The Sixth remains one of the composer's most popular works, and yet it is by no means easy to perform, requiring a complex blend of intellect and instinct to ensure success.

The six symphonies of Martinů are, of course, not the last word on the Czech symphony in the twentieth century. But of the three hundred and twenty or so works composed since 1930 they remain the most memorable and seem the most likely to form a twentieth-century equivalent to the symphonies of Dvořák even if, ultimately, Martinů's do not quite encompass the same variety. While most Czech composers attempting to write symphonies have rarely got beyond two, Martinů was by no means the most prolific. **Bartoš** (1908–1981), **Emil Hlobil** (b. 1901) **Modr** (1898–1983), **Podešva** (b. 1927) and **Řidký** (1897–1956) each composed seven symphonies. **Jan Kapr** (b. 1914) composed eight and **Jiří Válek** a resounding fourteen, all with titles. Picking a way through this extraordinary diversity is no easy task. The Czechs themselves are unlikely to provide in the next few years an overview of works with titles such as the 'Red Army' Symphony (*Rudoarmejská symfonie*, 1942) by **Josef Stanislav** (1897–1971), the 'Day of Victory' (Hlobil, 1951) or 'Lenin' (1943–54), by **Karel Janeček** (1903–1974). The range of style to be found in the post-1950 Czech symphony is also bewildering and shows little consistency. A fruitful exploration of a post-Martinů musical language is to be found in **Klement Slavický**'s (b. 1910) powerful *Symfonietta* No.4 for strings, keyboards, percussion, soprano solo and narrator subtitled 'Pax hominibus in orbi universo' of 1984. Echoes of Shostakovich are clear in **Vladimir Tichý**'s (b. 1946) effective second symphony for fifteen string instruments (1980). What the years after the Velvet Revolution will bring is anybody's guess, but the symphony does not appear to be at the top of the agenda. A list of first performances of works by Czech composers in 1990 up to July reveals only one symphony and that a recomposition made in 1988–89 of a work originally from 1940–42, and subsequently lost, by **Jan Hanuš** (b. 1915).

11

Russia before the Revolution

David Brown

Early in 1834 **Mikhail Glinka** (1804–57) began work on a symphony. He had just passed three years in Italy indulging his passion for Italian opera, but had become sated with the warmth and passion of this Mediterranean genre, and was already envisaging an opera thoroughly Russian in both subject and music. The trouble was that all Glinka's musical skills, like those of any Russian of his time who did not study in Western Europe, had been acquired haphazardly, and he realised he desperately needed a rigorous course in composition. So he paused in Berlin to study with the eminent pedagogue, Siegfried Dehn, and for nearly six months immersed himself in musical procedures that were basically German. Almost inevitably he tried his hand at a symphony – though not on invented material of a Germanic cast, but on two Russian folksongs. The slow introduction stated one of these, then varied it, and when the first subject of the *Allegro* introduced the second folksong Glinka again repeated his borrowed material against a series of different backgrounds, doing much the same thing in the recapitulation. But between these two stages he encountered problems. Trying to make his folksong generate the second subject also, he provided the wrong kind of accompaniment and the Russian character slipped away. As for the development, it was all Germanic counterpoint and tedious sequence. Disillusioned with the piece, Glinka abandoned it after the first movement.

Eighteen years later he set about composing a 'Ukrainian Symphony' based on Gogol's tale of the seventeenth-century Cossack hero, Taras Bulba. By now, 1852, with two imperfect yet (as music) vastly impressive operas behind him, together with a substantial clutch of excellent songs, and three splendidly novel orchestral pieces, Glinka had singlehanded laid the foundations of the Russian musical tradition. Yet his new attempt at a real symphony was no more successful than his previous ones. 'Not having the strength or the disposition to get out of the German rut in the development, I rejected my effort,' he recalled in his *Memoirs*. Never again did he tackle the form.

In Glinka's tussle with the symphony, and with alternative types of orchestral composition, is encapsulated the problems and the possibilities which confronted the Russian composer in tackling this most central of orchestral forms. The symphony was a West European creation, the perfect servant of the Austro-German masters who had evolved it, but problematic to those whose creative materials and mental workings were of a different nature. True, Glinka had used the sonata form blueprint for his First Spanish Overture, his *Jota aragonese* (1845), but he had simply filled the compartments with his borrowed Spanish melody, generating both subjects as a series of variations around this, concocting a development by combining it with arpeggio figures from the slow introduction, then compiling a recapitulation through yet more variations. It was all very engaging, but only rudely cobbled together; moreover, in his Second Spanish Overture, *Summer Night in Madrid* (1848; rev. 1851) and, even more, the brilliant little scherzo *Kamarinskaya* (1848), he had devised his own totally original schemes for deploying his Spanish and Russian folksongs.

Yet here is the paradox: it was not the First Spanish Overture but *Kamarinskaya* in which, Tchaikovsky was later to declare, lay the source of the whole Russian symphonic school 'just as the entire oak is in *the acorn*'. This was gross exaggeration, especially since Glinka had made no use whatsoever of symphonic form itself; but the remark was a pointer to the very nature of Russian creativity – that it was decorative and grew most naturally through various kinds of variation method (as Glinka's abortive 1834 attempt at symphonic composition had already shown) – through an often prodigious ability to repeat something with ever new significances. *Kamarinskaya* had demonstrated this brilliantly. Founded upon two Russian folksongs, it had unfolded as a swift series of continuous variations either to the tunes themselves or, far more often, to the backgrounds devised for them. Glinka's inventiveness is dazzling, but there is no sense that we have been taken on a carefully planned journey through a series of musical events that has finally brought us to a destination far from our point of departure. For the fact is that Russian decorative thought was static (or at least concentric) – whereas, of course, Western symphonic thought was dynamic. Much of the history of the Russian symphony was to develop from the tensions between these fundamentally opposing tendencies. It meant that the Russian symphony could rarely achieve that total identity of content and form, that sense of certain, even implacable, purpose which mark the best Western Classical symphonies. But what it did produce was a succession of very varied works, at their best of striking originality and creative vitality, occasionally of overwhelming physical and spiritual impact.

But for **Anton Rubinstein** (1829–94) there was to be no such tension between diverse creative urges, though this German-Jewish Russian would not be able entirely to escape the challenge of that more obvious, though more superficial, brand of nationalism: the employment of national subjects, and especially of native folksong (or folksong-conditioned melody). Born as Glinka was focussing his thoughts on his Italian trip, he and his younger brother, Nikolay, were also to study with Dehn, though the course they undertook gave Anton a technical command which ensured that his remarkable facility could supply an endless flow of competent music largely untroubled by the slightest sign of any true creativity. In general his symphonies are of less interest than his piano concertos. He composed six, of which No. 2 in C, the 'Ocean' (1851; rev. 1863 and 1880), gained considerable popularity. In its final form it grew to seven movements, but this is the only unusual feature in a watery Mendelssohnian piece. Insofar as a Rubinstein style may be identified, it is a compound of Mendelssohn and Schumann, the more radical of mid-century composers like Liszt and Berlioz being firmly excluded. His Fourth Symphony in E flat, the 'Dramatic' (1874), justifies its title only through its epic proportions, for sprawling a work across 65 minutes only serves to highlight the inconsistency, wanness (and sometimes downright feebleness) of Rubinstein's invention; the far more concise Fifth Symphony in G minor of 1880 is correspondingly more disciplined and even. Around this time Rubinstein was drawn briefly into the selfconsciously Russian world of the, by now, well established national school of composers, and this Fifth Symphony employs throughout quasi-folksong material, Rubinstein building from this a piece lively and resourceful enough for Gerald Abraham to suggest it would be 'worth a performance or two'. But the best of the symphonies is the Sixth in A minor (1886) which possesses real vitality and enough inventiveness to hold the listener through its first three movements and into a Finale which begins as the most frank of homages to *Kamarinskaya*: a slow introduction built from half a dozen statements of one folktune, followed by an allegro on a second repeated a score of times to a brilliant series of different backgrounds. The slow theme returns – but then, sadly, the material changes abruptly and leads the symphony to a more conventional (and over-delayed) conclusion.

Rubinstein was a solitary figure. No one could pretend that his symphonies merit even a modest toehold in our regular concert repertoire. That said, credit must be given for the enormous debt Russian music owed him. As a pianist second only in fame to Liszt, he brought glory to his native land; even more, as the spirit behind the foundation in 1859 of the Russian Musical Society, from whose classes the St Petersburg Conservatoire was to emerge in 1862 (with Rubinstein as its principal), he laid the foundations of that rigorous brand of musical education for which Russia remains noted. For most Russians in the third quarter of the nineteenth century Rubinstein was their greatest and most famed living musician. But history has judged him with harsh justice. The more important composers, who comprised the first generation of truly Russian symphonists, emerged in the 1860s, and mostly stood in opposition to Rubinstein and all that he represented. **Mily Balakirev** (1837–1910), **Alexander Borodin** (1833–87), **Nikolay Rimsky-Korsakov** (1844–1908), **Pyotr Tchaikovsky** (1840–93): all composed (or at least began) their first symphonies in this exciting decade. The first three were, like their hero Glinka, amateurs. Balakirev was a former maths student from Kazan University who had picked up what he knew of music in his native

Nizhni-Novgorod, and who had arrived in St Petersburg in 1855 in time to meet Glinka and be ordained by that great pioneer as the apostle who should continue the cause he had so boldly begun. Borodin (a scientist) and Rimsky-Korsakov (a naval officer) were to be first Balakirev's pupils, then the associates of this remarkable musical catalyst. Though professionally untrained, Balakirev devoted so much of his energy to teaching (Musorgsky and Cui were also his pupils) and concert activities that the time available for composition diminished sharply as the 1860s unfolded, and a personal crisis in the 70s was to drive him out of the Russian musical world for a number of years.

In 1864 Balakirev had begun his C major Symphony, then dropped it for nearly thirty years, completing it only in 1897. Yet it is impossible to be sure where composition was resumed, for Balakirev experienced no kind of inner development, and the music he wrote in the 1890s was no different from that of the 1860s. Nor was his Second Symphony (1900–08) to add anything new to his range of expression, though it is a neat and attractive piece. But Balakirev's importance as a seminal force was almost incalculable, and his First Symphony was a very notable achievement. The last three movements are filled with attractive music ranging from the sultry to the vigorously unbuttoned, but the most interesting movement is the first – a bold attempt to break the mould of traditional symphonic structure so that a thoroughly Russian mode of thought might unfold itself without undue constraint. Here Balakirev entwines Europe with Russia to weave his highly individual method, for while the motivic and contrapuntal workings stem from the West, the melodic repetitiveness against varied backgrounds derives from Glinka. The first six bars (Ex. 1a) of the slow

Ex. 1. Balakirev: Symphony No. 1

Ex. 1. cont'd

introduction encapsulate perfectly this stylistic divide, starting in a purely classical world with stalking counterpoint, in bar four passing to an equally clear Russian realm. These bars also foretell the two subjects (Ex. 1b and c), which reveal the poles of Balakirev's style yet more clearly, the first subject diligently working *x*, sometimes in augmentation, the second unfolding much more interestingly as nearly a score of statements of *y* with much variety in presentation and key. But any listener seeking the further outlines of sonata structure will be confounded. Rather, the movement goes on to reflect inventively on the themes, changing them, even effecting a thematic synthesis by incorporating *x* into the rhythmic matrix of *y* (Ex. 1d). No one could claim this movement as a model of structural coherence; yet its constant focussing on *x* and *y* (or derivatives thereof), coupled with the strength of Balakirev's resourcefulness, suffices to give it both expressive focus and a constant command of the listener's attention.

Thematic synthesis was to be yet more important in the two completed symphonies of Borodin; indeed, the device in various guises seems to have been one fundamental element within Russian creativity (it had also played a crucial role in *Kamarinskaya*). Borodin's method of thematic synthesis in his Second Symphony (1870–6) was to follow Balakirev's closely, but in the first movement of his First Symphony (1862–7) it is different, and is the very foundation of his symphonic strategy. Borodin composed the piece under Balakirev's close supervision. While the shade of Schumann is obvious in the Finale (the least interesting movement), in the Scherzo it is Berlioz's 'Roméo et Juliette' Symphony that provides the precedent, except that Queen Mab's gossamer fairies have become earth-bound goblins, and the Trio, with its perpetually changing metres and totally national melody, owes nothing to any western model. Nor does the slow movement. Borodin, the illegitimate son of a father with oriental blood in him, already discloses something of his ethnic origins in the mildly langorous opening theme and in the darkly sonorous harmonies, so often coloured by rich dissonance. But, individual as this beautiful, sturdy music is, it is the opening *Allegro* that is the most notable achievement. Though the conventional sonata scheme is followed, the motivic behaviour is highly individual, for here motifs and melodic line can become one. The bass line (Ex. 2a), which opens the *Adagio* introduction and is to become the first subject, is the repository of four motifs which separate off and assert their individuality when the *Allegro* arrives. The second subject (Ex. 2b) increases the fund by two, and the development builds textures which at times positively pulsate as these melodic particles jostle one another in that sharply clear orchestration so firmly based upon Glinka's practices. The recapitulation is mostly regular; the biggest surprise of all comes at the end, where the music slows to andantino and all six motifs are reordered, to be strung together into a single dolce cantilena for the cellos (Ex. 2c). The thematic fragmentation which had set the movement in motion has been complemented at the end by an even more comprehensive thematic synthesis.

Remarkable as this symphony is for a composer who had never before attempted so ambitious a piece or ever composed for the orchestra, its successor is an even more notable achievement, though again Balakirev played some part in its shaping. The B minor Symphony was begun

Ex. 2. Borodin: Symphony No. 1

after Borodin's first burst of work on *Prince Igor*, and it is possible that material from the opera was diverted into it (Borodin is reported as having in mind an assembly of Russian knights in the first movement, a bayan's (or minstrel's) song in the third, and a knights' feast with general jubilation in the finale). The trenchant opening theme (Ex. 3a) reveals a composer who can think instinctively outside the normal bounds of major and minor; a not unexpected corollary is that he would not incline to think naturally in terms of a structure that grew organically through the tonal dynamism of western sonata form, and we may see a consequence of this in the way the first subject ends, after nearly sixty bars, exactly where it began, requiring that the most explicit of transitions be stitched in to move to D major for the second subject (Ex. 3b). Yet all seems totally under control; after all, Borodin was a distinguished scientist with a highly disciplined mind. Indeed, the whole symphony is admirably to the point. Again in the first movement

Ex. 3. Borodin: Symphony No. 2

thematic synthesis is employed, first towards the end of the exposition, where the second subject grows back into the first (Ex. 3c), then early in the development where, in the answering phrase of Ex. 3d, the character of the first subject is stamped upon the second. Otherwise Borodin is content simply to build the tautest of developments by repeating material heard earlier, then amplifying the recapitulation with a new confrontation of first and second subjects (Ex. 3e). If the melody of the second movement's trio has a tinge of the exotic east, the beautiful horn melody of the third, with its changing metres, suggests it yet more strongly. But, as in the First Symphony's *Andante*, it is a masculine orient: warmly emotional, but always strong. Borodin's melodic virility is explicit in the sonata-patterned Finale. In the first movements of both this symphony and its predecessor Borodin had injected thrust through rhythmically patterned accompaniments; here the impetus is in the very material, and the result is one of the most entirely satisfying of Russian finales.

In 1886 Borodin began a Third Symphony, but sketches exist for only two movements; the outer portions of the second, a Scherzo in D, had been composed for string quartet in 1882, and these were worked up and orchestrated by Glazunov. Borodin's failure to devote more time to composition is one of the saddest facts in Russian musical history; except perhaps for Musorgsky, he was the most richly endowed of these amateurs. Rimsky-Korsakov was simply not in his class. Though the youngest of them, Rimsky was the first to finish a symphony. He began his First Symphony (1861–5; rev.1884) when he was only seventeen and still a student at the Naval Institute. Shortly afterwards he met Balakirev, who began setting his thoughts in order, then urged him to continue the piece during a two-and-a-half-year cruise on the clipper *Almaz* (the slow movement was written on the River Thames, where the ship had to wait some months for repairs, and was tried out on a piano in a restaurant in Gravesend). When revising it Rimsky raised the key a semitone to E minor, and reversed the order of the central movements so that the *Andante tranquillo*, which was founded on a folksong, came first. The symphony is clearly the work of a very young and inexperienced composer, and is only of documentary interest, even after revision. His Second Symphony, *Antar* (1868; rev. 1875 and 1897), written at Balakirev's and Musorgsky's suggestion to a programme drawn from a story by Osip Senkovsky, was simply an essay in exotic musical fantasy. Certainly it already revealed Rimsky's natural instinct for orchestration, but it was no more a symphony than the later and far superior *Sheherezade*. Rimsky himself came to admit this, renaming it at its second revision a symphonic suite.

Though painfully aware of the deficiencies in his technique, Rimsky had in 1871 accepted a professorship at the St Petersburg Conservatoire, and his Third Symphony (1872–3; rev.1886) is the clearest evidence of his desperate determination to prove himself worthy of his position. Recalling his labours on the first movement, he noted: 'I was trying to introduce a little more counterpoint, in which I was no expert, and in the effort of combining themes and motifs I significantly impeded my own spontaneous imagination . . . The same lot befell the third movement of the symphony, the *Andante*. The Finale came rather more easily; but in combining a lot of themes at the end I again got into difficulties.' The result is precisely what might be expected: a dutiful piece, lucidly planned both in its detail and its design, but melodically mostly lifeless and anonymous.

Of all Russian pieces with some claim to symphonic intentions Rimsky's Sinfonietta on Russian Themes (1880–4) – a transcription of three movements from a String Quartet on Russian Themes (1878–9) – is the one in which the *Kamarinskaya* principle is most consistently in evidence, for throughout one or another of the five folksongs is to be heard with accompaniments often enlivened by neat touches. Though Rimsky had none of Glinka's brilliant inventiveness, this Sinfonietta is certainly the most engaging of his symphonic works and, not being unduly difficult, would be worth the occasional performance by good amateur orchestras.

The titles Rimsky gave each of his Sinfonietta's movements are unconvincing and unnecessary, nor was there any stronger reason why the first two movements of Tchaikovsky's First Symphony (1866; rev.1874) should have been labelled 'Daydreams of a winter journey' and 'Land of gloom, land of mists' (and the whole symphony entitled 'Winter Daydreams'). Unlike Balakirev, Borodin and Rimsky-Korsakov, Tchaikovsky was professionally trained, and on graduating from the St Petersburg Conservatoire at the end of 1865, he was recommended by Anton Rubinstein to teach composition in the classes of the Moscow branch of the RMS which were soon to grow into the Moscow Conservatoire with Nikolay as its first principal. It is no surprise that the new professor should have decided his first task was to tackle the central form of that Western tradition in which he had been so thoroughly schooled. Yet his First Symphony proved one of the most arduous labours he ever undertook, bringing him close to nervous collapse, for he was determined to bend the form to his creative will. And so, though he used for the opening and close of the slow movement a portion of the love music from a student composition of 1864, *The Storm*, and employed the scherzo from a piano sonata of 1865 as the symphony's third movement (scrapping the original Trio, however, and substituting an engaging valse), the symphony is even more a forward-looking piece, the first movement pioneering many of those practices and procedures which were to permit Tchaikovsky's individuality to develop to the full. The formidable skill he already commanded enabled him to put together a convincing development section; the real challenge came in the exposition. True, for a composer of Tchaikovsky's melodic gifts the more lyrical second subject never posed many problems; the difficulty lay in the first subject (in classical practice a motif-generated, organic section) and in the ensuing transition (a carefully timed process of modulation from the tonic to the key of the second subject). Tchaikovsky's solution was bold indeed: he capitalized upon his thematic gift, expanding even further the first subject by unfolding it as a melodic strand spun from the interaction of two thematic threads, then added tonal colour by modulating distantly, returned to the tonic for a sonorous conclusion, and finally scrapped the transition except for five bars of dominant chord of the key to come. The result may be abrupt, and the seam certainly shows, but it was a price worth paying for a well-scaled exposition in which Tchaikovsky's inventiveness is never strangled by the need to do things nature had never intended it should.

Such hugely expansive subjects and economical transitions were to become Tchaikovsky's normal rule. The remainder of the movement well sustains the level set by this exposition. To gauge Tchaikovsky's success one need do no more than compare this movement with the sonata-schemed Finale, with its outbursts of undigested conservatoire counterpoint; neither the undeniable vigour of the music, nor its better stretches (especially parts of the slow introduction and second subject, in both of which a Russian folksong is the foundation) can conceal that this is a movement patched together. But the finest movement is the *Adagio cantabile ma non tanto*. Here melody alone could suffice, and the flow of living and very Russian invention, organized into a rondo scheme, sustains with total security the very formidable span of this lovely piece.

It is no surprise that many years later Tchaikovsky could affectionately judge this whole symphony to be 'better than many of my other more mature works', and the occasional performances it is now receiving are fully merited. In the 1874 revision Tchaikovsky replaced much of the first movement's second subject, and though no modification was required in the development, the coda had to be rewritten. But the revision he was to make to the Second Symphony ('Little Russian': 1872; rev. 1879–80) resulted in an almost completely new first movement except for its slow introduction and postlude. Tchaikovsky's conservatoire training had placed him within that tradition which Balakirev and his associates so vigorously spurned, yet which even they could not totally do without. Indeed, the rigid segregation of Russian composers into nationalists and westerners is historically an oversimplification; only Musorgsky contrived to maintain his nationalist purity, for Borodin even wrote string quartets (to Musorgsky's disgust), and Rimsky-Korsakov belatedly turned to the study of western method in an attempt to make good the deficiencies in his technique. As for Tchaikovsky, recognizing the honesty of these composers' aims (and as a fellow-Russian instinctively sympathetic to many of these), it is no surprise that he should have been drawn for a time into their orbit, and the Second Symphony is keen evidence of their influence. Employing three folksongs from the Ukraine (or 'Little Russia' as it was sometimes known; hence the symphony's nickname), it provides the strongest support for Tchaikovsky's perception of *Kamarinskaya* as the seed of the Russian symphonic school, for almost everywhere these folktunes are used (in the slow introduction and postlude to the first movement, the slow movement's centre, and the first subject of the Finale) they are, Glinka-like, repeated against changing backgrounds.

The Second Symphony is a further exploration of symphonic possibilities as Tchaikovsky saw them. Today, however, the version always played is the revised one with a shorter and simpler first movement. In fact, the original first movement is one of Tchaikovsky's meatiest creations, complex certainly (which was one reason he later turned against it), but often impressive, and sustaining its momentum admirably. It is no surprise that, after so substantial a piece, he should have felt that respite was necessary, and that the attractive but innocuous bridal march from his second opera, *Undine*, (composed in 1869, but destroyed after its rejection by the Imperial Opera in St Petersburg) would, with a new folksong-based centre, provide this well. The Scherzo was surely composed under the influence of that from Borodin's First Symphony, while the Finale is Tchaikovsky's most completely 'nationalist' movement. The first subject is almost pure *Kamarinskaya*, and the bold, even bizarre progress of the development is as daring as anything invented by Balakirev's company. In scale and weight the flanking movements of the 1872 version complement each other well, and the continuing neglect of Tchaikovsky's original conception of this fine symphony is one of the saddest facts in our concert life.

The Third Symphony ('Polish': 1875) is the most uneven of the series. In the original first movement of the Second there had been moments of self-conscious contrivance, but in the Third's opening *Allegro brillante* and concluding *Tempo di Polacca* Finale (hence the nickname the symphony acquired) Tchaikovsky's clear intention was to produce movements which reflected those 'correct' values of balance and technical diligence which he thought he perceived in the work of western symphonists. The result is music that is dogged in its procedures, stodgy in rhythm and textures, and melodically mostly second-rate. Schumann especially is the model not only in the first movement but for the overall design, which is in five movements like Tchaikovsky's favourite Schumann symphony, the 'Rhenish'. The middle three movements are a different matter. The second, 'Alla tedesca', might with equal justification have been marked 'Valse', and the fourth is a fleet Scherzo whose fascination lies as much in its textures as in its musical substance; for its centre Tchaikovsky salvaged part of the prelude to the Cantata he had composed in 1872 for the bicentenary celebrations of Peter the Great's birth. Between these two enchanting but lightweight conceptions lies the symphony's true heart, an *Andante elegiaco* in which Tchaikovsky's melodic flow is at its richest, producing one of the most ravishing of his slow movements. It is sad that this could not, in its turn, have been later rescued for a worthier context.

If Balakirev's creative style showed no evolution and Rimsky-Korsakov's changed only as the result of completely external factors (his interest in counterpoint during the 1870s, for instance, and later in Wagner), Tchaikovsky's evolved inexorably as the result of changes within the man himself. An event or decision in his personal life could precipitate such a change. Only something such as this can explain the stylistic and expressive gulf that divides the Fourth Symphony (1877–8) from its predecessors. Late the preceding year, 1876, Tchaikovsky had reached a moment of decision: in a desperate bid to defeat the main agent of his personal fate, his homosexuality, he resolved to marry. The Fourth Symphony reflects both the terrible inner turbulence that had precipitated this decision, yet at the same time a kind of hope that his torment might be assuaged (his disastrous 'marriage' took place only in July 1877, after the symphony had been sketched, though not scored). In 1878 Tchaikovsky described in detail – if not always very plausibly – the content of the symphony.* It imitated the 'fundamental idea' he thought was embodied in Beethoven's Fifth; fate (personified by Tchaikovsky in the strident opening theme which recurs dramatically not only in this first movement but in the Finale) controls all, and you can only submit to it – though by the end 'to live is still possible'. In addition, there is internal evidence that this symphony (and its two successors) deals with extra-musical issues. In fact, a feature that connects Tchaikovsky's last three symphonies is that each has at least one pointed thematic reference to another work. In the Fourth it is to two moments in Bizet's *Carmen*; to generate the opening theme of the *Moderato con anima* Tchaikovsky used the Toreador's Song (the entry of fate's agent in the opera) and then, it seems, Carmen's reading of the cards (the moment Carmen perceives what fate has in store for her), both already in F minor (Ex. 4a).

But even without Tchaikovsky's literary programme or knowledge of the *Carmen* connection, it is clear that the colossal first movement of the Fourth Symphony presents an experience of an unprecedented scale and intensity. The exposition in the first movement of the Third Symphony had contained three separate subjects; so does the Fourth, though the third subject is in part a transformation of material drawn from the preceding two. More significant, however, is the tonal scheme, for each subject rises a minor third above the preceding (F minor, A flat minor, B major), and the sequence is resumed in the recapitulation, the first subject (now drastically shortened) and the second being recapitulated in D minor, the third restoring the tonic. With two subjects having to share one key there was bound to be a very radical adjustment to the proportions of the movement – above all, a sense of progressive compression. When the coda, instead of rounding off the experience, seems to open it further, the sense of turmoil yet unresolved is complete.

After a movement of such sustained intensity, some respite is essential, and the two central movements are relaxed, the second of these arrestingly segregating the tone colours of pizzicato strings, woodwind and brass. The

* Tchaikovsky's programme is set out in my *Tchaikovsky: a biographical and critical study*, vol. 2 (London, 1982), pp. 163–6.

Ex. 4.

vigorous rondo-type Finale employs a folksong. Again the succession of backgrounds against which this is presented recalls *Kamarinskaya*, though the intrusion of the fate theme from the first movement is a forceful reminder of what governs everything. But though this Finale provides a rousing ending, neither in its scale nor in the quality of its thought is it a match for the first movement. To get the Finale absolutely right was to be not the least achievement of the last symphony.

The traumatic experience of his marriage clearly stunned the most personal side of Tchaikovsky's creative faculties, and for some eight years he mostly avoided pieces involving deep expressive issues. Full recovery came with the 'Manfred' Symphony (1885), based on a programme originally devised by the critic Vladimir Stasov some seventeen years earlier for Balakirev. Tchaikovsky found no problem in identifying with Byron's lonely figure who wanders in the Alps brooding upon the wrong (clearly one of incest) he had done his beloved Astarte, and though he was to turn against the last three movements, he recognized that in the first he had produced something that was as fine musically as it was truthful dramatically. The form is free; the slabs of dark, sometimes tempestuous music of the opening section projects Manfred himself, the slower *Andante* portraying Astarte in some of the tenderest, most beautiful music Tchaikovsky ever wrote. Images of the suffering woman were one of the most important recurring features in Tchaikovsky's work, especially after his marriage, and the appalling violence of Manfred's emotional response to Astarte's appearance no doubt carries something of Tchaikovsky's agony at his own sense of sexual guilt.

Berlioz was an important formative influence upon the remainder of the piece. As in *Harold en Italie*, the hero is represented by a theme which appears unchanged in all movements, while the two splendid central movements (a magical Scherzo representing the appearance of the Alpine Fairy in the spray of a waterfall, and an enchanting 'Pastorale' portraying the world of the mountain dwellers) owe a good deal to the Queen Mab Scherzo from *Roméo et Juliette* and the 'Scène aux champs' from the *Symphonie fantastique* respectively. The Finales of both the latter and *Harold* probably conditioned Tchaikovsky's last movement. But here the programmatic requirements (first an infernal orgy, then Manfred's appearance followed by Astarte's, and finally Manfred's death) weighed too heavily, producing a disjointed, uneven piece that flaws what is otherwise one of Tchaikovsky's masterpieces.

While Tchaikovsky's six numbered symphonies divide naturally into two equal groups, the first marked by vigorous stylistic as well as structural exploration, the second by a consistent and totally assured individuality, these latter still show a remarkable diversity. Brahms's music had no appeal for Tchaikovsky, but his respect for the German composer's integrity and mastery of his craft was unqualified. Early in 1888, during his first international tour as a conductor, Tchaikovsky came face to face with this greatest living representative of the western symphonic tradition, and the confrontation clearly decided him to demonstrate that he too could honour those qualities of balance and control which marked the German's work, yet at the same time remain uncompromisingly himself. Even more than the Third Symphony, the Fifth (1888) looks to western practice for its model. Though the presence of some extra-musical control is indicated by the motto theme (Ex. 4b) which is present in all four movements (this motto theme incorporates a phrase in the Act 1 Trio of Glinka's *A Life for the Tsar*; in addition, a fragment of a programme exists, indicating once again that fate is the ruling factor), and though the exposition has three subjects, the first movement observes an equilibrium between its sections such as its counterpart in the Fourth had deliberately avoided. Since the experience embodied in this strong, yet tightly disciplined movement does not drain the listener, there is no need for respite, and Tchaikovsky plunges yet deeper into profound expressive issues in what is one of the greatest of his symphonic slow movements. If the two incursions of the fateful motto theme are here violent, its entry at the end of the following Valse is so unassuming as to sound almost benign – and when, in the major key and with firm self-assurance, it provides the introduction for the Finale, any trace of menace has gone. Yet this Finale is the weakest movement, not because the sonata-structured *Allegro vivace* is poor in ideas or lacking in

Ex. 4. cont'd

[do not turn to sorrow]

drive, but because the bald reiterations of the motto theme (not one of Tchaikovsky's better tunes) in the *Moderato assai e molto maestoso* coda have an empty ring.

No charge of bombast or vapidity could possibly be levelled against the Finale of the Sixth Symphony (1893); indeed, it is the pain-filled key to the whole work. In fact, in 1892 Tchaikovsky had fully sketched a symphony in E flat, even scoring most of the first movement, but had then rejected it as unworthy. It is a faceless piece* and certainly had nothing to do with a programme he had outlined the previous year in which the Finale would present '*death* – result of collapse', then end 'dying away'. But there can be no doubt that Tchaikovsky returned to this part of his programme when composing his last great work, though the only pointer he gave to what the work is about is the title to which he agreed (*Pathétique*), and the inclusion in the first movement's development of the traditional chant from the Orthodox Requiem setting the words 'With thy saints, O Christ, give peace to the soul of thy servant' (see Ex. 4c). This first movement is the perfect collaboration of form and content, for the total certainty with which Tchaikovsky forges this creation of unprecedented range and forcefulness of expression is prodigious. As in the Fourth Symphony the exposition (again three-theme, but organized as two subjects) is vast, the development concise. But this time, after the recapitulation has been gathered up in the headlong rush, totally new music suddenly enters, heaves itself laboriously upward, then descends majestically in a gigantic scale (for Tchaikovsky a ubiquitous symbol of fate) and sinks into silence. After this outburst, as overwhelming

---

* A reconstruction of the E flat Symphony has been made by the Soviet musicologist, Semyon Bogatïrev, and is sometimes referred to as 'Symphony No. 7'.

as it is unexpected ('undoubtedly the climax of Tchaikovsky's artistic career,' as Tovey put it), the resumption of the recapitulation at the second subject comes as a relief, while the coda, as in the Fourth Symphony, provides the final stage of the experience, this time breathing a kind of resignation.

As in the Fourth Symphony also, the central movements are, of necessity, more relaxed, the first a kind of 'limping waltz' in 5/4 with a central section of pained melancholy, the second a brilliantly scored march, where the very vehemence and sustained energy of the music end by projecting a sense of a frenzied yet unavailing bid for happiness. The 1891 programme had specified that the third movement should represent 'disappointments', and the inescapable conclusion that, finally, happiness is unattainable stains the music of this third movement with increasing irony; the abrupt collapse into the despair of the Finale is both disconcerting yet inevitable. Music of such devastating eloquence as in this *Adagio lamentoso* requires no commentary; the whole symphony has been permeated by fateful descending scales, and it is with a broken scalic descent into the subterranean regions in which the work had opened that this Finale, surely the most original in any nineteenth-century symphony after Beethoven, finally dies to nothing.

No one could reasonably expect any of Tchaikovsky's successors to match, let alone surpass, the stupendous achievement of the *Pathétique*. Sadly, however, few of them could even on occasion rise to the level of Borodin; not until Shostakovich would the symphonies of a Russian working in his native land once again rightly command international attention. But it was not only that these successors were not in Borodin's or Tchaikovsky's league, for several were also pianists, the claims of this rival competence reducing to varying degrees the time each could give to composition. Nor was it simply their lesser endowments that account for their lower level of achievement. Rather, only one of them, Skryabin, was fired by a missionary conviction such as had driven Balakirev and Musorgsky (and Glinka before them) to blaze new trails; nor did any of the others have to make an alien tradition bow to the demands of their Russian creativity – a necessity that had stretched Borodin and, even more, Tchaikovsky to search out specifically Russian ways of thinking within Western symphonic forms. The new men had no need of Glinka as an icon for veneration – as a towering symbol of Russian creative independence (and sometimes even a route to musical salvation) such as he had been to the Balakirev/Tchaikovsky generation. In a way life was now almost too easy. Already the twin conservatoires had established that tradition of systematic musical education for which Russia has ever since been famed, and the generation that emerged in the last quarter of the century did so excellently equipped; with some clear models before them of how a Russian symphony might be written, most of these younger composers were content simply to extend such precedents (what is new in their symphonies is that the great majority are, in various ways, cyclic). This excellent preparation also meant that they could present themselves fully fledged when phenomenally young. Rimsky may have finished his First Symphony when only twenty-one, but it was a rough and inept piece compared to that with which his pupil, Alexander Glazunov was to bound before the Russian musical world when only sixteen. But, as Glazunov himself was to demonstrate all too painfully, there was no guarantee that prodigious competence would evolve into creative greatness. And so, while able professional composers were now thick on the ground, some are eminently forgettable as symphonists. No conductor, for instance, is ever likely to break a baton for the sake of the feeble E minor Symphony (1908) of **Mikhail Ippolitov-Ivanov** (1859–1935) or the dreary Second Symphony (1907–8) of **Reinhold Glière** (1875–1956) – though the devotee of programmatic symphonies who has an hour and a half to spare may find pleasure in following the fabulous adventures of the folk hero, Il'ya Muromets, as they are enthusiastically depicted in Glière's Third Symphony (1909–11). This epic piece must earn admiration if only for the enormous time span over which the pictorial vividness is sustained, despite the slender substance of the musical material. It is no surprise that Glière should have gone on to compose some successful ballet scores.

The gargantuan orchestra required for this work, as well as its time scale, will ensure it is almost never heard. Nor is there any very compelling reason why the First Symphony (1897) of **Sergey Lyapunov** (1859–1924) should ever be roused from slumber. It was as a miniaturist that this product of the Moscow Conservatoire, then close associate of Balakirev, showed his greatest flair, and his First Symphony is most memorable for its frequent suggestions of earlier composers, especially of Borodin (significantly it is in B minor). But Lyapunov's more ambitious, tightly cyclic Second Symphony (1917) is a rather different matter. Though it still resounds with echoes of the nationalists generally and, in its large and thoughtful first movement, of Tchaikovsky's 'Manfred' Symphony and even Liszt's 'Faust' Symphony, it is a piece which avoids easy, ready-made answers, even if by the end it commands respect rather than affection.

In the case of **Anton Arensky** (1861–1906) it is perhaps the reverse – at least, with the First Symphony (1883), like Lyapunov's, in B minor, for there is much fluency and inventiveness in this engaging piece, easily recognizable as by a pupil of Rimsky-Korsakov. Arensky's early career matched Tchaikovsky's exactly: study at the St Petersburg Conservatoire, then immediate transfer to the Moscow Conservatoire, where he was to be the teacher of Rakhmaninov, Skryabin and Glière. Problems within Arensky's character later led to a sad personal decline, and a failure to fulfil his earlier promise. But the young Arensky was full of ideas, well able to fill out the compartments of a symphonic structure engagingly. He had a marked liking for unusual metres, and the Scherzi of both his symphonies are written in five-beat bars. In the Second Symphony (1888) this makes for the best movement; otherwise the piece is markedly inferior to its predecessor.

The Finale of Arensky's First Symphony had been spiritedly folky, but the two symphonies of **Vasily Kalinnikov** (1866–1901) were more consistently coloured by a nationalist idiom, like Lyapunov's best described as post-Borodin. It was scarcely Kalinnikov's fault that his technique was not over-strong, for poverty forced him to withdraw early from the Moscow Conservatoire (though he did find alternative tuition in the Philharmonic Society's Music School). His First Symphony (1894–5) has much melodic liveliness, and retains the listener's attention by its invigorating energy, abundance of ideas, and occasional quirky but striking harmonic touches. This is a spirited cyclic piece, themes from all preceding movements recurring in the Finale. The Second Symphony (1895–7) is a more assured work, with a fine slow movement; regrettably, the Finale, which concludes by returning noisily to the work's opening theme, outstays its welcome. Though Kalinnikov showed no sign of becoming a major master, his death only nine years after completing his training was one of the saddest blows to Russian music at the turn of the century.

Four composers of greater significance remain: **Sergey Taneyev** (1856–1915), **Alexander Glazunov** (1865–1936), **Alexander Skryabin** (1872–1915) and **Sergey Rakhmaninov** (1873–1943). Of these, the odd one out was Taneyev, a pupil of Tchaikovsky at the Moscow Conservatoire and subsequently one of his closest friends. Russians seem to have an aptitude for composing 'horizontally', and they are one of the few races to have a folk tradition of oral heterophony (that is, building a rough accompaniment to a folktune by simultaneously improvising very free variations upon it). Russian composers have always shown a positive flair for devising countermelodies for existing tunes, and the Russians' facility for manipulating closed systems (is it accident that they are such accomplished chess players?) has always made counterpoint attractive to them, though building the creative substance of the music through contrapuntal method has usually proved more problematic, and the fugal passages that break out in Russian symphonies (in the Finales of Tchaikovsky's Third and Arensky's Second, for instance) are mostly no more than energetic but lifeless workings of a consummately mastered technique. For Taneyev, however, counterpoint was fundamental to his creative processes. Not being given, like so many of his contemporaries, to sudden impulses to be followed almost unheedingly, it was natural for him to start a composition with its details (often contrapuntal), which were then thoughtfully built into larger components until the whole piece had been assembled. And always everything was scrutinized remorselessly; few composers have been so self-critical.

It is no surprise, therefore, that Taneyev composed slowly – nor that his work is devoid of those characteristically Russian features that mark, and sometimes saturate, the work of other Russian symphonists. Officially he credited himself with only one symphony (1896–8); in fact, he composed four. His First (1873–4) was a student piece, his Second (1877–8: only three movements survive) earned some warm approval from Tchaikovsky, while his Third (1884) proved to be a deeply serious, even earnest piece, performed once, but denied publication.* The work he did finally let loose to the ears of the world at large is among the finest of Russian symphonies. Taneyev may never have been granted 'inspiration', but he had a superb natural musicianship which enabled him to build from his materials massive and richly filled structures. Not surprisingly, of all Russian symphonies Taneyev's in C minor is one of the most integrated, and at the root of this is a dense network of thematic relationships embracing all four movements (Ex. 5; the relationships charted here are by no means comprehensive).

The opening, tritone-strung motif (Ex. 5a), which will recur in all movements, is crucial: a striking gesture in itself, it is fundamental to what immediately follows, within a few bars modifying itself to round off the quaver phrase (Ex. 5b) which extends sequentially, this ending in retrograde inversion then launching the second theme of this first subject (Ex. 5f). And while such organic unfolding of the melody is thoroughly classical in spirit, pitting themes and thematic particles against one another is the very foundation of the development; if any such section is an 'argument', this is it. But there are some problems of texture; Taneyev's orchestration is efficient but without flair, and the almost unbroken complexity makes for a heavy, sometimes oppressive sound.

A composer of Taneyev's temperament and inclinations was unlikely to produce a highly defined personal style, and his Russian eclecticism encouraged constant echoes of other composers – almost always non-Russian. Shadows of Beethoven, Brahms, even Wagner, flit briefly across the music, though the method is very much Taneyev's own. Materials pass between movements. The opening phrase of the solemn and imposing *Adagio* (Ex. 5d) incorporates the symphony's first motif, builds its third phrase from another derivative of this motif (Ex. 5f) plus the second subject of the first movement (Ex. 5c), while the intervening phrase anticipates the Trio of the Scherzo (Ex. 5e). And if we feel the clear, untroubled woodwind theme that opens the centre of the movement sounds a little familiar, we are right, though where that same shape had first been heard (at the close of the first movement's exposition), its character had been very different.

This great *Adagio* is one of the most impressive of Russian slow movements, the Scherzo perhaps one of the most disarming. Its roots may still lie within the western tradition, but it has an element of harmonic capriciousness and melodic unexpectedness (and a relative textural fineness) which provides admirable respite; its opening is a delicate oboe transformation of a bass figure prominent in the first movement. In the Finale Taneyev's contrapuntal urges are given their head, and the process of

---

* The three surviving movements of the second symphony have been completed by the Soviet scholar, V. Blok, and have been recorded. The third symphony was published in 1947.

Ex. 5. Tanayev: Symphony No. 4

movement (Ex. 5f), and the transitional theme (Ex. 5i) rewrites an equally transitional theme in the *Adagio* (Ex. 5h). As this *Allegro energico* proceeds, ideas from preceding movements are drawn in, and the conclusion is an epic and remarkably comprehensive summary of earlier themes.

The dedication of this splendid symphony was given to Glazunov, no doubt in return for the latter's inscription of his Fifth Symphony (1895) to Taneyev. Yet it would be difficult to find a greater contrast than between the painstaking, unprolific pupil of Tchaikovsky and this extraordinarily fertile, technically fluent protégé of Rimsky who by the time he was twenty-five had produced three symphonies, a host of smaller orchestral works, and three string quartets. Glazunov was the Mendelssohn of Russian music in the nature of his talent, if not his musical character. In 1882 he had astounded a St Petersburg audience with his First Symphony (1881–2; rev. 1885 and 1929), and in his attractive Second (1886) he had gone on to confirm that his allegiance was still to the nationalist tradition generally and more specifically to the precedents set by Borodin's Second Symphony, unquestionably the most influential piece of its kind from the earlier generation. But it all sounds rather diluted besides Borodin's masterpiece. In the Third Symphony (1890) a clear shift is perceptible. By now it could not have been otherwise, for despite Tchaikovsky's pronouncement, there were severe limits to what even *Kamarinskaya* had to offer the symphonic composer. In fact the whole post-Glinka phase of Russian nationalism was passing, and Glazunov's Third Symphony proved to be a transitional work, less sure of its own character, and overlong. But when three years later its successor appeared Glazunov had found firmer ground. In its broadest terms, the model for this new style was the kind of 'lyrical' symphony such as Tchaikovsky had composed, and the melodic content of Glazunov's remaining symphonies suggests a search for a more individual style and utterance. The problem was that, whereas each of Tchaikovsky's symphonies had been formed by a unique creative impulse that had animated, sometimes with shattering force, the music through which it found expression, Glazunov mostly lacked such impulses, and his music's more generalized character could produce an impression of facelessness. But though it cannot be described as original, it is distinctive and, like Taneyev's, totally sure-footed. The opening of the three-movement Fourth Symphony (1893; Ex. 6) exemplifies this style at its best, the initial bars in their light ornamentation still suggesting something of an earlier oriental/nationalist idiom, the fifth and sixth bars shedding this for something more western, the seventh moving back to the opening manner, the remainder deftly fusing both styles. With its melody presented through the elegiac tones of the cor anglais, this is haunting indeed.

If the promise of such a beginning had been fulfilled, this might have stood among the finest of Russian symphonies. But it is not, for despite passages of much beauty or real enterprise, too much of the rest is filled out through an unfailing facility for devising second-rate ideas and for consummate note spinning. Often, too, a single movement will start well, then falter in quality,

Ex. 6. Glazunov: Symphony No. 4

and finally outstay its welcome. The Fifth Symphony (1895) is one of the most satisfactory of the series, not least because it is one of the most concise, and its noisily boisterous Finale knows when to stop – just. By contrast, the Sixth (1896) is the most inconsistent, following a powerful opening movement, one of Glazunov's finest, with two genial central movements, the first a set of variations, the second, labelled 'Intermezzo', a kind of minuet suggesting an intention similar to that which had prompted Tchaikovsky's rococo stylizations. The Finale is rhythmically stodgy and prolix.

Glazunov's two remaining symphonies belong chronologically to the twentieth century. A declaration made in a letter to Taneyev à propos the Seventh (1902) reveals much of where Glazunov's thoughts on symphonic matters had now reached. 'More by instinct than by premeditated intention I wanted to combine variation form (which latterly I have come to love passionately) with sonata and rondo forms and to build my music more on contrapuntal than harmonic bases.' Glazunov had already attempted something of the sort in the Sixth Symphony's Finale, and parts of the slow movement of the Seventh give the clearest evidence of the powerful attraction linear textures held for him (unlike so many other Russians, he was capable of devising fugatos with lives of their own, as the next symphony would show). This symphony is sometimes known as the 'Pastoral' because its key and first sounds pay explicit homage to a German model. But, in fact, the direct connections with Beethoven's Sixth Symphony become only intermittent in the opening *Allegro moderato* (certainly the best movement of the piece), and thereafter vanish. The Finale's aspiration to summarise much of what has gone before proves too ambitious, and the last movement of the Eighth Symphony (1906) also ends in being that work's least satisfactory movement, like so many of Glazunov's Finales overblown and overlong, though with some fine music in it and much emphasis on counterpoint. Its solemn opening chords remind us of those traces of an earlier Borodin-derived heroic manner that have persisted, though transformed, throughout many of the intervening works. But otherwise this symphony's musical ideas (and its sound world) are very much Glazunov's own, while the first movement is a truly noble piece, avoiding the facile patches which had reduced so many of his earlier movements to second-rank status, and the slow movement is one of the most impressive among pre-revolutionary Russian symphonies. In fact, the symphony had been gestating for at least two turbulent years, for during the 1905 disturbances Glazunov himself had been caught up in political events when he resigned from the St Petersburg Conservatoire in protest at the dismissal of Rimsky-Korsakov as director (when the authorities had made concessions Glazunov himself was elected director). It is easy to believe that the tensions of the times played their part in forming the deeply serious character of the Eighth Symphony, especially in this powerful slow movement. Striking is the way in which the strongly profiled first theme of this *Mesto* emerges naturally out of the ominous introductory sounds, and the quieter central section well maintains the level of achievement. In this magnificent movement Glazunov gets everything just about right, and nowhere more so than in its sombre conclusion.

In 1910 Glazunov began sketching a Ninth Symphony, then abandoned it, and though he was to live twenty-six more years, he never returned to the form. Perhaps after the Eighth he recognized that he had reached the ultimate of which he was capable. Glazunov was a supreme artisan composer, in his private life devoted to the interests of others (as his conservatoire years showed), making no effort to build his own cult, either personal or musical. His music may be eclectic, but the echoes of music by others are on the whole convincingly assimilated.

Rakhmaninov is altogether more readily recognizable. Yet as a symphonist he is far less important – and not merely because he composed fewer, for only one of his three can in any way match the best of his more famous works for piano and orchestra. The confrontation (or collaboration) of heroic soloist and combative (or supportive) orchestra afforded a special stimulus to Rakhmaninov's gifts for powerful rhetoric and strongly charged lyricism, and with the total establishment of his highly individual style in the Second Piano Concerto (1900–01) he found himself, paradoxically, in a kind of personal prison. In the massive post-Tchaikovskyan Second Symphony (1906–07) one is impressed by the highmindedness, and by Rakhmaninov's total control of his often complex, richly embellished textures. Yet it is a piece still in the grip, it seems, of the concerto's spell, driven to continue beyond that splendid piece, but leaving impressions of grand tunes now of less than first-rate quality and sometimes plain second-rate. Much of the slow movement is consummate note-spinning and a supreme example of how the last drop of yearning or languishment can be squeezed from very slight material when used in a massively prolonged sequence. The first movement is uneven but has some impressive passages, notably its nobly elegiac introduction and the vastly spanned *cantilena* of the second subject (especially in its recapitulated form) which does approach the melodic level of the Second Concerto. The weakest movement is the Finale, for all its surface energy and brilliance, the most satisfactory the Scherzo. When a couple of years later Rakhmaninov channelled the same creative urges into the fine Third Piano Concerto, the shortcomings of the symphony were highlighted. The Third Symphony (1935–6; rev. 1938) seems an attempt to blend the keen clarity and pointedness of the recently completed *Rhapsody on a theme of Paganini* (1934) with something of the full-blooded romanticism of the earlier works. The determination not to fall into formulae, even to break new ground, must earn respect, and fleeting moments remind us of what used to be, but the work remains a sad failure, for the creative forces are enfeebled and the springs of lushly surging melody now run weakly.

The good fortune of the First Symphony (1895) was to have been born before the Second Concerto, though ironically it is the symphony Rakhmaninov disowned, for he destroyed the score after the disastrous first performance, and it was unheard until it was reconstructed in 1945 from the recently rediscovered orchestral parts. Robert Simpson was later to declare that, had Rakhmaninov followed it 'with advancing successors, he would have been one of the great symphonists of the first half of the twentieth century'. This is nothing but the truth. Like its (non-advancing) successors it is a fully cyclic work, but the thematic integration goes far deeper than in most Russian symphonies. Themes and thematic fragments that have occurred in earlier movements are transformed, sometimes profoundly, to condition or generate new material. The opening sounds (Ex. 7a), which proclaim grandly that Borodin rather more than Tchaikovsky stands patron to this piece, presents two motifs crucial to the whole symphony, and *y* quickly reveals its potency by launching the first subject. However, the second theme of the second subject (Ex. 7b) is to prove equally important, its first bar (*z*) in collaboration with *x* opening each of the following movements, and in the Scherzo promptly generating the main theme (Ex. 7c, bars 6ff). Early in this movement a new repeated figure *a* appears (Ex. 7d), first to be heard separately, then in conjunction with the main theme, subsequently extending its activities into the following *Larghetto* to condition the beginning of the main theme (Ex. 7f, bars 4ff), then reveal itself openly in that theme's fifth bar, and subsequently become of yet greater importance (it is even to generate a semiquaver line (Ex. 7g) which proves to be something more than just an accompaniment figure). By borrowing two bars later a fragment of contour from the first movement's second subject (see bar two of Ex. 7b) a further connection with earlier music is established. And when this beautiful clarinet theme returns on strings for the *Larghetto*'s climax, it evolves into that very second subject.

Nor in all this has *y* been inactive. It had emerged in the middle of the Scherzo (Ex. 7e) and as a figure on the horns it had accompanied the dynamic climax of the slow movement; now at the Finale's opening, after *x* and *z* have done their combined duty (Ex. 7h), it fathers a march-like introduction (Ex. 7i), then stamps itself upon the first subject's opening (Ex. 7j) before *x* and *z* collaborate in yet another guise to provide the continuation (Ex. 7k).

But this is not simply a very thoughtful work; it is also an abundantly fertile one. The first subject of the first movement, like that of Tchaikovsky's First Symphony, unfolds expansively as a thread of melody full of motivic materials, while the second subject shows how well Rakhmaninov could invent melody devoid of heavy sentiment, yet as heart-stirring as it is fresh (variable metres contribute much to these touching tunes). The fugato which follows seems to promise disaster, but it is not to be; pedantry passes, and the development builds to an effective climax, with the whole-tone scale intervening just before the recapitulation to produce a touch of tonal vertigo. The Scherzo is magical, both in colour and harmony. It is another Russian memory, perhaps, of Queen Mab, but unique, with a basic phrase whose contour constantly varies. Rarely did Rakhmaninov show better textural judgement than here – or in the following *Larghetto*. In the Scherzo's centre *x y* and *z* had all contributed and had provided the movement's last fleeting sounds, but this lovely slow movement, with its light touches of Borodinesque sultriness, is thematically even more acquisitive, and the Finale sounds yet more comprehensive, not because every theme in the symphony is quoted, but because especially recognizable elements from many are incorporated into the central interlude that does service for a development. The second subject is new – a fine, broad theme that foretells the later, more familiar Rakhmaninov. But a powerful impression remains

Ex. 7. Rakhmaninov: Symphony No. 1

Ex. 7. cont'd

of the elemental rhythmic energy of so much else – that is, until the *Largo* coda reminds us (Ex. 7l) of what had been the three prime ingredients of the whole symphony, then drawing *a* in at the end.

There remains Skryabin. Nowadays this brilliant eccentric is frequently written off as an expendable curiosity. This will not do. Certainly we may feel suspicious of a composer who, while aspiring to a world-transforming (literally) individuality of achievement, should raid so explicitly other composers' styles. Yet in the end Skryabin did achieve a kind of musical originality; he had to, even though this originality sounds contrived rather than truly visionary, for he had taken upon himself the Nietzschean concept of the superman who would ultimately lead the elect, their spirits freed from inherited belief, into an ecstatic condition of free activity ('divine play') at one with the universe (to achieve this Skryabin envisaged involving also light, colour, dance, and in effect anything that would act upon the senses). And so he foraged through the styles of Chopin and Liszt, then Wagner and Debussy, before evolving his borrowed resources into a yet more tonally and harmonically emancipated music as he prepared himself to create the musical portion for the final 'mystery'.

It is no surprise, therefore, that so traditionally rooted a form as the symphony should have held only brief interest for Skryabin, and all three of his examples were composed within a five-year period. Yet it was in these that his very personal mission is first glimpsed. The E major Symphony (1899–1900) was virtually his first purely orchestral work. His music of the 1890s had been almost exclusively for solo piano, and though he now had three sonatas behind him, the tightly disciplined thought required by the symphony found him wanting; beside Rakhmaninov and Glazunov he seems inept. The Finale, which incorporates earlier material, introduces mezzo soprano and tenor soloists, plus a chorus, for a setting of a poem by Skryabin himself in praise of art; this declines into a fugue, as dreary as it is stylistically misplaced. The First Symphony is in six movements, its successor (1901) in five, thematically interrelated. Within a year Skryabin's grasp has grown significantly, but again it is the more lyrical movements and stretches that impress; the opening *Andante*, with its chromatic chord changes, unfolds far more naturally than the ensuing sonata-structured *Allegro*. The heart of the symphony is the extensive third movement – so much preferable to the post-Lisztian rhetoric of the following *Tempestoso*, or the grandiose but simple-minded Finale.

The Third Symphony ('Divine Poem': 1902–4) is a very different matter. The ghost of Wagner may constantly be discerned, especially in some of its melodic features and harmony, though now the music could rarely be confused with that of the German master; even the sudden eruption of the Tristan chord (bar 341: an 'écroulement formidable', as Skryabin dubs it in one of those increasingly ecstatic descriptions or directions with which he was now peppering his scores) seems only to liberate something yet more individual within Skryabin himself. The orchestra is huge, yet handled with much discrimination and sometimes ravishingly, whether delivering the most sonorous of textures, the cleanest of counterpoint or, in the middle of the slow movement, conjuring the birdsong of Skryabin's own magical 'forest murmurs'. The Third Symphony marked a great leap forward in all ways, for while in its preface Skryabin first confessed something of his more cosmic aspirations (the movements themselves are entitled 'Struggles', 'Delights' and 'Divine Play' respectively), the music itself shows him working purposefully towards an individual, more assured idiom, at the root of which

Ex. 8. Skryabin: Symphony No. 3

is a thoroughly Russian thematic integration. The student examining the score will observe a characteristically Russian use of tiny but distinctive thematic outlines which recur freely; the attentive listener will spot the thematic repetitions and perhaps some at least of the well-planned thematic engagements. The stern opening phrase (*x* in Ex. 8a) is incorporated into the first subject, whose opening contour (Ex. 8b) is itself conditioned by this same theme, and the first subject, in its turn, is to become what sounds like a new brass melody (Ex. 8c), after the Tristanesque 'fearsome collapse' in the development. Throughout the movement the fabric is tightly and richly woven from threads such as these (even so tiny an idea as Ex. 8d, which had emerged in the accompaniment of the first subject, has its importance). And there is integration between movements; the clarion call of *y* in Ex. 8a may crop up anywhere (it is to generate the first subject of the Finale: Ex. 8h), and the main theme of 'Delights' is prefigured during the first movement's development, then at the recapitulation (Ex. 8e) provides yet another counterpoint for the first subject while the second theme of the second subject provides a bass; in the Finale the second subject (Ex. 8g: as at bar 164) becomes an elaborate paragraph drawing in a double theme for brass from the slow movement (Ex. 8f) as counterpoints. At the symphony's end other themes prominent earlier are reintroduced.

Even this brief summary of some of Skryabin's thematic workings is sufficient to demonstrate the thoughtful and careful preparation that must have preceded composition (but, then, Skryabin was Taneyev's pupil). Couple this with the variety and inventiveness of his thought and the masterly control of musical space, and the 'Divine Poem' reveals itself to be as substantial musically as it is exciting dramatically.

Skryabin's further researches were to take him into a kind of music incompatible with the symphonic principle, and with the 'Poem of Ecstasy' (1905–8) and 'Prometheus' (1908–10), he had really passed out of the symphonic orbit (though both pieces have been labelled Symphonies). Transitional works are always at risk of neglect; the 'Poem of Ecstasy' may be more exquisitely and assuredly wrought, the 'Divine Poem' may be uneven and stylistically insecure, but it is one of the richest of all Skryabin's works, and its relegation to limbo is undeserved. With Rakhmaninov's First, Glazunov's Eighth and Taneyev's in C minor, it is one of the peaks of post-Tchaikovsky symphonism. The almost total absence of these symphonies from our concert halls is our loss.

12

The Symphony in the Soviet Union (1917–91)

David Fanning

On 21 November 1937 in the Great Hall of the Leningrad Philharmonic a half-hour ovation greeted the première of Shostakovich's Fifth Symphony. Was it musical qualities alone which so moved the audience? Was it the spectacle of Shostakovich's rehabilitation after the official criticism of his opera *The Lady Macbeth of Mtsensk District?* Or perhaps the audience had found an outlet for a kind of collective mourning for the victims of collectivization and the Stalin Terror. No composer in modern times provokes more unanswerable questions than Shostakovich, and no body of music is more difficult to assess than the Soviet/Russian Symphony. Sitting in a comfortable chair in a country unused to famine or mass persecution may not be the best place to start.

Composers make music. Performers make music. And in a third sense audiences make it too. Throughout their history the Soviets have experienced a hunger for culture beyond the Western creative artist's wildest dreams. In the mid-1930s, a time of terrifying personal experiences which it was perilous to write down or even talk about, listening to music could function as a gigantic safety-valve, an act of vicarious dissent, even a substitute for religious observance. At the same time the ideology of Socialist Realism placed restrictions on creative activity beyond the Western artist's worst nightmares. Defined as 'the truthful, historically concrete representation of reality in its revolutionary development', in practical terms Socialist Realism meant almost the exact opposite, its unspecified pre-condition being adherence to the Party Line. In the tension between official requirements and mass psychological cravings, Shostakovich and Prokofiev together produced eight or ten of the century's greatest and most enduringly popular symphonies.

This introduction will already have offended some readers (though certainly fewer than if it had been published ten years ago). It is based on personal intuitions, some would say fuelled by a Cold War ideology, supported only by the broadly similar views of émigrés and Western writers all of whom may have axes to grind. Ideologically pure or not, it projects dimensions on to music which are not verifiable in any strictly scholarly way and which beg all sorts of questions. The very fact that Shostakovich's Fifth Symphony can stir listeners who may never have heard of Stalin or the political events of the 1930s suggests that it transcends the circumstances of its production. Even so it has to be realized that Soviet music does not play the game by Western aesthetic rules (nor does pre-Soviet Russian music, for that matter). To pretend otherwise can lead to rash judgments – for example, the many scathing dismissals by Western commentators of Shostakovich's 'Leningrad' Symphony (No. 7, 1941) now seem remarkably arrogant and misplaced. If British music-lovers wonder why Elgar and Vaughan Williams do not 'travel', they have only to look at past critical attitudes to Russian and Soviet music in Britain and ponder the difficulty of assessing one culture from the standpoint of another. Not that we need to shy away from aesthetic judgment altogether; but it is as well to be sure that the historical basis for it is sufficiently firm and the imaginative basis sufficiently broad.

'Symphonism' has been a favourite topic in Soviet musicology. Indeed from 4 to 6 February 1935 the Union of Soviet Composers actually held 'Discussions about Soviet symphonism'.* These contained their fair share of banal, non-committal statements, as well as some sharp criticisms; but by comparison with the following year's discussions, in the wake of *Pravda's* diatribe on Shostakovich's opera *The Lady Macbeth of Mtsensk District*, it was a remarkably undogmatic affair. Shostakovich's close friend Ivan Sollertinsky spoke for many when he claimed that, for all its past failures and current problems, the prospects for the symphony in the Soviet Union were brighter than in the West. The only *caveat* was that composers must steer a careful course between the Scylla and Charybdis of 'formalism' and 'epigonism' (loosely speaking, over-intellectuality and lack of originality).† He was to be proved right, though probably not in the way he anticipated. The first eighteen years of post-Tsarist rule had produced only two 'repertoire' symphonies (Prokofiev's 'Classical' and Shostakovich's First), neither of which was conspicuously influenced by Socialist Reality.‡ Yet the next eighteen years would see a whole clutch of such works, *all* of them so influenced.

1935 is thus a handy demarcation point in the history of the Soviet symphony – beforehand relative pluralism of style and freedom of expression but few masterpieces, afterwards relative conformity and deference to

---

* Extensively reported in *Sovetskaya muzyka* 1935, parts 4, 5 and 6.
† The semi-official definitions of formalism as 'the separation of form and content' and 'exaggeration of form over content' again conceal a hidden political agenda. And since the terms of that agenda were themselves periodically redefined it is no wonder composers ran into trouble.
‡ Genrikh Orlov admits as much in the most comprehensive published study of the Soviet symphony, *Russkii sovetskii simfonizm*, Leningrad, 1966, p. 7.

authority, but a remarkable quota of masterpieces. Similarly, 1953 is an unmistakeable landmark, with the deaths of Stalin and Prokofiev (both on 5 March), the beginnings of a sporadic but progressive thaw in social and cultural policy, the appearance of Shostakovich's Tenth (which many Western commentators would hail as the finest Soviet symphony of all), and a gradual move away from stylistic orthodoxy. Between 1953 and the present it is more difficult to place such dividing-lines, but it is clear that by the mid-60s a further decisive re-orientation was under way.

1917 is the clearest dividing-line of all. In the words of Pasternak's Zhivago, 'The revolution broke out willy-nilly, like a breath that's been held too long'. In the musical world that breath all but extinguished the wilting flowers of the Russian symphonic tradition. A simple explanation for this would be the collapse of the 'privileged élitist' system upon which the production and consumption of symphonies had depended. In the first few years of the new régime there were those who would gladly have seen the demise of the symphony orchestra, along with the symphony and all associated genres. But since the death of Tchaikovsky in 1893 the Russian symphonic tradition had in any case shown only fitful signs of life, and those who might have carried the torch into the Soviet era had either died (Balakirev in 1910, Rimsky-Korsakov in 1908, Skryabin in 1915), or emigrated (Prokofiev in 1917, Rakhmaninov in 1918, Nikolay and Alexander Tcherepnin in 1921, Grechaninov in 1925) or stayed in Russia but stopped writing symphonies (Glazunov, Glière, Ippolitov-Ivanov). In the years of the Civil War from 1918 to 1921, a time of immense deprivation when food was desperately scarce and manuscript paper practically unobtainable, musicians in the main cities were directed towards the education of the proletariat and the composition of 'mass-songs' for propaganda purposes. Prokofiev's 'Classical' Symphony (1917) and Myaskovsky's Fourth and Fifth (both 1918) were all conceived before the Revolution; apart from these I can only trace two symphonies composed anywhere in Russia or its satellite states between 1917 and the end of the Civil War in 1921 – these being the first symphonies of the Ukrainians Levko Revutsky (1921, revised 1957) and **Boris Lyatoshinsky** (variously dated to between 1918 and 1922, revised in 1967). The latter work is strongly influenced by Skryabin's Wagnerian manner, as are Lyatoshinsky's later symphonies, the best-known being No. 3 of 1951, revised 1954. As a teacher Lyatoshinsky was much revered; his finest pupil is **Valentin Silvestrov**, whose Fifth Symphony of 1980–82 is in my estimation the greatest Soviet symphony still awaiting discovery in the West.

Of the pre-revolutionary symphonists who remained active, easily the most prolific and influential was **Nikolay Myaskovsky**. His first two symphonies (1908, 1912) map out the direction much of his later career would follow, the first being rather square and predictable, but solidly composed in the Glazunov mould, the second more adventurous and culminating in a remarkable fourths-based final chord in the manner of late Skryabin. Soviet commentators like to stress the move away from gloomy pessimism in Myaskovsky's post-revolutionary works. Certainly the E minor Fourth Symphony drives towards an affirmative E major coda, whereas the Third (1914) had subsided into wistful melancholy. No. 5, with its *amabile* opening movement, balalaika imitations in the slow movement, Galician carol and musette Trio in the third, is an altogether more memorable, and as it happens classically balanced, work. It is also a reminder that the symphony with folk-elements was by no means an invention of Socialist Realism, and with a degree of ideological slanting Myaskovsky's pupil Kabalevsky was later able to describe this as 'one of the first victories for the realistic direction in Soviet music'.* However, Myaskovsky was also fatally drawn to the César Franckian mannerisms of instant pathos. With their excessive sequential repetition of short units, and insufficient variety of harmonic pace, his structures tend to fill out space rather than moulding it dramatically. Notwithstanding moments of touching wistfulness, much of his music manages to sound at once short-breathed and long-winded.

The year 1921 marked the end of the Civil War and the beginning of Lenin's New Economic Policy, the first of many attempts to alleviate the effects of communist economics. It was only in this climate, and with the support of the relatively broad-minded Lunacharsky, People's Commissar for Public Education from 1917 to 1929, that symphonic composition became a realistic proposition at all. Contacts with Western music and performers were gradually re-established, and a Party resolution of 1 July 1925 gave official sanction to pluralism in the arts. Myaskovsky himself helped to establish the Moscow branch of the Association for Contemporary Music (ACM), an internationally-minded group, bitterly opposed by the Russian Association of Proletarian Musicians (RAPM). Both factions were established in 1923.

In this same year Myaskovsky completed his massive Sixth Symphony (revised in 1947), which was soon to be hailed as the first Soviet Symphony (as opposed to symphony composed in Soviet Russia). Certainly it engages with revolutionary themes, although with what ideological intent may be open to debate. The Finale is based on two songs of the French Revolution – the *Carmagnole* and *Ça ira* – but these are heard only in the orchestra. The chorus enters much later with an old Russian chant, 'The parting of body and soul', while the *Dies irae* looms large here and in the slow movement. A recall of the slow movement, the most moving of Myaskovsky's many Franckian cyclic reminiscences, concludes the work on a note of intense pathos. According to Soviet commentators, the tragedy is that of the old intelligentsia whose world was turned upside down by the Revolution. Given the layout of the Finale, however, it can just as easily be read as the tragedy of revolutionary

* Introduction to score of symphonies 4 and 5, Moscow, 1953.

fervour betrayed by later events. Whatever the intention, Myaskovsky was here fired to levels of inspiration he would rarely approach again. The *allegro feroce* first movement has an Elgarian energy which offers considerable compensation for the repetitiveness of the structure; above all there is the visionary stillness and sense of loss which comes over the Trio section of the second movement (Ex. 1). This violin and celesta chorale is one of several passages in this symphony suggesting a knowledge of Mahler's Sixth (Mahler in turn lifted his version of the idea from that most archetypal of Russian sources, Glinka's *Ruslan and Lyudmila*). The basic E flat minor tonality of Myaskovsky's Sixth, extremely rare in non-Russian music, brings to mind the most funereal and despairing moments of Musorgsky's *Boris Godunov* and *Khovanshchina*, and it established an archetype of mournful protest to be taken up by a number of later Soviet symphonies, e.g. Prokofiev 6 (1945–7), Ovchinnikov 1 and 2 (1955–7, 1956 revised 1972–3), Shchedrin 1 (1957), and Eshpai 1 (1959).

Ex. 1. Myaskovsky: Symphony No. 6

By his death in 1950 Myaskovsky had produced a total of twenty-seven symphonies, many of them examples of solid musical construction and dignified character at a time when such qualities were at a premium. A minor landmark is the Twelfth of 1931–32, the so-called *Kolkhoz* Symphony, whose ostensible dedication to the ideals of collectivization has no musical symptoms other than the rather empty tunefulness and would-be affirmative tone of the Finale. This reflects the temporary ascendancy of the RAPM from 1929 until the founding of the Union of Soviet Composers in 1932. Prior to that, in accordance with his ACM position, Myaskovsky had been following up his semi-experimental interests in Symphonies 7 to 10 (1922–27), trying his hand at more of the harmonic tricks of late Skryabin, notably in the two-movement No. 7, and at a discreet formal experimentation, notably in multi-thematic Scherzos such as that of No. 9. In No. 10 he produced a genuine one-movement symphony for the conductorless orchestra Persimfans;* in the wild, almost expressionistic tone of this work he came as close as he ever would to the contemporary Parisian idiom of Prokofiev. Prokofiev and Myaskovsky were in fact lifelong friends, and their important correspondence deserves to be translated (and preferably de-expurgated). After No. 13 of 1933, another single-movement symphony, Myaskovsky's relatively adventurous vein dried up for good.†

In common with virtually every other Soviet composer Myaskovsky could trace his lineage back to Rimsky-Korsakov. From Rimsky-Korsakov the pedagogic line passes through Lyadov to Myaskovsky and thence to Shebalin in Moscow and to composers of the present day; it passes through Steinberg to Shcherbachev in Leningrad (and thence to the Georgians) and Shostakovich (Leningrad, later Moscow), through Kalafati to Eller and the Estonians, through Arensky to Glière and thence to the Ukrainians and Armenians, through Vitols to the Latvians. The line also passes directly to most of the émigré Russians as well, above all, of course, to Stravinsky.

By coincidence the three major symphonist-pedagogue contemporaries of Myaskovsky each composed five symphonies, each arriving at No. 4 in the early thirties when topical subject-matter was much in demand. **Maximilian Steinberg**'s 'Turksib' (1933) celebrated the opening of the Turkestan-Siberian railway, **Vissarion Shebalin**'s 'Perekop' (1935, revised 1961) commemorated a decisive 1920 defeat of the White Army in the Civil War, and **Vladimir Shcherbachev**'s 'Izhorsk' (1932–5) took its title from a factory whose workers joined in the 1905 revolutionary upheavals. None of these managed to find the magic formula for reconciling the propaganda element (generally in the musical incarnation of the heroic Mass Song) with their own established symphonic style (square and predictable in Steinberg's case, highly chromatic, near-expressionist in Shebalin's, and structurally experimental in Shcherbachev's – his Third Symphony of 1926–31 is one of the few Soviet symphonies pointing the way ahead to Shostakovich's Fourth).

Much the same problems faced the various oratorios-cum-symphonies – notably Shcherbachev's monumental apocalyptic Second of 1922–6 (incorporating verses by Blok), **Mikhail Gnesin**'s *Symphonic Monument* of 1925, Shebalin's un-numbered 'Lenin' Symphony of 1931 (revised 1959) for four soloists, chorus, reciter and orchestra – on a dreadful Mayakovsky poem whose musical setting at least has the grace to be totally uninspired – and **Yuri Shaporin**'s Symphony of 1933 with wordless chorus. And the same applies to the so-called song-symphonies which represented the

---

* The PERvyi SIMFonicheskii ANSambl (First Symphonic Ensemble) was conductor-less not only for ideological reasons – there was also a chronic shortage of competent conductors, see Fred Prieberg, *Musik in der Sowjetunion*, Cologne, 1965, p. 51.

† The first single-movement Russian symphony known to me is Vladimir Shcherbachev's First (1914), although Skryabin's orchestral poems are sometimes described as symphonies and are clearly the model for such works.

other significant attempt to give the Soviet symphony a relevance at once contemporary and proletarian, e.g. **Alexander Kastalsky**'s 'Agricultural Symphony' of 1923, **Klimenti Korchmarev**'s three vocal symphonies, 1923–35, and the young **Dmitri Kabalevsky**'s Third Symphony of 1933, known as the 'Lenin Requiem'. Nearer than any of these to a lasting success was **Lev Knipper** in his Third Symphony (the 'Far-Eastern', 1932) and especially his Fourth ('The Poem of the Komsomol Fighter', 1933, revised 1965). Both of these are somewhat rambling assemblages of Hindemithian neo-classical counterpoint, Tchaikovskian fate-themes, and mass songs. The partial saving grace of No. 4 is its smash-hit song 'Meadowland', an original composition which became one of the Red Army Ensemble's favourite showstoppers. But the song-symphony soon died out – Shostakovich's Fifth dealt it the *coup de grâce* in 1937. Knipper went on to complete twenty-one symphonies in all before his death in 1970. None of his later works hit the headlines, though they were occasionally given a ritual nod of disapproval for their supposed 'excessive individualism', a remarkable inversion of the truth.

The common factor in virtually all these now largely forgotten works, and a large number of Myaskovsky's too, is the absence of musical surprise. They may not always take the obvious structural path, but generally the presentation of themes is as unimaginative as the paragraphing is predictable. Of course surprise can come in many varied guises; it has to, if the opposite kind of tedium is not to ensue. But in this respect the first symphonies of **Sergei Prokofiev** (the 'Classical') and **Dimitri Shostakovich** (1924–25) are paragons. They are also marked out by wit, a sub-category of surprise and another rare commodity in Soviet or indeed any other category of twentieth-century symphonies.

Trying to imagine the kind of symphony Haydn might have written in the twentieth century, Prokofiev took a new broom to the cobwebbed corners of Russian late-Romanticism. There is hardly a trace of pathos – just a whiff of it in the plagal cadences of the slow movement – or of conflict (though given a degree of insistence the first movement development section could easily have been nudged that way). Structural initiatives are minimal, though the first and second movement recapitulations are rather subtly dovetailed. Instead the presentation of material is freshened up, textures aerated and all four movements infused with the spirit of the ballet. The slow-polonaise(!) second movement crosses the first interlude of Glazunov's *Raymonda* with Ponchielli's 'Dance of the Hours', and the second subject in the first movement (on points, as it were) is harmonised in the manner of the Ballerina and Moor's Waltz from the third tableau of Stravinsky's *Petrushka*. The famous gavotte third movement is a *locus classicus* for Prokofiev's harmonic dislocations, whereby harmony side-slips only to be picked up by the scruff of the neck and put back on the right track. Writ large, the same technique will enable Prokofiev to open up broad harmonic vistas in his symphonic masterpieces of the 1940s.

The very first note of Shostakovich's First, scored for muted trumpet, catches the ear. Imagine a slight crescendo on it and continue into the second bar and you are immediately in the world of *Petrushka*. In fact no single piece of music had a greater influence on Shostakovich than Stravinsky's puppet-ballet; its character-archetypes can be found all over this symphony and its musical implications were to be explored in many later works. The remarkable introduction is a nervy search for a home key and a viable main theme (a bemused Glazunov tried to 'correct' the 18-year-old student's harmonies at the end of the first phrase). The structure thereafter is fuelled by transformation of themes – for example, the peg-leg waltz of the second subject is rhythmically ironed out into aggressive quavers in the development, and the funereal oboe theme in the slow movement proves equally poignant as a Finale episode in its strict inversion on the solo violin (Ex. 2). This kind of thematic transformation is the powerhouse for most of Shostakovich's symphonies, large-scale tonality tending to be a passive rather than generative force. The slow movement of the First Symphony seems to remind many writers of Tchaikovsky or Skryabin, but it is even more clearly akin to Bruckner and Mahler (compare the first theme with the main idea of the *Adagio* of Mahler's Tenth; perhaps coincidentally the latter was first published and performed only months before Shostakovich began work on this movement). If Shostakovich's First Symphony is more discomfiting and psychologically intriguing than Prokofiev's, that is largely because of the duality between the Stravinskian and Mahlerian tones. And it is noteworthy that these overriding influences come from the two supreme masters of irony in music.

Ex. 2. Shostakovich: Symphony No. 1

Perhaps the most important historical consideration in these two symphonic debuts is that they held out the prospect of stylistic renewal of the symphony by means of images from 'low art' (the dance-hall, theatre-revue, silent film comedy), comparable to Vsevolod Meyerhold's renewal of theatre through the *commedia dell'arte*, circus and folk traditions. The risk was of throwing out the symphonic baby with the academic bathwater, and it is noteworthy that neither work founded a tradition, although the popular sub-genre of the 'Youth' symphony may owe something to Prokofiev's example – e.g. **Andrei Pashchenko** No. 4 (1938, revised 1956), **Artur Kapp** No. 4 (1949), **Otar Taktakishvili** No. 1 (1949), **Rauf Gadzhiev** No. 1 (1953), **Nikolai Rakov** No. 2 (1957), and **Vadim Salmanov** 'Children's' (1962). Nor did Prokofiev and Shostakovich's achievements protect them from acute problems with their next efforts at symphonic composition. Their Second Symphonies both displayed an upsurge of enthusiastic modernism; this was followed by a partial *rapprochement* with traditional values in their Third and Fourth and finally the 'classic' statements of their Fifth Symphonies. The numerical correspondence is again entirely coincidental, but the general trend is not – it reflects a widespread, indeed international, tendency in music of the time.

The environment was rather different in each case, of course. In 1920 Prokofiev had settled in Paris after 18 months in the USA. In the home of Cocteau and *Les Six* he found a seething artistic ferment whose only real focus was the idea of anti-Romanticism. This suited that part of Prokofiev's personality which had always been drawn to motor rhythms and innovation – as early as his 'Scythian Suite' of 1915 he had set out to beat Stravinsky's *The Rite of Spring* at its own game. In 1924 Prokofiev embarked on a symphony 'made of iron and steel'; the result, as he later admitted, proved incomprehensible not just to the audience but to himself. Admittedly, a carefully balanced performance of the Second Symphony can probably give a more coherent impression than any audience would have received in the twenties; much of the writing is tremendously exciting, and the more restrained second movement variations have many attractive moments. It is a vastly more talented score than, say, the First Symphony of a fellow émigré to Paris, **Alexander Tcherepnin**, (1927 – with a Scherzo for percussion alone). Indeed, Prokofiev thought highly enough of the work to consider revising it towards the end of his life. But the piled-high complexities and sporty exhibitionism found a more appropriate outlet in his piano concertos, and in the absence of stage action or a solo combatant the Second Symphony feels more like a manifesto than a work of art. It is difficult to avoid the consensus verdict that its studied complications offer diminishing returns.

Russia had exported a sizeable portion of its avant-garde artistic community at the time of the Revolution – the painter-composer **Efim Golyshev**, for instance, had joined a Berlin Dadaist group, where he presented his 'Anti-symphony (Musical circular-guillotine)' in three parts in 1919. But St Petersburg (from 1914 Petrograd, from 1921–91 Leningrad) retained powerful modernist factions; in the visual arts Constructivism flourished and literature boasted a self-declared Formalist movement. The most internationally famous example of the constructivist ethic in music was Alexander Mosolov's 'Iron Foundry' of 1927, a 'symphonic episode' based technically on Honegger's 'Pacific 231' and the 'Procession of the Sage' from *The Rite of Spring* and celebrating the notion of the heroism of modern industry. This four-minute orchestral toccata seems to encapsulate most of what the first movement of Prokofiev's Second was trying to say. By this time noise orchestras had been founded and silent films were sometimes accompanied with percussion ensembles; the post-Skryabinist Pashchenko, who produced sixteen symphonies between 1915 and 1972, composed a 'Symphonic Mystery' in 1923 including a part for Leo Termen's recently invented Theremin (the electronic instrument later responsible for the 'headache' music of many a Hollywood score). Perhaps most ambitious of all, a 'Symphony of Horns' by the Taneyev pupil **Arseni Avraamov** was performed in Baku on 7 November 1922 by an 'orchestra' of factory whistles, the Caspian fleet, artillery, seaplanes and machine guns, coordinated by a conductor waving flags from the rooftops. Regrettably, no score or recording survives.*

So the factory whistle in F sharp (optionally scored for brass) which interrupts the anarchic progress of Shostakovich's Second Symphony (1927) is not entirely without precedent. And there is a model for this work's opening carpet of string sound, and for the thirteen-part massed polyphony of the central section, in Berg's *Wozzeck*, which Shostakovich heard in Leningrad only weeks before embarking on the composition.†
As with a number of his 'post-graduate' works these sections turn out to be more carefully composed than the innocent ear might suspect. As the words of the concluding rabble-rousing chorus confirm, the early phases are intended to represent pre-revolutionary chaos (the thirteen-part episode has been plausibly related to the babble of impassioned street-corner orations) which is destined to yield to the new order. Shostakovich's Second has been called 'an ACM Symphony with an RAPM finale', and its stylistic mix drew adverse comment almost immediately. It satisfied neither as propaganda (the work had been a commission for the Tenth Anniversary of the October Revolution) nor as music – a familiar story. It is a much stronger work than its present standing suggests, however; and however rapidly it was composed it is difficult to accept that it was tossed off with little or no commitment to the revolutionary subject-matter.

Shostakovich's Third Symphony of 1929 has a similar groundplan to the Second and culminates in a tub-thumping chorus in celebration of the First of May. It teems with strong thematic ideas, around forty of them at a conservative estimate, in a single twenty-seven-minute movement – no wonder so many of Shostakovich's fellow-composers were jealous of his talent. Ultimately, however, it leaves less to chew on than the Second Symphony. Six years later, wearying of a routine of film scores and incidental

* Prieberg, op. cit., p. 42, p. 70 and Eckart Kröplin, *Frühe sowjetische Oper*, Berlin, 1985, p. 39.
† See Detlef Gojowy, *Neue sowjetische Musik der 20er Jahre*, Laaber, 1980, pp. 420–41 for a useful calendar of performances in the Soviet Union 1922–1930.

music for plays, but nonetheless prepared to let their manner infiltrate his concert works, Shostakovich was ready to embark on his Fourth Symphony. He announced that it would be his 'symphonic credo'.

Prokofiev meanwhile had been developing an even closer relationship between stage and symphonic music. His Third Symphony of 1928 is based on material from his lurid opera *The Fiery Angel*, the story of a woman's obsession with an angelic vision which she seeks to discover in human form; and his Fourth of 1930 uses material from *The Prodigal Son*, the last ballet mounted by the Ballets Russes before the death of Diaghilev and the disbandment of the company. In both instances Prokofiev was able to take over long passages that were already 'symphonic' in the loose sense of being musically self-sufficient. Another encouraging factor was the realization that there was some excellent music here which was destined only rarely to be heard in the opera house or theatre.

The limited success of both works, in terms both of audience popularity and critical approval, comes down to the stricter sense of the word 'symphonic'. Themes and paragraphs are almost uniformly strong, and their disposition makes a not implausible simulacrum of symphonic proportion. But for all their striking impact they tend to remain on separate terraces, sometimes quite artfully bridged, but not transformed into something more than the sum of their parts. To a certain extent this is a problem endemic in the entire Russian symphonic tradition, and it is arguably not the worst drawback in the world – there are plenty more 'symphonically' conceived symphonies which are nevertheless stillborn. Nor did Prokofiev's Fifth Symphony (1944) entirely dispose of the problem by de-emphasizing the balletic and highlighting the lyrical. Nevertheless the Fifth and Sixth are conceived as symphonies from the roots up in a way that the Third and Fourth are not – and it shows. The revision of No. 4 in 1947 broadens the whole design, in particular by the addition of a more or less heroic, Soviet-*nobilmente* vein to the first movement. It reflects something of the greater symphonic wisdom achieved in the Sixth Symphony (completed earlier the same year), but it cannot turn an attractive work into a masterpiece. Nevertheless there are marvellous things in the inner movements of Nos. 3 and 4. The Scherzo of No. 3, using material from the sorcery episode in Act Two of *The Fiery Angel*, is an astonishing feat of virtuoso aural imagination – wholly unsystematic so far as analysts have been able to discover, and yet absolutely precise in its calculation of effect (how precise may perhaps be judged from Andrei Eshpai's only half-successful attempt to emulate it in his Second Symphony of 1962). At the other extreme the quasi-gavotte slow movement of No. 4, from the scene of the seductive Maiden's Dance, is one of Prokofiev's most simple and charming inspirations, an example of the restraint which he himself came increasingly to value and which would help smooth his path after his final return to the USSR (at the beginning of 1936, after many shorter visits).

By 1935 the Soviet Union's bitter artistic feuds had been settled, albeit forcibly. The Party Resolution of 23 April 1932, 'On the Reconstruction of Literary and Artistic Organizations', dissolved all proletarian arts associations, including RAPM, and led to the founding of the Union of Soviet Composers (from 1957 the Union of Composers of the USSR).* Many musicians were relieved to see the back of militant proletarianism as represented by RAPM, which had been in the ascendant since 1929, and the establishment of a more orderly infrastructure was broadly welcomed. In 1934 official fees of 6–8,000 rubles were set for 'accepted' symphonies and in 1935 the newspaper *Komsomolskaya Pravda* instituted a competition for the best new symphony.† The horrors of collectivization and the first purges were stark enough, but it was not until the *Lady Macbeth* affair of 1936 that the full implications of the new authoritarianism in the arts were realized.

At the February 1935 conference on Soviet Symphonism the question of 'where we go from here' was hotly debated. Those who sought to reconcile history and ideology drew attention to Paul Bekker's booklet *Die Sinfonie von Beethoven bis Mahler* (published 1918 and translated into Russian, with a preface by the doyen of Soviet musicologists, Boris Asafyev, in 1926). Bekker's main aim was to show that the principal post-Beethovenian symphonic trends (mid-German, Austrian, and cosmopolitan-Lisztian) had been re-synthesized by Mahler, who in the process had arrived at a new idealism. But Soviet commentators were more interested in Bekker's emphasis on the symphony's essential 'community-forming' [*gemeinschaftsbildend*] power, supposedly cultivated by Beethoven under the influence of French Revolutionary ideals. The similar views of Romain Rolland were also widely cited.

How that power was to be reinstated in the twentieth-century symphony was a matter for dissension, though it was generally agreed that the 'urbanism' of Prokofiev's Paris symphonies or of the neo-classical Stravinsky would have no part to play. (Interesting that 'urbanism' should have been preferred to the more abstract 'modernism'; the term was variously used by Soviet commentators as a straightforward pejorative or as a more or less neutral description.) Still, the community-forming ideal was one that virtually all speakers at the 1935 conference espoused and that a number of symphonists had already tried to address, with mixed success as noted above. Only the 'graduation-piece' debut, in which the fledgling composer could be said to be trying his wings, was more or less exempt from the demand for social relevance – witness the First Symphonies of Kabalevsky (1932 – a remarkably ambitious and unstable work by his later standards), **Aram Khachaturian** (1934, revised 1960 – an attractive score, characteristically full of eastern promise) and **Tikhon Khrennikov** (1935 – dedicated to Shostakovich, and by no means a negligible work).

---

* See Boris Schwarz, *Music and musical life in Soviet Russia, 1917–1981*, Bloomington, 1983, p. 111ff.
† Prieberg, op. cit., p. 130, p. 143.

In some ways the 1935 conference perpetuated the old battle lines of the mid-nineteenth-century Westernizers and Slavophiles – those who thought that Russia had better learn from the West, and those who thought it should look to its own traditions, especially to folk music, and come up with an invigorating counterblast to Western decadence. Many spoke of the terminal decline of the symphony in the West and of the opportunity for Soviet composers to pick up the torch. Their arguments rested probably more on a selective reading of German musical journals than on a proper awareness of the musical scene (Elgar, Honegger, Roy Harris and Walton were referred to in passing; Sibelius and Nielsen seem to have been virtually unknown). But it is worth bearing in mind that Elgar, Sibelius and Nielsen had indeed experienced very real difficulties in coming to terms with the creative climate of the twenties. The Soviet analysis of the symphonic crisis was an exaggeration but not a total falsification, just as the demand for a new simplicity was only a slight distortion of an international trend, already voiced and put into practice by Bartók, Copland, Hindemith, Prokofiev, Berg, even to a degree by Schoenberg. The main distinguishing factor was the Soviets' determination to harness such programmes to ideological propaganda, plus their willingness to enforce them, ruthlessly if necessary. Similarly the call for symphonies reflecting the heroic spirit of the times may seem naïve, even cynical, and it was almost certainly pronounced with half an eye on Maxim Gorky's prescriptions for the Writers' Union the previous year; but it could also claim roots in nineteenth-century Russian attitudes to the symphony, which always leaned towards the programmatic and therefore always had major problems with the symphonies of Brahms. Basil Lam's view on the *Eroica*: 'the greatest human being would be unworthy of the "Eroica" . . . as we shall be if we let our experience of it be distorted by reflections on the French revolution . . . or anything apart from the miraculous structure in sound',* is one to which virtually no pre-Soviet Russian musician would have subscribed, and to which no Soviet musician in the 1930s would have dared subscribe.

It was, as Asafyev later put it, a period of 'intonational crisis' (a euphemism, but an intelligent one).† Shostakovich's music, with its highly developed sense of irony, backed up by his strong affinity with Mahler and Stravinsky, was particularly well equipped to survive it. If Shostakovich had already struck out for his own brand of new simplicity (in the Cello Sonata of 1934) he had done so in such an ambivalent way that it could just as easily be called anti-heroic as heroic. His downfall came with *Pravda's* notorious denunciation of *The Lady Macbeth of Mtsensk* as 'Muddle instead of Music' (28 January 1936). Pronounced in the middle of Stalin's Great Terror, which disposed of an estimated ten million of the country's political and

---

* In Robert Simpson (ed.), *The Symphony 1: Haydn to Dvořák*, London, 1966, pp. 120–1.
† Orlov, op. cit., p. 9.

intellectual élite, this was a terrible warning to all serious Soviet composers and a tremendous encouragement to a host of jealous third-raters.

For a brief period Shostakovich seriously contemplated suicide. Nevertheless he brought his Fourth Symphony to a conclusion by April of the same year, although it was withdrawn in rehearsal and not performed until 1961. This colossal three-movement work has long had the reputation for a sprawling lack of discipline. As regards the first movement, an expanded sonata form fuelled by prodigious thematic transformations, this is totally unfounded; while the Finale, a funeral march sandwiching an extended brutal Scherzo and a modern dance-suite, invites explanation as a reflection of the times, using quasi-theatrical means. For all its far-flung contrasts Shostakovich's Fourth Symphony is a more psychologically focused work than his Third, and it throws back the conservatives' recipe for symphonism in their faces. For it is Shostakovich who truly 'hands down to future generations memorials of our great unparalleled epoch'.*

It is worth observing that however wide of the mark former Western evaluations now appear to be, most Soviet musicological and critical commentary from 1936 until about 1962 is worthless from the point of view of critical or analytical assessment. Soviet critics were forced to take on a special function, mediating not between composer and audience as in the West, but between composer and officialdom. In this sense their contributions might be far from worthless – they could suggest to the composer ways of courting official approval, and they could interpret artistic productions in ways which, however intrinsically absurd, might make that approval more readily forthcoming. But the restrictions on honest value judgment, and above all the compulsory humanist-hermeneutic tone and insulation from Western thought, led to a catastrophic decline in journalistic and scholarly standards, from which Russian writers have only recently begun to recover. At the time, of course, survival was a more immediate priority than intellectual integrity.

Composers also adopted a self-preservatory language. Shostakovich described his Fifth Symphony (1937), the work which ensured his temporary rehabilitation, as 'a Soviet artist's practical creative reply to just criticism'. Or rather he attributed the description to an anonymous reviewer – so anonymous in fact that the original review has never been identified and in all probability never existed.† And he 'accepted' novelist Alexei Tolstoy's assessment of the basic idea of the work as 'The growth of a personality' – doubtless aware that this was one of those intelligent-sounding, vague phrases which could conveniently be read in contradictory ways.

Whatever the intentions underlying it, the Fifth was a famous success, at a stroke transforming Shostakovich's standing, and giving Party officials

---

* Yuri Ogolevtsev in *Sovetskaya muzyka*, 1935, part 6, p. 39.
† 'Moi tvorcheskii otvet' [My creative answer], in *Vechernyaya Moskva*, 25 January 1938, p. 3. German translation in Kröplin, op. cit., pp. 558–60.

the chance to crow at the wondrous effects of their wise counsel. It also spared him the indignity of having to celebrate the twentieth anniversary of the Revolution (in which capacity Prokofiev's *Cantata* signally failed to please).

No doubt the move towards a more balanced, traditional symphonic layout was accelerated by the pressure of events. But the change of orientation between the Fourth and the Fifth Symphonies is not quite so drastic as it might first appear. Many characteristics of the Fourth's 'dramaturgy' (a favourite term in Soviet musicology) are slightly modified and re-allocated among the movements of the Fifth. A dramatic opening gesture is retained, but the stamping first group of the Fourth is transplanted to the Finale of the Fifth, where it takes on a heroic, summatory aspect; the restrained narrative of the transitional section in the earlier work now characterizes the first subject area, and the lyrical second group is retained and shorn of its bizarre elements; the development section is now made more unidirectional, driving towards a single crisis point and with transformations of a now predominantly lyrical exposition taking on the character of violation; this tumbles into a recapitulation on similarly compressed lines to those of No. 4. The Scherzo of No. 5, placed second, draws off the Scherzo and divertimento music from the Finale of No. 4; the slow movement forms a new emotional lyrical core (owing much to the experience of the Cello Sonata); and the Finale, as mentioned, redirects the expository material of the first movement of No. 4, with the funereal tone now modified as a reflective central episode.

Soviet scholars, following Bekker, conceptualize the overall dramaturgy of the symphonic genre as unfolding between archetypes of 'action, meditation, play and the communal'.* This perhaps helps to clarify the particular contribution of Shostakovich's Fifth in shifting something of the meditative element to the first movement, placing the Scherzo second so as to space the first movement from the more extensive meditation of the slow movement, and increasing the Scherzo's threatening aspect whilst transferring some of its playfulness to the Finale. This is a useful template by which to measure not only Shostakovich's later modifications of the four-movement plan but also the uniqueness of Prokofiev's later symphonies.

It does not solve the classic problem case of the Finale of Shostakovich's Fifth, however. Regarded by many, both in Russia and the West, as a distinctly hollow victory, it is claimed in Shostakovich's disputed memoirs to be calculatedly so: 'It's as if someone were beating you with a stick and saying, "Your business is rejoicing, your business is rejoicing" and you rise, shakily, and go marching off muttering, "Our business is rejoicing, our business is rejoicing."'† The controversy surrounding these memoirs continues. Solomon Volkov apparently reconstructed them from shorthand

---

* Mark Aranovsky, *Simfonicheskie iskaniya*, Leningrad, 1979, pp. 14–39.
† Solomon Volkov, *Testimony: the memoirs of Shostakovich*, London, 1979, p. 140.

notes taken during conversations during the last decade of the composer's life, incorporating a number of passages from previously published articles, before publishing them on his emigration to the West. Corroboration of a general nature from émigré Russians who knew Shostakovich is extensive; but in Russia, even under *glasnost*, rejection continues to be voiced – Boris Tishchenko, noted by Volkov in a footnote as 'Shostakovich's favourite student', continues to describe the book as a forgery,* and both he and the composer's son Maxim consider parts of the book to be based on rumour rather than actual conversations.

Accurate or not in its details, *Testimony* certainly rings true in its general thesis of human art created under the most appalling human conditions, and as such it is accepted by practically all who knew Shostakovich. It is a document no-one can afford either to ignore or to take at face value. The old view of Shostakovich as a good communist who tried seriously but with limited artistic success to fulfil the dictates of Socialist Realism, has taken such a battering that it is no longer recognizable as a serious proposition. Even before *Testimony* Russian commentators felt the need to address the question of Shostakovich's ambivalence, coming up with another intelligent evasion in the 'Hamlet figure' (the Fifth has been widely known in the Soviet Union as his 'Hamlet Symphony').

The argument remains that if music needs this kind of explanation it is somehow deficient. The counter-argument is that it is only dunderheads, arrogant aesthetes, or blinkered adherents to discredited ideologies who have ever needed it – open-eared and open-minded listeners got the message long ago. But Shostakovich's rôle as chronicler of his time should be borne in mind when it comes to the unusual features of the succeeding symphonies. The Sixth (1939), with its profound lamenting *Largo* followed by a hard-driven scherzo and a circus-galop Finale, does not 'add up' as a traditional symphonic scheme; but it does if heard in the context of a country enduring horrific suffering but forced to pretend that 'Life is getting more enjoyable'. The 'invasion' episode of the first movement of the Seventh (the 'Leningrad', 1941) has been repeatedly cited as a colossal lapse of artistic judgement – yet what more potent image of naked totalitarian evil is there than this instance of the trivial elevated to the cataclysmic? The Finale of the Eighth (1943) is often thought of as something of an anti-climax, and this is not a claim that can be lightly waved aside, not even by the ingenious argument that sees the Finale as a restoration of artistic balance through bitter irony, after artistry has been all but overwhelmed by the agonies depicted in the previous movements.† But a consideration of what happens to this Finale's frivolity on the way may supply one part of the answer – for Shostakovich, looking to the future may be as bleak

* Ibid., p. 226. For Tishchenko's remarks on Volkov see *Music in the USSR*, July/September, 1989, p. 35.
† Ian MacDonald, *The new Shostakovich*, London, 1990, 171–2.

a scenario as brooding on the past. How the Ninth Symphony with all its sarcasm and terror could ever have been described as light-hearted (or still worse, played that way) is beyond comprehension, certainly to anyone who has heard performances conducted by Kirill Kondrashin or Gennadi Rozhdestvensky. Even the Finale of the Tenth, which most commentators are happy to take straight, has psychological depths beneath its veneer of boisterousness.*

Seen in this light Shostakovich turned the tables not just on officialdom, but also on the 'finale problem' and on Western critics of his supposedly old-fashioned style. An apparently joyful conclusion, especially if the smile is artificially prolonged into a grimace, can be an even more horrific outcome to a tragic symphony than an overtly tragic one, at the same time as being irreproachable for the purposes of official acceptability and more 'modern' in its psychological complexity than any stylistically consistent ending, however 'advanced' the style.

In all this Shostakovich was paradoxically helped by the appalling circumstances of wartime, not least because tragic, violent, even modernistic music, could now be 'explained away' as depicting the external aggressor (and also for the simple reason that the energies of officialdom were otherwise engaged). Again it is worth stressing the supreme irony, that all Shostakovich's symphonies from Nos. 2 to 9 are faithful to the letter of Socialist Realism, and yet in 1948, when Stalin took the reins again through his henchman Zhdanov, they could be castigated for 'formalism' – the last thing they should have been accused of.

Not that all the special qualities of these symphonies need to be understood in this way. The sheer compositional resourcefulness underpinning the epic first movement structures is profoundly impressive. And Shostakovich wrestled mightily with the problem of how to *absorb* sustained tragic expression. In the first movements of Symphonies 7 and 8 he does so by means of mournful woodwind recitatives. In the latter case this transforms the function of the first subject recapitulation and thereby side-steps another problem area for the late-Romantic symphony (the Tenth, with its subtler tonal processes, could be said to solve the problem rather than merely side-stepping it). The Eighth also has to absorb the shock of two successive violent scherzos, which it does by means of a passacaglia slow movement – an ideal choice of genre given its associations of lamenting and obsessiveness, and the imposition of strict discipline on limitless grief. Shostakovich's first passacaglia, in *The Lady Macbeth of Mtsensk District*, performs much the same tragedy-absorbing function, and with his enforced turn away from the musical stage, opera's loss was clearly the symphony's gain. The influence of film music should also be borne in mind. The first of Shostakovich's epic mourning scenes may be found towards the end of his score for

---

* As I have tried to explain in *The Breath of the Symphonist: Shostakovich's Tenth*, London, 1988.

Kozintsev and Trauberg's *New Babylon* (1929), and Prokofiev's *Alexander Nevsky* (1939) supplied a compelling film version of the embattled scherzo followed by immeasurable sorrow ('The battle on the ice' and 'The field of the dead').

The years 1936–53 were not vintage ones for the second division of Soviet symphonists. Old wine in old bottles was the norm. Shebalin was largely preoccupied with pedagogic duties – he was a professor of composition from 1935 and Director of the Moscow Conservatoire from 1942 until 1948 when the Zhdanov 'formalist' condemnations sucked him into their wake – his Fifth and last symphony was delayed until the more favourable climate of 1962; it is dedicated to, and modelled on, his teacher Myaskovsky. Shcherbachev's Fifth (1942–8, revised 1950) backtracks smartly from his relatively adventurous pre-war style – like Rakov's First (1940, revised 1958) it contains little that would have surprised Borodin or Kalinnikov. It was still not conservative enough to win official approval, but the Scherzo did have a demonstrable influence on the corresponding movement of Shostakovich's Tenth. Steinberg's Fifth (1942) takes the cultivation of folk culture to considerable lengths; subtitled 'Rhapsody on Uzbek themes' it includes music for Uzbek instruments and is structured as a narrative on more or less the entire known history of Uzbekistan. Khachaturian's Second (1943), subtitled 'The Bell', is a massive wartime epic, and its direct, straightforward, and extremely loud manner serves to highlight the greater emotional depth and ambivalence of Shostakovich; his Third of 1947, a 'Symphony-Poem' with obbligato organ and 15 trumpets, proved yet another failure to celebrate the October Revolution in acceptable fashion. Myaskovsky continued on fairly predictable lines, producing a topical symphony (No. 16 of 1933–4, 'The Aviators', based on the ill-fated voyage of the airliner *Maxim Gorky*), a cheerful one for military band (No. 19 of 1939), one supposedly reflecting wartime experiences (No. 22 of 1941), ones based on folk material (No. 18 of 1937, No. 23 of 1941 on Kabardinian tunes, No. 26 of 1948 on Russian themes), a stormy and rather impressive one (No. 24 of 1943) and a quiet and less impressive one (No. 25 of 1946). He finally bowed out with the characteristically wistful No. 27 (1949–50). His greatest success in these years came with his shortest and arguably best-proportioned symphony, the single-movement 'Symphony-fantasia' No. 21 (1940). This was a commission from Chicago, where his earlier symphonies, in particular No. 6, had enjoyed considerable success; there is a strikingly mid-Atlantic, even Waltonian tone to No. 21 – perhaps an indication of the milder side of Hindemith entering the international vernacular.

Almost alone among the minor figures, **Gavriil Popov**, pupil of Shcherbachev and Steinberg, managed to write individual and craftsmanly symphonies, even if they were subtitled 'Motherland' (No. 2, 1943) or programmatically related to the Spanish Civil War (No. 3 for strings, 1946). Popov's jazzy Chamber Symphony of 1927 is a marvellously inventive piece (originally and more properly called Septet), and his five-movement Fifth Symphony (1969) is another highly individual work, almost unique among Soviet symphonies in ending with a slow movement. At least one significant new talent emerged in the Polish-born **Moshei** [since 1985 Mieczyslaw] **Vainberg**. The eight out of twenty-two symphonies I have managed to find (dating from 1941 to 1988) suggest a steady flow of expressive, inventive and expertly controlled music, much indebted to, but never wholly overshadowed by Shostakovich. Vainberg's Second Symphony of 1946, like Popov's Third of the same year, is for strings alone, a medium possibly suggested by Honegger's Second of 1941. Honegger was one of the few Western symphonists whose work was known and respected in Russia at the time, for his ethical stance as much as his musical qualities. The string symphony was to prove one of the more fruitful sub-genres in the Soviet Union – **Ovchinnikov**'s Second is a strikingly impressive example.

More significant than any of these was the achievement of Prokofiev. After many short visits he had finally returned to settle in Moscow just before New Year 1936, no doubt in expectation of the kind of sympathetic treatment Gorky had received on his return from exile in 1931. For a while his newly restrained style was held up as an example of the benefits of a return to the homeland, but his attempts at official patriotism found little favour, and perhaps recalling the opprobrium that the Soviets had heaped on his 'Symphonic Song' in 1934, he waited until 1944 and the tragic conduciveness of wartime before returning to the field of the symphony.

Prokofiev's Fifth starts with a long-breathed tune, flexibly phrased, economically accompanied, in a warm B flat major whose heroic associations are confirmed by Kutuzov's music at the end of the opera *War and Peace* which he was working on at the time (Ex. 3). This was the tune, this indeed was the lyrical symphony, for which Soviet composers seemed to have been striving for twenty years. Prokofiev called it 'a symphony of the grandeur of the human spirit', and one is more disposed to take his comments seriously than Shostakovich's, partly because they are less obviously evasive, and partly because they seem to reflect the music more accurately. On the other hand due weight should be given to passages such as the menacing first-movement coda, the funereal middle section of the slow movement, and especially the

Ex. 3. Prokofiev: Symphony No. 5

very end of the work where the 'grandeur of the human spirit' is faced with almost its precise antithesis in a remarkable resurrection of 1920s machine music. Without such passages all the profuse lyrical invention would lack emotional perspective.

The Sixth Symphony (1947) brings the darker elements of the Fifth more consistently to the surface. With the First Violin Sonata this is the most painful music Prokofiev ever wrote, laconic in expression and yet operating over broad, inter-dependent paragraphs and concluding with one of the most anti-heroic bursts of E flat major imaginable. All three movements are based on sonata-form principles, and in all three every stage in the structure is deeply thought out and felt through. The cyclic return of the first movement's melancholic second subject just before the anti-heroic coda is shatteringly poignant in its simplicity. No Soviet symphony is more impressively controlled; few are as profound.

Shostakovich's reaction to the 1948 formalist condemnations was to feign total submission and produce pot-boilers such as 'The Song of the Forests' (in celebration of Stalin's ill-conceived re-afforestation plans) whilst keeping 'genuine' works (the First Violin Concerto, the Fifth String Quartet, the song-cycle *From Jewish Folk Poetry*) unperformed in a drawer. In this he followed the example of the poetess Anna Akhmatova. Prokofiev, rather in the manner of the satirist Mikhail Zoshchenko, was apparently more anxious to protest his innocence, and he continued to search for a single acceptable and more or less integrated style. In this attempt he was able to draw on the chaste lyrical vein that had served him well in such works as *Peter and the Wolf* and the Flute Sonata, and he did finally win approval with his last symphony, No. 7 of 1951–2. The melodious simplicity of this gentle work comes complete with echoes of Russian fairytale music and recurring references to the Astrologer's music from Rimsky-Korsakov's satirical opera *The Golden Cockerel*. There is a touching wistfulness and sense of wonder to this symphonic swansong.

Zhdanov died in the same year as his castigation of Soviet composers, but his directives were enthusiastically followed up by the newly appointed head of the Composers' Union, Khrennikov. Even before Stalin's death on 5 March 1953, the same day as Prokofiev's, some voices were raised against the harmful effects of 1948 – euphemistically summed up as the 'No conflict' theory – among whose symptoms were such tepid efforts as Julius Juzeliūnas 2 (1949), Lyatoshinsky 3 (1951, revised 1954), Knipper 13, Mshvelidze 3 and Pashchenko 5 (all 1952). Any artistic statement which drew too much attention to itself, however well-meaningly mediocre, could run into trouble, as **Vano Muradeli**, author of two feeble symphonies in 1938 and 1945 (revised 1946), had discovered when his no less feeble opera *The Great Friendship* inadvertently triggered off the 1948 condemnations.

How Prokofiev might have reacted to the post-Stalin Thaw we will never know. Shostakovich's first reaction came very quickly in the shape of the Tenth Symphony (1953). If *Testimony* is to be believed, the Tenth is 'about Stalin and the Stalin years' and includes a 'portrait of Stalin' in its Scherzo second movement.* In fact this movement, for all its concentrated fury, is not conspicuously more Stalinoid than, say, the Scherzos of the Eighth Symphony. But it is certainly a more rigorously disciplined composition, as is the whole symphony. The first movement is at once the most sophisticated of its kind in the inter-dependence of its paragraphs, and the smoothest, the least gestural, the most archetypal in its thematic material. This is one important symptom of the universality of the message, of its absorption to the highest levels of philosophical reflection. The third movement includes the first overt appearance in Shostakovich's music of his DSCH monogram (using German note-spellings), which cries out to be understood as the assertion of his personal creative survival (Ex. 4).

Ex. 4. Shostakovich: Symphony No. 10

(Es = German for E flat
H = German for B natural
Dmitrij SCHostakowitsch)

For all its mastery, Shostakovich's Tenth was as much the end of an era as it was a new beginning. The 1950s saw a number of admirable successors – such as the First Symphony by Aram **Khachaturian**'s nephew **Karen** (1955, revised 1963), Ovchinnikov 1 (1955–7), Popov 4 (1956), Vainberg 4 (1957, revised 1961), Rodion Shchedrin 1 (1957) and **Andrei Balanchivadze** 2 (1958). At the same time there were many less admirable ones – such as Kabalevsky 4 (1954), the long-winded Fourth of the Shostakovich pupil **Akhmed Dzhevdet Gadzhiev** (1955), and the excessively square Second of Rakov (1957). But Shostakovich himself, having brought the non-programmatic epic symphony to its apogee, turned his attention elsewhere. Before long a new generation of composers and audiences would be looking askance at the whole notion of epic symphonism.

Shostakovich's Eleventh (1957) incorporates some nine revolutionary songs and follows the events of the 1905 Winter Palace shootings (Bloody Sunday) with cinematographic closeness; yet it can just as easily 'read' as a covert commemoration of the Soviet invasion of Hungary in 1956. The Twelfth (1961) supposedly depicts the revolutionary events of 1917 without resorting to borrowed material; it is both Shostakovich's most 'objective'

* Volkov, op. cit., p. 107.

symphony and in many people's view (mine included) his least successful musically. The Thirteenth (1962), in effect a symphony-cantata for bass, male chorus and orchestra, marks Shostakovich's last major brush with authority. Yevtushenko's poems place the most transparent of masks on the unacceptable faces of Soviet society – anti-Semitism, institutional brutality, oppression of women, fear, and careerism. Shostakovich's five-movement scheme has vestiges of the traditional symphonic layout (with two inner slow movements), but the eleven movements of No. 14 (1969), on the subject of death, are a more radical departure. In principle this song-cycle is no more symphonic than the eleven movements of the *Suite on Verses of Michelangelo* (1974), which Shostakovich could well have called his Sixteenth Symphony. The Fourteenth is notable for its instrumentation, for soprano, bass, percussion and a small body of strings. It is also the main repository of Shostakovich's twelve-note themes – a strong hint at their symbolic association with the idea of death. Behind both works stands the example of Mahler's *Das Lied von der Erde*, and by this time there is also a strong reciprocal influence with the vocal cycles of that other ardent Mahlerian, Britten. When Shostakovich did return to the four-movement, non-vocal, non-programmatic symphony (No. 15, 1971) he did so in a decidedly non-epic way, hedging the central message around with cryptic quotations from Rossini and Wagner, and near self-quotations from almost all his own symphonies. His symphonic career ended in a hovering, watchful, thoroughly ambivalent, percussion-dominated A major.

Shostakovich's last three symphonies may be the finest of their kind, but they are not the first. As mentioned above, the forces involved in symphonies 13 and 14 are by no means without precedent; neither is the multi-movement layout of No. 14 (see Vainberg's ten-movement No. 8 with tenor solo and mixed choir, 1964). Indeed Shchedrin, the USSR's first 'licensed' modernist in music, had gone so far as to make his Second Symphony of 1962–65 (revised 1967) a sequence of 25 Preludes, albeit grouped into five larger movements. The fourth movement of Vainberg's Eighth also looks forward to the enigmatic tranquillity of the Finale of Shostakovich 15, and Vadim Salmanov's fine Fourth Symphony (1972–76) echoes that same mood; while in **Boris Chaikovsky**'s Second of 1967 there is even precedent for the incorporation of unexplained quotations – in this case a medley from Mozart's Clarinet Quintet, Beethoven's String Quartet Op. 18, No. 4, Bach's *St Matthew Passion*, and Schumann's piano piece 'Des Abends'. Chaikovsky's Second is a symphony of the highest calibre; his Third, 'Sevastopol', of 1980, is less consistently inventive.

In fact the quotation-symphony is part of a broader tendency in recent Soviet/Russian music to question not just the external layout of the symphony and its instrumental forces, but also its integrity of style. This trend can be followed through the three symphonies of the Estonian **Arvo Pärt** and the five of **Alfred Schnittke**. An early sign of the shake-up came with the selective adoption of twelve-note techniques, of which there were already signs in an 'underground' way in the years around 1960, stimulated by official visits such as Glenn Gould's in 1957, Stravinsky's in 1962, and Luigi Nono's in 1963. Pärt's First Symphony ('Polyphonic', 1963) is exceptionally thorough in its 12-note construction; indeed its polyphonic and twelve-note elements seem rather tautologous and fail to generate much tension. More typical, and more artistically successful, was the blend of tonal and twelve-note styles cultivated by the Shostakovich pupils **Kara Karaev** and **Boris Tishchenko** in their Third Symphonies (1965, 1966 respectively), by **Nikolai Peiko** in his Fifth (1969) and by Vainberg in his Tenth (1968). But perhaps only **Edison Denisov**, the most experienced and committed of the Soviet Union's twelve-note composers, has managed to find both poetry and structural integrity in the technique, as for instance in his Chamber Symphony of 1982, which also owes a good deal to Ligeti. The massive symphony of 1987, with its radiant D major conclusion, suggests that Denisov is joining the growing ranks of the new symbolist-spiritualists in Russia.

Pärt's Second (1966) is again twelve-note-based, and much of it continues to sound something like the aural equivalent of brutalist sixties architecture. It also typifies a rather sad trend among Soviet composers to swoop on 'advanced' Western techniques like children on a formerly out-of-bounds sweetshop. In this instance the orchestra is supplemented by a group of toy instruments, and various paraphernalia of the new Polish school are featured, such as tapping with the wood of the bow on seven different specified parts of the violin body. There is a certain appeal in this wild throwing-off of constraint, but little lasting reward for the listener. Similar doubts arise apropos the Fourth Symphony of Juzeliūnas (1974) and the Second and Fourth of Tishchenko (1965, 1974 – lasting fifty and a hundred minutes, respectively) whose massive dimensions nevertheless have an unmistakably communicative force behind them. Tishchenko's *rapprochement* with the style of his teacher has produced a more finished work in the Fifth Symphony (1976), the most impressive of a number of symphonies dedicated to Shostakovich's memory; but even this is surpassed, in my view, by his superb Second Violin Concerto of 1982. Perhaps the most significant feature of Pärt's Second is its apparently innocent quotation from Tchaikovsky's *Album from the Young*, which is then vomited back in disgust by the full orchestra – like a hand grenade thrown into a children's party. Here is Schnittke's 'polystylism' in embryo. In his most recent symphony, the Third of 1971, Pärt turned away from serialism and avant-garde trappings in the direction of archaism and ascetic spirituality, the qualities which have marked his works since his emigration to Berlin in 1980 and which have helped make him something of a cult figure.

Given the proximity of the Baltic states to Poland it might be expected that the more radical Western developments would take root there. On the other hand these countries have also been home to a new brand of conservatism, the post-Glazunov line having effectively dried up by

1962. From the cross-section of works I have been able to examine, the symphonies of the Estonian **Jaan Rääts** (eight up to 1985 – he is sometimes referred to as the Russian Hindemith) and the Latvians **Janis Ivanovs** (twenty-one up to 1983), **Adolfs Skulte** (nine up to 1986) and **Romualds Kalsons** (four up to 1981) are more competent than inspired. Rääts and Skulte both produced decidedly un-cosmic 'Cosmic' symphonies (No. 4 of 1959 and No. 3 of 1963, respectively) in celebration of the first Sputnik and of Yuri Gagarin's space-flight. These were among the last of the Socialist Realist topical symphonies, although there was still the Lenin centenary to be celebrated – Vainberg 11 (1969), Knipper 17 (1970).

The radical direction was most searchingly opened up by Schnittke. Of mixed German-Russian parentage but brought up in Moscow, Schnittke has long been heralded in the West as the natural successor to Shostakovich – partly for the simple reason that more of his music has been played outside Russia than that of his colleagues. The accolade is understandable, given that his polystylism (his own term) reflects strong interests in the work of Stravinsky and Mahler – Shostakovich's early idols. Schnittke's First Symphony (1969–72) is a massive sixty-five-minute work. It contains a whole lexicon of 'advanced' devices – the theatricality of American happenings, with the players entering one by one and leaving at the end only to enter again as if to restart the whole process, the aleatory (chance elements) of the Polish school, and the multiple quotations of Berio's *Sinfonia*, plus a cadenza for jazz violin. In general it would be difficult to over-estimate the importance of the Poles Penderecki and Lutosławski for recent Soviet/Russian music – they set examples of direct emotional impact in an essentially nonconformist, contemporary manner.

Other recent jazz-influenced Soviet symphonies include Eshpai 4 (1980), **Sergei Slonimsky** 2 (1978), and **Vyacheslav Artyomov**'s 'The Way to Olympus' (1984). Schnittke's Second and Fourth Symphonies (1979, 1984) invoke religious themes. The Second, entitled 'St Florian', is a homage to Bruckner and follows the sections of the Roman Catholic mass; the Fourth symbolizes multi-cultural unity in combining the chant styles of Orthodox, Catholic, Protestant and Jewish traditions. The Third Symphony of 1981 is a more focused essay in the manner of No. 1, with a tribute to the commissioning city of Leipzig in the form of musical monograms of thirty-four German composers (e.g. BACH, SCHumAnn). For all their frantic surface activity these are all essentially static works, from the Western technical point of view often startlingly naïve. But Russian musicians appreciated their boldness and responded eagerly to their professed spiritual content. The First Symphony, despite being exiled to Gorky for its première, excited enormous interest, not least because it seemed to look right into the abyss at the symphony's possible demise as a genre.

The Soviet Union has been the chief breeding-ground of the double-barrelled symphony – the symphony-poem (Khachaturian 3), symphony-fantasia (Myaskovsky 21), symphony-ballade (Myaskovsky 22), symphony-suite (Myaskovsky 23), symphony-rhapsody (Steinberg 5), symphony-dialogue (Ter-Osipov), symphony-ballet (Eshpai 4) and even the Miracle-symphony (Valeri Gavrilin's very Orffian 'Chimes' of 1982 for *a cappella* chorus and oboe). Most spectacularly double-barrelled of all is Schnittke's Concerto grosso No. 4/Symphony No. 5 of 1988. This starts in a neo-classical manner recalling Stravinsky's Violin Concerto and later on Prokofiev's Fourth Piano Concerto; it then moves through a pastiche-variation on Mahler's early unfinished Piano Quartet, towards a dramatic *Allegro* and a long-drawn *Adagio*, both strongly influenced by Mahler's mid-period symphonies. Thus it starts as a concerto grosso and finishes as a full-blown tragic symphony. This work represents a major advance on Schnittke's previous symphonies, both in conception and realisation; indeed it is probably one of the select few Soviet/Russian symphonies since Shostakovich to stand a real chance of survival.

If Schnittke is currently undisputed king of polystylism he still has some healthy competition for the title of high priest(ess) of the new spirituality. A strong contender here is **Sofia Gubaidulina**, whose 1986 symphony 'Stimmen-Verstummen' (Voices-silence) uses proportions based on the Golden Section and includes a cadenza for conductor (not entirely unaccompanied). Here a connection between spirituality and mathematical construction is proposed which recalls the Pole Panufnik (and which has an equally hit-or-miss experimental feel). Dark horses in the spiritualist stakes are **Avet Terteryan**, whose Fifth of 1978 evokes Armenian church ritual in a stark post-Pendereckian style, and **Galina Ustvolskaya**. The latter, another Shostakovich pupil, has evolved an extraordinarily hard-hitting, agonized style; her symphonies have been getting progressively shorter and more sparsely scored (the twelve-minute Fifth of 1990 is for oboe, trumpet, tuba, violin, and thick plywood cube played with wooden hammers).

Along with Ustvolskaya's Second Symphony of 1979 ('True, eternal bliss') I would single out Silvestrov's radiant and profoundly restful Fifth of 1980–82 as the best examples of the spiritual or contemplative trend in Soviet music. A little to one side of this are the symphonies of the Georgian **Giya Kancheli**. Since his semi-conventional First of 1967, Kancheli has produced a series of single-movement works, all slow-moving, lasting twenty to thirty minutes and built up in mosaic fashion from short, often violently opposed fragments. His Third Symphony (1973) is characteristic in opening with a wordless chant motif for solo tenor, the refrain of a ritual Georgian folk lament which registers as a kind of symbol of eternity (Ex. 5). This is immediately impacted into a Stravinskian pandiatonic cluster; indeed Kancheli's whole style, like that of the Mari-born Eshpai, shows the continuing capacity of Stravinsky's Russian ballets to inspire symphonic thought.

Ex. 5. Kancheli: Symphony No. 3

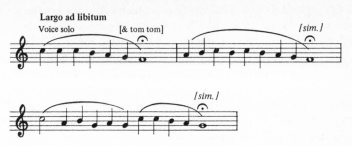

As everyone knows, Russia is currently embarked on one of its periodic attempts at self-reform, whose consequences for music remain to be seen. Some previously forbidden areas are undeniably starting to open up. The 1922 symphony by Nikolay Roslavets has been discovered and is in the process of reconstruction; publication of this and who knows how many other 'lost' symphonies may change our perspectives on the whole history of Soviet music.* Movements for 'catching up with the West' have been as strong as ever. The danger here, if recent history is anything to go by, is of latching on to 'advanced' Western developments at about the time Western composers admit they never really believed in them in the first place.

Remarkably, in April 1991 the seventy-seven-year-old Khrennikov was re-elected as head of the Composers' Union, the post he has held since 1948; but the extent of the Union's power has greatly diminished. At the time of writing (February 1992) those composers who apparently would have most to contribute to the symphonic tradition are living abroad on temporary visas. These include Kancheli, Gubaidulina, Shchedrin, Schnittke and Silvestrov, all in Germany, and Dmitri Smirnov and his wife Yelena Firsova in England. Many of the finest Russian performers and teachers preceded them and now hold posts in the United States, Holland or Germany. Chaos in the economy means that there is little sign of an improvement in the availability of musical scores for export – rather the reverse, although agreements with Western record companies have at least made a sprinkling of valuable recordings available.†

Parallels with the years following the October Revolution are unmistakable, except that now those Russians who remain report that the concert halls are empty and the porn cinemas full. Even in a best-case political and economic scenario, those composers who eventually return home may find that free speech and prosperity breed the kind of audience apathy their Western colleagues have had to live with for generations, and dwindling

* For instance, there are apparently six symphonies by Mosolov, variously dated in different Soviet works of reference, which I believe remain unpublished.
† I should like to thank Julia Wright of Boosey & Hawkes Ltd, London, for kindly obtaining a large number of scores from the USSR, and Robert Layton and Onno van Rijen for copies of some rare and valuable recordings.

state subsidies are unlikely ever again to support a massive industry of symphonic composition. The worst case scenario does not bear thinking about. On the other hand, which Western commentator writing in 1920 could have predicted the emergence of a Shostakovich?

As ever, Russian (or Commonwealth of Independent States?) composers will probably have to wrestle with the difficult balance between truthfulness to their own culture and acknowledgment of Western developments. It is a dilemma which many have been unable to resolve in the past, but which from time to time has produced profoundly stirring human documents. We can only hope that it will do so again.

Chronology

1900	Skryabin 1	
1901	Rakhmaninov 2, Skryabin 2	
1902	Glazunov 7, Maliszewski 1, Zolotarev 1 ('Symphony of Anger')	
1903	Gedike 1, Maliszewski 2	
1904	Skryabin 3 ('Divine Poem'), Vasilenko 1	
1905	Gedike 2	Winter Palace shootings (Bloody Sunday) Revolutionary flare-ups
1906	Steinberg 1	
1907	Glazunov 8, Ippolitov-Ivanov 1, Maliszewski 3, Stravinsky 1	
1908	Lemba 1, Myaskovsky 1 (rev. 21), (Skryabin *Poem of Ecstasy*), Balakirev 2	
1909	Grechaninov 2 ('Pastoral'), Steinberg 2, Glazunov 9 (inc.)	
1910	(Skryabin *Poem of Fire*)	
1911	Glière 3 ('Il'ya Muromets'), Myaskovsky 2	
1912	Kalafati 1	
1913	Shcherbachev 1, Vasilenko 2	
1914	Myaskovsky 3	
1915	Hartmann 1, Pashchenko 1	
1916		
1917	Prokofiev 1 ('Classical')	'FEBRUARY' AND 'OCTOBER' REVOLUTIONS
1918	Myaskovsky 4, 5	Civil War, first terror (anti-bourgeois)
1919	Golyshev 'Anti-Symphony', Lyatoshinsky 1 (rev. 67),	
1920		
1921	Revutsky 1 (rev. 57)	Lenin's New Economic Policy (NEP), Civil War ends, Famine kills five million Stalin General Secretary
1922	Avraamov ('Symphony of Horns'), Gedike 3, Mediņš 1, Myaskovsky 7,	

Pashchenko 2 ('Hymn to the sun', rev. 39), Roslavets 1

1923	Grechaninov 3, Kastal'sky ('Agricultural'), Korchmarev 1 ('Holland'), Lemba 2, Myaskovsky 6 (rev. 47)	Association of Contemporary Music (ACM) and Russian Association of Proletarian Musicians (RAPM) founded
1924	A. Kapp 1 ('Quasi una fantasia: in memoriam Beethoven'), Grechaninov 4 (dedicated to P. I. Tchaikovsky)	Lenin dies
1925	Evseev 1, Gnesin *Symphonic Monument*, Krein 1, Maliszewski 4, Myaskovsky 8, Pashchenko 3 ('Heroic'), Prokofiev 2, G. Rimsky-Korsakov 1, Shebalin 1, Shostakovich 1	
1926	Shcherbachev 2 ('Blok')	
1927	Abramsky 1, A. Cherepnin 1, Myaskovsky 9, 10 ('The Bronze Horseman'), Popov Septet Op. 2 (Chamber Symphony), Revutsky 2 (rev. 40 and 70), Shostakovich 2, Tikotsky 1	
1928	B. Aleksandrov 1, Litinsky 1, Mosolov 1, Prokofiev 3, Steinberg 3	FIRST FIVE-YEAR PLAN, collectivization
1929	Chulaki 1, Knipper 1, Maliszewski 5, Polovinkin 1, Revutsky 3 ('Little Cossack'), Shebalin 2 (rev. 59), Shekhter 1, Shostakovich 3, Zolotarev 2 (rev. 55)	Liquidation of Kulaks (three million?)
1930	B. Aleksandrov 2, Lur'ye 1 ('Sinfonia dialectica'), Prokofiev 4 (rev. 47), Zhelobinsky 1	ACM suppressed, Proletarian groups supreme
1931	Brusilovsky 1, Knipper 2, Korchmarev 2 ('October'), Polovinkin 2 (rev. 39), Shcherbachev 3, Shebalin ('Lenin', rev. 59), Veprik 1	Party purges begin
1932	Brusilovsky 2, Kabalevsky 1, Knipper 3 ('Far Eastern'), Myaskovsky 11, 12 ('Kholkhoz'), Mosolov 2, Polovinkin 3 ('Romantic'), Popov 1, Roslavets 2 ('Uzbek'), Zhelobinsky 2	Famine (five million?), Proletarian arts groups dissolved, Union of Soviet Composers founded
1933	Evseev 2, Golubev 1, Ivanovs 1, Kabalevsky 2, Knipper 4 ('Young Komsomol', rev. 65), Myaskovsky 13, 14, Pashchenko 3 ('Heroic'), Polovinkin 4, Račiūnas 1, Shaporin 1, Steinberg 4 ('Turksib')	SECOND FIVE-YEAR PLAN, Famine in Ukraine (seven million?) More collectivization (eight million?)
1934	Gladkovsky 1, Gol'dshtein 1, Kabalevsky 3 ('Lenin Requiem'), Khachaturian 1 (rev. 60), Kozlovsky 1 ('Choreographic'), Myaskovsky 15, 16 ('Aviators'), Shebalin 3, Tubin 1, Vasilenko 3 ('Italian', for balalaika-domra	Socialist Realism proclaimed at Writers' Congress, Great Terror begins

ensemble), 4 ('Arctic'), Zolotarev 3
('Chelyushinsky'), 4 ('Belorus')

1935   Ippolitov-Ivanov 2 ('Kardis'),   Conference on Symphonism
        Khrennikov 1, Knipper 5,   Stakhanovitism
        Korchmarev 3 ('People of Soviet
        Land'), Kozlovsky 2, Nadezhdin
        1, Shebalin 4 ('Perekop', rev. 61),
        Shcherbachev 4 ('Izhorsk')

. . . .

1936   Eller 1 ('Mixolydian'), Gol'dshtein 2,   *Pravda* ATTACK ON
        Grechaninov 5, Ivanovs 2, Knipper 6   SHOSTAKOVICH
        ('Red Cavalry'), Lyatoshinsky 2 (rev.
        40), Mokrousov 1 ('Anti-fascist'),
        Shirinsky 1, Shostakovich 4,
        Zolotarev 4

1937   Gladkovsky 2, Golubev 2, Ivanovs   Height of Terror
        3, Knipper 7 ('War'), Medinš 2,
        Myaskovsky 17, 18, Shostakovich 5,
        Sviridov 1, Tubin 2, Zhiganov 1

1938   Asafyev 1 ('In memoriam Lermontov'),   December: Terror abates
        2 ('From age of peasant uprisings'),
        Gurovi 1, Muradeli 1, Pashchenko
        4 ('Youth', rev. 56), Shirinsky 2,
        Veprik 2

1939   Lur'ye 2 ('Kormchaya'), Mosolov 3   Molotov-Ribbentrop pact. Hitler
        (?), Myaskovsky 19, Shostakovich 6,   and Stalin share out Poland
        Zhelobinsky 3

1940   Myaskovsky 20, 21, Polovinkin 5,   Baltic states annexed
        Rakov 1 (rev. 58), Sviridov (str.)

1941   Ivanovs 4, Medinš 3, Myaskovsky 22,   HITLER INVADES. Siege of
        23, Shostakovich 7 ('Leningrad'),   Leningrad
        Tikotsky 2 (rev. 44), Zeidman 1

1942   Asafyev 3 ('Homeland'), 4, 5 ('The
        Seasons'), Ashrafi 1, Golubev 3,
        E. Kapp 1, Khrennikov 2 (rev. 44),
        Mosolov 4, Polovinkin 6, Steinberg
        5 ('Uzbek'), Shtogarenko 1, Tubin 3,
        Vainberg 1 ('Red Army'), Zhelobinsky
        4, Zolotarev 5 ('1941')

1943   Bunin 1, Evseev 3, K. Karaev 1   Battle of Stalingrad 1,
        Khachaturian 2, Knipper 8,
        Mshvelidze 1, Mayaskovsky 24,
        Polovinkin 7, 8, Popov 2
        ('Homeland'), Shekhter 2,
        Shostakovich 8, Stepanyan 1,
        Tubin 4 (rev. 78), Zolotarev 6 ('My
        Motherland')

1944   Ashrafi 2, Balanchivadze 1,   Liberation of Leningrad
        Brusilovsky 3 ('Golden Steppe'),
        Dzegelenok 1, Gadzhibekov 1,
        A. D. Gadzhiev 1, Gol'dshtein 3,
        Hartmann 2, Knipper 9, Mshvelidze
        2, Polovinkin 9, Prokofiev 5,
        Zhelobinsky 5

1945 Bunin 2, Chulaki 2, Gladkovsky 3, Ivanovs 5, A. Kapp 2, Krein 2, Muradeli 2 (rev. 46), Peiko 1, Shekhter 3, Shostakovich 9, Stepanyan 2	Five million returning p-o-w's sent to labour camps
1946 Bogatyrev 1 (rev. 56), Evlakhov 1, Gadzhibekov 2, A. D. Gadzhiev 2, Gurovi 2, K. Karaev 2, Knipper 10 ('Scenes from Great Patriotic War'), Meitus 1 ('Turkmenian'), Myaskovsky 25, Peiko 2, Popov 3 (str.), Račiūnas 2, Shtogarenko 2, Tubin 5, Vainberg 2 (str.), Zhelobinsky 6	Zhdanov attacks writers and film-makers
1947 Amirov 1 (str., rev. 64 and 83), Bogatyrev 2, B. Chaikovsky 1, Eller 2, A. D. Gadzhiev 3, Golubev 4, A. Kapp 3, V. Kapp 1, Khachaturian 3 (Symphony-poem), Machavariani 1 (rev. 60), Mosolov 5 (?), Prokofiev 6, Shekhter 4, Vasilenko 5	Attempt to claim all inventions as Russian
1948 Juzeliūnas 1, Levitin 1 ('Youth', rev. 55), Myaskovsky 26, Shcherbachev 5 ('Russian', rev. 50), Tikotsky 3 (rev. 55)	ZHDANOV ATTACKS COMPOSERS
1949 Ivanovs 6, Juzeliūnas 2, A. Kapp 4 ('Youth'), Knipper 11, Popov 4, Sviridov 2 (incomplete), Taktakishvili 1 ('Youth'), Vainberg 3	
1950 Karetnikov 1, Knipper 12, Mosolov 6 (?), Myaskovsky 27, Račiūnas 3	
1951 A. Cherepnin 2, Lyatoshinsky 3 (rev. 54), Shekhter 5 (rev. 53)	
1952 Gol'dshtein 4, A. Kapp 5 ('For Peace'), Knipper 13 ('In memoriam Myaskovsky'), Mshvelidze 3, Pashchenko 5, Prokofiev 7, Salmanov 1, Tsintsadze 1	
1953 A. Cherepnin 3, R. Gadzhiev 1 ('Youth'), Hartmann 3, Ivanovs 7, Shostakovich 10, Stepanyan 3, Taktakishvili 2	Doctors' Plot, DEATH OF STALIN. Triumvirate, but then Khrushchev takes over from Beria. First thaw
1954 Kabalevsky 4, E. Kapp 2, Klyuzner 1, Knipper 14, Pashchenko 6, Skulte 1 ('For peace'), Tubin 6	First thaw ends
1955 Denisov (in C), A. D. Gadzhiev 4 ('Lenin'), Grinblats 1, Hartmann 4, V. Kapp 2, Karetnikov 2, K. Khachaturian 1 (rev. 63), Tikotsky 4, Ustvolskaya 1, Zagorsky 1	Warsaw pact formed
1956 Ivanovs 8, Ovchinnikov 2 (rev. 73), Pashchenko 7, Pirumov 1, Popov 4	Second thaw. KHRUSHCHEV DENOUNCES STALIN. Hungarian uprising. End of second thaw

1957   Arutyunyan 1, 2, Brusilovsky
       4, Bunin 3, A. Cherepnin 4,
       Grinblats 2, Mirza-Zade 1, Nasidze
       1, Ovchinnikov 1, Pashchenko
       8, Peiko 3, Rääts 1, Rakov 2
       ('Youth'), Ramans 1, Shchedrin 1,
       Shostakovich 11 ('1905'), Ter-Osipov
       1, Ter-Tatevosyan 1, Vainberg 4 (rev.
       61), Vainiūnas 1

1958   Balanchivadze 2, Basner 1, Glebov   *Doktor Zhivago* affair
       1 ('Partisan'), Gubaidulina 1,
       Karetnikov 3, Kolodub 1, Lokshin
       1, Melikov 1, Pashchenko 9, Rääts 2,
       Slonimsky 1, Tishchenko ('French'),
       Tikotsky 5, Tubin 7

1959   Bunin 4, Chulaki 3, Eshpai 1, Rääts   Dissidence begins. Détente
       3, 4 ('Cosmic'), Salmanov 2, Skulte
       2 ('Hail to the sun!'), Tamberg
       (Ballet-symphony), Ter-Tatevosyan 2

1960   Egiazaryan 1 ('Razdan'), Golubev 5,   Use of psychiatric hospitals for
       Ivanovs 9, Nikolaev 1, Račiūnas 4   dissidents

1961   Bogoslovsky 1, Brusilovsky 5, Bunin   Berlin wall erected, Gagarin. Third
       5, Eller 3, Ivanovs 9, Klyuzner 2,   thaw begins, Khrushchev again
       Nikolaev 2, Račiūnas 5, Shostakovich   speaks against Stalin
       12 ('1917'), Tishchenko 1, Tormis 1

1962   Agafonnikov 1, A. Ali-Zade 1,   Cuban missile crisis. End of
       Denisov (two str., orch + perc),   third thaw
       Eshpai 2, Knipper 15 (str.), Mirzoyan
       1, Nikolaev 3, Rakov 3 ('Little'),
       Salmanov (Children's), Shebalin 5,
       Shostakovich 13 ('Babi Yar'), Vainberg
       5, Zolotarev 8

1963   Barkauskas 1, Bogoslovsky 2, Evlakhov
       2, Falik 1, Glebov 2, Ivanovs 10,
       E. Kapp 3, Karetnikov 4 (rev. 73),
       Lokshin 2, Lyatoshinsky 4, Nasidze 2,
       Pärt 1 ('Polyphonic'), Pashchenko 10,
       Pirumov 2, Salmanov 3, Silvestrov
       1, Sink 1 (Chamber), Skulte 3
       ('Cosmic'), Tikotsky 6, Tsintsadze 2,
       Vainberg 6

1964   Bajoras 1 (rev. 68–70), Eshpai 3,   Khrushchev deposed, BREZHNEV
       Grinblats 3, Glebov 3, Kalninš 1,
       Ovchinnikov 3 (rev. 82)

1965   A. Aleksandrov 1, Bogoslovsky   Daniel and Sinyavsky
       3, Brusilovsky 6 ('Kurmangazy'),
       Ivanovs 11, Juzeliūnas 3, Kalninš 2,
       Kalsons 1, K. Karaev 3, Peiko 4,
       Pirumov 3, Ramans 2, Shchedrin 2
       (rev. 67), Sidel'nikov 1 ('Romantic
       Symphony-Divertissement in Four
       Portraits – Vivaldi, Ravel, Berg,

Stravinsky'), Silvestrov 2, Skulte 4, Tishchenko 2

1966 A. Ali-Zade 2, Bibik 1, Bunin 6, Golubev 6, Klyuzner 3, Lokshin 3, Lyatoshinsky 5, Pärt 2, Pashchenko 12, Rääts 5, Račiūnas 6, Shtogarenko 3, Sidel'nikov 2 ('Song about the Red Banner'), Silvestrov 3 ('Eschataphony'), Ter-Osipov 2, Tishchenko 3, Tubin 8, Uspensky 1, Zeidman 2 ('Songs of Struggle') — Moves to rehabilitate Stalin

1967 Akhinyan 1, B. Chaikovsky 2, Chamber Symphony, Evlakhov 3, Golubev ('Choreographic'), Grinblats 4, Ivanovs 12, Kancheli 1, Rääts 6, Sink 2 (Chamber), Vainberg 9, Vustin 1

1968 Banshchikov 1, Gabichvadze 2, Glebov 4 (str., rev. 74), Kalninš 3, Kalsons 2 ('in modo classico'), Karetnikov, Chamber, K. Khachaturian 2, Knipper 16 ('Dramatic'), Lokshin 4, Mshvelidze 4, Nikolaev 4, Peiko 5, Rybnikov 1, Sidel'nikov 3 ('Hymn to Nature'), Vainberg 10, Zagortsev 1, Zhiganov 2 — Prague spring, invasion

1969 Arsumanov 1, Bibik 2, Brusilovsky 7, Bunin 7, Khagagortyan 3, Nasidze 3, Pashchenko 13, 14, Popov 5, Rabinovich 1 ('Serait-il impossible?'), Račiūnas 7, Shostakovich 14, Stankovich ('Mountain Symphony'), Terteryan 1, Tsintsadze 2, Tsytovich 1, Tubin 9, Vainberg 11 ('Lenin centenary'), Volkov 1 — Solzhenitsyn expelled from Writers' Union

1970 Bajoras 2, Bibik 3, Bunin 8, Ivanovs 13, Kancheli 2 ('Chants'), Knipper 17 ('Lenin'), 18, Lokshin 5 ('Shakespeare Sonnets'), Melikov 2, Mirza-Zade 2, Pashchenko 15, Popov 6, Račiūnas 8, Ramans 3, Rybnikov 2, Suslin ('Sinfonia piccola'), Ter-Osipov 3, 4, Tishchenko ('Sinfonia robusta') — Jewish emigration movement

1971 Barkauskas 2, Falik 2, Ivanovs 14, Knipper 19, Lokshin 6, Nikolaev 5, Pärt 3, Shostakovich 15, Volkov 2 ('In memoriam Myaskovsky'), Zeidman 3 ('Songs of Spring'), Zhiganov 3, Zhubanova 1 ('Energy')

1972 Bajoras 3 (rev. 76), Brusilovsky 8, Butsko 1 (rev. 78), A. D. Gadzhiev 5 ('Man, the earth, the cosmos'), Golubev 7 ('Heroic'), Ivanovs 15, Kalninš 4, Kalsons 3, Klyuzner 4,

Knipper 20, Lokshin 7, Meerovich
1, Pashchenko 16, Peiko 6, Popov
7 (inc.), Schnittke 1, Shtogarenko 4,
Ter-Osipov 5, Terteryan 2

1973 Balakauskas 1, Butsko 2, Dzhaparidze
1, Kancheli 3, Khrennikov 3, Lokshin
8, Machavariani 2, Pirumov 4, Rääts
7, Ramans 4, Shut' 1, Sidel'nikov 4
('The rebellious world of the poet'),
Stankovich 1 ('Verkhovina'; 'Largo'),
Chamber 1, Ter-Osipov 6, Tubin 10,
Zhiganov 4

1974 Balasanyan 1, Ivanovs 16, Juzeliūnas   Solzhenitsyn exiled
4, Karabits 1, Knipper 21, Mshvelidze
5, Pirumov 3, Sidel'nikov 5 ('The
duels'), Skulte 5, Stankovich 2
('Heroic'), Ter-Osipov 7, Tishchenko
4, Tolstoy 1 ('A thought about the
motherland'), Tsytovich 2, Zhiganov 5

1975 Ermolaev (Eight spiritual symphonies),   Helsinki agreement
Kancheli 4 ('In memoria di
Michelangelo'), Karabits 2, Korndorf
1, Lokshin 9, Nasidze 4, Shut' 2,
Ter-Osipov 8, Terteryan 3, Vainberg
12 ('In memoriam Shostakovich'),
Zhiganov 6

1976 Akhinyan 2, F. Ali-Zade 1, Bibik
4 ('In memoriam Shostakovich'),
Boiko 1, Filippenko 1, Gabichvadze
4, Chamber Symphony, Ivanovs
17, Kancheli 6 (rev. 80), Kangro
('Simple Symphony'), Lokshin 10,
Melikov 4, Salmanov 4, Shtogarenko
5, Silvestrov 4, Stankovich 3 ('Self-
assertion'), Terteryan 4, Tishchenko
5 ('In memoriam Shostakovich'),
Vainberg 13, 14, Zhiganov 7

1977 Artemov ('Symphony of elegies'),
Balsys (Symphony-Concerto),
Banshchikov 2, Erkanyan 1
('Introspection'), Ivanovs 18, Kancheli
5, Lobanov 1, Nasidze 5 ('Pirosmani'),
Peiko 7, Ramans 5, Z. Shakhidi
'Symphony of makoms'), Skulte 6,
Stankovich 4 ('Lyric'), Vainberg 15 ('I
believe in this earth'), Zhiganov 8

1978 Akhinyan 3, A. Aleksandrov 2,
Bibik 5, Boiko 2, Erkanyan 2 ('Aik
and Bel'), Kefalidi 1, Khagagortyan
4, Nasidze 6 ('Passione'), Petrov
('Pushkin' – vocal-poetic symphony),
Shut' 3 ('Sinfonie da camera'),
Slonimsky 2, Tamberg 1, Terteryan 5,
Zagortsev 2, Zhiganov 9

1979	Balakauskas 2, Barkauskas 3, Bogoslovsky 4, Dmitriev 1, 2, Ivanovs 19, Kalninš 5, Karabits 3, Korndorf Chamber, Melikov 5, Narbutaite 1, Nasidze 7 ('Dalay'), Pavlenko 1, Ramans 6, Schnittke 2, Shtogarenko 6, Tsintsadze 4, Ustvolskaya 2 ('True, eternal bliss'), Zhiganov 10	Invasion of Afghanistan
1980	Bibik 6, B. Chaikovsky 3 ('Sevastopol'), Eshpai 4, Korndorf 2, Smirnov 1 ('The Seasons'), Stankovich Chamber 2, Pastoral Symphony	
1981	Bogoslovsky 5, Boiko 3, Ivanovs 20, Izraelyan 1, Kalsons 4 ('New dreams from old tales'), Kuprevičius 1, Lobanov 2, Schnittke 3, Shut' ('Largo Symphony'), Sidel'nikov Symphony-Sonata for violin and piano, Skulte 7, Slonimsky 3, Sumera 1, Terteryan 6, Vainberg 16, Vlasov 1, Zhiganov 11	
1982	A. Ali-Zade 3, Balanchivadze 3, Bibik 7, Denisov Chamber, R. Gadzhiev 2, Gavrilin ('Chimes'), Juzeliūnas 5 ('Hymns of the Plain'), F. Karaev ('Tristezza I – Farewell Symphony'), K. Khachaturian 3, Ovchinnikov 4, Pavlenko 2, 3, Silvestrov 5, Slonimsky 4, Smirnov 2, Stankovich Chamber 3, Tarnopolsky 1, Zhiganov 12	Brezhnev dies, Andropov succeeds
1983	Chulaki 4, Ivanovs 21, Machavariani 3, Slonimsky 5, Ustvolskaya 3 ('Jesus Messiah, save us'), Zhiganov 13	Andropov dies, Chernenko succeeds
1984	A. Ali-Zade 4 ('Mugam'), Artemov 'Way to Olympus', Balanchivadze 4 ('Forest'), Banshchikov 4 ('Eternal fire'), Erkanyan 3 ('Voices of the fallen'), Grinblats 5, Juzeliūnas (Organ), Kangro ('Sinfonia sincera'), Kasparov 1 ('Guernica'), Machavariani 4, Melikov 6, Schnittke 4, Skulte 8, Slonimsky 6, 7, Sumera 2, 3, Tüür 1, Vainberg 17, Zhiganov 14	
1985	Bajoras ('Symphony-Diptych'), A. Chaikovsky 1, Erkanyan 4 ('Nemesis'), Eshpai 5, Pavlenko 4, Rääts 8, Slonimsky 8, Tishchenko ('Chronicle of the blockade'), Tsintsadze 5, Vainberg 18, 19, Zhiganov 15	Chernenko dies, GORBACHEV succeeds. Drive against alcoholism
1986	Balasanyan 2, Barkauskas 5, Butsko 3, Gubaidulina ('Stimmen-Verstummen'), Kangro (Tuuru Tubasümfoonia'), Kancheli 7 ('Epilogue'), Kasparov 2 ('Symphony of the Cross'), Rogalev	CHERNOBYL

1, Skulte 9, Stankovich ('Symphony-
Diptych'), Tamberg 2, Tüür 2,
Zhiganov 16

1987   Balasanyan Chamber, Butsko 4
(Chamber), Denisov [2], Machavariani
5, Sergeeva (Organ), Silvestrov 6
('Exegi Monumentum'), Slonimsky 9,
Stankovich Chamber 4, Terteryan 7,
Ustvolskaya 4 ('Prayer'), Vainberg 20

1988   Banshchikov 3, Machavariani 6,
Sergeeva 1, Schnittke 5,
(= Concerto grosso 4), Tishchenko 6,
Vainberg 21, 22, Zagortsev 3
('Symphony of Alarms')

1989   Dmitriev 3, Eshpai 6, Grinblats 6   COLLAPSE OF COMMUNISM
('Intervals'), Ikramova 1, Korndorf 3,   IN EASTERN EUROPE
Tamberg 3, Terteryan 8   Lithuania declares independence

1990   Ustvolskaya 5

1991   Soviet Union dissolved; Gorbachev
loses power; Commonwealth of
Independent States formed.
New exodus of composers to
the West.

13

The Symphony in Scandinavia

Robert Layton

So strong is the hold exercised over our consciousness by the great central European composers that we tend to know rather little about composers on the periphery. Indeed, even keen music-lovers are often hard pressed to think of any Scandinavian composers apart from the really major figures – Grieg, Sibelius, Nielsen and, perhaps nowadays, one can add Stenhammar. But there is Danish music before Nielsen just as there is Swedish music before Berwald though not always with a distinctive enough voice for it to make itself really felt in the wider world. Norway before Grieg and Finland before Sibelius are rather different cases: Norway was predominantly Danish in cultural sympathies in the eighteenth century though in the 'Bergen Harmonien' it boasts Europe's oldest orchestra; Finland was predominantly Swedish in culture even after it came under Tsarist hegemony as a result of the Treaty of Tilsit. Sweden was the great power in the seventeenth century but no great musical tradition emerged. True, some of the great Flemish masters of the Renaissance were heard at the Swedish court and King Erik XIV actually wrote a piece of eight-part polyphony but there was nothing comparable to the splendour of the Court of King Christian IV of Denmark: Dowland, Praetorius and, more importantly, Schütz were on his musical establishment. The 'Father of Swedish music' (the title was in currency long before it was used by his first modern biographer, Patrick Vretblad) and its first 'symphonist' was **Johan Helmich Roman** (1694–1758). Before that, in the seventeenth century, Sweden imported talent, as did the Tsarist Court in the eighteenth. Queen Christina had invited Abrici, Alessandro Scarlatti, Cesti and Carissimi to the Court. Roman still speaks the 'lingua franca' of his day; the Court sent him to England in 1716–21 where he probably studied with Pepusch but the musical language of his sinfonias, the best of which is fully commensurate in quality with Geminiani or Telemann, is essentially as Handelian as is that of his concertos.

Johan Agrell (1701–65) whose Op. 1 Sinfonias are in the tradition of the Italian opera overture (and who at one time was thought to have studied with Roman), settled in Nuremburg but for the most part the movement was in the other direction. **Johan Daniel Berlin** (1714–87) from Memel went to settle in Trondheim in Norway (such of his music as I have heard is spectacularly anonymous) but in Sweden, in the enlightened reign of Gustav III, **Joseph Martin Kraus** (1756–92) is the first symphonist of importance. Kraus studied in Mannheim, later reading law and philosophy at Göttingen and was very much a man of ideas. He was a fervent admirer of Klopstock, and published a set of poems (*Herdedikter* or *Idylls*, Mainz 1773), a tragedy, *Tolon, Trauerspiel in 3 Acts* (Frankfurt, Leipzig, 1776) and a theoretical pamphlet on opera in his early twenties. His musical language inhabits much the same world of sensibility as Carl Philipp Emmanuel Bach though without his wild, unpredictable modulations. The Symphony in C minor (1783) is modelled on an earlier symphony in C sharp minor,* composed some time before he left Sweden on a tour of study (1782–86) is very much influenced by Gluck and Haydn, who admired it enough to conduct it in Eszterháza, and it embodies the same 'Sturm und Drang' spirit of Haydn's own symphonies of the 1770s.

But if Roman or Kraus do not differ stylistically from major European contemporaries, by the nineteenth century there were more distinctive voices: Berwald in Sweden, and Svendsen and Grieg in Norway. In the Baroque and Classical eras, composers, in their very different individual accents, laid greater stress on those qualities that we all have in common and that unite us, while in the nineteenth century when Romanticism was gathering force, artists tended to concentrate more on those qualities which mark us off from each other. **Franz Berwald** (1796–1868) is the leading Scandinavian symphonist before Sibelius and the most commanding figure of his day, though this is not how it would have seemed at the time. The discovery of Berwald belongs to the early years of our present century. Of course, there are others: **Niels Gade** (1817–90) in Denmark and **Adolf Fredrik Lindblad** (1801–78) in Sweden were symphonists of note, but neither offers quite the same individual profile. Lindblad's First Symphony in C minor (1832) is a work of quality very much in the Viennese classical tradition in which (from the vantage point of hindsight) one can almost delude oneself into discerning a foretaste of Berwald. Only Svendsen in his two much later symphonies might be said to offer a challenge but he is nowhere as personal in his approach to form.

Berwald was born in Stockholm the year before Schubert and died the same year as Rossini, so that his career encompassed those of Chopin, Schumann, Mendelssohn and, save for one year, Berlioz. The family was of German stock, Berwald's father settling in Stockholm in the 1770s, a few years before Kraus, where he joined the orchestra of the Royal Opera. In his youth Berwald also served the the Royal Opera as violinist and violist but his gifts were many-faceted and he possessed a fertile and resourceful intelligence. He spent many vital years on non-musical projects, founding

---

* Birger, Anrep-Nordin, *Studier över Josef Martin Kraus*, Stockholm, 1924, p.114.

a successful orthopaedic enterprise in Berlin (1835–41) based on the most highly developed techniques.* In 1841 he went to Vienna where success, albeit shortlived, released a burst of creative energy: all four symphonies come from the same productive years (1842–45). By the 1850s Berwald had given up hope of advancement in the Swedish musical establishment. He had been passed over for two posts to which he felt his talents entitled him and he turned to other non-musical activities, this time in the north of Sweden as manager of a saw mill and a glass works!

Only one of Berwald's symphonies, the *Sinfonie sérieuse* (1842) was performed in his own lifetime: his masterpiece, the *Sinfonie singulière* (1845) waited sixty years for its première. But the *Sérieuse* was not his first effort in the genre. The Symphony in A major (1820), which survives only in fragmentary form, has Beethovenian touches and the shadow of the *Eroica* surfaces in the second group of the Finale of the *Sérieuse*. Yet, as so often in Berwald, what one at first takes for resonances of earlier composers turn out to be prophecies of things to come. There is in the same symphony a faint whiff of Bruckner in the slow movement, and the main idea of the G minor section of the Finale has overtones of Dvořák. (In much the same way, the A minor String Quartet (1849) seems almost to foreshadow Reger and Nielsen.) Yet, for all that, much of his music sounds like no one else. This certainly holds good at the opening of the *Sinfonie singulière* (1845) which is quite unlike any other music of its time – or for that matter, any other! The harmonies may not be in advance of Mendelssohn or Schumann but their treatment reveals a fresh and novel sensibility, and it is not too fanciful to attribute its transparent texture to the quality of light in these northern latitudes. There is no doubt as to his keen classical instincts: the influence of Beethoven can still be discerned in the transitional passages where Berwald hammers away at a short pregnant motive with insistent tenacity.

Berwald enfolds the light and mercurial Scherzo into the body of the slow movement, an experiment that he first tried in the Septet (1828), and one that he developed still further in the E flat String Quartet (1849) when both the slow movement and Scherzo are embedded in the body of the first movement! The Finale has tremendous fire and its robust, spirited main theme makes a splendid contrast to the languid poetry of the *Adagio*. There is a refreshing vigour that steps outside the pale Biedermeier atmosphere of the Swedish musical world of the 1840s and stands in striking contrast to such Scandinavian contemporaries as Gade.

All four symphonies plunge directly into the musical argument without any introductory preamble, the only exception being the *Capricieuse*. The *Sérieuse* has greater contrapuntal interest than its companions as its noble first subject shows. The tonal plan of its first movement is also worth

* Some of the apparatus that he himself devised for the treatment of patients was in all practical essentials still in use as a basis for therapy until the present century, which is all the more remarkable in that he had no scientific training and indeed precious little formal education of any kind.

Ex. 1. Berwald: Sinfonie singulière.

Ex. 2.

comment: the home key is G minor and the bridge subject which plays an important part in the development appears in the subdominant before modulating to the relative major, B flat, where the second group begins. At the reprise the first group is restated in A minor and the tonic major is established only with the second group. The slow movements of the symphonies all follow more or less ternary outlines and the Scherzos (except in the *Capricieuse* where there is none) follow traditional lines. At the beginning of the Finale the material of the slow movement returns. The Finale itself is in sonata form though the beginning of the reprise telescopes the first subject. The *Sinfonie capricieuse* has a more complex history than its companions. The bound volume of the autograph disappeared at the time of Berwald's death but a short score survives whose title-page bears the titles, 'Sinfonie singulière', 'Sinfonie pathétique', both crossed through, and finally 'Sinfonie capricieuse'. The *Capricieuse* was the last to reach the public: a performing edition prepared by Ernst Ellberg was given in Stockholm early in 1914 under the baton of Armas Järnefelt, Sibelius's brother-in-law.* The opening *Allegro*, like the first movement of the Schumann Piano Concerto which it predates, is virtually monothematic: its two main ideas are so closely related rhythmically that they can hardly be regarded as independent. Although not the finest of the symphonies, the *Capricieuse* has the freshness that distinguishes Berwald and the slow movement has a distinctive eloquence.

Berwald's Fourth and last Symphony was finished only a month after the *Singulière* and is the only symphony without a title, though he did at one time consider calling it *Sinfonie naïve*. The Symphony in E flat is one of the sunniest of Berwald's scores and its invention is both fertile and subtle. The opening *Allegro* is wonderfully spirited and brilliantly scored, and its second subject delightfully fresh. The *Adagio* is based on a theme from 'En landlig bröllopsfest' ('A Rustic Wedding') dating from 1844, for organ or 'piano' four-hands! Its symmetrical phrases reflect something of the well-regulated emotional temperature in which Berwald's inspiration was conceived, and yet at the same time radiate great warmth and humanity. There is a touch of considerable novelty in the Finale that is worth mentioning. At the beginning of the recapitulation when one expects the first group to be restated, Berwald surprises us with an entirely new theme – and a charming one at that! Although the formal innovations of Berlioz, Chopin and others often occur at this point, the first subject being telescoped or the order of the two main themes reversed, this particular innovation has few if any precedents. Interesting though these departures from convention may be, it is the quality of Berwald's thematic invention, his transparent textures and expert orchestration, and the generosity of spirit that informs his musical personality that make his music engage both our sympathies and our affection.

Berwald does to some extent sound Swedish or at any rate Nordic; and there is no doubt that, say, the First Symphony of Nielsen sounds distinctively Danish in much the same way that the paintings of Christen Købke look Danish. **Niels Gade** is, however, another matter: he composed his First Symphony in 1841, the year before Berwald's *Sérieuse*, and he went on to compose eight in all, the last in 1870, and although he was to live for another twenty years he never returned to the genre. Gade studied in Leipzig: just as Rome had been the Mecca of Danish painters of the Golden Age, to which such artists as Bertel Thorvaldsen and Christen Købke had made their pilgrimage, so Leipzig was the centre for musicians. Even Grieg

---

* A subsequent edition by the doyen of Berwald scholars, Nils Castegren, was prepared for the Berwald Centenary Celebrations in 1968 and it is this that is now in general currency.

studied there though he was not particularly happy in such an academic and conservative climate. Later while still in his teens he went to Copenhagen (Oslo or Christiania, as it was then known, would have been too provincial) and studied with Gade and it was as a result of his promptings that he wrote his early Symphony in C minor. Gade was to Danish music what Eckersberg was to painting, a positive force but essentially an academic.

Gade was born two years after the end of the Napoleonic wars, in 1817, the son of an instrument-maker, and lived until 1890. Mendelssohn was so taken with his First Symphony (*På Sjølands fagre sletter*)* that he conducted its first performance – and Gade also had the good fortune to have Schumann's pen active on his behalf, and that set the seal on his international reputation. He briefly succeeded Mendelssohn at the Gewandhaus in Leipzig but in 1848 the outbreak of war between Prussia and Denmark forced Gade to resign his conducting post and return home. In 1851 by the time he was thirty-four he held several key positions in Copenhagen musical life, and felt secure enough to marry: his fiancée was the daughter of Denmark's senior composer, **Johan Peter Emilius Hartmann** (1805–1900). Gade's wedding present to his wife was his Fifth Symphony in D minor (1853), a captivating score for piano and orchestra with a marvellous main theme. The piano assumes a prominent obbligato rather than a solo role, and there is none of the tension between piano and orchestra that you find in such concertante works as the d'Indy *Symphonie sur un chant populaire montagnard* or the Franck Symphonic Variations, which it predates. Formally these symphonies offer no surprises although they are full of fresh attractive ideas: they are, too, beautifully proportioned and crafted; new ideas enter when we feel they should (as in the finely paced Third Symphony in A minor) and rarely outstay their welcome. However, they inhabit a polite and well-regulated world and never succeed in making any significant escape from the orbit of Mendelssohn; any Nordic dialect is muted. If we are looking for a distinctive voice, one that heralds Carl Nielsen, this is not it, any more than is Hartmann. Like his son-in-law, he was a fine craftsman, as indeed was his contemporary, **Christian Frederick Emil Hornemann** who is said (by Nielsen himself) to have influenced him. Be that as it may, neither of his symphonies have a more than peripheral hold on the repertoire.

Of course, just as Danish music before Nielsen had been enriched by either German or German-trained composers such as Christoph Ernst Friedrich Weyse and Friedrich Kuhlau, the same holds true of the other Scandinavian countries: the German-born Pacius in Finland and, as we have already seen, Kraus and Berwald in Sweden. But as the nineteenth century wore on, and the individual traditions grew stronger, the Scandinavian countries came to influence each other; Grieg was certainly one of the influences on the early music of Sibelius and Nielsen owes

* Probably best translated as 'From the beautiful plains of Sjøland'.

much to **Johan Severin Svendsen** (1840–1911). In the 1870s Svendsen abandoned Christiania to settle in Copenhagen where he was conductor of the Orchestra of the Royal Theatre. (Indeed Carl Nielsen played under him during the 1890s and it was Svendsen who conducted the first performance of the First Symphony. And it is to Svendsen as much as any one individual composer to whom we must look for some of the roots of Nielsen's style.) Not that one can regard Svendsen as anything other than Norwegian, any more than you could C. F. Dahl among nineteenth-century painters, but his years in Paris and Germany (*Carnival in Paris*, 1872, was written in Bayreuth of all places) made him far more cosmopolitan than many other Scandinavian composers of his time.

As befits a conductor, Svendsen was a master of the orchestra, for which Grieg had no particular flair. Yet Svendsen's First Symphony, like that of **Edvard Grieg** (1843–1907), was a student work written while he was still at the Leipzig Conservatory; when he first heard it in Christiania in 1867, Grieg thought it a revelation (he called it a work of 'scintillating genius, superb national feeling and truly brilliant handling of the orchestra') and its excellence made him more than ever aware of the inadequacies of his own C minor Symphony. Certainly Svendsen's symphony is a work of astonishing assurance and freshness. Even though he and Grieg were good friends, Svendsen did not involve himself in the folksong movement to anywhere near the same extent as had Grieg (the four Norwegian Rhapsodies were probably as close as he ever came to it). His basic sympathies remained predominantly classical and he continued to work within sonata-form structures (three of its four movements are in sonata form), yet there is a distinctive Norwegian feel to his melodic ideas. After he gave up the direction of the Christiania Orchestra in 1877, which he had shared with Grieg, he became more of what nowadays we would call a 'star' conductor. He appeared in London, Paris, Leipzig and then from 1883 onwards he went to Copenhagen as conductor of the Orchestra of the Royal Theatre, where he remained until ill-health forced his retirement in 1908. Alas, the creative fires burnt themselves out long before that, and after the famous Romance in G major for violin and orchestra, he more or less gave up composing. The Second Symphony, completed towards the end of his five-year spell (1872–77) in the Norwegian capital, was his last large-scale work and has the charm of its predecessor though its Scherzo does not have the effervescent quality of No. 1.

Svendsen succeeded in fusing the legacy of the Viennese classics with the Norwegian folk tradition. His invention blends liveliness and exuberance with a vein of poetic fantasy not unworthy of the best Grieg. Even if he may have been unduly harsh on the piece*, the Symphony is far from Grieg at his best or even most characteristic. He withdrew it after hearing Svendsen's First Symphony and bequeathed the score to Bergen Public

* Finn Benestad and Dag Schjelderup-Ebbe, *Grieg*, Oslo, 1980.

Library on the understanding that the injunction on its title-page, 'Never to be performed', was observed. All the same he thought sufficiently well of the inner movements to publish them in piano-duet form. But performances of the complete symphony remained under embargo. Then a photocopy of the autograph score was surreptitiously spirited away to the Soviet Union and played on Moscow Radio so that the case for upholding Grieg's ban really went by default. It was performed at the 1981 Bergen Festival and subsequently recorded, and is included in the Grieg Gesamtausgabe currently being published.

But in this same decade, the two giants of the Scandinavian symphony were born and their roots are very different. Nielsen has his in Danish song: his lines are sturdy, diatonic, firmly rooted in classical major-minor tonality. From Svendsen he learned much of his harmonic subtlety and mastery of the orchestra: but time had moved on since the days of Gade when Mendelssohn was the commanding figure, for Carl Nielsen it was Brahms and Dvořák. By the 1860s and 1870s nationalism was becoming a major force in Scandinavia, particularly in the two countries subject to alien domination – Norway then under the sway of Sweden, and Finland which was an autonomous Grand Duchy of the Tsarist Empire but was still dominated culturally by Sweden. Yet in spite of the discovery of the Kalevala, the Finnish mythology, exemplified in Gallén-Kallela's paintings and Sibelius's music, there are classical models. Jean Sibelius was writing in a much less well-developed national tradition, and it was to Haydn and Beethoven that he turned in his youth and, of course, among modern composers, Tchaikovsky. There was no indigenous musical tradition in Finland comparable with those of Sweden and Denmark. Johan Filip von Schantz (1835–65) had written a symphonic poem entitled 'Kullervo' thirty years earlier but the first Finnish symphony proper was composed by Aksel Gabriel Ingelius (1822–68). The conductor, **Robert Kajanus** (1856–1934) had composed his *Aino* Symphony in the 1880s. This fired Sibelius's imagination when he heard Kajanus conduct it in Berlin during the year (1889–90) that he was studying with Albert Becker. But *Aino* is more accurately described as a symphonic poem with a choral apotheosis than a symphony. It is a shortish work of about fifteen minutes' duration and shows a certain indebtedness to Wagner. It does not show any strong creative identity, though one can well understand the impression it would have made on a young composer of Sibelius's then circumscribed musical experience. But in ambition, scale and originality, his own *Kullervo* Symphony had no real precedent in the then provincial world of Finnish music or for that matter, in her Scandinavian neighbours.

14

Sibelius

Philip Coad

'It stands as a protest against present-day music. It has nothing, absolutely nothing of the circus about it,'* wrote Sibelius of his Fourth Symphony shortly after its première in 1911. If Sibelius was deliberately isolating himself from the overripe romanticism and opulent extravagance of much pre-war music, it certainly resulted in a work which puzzled many. One critic wrote: 'Everything seems strange. Curious, transparent figures float here and there, speaking to us in a language whose meaning we cannot grasp. Posterity must decide whether the composer has overstepped the boundaries dictated by sound, natural musicianship in overstraining the functions of various intervals in a melody'.† Yet the bewildered public and critical reaction following its first performance may well have seemed preferable to one press cliché which had been circulating for years. In exasperation Sibelius had written in 1910: 'How much more nonsense am I expected to endure? Yet again I read of my spiritual legacy from Russia and Tchaikovsky. I haven't developed a thick enough skin yet, and remain over-sensitive. It all pains me.'‡ No doubt this particular train of critical thought was all the more irksome as Finland was under Russian rule, and Sibelius – even before the composition of *Finlandia* in 1899 – had been upheld as a national hero.

There is no point denying that Sibelius' individuality in the First Symphony of 1898 was tempered with his discovery of Tchaikovsky's later symphonies. Earlier, in *Kullervo* (1892) – a five-movement symphonic work whose central part is like an operatic scena – it had been rather the influence of Bruckner and the modal inflexions of Finnish runic song which had combined, in a powerful representation of part of the *Kalevala*. This national epic was to be the inspiration behind nearly all his tone poems.

But the Tchaikovskian element of the First Symphony is certainly

---

* Erik Tawaststjerna: *Sibelius*, tr. Robert Layton, London, 1986, Vol. 2, p. 172.
† Op. cit., Vol. 2, p. 170.
‡ Op. cit., Vol. 2, p. 138.

exaggerated. Two admittedly obvious parallel areas, one with Tchaikovsky's Fifth and one with the Sixth, both reveal with hindsight quite distinctive Sibelian traits at the same time.

Sibelius' First and Tchaikovsky's Fifth are both in E minor. Both begin with a slow introduction and a theme for solo clarinet which is recalled in more full-blooded fashion at the opening of the Finale. But Sibelius' opening melody is unharmonized and tonally elusive – appearing to be closer to the Dorian mode than the minor scale – and its irregularity of phrasing is quite unlike Tchaikovsky's clear-cut melodic structure. Furthermore, Sibelius' melody contributes importantly to the motivic material of the first movement instead of being used simply as a motto theme. Its partial return at the beginning of the Finale marks an atmosphere of stark and passionate tragedy, while Tchaikovsky's theme basks at length in the major key within a luxuriant orchestral texture. Sibelius, unlike Tchaikovsky, allows no further triumphant peroration.

Secondly, Tawaststjerna has demonstrated* how a particular harmonic progression recurs in all four movements of the First Symphony, and traces it to the opening of the central section of the second movement of the *Symphonie pathétique*. This is perhaps the single feature which was most to blame for Sibelius' 'Tchaikovsky label': a diminished seventh chord decorated by an appoggiatura which resolves over a mediant pedal point.

The use of mediant pedal-points in a minor key is certainly a feature of Sibelius' earlier works as it is of Russian music of the period; but Sibelius is already exploiting them in an individual way. As the clarinet theme fades in G minor, the second violins introduce the first main *Allegro* idea with a tremolo on G and B. The theme itself (see Ex. 1b) appears to begin in G major, but the tremolo between B and G fits the prominent Es at the end of the first phrase and the beginning of its extension. Is this E minor or G major? Ex. 1 does not resolve the issue, despite its D sharp, because the G pedal preserves an ambiguity; and, indeed, when the pedal ends after seven bars, it is beneath G major harmony.

All this might seem over-indulgently fastidious, were it not for the fact that it illustrates at a very early stage in Sibelius' symphonic career his quite individual approach to tonality. Here the music is both static – the journey from minor to relative major is denied as the two keys seem to co-exist – and fluid – as the balance between the two shifts with some subtlety. When the theme returns in the recapitulation, it leads into a slow passage lingering around G for some time before the inevitable return in the coda to E minor. The same ambiguity is in evidence at other points in the symphony where the Ex. 1 progression

* Op. cit., Vol. 1, pp. 210–211.

is used. The opening of the slow movement hovers at first between E flat major and C minor over an E flat pedal point, and the Finale's second subject is poised between C major and A minor in the same way. But in Tchaikovsky's *Pathétique*, though a D pedal runs throughout that Trio section, there is never any doubt about the supremacy of B minor.

Ex. 1.

Other signs in the First Symphony of the mature Sibelius are mainly to be found in the opening movement. There is evidence of Sibelius' methods of evolving one idea organically from another. The first three notes of the opening clarinet melody are elongated into a luxuriant G major theme later in the first *Allegro* group (Ex. 2a and b): another clarinet figure reappears, enlivened and fragmented, in the second group when it is given, typically, to a pair of flutes in thirds (Ex. 3). The principal ideas of the two exposition groups both begin with a long note and end with a triplet flourish: these features are utterly characteristic of Sibelius' melodic writing.

Ex. 2.

Ex. 3.

If Sibelius' woodwind pairs often consort in thirds, the apparently endless reiterations for strings at the end of the exposition look forward to many string background textures in later works. Above the bass pedal point, the woodwind add a hypnotically repetitive procession of crotchets. Hypnotic effects in Sibelius are commonly brought about by repetition of circular melodic patterns, but are also often an indication of a large-scale thinking and basically slow pace unusual in works of modest length. In the development section, the strings build an intrinsically more interesting 'backcloth' out of motivic fragments; and this too becomes a standard procedure. But after a while the woodwind take on this role with the low strings. Instead of leading into the recapitulation conventionally with the first *Allegro* idea, the upper strings superimpose Ex. 2b on to this backcloth, so that by the time it resumes its original pitch without the woodwind, it is already quite established. This overlapping technique is a most intriguing aspect of Sibelius' methods and complements his balancing of E minor and G major earlier on.

The second movement may contain hints of Wagner's *Rheingold* (at letter F in the score) and Tchaikovsky's ballet music (letter G), but there are some impressively original features here too. A prominent motivic fragment (Ex. 4a) turns out to be the inverted form of Ex. 3's opening, and is also related to the third bar of the movement's first idea (Ex. 4b). A dramatic fast-moving development is built on this fragment; but the vigorous *moto perpetuo* is eventually pitted against the return of a slow theme, and we hear it in a new context as the realization dawns that the pulse has halved in pace (letter O). Already in his First Symphony Sibelius is overlapping tonalities, thematic material and now speeds, instead of moving more conventionally from one state to another.

Ex. 4.

After its blunt opening, the C major Scherzo also calls on imitative *moto perpetuo* textures. Movement into E major for the slow Trio is accomplished through a variant of the *Pathétique* progression. It is an E major predictably clouded by hints of C sharp minor; just as the flute seems to be leading to the relative minor convincingly, low strings and bassoon outline an E major triad and the accompanying texture dwindles to a clarinet trill and a bass drum roll. It is a bewildering moment, but how typical of Sibelius to draw us up short when we think that the music is 'under control'. There is another such moment just before the coda of the Finale, which is otherwise the most backward-looking movement of the four. Its two quite contrasting thematic groups – the first energetic, the second wiltingly lyrical – in a perfunctory sonata design make it a typical nineteenth-century product. Indeed, Sibelius seems almost to apologize for its slack structure in his use of the heading *Quasi una fantasia*, although it is no less coherent than many nineteenth-century Finales. The first group develops itself in Tchaikovskian chromatic sequences, but does use a further variant of the first four notes of Ex. 3 in the process. The second group is certainly a 'big tune', but – especially on its extended return – quite cramped in its contours with very few melodic leaps. Sibelius goes through the Romantic motions effectively enough, but his melodic gift is of a different order from that of

Tchaikovsky or Rakhmaninov. Sibelius never tried to 'swoon' like this again in later symphonies, nor does he ever write so opulently for the harp again. The sombre coda is slow, despite rapid string figuration; it refers briefly to the first group before ending, like the first movement, with two pizzicato chords.

The Second Symphony in D major, written in 1901, dispenses with harp and untuned percussion as well as with most of the Russian associations. There are still hints of Tchaikovsky and Wagner in the more febrile moments of the second movement; the Finale's second subject is linked to the motto theme of Tchaikovsky's Fifth in contour; and the use of two successive falling or rising steps as a starting-point for much of the work's thematic material is true also of the *Pathétique* (Tchaikovsky is rarely given due credit for symphonic coherence in this work). But Sibelius' individuality is intensified further in the Second. The structure of the opening movement is a case in point. Although the First Symphony's first movement seemed initially to be as much in G major as E minor, it could be analysed in terms of traditional sonata structure. The Second Symphony's opening movement poses problems for the more blinkered analyst looking for sonata form. Where is the thematic duality so obvious in the Finale of the First? Where do we reach a related key for the second group – and which of the dozen or so fragmentary ideas is first group, which transition, which second group? Before the coherence of the final cadential section of the exposition, Sibelius plays cat and mouse with the dominant key, and the discontinuity of the music is of a new order in the context of a symphonic exposition.

The development of these various ideas is ingenious and the music more continuous, though not so reliant as is usual in Sibelius on remorseless background reiterations from the strings. The return to D major and the arrival of the recapitulation is a subtle process. The brass provide a climactic transformation of a tonally ambiguous idea, originally for unaccompanied unison violins, but here fully harmonized and accompanied by a rising string tremolo. Brass power and the return of this idea at its original pitch give the music a recapitulatory air; but the impression of recapitulation is stronger still when the first of the opening melodic ideas for woodwind reappears, virtually as at the outset. It is less important to pinpoint the exact beginning of the reprise than to observe Sibelius' methods as it progresses. The woodwind phrase may be familiar, but not the manner in which it is successively combined with two ideas, for horns and strings respectively, which came later in the exposition. Immediately afterwards, another more positive gesture for strings from the exposition shows its ability to pitch in simultaneously with the woodwind idea. Sibelius is compressing the discontinuous part of his exposition not by omission or shortening ideas as much as by reordering his material and by combining his ideas vertically. Nothing is left out. The effect is still to some extent discontinuous, but there is a real sense of progress from one state to another in these ingenious reworkings. The final section provides the only reassurance for the inflexible analyst in its straightforward recall, in the tonic, of the exposition's cadential paragraph.

If the other movements are less innovative structurally, they are no less characteristic. The *Andante*, like its counterpart in the First Symphony, has great variety of pace and mood. It begins with an apparently directionless line of pizzicato quavers from basses and 'cellos in alternation, which eventually becomes an accompaniment for a bassoon tune which cannot pull itself away from the tonic D. The pace quickens; then typical *largamente* markings introduce a series of massive brass chords with a Tristanesque fall. A beautiful slow transformation, for divided strings in F sharp major, of a previously frenetic motive, decorated by woodwind thirds, leads into an intensified repeat of the action. F sharp major radiance eventually becomes D minor gloom (a nod in the direction of the Finale of the *Pathétique?*) before a coda of strange ejaculatory dialogue between strings and wind causes the movement to end as oddly as it began.

The compound time of the Scherzo tends to revert to groupings of two and four, an element which links it to the first movement. This is especially true of the second idea, given almost always to the wind; while the *moto perpetuo* scurryings of the opening idea are typically reserved for the strings. The slower Trio section has a pastoral quality: horns and bassoons provide a sustained background for the oboe melody which begins, remarkably enough, with nine B flat crotchets, and only at length extends itself beyond the range of a perfect fifth. Sibelius' growing mastery of transition is shown at its clearest when the Trio section returns later. Two comparatively insignificant complements to the oboe theme – a rising broken chord figuration from the strings, and a sequence of five rising steps for clarinets found between the oboe phrases – grow into prominence and are subtly altered as the music leads seamlessly into the Finale. The broken chords fade into background anonymity; but the rising steps, split into two groups, build the first subject's main element, at the same time recalling the very opening of the symphony. Here is an indication of the organic processes which were to find their culmination in the one-movement form of the Seventh Symphony.

In outward shape, the popular Finale conforms firmly to nineteenth-century reappraisals of sonata form. There are two big melodic periods with a transition theme between them, and the most perfunctory of tonal adjustments in the recapitulation. But within this structure are individual elements. Both themes begin in fragments and reach their fullest phrasing later. The first opens over a long pedal point; the second, in the minor, is underpinned throughout by a scalic ostinato. The development displays the three rising notes exhaustively; they gradually gain ground over a laboriously ascending chromatic quaver movement for strings. The second theme is extended in the recapitulation, like its counterpart in the First Symphony; and it is only here that we sense fully the static quality of the music. The ostinato turns over and over while its theme, unable to escape from its dominant note, piles on remorseless repetitions. Eventually there is a heave back into the major. The *Molto largamente* coda, fixed firmly on a tonic pedal, is not only the slowest part of the movement: it also contains its motivic culmination. The three rising notes (D, E, F sharp), so prominent in both outer movements, find their logical continuation (G) at last in the brass. The final vast slowness has provided the single most significant and progressive event in the whole work.

The first two symphonies may refer to structural models and have their transparently derivative moments; but these have tended to disguise their obvious individuality. No one has ever denied the originality of the three middle symphonies, which occupy the years 1904–1919 between them; but they contain further developments of many procedures in the first two. Each, for instance, contains further progress towards an organic linking of movements. The Third Symphony (completed in 1907) is in three movements only: the Finale begins with the kind of motivic activity found in the Second Symphony's Scherzo, develops it and then culminates in a heroic theme hinted at earlier, based on a hypnotically repetitive rhythmic cell. The Fourth Symphony (1911) appears to follow a straightforward four-movement plan, but both pairs of movements are subtly linked by the prominence of a single note. A high A joins the first and second movements, and lower C sharps finish the slow movement and begin the Finale. There are dark woodwind hints of the Finale's opening theme towards the end of the slow movement too.

The Fifth Symphony was originally cast as four movements in 1915, but the second revision – the version always heard today – finds the first two movements telescoped convincingly into one. The second section of the composite movement is much faster; but the new tempo is eased in so smoothly amongst familiar material, and elements of reprise at the end of the whole movement are so clear that there is no lack of coherence. The contribution of the double basses in Sibelius is so often remarkably imaginative and unexpected: twice in the central movement they anticipate in pizzicato octaves the powerful swinging ostinato of the second Finale paragraph.

There are, however, two features in the musical language of these three symphonies which find no real precedent in the first two. One is a brief but potent melodic shape common to all three works. It is first heard in this phrase on the violins in the Third:

Ex. 5.

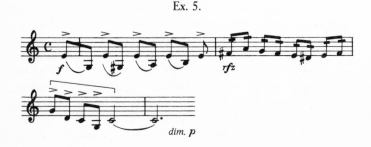

The four accented notes at the end are increased in significance by the fact that they are used immediately in the woodwind sequel. In the Finale they return as a woodwind ostinato accompaniment to the horns' version of the culminatory theme; this provides the most aurally obvious link between the two outer movements. In the second movement of the Fourth Symphony it is again the violins which introduce the four-note fragment, this time in ascending form and more positive thematically; the slow movement alters the sequence of notes slightly in another ostinato, this time for strings.

But all this is a mere preparation for the four-note motive's dominance in the Fifth Symphony in E flat major. Aligned immediately to a memorable rhythmic contour in the opening horn phrase (Ex. 6a), it is thoroughly developed as a theme and as an accompanimental ostinato in the first movement before its virtual saturation of all parts in the coda. The prominence of falling and rising fourths in the central movement suggest the motive strongly. In the Finale, it is clearly in evidence in a gesture as symphonically conclusive as the trumpets' and trombones' extra rising step at the end of the Second Symphony. The brass banish once and for all the A natural (which has tended throughout the work to unsettle E flat major) with a resounding affirmation of A flat harmony (Ex. 6c), while at the same time linking the memorable Finale ostinato (Ex. 6b) with the work's opening thematic idea.

The unsettling A naturals in an E flat major context are indicative of a still more prominent characteristic of the three middle symphonies: their use of the tritone or augmented fourth as a melodic force. The melodic tendency to sharpen the fourth degree of the scale often links the music to the Lydian mode (see Ex. 5 for instance) – but this is only the tip of the iceberg. Sibelius is already the kind of thoroughbred symphonist who will allow a melodic characteristic to inform his use of harmony and tonality.

The Third Symphony's opening paragraph is rooted almost exclusively to C major harmony, reinforced by C pedal points. Although – as has often been remarked – its sound is energetically classical, it is harmonically a static beginning, and even the F sharps of Ex. 5 do not give rise even to a glimmer of C major's dominant chord, let alone the dominant key. Instead of being treated as the leading-note to the expected secondary key of G major, the note F sharp is deprived of its most obvious tonal function. If it had succumbed to a modulation into G major straightaway, the potent melodic quality of the Lydian inflexion would of course have vanished. F sharp eventually finds its tonal function as the dominant note of B minor, in which key a second group begins, with one of Sibelius' most circular, cramped melodic ideas. The exposition ends with a suggestion of G major – but only over a B pedal. It is a pedal point on B, rather than the dominant G, which introduces the recapitulation, too. The second group reappears in E minor, with F sharp in full tonal focus, and so a slow coda placing weight on B flat restores the balance.

Ex. 6.

In the Finale, Sibelius continues to ignore the traditional claims of the dominant key in this individual way. The first 170 bars never escape a C pedal for long. The pedal point is accommodated within A minor and F minor before a kaleidoscopic development admits of no tonal security at all. Gradually the final theme emerges in a confident C major, but with F sharps which once send the music off into E minor again. In the symphony's last moments, there is further evidence of neglect of the dominant chord, as the strings' alternation of the notes B and C battles against a C pedal and a C major chordal background as obdurate as those with which the work began.

The Fourth Symphony moves beyond the implications of any Lydian inflexion into a tonal battleground. The first movement's opening four notes hint at a Lydian-inflected C major, which then seems to veer towards E minor for a 'cello solo. C major seems to be battling tortuously back when it is overthrown at the last minute by F sharp and C sharp pedals, and a second group takes shape in F sharp major instead. Eventually the real key centre of A (midway between F sharp and C) asserts itself conclusively. In the second movement, a mildly Lydian inflexion gives way to aggressive falling tritones which stifle a proper return of the opening section. The slow movement finds a noble melody based on two rising perfect fifths gradually gaining ground over diminished fifths and the rhythmic instability which they bring. But the real battle is yet to come.

The Finale begins disarmingly enough with gentle Lydian D sharps in A major; but a continuous *pianissimo* texture for strings in A major becomes the backcloth for a woodwind interjection in E flat major. The strings (and horns) eventually take the hint and move towards E flat themselves, only to find that the woodwind have also changed allegiance. E flat major and A major argue over neutral, rhythmically unstable bass lines until their incompatability is seen at its plainest in a straight chordal alternation. The argument is diffused by new material in a subtly disguised tonality, and then exactly neutralised by a block of C major harmony shot through by a trumpet F sharp.

After development, the second encounter of A major and E flat major makes the first seem like an amusing skirmish. The atmosphere is similar at first: the strings now begin their backcloth in E flat, the wind interject in A. But this time the destructive force of the tritone sounds terminal. The strings' *moto perpetuo* teeters into uncertain triplets as familiar motives wander around in a texture of chaotic polyphony, with no apparent rhythmic stability or tonal direction. The diffusing agent adds its voice, but this time it is too late; the music has gone beyond argument. The glockenspiel makes a brief attempt to recall the opening A major before being brushed aside by the disembodied fragments which make up the coda. At first vigorous and chromatic, this final section gradually resigns itself to an A minor stripped of all melodic pretension. It is, in one sense, too negative an ending to imply any sort of victory – for A over E flat, for instance; but in its inspired individuality there is a positive quality, and certainly a freedom from the bombast or 'circus' against which Sibelius claimed to be protesting. For all its air of disintegration, there is a kind of coldly passionate intensity, especially in the string writing, which looks forward to the Sixth and Seventh Symphonies. And finally: what other symphony ends *mezzo forte*?

If the Fifth Symphony is less totally governed by the tritone than the Fourth, it is certainly as full of pedal-points and as bereft of the dominant key as the Third. The Third and the Fifth also have rhythmically repetitive, tonally static middle movements in common. There are further static elements in the Fifth's Finale. Both principal ideas are grounded firmly on their tonic chord: the second is so reluctant to employ a related key that it only achieves it halfway through its course by a straightforward sidestep from E flat major to C major. Later the recapitulation chooses to begin in G flat major, presumably so that it can return to E flat major without further alteration (a link with the Schubertian ploy of beginning the reprise in the subdominant). But the slow culminatory final section, its rhythmic polyphony for brass a degree more complex and dissonant than the equivalent passage in the Third, does of course show that Sibelius was not going to content himself with mere perfunctory repetition (see Ex. 6).

By now it has become quite clear how closely Sibelius' imagination is allied to his use of the orchestra, and, in particular, how separate from each other the three main instrumental groups can seem, even in a *tutti* passage. 'Look at his orchestration, that mass of different instruments in unison!' Sibelius once commented, in disparagement of Wagner's methods.* If the end of the Fifth's Finale demonstrates Sibelius' sonorous use of the full brass section at moments of culmination, the first movement of the Fifth shows at several points how readily his string section retreats into background figuration, and how often his woodwind instruments are found in pairs a third apart. The Fourth Symphony separates the groups even more severely, and in the Finale (as we have seen) gives strings and wind opposing tonal roles. The expansion of the significance of instrumentation is an important factor in the tonal argument of Sibelius' Sixth Symphony.

The symphonic challenge of the tritone was wholeheartedly faced in the Fourth; in the Sixth (1923) the main discussion is between tonality and modality. Sibelius exploits the properties of the Dorian mode with twentieth-century tonal hindsight, and probably in a more symphonic manner than ever before. He shows how the Dorian mode beginning on D, with its raised sixth degree (B natural) but flattened seventh (C natural), lies with perfect ambiguity between C major and D minor. The notes which characterize the mode – here B and C – pull strongly towards C major, unless D is felt to be the starting or stopping point, which of course it often is. And the note C sharp may pull D Dorian towards D minor. The first evidence that instrumentation is going to play an important part in this discussion takes the form of a harmonic superimposition, of a kind found also in the Fourth and Fifth Symphonies. An opening paragraph for strings and wind, poised inimitably between D Dorian and the 'neutral' F major, reaches – surprisingly – a seventh chord on C sharp. This chord is reiterated with increasing conviction, until trumpets and trombones, heard for the first time, slide in underneath with the work's first C major chord. The final bars of the movement find the brass interrupting again to proclaim C major, before strings and wind have the last quiet word in D Dorian. The brass identification with C major is emphasized again in the Finale at two important points; and it is significant that they are silent in its coda, as the work settles for D Dorian at the end.

Instrumental involvement in the rivalry between C and D compensates for the understated quality of their relationship, anticipated in earlier works by Sibelius' tendency to allow two keys to co-exist. But there is still definition in his structural schemes. The D Dorian of the outer movements and most of

* Bengt von Törne, *Sibelius, a close-up*, London, 1937, p. 60.

the third, is met by a balance between the G Dorian of the second movement, and use of A Dorian in the third. The A Dorian reinstates F sharp, which had been of tonal significance in the first movement, combining in the second group and developmental backcloth with C to provide still more tritone suggestions. The first movement does display a clear duality of key and mode in its two groups of material (and, in the exposition only, the illusion of different tempi). The sonata structure of the third movement is paradoxically more thoroughly Dorian and nearer to tonal convention: it uses A Dorian, the 'Dorian dominant', instead of C major as its secondary 'key'. The second movement, no more a genuine slow movement than the middle movements of the Third and Fifth, makes few concessions to symphonic normality: it virtually dispenses with a return to opening material, as the second movement of the Fourth had done. The Finale finds a new kind of balance. Three 'waves' of material oscillating between C and D are placed between an opening antiphonal exchange, fairly firmly in C major, and its return which ends poised in the neutral area of F. The most chromatic areas of both outer movements are the codas, which clear the air for the final gentle insistences of D Dorian. An important link between all the movements is the scalic descent of four notes with which the work begins, which characteristically finds culmination in the Finale's slow coda.

Although much admired by Sibelius enthusiasts, the Sixth has never become a popular work. This it has in common with the Fourth – but the Fourth is distinctly 'unpopular' in character. The Sixth is not deliberately uningratiating, but it is perhaps deliberately self-effacing. It does in fact use a slightly larger orchestra than the Fifth, but the bass clarinet and harp are not used in a flamboyant fashion: compare the harp writing in the First Symphony. Unusual instrumental effects are generally found low down in the texture – the four-part tremolo for 'cellos at the end of the first movement, for instance. A lot of the thematic material is scalic and intrinsically very plain; there are no dramatic leaps in its contours. Sometimes it is hard to tell foreground ideas from background: for instance, the return of the opening subject of the first movement is found almost note for note in the figuration which accompanies it. Ideas are not developed in a muscular way; instead Sibelius uses with great ingenuity devices such as canon (especially in the third movement), augmentation, diminution and inversion, which do not give the impression of developmental argument. The outer movements employ sequence a good deal, but it is invariably sequence descending in whole tones, which has a relaxing rather than an intensifying effect. When the music is static, it is not static in that monumental sense of being based on immense pedal points. Even the strongly rhythmic gestures of the last two movements tend to repeat themselves until they become hypnotic rather than vital; while in the opening sections of the first two movements and again at the very end of the symphony, the rhythmic subtlety is such that it sounds as if the music has been composed without barlines. Not all these qualities are entirely new, but they are certainly pronounced in the Sixth.

The complementary outer edges of the symphony have often attracted comparisons with Palestrina and sixteenth-century polyphony. The barline-less quality is certainly a link; but entries at unexpected parts of the bar are found in all Sibelius' significant works. What draws our attention here in particular is the polyphonic balance of the string writing, often involving contrary motion between outer parts. This is certainly one of several features which unite the Sixth and Seventh Symphonies, and set them apart from earlier works – the last two symphonies were, after all, conceived at around the same time. There is also a greater interest in antiphonal exchanges in these works, usually between instrumental groups. Partly for this purpose, the woodwind are often split into two further groups, flutes and bassoons alternating with oboes and clarinets. Here then are three new aspects of balance: in polyphony, antiphony and instrumentation. Introduced in the Sixth Symphony, they are used further in the Seventh to help Sibelius meet the demands of the one-movement form, in which an overall balance needs to operate on many levels for the structure to succeed.

Although it was originally titled *Fantasia Sinfonica*, Sibelius soon decided that his new one-movement work (1924) was worthy of the name Symphony No. 7. It is in C major; and a look back over the previous four symphonies will reveal how great the domination of C major has been. It is the key of the Third, the relative major of the Fourth and the important 'neutral agent' in its Finale, the key which first forces away the tonic in the Fifth's Finale, and the principal opposition – the key of the brass – in the Sixth. Although it is now the tonic key, C major is also strongly associated with the brass in the Seventh Symphony. The principal structural feature of the work takes the form of a slow trombone theme in C, which appears three times, the second time in the minor. Slow sections begin and end the work, building up to and climbing down from this theme; and the two central sections between trombone statements both reveal their fastest speeds just before the trombone returns.

This simple symmetry is complemented in other ways. One element, still aurally obvious, is emphasized by instrumentation: fragments for flutes, clarinets and bassoons beginning in the seventh bar are heard again up to seven bars before the end; and immediately within these fragments are passages of string polyphony – expansive and calm early on, intense and short-lived towards the end. Balance between woodwind and string contributions is displayed through antiphonal writing, especially in the two fastest passages, and to a far greater extent than any of his previous works.

The most all-pervading element of balance, however, derives directly from the polyphonic integrity which was also apparent in the outer edges of the Sixth Symphony: with contrary motion between outer parts, and melodic movement in one direction being immediately followed by movement in the other. An astonishing proportion of the thematic material in the Seventh is based on the encircling of tonic and dominant notes in this manner:

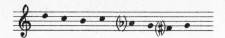

There are less obvious references to these 'cells'. The first appearance of the trombone theme, for instance, begins with the notes D – C and ends with B – C at around the same pitch. If the final B – C movement is disguised in the two later versions of the theme, it may be in order to save something for the final culmination of the motive. The encircling of both tonic and dominant is disguised in a passage for flutes, bassoons and horns involving contrary motion between outer parts, soon after that first trombone utterance:

Ex. 7.

Its passionate re-emergence for upper strings marks the beginning of the final slow section, in which the dominance of the shape in its two forms is at its plainest. After the violins have dwelt with great intensity on F sharp – G – A flat – G, the final bars grind out D – C – B – C in a way which demonstrates Sibelius' instinctively individual use of dissonance: first D and then B are squeezed into C with an almost tortuous finality.

If the three trombone statements and this ending indicate the supremacy of C, this is certainly not how it appeared at the outset. A rising scale figure (with Sibelius' remarkable double basses dragging a quaver behind) leads to the work's first chord: A flat minor. Sibelius, the instinctive symphonist, makes use of this surprise, ensuring that the second central interlude uses the key centres A flat, C flat and E flat prominently; but no key really ever looks like challenging C. The battle of the Fourth's Finale and the gentler vacillating of the Sixth are not to be repeated. Once again Sibelius has created a new symphonic context to explore.

For all its novelty, the Seventh does draw together a great many elements from the earlier symphonies in a consummation of his highly individual methods. His control of all kinds of transition is evident here: the two fastest tempi of the work give way to the trombone theme by means of ostinato patterns which at first seem fast, but soon accommodate monumental slowness. His string ostinati, here as elsewhere, do strictly speaking belong to the background, but they invariably contain such cumulative potential that they are quite capable of rising up to overwhelm their surroundings.

Huge pedal points are less in evidence in the last two symphonies, but long held notes in all parts of the texture, often growing in prominence after an inconspicuous start, continue to feature widely. The motive which linked the three middle symphonies (see Exx. 5 and 6) returns in the second central interlude; and it is remarkably close to the C minor version of the trombone theme. The Lydian F sharps which do not lead to dominant chords, the Bs not harmonised by dominant chords – the very end is a striking example – also remind us of the middle symphonies, especially the Third. Indeed, the Third's tendency towards E as a tonal centre is once again in evidence: note the decisive cadences in E as the trombone is shaken off after its second and third appearances (before letter N and at letter Z respectively). Not to be outdone, the Dorian mode of the Sixth (but also notable in works as far back as *Kullervo*) is clearly present in the earlier part of the first central episode. If the strings' polyphony of the last two symphonies sounds a new note, the brass's rhythmic interactions around the solo trombone provide a clear reminder of the brass polyphony in the final stages of the Third and Fifth. Perhaps above all, the ending of the Seventh shows again how masterful Sibelius was in his achievement of genuine motivic culmination, and how invariably he achieves this genuine symphonic finality at a slow pace. This of course is indicative of the slow momentum which lies deep beneath all his important works.

Tapiola, Sibelius' greatest and most thematically close-knit tone poem, followed a year after the Seventh Symphony in 1925. Sibelius never changed his mind about its title as he had done with the *Fantasia Sinfonica*. The score is after all prefaced by a descriptive stanza, while the seven symphonies are entirely abstract in content. Furthermore, it is virtually monothematic: its intense obsession with a single melodic strand of stepwise motion makes even the Seventh seem profligate in motivic variety. After *Tapiola*, and for over thirty years until Sibelius' death in 1957, there was conjecture over a real Eighth Symphony, which Sibelius told Basil Cameron in 1945 had been 'finished' many times, but not to his satisfaction. At his death it was announced that the Eighth did not exist.

Why did the Eighth never emerge? It is possible that the intellectual processes required to get a symphony of Sibelian density down on paper were by now beyond him; but we can speculate more positively than that. The Seventh and *Tapiola* reveal a level of motivic resource and organic symphonic development which perhaps not even Sibelius could ever have surpassed. His recorded frustrations with the Eighth Symphony plans may have been in part an acknowledgement that he had achieved his own kind of consummation sooner than he would have liked. In those post-war years he had grown beyond the Fourth Symphony's element of protest, but with no sense of compromising his utterly distinctive musical personality.

15

Nielsen

David Fanning

The Danes, masters of self-deprecation, speak of some of their achievements as being 'world-famous in Denmark'. But it would seem that their national composer actually has become world-famous in the world – and this virtually behind their backs, for they themselves have never gone out of their way to promote his cause. The article on 'The Symphony' in the 1980 *New Grove Dictionary of Music and Musicians* discusses Carl Nielsen (1865–1931) on an equal footing with Mahler and Sibelius; there are currently six complete or near-complete cycles of the symphonies available on CD. Here are indications of a degree of recognition which few would have predicted twenty years ago.

From the seventh of twelve children born in 1865 to a village house-painter, to Denmark's national composer, and now to internationally acclaimed symphonist, is some story. And whatever the risk of fairytale cliché, the importance of Nielsen's humble background has to be stressed. The mother's singing, the father's violin and cornet-playing in the village band, the four-year-old Nielsen's makeshift outdoor xylophone, the eleven-year-old's improvised descants at wedding feasts, all these, combined with the sights, sounds and personalities of the island of Fünen, implanted a reverence for the 'simple original' which was to become a lifelong artistic creed.*

Nielsen's early musical experiences, whether in village dance-bands or in the local amateur orchestra, were predominantly of Viennese Classical or classically-derived idioms. In the impressionable years of adolescence he was therefore shielded, as a city boy would not have been, from the Romantic high-art music of the day. As a student at Copenhagen Conservatoire and afterwards with the pedagogue Orla Rosenhoff, he was schooled in solid mid-nineteenth-century Germanic compositional values; but his deepest attachments, for Bach and the Viennese Classics, had already been formed. He rapidly came to respect Brahms, who with Dvořák is a

---

* See the essay 'Musical Problems' in *Living Music*, London, 1953, p. 42. Nielsen's early life is delightfully recounted in *My Childhood*, London, 1953.

conspicuous stylistic influence on his first large-scale compositions; but he had little enthusiasm for the academically smoothed-over Romanticism of Niels Gade – the Grand Old Man of Danish music at the time – and at the other extreme, his initial enthusiasm for Wagner soon cooled. Nielsen's opinions on his contemporaries frequently hinged on whether he felt their music to be 'healthy'.

His own First Symphony, composed 1891–94, exudes a tremendous sense of confidence and well-being. As well it might. After a couple of years of freelance playing and teaching he had secured a post as second violin in the Royal Theatre Orchestra, had won a scholarship and travelled to Dresden, Berlin, Leipzig, Paris and Italy, had met and married the sculptress Anne Marie Brodersen, and had scored a gratifying success with his Little Suite for Strings, Op. 1 (FS6).* He had already made one attempt at a symphony in 1888, and the single completed movement had been successfully performed. This was a 3/4 sonata *Allegro* in F major with some traces of the familiar Nielsenish geniality and some more obvious ones of simple inexperience – timing and proportions are rather hit-and-miss and the music rarely succeeds in driving itself forward over a long span. Recognising the excessive stylistic debt to Johan Svendsen (especially to his Second Symphony of 1880–83) Nielsen left the movement unpublished. Under the somewhat misleading title of 'Symphonic Rhapsody' it is occasionally played and has been recorded. In this movement and in a number of string quartets (two of them unpublished and unnumbered) Nielsen began to fashion the tools of his symphonic trade. And of all his many learning experiences around 1890, perhaps the most decisive was his encounter with Beethoven's Fifth Symphony, whose first movement so impressed him that he set about copying it out note for note. With all these things behind him, Nielsen could now see his way clear to the large-scale co-ordination and enhancement of his ideas.

An early review of the First Symphony summed it up as 'a child playing with dynamite'† – an overstatement no doubt, but one which accurately reflects the fusion of wonder and energy. The dynamite is in the small rhythmical units – the three elements marked in Ex. 1 have something very close to a Beethovenian generative force, far removed from the then more common melody-based conception of symphonism. The interruption of harmonic flow just before the second subject is again Classical in principle if not in practice, and it enables Nielsen imaginatively to redirect conventional harmonic sequences and to freshen the effect of the conventional relative major when it eventually appears in the codetta.

* Nielsen's opus numbers are chaotic and misleading and his works are now generally referred to by FS numbers, after the catalogue published by Dan Fog and Torben Schousboe, Copenhagen, 1965.
† Charles Kjerulf in *Politiken*, cited by Knud Ketting in liner notes to BIS CD 454 (1990).

This kind of delayed fulfilment will become a vital ingredient in his later symphonies.

Ex. 1.

Here is a composer winning his symphonic spurs, and there are many similar examples in this symphony of poetry and drama expressed by fundamental musical interactions, rather than by exotic textural or programmatic means. The beginning of the first movement development section is perhaps even more noteworthy. Here Nielsen quietly probes the common ground between his themes whilst his harmony marks time. This magical moment of alert tranquillity enhances the dramatic intensifications to come and fosters a special kind of intent listening; it tells the audience that this is something more than just a major talent at work.

The very first phrase of the symphony has to wrest its G minor home key from the clutches of a bold C major chord (see Ex. 1), and this tension is reinforced at the exposition repeat by a perfect cadence. Here is forecast the eventual C major destination of the entire work. An initial area of tonal instability and its consequential follow-through is a wholly Beethovenian concept (Beethoven tended to reserve it for finales, though); nor is it all that rare for a work to end in a key other than that of its opening. But for a symphony to display these features does seem to be unprecedented (Beethoven's First derives remarkable consequences from its initial oscillation to the flat and sharp sides of the tonic, but the final tonic destination is never in doubt). The conclusion of Nielsen's First Symphony in C major is no mere token gesture to his opening chord (nor *vice versa*). It reflects a daring inter-penetration of structure and style, worked out in the mid-range time-spans of the music. The point-to-point progress of that working-out can be followed in Robert Simpson's study of Nielsen,* to which one general observation might be added. Even as late as the Finale coda there is no reason why the conclusion *has* to be in C major. But the potential excitement of a coda in the conventional G major is vitiated by the fact that the slow movement has been in this key and that the scherzo-substitute third movement (in E flat) has repeatedly dwelled on G minor. The C major conclusion is in this sense a kind of enhanced *tierce de Picardie*, and the harmonic processes throughout the work ensure not that it will be inevitable, but that it will be fresh without sounding arbitrary.

The great symphonies have a quality of spiritual discovery. Nielsen's First has it, if not in the obviously striking ways of near-contemporary symphonies (Mahler 1, Tchaikovsky 6, Dvořák 8 and 9). What it discovers is the possibility of a new vigour, expressed in post-Classical rather than anti-Romantic terms. Nielsen greatly admired the rhythmic verve and vivid orchestral colouring of Johan Svendsen's music, and traces of his influence remain. The progression shown in Ex. 2, heard in all four movements, also features in Svendsen's *Carnival in Paris*, a kind of Scandinavian-accented Berlioz overture, which Nielsen heard and was captivated by in 1890. Even this progression is absorbed into his overall tonal argument, as a means of leaning towards C major, and it is retained as a Nielsenish fingerprint in the first movements of his Second and Third Symphonies.

Ex. 2.

Nielsen's first three symphonies came at nine-year intervals. This was partly for practical reasons – his work in the Royal Theatre Orchestra from 1887 to 1905 was time-consuming (at times soul-destroying) and the demands of a young family were considerable (three children were born between 1891 and 1895), especially as his wife was actively pursuing her own artistic career. But no less important was the need Nielsen felt to wait for what he called the 'undercurrent'.

In the event it was a chance encounter which set the current in motion for his Second Symphony (1901–02). In a village pub in Zealand he saw

---

* *Carl Nielsen: Symphonist*, London, 1952; 2nd rev. ed. London, 1979. This masterly survey is an essential point of reference for an understanding of Nielsen.

a painting personifying the Four Temperaments – Choleric, Phlegmatic, Melancholic and Sanguine – which in medieval theory make up the human personality. The exaggerated portraits caused him great amusement, but he realized on reflection that they might also provide the germ of a symphonic concept. They also chimed in with his growing fascination for character types. Nielsen's father had been renowned for the subtlety of his character impersonations,* and the young Carl inherited something of the gift (as some photographic portraits from about 1885 suggest).† The ability to identify with another personality as though from within surfaces constantly in his verbal descriptions (notably of the elderly Brahms, whom he met in 1894).‡ It was a quality Nielsen found and treasured in the operas of Mozart and which he endeavoured to emulate in his own first opera, *Saul and David* (composed 1898–1901 and first performed a couple of weeks after the Second Symphony). If his concept of the symphony was to expand and yet avoid false pathos and theatricality, the idea of character archetypes offered the ideal stimulus.

The first movement of the First Symphony already bore the unusual designation *allegro orgoglioso* [proudly].§ This was the first in a succession of esoteric Italian terms that were to become a hallmark of Nielsen's scores. They are also an external symptom of his distance from the issues of subjective versus objective, programmatic versus absolute, post-Romantic versus neo-Classical, which dominated musical aesthetics and criticism during his lifetime. More than any of those labels the essence of Nielsen's art is empathy. Empathy could broaden through character-types (Symphony 2, 'The Four Temperaments') into an identification with elemental life-forces (Symphonies 3 and 4, *Sinfonia espansiva* and 'The Inextinguishable'); those forces could in turn gain in perspective from the need to assert and defend them in the context of life-threatening opposition (Symphonies 4 and 5); and one way of approaching the problematic Sixth Symphony (*Sinfonia semplice*) is to see it as an agonized questioning of the victory-through-struggle ethic of its predecessors – another broadening, of a kind.

A vital feature of 'The Four Temperaments' is the quality of controlled excess. The Choleric first movement and the Melancholic third have passages of exceptional contrapuntal density, respectively manic and depressive, which pay scant regard to aesthetic norms. No less strikingly, the Phlegmatic second movement and the Sanguine Finale indulge in passages of idleness and recklessness which circumvent conventional symphonic decorum, but which require only a modest exercise of empathy on the listener's part to be understood and relished.

The expansion of Nielsen's technique to accommodate these extremes is

---

* See *My Childhood*, pp. 76–77.
† See Mina Miller, *Carl Nielsen: A Guide to Research*, New York and London, 1987, pl. 3.
‡ Simpson, op. cit., 2nd ed., p. 19.
§ The original heading had been *allegro marcato*.

impressive. His instinct for motivic and thematic working now extends to a wellnigh virtuosic spanning of the contrast between main subject areas in the first movement exposition, and the wide-ranging chromaticism of the third movement is a potent individualization of the language of Franck and Reger. Even when moderation is the order of the day individual details are intensely memorable – rather like someone who sees the same things as the rest of us but with a penetration and freshness we can only rarely glimpse.

Each movement in 'The Four Temperaments' is centred on a tonality a major third below its predecessor (except that the Finale *rises* a third from the end of the third movement) and in each case it takes up the previous movement's subsidiary tonality as its own home tonic. Later in life Nielsen claimed never to have planned out the complex designs his pupils and commentators discerned in his music; but the designs he referred to were probably thematic rather than tonal ones, since it was not until the appearance of Robert Simpson's study in 1952 that Nielsen's 'progressive tonality' was analysed with any degree of thoroughness.* Even allowing for an element of contentiousness in such analyses it seems clear that key-evolution within a work was a conscious part of his compositional technique. And even if aspects of that evolution seem to over-estimate the faculties of most listeners, their presence would be largely justified by the composer's belief in them – in that such belief would encourage his creative imagination to flourish in other, allied musical dimensions.

The D major Finale of 'The Four Temperaments' is capped by a coda in A major. To this sharpwards progression in tonality is allied a transformation of the main theme into a march, reflecting the Sanguine temperament's ability to learn from experience – 'more dignified and not so silly and self-satisfied as in some of the previous parts of his development', as Nielsen put it.† Roughly the same tonal progression underpins the whole of the *Sinfonia espansiva* of 1910–11; five years later the Fourth Symphony rests on a double sharpwards progression – from D to A major in the first movement, from A to E in the Finale; and there are vestiges of the same terracing in fifths in the first movement of No. 5 (1921–2). In each case the implication, resting on the Classical heightening of tension in a sharpwards modulation, is of psychological growth or enhancement of awareness.

In 1906, midway between the Second and Third Symphonies, Nielsen scored a huge success with his comic opera *Maskarade*, an immensely tuneful and good-natured score which was to become virtually *the* Danish national opera. This was also the period of the genial Fourth String Quartet and of some of his most popular strophic songs. Nielsen was coming into his

* The term 'progressive tonality' had been in circulation for some time before then, mainly as applied to Mahler. Simpson later expressed a preference for the term 'emergent tonality' – see his 'Carl Nielsen and Tonality', *Dansk musiktidskrift* x1/4 (May 1965), pp. 89–93.
† Nielsen's programme note for 'The Four Temperaments' is given in full in Simpson, op. cit., 2nd ed., pp. 33–35.

prime, and from this time on growing recognition of his talents brought increasing numbers of commissions for incidental music and cantatas. In 1908, three years after resigning as a violinist, he was appointed second Kapellmeister at the Royal Theatre, a post he would hold until June 1914. Among many significant musical impressions at the time was Sibelius's Second Symphony. A letter to Sibelius of 9 February 1909 testifies to its effect on Nielsen,* and bearing in mind that work on the *Sinfonia espansiva* was soon to begin, it may be that the long pedal-points and high string writing of the second movement owe something to that impression.

The pedal-points are one aspect of the 'expansive' in the Third Symphony, but not the most important. The fundamental meaning for Nielsen is, as Simpson writes, 'the outward growth of the mind's scope and the expansion of life which comes with it'.† By the same token the musical paragraphs are not just longer than in the previous two symphonies, but also, at least in the first and third movements, more explosive and centrifugally directed.

The opening *Allegro espansivo* marks the first appearance in Nielsen's symphonies of the swinging, athletic triple time for which he is famous. This is a fusion of elements of classical Scherzo and first movement momentum, which may swing towards a waltz transformation or towards energetic *fugato* counterpoint, but whose main mood can only be summed up by the particular connotation of 'expansiveness' noted above. With its highly arched contours, thrusting rhythms and propulsive harmony this kind of writing gives the sensation of being composed in the future tense, always forward-looking (Ex. 3). Its most obvious progenitor is the opening movement of Schumann's Third Symphony, 'The Rhenish', and its debut in Nielsen's output is in the opening scene of *Saul and David*, where the Israelites are anxiously awaiting the delayed arrival of Samuel.

Ex. 3. Symphony No. 3

* See Erik Tawaststjerna, *Sibelius*, Volume II, 1904–1914, London, 1986, p. 235.
† Simpson, op. cit., 2nd ed., p. 57.

Apart from this special brand of expansiveness the first movement is also Nielsen's hitherto most emancipated with respect to sonata-form layout and functional harmony; and the measure of his creative evolution is the assurance with which he makes the emancipated elements interact. Also swept aside is the dominance of the four-bar phrase which was the main sign of a residual caution in the first two symphonies. The pastoral slow movement irresistibly evokes the rolling countryside eulogized in the essay 'The Song of Fünen' in *Living Music* (virtually the only example of Nielsen's literary style going 'over the top'). Wordless vocalises for solo soprano and baritone are brought in to heighten the lyrical ecstasy, and Nielsen's sketches reveal a partial texting for this section which he later suppressed: 'All thoughts disappear. Ah! All thoughts disappear[,] I lie beneath the sky'.

If the tranquillity of the slow movement conclusion explores one aspect of the 'expansive', the third movement counters it with activity and assertive will-power. Already in the First Symphony this was the point where Nielsen was most willing to allow an unfolding psychological drama to override formal conventions. The third movement of the *Espansiva* is less of a scherzo than ever (not least because so much scherzo-like momentum has been transferred to the first movement). This movement forges a vital link in the tonal argument – the key of D major, from which the Finale will spring towards the eventual goal of A major. The Finale is at once the easiest movement to grasp and the most problematic in context. It is openhearted and virtually free from shadow or conflict, yet for precisely that reason difficult to reconcile as a conclusion to such a dynamically conceived work. Even Simpson suspects an element of irony in the opening theme,[*] which the composer's description seems not to allow: 'the orchestra sings its introductory theme in so commonplace a fashion that you might well call this theme "healthy-popular" ["sundt-populært"]. After a development which touches on other moods in the middle of the movement the Finale closes with its first theme, like a man who uninterested, but soundly and at his ease, nears the objective of his travels.'[†] In the long run the Finale can be felt as wholly characteristic of Nielsen and his view of life, but unless it is taken (and of course played) in the same open-hearted spirit in which it is offered, it can seem homespun or even patronizing. In that sense the apparently more challenging Finale of the Fourth Symphony is easier to relate to.

Up to this point it is possible to view Nielsen's symphonism as a steady expansion of horizons, with compensating stylistic adjustments on the way. The process does continue in the Fourth Symphony (1914–15), with the linking of the four traditional movements into a continuous whole, with an idyllic slow movement as it were in parentheses, with the forging of the

[*] Private communication.
[†] Torben Schousboe, 'Tre program-noter af Carl Nielsen om "Sinfonia espansiva" ', *Musik og Forskning*, 6, 1980 p. 5–14 p. 12.

Finale's opening key in a tensely dramatic third movement, and with the 'terracing' of keys as a means to organising their mid-term progression. Even the preface to the score suggests a logical broadening of scope – 'With the title "The Inextinguishable" the composer has sought to indicate in one word what only music has the power to express in full: *The elemental Will of Life*'. (The grammatical sense of the title is 'that which is inextinguishable', rather than 'the inextinguishable symphony'.) But there are other respects in which the years between the Third and Fourth symphonies mark a major re-orientation in Nielsen's style. A significant toughening is already evident in the Second Violin Sonata of 1912, and a number of Danish scholars attribute the asperity of the Fourth Symphony to the crisis in his personal life at the time – Nielsen and his wife were separated from 1915 to 1922. In the Finale of 'The Inextinguishable' the element of antagonism comes to the fore, embodied in two competing sets of timpani; but it is also inherent in the streams of linear writing which obscure the tonality of the very beginning of the work and which turn the first part of the development section into something of a battlefield too. Not only is the norm of dissonance several degrees higher, but there a jaggedness of continuity beyond anything to be found in the *Espansiva*.

'The Inextinguishable' is Nielsen's most often-played and recorded symphony; yet it can also provoke the most resistance. Are the contrasts of style not too programmatically blatant? Is the long stream of Sibelian thirds which first brings order out of chaos capable of sustaining the extreme demands placed on it? Is the dissonant counterpoint in the first movement precisely heard? The last of these queries tends to evaporate in the concert hall, where the textures have more space to breathe than in even the finest recording; and the Finale pulls the threads together in a way which drives previous uncertainties from the mind. But it needs to be a very special performance to carry conviction from first note to last; it is indicative that one of the major revisions in the second edition of Simpson's book is an additional page outlining traps for the unwary conductor in this work.*

The impact of the Fifth Symphony can also vary dramatically from performance to performance. Just as there is a fine line between the elemental and the banal, between the revelatory and the naïve, so Nielsen's symphonic battleground of opposed forces, with a side-drum in the first movement instructed to improvise 'as if at all costs he wants to stop the progress of the orchestra', can be made to seem simple-minded. He himself stressed the contrast between passive-idyllic vegetating and positive action: 'There is something very primitive I wanted to express: the division between dark and light, the fight between good and evil. A title such as "Dream and Deeds [Drøm og Daad]" might perhaps convey the inner picture I had in mind during the composition.'† What he did not mention were the shades

* Simpson, op. cit., 2nd ed., pp. 88–89.
† L. Dolleris, C. Nielsen, *En Musikbiografi*, Odense, 1949, pp. 260–1.

of expectation he composed into those oppositions and which display an extraordinary range of harmonic resourcefulness. In the first movement in particular he seems to crawl through the gaps between traditional harmonic functions and discover a strange new world of wandering, hovering, and superimposed tonalities and modalities, all subtly animated and inter-related. On the conductor's instinctive response to this, plus the ability of the solo clarinettist and side-drummer to hold the stage rather than politely integrating themselves into the texture, hangs the drama of the first movement.

For the only time in his six symphonies Nielsen abandons the four-movement layout. The second movement of the Fifth can admittedly be thought of as a three-in-one design enclosing Scherzo and slow movement (both fugal) in an interrupted Finale, and so as an extension of the kind of telescoping of middle movements favoured by Berwald. But the overriding point is to embody a conflict every bit as terrifying as that in the first movement and a resolution even more invigorating – this time it is the undermining of regenerative forces, countered not by matching force with force but by responding to despair with reason. The conductor has a responsibility here, too. The opening needs to go at or close to its fast metronome mark (dotted minim = 72–76) if it is to pack the right dramatic punch; and the same goes for the following *presto* F minor section – to hell with the strings, because that is where this Witches' Sabbath of a fugue is taking us anyway. In a performance where everything clicks Nielsen's Fifth can indeed seem, as Deryck Cooke once proposed, 'the greatest symphony of the present century'. Not that such things should be reduced to league tables, but if only a dozen symphonies were destined to survive from the twentieth into the twenty-first century Nielsen's Fifth, by the scope of its humanity and musicality, would have a good claim to be among them.

'The Inextinguishable' and the Fifth Symphony brought Nielsen the greatest measure of international recognition. Indeed it is somewhat ironic that Scandinavian critics who had found a vein of wilful experimentation in his earlier works were bowled over by these apparently far more challenging masterpieces. Nevertheless for Nielsen himself some of the edge was taken off his creative triumphs by the realization that his music had not made the headway outside Scandinavia that it deserved. He found little to admire in the European musical scene in the twenties, and to make matters worse his own health was being undermined by heart problems which first manifested themselves after his intense hard work on the Fifth Symphony.

To what extent any or all of these factors colour the Sixth Symphony (1924–25) is a moot point, and the intention behind its subtitle *Sinfonia semplice* is similarly open to question. Nielsen's own comments on the work give little clue, except as regards the 'Humoreske' second movement: 'Times change. Where is music going? What is permanent? We don't know!'[*]

---

* Simpson, op. cit., 2nd ed., p. 113.

Even this is a pale indication of the music's withering sarcasm, and if the 'Humoreske' is a parody then the object would seem to be not so much the casual dissonance of the 1920s vernacular as the experiences set out in his own intensely tragic first movement. Tonalities, progressions, themes and instrumental timbres are taken over and wilfully distorted, while a trombone delivers yawns of contempt (specifically identified as such in the first edition of the score). The change of style from previous symphonies is evident throughout the symphony in the almost total purging of the element of song (one reason, perhaps, why the brief lyrical phrase for the trombone in the *minore* Variation of the Finale carries such intense pathos).

Robert Simpson's first analysis of the *Sinfonia semplice* was made from the score, without the benefit of even having heard the work. It stressed the tragic power of the first movement's 'loss of and fruitless search for a state of childlike joy', but considered the remainder of the work as a 'kind of appendix in which Nielsen descends from objectivity to subjectivity'.* By 1979 his view had been radically revised to stress the catastrophe of bars 171ff. in the first movement ('almost literally evocative of a heart attack'),† followed by various avoidances and the eventual acceptance of the B flat tonality associated with the onset of that catastrophe. The degree of selectiveness which sustains this analysis is worrying and its anecdotal reference seems too pat. To take a different, no more selective approach, at least as much local and global musical significance is concentrated in the *culmination* of that same catastrophe (bars 184ff.). In any case some big musicological guns are currently being trained on the *Sinfonia semplice* and it may be that new perspectives will emerge from that. For the moment it seems prudent to continue to view the work as an unsolved enigma. Certainly it marks a radical change of tack, and in this it is comparable to the last symphonies of Bax, Vaughan Williams, Prokofiev and Shostakovich. Indeed if there was the slightest shred of evidence that Shostakovich was acquainted with Nielsen's music I would seize on it, for so much that is distinctive in the *Sinfonia semplice* – the brutalization of virtually every theme in the first movement, the post-*Petrushka* antics of the second and fourth movements – looks forward to the Russian. Indeed the commencement with quiet repeated notes on the glockenspiel, plus the very notion of a symphony conceived as simple and childlike, yet warped by experience, calls to mind Shostakovich's Fifteenth Symphony.

Having been born in the same year as Sibelius, Nielsen ceased his symphonic output at almost exactly the same time. Sibelius had thirty years still to live and his creative silence was absolute, whereas Nielsen had only six more years, during which he produced two of the century's greatest concertos (for flute and for clarinet) and much other music of the highest quality. But for all sorts of cultural reasons the late twenties

* Simpson, op. cit., 1st ed., p. 115.
† Simpson, op. cit., 2nd ed., p. 122.

were one of the most inimical periods to humanistic symphonism since the birth of the genre. I have come across no statement of Nielsen's about 'the future of the symphony', other than a general expression of impatience with inherited movement-schemes (which certainly throws light on the two late concertos); but neither have I come across any mention of a projected Seventh Symphony.

As it is, Nielsen's symphonic career ends enigmatically, rather than with a summing-up comparable to Sibelius's Seventh. But the very questioning of values – Nielsen's own values – in the *Sinfonia semplice* could be said to constitute a courageous advance from the Fifth Symphony. Perhaps most moving of all is the *Proposta seria*, which sets out with much the same passionate determination as the third movement of 'The Inextinguishable' but wins through not to optimistic assertion but to resigned acceptance. In my view the 'facing-up-to-B-flat' explanation is limiting and over-ingenious (as in a sense all analyses tend to be), and it may even be unhelpful to look for the same degree of purely musical coherence as in the previous symphonies. Rather like 'The Inextinguishable', the Sixth shows Nielsen willing to take the risk of a concept outstripping his technique.

Whatever we make of the *Sinfonia semplice* we are left with an immensely invigorating symphonic legacy, as powerful a reminder of the ethical dimension of symphonism as the works of Shostakovich or Tippett. Nielsen helps us to discover the Scandinavian in ourselves, the specifically Danish-Scandinavian in terms of vigour, generosity and empathy. That may sound too good to be true. But for Nielsen the ideal and the real co-existed in a rare harmony, and that too is something that makes his music extraordinarily uplifting.

16

After Sibelius and Nielsen

Robert Layton

Sibelius possessed so powerful a symphonic instinct and so highly developed a feeling for form that he overshadowed all his younger contemporaries as had Grieg in Norway, and the broader history of both Finnish and Norwegian music is the reaction of successive composers to their dominance. Similarly Carl Nielsen exercised a dominant influence not only on younger Danes like Vagn Holmboe and Niels Viggo Bentzon but outside its borders on Swedish composers such as Dag Wirén and Lars-Erik Larsson, and the Norwegians Harald Saeverud and Olav Kielland. What distinguishes their music – as it does that of Falla, Vaughan Williams and Copland – is a strong sense of place. The cool, open textures of the opening of Nielsen's Fifth Symphony seem to spring naturally from the Nordic landscape, just as the cross-hatched string writing and woodwind in thirds that Sibelius made so completely his own seem to be in the air. And this goes for less celebrated Nordic composers too. The luminous woodwind writing of Holmboe, and the gentle melancholy you find in his Swedish contemporaries, Hilding Rosenberg and Lars-Erik Larsson, instantly proclaim their provenance. Their music could be conceived in no other latitudes, for it is the quality of light one finds in the north, the dark winters and the long white summer nights, that conditions their imagination. This pale short-lived summer is central to the Scandinavian sensibility, and the sense of a heightened awareness of the evanescence of life that it brings reinforces the gentle but intense feeling of nostalgia present in so much Nordic music.

But it is not only the natural landscape they inhabit that determined their musical physiognomy. Grieg dominates in Norway because his musical personality was so steeped in the folk melody, speech rhythms and poetic sensibility of his countrymen, while in Finland, Sibelius dominates because his musical inspiration sprang from the very soil of Finland, its rich and wholly individual repertory of myth and its speech rhythms. Words obviously influence the metres and cadences of folksong and if we are to believe the Finnish conductor, Simon Parmet*, the influence in Sibelius's case goes

---

* Simon Parmet, *The Symphonies of Sibelius*, London, 1959.

deeper, for the inflections and speech patterns of Finnish mould the melodic lines, albeit in a subtle fashion, of such works as the First Symphony and 'The Swan of Tuonela'. Nielsen's musical language was enriched by the diatonicism of Danish folk melody and the broader symphonic tradition of Brahms, Svendsen and Dvořák.

Post-nationalism in Sweden

The symphony took second place to opera in late nineteenth-century Sweden and enjoyed relatively frail health. The four symphonies of Ludvig Norman (1831–85) reflect a predominantly Leipzig schooling but have not maintained a foothold on the repertory.* By far the strongest figure to emerge in Berwald's wake was **Wilhelm Stenhammar** (1871–1927). In him three Nordic symphonists met: he was a friend and champion of both Nielsen and Sibelius, and with Tor Aulin, played a leading part in the Berwald revival in the early years of the century. Stenhammar's Symphony in F major (1902–03), written when he was in his early thirties, is an ambitious piece and almost Brucknerian in scale. During this period and in the wake of his opera, *Tirfing* (1898), Stenhammar was undergoing something of a crisis, and struggling to free himself of the dual influences of Wagner and Brahms. The opening horn sextet offers more than a whiff of Valhalla yet a distinctive sensibility can already be discerned. The score betrays sympathies with such composers as Brahms, Bruckner (Stenhammar himself even called the work 'idyllic Bruckner'), and Berwald, and in the slow movement, there is even an affinity with Elgar. However, it is less the fleeting reminders of others that resonate in the mind, but the emerging individuality. Shortly after its Stockholm première, there were plans for Hans Richter to conduct it with the Hallé Orchestra (Richter had conducted his Overture, 'Excelsior!' with the Berlin Philharmonic as early as the 1890s and Stenhammar himself had played his First Piano Concerto under his baton in Manchester). But not long afterwards Stenhammar heard the Second Symphony of Sibelius, and was so bowled over by it that he decided to withdraw his own for revision, and wrote to Richter asking for a postponement. He then became side-tracked by work on other projects, his Second Piano Concerto, the Serenade for Orchestra and his Third and Fourth Quartets – not to mention all his work as a conductor and chamber-music player. Vaclav Talich revived it in Stockholm in 1931, after Stenhammar's death, embodying some of the minor revisions in orchestration which the composer had found time to make. However, the fact remains that Stenhammar had doubts about all but the slow movement, which he had thought of publishing separately under the title 'Nenia'. Indeed when he came to publish the Second over

---

* Nils Castegren, the doyen of Berwald scholars, makes strong claims for No. 3 in D minor.

a decade later, it was simply called 'Symphony in G minor, Op. 34'. By this time Stenhammar had freed himself of Wagnerian influence: indeed, he wrote to Nielsen in 1907:

> I know that you have always striven, successfully, to remain free of Wagner's influence, and I am more and more convinced that this is the only way for us northerners to create a style of our own. For if we go on from where Wagner left off, we will only arrive at Strauss and those who copy him.

Stenhammar himself said of the Second Symphony that he had tried to compose 'sober and honest music free from frills', and the directness of the score is obvious from its very opening. He began work on it in 1911 while at the Villa Borghese, Rome, and finished the first movement in Gothenburg the following year. It took some time before reaching its final shape in 1915 and so became an almost exact contemporary of Nielsen's Fourth and Sibelius's Fifth – in its first version. His handling of sonata design is far more sure-footed than previously, and folk elements and modal polyphony are both elements in its profile. Stenhammar's assimilation of folk material into the bloodstream of his musical being is more complete than any of his Swedish

Ex. 1. Stenhammar: Symphony No. 2

contemporaries. The opening idea is a kind of dancing-song, a robust idea on violas, cellos and bassoon whose folk origins can be seen above (Ex. 1).

Almost immediately there is a wind riposte and the music gradually gathers power, giving way to a gentle and alluring second group which subsides into a quiet dreamy passage. The development is powerful and imaginative, one of its most inspired passages occurring towards the end when the tonic is reasserting itself and the original wind idea from the very opening recurs – this almost sounds prophetic of Moeran's Symphony in the same key! The *Andante* has a processional character: the initial idea on the strings is elegiac, and after it reaches a climax, the opening rhythm serves to introduce a variant of the main idea on the wind. In the 1920s Stenhammar said it had been inspired by the Prometheus of Aeschylus. The Scherzo has the character of a folk-dance, in which the strings carry the burden of the musical argument: the contrasting Trio paid homage to the wind players of the Gothenburg orchestra, to whom the piece is dedicated. The Finale, the longest of the four movements, is perhaps the most ambitious and for all the eloquence of the powerful cantilena on strings in its closing pages, the least convincing. It opens with a *Grave sostenuto* which quickly leads into a fugal Allegro section; then follows a section marked 'tranquillemente', also fugal; a quicker episode ('*poco a poco animando*') can be thought of as a kind of development, in which both fugue subjects play a part. But whereas in the Serenade for Orchestra, the relationship between the part and the whole is perfectly judged, this movement for all its generosity of feeling, seems just a little overblown.

Stenhammar's nationalism was not so overt as that of **Hugo Alfvén** (1872–1960) or **Wilhelm Peterson-Berger** (1867–1942), both of whom drew on the repertory of Swedish folk music for their inspiration, yet he seems more deeply attuned to the Swedish spirit – or the best of it. His was an aristocratic cast of mind and the best of his music has an Elgarian dignity and noblesse, and he has something of the delicacy and poignancy, though not the tragic intensity, of his more immediate contemporary Josef Suk. He certainly possesses the same awareness of the evanescence of life that distinguishes the late Romantics such as Mahler, Elgar and Delius. Together with the Symphony No. 2 in G minor, the glorious Serenade for Orchestra is his masterpiece, almost symphonic in scope and character and rich in atmosphere.

Wilhelm Peterson-Berger made overt and often highly successful use of folk material. The Second of his five symphonies (*Sunnanfärd*, 1910) is a kind of Nordic *Aus Italien*, soaked in a post-nationalist Straussian ethos and the Third (*Same Ätnam*, 1915) draws on Lapp folk material to often picturesque effect. Hugo Alfvén drank even more deeply at the fountain of Swedish folk music and flew the colours of nationalism at his masthead. In his eighties he claimed that 'my symphonic predecessors in this country were all strongly influenced by German or Danish music' and spoke of his F minor Symphony (1897, rev. 1903–04) as 'the first to be written in the Swedish language'. Whether that quite does justice to the opening of Berwald's *Sinfonie singulière*, or whether his own strikes quite the strong nationalist tone he himself perceived, is perhaps more open to question. The shades of Dvořák are occasionally to be discerned and the main ideas of the first movement have quite strong overtones of Svendsen. But if it is a young man's work, it is well crafted and has a good feeling for the received formal conventions. The ideas are attractive without being strikingly individual and there is a particularly endearing Scherzo and Trio. But it was the Second Symphony (1899), which served to put Alfvén firmly on the Swedish musical map. It was first performed the day after his twenty-seventh birthday and conducted by Stenhammar, no less. Again the idiom is rooted in Dvořák and Strauss and nowhere as characteristically Swedish or as fresh as his masterpiece, 'The Midsummer Vigil' (1903). This draws on folk material from Dalecarlia, is a brilliant repertoire piece and in a sense the Swedish equivalent of Svendsen's Norwegian Rhapsodies. The best of the symphony is to be found in its first movement and its Scherzo; the Finale is let down by a rather dreadful fugue. The Fourth Symphony (*Från Havsbandet*) of 1919 evokes the otherworldly atmosphere of the beautiful archipelago that stretches out from Stockholm into the Baltic, surely one of the most magical waterways in the world. Its subtitle is probably best translated as 'from the outermost skerries of the archipelago', hardly snappy or practical, and there is a highly romantic programme which plots the emotions of two lovers and which rather shocked contemporary opinion in Sweden as being excessively sensual, though it is difficult to imagine that it would shock anyone nowadays! The score is opulent, sumptuous and at times derivative: Strauss, Reger and Debussy pass briefly through our minds. Its lavish scoring (quadruple woodwind, eight horns, two harps, celeste and piano etc.) calls to mind the Alpine Symphony. It is no masterpiece though there are some rich sonorities and colours. The wordless vocalise was probably prompted by the example of Nielsen in the *Sinfonia espansiva* (1911) but lacks its purity and inspiration. Probably the most consistent in quality (and certainly the most coherent formally) is No. 3 in E major.

Of the next generation, Sweden's 'generazione dell'Ottanta', are **Ture Rangström** (1884–1947) and **Kurt Atterberg** (1887–1974). Rangström was at his best as a miniaturist and above all, as a master of the *romans* (the Swedish equivalent of *Lied*), he is almost unsurpassed. But he is a good deal less comfortable on a larger canvas and his four symphonies lack concentration and sinew. Like Alfvén, Atterberg also drew much inspiration from folk sources: the Fourth of his nine symphonies, in G minor (*Sinfonia piccola*, 1918) is the most exclusively folkloric and the slow movement of his Sixth (1928)* has a strongly national flavour. Atterberg was

---

* This is the so-called 'Dollar' Symphony, which won the 10,000 dollar prize offered by the Columbia Graphophone Company (as Columbia was then known) on the occasion of the Schubert Centenary in 1928 and was subsequently recorded by Sir Thomas Beecham.

slow to turn to music, and was still an engineering student at the time of his Second Symphony (1912). There is no doubt as to the expert craftmanship and his vivid feeling for colour in the Third (*Västkustbilder* – 'West Coast Pictures') or the breadth of its romantic gestures. Though his is perhaps a less distinctive profile, he embodies something of the romanticism of Arnold Bax in England or Leevi Madetoja in Finland. The Sixth Symphony has genuine sweep and (in its Finale) a robust sense of humour and its neglect even in Sweden is puzzling.

Norway after Grieg

Norwegian nationalism was a stronger force in the nineteenth century for obvious historical reasons, until the 'upplösning' (the dissolution in 1905 of the Union with Sweden that had been imposed after the Treaty of Tilsit). Most composers after the generation of Grieg and Svendsen are steeped in the folk inspiration on which Kjerulf, Grieg and Svendsen first drew: **Johan Halvorsen** (1864–1935) and **Ludvig Irgens Jensen** (1894–1978) are two instances. The exception is **Christian Sinding** (1856–1942), of 'Rustle of Spring' fame, who was a contemporary of Elgar, and the leading figure to emerge after Grieg and Svendsen. His musical language is frankly neo-Romantic and has its roots in Wagner, Liszt and Strauss. There is little evidence of interest in Norwegian folk music, though his music still bears a Scandinavian stamp. There are four symphonies, the first of which reflects not only the legacy of Viennese classicism but is also attuned to newer trends on the continent – one passage almost foreshadows the choleric movement of Nielsen's Second Symphony. In the 1890s to 1920s Sinding along with Grieg and Svendsen symbolized Norwegian music for the rest of Europe but he does not seem to possess a tithe of the freshness and quality of either. The symphonies of Johan Halvorsen are of greater interest. He did not turn to the genre until relatively late in life: his First in C minor (1923) is highly conservative in outlook, and the Second ('Fate'), begun on his sixtieth birthday the following year, belongs to an earlier age. Many of its gestures are predictable in much the same way as are those of Taneiev, Josef Bohuslav Foerster and Madetoja. But if it is not exploratory in its musical language, it leaves a far more positive impression than the symphonies of Sinding. Not only is its opening arresting and within the limits of a post-nationalist idiom quite individual, but its ideas are generally well sustained. Ludvig Irgens Jensen, best known for his songs, is underrated and makes most effective and original use of a national folk-derived, diatonic idiom in his Partita Sinfonica (1937) and his finely-wrought Symphony in D minor (1945).

Harald Saeverud (1897–1992) is a figure unique in Norway: in terms of sheer personality (in particular, a dry, laconic wit), he outstrips almost all his younger countrymen. Saeverud used to show his visitors with some pride caricatures of him as a drayhorse, and this note of self-mockery can be clearly discerned in his music. He first attracted attention here with his music to a post-war production of *Peer Gynt* but works such as *Kjæmpeviseslåtten* ('The Ballad of Revolt') with its dark, combative, inspiriting character rallied Norwegian spirits during the Nazi occupation. His short but powerfully lyrical Sixth Symphony (*Sinfonia dolorosa*, 1942) and its successor, *Salmesymfoni* (1944–45), betray a strong sense of the Norwegian landscape. The Ninth (1966) is rugged, craggy, and full of imagination: it opens with a resourceful movement that combines sonata form and passacaglia, the mood of its *Andante* is powerfully concentrated, the waltz movement is splendidly tangy and characterful. Although the sad, gentle world of **Fartein Valen** (1887–1952) is highly distinctive, I know no more original Norwegian composer than Saeverud, whose craggy independence of outlook makes him so attractive.

Valen was something of an outsider in Norwegian musical life, what one might nowadays call a 'loner'. As early as the 1920s he developed a kind of twelve-note technique, which he used for the remainder of his creative career. At its very best Valen's music has a strong sense of the open air and a keen sense of nature. Occasionally its textures prompt the thought that he is a kind of dodecaphonic Delius, but at the same time there is a feeling of claustrophobia as if the fjords are inhibiting vision and light. However, despite these haunting moments, his writing suffers from congestion and the ear tires of the concentration of activity above the stave. Like Halvorsen, he turned to the symphony late in life: the First began life as a piano sonata but was finished in its definitive orchestral form two years later in 1939. Some of it is dense in texture but the opening of the second movement of the First Symphony is an exception: here the textures are limpid and transparent, and the pale luminous colours are distinctively northern, though its source of inspiration is El Greco's *Christ on the Mount of Olives*. The Second Symphony was written in 1941–44 during the German occupation of Norway, which had plunged him into the darkest depression, and its somewhat arid successor occupied him for another two years, but by the time of the Fourth (1949) Valen was emerging from seclusion and was beginning to enjoy some recognition. Its middle movement has a keen poetic intensity and an affecting elegiac quality but overall the symphonies still remain problematic. They have a powerful atmosphere and a strong sense of identity; there is an individual if neurasthenic sensibility and much delicacy of feeling but over a long time-span they reveal a deficiency in rhythmic vitality and line. They are ultimately too amorphous to offer a completely satisfying musical experience.

But what strikes you at first when you start exploring Norwegian music after Grieg is the sheer profusion of music by composers who are barely even names outside their native country – and how good so much of it is! The First Symphony (1935) of **Olav Kielland** (1901–85) is a bracing, finely paced and invigorating score with a strong Nielsenesque sense of momentum – but this is a Nielsen with distinctively Norwegian acccents. **Klaus Egge**

(1906–79), who liked to sign his scores with the notes e.g.g e., reveals in his First Symphony (1942) an ability to sustain a symphonic argument but an insufficient diversity of musical substance, and though his craftsmanship is unfailingly assured (he was a pupil of Valen), inspiration is intermittent. **Bjarne Brustad** (1895–1978) also composed in a traditional diatonic idiom – his Second Symphony (1952) may not have the strong personality of Saeverud but its material is well held together. **Finn Mortensen** (1922–83) who used a modified twelve-note technique (he briefly studied with Niels Viggo Bentzon in the mid-1950s) showed impressive command of long term structures and a far from negligible breadth in his Symphony, Op. 4, and there are many other Norwegians who have contributed to the medium such as **Conrad Baden** (b. 1908), who studied with Honegger and Jean Rivier whose short one-movement Sixth Symphony (*Sinfonia espressiva*, 1980) is a most beautiful work, sensitively scored and distinguished by much refinement of feeling and atmosphere and **Edvard Fliflet Braein** (1924–76), another Rivier pupil, and a composer of strong lyrical instinct.

Of the younger generation **Halvor Haug** (b. 1952) is another composer at one with the sounds and the landscape of the northern latitudes. The two outer movements of the First Symphony (1981–82) are long and of considerable substance: the first in E flat minor has great concentration of atmosphere and a breadth that is almost Sibelian, though without perhaps having the sense of movement that distinguish Sibelius, Nielsen or Holmboe. Its opening chorale-like progression almost recalls Reger or Bruckner and there is a brooding intensity that betokens a kinship to the great symphonic *Adagios* that open Shostakovich 6 and 8. Robert Simpson with whom he briefly studied spoke of his 'single-mindedness and his determination to stick to his own line', and of 'a fine ear for sonorities and, even more important, a coherent sense of design'. There is a concentration about his writing and he creates his own sound world.

Sweden after Stenhammar

In the aftermath of Stenhammar, whose pupil he briefly became, **Hilding Rosenberg** (1892–1985) was a standard bearer of the reaction against the national romanticism of the 1910s, to his seniors like Alfvén and Atterberg, and the first Swede to respond to the new modern music on the continent: to Schoenberg, Hindemith and to the French school and in particular Honegger. His eight symphonies bestride six decades: Rosenberg was not particularly happy with his First Symphony, which he wrote in the early 1920s and he wrestled with its successor (*Sinfonia grave*) for many years. Its first version was ready in 1928 but when he heard it at rehearsal, Rosenberg was seized with doubt and laboured over it for a further seven years. Even as late as 1980 when he was in his late eighties, he refashioned the first movement of a large choral work which he had called an Eighth Symphony as a single twenty-minute work for orchestra. But the *Sinfonia grave* can be seen as a watershed in his career: it has the breadth of a symphonist with long sweeping lines and a real sense of forward movement; there is an unmistakably Nordic stamp to it but a wider cosmopolitan vision. His larger symphonies embrace other forms or programmes: the Third (1939) originally bore the subtitle, 'The Four Ages of Man' and drew on Romain Rolland's *Jean Christophe* for its inspiration. Indeed at its first performance it was given with narration between each of the four movements but Rosenberg subsequently had second thoughts, withdrew the title and made some revisions excising a fugal section in the Scherzo. The first movement opens with a rather angular motive that makes use of all twelve notes of the chromatic scale but arranged in such a way that the sense of key is not undermined* and generates writing

Ex. 2. Rosenberg: Symphony No. 5

of great expressive power, and the second group with its muted colours and transparent scoring is one of his most delicately-imagined inspirations. The Fourth (*Johannesupfenbarelse* – 'The Revelation of St John the Divine',

* See Robert Layton: 'Vagn Holmboe and the Later Scandinavians' in volume two of *The Symphony*, London, 1967, p. 240.

1940) is more oratorio than symphony, whose opening has the striding fourths of Hindemith or Walton – or the Honegger of *Le roi David*. The Fifth, subtitled *Örtagårdsmästaren* 'Hortolanus', 1944, for soprano, chorus and orchestra is arguably his masterpiece. The open textures and serenity of its beginning are deceptive, for from this unpromising material evolves a distinct and individual world (Ex. 2).

Rosenberg is often open to the charge of note-spinning, and there are moments even in the often inspired Sixth Symphony (*Sinfonia semplice*, 1951) where the powerful sense of direction generated at the beginning momentarily falters. Like Hugo Alfvén, who was a gifted watercolourist, **Gösta Nystroem** (1890–1966) was an accomplished painter (a great admirer of the Cubists and Matisse) and only settled decisively on a musical career in the early 1920s when he became a pupil of d'Indy and Sabaneiev. His outlook is predominantly Gallic and Honegger was a strong influence in the *Sinfonia breve* (1929–31), composed during his Paris years, and in the powerful *Sinfonia espressiva* (1935), arguably his finest work. This has an organic feeling and a sense of direction which somehow failed him in the *Sinfonia del mare* (1947–48), which enjoyed quite a vogue in the early 1950s. Its inspiration was fuelled by his lifelong love of the sea; there is a large orchestra and a wordless soprano part but it is conspicuously deficient in thematic vitality and repeats to the point of exasperation a miserably insignificant semitonal idea. Nor does the *Sinfonia seria* (1962) for all its moments of atmosphere, leave a much stronger impression. The three symphonies of **Lars-Erik Larsson** (1908–86) are exercises in the received tradition: the composer himself had doubts about both the Second (1937) and the Third (1944–45) and only permitted their revival late in life, and the five symphonies of **Dag Wirén** (1905–1986), the most natural lyricist of his generation, have not established a firm hold on the repertoire. There are always characteristic touches and at one point in the monothematic Fourth (1955) a passing hint of Honegger's *Deliciae Basiliensis* at one point. But both here and in the Symphony No. 3 (1944) the melodic span is too short-breathed.

The next generation was dominated by the figure of **Karl-Birger Blomdahl** (1916–68), a Rosenberg pupil, who responded strongly to the influences, first of Bartók and Hindemith, and then of Schoenberg and the post-serialist school. His Second Symphony (1946) shows him to possess a good feeling for structure while the Third (*Facetter* or 'Facets', 1951) exhibited considerable resource in its transformation of its opening twelve-note series on the flute. This was the time when Bentzon and Holmboe had proclaimed 'metamorphosis' as 'vår tids form' ('the form for our time') but they were predominantly tonal in outlook. Blomdahl on the other hand, while distancing himself from the expressionism of Schoenberg* was fascinated by the twelve-note technique, and in its handling both of key

---

* Blomdahl in *Modern Nordisk Musik*, Stockholm, 1957, p. 169.

and the principle of metamorphosis the symphony exhibits ingenuity and imagination. During its course various 'facets' of the opening idea emerge, and throughout the scoring is dark (the writing for the wind is particularly strong) and a powerful atmosphere generated.

Pettersson and Tubin

Like the Estonian-born Eduard Tubin, **Allan Pettersson** (1911–80) was rather cold-shouldered by the Swedish musical establishment during the 1950s and 60s but he captured the public imagination with his frankly Mahlerian, post-Romantic one-movement Seventh Symphony (1967), which came as a huge relief to audiences force-fed on a serial and post-serial diet. Here was a composer who steered an independent path from the then fashionable trends. Its success led to an upsurge of interest in the other symphonies, which number no fewer than sixteen. Pettersson studied at first with Blomdahl and then with Honegger and that genial apostle of the twelve-note faith, René Leibowitz, and his best music has a certain dark eloquence, even if the thematic material is not always of the highest quality. Most of the symphonies are long though nearly all of them seem longer than they are. The Fifth (1960–62) can serve as a kind of archetypal Pettersson symphony. It is a loosely held together structure playing without a break for some forty minutes, but the brooding atmosphere of its opening paragraphs arouses expectations which are only intermittently realised: there are powerful ostinato figures which lead one to expect the entry of significant motivic material but little of real substance or distinction ever emerges. There is considerable expertise in the handling of the orchestra (Pettersson played for a time in the Stockholm Philharmonic), but the symphony remains deficient in thematic vitality and density of incident. As so often with this composer, the whole is very much less than the sum of its parts. Where he manages to sustain his invention, as in much of the Seventh Symphony, he is persuasive but even here there is a streak of self-pity that is unappealing, and the later symphonies are inflated and garrulous.

Eduard Tubin (1905–82) only came into his own after his death and is in a totally different league. Right from the very beginning we are aware of an original and highly inventive musical mind with an intuitive grasp of the symphonic process. His musical language is direct, tonal and, once one has got to grips with it, quite personal. Here is a composer with a real sense of scale, and an ability to conceive music in long-breathed paragraphs. Tubin began his First Symphony (1931–34) when he was still a pupil of Heino Eller, the first Estonian composer of quality, and what is so striking is the fact that it does not really sound much like anything that has gone before; nor are there many of the fingerprints that were to emerge in the later symphonies. The opening almost calls to mind Bax and there is a Sibelian breadth, but the overall impression is of a symphony 'apart' from its fellows, perhaps in a way that *Kullervo* is 'apart' from the seven Sibelius symphonies. Yet the feeling for form is already strong, the musical argument unfolds naturally and its presentation is astonishingly assured. The Second Symphony ('The Legendary', 1937) was written on the high north-eastern coastline of Estonia, and despite its title there is no specific programme. The opening is quite magical: there are soft luminous string chords that evoke a strong atmosphere of wide vistas and white summer nights, but the music soon gathers power and reveals a genuine feeling for proportion and of organic growth. In some ways this makes a more attractive entry point into Tubin's music than the Fourth Symphony (1944, rev. 1978), which he took to Sweden with him when he fled from his native Estonia. In the Fourth the atmosphere is predominantly pastoral, a mixture of the Slavonic and the Nordic. The Fifth (1946), the first he composed in Sweden, is perhaps the tautest and most neo-Classical and with it Tubin enjoyed brief celebrity. It was the only one of his symphonies to be published in his lifetime. The Sixth (1952) has obvious resonances of Prokofiev even down to instrumentation; and yet his rhythmic vitality and sense of movement are striking. The music is always pursuing a purposeful course and the ear is always engaged by the diversity of musical incident and this is true of the darker, more inward-looking Seventh (1961). The Eighth (1966) is possibly his masterpiece; it is as different from Nos. 5 and 6 as it is from its successor. It is darker in colouring and intense in feeling. There is none of the pastoral symphonism of the Third and Fourth symphonies but an astringency and a sense of the tragic that leaves a strong impression. The Ninth Symphony (*Sinfonia semplice*, 1969) is strongly elegiac in mood and the gently restrained melancholy of its slower sections is all the more powerful for its understatement. Incidentally I am not alone in sensing an affinity to Bax in this or other symphonies; Arved Ashby wrote: 'Tubin's orchestration and fluid harmonies at times remind one of Honegger or Bax, some rhythms recall Prokofiev, his woodwind writing in thirds and octaves suggesting Sibelius, some of his wind doublings resembling those of Shostakovich.'[*]

All these occasional affinities are worth mentioning to help 'place' Tubin for those who have not encountered the actual sound of his music: Tubin is very much his own man with distinctive musical fingerprints, whose spiritual landscape is unlike any other. In the finest of his works, like Symphonies 7–10, there is not one wasted gesture, nor is the invention touched by routine. The ideas could not be by anyone else and the music unfolds with seeming inevitability and a powerful logic. The Tenth Symphony (1972) was commissioned – to its eternal honour – by the Gothenburg Orchestra, and is quite unlike its elegiac predecessor. It begins with a sombre string idea which is soon interrupted by a horn call that periodically recurs and which resonates in the mind long afterwards. It shows that Tubin's imaginative

---

[*] Arved Ashby, 'Eduard Tubin – An Overview'. Conference on Baltic Studies at Wisconsin University, 1986.

vitality and strong feeling for structure remained unimpaired until the last year of his life when he was working on his Eleventh Symphony.

Denmark after Nielsen

Nielsen was so strong a voice in Denmark that few of his contemporaries have made much of an impression. The six symphonies of **Louis Glass** (1864–1936), for example, a composer of distinct quality, remain on the outermost periphery of the repertoire, though they have recently been recorded, while the three of **Peder Gram** (1881–1956) are totally neglected. A cult figure in the 1960s was **Rued Langgaard** (1893–1952), the most eccentric of the Danish composers post Nielsen. (He has been compared with Ives in America and not without some measure of justice.) Langgaard was enormously prolific and his output numbers some four hundred works including sixteen symphonies. Stylistically there is little consistency in his output; there seem to be many personalities struggling to get to the surface. Works such as the *Sfaerernesmusik* ('Music of the Spheres'), with its tone-clusters, the piano played directly on the strings, repetitive chants and sundry forward-looking techniques, have moments of real vision, but elsewhere he offers music of some considerable banality, as in the Sixteenth Symphony (1950). Even the best known of them, the Fourth (*Løvfald* – 'The Falling of the Leaves', 1916) and Sixth (*Det himmelrivende* – 'The Storming of the Heavens', 1919) which derives its inspiration from a poem by Hans Adolf Brorson and St Paul's letter to the Ephesians ('Then Jesus used force and drove the storming armies of evil under the canopy of heaven') offer moments of inspiration rather than a wholly coherent symphonic experience, the raw materials of art rather than the finished work.

But by far the most commanding Danish composer of the post-Nielsen era is **Vagn Holmboe** (b. 1909). He speaks a language that has its roots first in the music of his great countryman, and secondly, in what one might call neo-Classicism. He has followed his own star and remained unresponsive to the fashionable changes in the stylistic barometer that affected so many Nordic composers in the 1950s and 60s. Holmboe's symphonies have an unflagging sense of direction and purpose, logic and momentum. Much of his music employs the principle of metamorphosis – the thematic matter defines its own development and undergoes constant change. To paraphrase his own words, a work has its own particular laws and if the composer tries defiantly to force its path or 'follow his own head, he will soon be taught a lesson!' His Fifth Symphony (1944) and the Seventh (1950)* brought him attention outside Denmark, as did the first of his twenty published string quartets (1949). Like Shostakovich, Holmboe has concentrated on classical

* For a discussion of Holmboe's Symphonies 5–8 see Robert Simpson *The Symphony*, London, 1967, Vol. 2, pp. 232–36. Holmboe himself discusses Symphonies 6–8 in *Modern Nordisk Musik*, Stockholm, 1957, pp. 154–66. There is a helpful analysis of the Seventh Symphony in Paul Rapoport's *Opus Est*, London, 1978, pp 56–62.

forms but whereas his preoccupation with the quartet medium has been constant, there have been long gaps in his symphonic production. After the Eighth Symphony (1952–53) there is a gap of more than a decade before the Ninth (1969) and Tenth (1970–71) and further gaps before the Eleventh (1981) and Twelfth (1989). Holmboe's music is never static, not even when it is at its most tranquil (as in the opening arabesques of the Eleventh Symphony). It relies on the cumulative effect of a musical argument rather than on isolated details of colour and texture. The Tenth (1970–71) prompted the Swedish critic, Lennart Riemers to write, 'in long, vast dynamic crescendos, reminiscent of Bruckner, the masses of sound swell to a gradual explosion ... the impression is of fierce, rotating sun-flames, of protuberances flung out in whirling heat from a boiling centre'. The hallmark of symphonic thinking is to generate an argument from the most apparently unpromising motivic ideas. The simplest of ideas open the Tenth: an explosion from woodwind and percussion, then a menacing pedal-note on double basses and cellos after which wisps of ideas begin to form on muted strings sounds:

Ex. 3. Holmboe: Symphony No. 10

Like its predecessors the Twelfth Symphony evolves from the ideas thrown out in the opening bars (a small cell of four notes, G, F sharp, C and G) whose power generates the bulk of the movement's activity. It carries a capacity for diversity; for example, after the bassoon idea, barely a minute into the music, there is *pianissimo* string passage (not dissimilar in character to a pensive idea in the Cello Concerto), quite different in character yet obviously the same thought as the opening. When the pace changes a little later there is an example of the luminous writing for winds that gives Holmboe's music so distinctive a personality. But the music is carried on its own current, whose logic is more easily discerned by the ear than described in words. The middle movement, *Andante sereno*, is, as its tempo indication implies, tranquil in mood, yet concentrated in feeling. It is music of grave and haunting beauty whose ideas are related to the world of his *Requiem for Nietzsche*. There is an organic coherence in all the Holmboe symphonies that place him in the tradition of Sibelius, yet there is no trace of his influence in his sound world. The finest of the symphonies have an impressive clarity and distinction of mind, while his scoring is of comparable translucence. Where the awareness of nature is strongest, the Nordic sound is at its most deeply characteristic.

This luminous wind writing and marvellous sense of space is present in the early symphonies of **Niels Viggo Bentzon** (b. 1919). Bentzon, incidentally, is a direct descendant of the composer J. P. E. Hartmann (1805–1900) and more distantly of Niels Gade (and his cousin Jørgen (1897–1951) was also a composer of no mean accomplishment and finesse). He is enormously prolific and a catalogue published in 1980 already listed 429 opus numbers: there are at least twenty symphonies and as many piano sonatas, and fifteen piano concertos. (There are dozens of sonatas for various instruments and even a Well Tempered Clavier – 24 Preludes and Fugues, Op. 409, in all the tonalities!) In his high-spirited fashion he fuses during the late 1940s and early 1950s the lean rhythmic neo-Classicism of Stravinsky, the contrapuntal vitality of Hindemith and the brashness and energy of Shostakovich and Copland. It would be idle to pretend that his creative hyperactivity is matched by consistency of inspiration. However, the early symphonies from No. 2, for piano and orchestra (1944), through to No. 7 (1953) are all marvellously rich scores teeming with invention. The pastoral opening of No. 3 (1947) opens up a flow of varied ideas (Ex. 4).

At about this time Bentzon had spoken of metamorphosis, as being the basic structural principle of the music of our time. The Fourth Symphony (1948) is a masterly example of thematic metamorphosis. It offers music of real vision whose textures glow luminously. As to its orchestration Bentzon writes that the study of the interludes from Benjamin Britten's opera, *Peter Grimes*, revealed many instrumental effects such as muted horns combined with harp glissandi, an effect he uses in the second of the work's three movements. The Sixth Symphony is remarkably classical in its outlook and proportions.

Ex. 4. Bentzon: Symphony No. 3

A more peripheral but gifted figure whose musical outlook was formed by the diatonicism of Nielsen is **Leif Keyser** (b. 1919) whose remarkable First Symphony was first performed in Gothenburg when he was only twenty and whose Second, composed a year later, is hardly less impressive in its sense of pace and feeling for organic growth. However, the enormous promise of these early works does not seem to have developed into a comparable fulfilment, and creative work was for a time interrupted by his call to the priesthood. These two symphonies (there are apparently six in all) should not be permitted to fall into oblivion.

Of younger Danish composers **Per Nørgård** (b. 1932) has enjoyed the most exposure and his early music was greatly influenced by the teaching of Vagn Holmboe and the principle of metamorphosis. However, by the late 1960s he had broken loose from this tradition into a more mystical world of infinity rows as in his Second Symphony (1971) or the Fourth (1981) whose two movements, 'The Indian Rose Garden' and the 'Chinese Witches' Lake', explore the theme of polarization between idyll and catastrophe. His extra-musical inspiration and often pleasing sound world has served perhaps to draw wider attention to his music than its substance justifies and has overshadowed the seven symphonies of Ib Norholm (b. 1931).

Finland after Sibelius

In the 1940s and 50s, when Sibelius reigned supreme in the Anglo-Saxon world, interest naturally extended to other Nordic figures, but as his fortunes declined in the 1960s and a Sibelius symphony became (comparatively speaking) a rarity in concert and radio programmes, so lesser figures temporarily dipped under the horizon. **Leevi Madetoja** (1887–1947) was probably the best-known of the Finnish symphonists to emerge in Sibelius's wake and certainly the most gifted.* Along with Toivo Kuula (1883–1918) he was one of Sibelius's two pupils and briefly studied with Vincent d'Indy. Although in the Second Symphony (1917–18) his musical personality embraces strong suggestions of Sibelius and the post-nationalist Slavonic symphonists, his distinctly Finnish outlook is tempered by a feeling for French culture. The French critic, Henri-Claude Fantapie, speaks of the Third Symphony (1925) as 'Gallic in its classicism, in its elegiac character, in its refusal to seek an easy effect, in its effort to be "musique pure", . . . in its affinity with a little known but important branch of French music of the day which evolved in the shadow of triumphant impressionism and was represented by the likes of an Albert Roussel, an Alberic Magnard or a Paul le Flem'. Though he has a distinctive voice, he does not possess the extraordinary intuitive grasp of form that Sibelius had at his command.

The Fifth Symphony of **Erkki Melartin** (1875–1937) has attractive post-nationalist colourings but none of his seven symphonies nor the three of **Ernst Pingoud** (1888–1942), best known for his orchestrations of some of Sibelius's songs, have succeeded in holding the stage. Pingoud was a pupil of Siloti and Reger whose music looks more towards Skryabin than Sibelius. Indeed given the latter's dominance, the Finnish composer could either succumb or look outwards, as did Uuno Klami (1900–61) who was also indebted to the French or **Aarre Merikanto** (1894–1959). His music has echoes of Szymanowski and Schreker as well as Skryabin and Debussy. Merikanto also studied with Reger before the First World War but, like Rued Langgaard in Denmark and Fartein Valen in Norway remained very much an outsider and suffered neglect for much of his creative career. He is every bit as interesting as they are, and in many ways more substantial though neither of his two symphonies has established themselves in the repertory.

Joonas Kokkonen (b. 1921) belongs to the same generation as Bentzon in Denmark or Simpson in England, and first came to wider prominence outside Finland with his Third Symphony (1967). His style is essentially

* For a more detailed discussion in English of Madetoja's music see Juoni Kaipainen: 'Comments on the Orchestral Works of Leeve Madetoja', *Finnish Music Quarterly*, 3–4 (1985), pp. 45–57.

neo-Classical and he has fully assimilated the examples of Hindemith and Bartók without resembling either. His music is informed by a powerful sense of logic and finely disciplined craftsmanship; both the Third and Fourth (1971) show a symphonist of real power and no mean personality, though there is not the immediate openness and effortless facility of **Einar Englund** (b. 1916) whose five symphonies have enjoyed little exposure outside his native country. Both have been overshadowed in recent years by **Aulis Sallinen** (b. 1935) who first came to international attention with *Mauermusik*, written in 1962 as a memorial to a young German victim of the Berlin wall. In recent years he has gained celebrity as one of the leading forces behind the revival of opera in Finland. Sallinen now has six symphonies to his credit, the Fifth, subtitled 'Washington Mosaics', being commissioned by Rostropovich. The sustained eloquence of the one-movement First Symphony (1971) made a strong impression and put Sallinen on the map. Although the atmosphere in Sallinen's music is powerfully charged, it seems at first wanting in the kind of concentration that you find in, say, Holmboe's Seventh. At times the melodic ideas themselves seem to lack distinction and the invention is wanting in substance. Yet the listener always wants to return to his music, and it is not very long before new detail that seemed insignificant at first hearing comes to the surface. Perhaps the very accessibility of his musical language, with its overtones of Shostakovich, Puccini and Britten, is in itself deceptive.

The Third Symphony (1975) makes a good entry point into Sallinen's music. Composed on an island in the Baltic, the first of its three movements resonates with sounds of nature: the woodwind cries seem like gulls while the surging strings reflect the changing moods of the waters. It seems to evoke the world of Sibelius's *Tempest* music or Britten's East Anglian landscapes. In its Finale 'the gull-cries return at the climax', as Ronald Weitzman* puts it, 'before a massive tidal-wave engulfs all attempts to gain mastery over the elements.' Again in the Fifth (1985) there is a strong sense of nature and the sonorities are recognizably characteristic. The overall form is symmetrical: the outer movements (Washington Mosaics I and II) are the most substantial and frame three shorter middle movements, all called intermezzi. The first movement has some Stravinskian overtones and there is some sense of movement even if much of the work is static, and the musical argument is wanting in density. Yet for all that, one is always drawn back into its sound world. There are passing affinities with Britten and Shostakovich: the opening of the first intermezzo even has mild echoes of Berg in much the same way as does his countryman, Aarre Merikanto.

Sallinen has also overshadowed outside Finland the achievement of **Einojuhani Rautavaara** (b. 1928) who first attracted attention in the early 1950s with his *Requiem for our Time*. His five symphonies inhabit

* Ronald Weitz, 'Sallinen's Orchestral Music', *Finnish Music Quarterly*, 3–4 (1985), pp. 29–39.

an individual sound world: the First has an almost Sibelian sense of pace and there is a seriousness about his art that is impressive and even the serial Fourth Symphony (1962) retains a distinctive accent. His pupil **Kalevi Aho** (b. 1949) is also a remarkable talent: the serious tone of his First Symphony (1969) undoubtedly betokens a composer of some substance. The first movement is (to quote the composer) 'formally a fugue, for this form gives the movement the psychological expressiveness which I had sought'. It has something of the gravity of Nielsen, Bartók or Shostakovich and is both powerful and compelling. In the second movement Aho transforms the fugal theme into a 'tragi-comical, limping waltz melody'. He has something of Shostakovich's macabre sense of humour, perhaps with a touch of Britten. I find the 'surrogate Baroque world' of the third movement, which the composer tells us 'rips itself apart like a nightmare', less convincing. The Finale, also a fugue, is the most ambitious part of the work and has an impressive eloquence. His subsequent music has not spread widely beyond the shores of his native Finland but like Ketil Hvoslef or Halvor Haug in Norway, his is a name that gives hope for the future.

17

After Mahler: the Central European Symphony in the Twentieth Century

Stephen Johnson

'Young people love Mahler and his art, and thus his right to the future cannot be taken from him.' Thus wrote Guido Adler in 1913, two years after the composer's death. Readers who have grown up since the Mahler boom began in the 1960s may find the tone of that statement surprising: was Mahler's 'right to the future' ever in doubt? Nowadays we are so accustomed to hearing him spoken of as the twentieth century's foremost musical prophet – the *vox clamantis* announcing cataclysms long before most of his contemporaries got wind of them – that Adler's defensiveness seems unnecessary. In fact the number of musicians who sensed the future in Mahler's music in 1913 was relatively small. Even such a dedicated advocate as Adler felt it necessary to stress that Mahler's works 'range themselves beside those of his progressive contemporaries' – he names Richard Strauss and Max Reger – though 'Schoenberg and his followers' are plainly another matter, remote in their aims from Mahler's striving after 'the sublime'.

Certainly if one looks at the history of the Central European symphony after Mahler, it is striking how few works bear the mark of his influence in any significant way. Granted, the age of the big Romantic symphony was already in decline before the outbreak of the First World War, and in the reaction against late-Romantic inflation that set in soon afterwards the composer of the 'Symphony of a Thousand' would have been an obvious target. But to today's educated listeners it is disturbing to think of Mahler's achievement being dismissed on such superficial grounds. Surely the challenge of his 'world-embracing' aesthetic reverberates on just about every compositional level? – and yet the Austro-German symphony seems to have flowed on largely unaffected. It is possible that if Alban Berg had finished the symphony he was working on in 1912–13,* or if Schoenberg's symphony (1915) had not transformed itself into a preparatory study for the oratorio *Die Jakobsleiter*, things might have turned out differently – but those are very big 'if's. What Berg and Schoenberg were soon to discover was that, great symphonist as he was, Mahler had also pointed out paths that led in new directions, beyond the Romantic humanist premises of the post-Beethovenian symphony. Alder's comments notwithstanding, it was Schoenberg and his followers who took Mahler's lead, and the line of descent remained with them until the Mahlerian narrative symphony was re-born in the Fourth and Fifth Symphonies of Shostakovich.

There have been those who have found Mahlerian elements in the symphonies of **Franz Schmidt** (1874–1939) – which only goes to show how loosely the term can be applied. Resemblances between the two are rare, fleeting and largely superficial. In fact soon after the success of his First Symphony (1896–9) Schmidt found himself being taken up by Viennese critics as a stick to beat Mahler. Not surprisingly he seems to have found this embarrassing: for one thing it soured their professional relationship (for a while Schmidt was Mahler's principal cellist in the Vienna Opera Orchestra); and for another Schmidt's attitude to Mahler was by no means as determinedly hostile as that of some of his champions. It is true that on one occasion he dismissed Mahler's symphonies as 'cheap novels', but there were times when he was more respectful – even if one still gets the impression that for Schmidt, as for many of his generation, Mahler's achievement as a conductor was of greater significance than his legacy as a composer.

A glance at the orchestration of Schmidt's Second Symphony (1911–13) might suggest a connection: there are the eight horns, the big percussion section and the expanded and colouristically enriched woodwinds (particularly the clarinets). But not only is the thematic material unlike anything in Mahler, the processes by which it is developed grow from very different roots. Take the Bach-like opening idea (Ex. 1a): this is no Mahlerian invocation of the past; Schmidt's imitation of the Baroque is fresh and completely without irony.

In terms of the famous Mahler-Sibelius exchange Schmidt stands closer to Sibelius. Severity of style may not be the first words that come to mind when one thinks of Schmidt: like his teacher Bruckner he is quite capable of putting goal-directed movement on hold and simply enjoying the musical landscapes he creates – and there are places in the Second Symphony where momentum sags; but 'inner connection' of motifs is a constant preoccupation. The theme of the variation second movement (Ex. 1b) derives quite naturally from Ex. 1a – in fact its first phrase seems like a *distillation* of the

---

* Berg's Symphony was to have been a four-movements-in-one structure, ending with an off-stage boy soprano singing words from Balzac's novel *Seraphita*. Ideas for the work reappeared in the *Präludium* from the *Three Pieces for Orchestra*, Op. 6, and the D minor interlude from Act III of *Wozzeck*.

earlier shape – and the germinal idea of the Finale is another offshoot (Ex. 1c). When Ex. 1b finally reappears as a sonorous brass chorale, at last in the tonic major, it brings a sense of fulfilment: what was once a simple hymn-like tune now stands revealed as both the culmination and the source of so much of the symphony's leading material. Even so there is no pressing demand for interpretation; the musical experience is absolute.

Ex. 1. Schmidt: Symphony No. 2

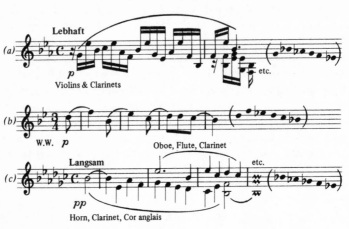

Fourteen years passed before Schmidt began work on the Third Symphony (1927–8), but despite the long pause it is possible to see in it a reaction to the Second. The orchestra is Schumann-like in composition: double woodwind, no tuba, trombones used sparingly, the only percussion a pair of timpani. The broad layout is familiar too: a sonata-form *Allegro molto moderato* (complete with exposition repeat), an *Adagio* with suggestions of variation and sonata forms, a Scherzo and Trio (with straightforward *da capo*) and a sonata-based Finale with a slow introduction. The musical landscape is a distinctly Austrian Arcadia (strong hints of Schubert and the bucolic Bruckner); however the serene smile conceals some original thinking, especially in the first movement. The exposition seems to flow effortlessly forward in a sustained outpouring of song, but in fact the structure is carefully and subtly articulated. Like Brahms, Schmidt makes sure that his opening phrases carry strong motivic impetus (Ex. 2). Note the rising fourths and thirds; so much is to grow from them – the strings' answering phrases for instance.

The interval of the perfect fourth also plays an important rôle in the Fourth Symphony's germinal theme (Ex. 3a) – only where the Third's opening phrases aspired, here there is a marked tendency to fall. There is much more to this than a simple difference of colouring: the dying fall is essential to the character of the theme and of the work that grows

Ex. 2. Schmidt: Symphony No. 3

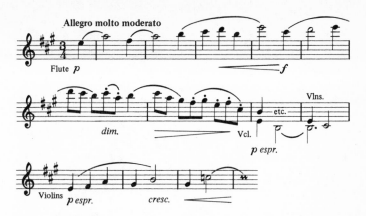

from it. For Schmidt this is new territory. In the other three symphonies the mood is fundamentally buoyant and positive; but in early 1932 Schmidt suffered a terrible shock when his much-loved daughter Emma died in childbirth. The Fourth Symphony, begun not long afterwards, was in his own account a 'requiem' for her, and there is no mistaking the feeling of loss in the *Adagio* second movement, and still more in the final pages. But despite the strongly personal motivation, the focus remains objective. Not only is this the most deeply-felt of Schmidt's symphonies, it is also the most carefully constructed.

Take those fourths for instance (Ex. 3a):

Ex. 3. Schmidt: Symphony No. 4

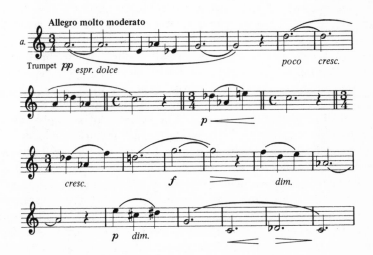

Ex. 3. cont'd

The *Adagio*'s solo cello theme (Ex. 3b) also makes prominent use of this interval, as does the Scherzo theme Ex. 3c, a thinly disguised variant of Ex. 3b. There are tonal consequences too: Schmidt's very original solution to the Romantic 'Finale problem' is to make his last movement the proper full recapitulation of the first, only here the keys are a *fourth* higher: C – F♯ becomes F – B, followed by a big coda in the tonic C. The C – D♭ – C alternation at the end of Ex. 3a is also important: harmonically the whole first group is built upon it, D♭/C♯ eventually leading to F sharp major-minor for the second subject.

Still more original is the adaptation of the classic arch form to Schmidt's dramatic purposes. The close similarity of Exx. 3b and c may suggest that the Scherzo is to be a huge variation on the *Adagio*. It isn't – but the signal is important. What happens is that material from the first movement begins to creep back, though at the Scherzo's much faster tempo. Then comes the Finale-recapitulation – right tempo, wrong keys, and with Ex. 3a presented hauntingly by a choir of horns. Ex. 3a only returns in the right key and on the right instrument at the very end. The effect is of a steady *crescendo* of recapitulation – a rising tide, bringing the music back inevitably to its starting point; but where in the beginning Ex. 3a had seemed heavy with dark possibilities, it is now unmistakably final.

Extravagant claims have been made on Schmidt's behalf: for instance Harold Truscott's proclamations that he is 'one of the greatest and most independent of symphonists', and that the *Adagio* of the Fourth contains 'perhaps the greatest lament in twentieth-century music'. Such overstatement does a relatively little-known composer's case more harm than good. But one doesn't have to go nearly so far to be impressed by Schmidt's achievement in this, his last symphony – or to be moved by it. Compared with an outstanding musical tragedy like Sibelius's Fourth it may seem to lack tautness in places*, but tragic it is, in a powerful and entirely individual way.

It is intriguing to compare Schmidt with his close contemporary **Alexander von Zemlinsky** (1871–1942). Not one of Zemlinsky's three purely orchestral symphonies (1892, 1897 and 1902) was ever dignified with an opus number, but the Second, in B flat, has been published and recorded, and it shows him – like Schmidt in his First Symphony (finished two years later) – pursuing a safely traditionalist course. Dvořák is unmistakably a leading influence here, and in the last movement comes a monumental tribute to Brahms: thirty variations on a ground bass in the tonic minor – a direct imitation of the passacaglia-finale of Brahms's Fourth Symphony.

Then, at about the turn of the century, Zemlinsky entered a long period of stylistic crisis. First he leaned towards Wagner, but then came the problem of facing up to post-Wagnerian developments, particularly those represented by his brother-in-law, Schoenberg. Unlike Schmidt, who seems to have been relatively sure of his course, Zemlinsky spent a lot of time wavering between stylistic positions (especially as regards tonality), and in later years his intense self-consciousness appears to have had an increasingly inhibiting effect. But there was a stage – from just before the death of Mahler to the early 1920s – in which the tensions were productive. Some very impressive works date from this period: the opera *Der Zwerg*, 'The Dwarf' (1920–21), the Maeterlinck songs (1910–13), the Second and Third String Quartets (1914 and 1923) and above all the *Lyrische Symphonie* ('Lyric Symphony') of 1923. Mahler is a liberating influence here, and one work in particular: the symphonic song-cycle *Das Lied von der Erde*. Zemlinsky's description of his work as a 'song-symphony' underlines a connection already apparent in the alternation of male and female soloists and the choice of exotic texts – in this case poems by Rabindranath Tagore.

But Mahler provided Zemlinsky with more than just a formal pattern or a clue as to where to look for subject-matter. In both fields Zemlinsky is no mere imitator. Unlike Mahler, who in his first and last songs integrates song and symphony with remarkable skill, Zemlinsky allows the elements to separate, alternating dynamic orchestral sections with settings which, despite fleeting memories of strophic form, come close to yielding completely to the text. Zemlinsky's subject is different too: perfect love, and how its dream – in the words of the sixth song – 'can never be made captive'.

No, the most valuable lesson Zemlinsky learned from Mahler was how seemingly incompatible styles can be fused or contrasted in meaningful ways. At first hearing, the 'Lyric Symphony' may seem to veer confusingly between warmly expressive 'late' diatonicism and something much closer

---

* Though it is worth bearing in mind that Schmidt's own performance of the Fourth Symphony in February 1935 took only thirty-nine minutes – about ten minutes less than in the commercial recordings by Zubin Mehta and Ludovit Rajter.

to the expressionist Schoenberg or Berg. But there is a purpose: 'Let it not be a death, but completeness' sings the baritone in the seventh and last song. When the poem is finished, the orchestra raises itself to a grindingly dissonant climax, and then, at a signal from the tamtam, tonality – already precarious – seems for a few bars to dissolve. But the bass A continues, and slowly – magically – the song's 'tonic' D re-emerges to form a radiant added sixth chord, enriched in its final bars by the passing inclusion of every note of the D major scale (the fourth sharpened). The threat of harmonic dissolution – 'death' – is balanced by a richly expanded tonality – 'completeness'. So is Zemlinsky's answer to Tagore's plea affirmative? Is love – in the words of the *Song of Solomon* – 'strong as death'? It is possible to read this message in the closing pages; and yet the note of longing persists to the end, notably in the great Mahlerian sigh that introduces the final chord. Perhaps the real answer is, 'if only . . .'

The case of **Karol Szymanowski** (1882–1937) is different again. While Zemlinksy's parents were Polish, culturally he was very much a product of his native Vienna; Szymanowski was Polish to his heart's core. As Andrzej Panufnik has observed, even his love of Arabic music may have been a kind of atavism: many authorities, including Bartók, have found Arab roots in Slavonic folk song and dance. As a young pianist Szymanowski made contact with Austro-German music via Bach, Beethoven and Brahms, but at the same time other enticing possibilities were opened up by Chopin and, later, Skryabin. When eventually Szymanowski acknowledged the pull of Vienna in 1907, it was Strauss and Reger, rather than Mahler or Brahms, who exerted the strongest fascination. With these two as guides – and with echoes of Skryabin still reverberating – he set out to write his First Symphony, a work which soon afterwards he was to dismiss (with some justice) as a 'contrapuntal-harmonic-orchestral monster.' These same influences can be felt at work in the two-movement Second Symphony (1909–10), but here Brahms seems to have had a salutary effect. The formal thinking is more original and more purposeful, the textures clearer. While in the First there is a great deal of ranting and gesturing to very little effect, here Szymanowski's relative economy makes his big moments far more telling.

Still, despite the greater sureness, and despite the strong foretastes of the voluptuous sound worlds of the First Violin Concerto (1916) and the Third Symphony, the Second is not a complete success. Szymanowski still seems over-anxious to prove his contrapuntal mettle – particularly in the concluding fugue – and not all his developments fit the material they are imposed upon: as Christopher Palmer says, the gorgeous violin solo that opens the work is 'quite happy just to "be"; it does not want to "do" or "become" anything'. If this sounds rather like the old Russian problem of the 'folksong symphony', that may be another indication of how deeply Slavonic his musical inclinations were.

After this Szymanowski turned his back on traditional symphonic form. The work occasionally programmed as 'Symphony No. 4' (1932) is much better described by its alternative title, *Symphonie Concertante*, while the single-movement Third (1914–16), subtitled 'Song of the Night' and based on a poem by the thirteenth-century Persian mystic Jalal'ad-Din Rumi, is less like the conventional idea of the symphony than anything considered in this chapter so far. Scored for tenor solo*, chorus and huge orchestra (including organ), it is a work which seems to defy the Beethovenian idea of movement, yet here Szymanowski's thinking is at last completely in focus. Behind the profusion of ideas one is aware of a framework of great subtlety and strength – essential in a work which views night and the senses not merely as goals in themselves, but as gateways to knowledge of The Divine.

We seem to be straying back in the direction of Skryabin – and where else would Szymanowski have got the idea of giving a pivotal role to a single non-diatonic chord (Ex. 4a)?

Ex. 4. Szymanowski: Symphony No. 3

The way the violins tease their melody (Ex. 4b) out of the chord is also reminiscent of the composer of 'Poem of Fire' and 'Poem of Ecstasy'; and yet the effect is quite different. Even at this early stage it is evident that Szymanowski can treat Ex. 4a as a power-source without being chord-fixated in the way Skryabin sometimes is; and what follows is emotionally far removed from the Russian's relentless pursuit of the ultimate high. The range is immense, from the ominous excitement of the introduction, to the convulsive climax that follows, to the wonderful hushed tenor solo at the words 'How quiet it is. Others sleep. God and I are alone in this night!' – the accompaniment a barely audible cymbal roll punctuated by bell-like *pianissimo* chords for strings, piano and harps. With this last passage we reach the heart of the work. The music seems to pause, awestruck, before the possibility of something greater than itself and its creator – something one could never say of Skryabin.

* The autograph clearly says 'tenor'. The practice of substituting a soprano solo does not appear to carry the composer's authorization.

Nor could Skryabin – or Zemlinsky – have created anything like Szymanowski's coda. Ex. 4a has been a recurring presence: the three great climactic transfigurations of Ex. 4b by six unison horns are rooted in it, though in the last two cases with 'dissonant' bass pedals. The unmistakable reference to the yearning motif from the opening of *Tristan* that marks the symphony's emotional high point also grows from Ex. 4a's whole-tone configuration. Then, as the chord fades, its pedal C remains, until at the close it becomes the basis of a widely-spaced perfect fifth, coloured by the open harmonics of the violas' and cellos' C strings. It is a strangely cool, 'natural' sound, like the free-floating consonance of the aeolian harp. This may not be a resolution of Ex. 4a in anything like the orthodox Western sense, but after the release of the *Tristan* climax, its pureness and stability suggest that equilibrium too has been reached. While for Zemlinsky completeness appears to have been attainable only in dreams, here we glimpse its actuality.

From Szymanowski to **Kurt Weill** (1900–50) is no small step. A few bars from the opening of either of Weill's two numbered symphonies reveal a sound world far removed from the fantastic fertility of the *Song of the Night*. But the difference is more than a matter of texture or orchestration. It comes as something of a jolt to discover that Szymanowski was writing his Third Symphony while Europe was in a state of bloody turmoil. But the more one knows of the music and the man, the easier it is to understand. This is the introvert's response to crisis: Szymanowski searches within himself for that which will bring him strength at a time when, in Yeats's words, 'things fall apart'. None of Weill's music from the years of the First World War has survived, but the works written up to the time he fled Germany in 1933 show a composer deeply concerned with the leading issues of his day. Even in the few pieces without texts the imprint of the times is unmistakable.

Weill wrote his one-movement First Symphony (1921) during his period of study with Busoni (an earlier effort, dating from the previous year, is lost), and the influence of that formidable teacher is clear, particularly in the fugal writing that begins the third section – though it has to be said that this is the least impressive part of the work, and it's easy to understand why Busoni felt the need to send Weill off for intensive counterpoint lessons with his assistant Philipp Jarnach. But despite the odd awkwardness here and there, it is a remarkable piece of work for a twenty-one year-old composer. Of course there are resemblances to other composers: hints of Mahler in some of the more impassioned outbursts, of Schoenberg's Chamber Symphony (1906), especially in the fourth-based opening gesture, and of then-fashionable figures like Reger and Franz Schreker (whose own Chamber Symphony had appeared in 1916); but Weill manages to draw these together into something very personal. A powerful unifying factor was Weill's characteristic desire to communicate a vision – in this case contained in some lines* from a mystical socialist play by Johannes Becher: *Arbeiter, Bauern, Soldaten – Der Aufbruch eines Volkes zu Gott*, 'Workers, peasants, soldiers – the awakening of a people to God'.

Apart from the fine Concerto for violin and wind instruments of 1924 and the rather less successful String Quartet of the previous year, Weill wrote virtually nothing without texts until the Second Symphony, which he began in Berlin in January 1933. Date and place are important: Adolf Hitler became Chancellor of Germany on 30 January 1933. There could be no doubt about what this meant for Weill – a Jew, a notorious leftist and for the Nazis a prime example of *Entartete Musik*, 'degenerate music' – and on 14 March he fled for Paris. Despite the upheaval, and despite the strong competing demands of *Die Sieben Todsünden* ('The Seven Deadly Sins'), the idea of the symphony kept its grip on Weill, and he went on to finish it the following February in France.

The result is one of Weill's finest works – in fact the Second Symphony is sometimes paired with *Die Sieben Todsünden* as representing the summit of Weill's achievement. Dr Johnson spoke of how a man under the threat of death 'concentrates his mind wonderfully'; even in the relative safety of Paris Weill's terrible experience seems to have had precisely that effect. Superficially the work appears neo-Classical: a sonata-form first movement with slow introduction, a march-like *Largo* and a rondo Finale, the whole scored for a typical early nineteenth-century orchestra plus two trombones; and the surprisingly successful marriage of Weill's streetwise lyricism and sonata energy suggests that he had learned a few things from Schubert. But what impresses most is the rhythmic urgency, sometimes driving the music forward, sometimes – as at the height of the *Largo* – erupting into what sounds like impassioned protest.

And then there is the question of the ending: is it, as one commentator initially remarked, 'joyful'? To these ears at least there is something distinctly thuggish about the jaunty C major transformation of the *Largo*'s first theme. We should not forget that we are dealing with an accomplished ironist here: one who, no less than Mahler, could use popular styles to poignant, disturbing or even downright brutal effect. Weill refused to offer any explanation, saying that the symphony was 'conceived as a purely musical form'. In its elegant and concise construction it certainly seems far removed from Mahlerian narrative – and yet there are passages in which it is difficult not to be reminded of Weill's ordeal: the nervously searching introduction, that very ambiguous

* What the lines were is unknown: when the score was rediscovered after the composer's death its title page had been removed.

ending, or this achingly sad flute solo from the heart of the *Largo* (Ex. 5).

We know only too well what, politically speaking, Weill left behind him. But what of the symphony? On 23 March 1933 – nine days after Weill's hurried departure from Germany – Munich saw the first performance of

Ex. 5. Weill: Symphony No. 2

the Symphony No. 1 by **Hans Pfitzner** (1869–1949). Neither this work nor its successor has survived in the post-war world, and it is not difficult to see why. The First is actually an arrangement of the String Quartet in C sharp minor of 1925 – and once one knows this it is virtually impossible to hear it in any other way. The orchestration, though sometimes impressive, more often seems merely applied to the original textures. The Second Symphony, in C major (1940), does exhibit a genuine orchestral sense, but the three-movements-in-one structure is not worked through with any real conviction, and much of the material – especially the hearty brass tune that opens the initial *Allegro moderato* – is resoundingly hollow. With this work the unthinkable has happened: the German symphony has become provincial.

In September 1932, while Pfitzner was labouring to transform Quartet to Symphony and Schmidt was at work on his Fourth, **Anton Webern** (1883–1945) was lecturing on a symphony he had written four years earlier. The talk, which would have horrified Pfitzner and probably baffled Schmidt, explained how the manipulations of the basic twelve-note row had replaced the role of tonality, and how considerations of symmetry and regularity were now paramount. 'For the rest', said Webern, 'one works as before.' Accordingly the first of the two movements duplicates all the main landmarks of Classical sonata form: exposition and development-recapitulation repeats with first and second time bars *und so weiter*. Fascinatingly, behind the ghostly, fragmented surface, a trace of the old pattern of presentation-intensification-release remains; and yet, weirdly beautiful as it is, there is something unsettling about it – rather like watching a robot imitating the most personal actions of a human being. For the post-war avant-garde, particularly the total-serialist camp, Webern's Symphony acquired immense significance – the threshold of a new way of composing. For the symphony as a genre, however, it was as much a *cul de sac* as the efforts of Pfitzner.

There was still one outstanding work bearing the title 'symphony' to appear in Germany between Hitler's accession and the outbreak of war: the Symphony *Mathis der Maler* ('Mathis the Painter') by **Paul Hindemith** (1895–1963). There are two possible arguments against its inclusion here. First, the material is largely taken from the opera of the same name (1933–5) – the first two movements are in fact the prelude, *Engelkonzert* ('Angel Concert'), and a later interlude, *Grablegung* ('Entombment') from the opera – and thus the work could just as adequately be entitled 'Suite: Mathis der Maler'. Secondly there is the argument put forward by Robert Simpson:* that here and in Hindemith's other so-called symphonies there is 'the same kind of calm solidity as an early suite; the tonalities move round like the spokes of a wheel, rotating about a fixed centre that is never seriously in doubt ... This

* In volume 2 of *The Symphony*, London, 1967, p. 12.

is impressive, but the music does not "travel" like symphonic invention.'

It is difficult to disagree with this as a description of Hindemith's practice
in general. The basis of his art is, as Simpson says, 'nearer to that of Bach
than to Beethoven's'. But we have already looked at works in this chapter
which do not 'travel' in the Beethovenian manner; moreover it has to be
said that a very high proportion of Hindemith's most inspired music is to
be found in the works he called symphonies; and here is the beginning of
the response to the first argument: the *Mathis der Maler* Symphony may
have grown out of the opera, but there is a strong case for regarding it as
an even finer achievement – perhaps in itself Hindemith's greatest work.
And while one may recognize the stately progress of Baroque concert music
in the wonderful folksong variations of *Engelkonzert*, the slow processional
of *Grablegung* or the ingenious combination of passacaglia and chorale
prelude that makes up the final crescendo of *Versuchung des heiligen
Antonius* ('Temptation of St Anthony'), the work does have its moments
of quite un-Baroque drama, like the re-emergence of the tune *Es sungen
drei Engel* ('Three angels sang') in a blazing tutti (complete with cymbal
roll) at the climax of the first movement.

The grandeur and intensity of the writing made the *Mathis* Symphony a
huge success at its première in 1934 (Furtwängler, who had commissioned
the work, conducting), but the association with the liberal, anti-totalitarian
message of the opera made the authorities uncomfortable, and eventually
Hindemith found himself officially suppressed. After a two-year visit to
Turkey – a timely invitation to help set up a music school in Ankara –
he too left Germany, eventually settling in the United States. But, in
contrast to Weill, Hindemith made no drastic musical change of direction.
Not long after his arrival in America he completed another symphony:
the Symphony in E flat (1940). This time the layout is traditional – a
lively first movement, a solemn *Sehr langsam*, and a Scherzo-plus-Trio
linked to a truly climactic Finale – and yet it comes closer even than the
Mathis Symphony to Simpson's description: the first movement in particular
has something of the regular, chugging vitality of an eighteenth-century
concerto grosso. The Symphony in E flat may fall short of its predecessor
in terms of originality and melodic distinction, but it is an impressive
and in places appealing work, and one that does not deserve its current
neglect.

Much the same could be said of the *Sinfonia serena* (1946) – not
perhaps as consistent as the Symphony in E flat, but a work with
many imaginative touches: the piccolo's quietly persistent birdsong figure towards the end of the Finale is a good example of the gently
humorous side Hindemith showed perhaps too rarely. The opening of
the Symphony (Ex. 6) is as beautiful as anything in *Mathis der Maler*,
and the crescendo Hindemith builds upon it sustains the inspiration
magnificently.

Ex. 6. Hindemith: *Sinfonia serena*

Still more inconsistent is the Symphony *Die Harmonie der Welt* ('The Harmony of the World', 1951), once again closely linked to the material of an opera, this time based on the life of the astronomer Johannes Kepler. In this case, however, the symphony seems to have come first. The titles of the three movements – *Musica instrumentalis*, *Musica humana* and *Musica mundana* ('Music of the spheres') proclaim a relation to the writings of the early Christian philosopher Boethius – though what the details of that relationship might be are hard to say without the help of the opera, and that dropped out of the repertory long ago.

That the flame could still burn high is evident right at the start, where against an accompaniment of shrill high strings, brass blare out an arresting motif in canon. The slow quasi-fugal introduction to the Finale has a quality – typical of Hindemith at his best – for which only the word 'noble' seems adequate. The Passacaglia that follows begins very promisingly, but after a while it becomes obvious that what we are going to hear is not so much variation as an immensely long process of decoration. The theme doggedly holds centre-stage: even in the imaginative recitative-like variation for flute and bassoon the glockenspiel will keep reminding us of it, note for note. It is worth persisting for the Brucknerian final climax – if only more had happened between this and the introduction.

Before we go on to look at what happened to the Central European symphony after the Second World War, there is one more important figure to be considered. **Igor Stravinsky** (1882–1971) was of course born in Russia, but after the 1917 Revolution he chose to stay in France, retaining Paris as his base until the outbreak of war when he too sought safety in

America. Stravinsky had already composed works whose titles included the word 'symphony' (or 'symphonies') before this second forced deracination, but aside from the early and very Rimskyan Symphony in E flat (1905–7), he had determinedly avoided anything that suggested the familiar model. The 'Symphony of Psalms' (1930) is certainly more than a collection of psalm-settings: the inevitability with which the three movements follow each other is a reminder that this was intended as a concert work rather than a liturgical offering. But in the Symphony in C (1938–40) and the Symphony in Three Movements (1942–45) Stravinsky shows an involvement with the Austro-German symphony unprecedented in his career – fascinating that he should have felt the need to make this engagement at such a time.

Engagé it may be, but the Symphony in C remains like nothing else in the repertory. It is here, and not in Sibelius, that we at last reach the true antithesis of Mahler. However much one may admire the control – the 'severity' of Sibelius's Fourth Symphony, its mood is as directly relatable to contemporary events in its composer's life as in any of the Mahler symphonies. The Symphony in C, however, gives not a hint that it was begun in what Stravinsky called 'the most tragic year of my life'. Between November 1938 and June 1939 – as war became increasingly inevitable – he lost his elder daughter, his first wife and his mother, and then found that he himself was seriously ill. But then, as we have seen with Szymanowski and Weill, there is more than one way of responding to crisis. Stravinsky's creative solution was to look hard at symphonic scores (he mentions Haydn, Beethoven and Tchaikovsky's First) and apply his penetrating intelligence to what he found.

The result is a piece which, rather than sounding intrinsically symphonic, gives the impression of being about the *idea* of the symphony – an idea which Stravinsky proceeds to deconstruct with characteristic relish. In the first movement the familiar landmarks of sonata form are all present, but the way they are related is quite new – sometimes it is as though the movement were being built up in independent 'blocks' – and teasing ambiguities abound. What we sense is, in Peter Evans's words, the 'simultaneous acknowledgement and denial of classical precedent'. And if the word 'Symphony' in Stravinsky's title seems to call for quotation marks, so too does the remaining 'in C'. Nowhere in the work is there anything like an emphatic C major triad in root position: the first and last movements end with chords which, though they incorporate only the correct 'white' notes, are both built up from a bass E; the pounding Bs of the opening could be leading notes of C – but the implication of the dominant of E minor is stronger, at least at first. Perhaps it would be truer to say that the symphony is about the scale of C, in which C, E or G can be felt as alternative centres of gravity.

In later years Stravinsky complained that the Symphony in C was divided down the middle – that there was a European half and an American half. The first movement, he pointed out, sticks untypically to one metre throughout, 'whereas the third movement's metrical irregularities are among the most extreme in any of [my] compositions'. True – but variety can be as much the spice of symphony as of life, and the Finale clearly takes its cue from the harmonic tensions of the first movement, bringing them to a satisfying conclusion. It has to be said though that it is only in the middle two movements – the florid *Larghetto concertante* and the unashamedly balletic *Allegretto* – that the music is totally free from the suggestion of intellectual exercise.

The Symphony in Three Movements is a very different proposition. It was written, said Stravinsky, 'under the impression of world events. I will not say that it expresses my feelings about them, but only that . . . they excited my musical imagination'. As to what the specific events might have been he was surprisingly specific: the strident march-opening of the Finale was 'a musical reaction to the newsreels and documentaries that I had seen of goose-stepping soldiers'; the initial 'comic' immobility of the following fugue paralleled 'the overturned arrogance of the Germans when their machine failed', while the final 'albeit rather too commercial D flat sixth chord – instead of the expected C – tokens my extra exuberance in the Allied triumph.' Then, sensing perhaps that he had gone further than he should, Stravinsky adds that 'the Symphony is not programmatic. Composers combine notes. That is all.'

Up to a point of course he is quite right. The Symphony in Three Movements can be enjoyed for the exhilarating, brilliantly colourful thing it is without the aid of programmes – and how would one fit into any 'war' scheme the fact that the *Andante* middle movement was derived from an incomplete film-score for Franz Werfel's *The Song of Bernardette*? What is undeniable is that the stimulus of world events set Stravinsky's imagination working at full power. The musical argument is intensified by something more like Beethovenian tonal conflict – the clash of G and A flat in the first movement, and of C and D flat in the Finale. At the same time there are *concertante* elements:* the piano moves into the spotlight for parts of the first movement, the harp in the second, and both make important solo and duo contributions in the Finale. The building-block technique from the Symphony in C remains too, so that we may wonder whether the Finale has actually progressed, or simply gone through a sequence of more or less arresting musical images – as, indeed, in 'newsreels and documentaries'. Whatever the case, it is a uniquely compelling work – and one of the few uncontested masterpieces of Stravinsky's post-European career.

Whether any of the symphonies written in post-war Germany will achieve similar masterpiece status is still an open question, though the list of contenders is getting smaller. For a while there was widespread championship for the cause of **Karl Amadeus Hartmann (1905–63)**,

---

* According to Alexander Tansman, the first movement began life as 'a symphonic work with a *concertante* part for the piano'.

a figure who during the 1950s came to represent the acceptable face of German modernism. Here was a composer who could acknowledge the innovations of the Second Viennese School (he had been a pupil of Webern), but at the same time maintain a way of thinking that was fundamentally recognizable. Atonal the later symphonies may have been, but they were still recognizably symphonies – dark, often violent, but undeniably expressive. Hartmann's deliberate withdrawal from the musical scene during the period of Nazi rule gave him the added advantage of political acceptability; he had even written a work in protest at the invasion of Czechoslovakia – the *Concerto funèbre* for violin and strings (1939) – which had been performed in St Gallen in 1940.

Hartmann's path to full engagement with symphonic form was slow. The First (1936, revised 1948) was also described by Hartmann as 'Essay for a Requiem', and its five movements include settings of lines from Walt Whitman's *Leaves of Grass* for contralto and orchestra. The one-movement Second (1946) and the Third (1948–9) edge closer, though the manner does not yet seem quite focussed – too many influences pulling in contrary directions, perhaps. The suite-like Fourth, for strings alone (1947), and the *concertante* Fifth (1950) – a reworking of an earlier concerto for trumpet and wind – are more successful musically, but in terms of Hartmann's struggle to come to terms with the symphony these are retrograde steps.

Then in 1953 Hartmann completed a work whose claims to the title were much more impressive – the Sixth Symphony. What stands out in comparison to the earlier symphonies is the much greater sureness and directness of the manner. The two movements – an intense, melodic *Adagio* and a rapid *Toccata variata* including three brilliant fugues – bring together many sides of Hartmann's musical personality: the frenetic or brooding Bergian lyricism, the Brucknerian long-term planning and the driving rhythms that he so admired in Bartók; there are even echoes of the neo-Classical *concertante* style of the Fifth in the fugal writing. But there is a recurring problem: Hartmann's melodic lines may be expressive, his counterpoint muscular, but what the symphony often fails to achieve is convincing harmonic dimension. Hartmann seems to have wanted to retain something of the functional character – the feeling of tension and resolution – of tonal harmony while rejecting key centres. It can be done, of course, and in some parts of the symphony Hartmann comes close to success – the winding-down of the first movement on to a widely-spaced C sharp-centred chord is a good example – but there are places, particularly towards the end of the Finale, where densely dissonant chords succeed one another arbitrarily. Instead of surging forward, the music frantically treads water.

The Seventh Symphony (1957–8) is in some ways a step in the right direction – the paring down of the Sixth's rich textures helps in the achievement of harmonic focus – but the work lacks the strong profile of its predecessor, and again there are long stretches in which the only activity is a rather self-defeating busyness. With the Eighth Symphony (1960–62), however, there is a feeling that at last the elements have begun to fuse. The final climax of the opening *Cantilène* may overstate its case, but on the whole this movement shows Hartmann's non-tonal melodic writing at its most mellifluous, and the harmonies really do seem to grow from it. The vertical dimension is still the weakest aspect of the following *Dythrambe: Scherzo – Fuga*, but the spirit of Dionysus is present, particularly in the pounding dance-rhythms of the *Fuga*. Perhaps if Hartmann had lived, he might – like his slightly older contemporary Roberto Gerhard – have gone on to a brilliant late flowering. From his symphonic output, however, the overall impression is of great promise never quite fulfilled.

'*Es lebt, die Symphonie!*' ('The Symphony Lives!') read a headline in a Berlin newspaper after the première of the Seventh Symphony by **Hans Werner Henze** (b. 1926) – the note of surprise is significant. 'Old forms', Henze has written, 'appear to me as Classical ideals of beauty, no longer attainable but still visible from a great distance, arousing memories like dreams'. Each of his symphonies attempts to find fresh ways of bringing together the old and the new. The First (1947, revised for chamber orchestra 1963) finds an appealing line of fantasy in a fusion of neo-Classical Schoenberg and Stravinsky, but with the Second (1949) Henze at last acknowledges his Austro-German inheritance: the intensely expressive string writing of the *Adagio* invites comparison of Mahler, even if it is Mahler viewed through Schoenbergian eyes. Still more Mahlerian is Henze's increasing desire to widen his embrace. Invocations to jazz and the gods of ancient Greece form the basis of the highly balletic Third Symphony (1951); the forest sounds of the opera *König Hirsch* combine with traditional forms in the Fourth (1955); the Fifth apparently portrays 'the sensuous happiness of 20th-century Rome', while in the avowedly communist Sixth (1969) 'bourgeois (European) new music and my own resist and fragment. A conflict is depicted'.

The colour, atmosphere and range of reference in Henze's symphonic works is undeniable. The question is, how meaningful is the resultant *mélange*? For this writer, initial interest has in each case been followed by a steady process of disappointment. Attractive or exciting sounds drift past, seeming to promise much; but further acquaintance fails to establish any deeper connections. It could be argued that such fragmentation accords with the remark quoted above: that the music illustrates Henze's contention that old forms and ideals of synthesis are 'no longer attainable'. Or perhaps the truth is more simply that Henze's symphonies are prime examples of the whole adding up to less than the sum of the parts.

The Seventh Symphony (1983–84) illustrates this problem as well as any of its predecessors. According to Henze, the third and fourth movements were inspired by disturbed, fragmentary later poems of Friedrich Hölderlin. Again, Henze sets out to capture something of the half-logic of dreams, but against the background of the traditional symphony. The question is whether the tension between the two is strong enough to sustain a forty-five-minute structure – and 'structure' is plainly how Henze wishes it to be perceived, for all his protestation of ironic 'distance'. So how does the Seventh Symphony evolve? The opening movement, *Tanz* ('Dance'), begins promisingly, and keeps up its air of anticipation almost to the end. There is tension too in the opening of the slow movement, plus some of Henze's most beguiling sounds, but the lyricism falters, and still more than in *Tanz* there is a tendency for climaxes to degenerate into an all too typical expressionist bombast – the most common manifestation being the reiterated *ffff* brass dissonances that take their cue (but unfortunately not their *raison d'être*) from the Funeral March of Webern's 'Six Pieces for Orchestra.' In the slow final movement the promise and frustration are both at their most intense. The viola melody of the coda is a late reminder that Henze can write convincing long lines – but it is soon eclipsed by the dense tutti of the coda.

After the war and the ensuing communist takeover, Poland's musical ties with Austria and the greater part of Germany were severed. The conditions under which Szymanowski could regard Vienna as a second home were replaced by an enforced Soviet-orientation. In recent years, however, as liberalization has increased, there have been signs of a cultural drift back to the west. Two members of the once exuberant and very fertile Polish avant-garde – **Krzysztof Penderecki** (b. 1933) and **Witold Lutosławski** (b. 1913) – have been drawn increasingly towards the traditional symphony. Penderecki's Second Symphony (1980) was one of the first signs of an extraordinary stylistic volte-face, in which he turned his back on radical experimentation and threw himself into neo-romanticism – with far from convincing results. But Lutosławski's Third (1983) is a much more interesting attempt to make sense of the changing relationship of old and new. In the early stages of the work the familiar intertwining

Ex. 7. Lutosławski: Symphony No. 3

textures and semi-aleatory devices are combined with a growing forward movement in which, from time to time, longer lines strive to emerge. Then at the height of a characteristic whirlpool tutti, the music suddenly plunges headlong into this:

We have heard Ex. 7 before, but its presentation here on full strings, *ff*, is startling, as is its impassioned continuation. If this sounds like an invocation of Mahler, the Symphony's final grand crescendo, with its tolling low harp and piano and expanding horn calls, comes close to direct imitation. Modernism confronts the past. But how effective is this juxtaposition? Is Lutosławski making a statement about the symphony then and now, or is Ex. 7 merely a gesture to the gallery? We may have our suspicions, but it would be rash to try to guess how future generations will view the ambiguous monuments of our time. Germany, Austria, Poland – indeed all of Europe – has entered another period of momentous change. What the results will be, politically and musically, is anybody's guess. Whether the extraordinary rise in popularity of **Henryck Gorecki's** 'minimalist' Third Symphony (1976) will turn out to be an event of lasting significance or a commercial flash in the pan is impossible to say. It is possible that a work like Lutosławski's Third may come to be seen as prophetic of a new era in the history of the symphony. It is also possible that posterity will judge it as Debussy once judged Wagner: 'a beautiful sunset mistaken for a dawn'.

18

The American Symphony

John Canarina

The American symphonic tradition is understandably less venerable than its formidable European counterpart. William Billings (1746–1800) is the earliest American composer performed with any regularity today, but he is not part of that tradition. The bulk of his work is choral music in the form of hymns, anthems and patriotic songs that attained great popularity during the American Revolution. But it was not until 1837 that one of the earliest American works to bear the designation 'symphony' appeared, 'The Columbiad: Grand American National Chivalrous Symphony' by the Bohemian-born **Anthony Philip Heinrich** (1781–1861), who had emigrated to the United States in 1810. Its incorporation of such American national airs as 'Hail Columbia' and 'Yankee Doodle' can be said to have led the way to the more far-reaching scores of Charles Ives.

In his day Heinrich was called the 'Beethoven of America', and other examples of his symphonic catalogue are the 1845 'Manitou Mysteries; or The Voice of the Great Spirit' (*Gran sinfonia misteriosa – indiana*) and the 1857 ornithologically inspired 'Migration of American Wild Passenger Pigeons' (A Characteristic Symphony in two parts), again including 'Hail Columbia' and 'Yankee Doodle'. It is ironic that Heinrich, a transplanted European, spent much of his time writing music overtly American in flavour, both in subject matter and in the use of familiar national tunes, while more than an entire succeeding generation of native-born Americans went out of its way to compose music based on European, specifically German, models.

The best-known internationally of nineteenth-century American composers is the colourful **Louis Moreau Gottschalk** (1829–69). Celebrated for his Latin-flavoured piano music, he also wrote two similarly tinged orchestral works designated as symphonies: the two-movement 'A Night in the Tropics' (*Symphonie romantique*) and the one-movement, seven-sectioned 'To Montevideo' (*Symphonie romantique pour grand orchestre*), which contains not only an arrangement of the Uruguayan national anthem but also the ubiquitous 'Hail Columbia' and 'Yankee Doodle'. Of course, neither of these scores is a true symphony in the classical sense, any more than their predecessors are. The term was used rather loosely to embrace a wide variety of orchestral compositions (still the case even today, and not only in America).

Most intriguing of all nineteenth-century American works is the 1853 'Santa Claus' Symphony by **William Henry Fry** (1813–64), a controversial piece thought to be of greater entertainment value than artistic merit and written for the French showman conductor Louis Antoine Jullien, who in that year brought his celebrated orchestra to America. Revived in 1958 by the American conductor Howard Shanet with his Columbia University Orchestra, it is probably the first American work to employ a saxophone, and includes a whip, sleigh bells and a toy trumpet among its instrumentation, while the string players are called upon to produce *glissandi* to depict the howling and whistling of the wind.

Other than Gottschalk's 'A Night in the Tropics', the earliest American symphonies one can hear today, thanks to recordings, are the two by **John Knowles Paine** (1839–1906). Paine is the first in a long series of composers based in the Boston area that have come to be known as the 'Second New England School', to distinguish the group from Billings and his contemporaries. These composers felt the need to study in Germany and write according to established methods and styles. While they produced a considerable body of work, much of it of great merit and well worth exploring today, it cannot be said that they achieved a distinctive national style (perhaps not their objective, though the formative stages of such a style can be detected in the work of the best of them).

Paine's First Symphony in C minor (1872–75) is a remarkable achievement, a work steeped in the tradition of Beethoven and Schumann, yet one that looks ahead to Brahms (whose own First Symphony in C minor was not completed until 1876) and, in its warmly tender *Adagio*, even Mahler. The *Allegro con brio* first movement opens with an arresting *agitato* figure in the cellos and basses, and contains references to the motto theme of Beethoven's Fifth with descending sequences similar to those found in that score. This is a movement of intense dynamism, but it lacks Beethoven's terseness. The tripping scherzo in ternary dotted rhythm – the Beethoven Seventh first movement rhythm – is also reminiscent of the Seventh's Scherzo. After the *Adagio*, there is a vigorous and jubilant Finale with some bows in Schumann's direction, in which the Scherzo's dotted rhythm returns to bring the work to a triumphant close. Throughout the symphony one is impressed by the complete assurance of Paine's orchestral writing, not only in the dynamic sections but in the many felicitous woodwind and horn solos. The lyrical secondary themes are marked by a sweetness and naïveté not found in Beethoven, a trait that will continue to manifest itself in American music for some time. The only element preventing this symphony from achieving repertory status is the lack of truly distinctive thematic material – unfortunate because its development is so striking.

The same can be said of Paine's Second Symphony in A major (1880).

If the subtitle 'In Springtime' evokes Schumann, so does the score's more ingratiating manner in comparison with the First Symphony. Again we have those dotted rhythms (characteristic of Schumann as well as Beethoven) and the sweetness and naïveté of the lyrical themes. What makes this symphony ultimately less successful than its predecessor is the composer's inability to sustain interest in his thematic material over the score's protracted length (about fifty minutes) – and a certain blandness of expression. Still, one can say, on the basis of these two symphonies, that Paine's music, while inspired by Beethoven and Schumann (with a touch of Dvořák and even a hint of Elgar in No. 2 – before their major works), doesn't really sound like those composers. He was finding his own voice within the established limits of mid-nineteenth-century German style, and was obviously a master orchestrator within that genre.

In 1876 a young man named **George Whitefield Chadwick** (1854–1931) attended the première of Paine's First Symphony in Boston. He was very excited by this 'great event', as he called it, feeling that at last America could lay claim to a great composer. Chadwick, too, was to study in Germany, though his music is more in the spirit of Dvořák than of any German model, the Second Symphony in B flat (1883–86) contemporaneous with the Czech master's Seventh Symphony and predating the last two by several years. Essentially a good-humoured score, the Second Symphony, like Paine's, suffers from a lack of thematic distinction, though its Scherzo does have a slight American Indian flavour.

The Third Symphony in F major (the same key as Brahms's Third) is a more sophisticated, more 'European' score, but also a less inspired one, notable primarily for having won a competition of which Dvořák was a judge. Its high point is a sprightly and engaging Scherzo, demonstrating that the New England composers were very good indeed at evoking the world of 'woodland goblins' and the like (shades of Schumann again). A symphony in all but name, Chadwick's most attractive and original work is the Symphonic Sketches (1895–1907), of which the first section, 'Jubilee', has often been performed separately. Though lighter in mood than the symphonies, this score contains everything that they lack – ingratiating tunes, buoyantly inventive rhythms and sparkling orchestration, though also some thematic material evocative of the American Indian, which is found in the other works. Remember that it was Dvořák who encouraged American composers to look to their own roots in forging a national style, yet much of Chadwick's work predates the 'New World' Symphony, which Dvořák wrote as an example of how this could be done.

In **Amy Beach** (1867–1944) he found a willing and responsive echo, though her only symphony (1896) draws not on American Indian music but on a collection of old Irish melodies: hence the subtitle 'Gaelic'. Mrs Beach, as she is often known (though one doesn't speak of Mr Chadwick or Mr Ives), was largely self-taught and learned her orchestration from Berlioz's treatise, which she translated. There is nothing particularly original or specifically American about it: the opening is rather Lisztian or Tchaikovskian, whereas the delightful slow movement has Dvořákian touches. But it is a well-schooled symphony of enormous accomplishment and the best of it has great charm.

Most Americans agree that their first certifiably great native-born composer was **Charles Ives** (1874–1954). His father was a progressive Connecticut bandmaster who taught his family to sing hymns in one key while he accompanied them at the piano or organ in another, thus expanding their aural horizons. Just as Mahler, who grew up near a military barracks, incorporated martial fanfares into many of his works, so did Ives include the musical artefacts of his childhood in virtually everything he wrote – the patriotic airs and marches associated with his father's band, the hymns sung in church. But whereas Mahler was content to make passing reference to this material, Ives based entire compositions on it with, in many cases, several hymn tunes and patriotic songs sounding simultaneously, often in different tempos. In his First Symphony in D minor (1897), completed as an academic exercise while he was a student of Horatio Parker, Dvořák is still a presence (there is even a cor anglais theme in the slow movement that calls him to mind), but despite its traditional formal layout there are many portents of what is to come.

Ives's Second (1897–1902) is the earliest American symphony regularly performed today, a situation that has obtained only since 1951, for it was not until then that the work received its first performance, with Leonard Bernstein conducting the New York Philharmonic. Not complex at all, this lovable score is at once a pastiche and a work of striking originality. While it is true one can find in it allusions to Bach, Handel, Brahms, Wagner and other great composers, plus a lively assortment of American hymns, folksongs, marches and patriotic tunes (most notably Ives's favourite, 'Columbia, the Gem of the Ocean,' blared forth stirringly by the trombones at the end, just after the Army *reveille* bugle call), they are all combined and filtered in such a way as to form a commentary on the evolution and state of European and American composition up to that point. When the symphony seems about to conclude in the traditional European repeated-chord manner, *reveille* returns, to be followed by a final nose-thumbing chord containing all twelve notes of the chromatic scale. With that one gesture Ives seems to be proclaiming: 'Enough of that old-fashioned prettiness – let's enter the twentieth century!'

The Third Symphony ('The Camp Meeting', 1902–04) is an attractive work of slighter dimensions both instrumentally and formally. It remained unperformed until 1946, winning the prestigious Pulitzer Prize the following year. While it contains its share of hymn tunes, they are less obviously presented than in No. 2. The second movement, 'Children's Days', is a naïvely joyous romp and the concluding 'Communion' is an unusual example of Ivesian austerity.

Most remarkable is the Fourth Symphony (1910–16), of which Leopold

Stokowski gave the posthumous première in 1965 with his American Symphony Orchestra. 'Completed' work is also applicable, for Ives had left the score and parts in a state of disarray, with no clear indication of the proper sequence of pages or, at times, even which lines of music belonged with other lines, all of which had to be carefully collated and edited by the composer Henry Cowell, a long-time friend and associate of Ives. According to Ives, 'The aesthetic programme of the work is that of the searching questions of "What?" and "Why?" which the spirit of man asks of life. This is particularly the sense of the Prelude. The three succeeding movements are the diverse answers in which existence replies.'

That brief Prelude, imposing and mystical, is a setting of the hymn 'Watchman, Tell us of the Night'. A small chorus is called for, though Ives, with characteristic humour, wryly notes that it would be preferable to omit it. The second movement is Ives at his most complex, an apotheosis of everything he had written previously, recalling but outdoing the 'Putnam's Camp' section of his *Three Places in New England*. All the familiar tunes are there, but often in such a dense conglomeration as to make it virtually impossible to hear any of them clearly. At other times they float by as if in a dream. After this the third movement is simplicity itself, a double fugue on the hymns 'From Greenland's Icy Mountains' and 'All Hail the Power', ending with a phrase from Handel's 'Joy to the World'. The final *Largo maestoso* movement brings back the Prelude's mystery, with opening and closing distant percussion and a wordless chorus towards the end.

So complex is the writing in portions of this symphony, in terms of simultaneous metrical and tempo variance among different sections of the orchestra, that, in the manner of the Stokowski-led première, it is often performed with two sub-conductors in addition to the principal conductor. Editions have been made enabling one conductor to direct the score throughout, but something is inevitably lost in the process, if only its theatrical value.

The first American composer to write entirely in this century and to create a substantial body of symphonies was **Howard Hanson** (1896–1981). He was also widely known as a music educator (first director of the Eastman School of Music, 1924–64); his music was championed by Serge Koussevitzky with the Boston Symphony Orchestra. An unabashed romantic, Hanson was for many years thoroughly out of fashion with the American musical establishment, but recent years have seen a gradual reawakening of interest in his work, of which the early scores especially pay homage to his Swedish ancestry.

In all, Hanson produced seven symphonies; the 'Nordic' First in 1924, the final choral 'Sea Symphony' shortly before his death. Of these, the 'Romantic' Symphony (No. 2) is quite possibly the most performed of all American symphonies, for though it rarely appears on the programmes of American major orchestras, it has long been a great favourite with lesser ensembles, such as amateur and youth orchestras, of which there are many.

The 'Romantic' was one of that celebrated group of works composed to commemorate the Boston Symphony's fiftieth anniversary in 1930. After the première under Koussevitzky, it was also performed by Arturo Toscanini with the New York Philharmonic.

The first movement's slow introduction is based on a reiterated rising three-note figure that builds to a climax and subsides, after which a horn fanfare leads into the movement's principal descending theme, heard first from the brass. After an extended transition, a tenderly nostalgic and yearning second theme appears in the strings, which is ultimately to dominate the entire symphony. This theme is truly 'Romantic' in character, even a bit sentimental, and if one is to accept the work one must surrender to it for, once heard, it tends to remain in one's consciousness, particularly as the composer brings it back in the remaining two movements, each time with greater emphasis.

A gentle woodwind theme dominates the second movement, and two horn themes of American Indian character (Hanson was from Nebraska) animate the Finale, the second over vigorous ostinato string pizzicati. The closing pages, with both themes from the first movement returning, are quite triumphal, and if one is reminded of Hollywood, it should be remembered that the work was composed before any of the major Hollywood film scores.

The Third Symphony in A minor (1938) opens with a finely paced and expertly laid out first movement, and its slow movement shows particular generosity of lyrical feeling. Also of interest, because atypical, is Hanson's Fourth Symphony (1943), the four movements of which derive their titles from the Roman Catholic requiem Mass: 'Kyrie', 'Requiescat', 'Dies Irae', 'Lux aeterna'. This is a more solemn, austere and concise Hanson, the second movement's bassoon solo over pizzicato cellos and basses bringing Sibelius's Second to mind. Particularly notable is the 'Dies Irae' with its sardonic woodwind theme, snarling muted trombone, throbbing timpani and insistent Polovtzian side-drum rhythm.

The Fifth ('Sinfonia Sacra', 1954), which is inspired by the story of the Resurrection as recounted in the Gospel according to St John, is a concise one-movement piece lasting under a quarter of an hour, falling into three sections, with a distinctly Nordic flavour to its middle pastoral section and a final section of some eloquence, whose power rests on an effective juxtaposition of chords of E major and D minor.

Another of the composers championed by Koussevitzky was **Roy Harris** (1898–1979), who has been termed an 'American Musorgsky' because of the generally rough-hewn, craggy character of much of his work and his indomitable striving to express the American spirit in his music. By the same token, he could also be thought of as an 'American Janáček'. His 'Symphony 1933', the first of fourteen, has the honour of being the first American symphony ever recorded, a live recording of a concert performance by Koussevitzky and the Boston Symphony. Although somewhat uneven in workmanship, the score is already in the 'Harris style' with its exuberant horn passages and timpani ostinatos. Harris was, in fact, the first American composer of prominence to write soloistically for the timpani, a practice adopted with even greater relish by his pupil William Schuman.

For many years Harris has been unjustifiably regarded as a one-work composer, that work being his Third Symphony. Premièred by Koussevitzky and the Boston Symphony in 1939, this was the first American symphony to capture the imagination of conductors, critics and audiences, and thus the first to enter the standard repertoire both in the United States and internationally. For a time it may have been the American symphony most frequently performed by the world's major ensembles.

With Sibelius's Seventh as a precedent, Harris cast his Third in a single movement with several subsections. He was not the first American to adopt this format, for Samuel Barber's First of 1936 (of which more anon) is similarly ordered. In the first section Harris wishes to evoke the vast spaces of America's great prairies. The opening passage (Ex. 1) for cellos alone, with occasional viola reinforcement, is in the manner of a plain-chant, and as the violas begin to add more significantly to the texture, the harmonies of bare fourths and fifths succeed admirably in achieving the composer's vision.

Ex. 1. Harris: Symphony No. 3

Dark chords by the trombones usher in the more broadly paced second section, written almost entirely in minims and breves. Long unison lines by the woodwinds dominate as the tempo increases and then relaxes into an extended *pastorale*. Here soft folk-like woodwind melodies, starting with the cor anglais, are accompanied by incessantly rising and falling string arpeggios. (Among American orchestral musicians this episode has come to be known as the 'wallpaper section' because the pages and pages of arpeggios in the string parts look like a wallpaper design.) Delicate punctuations by the vibraphone add a touch of colour. With the gradual entrances of the brass, the music becomes more animated, swirling woodwinds and descending strings ultimately leading to a vigorous section which the composer has described as a fugue. While it may be fugal in the sense that its arresting theme (Ex. 2) is reiterated many times, often canonically, it is hardly a fugue in the traditional sense, being virtually devoid of linear counterpoint. The brass come to the fore in this section, as do the timpani, whose pounding punctuation of the main theme adds so much to the work's vitality. Also notable is the insistent three-note accompanying figure so characteristic of Harris, which reappears throughout:

Ex. 2. Harris: Symphony No. 3

The fugal section culminates in long sustained canonic string and woodwind lines encasing rhythmic passages by the brass and timpani, leading into the symphony's conclusion. Over throbbing timpani on the note D, the brass intone a chorale-like theme and are soon joined by woodwinds and strings, each playing a separate line. The mood of this section is one of tragedy, so often an underlying element in Harris's works. Intensity mounts, to be released by two ominous outbursts on the timpani and bass drum. As much of the work's harmony has been based on intervals of fourths and fifths, the final unequivocal G minor chord comes as something of a catharsis.

The Third remains the quintessential American symphony, a work of enormous power and real stature. Try as he might, Harris was never able to duplicate its success, though certain of its successors are by no means negligible. No. 4, called 'Folk-Song Symphony', is a choral work in which American folksongs are presented fairly straightforwardly with ingenious orchestral accompaniments (there are also two purely orchestral interludes). No. 5 offers a vigorous first movement of remarkable terseness based on that Beethoven Seventh rhythm (shades of Paine!) and also incorporating the three-note figure from the Third Symphony. The second movement is dirge-like and tragic, also reminiscent of No. 3, with a regular throbbing pulse in the cellos and basses supporting long melodic lines. The Finale has an impassioned opening by the strings, then becomes vigorous, even a bit strenuous, with prominent trumpet fanfares.

The four-movement Sixth Symphony, subtitled 'Gettysburg', is Harris's tribute to Abraham Lincoln, with whom he felt a spiritual kinship, having been born in a log cabin (so he said) on Lincoln's birthday in Lincoln County, Oklahoma. It is a remarkable combination of tragic and optimistic elements, with a marchlike second movement, horns whooping and drums pounding, which could also earn the composer the title of an 'American Shostakovich'.

The Seventh (1955) is probably Harris's most performed symphony after the Third. Like the earlier score, it is in a single movement. The composer has described it as a 'dance symphony' and 'a study in harmonic and melodic rhythmic variations'. Opening with a passacaglia with five variations, the work continues with contrapuntal variations both in asymmetrical and symmetrical metres, followed by development of these sections in which the passacaglia theme returns in augmentation. Rhythmically more complex than the Third Symphony and more sumptuously orchestrated, the Seventh, too, presents thematic material of folkish character, such as occurs in the section in 11/4 metre. Tragic overtones also permeate this work, only partially dispelled by the buoyantly rhythmic coda.

William Schuman (1910–92) is undoubtedly the most universally respected of all the American symphonists, also known as an educator (president of the Juilliard School 1945–62) and arts administrator (first president of Lincoln Center, 1962–69). He has produced ten symphonies, of which only eight are in his active canon, the first two having been withdrawn by the composer shortly after their respective premières.

Like several of his colleagues, he thus made his mark with a Third Symphony, first performed in 1941 by whom else but Koussevitzky and the Boston Symphony – and what a powerful work it is! It remains Schuman's most popular symphony, second only to the Harris Third in frequency of performance by American major orchestras (and only major orchestras can do justice to the bulk of Schuman's music, so great are its technical demands). 'Now you must learn to hate Roy Harris,' said Koussevitzky to Schuman, implying that the younger composer should free himself of the musical influences of his teacher. Schuman obviously took his advice to heart, for his Third Symphony displays many traits that have come to be recognized as hallmarks of his style: a harmonic language revolving around frequent use of the 'major-minor' chord (major and minor triads sounded simultaneously); blocklike scoring (extended passages for only brass, woodwinds or strings); long-breathed, arching melodies; nervous, almost telegraphic rhythms; important solo passages for the timpani; craggy, jagged writing for the brass (such as is found in the later works of Michael Tippett); above all, a feeling of buoyancy and optimism, perhaps a bit brash here, that could only have come from an American who had grown up with jazz, as Schuman had (although his music can seldom be termed jazzy).

Schuman's Third is unusual in that it is in two movements, each divided into two parts. (There is precedent for this format in the Third Symphony of Saint-Saëns, though it is doubtful that Schuman had this work in mind as a model.) The two movements pay homage to the Baroque: passacaglia and fugue, chorale and toccata.

The passacaglia begins with the theme presented not in the traditional manner by the bass instruments, but by the violas (Ex. 3). It is a pensive, lyrical theme opening with an upward octave leap, after which fourths and fifths are important in shaping its contours. No ordinary passacaglia this, however, for each successive entry of the theme is stated a half-step higher, the sequence ranging from E to B flat.

Ex. 3. Schuman: Symphony No. 3

Similarly, with the commencement of the vigorous fugue, each entrance of the angular subject (Ex. 4) begins a half-step higher than the preceding one, starting with B flat, where the passacaglia theme had left off, taking us back to E. At this juncture a canonic passage for four trumpets ushers in a more reflective second fugal section in which woodwinds predominate. A sudden highly rhythmic timpani solo, begun *fff*, ushers in the dynamic coda.* Over extremely jagged dotted rhythms in the strings, the four horns (marked 'brassy') intone the passacaglia theme in augmentation, followed by trombones and double basses, woodwinds and trumpets. During this sequence the strings' dotted rhythm has evolved into a three-note figure, demonstrating that Schuman didn't really hate Roy Harris after all. Chattering triplet woodwind figures along with plucked and bowed string quavers accompany fragments of the passacaglia theme in the brass, after which a brief trumpet fanfare, based on the three-note figure, introduces the closing section. Here the trombones and double basses intone the second fugal subject *fff* in augmentation, the horns and trumpets playing strongly accented chords above them. All the brass are instruced to play *fff* with their bells in the air, as the full orchestra joins in to bring the movement to a massively sonorous conclusion.

Ex. 4. Schuman: Symphony No. 3

By contrast, the chorale presents a contemplative opening played by divided cellos and violas, by way of introduction to the main theme, given as an extended quietly plaintive solo on the trumpet. It was only in the early twentieth century that the trumpet gained respectability as a solo instrument within the orchestra, and its prominence in jazz surely had much to do with that development. Again, Schuman's solo is not jazzy, but its melancholy feeling certainly derives from the blues.

A solo flute takes over, fourths and fifths important in its thematic presentation. Eventually the trumpet theme is sounded *fff* by the full woodwind and string sections, ultimately subsiding to a mysterious, distant-sounding passage for the four horns, muted, playing *pianissimo*. The divided cellos and violas return, but as an accompaniment to muted trumpets and then three ascending notes by the solo oboe with a sustained B flat underpinning by the cor anglais. As the movement appears to be dying away on the oboe's and cor anglais' bare fifth of B flat and F, we are brought up with a start by a sudden wrenching B flat pizzicato by the cellos, marked

---

* To a non-American listener this may seem essentially urban in character, its landscape that of skyscrapers but powerfully atmospheric and full of poetic feeling.

sfffz (*sforzandississimo*), the double basses attacking the same note *arco* and sustaining it in a diminuendo. The effect is not unlike the pizzicato that ends the first movement of Mahler's Fifth Symphony.

The toccata follows without pause, the double bass B flat having been surreptitiously co-opted by the bassoons and double bassoon, who sustain it under a soft extended solo by the side-drum, tapping out the nervous dotted and triplet rhythm of the toccata's main theme, soon to be introduced by the bass clarinet. It is a stunning virtuoso solo for that instrument, extending rapidly over its entire range. This movement is in every sense an orchestral *tour de force*, making breathtaking demands on all the sections and instruments. Tension relaxes for a time in the central portion, which begins with what amounts to a cadenza for the cello section, slowly at first, then gradually accelerating, with deeply sonorous pizzicato chords. Soon the other strings join in – a cadenza for them all. When the original tempo resumes, the strings furiously play their three-note figure as the bassoons, bass clarinet, horns, trombones, tubas and double basses (pizzicato) sound *fff* the beginning of the toccata's main theme in double augmentation. After this point the movement becomes a whirlwind to the end, with swirling woodwind triplets, furious string triplets, trumpet calls, rim-shots on the side-drum, incessant dotted triplet rhythms, another timpani solo, and finally a series of massive E flat major chords that bring the work to an exuberant and jubilant conclusion.

Though composed during the early stages of World War II, William Schuman's Third Symphony is a work of unbridled optimism and exhil-aration. As such, it is an expression of the spirit of its time in so far as American music is concerned, for it heralded a period when American composers became accepted, performed and appreciated in their own country to a previously unprecedented degree. In a way the war was responsible for this, with patriotism in the United States reaching a new high, the fostering and encouragement of all things American, even 'serious' music, a natural outgrowth of this development. The favourable atmosphere thus created was to continue throughout the 1940s and 1950s, slackening in the 1960s as the tonal music of the composers prominent during that period began gradually to fall from favour, to be supplanted by more cerebral, less immediately attractive music. The pendulum has begun to swing back, however, for recent years have seen a reawakening of interest in the American symphonic music of the 1940s and 1950s.

Of Schuman's remaining symphonies, special mention should at least be made of Nos. 5 and 6. The former is the Symphony for strings (1943), second in popularity to No. 3, and yet another Koussevitzky-premièred work (and commissioned by the Koussevitzky Foundation – where would American music be without him?). It is in three movements: an energetic and athletic opener, a *Larghissimo* slow movement of extreme beauty that rises to an impassioned climax, and a *Presto* finale both vigorous and playful, opening with one of Schuman's characteristically nervous rhythmic patterns.

In this case the rhythm, in *alla breve* time, seems to evolve quickly into 3/8 metre, yet the *alla breve* remains constant. Like the Third Symphony, the piece is extremely buoyant and positive in feeling.

What a change awaits us in No. 6! Here is a side of Schuman hitherto unencountered. Cast in a single movement of approximately twenty-eight minutes' duration, this is a starkly serious score that makes no concessions to either performers or listeners. Its moods are sombre, tragic, even violent at times. It is Schuman's most difficult orchestral work, performances of which have been relatively infrequent since its 1949 première by Antal Dorati and the Dallas Symphony Orchestra. It has been recorded by Eugene Ormandy and the Philadelphia Orchestra and programmed in recent years by Leonard Slatkin and Edo de Waart. When performed with the proper technical flair and emotional intensity, Schuman's Sixth is a truly stunning work.

Schuman returned to the medium twelve years later, though in the Seventh (1960) he does not kindle the same fires. The Eighth (1962) was commissioned by the New York Philharmonic for the inaugural season of the Lincoln Center, and is a work of much greater power and eloquence, whereas the Ninth (1968) (*Le Fosse Ardeatine*), the first to make use of an extrinsic or nonmusical programme element, is a response to a wartime atrocity, the massacre by the Nazis of some 300 Italians in the Ardeatine Caves. There is as always in Schuman's music enormous ingenuity, a complexity yet at the same time directness and a strong sense of formal coherence.

If Roy Harris can be termed the 'American Musorgsky', then surely a case can be made for thinking of **Walter Piston** (1894–1976) as the 'American Roussel'. Like Harris, Piston was one of many American composers who made the trip to Paris to study with the by now legendary Nadia Boulanger. Unlike Harris, Piston shows evidence of this tutelage in his music. We do not find there the stamping rhythms of Roussel, but we do find a particularly Gallic fastidiousness of workmanship, extremely lean and clean scoring in which every note tells, and an utter lack of pretension (Piston never seems to be striving to make a 'big statement'). His themes are usually graceful and fall pleasantly upon the ear; his harmonic language is mostly tonal, his rhythms snappy but uncomplicated. He was the author of highly respected books on harmony, counterpoint and orchestration. By the same token, in his less inspired moments a certain aridity creeps in and he seems to be going through the motions. The composer was once quoted as saying: 'Every time I begin a piece I try to put something new into it, but in the end it comes out the same old Piston!'

His long tenure as professor of composition at Harvard University put him in the enviable position of being a virtual 'court composer' to the Boston Symphony, which gave the premières of five of his eight symphonies, not only under Koussevitzky, but under his successors Charles Münch and Erich Leinsdorf as well. (Piston's most popular score, the ballet *The*

Incredible Flutist, was first given by Arthur Fiedler and the Boston Pops Orchestra – the Boston Symphony in disguise.)

The Piston symphonies are remarkably consistent in format and crafts-manship, and there is little outward evidence of a work's being early, middle or late, though the composer did flirt with the twelve-tone system at odd moments in some of his later works. The three-movement symphonies invariably follow a moderate-slow-fast sequence, those in four movements a moderate-fast-slow-fast ordering, while the orchestration is virtually identical from one work to the next, give or take a harp or two.

No. 4 will suffice for our purposes, as it is perhaps the most attractive of all. It was first given in 1951 by Dorati and the Minneapolis Symphony (now the Minnesota Orchestra), and is in four movements, the first marked *Piacevole* (pleasantly). It opens with one of Piston's most appealing melodies:

Ex. 5. Piston: Symphony No. 4

As in the themes of many of his colleagues, the interval of a fourth plays an important part. It is not a theme that the composer chooses to develop significantly, however; rather, it returns intact from time to time. Between these statements, busy contrapuntal passages animate the movement. The Scherzo, marked *Ballando* (dancing), presents a jaunty theme initially in the woodwinds, characterized by frequent metric irregularities – in fact, much of the movement is in 5/8 and 7/8 time. An exception is the lilting, waltz-like second theme (actually in 6/8), really quite tuneful, if bordering on the banal, somewhat in the manner of the second theme of the second movement of Saint-Saëns's Second Piano Concerto. Also rhythmically regular is the Scherzo's central section (the equivalent of the Trio in a classical Scherzo), where we have what amounts to an American square dance – not an actual square dance, of course, but the stylized effect of one as might be played on the stage of Carnegie Hall. The Scherzo's return brings added emphasis of the irregular metres, and the movement concludes with several vehement bars in 5/8. The contemplative slow movement is Piston at his most broodingly introspective, the 6/8 *energico* Finale 'rugged and rhythmic' (the composer's words) in its first theme. A *cantabile* second theme takes over and dominates the movement towards the close as it rises from the lower depths of the orchestra and sings its way to a lusty climax.

Emphatic reiterations of the opening motif pave the way for the exuberant final chords.

Piston's Sixth Symphony (1955), also in four movements, is very similar in manner to No. 4, save for a soft, wispy Scherzo featuring fleet perpetual motion-type muted violin passages and delicate percussion. One is reminded of the Scherzo of Lutosławski's Concerto for Orchestra (1954), which Piston could not have known at that time.

Highly respected yet rarely performed are the eight symphonies of **Roger Sessions** (1896–1985). A pupil of Horatio Parker and Ernest Bloch, Sessions himself achieved renown as a teacher, most notably at the University of California at Berkeley, at Princeton University and, in his later years, at the Juilliard School. During the 1920s he and Aaron Copland were active in promoting New York's Copland–Sessions Concerts, which featured international avant-garde music of the period. With many pupils who are prominent today, Sessions has had a profound influence on much of the American music that came after the bulk of the works discussed in this chapter.

Sessions's symphonies are tough nuts to crack for orchestras and audiences alike (and no doubt for conductors as well). The New York Philharmonic, for example, has performed only three of them since 1950, one of which (No. 8) it commissioned. The music of Sessions is extremely serious and intellectually rigorous, his orchestral compositions often densely scored. His later works embrace the dodecaphonic principles of Arnold Schoenberg, though if Sessions bears musical resemblance to any composer, it is to Alban Berg.

Sessions's quite tonal Second Symphony (1944–46) was first performed in 1947 by the San Francisco Symphony under Pierre Monteux (not the type of repertoire one associates with him), and recorded in 1950 by Dimitri Mitropoulos (with whom one does associate it) and the New York Philharmonic. It is one of the composer's more accessible works, though by no means easy going for the uninitiated. Whether intentional or not, the influence of *Wozzeck* is quite strong. A quite agitated and turbulent opening presents its basic material in the first twenty-one bars. After some development, a second section, *tranquillo e misterioso*, offers its own ideas, the two moods alternating in A-B-A-B-A form. Atypical of Sessions is the extremely brief, dancelike second movement, *Allegretto capriccioso*. Only sixty-five bars long, it shows the composer in a rare carefree and humorous mood, the entire piece based on the jaunty opening oboe and cor anglais theme (Ex. 6) – a tune that a listener can actually take home. The heart of the symphony is its brooding, darkly coloured *Adagio* third movement, on which the composer was working at the time of the death of President Franklin Delano Roosevelt. This tragic event affected him deeply, and greatly influenced the emotional content of the score. The *Allegramente* Finale threatens to become populist in tone with its romping opening 5/4 trumpet theme, but it never descends to that level. The extreme busyness of the writing ensures against this, and the theme, which recurs quite often in full or in part, is really something of a signpost between more complex material. Sessions's Second Symphony is definitely a masterpiece of its period, deserving of more frequent hearings.

Ex. 6. Sessions: Symphony No. 2

The composer began incorporating twelve-tone elements into his scores in the 1950s, an approach that became solidified in the Third and Fourth Symphonies (1957, 1958). The latter, with its movement headings of Burlesque, Elegy and Pastorale, transcends the implications of those titles by virtue of its expressive and structural complexity. At the time of writing all the Sessions symphonies except No. 6 have been recorded. No. 8 (the New York Philharmonic commission of 1967–68) is in two movements played without pause. Dodecaphonic in its notational and structural techniques, the work adheres to the principle of non-literal repetition of thematic material.

Like Hanson, Schuman and Sessions a distinguished educator, **Peter Mennin** (1923–83) served as president of the Juilliard School from 1962 until his death. As was the case with Harris and Schuman, it was a Third Symphony that established him on the compositional scene and his first two symphonies, like Schuman's, remain unpublished. Mennin was all of twenty-three when the Third received its 1947 première by the New York Philharmonic under Walter Hendl's direction. Hendl was the orchestra's assistant conductor at the time, and if Mennin can be said to have had a champion it would be Hendl, who went on to conduct further premières and other important performances of the composer's works. (Mennin was just a bit too young to fall within the Koussevitzky sphere.)

A pupil of Hanson at the Eastman School, Mennin does not exhibit his teacher's expansive Romantic tendencies. His early work owes to William Schuman its use of major-minor sonorities, and to Hindemith the dynamic motoric rhythms and momentum of its fast movements. In fact, Mennin's running bass lines actually owe a lot to Bach, as do Hindemith's. As for the slow movements, the winding modal melodies bring to mind none other than Vaughan Williams, the tone of whose Fourth Symphony also permeates Mennin's Allegros – and Walton. But for all fine composers, influences are one thing, what is done with them another. Mennin was able to fuse these disparate elements into his own highly personal style.

The Third Symphony is a remarkable work for one of such tender years. It evinces a terseness of expression that was to remain with the composer. Whatever else one may say about a Mennin symphony, it never outstays its welcome. The *Allegro robusto* first movement is based upon the declamatory five-note motto theme sounded immediately by the brass. It is then taken up in an intense and vehement manner by the entire string section and expanded into a ten-bar phrase. Three subjects ultimately animate the movement, with such time-honoured devices as ostinato and canon playing an important part. It is in the *Andante moderato* second movement that Mennin's debt to Vaughan Williams becomes apparent, while the *Allegro assai* Finale brings a return of the opening's dynamism, but with increased intensity. One of Mennin's characteristics, evident here, is the sounding of long, sustained melodic lines over very busy ostinato accompaniments.

The Fifth Symphony (1950) is very similar in style and form to the Third, the composer's use of counterpoint and polyphony based upon principles that go back to the Renaissance. With the Seventh (1963), called 'Variation Symphony', the influence of Béla Bartók makes itself felt. Again, however, Mennin puts it to his own use. No. 8 (1973) is unique in Mennin's output in that, as in Hanson's Fourth, each movement bears a biblical inscription: 'In principio', 'Dies irae', 'De profundis' and 'Laudate Dominum'. In this work can atypically be found dense clusters of chords, wildly swirling thematic fragments and powerful explosions of sound. His final Symphony, No. 9 (1981), originally called 'Sinfonia capricciosa', has a basic feeling of anger quite at odds with that title (which is undoubtedly why it was deleted). The final *Presto tumultuoso* is an apt conclusion to the work of perhaps the most viscerally exciting of all American symphonists.

Starting with Hanson, our discussion has focused upon those composers for whom the writing of symphonies has been central to their creativity. There are others that merit attention. **Paul Creston** (1906–85), though he was a New Yorker of Italian origin (his real name was Giuseppe Guttoveggio), was essentially Gallic in outlook. He was self-taught and originally planned a literary career. His musical language is much influenced by French music (in particular Ravel and Roussel) and his scoring is masterly. The Second (1944) of his six symphonies was much played at one time and its exotic dance movement may well be the single most infectiously attractive movement of any American symphony. Serial and post-serial techniques were foreign to his nature, as they are to **David Diamond** (b. 1915), another composer promoted by Koussevitzky. His music was much in vogue during the immediate post–World War II years. After quite a lengthy period out of the spotlight, he would appear to be making a comeback. His Second Symphony (1944) is a powerful statement deftly combining the tragedy and optimism of its time, while the Fourth (1945), more slender and concise, is an excellent example of his considerable refined sensibility and impeccable craftsmanship. Nor should **Vincent Persichetti** (1915–87) be overlooked. He was a composer of generally lively and engaging works who often displays a rather quirky sense of humour. The Fourth Symphony (1951) is a good example of this style, while the Symphony for Strings (No. 5, 1954) shows a more serious side and represents him at his very best.

Henry Cowell (1897–1965) wrote nineteen completed symphonies. His music seems largely forgotten today, but the best of it reveals a composer of gentle lyricism and puckish humour, at times drawing on his Celtic heritage.

At the last count **Alan Hovhaness** (b. 1911) had notched up fifty-two symphonies, though his reputation is based primarily on No. 2, 'Mysterious Mountain'. Most of his works employ principles of Eastern music, such as the use of other scales than the conventional major, minor and chromatic. His Armenian heritage also plays an important role in his music.

There remain those composers whose primary reputation lies in areas other than the symphony, but who produced important works in that genre. **Samuel Barber** (1910–81) is one such. His musical orientation was thoroughly Romantic, with broad, sweeping themes and sumptuous orchestration. What distinguishes his music from Hanson's, the factor most likely responsible for keeping it in the repertoire at a time when Hanson's had faded from it, is its cutting edge and rhythmic vitality. Put another way, Barber's music contains just enough dissonance to satisfy the modernists, but not so much as to drive away the traditionalists, while the rhythms are quite contemporary and, in the ballet *Medea*, even jazzy.

The first of Barber's two symphonies appeared in 1936, with the revised version known today made in 1943 and premièred by Bruno Walter with the New York Philharmonic. This is a score that, even more than the Harris Third, follows the model of the Sibelius Seventh. In one movement with four subdivisions, it is a more unified work than the Harris in that it is based almost entirely upon a single theme that occurs in various guises throughout the piece. After an arresting opening of timpani and syncopated brass entrances, that theme is first stated by strings and woodwinds in the symphony's second bar (Ex 7).

In rapid 6/8 quaver form it becomes the basis of the fugal Scherzo, where it is often accompanied by an ingeniously syncopated rhythm that itself ultimately dominates the section when it is pounded out by the full orchestra at the climax. The Scherzo ends in true Sibelian fashion with quiet solo taps on the timpani. An *Andante tranquillo* introduces a new theme, a soaring oboe melody over quiet undulating strings. As the strings passionately take up this melody, a dramatic high point is achieved, only to subside quickly as the final passacaglia section begins softly, its theme taken from the work's opening motif. Over this ground bass Barber constructs a series of flowing variations featuring a rising, yearning theme, first presented by oboes and bassoons, and building to one of the most powerfully dramatic conclusions of any American symphony.

Ex. 7. Barber: Symphony No. 1

A three-movement Second Symphony appeared in 1944, probably the only such work dedicated to a military organization (the United States Army Air Force). Barber revised it in 1947 and subsequently recorded it but some twenty years later, in a fit of depression at its total neglect, withdrew it, save for the slow movement, which he published separately as 'Night Flight', Op. 19a. Despite the rather contrived rhetoric at the opening of the Finale, it has much to recommend it. The first movement has a fine sense of forward movement and the beguiling second group is a lyric pastoral idea with an innocent freshness reminiscent of 'the folk songs that once floated across the Appalachian hills'.

Surely, at this stage, no preliminary words are necessary concerning **Aaron Copland** (1900–90). His symphonies number three, but there are in fact four such works (or perhaps four and a half). The composer chose not to include in his symphonic canon the perky and jazzy 'Dance Symphony'

(1930), based on music from an earlier ballet. In any case, the earlier 1924 Symphony for Organ and Orchestra, composed for Nadia Boulanger, is Copland's actual first symphony, though it received the official designation of No. 1 only in 1928, when he revised it as a purely orchestral work without organ. And so, while the music is the same, its effect is different.

1933 saw the completion of the 'Short Symphony', the official No. 2. This spiky Stravinskyan neo-Classical work, premièred in Mexico by Carlos Chávez in 1934, was not heard in the United States for ten years. Projected performances by Stokowski in Philadelphia and Koussevitzky in Boston were cancelled because of insufficient rehearsal time for the orchestras (and perhaps the conductors) to master the work's exceedingly complex irregular rhythms. In 1944 Stokowski succeeded, more or less, with the NBC Symphony, but a planned 1954 Mitropoulos New York Philharmonic performance was aborted for the same reason. It remained for Leonard Bernstein to succeed in 1957 in New York where Mitropoulos had failed, and the piece has held few if any problems for orchestras and conductors ever since. Meanwhile, perhaps in desperation, Copland had arranged the work as a sextet for clarinet, piano and strings, in order to ensure more frequent performances. It was the Third Symphony (1946) that brought Copland attention and acclaim as a symphonist.

The Third is the one symphony mentioned in this chapter that can truly be called an epic work, both in terms of length (about forty minutes) and musical content, often achieving moments of grandeur. Once again, it was Koussevitzky who provided the impetus for the work's creation, having commissioned it through his Foundation, and who directed the première. In the composer's own words:

> It's true that the Third Symphony is fully scored. And I certainly was reaching for the grand gesture. The writing was much influenced by Serge Koussevitzky and by the Koussevitzky aura. We were close friends, and I knew exactly the kind of music he enjoyed conducting and the sentiments he brought to it. I was also very familiar with his orchestra, the Boston Symphony – I've been closer to that orchestra than any other because of the many summers I spent at Tanglewood . . . After all, in composing you are aware, almost unconsciously, of who you are writing for, who is going to play a piece first, and who is going to be pleased or not pleased by it.*

The symphony is a skilful amalgam of the composer's folksy style, as epitomized in the popular ballets *Billy the Kid*, *Rodeo* and *Appalachian Spring*, and the more austere and dramatic idiom (what Copland called his 'laying-down-the-law' style) of his Variations and Symphonic Ode. Its opening movement, *Molto moderato*, in E major, dispenses with traditional sonata *Allegro* form by presenting three successive themes with very little development. The first

* From a conversation with Phillip Ramey, quoted on the sleeve of the composer's CBS recording of his Third Symphony (M-35113).

of these, played by the strings, begins the work simply and directly and is to play an important role in the symphony's conclusion (Ex. 8):

Ex. 8. Copland: Symphony No. 3

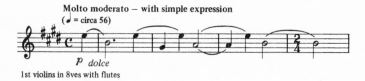

Molto moderato – with simple expression

1st violins in 8ves with flutes

As in so many of the themes discussed in this chapter, the intervals of the perfect fourth and fifth are prominent. The Scherzo, in A-B-A form, is based on a jaunty subject also in fourths and fifths. This movement, with its lyrical and often canonic Trio, is most reminiscent of the composer's western ballets. The *Andantino quasi allegretto* slow movement opens with the violins alone in the stratosphere, their theme a transformation of the first movement's third theme. This is an intensely personal, even austere utterance, its solitary mood mitigated by the entrance of the solo flute and a delicately scored dancelike central section.

As a transition between this movement and the Finale, Copland presents his familiar 1942 'Fanfare for the Common Man', played softly at first by the woodwinds, then in its full panoply of brass and percussion. The Finale proper ensues, first with an animated theme in semiquavers, then a broader and more lyrical theme, both of which are developed and recapitulated, with elements of the fanfare included. An unusual procedure is Copland's placement of his second subject within the development section rather than in what would be its customary place in a sonata *Allegro* movement.

The coda reintroduces the fanfare in full splendour, and also brings back the opening movement's first theme in majestic fashion in what must surely be the grandest (and loudest) conclusion of any American symphony. Of other twentieth-century symphonies, probably only the Shostakovich Fifth comes close. Copland wisely authorized, and himself adopted, a small cut in the final pages, lest the ending (and perhaps the listeners) be overcome by a too protracted high-decibel level. Although he was to compose for over twenty years more, Copland did not write another symphony.

Special mention should be made of the first two symphonies of **Leonard Bernstein** (1918–90). He was only twenty-four when he composed the 'Jeremiah' Symphony and twenty-five when he conducted its première with the Pittsburgh Symphony Orchestra in January 1944. Jennie Tourel was the mezzo-soprano soloist in the last movement. Like many of Bernstein's compositions, it reflects and celebrates his Jewish faith. The themes of the three movements, 'Prophecy', 'Profanation' and 'Lamentation', derive from Hebraic sources: the cantillation of the Bible and liturgical chant of the synagogue. Almost all the themes are outgrowths of immediately preceding material. In the words of Bernstein's annotator, Jack Gottlieb, 'the entire symphony is a giant sonata form wherein the movements are, successively, the exposition, development and recapitulation'.* The 'Profanation' Scherzo is an especially fascinating and exciting movement. Its irregular rhythms and occasionally violent outbursts obviously owe something to Stravinsky's *Le Sacre du Printemps*, but the debt is amortized by the force of Bernstein's own personality, even at that young age. In the emotionally intense Finale, the mezzo-soprano soloist sings in Hebrew from the Book of Lamentations, ending with the words: 'Lord, wilt thou forget us forever? How long wilt Thou forsake us? Turn us unto Thee, O Lord.' (The precedent for a Finale built around a single vocal soloist had been set by Gustav Mahler in his Fourth Symphony of 1892.)

Bernstein's Second Symphony (1949) bears the title 'The Age of Anxiety', after the poem by W. H. Auden. It is at once a symphony and a sort of piano concerto, for which there are numerous precedents – Vincent d'Indy's 1886 Symphony on a French Mountain Air or Szymanowski's Fourth (most likely not in Bernstein's thoughts when he wrote this piece). Koussevitzky led the première in 1949, with the composer as piano soloist. The work is in two parts, each with three sections. Bernstein has written:

> I regard Auden's poem as one of the most shattering examples of pure virtuosity in the history of English poetry. The essential line of the poem (and of the music) is the record of our difficult and problematical search for faith. In the end, two of the characters enunciate the recognition of this faith – even a passive submission to it – at the same time revealing an inability to relate to it personally in their daily lives, except through blind acceptance.

He also states that his idea of a symphony with piano solo emerged

> From the extremely personal identification of myself with the poem ... the pianist provides an almost autobiographical protagonist, set against an orchestral mirror in which he sees himself, analytically, in the modern ambience.†

While the score displays the influence of Copland, it again demonstrates Bernstein's ability to assimilate another composer's traits into something meaningfully his own. In particular, the riotously infectious use of jazz elements in the *Masque* section could not have been written by anyone else. The majestic Epilogue, in which the pianist is more an observer

* From New York Philharmonic programme notes.
† From the composer's own note appended to the score.

hearing, as is the First of **Easley Blackwood** (b. 1933). Nor should the finely crafted, slightly Hindemithian 'Triumph of St Joan', a choreographic symphony by **Norman Dello Joio** (b. 1913) composed for Martha Graham, be overlooked, nor such names as **Wallingford Riegger** (1885–1961), a rare example of a twelve-tone composer with a sense of humour; the Austrian-born **Ernst Toch** (1887–1964); and the West Coast symphonist **Andrew Imbrie** (b. 1921). The Second Symphony of **Randall Thompson** (1899–1984) was much played in the 1940s and 1950s, and such a lovable score does not deserve to slip from the repertoire, any more than does the quirky and amusing Symphony on a Hymn Tune by **Virgil Thomson** (1896–1989). **Robert Ward** (b. 1916) has composed six symphonies and **Ellen Taaffe Zwilich** (b. 1939) two: she was the first woman to win the Pulitzer Prize with her Symphony No. 1.

No American symphony of recent years has received as much attention and general critical acclaim as the First of **John Corigliano** (b. 1938). Premièred in 1990 by Daniel Barenboim and the Chicago Symphony Orchestra, the work is an anguished response to the AIDS epidemic, from which the composer has lost many friends. From the opening anvil stroke and intensely sustained A on violins and violas, through the frenzied antiphonal brass fanfares and throbbing timpani strokes, and the fitful and macabre tarantella (seemingly based on a phrase from Siegfried's horn call), to the serene conclusion, the score alternates extremely violent and elegiac moods in a very personal manner.

Striking use is made of Leopold Godowsky's piano transcription of Albéniz's Tango, heard hauntingly from offstage in the first movement and returning in the last. This piece was a favourite of one of the friends memorialized in the symphony, and the third movement contains remembrances of others. It is possible to be affected by Corigliano's symphony without any knowledge of its programmatic intent, for it is obviously a work dealing with great catastrophe. Awareness of that tragedy, however, makes one's appreciation and response all the keener.

If American composers appear to be writing fewer symphonies today than their counterparts in previous generations, this is not a situation restricted to the United States. Suffice it to say that the composers discussed in this chapter have combined to produce, in a relatively short time, a remarkably rich American symphonic tradition.

19

The Symphony in Britain

Robert Layton

Island cultures develop differently from those with mainland frontiers; artists insulated from the mainstream evolve distinctive accents and idioms, much in the same way that an isolated community develops its own dialect and patois. In past centuries a composer's knowledge of the literature of music did not extend beyond a circumscribed geographical area and a limited period of time (in the case of J. S. Bach not much more than a century), and these constraints were further compounded on the outer periphery, far from the great musical centres of mainland Europe. Isolation can throw both an individual artist and a community on their own inner resources, for, as Hofmannsthal once put it, 'the deeper a man's solitude, the more powerful his language'. The isolation wrought by his deafness certainly forced Beethoven in on himself, and when we listen to one of the late quartets or sonatas, we think of the spiritual truths that hold good for all mankind irrespective of time and place, not just the 1820s in post-Congress Vienna.

Although some great works concern themselves with truths that hold good for us all, and that step outside time, others enshrine the spirit of a period or a place and have the power to convey it with the simplest musical gesture. You have only to hear a bar of Vaughan Williams or Delius to know exactly where you are in the world; but the same could not be said about Parry. What is it about their musical language that so clearly conveys their national identity? For surely there is no doubt about the Englishness of Delius, whose music immediately transports us to the luxuriant summer gardens of England, or of Vaughan Williams, whose symphonies breathe the very air of rural England. Think, too, of Elgar, whose harmonic vocabulary and orchestral apparatus are in many ways close to those of Richard Strauss and yet at the same time so far. The overture 'In the South' sounds like neither Strauss nor the Italy of Alassio which it seeks to depict, but turn-of-the-century England. With the 'Cockaigne' overture, we can see Edwardian London alive before our very eyes in all its imperial confidence, just as in 'Falstaff' and the Cello Concerto, the first notes of a national self-doubt that was to grow apace in the post-war imperial sunset begin to resonate. And what is it about the the symphonic tradition on these isles that marks it off from those, say, of Scandinavia and France?

For years, nineteenth-century England was dismissed as *Das Land ohne Musik*, though it would, perhaps, have been more accurate to say 'the nation without composers', for at a time when such masters as Berlioz, Brahms, Dvořák and Wagner were flourishing in continental Europe, England could boast no major figure. True, Beethoven thought highly of Cipriano Potter and Mendelssohn acclaimed Sterndale Bennett, but their music did not make much more than an ephemeral impression. Yet, even in the fallow period between the death of Handel and the emergence of Elgar, there was an omnivorous appetite for music. Indeed, at a time of chauvinism and imperialist expansion, it was welcoming and outward-looking. If nineteenth-century England virtually adopted Mendelssohn as her forefathers had Handel (or should one, perhaps, say Handel *conquered* them?) in the preceding century, Berlioz and Dvořák had no less strong a following in later years. So there is no more doubt about the English appetite for music in the Victorian era than there is now.

In a lecture published at the end of World War II, 'The Unity of European Culture', T. S. Eliot spoke of English as having the richest vocabulary, 'a vocabulary so large that the command of it by any one poet seems meagre in comparison with its total wealth.' But he went on to argue that this in itself is not why it is the richest language for poetry, rather 'it is the variety of elements which comprise it: the German foundation, the Scandinavian element and the Norman French'. He did not argue that for this reason England must have produced the greatest poets but that 'no one nation, no one language, would have achieved what it has, if the same art had not been cultivated in neighbouring countries and in different languages'. This also applies to the other arts: and if I paraphrase him, it is to say that to renew itself and proceed to new creative activity and make new discoveries in the use of sonority, any musical tradition must, firstly be able to receive and be enriched by influences from abroad and, secondly, have an ability to go back and learn from its own sources. And so perhaps the long periods of assimilation served in the end to nourish an individual voice.

Even in the generation before Potter, **Samuel Wesley** (1766–1837) had shown in his four youthful symphonies composed in the 1780s that he had not only absorbed Johann Christian Bach but added his own individual accent, and in his B flat Symphony (1802) had a lucidity and freshness that testify to a far from negligible talent. The symphonies of **William Sterndale Bennett** (1816–75) have not stayed the course but the youthful Symphony of **Arthur Sullivan** (1842–1900) has. Sullivan was a fellow pupil of Grieg at the Leipzig Conservatoire and an exact contemporary. His Symphony in E minor (1864) was also his sole contribution to the genre. It has great fluency and shows real assurance in its handling of form. When placed alongside other contemporary works from the mid-1860s, such as the Svendsen D major Symphony, Op. 4, Dvořák's First ('The Bells of Zlonice'), and Tchaikovsky's First ('Winter Daydreams'), the Sullivan is more eclectic, less distinctive in profile and more modest in ambition. Yet it has an effortless Schubertian fluency and grace.

Certainly the symphonies of **Hubert Parry** (1848–1918) and the Irish-born **Charles Villiers Stanford** (1852–1924) come at the end of these assimilative years, and the recent renewal of interest in them shows how unjust has been their dismissal from the repertoire. Parry's symphonies rated little more than a passing mention in Ernest Walker's *A History of Music in England** – where the Second ('Cambridge', 1883, revised 1887) is singled out for praise – and hardly more than that in a relatively recent symposium,† where (as in *Grove*) they are said to number four. The Third in C major ('English') (1888–89) was at one time the most often played British symphony and, like its companion, the Fourth (1889, revised 1910), has an undoubted Classical lineage. It breathes essentially Brahmsian air, yet it is at the same time more skilfully crafted and finely paced than, say, any of the Fibich symphonies. Though the same might be said of the Fifth (1912), there is a depth and eloquence that serves to explain the allegiance he inspired in such figures as Elgar and Vaughan Williams. The seven symphonies of Stanford are elegantly crafted, and the product of a cultured and fertile musical mind, but although he had recourse to the use of Irish melodies, the folk elements are grafted on rather than integrated into a highly personal style. His symphonies offer intelligent and civilized discourse but do not project the powerfully concentrated argument or strong musical personality of a great composer.

Much the same could be said of his contemporary **Frederick Cowen** (1852–1935), whose music is fluent, unpretentious and charming. The Third Symphony ('Scandinavian', 1880) serves to confirm Hanslick's verdict that he was well schooled, with a lively sense of tone-painting, great skill in orchestration – and no individuality! Forging a national voice is more than the integration of folk elements into art music or, as in Smetana's tone poems, the use of patriotic legend as a programmatic source of inspiration. The folk

* Ernest Walker, *A History of Music in England*, ed. J. A. Westrup, Oxford, 1953, pp. 330–31.
† *Music in Britain – The Romantic Age 1800–1914*, ed. Nicholas Temperley, London, 1981, p. 373.

element is but one strand; texture is another, and speech patterns a third.*
One explanation for the slow awareness of its rich folk resource is that, far
from suffering domination, Britain was at the height of an ugly period of
imperial and industrial expansion, and busy imposing its hegemony on other
continents. The English composers of the period, from Potter to Stanford,
were figures of considerable culture and taste, but they did not inhabit a
wider world that could encompass vulgarity.

But with **Edward Elgar** (1857–1934) a major figure emerged. Of course
there are other composers of quality of this generation but none who so
completely sums up an age as he does. For with him began a renaissance
almost as rich as that of Elizabethan times. In a sense Elgar was also a
European master, and recognized as such before the First World War; and
a measure of his recognition can be seen in the fact that his First Symphony
received no fewer than a hundred performances in the first year of its life.
His achievements in the 'Enigma' Variations, *The Dream of Gerontius*, the
two symphonies and the Violin Concerto loom all the larger when one thinks
of the relatively barren creative soil from which they sprang. Not only do
they reveal a highly original, individual sensibility tinged with melancholy,
but they speak for an epoch. Of course, there is the less appealing 'public'
side, the 'Pomp and Circumstance' marches and the 'Coronation Ode', but
this is more than offset by the keen poetic feeling, the sheer mastery of the
symphonic canvas and the acute poignancy in such pieces as *Sospiri*, the
Cello Concerto and the Piano Quintet.

Inevitably, some observers have argued that Elgar's world is in some sense
closed to those unfamiliar with the background. In the 1930s, believe it or not,
the essential 'Englishness' of this music was thought to elude even Casals and
Toscanini. (No study of Toscanini's records of the 'Enigma' Variations could
possibly support that!) Yet there is always some element in any composer
that remains closed or lost: Rakhmaninov's music must enshrine much of
the world of imperial St Petersburg that outsiders cannot fully perceive,
and some part of Proust's world must elude a later generation reading it in
translation. However, providing that it transcends parochial limitations, the
art that is most strongly national is often the most universal – Musorgsky is

---

* Different languages, with their different speech patterns and rhythms, shape musical
thinking; they fashion the melodic contours and rhythmic inflections, the habits of musical
speech. Words obviously influence the metres and cadences of folksong and as long as
Latin, albeit with local variation in pronunciation, was the *lingua franca* of the Mass and
the Motet, easily recognizable individual national styles were slow to develop. Yet even
so, there is an undoubtedly English flavour to the music of the Renaissance; much
of this impression may be due to the English predilection for false or cross relations.
These result from following the modal logic of one line even if it involves a harmonic
clash with another line in the texture. This kind of harmonic effect permeates English
composers from Tallis through to Purcell, though, of course, it is also to be found
in many other important composers from Frescobaldi and Monteverdi among others.
But these poignant dissonances sound quite different from those cultivated south of
the Alps.

an obvious instance. With Elgar there is an additional complication in that his music breathes the atmosphere of its period to a greater extent than that of such contemporaries as Mahler, Strauss or Sibelius. Strauss may represent some of the bourgeois values of Wilhelmine Germany, but he did not record the whole period with such fidelity or such an all-pervasive sense of atmosphere as did Elgar for England. Here is the most intense evocation of Edwardian England, at the zenith of its imperial power. For the generation growing up in the wake of the 1939–45 war, impatience with the established order may have spilled over into an impatience with Elgar, who had captured its ethos so well and, on the face of it, seemed so totally in tune with its values. In any event, there is far more to Elgar than this; he possessed an awareness of the transience of experience, the vulnerability of the human condition, and conveys a nostalgic intensity unsurpassed even by Mahler and Delius.

Not only are the Elgar symphonies larger in scale, grander in ambition and more searching than anything that had gone before in England, but their greater breadth of vision is exemplified in their breadth of utterance: phrases are longer, the canvas larger and filled with a far greater density and variety of incident. Think of the quality and diversity of the ideas that pass before one's eyes in the Scherzo of the First Symphony (1908), and the mastery with which in the first movement he plunges from the security and simplicity of the opening A flat theme into the restless, anxious world of the *Allegro*, as strongly contrasted in character as it is in key (A flat major and D minor). At the restatement, the D minor theme strongly suggests A minor while the bass line has a predominantly G major flavouring, prompting Elgar to remark in a letter to Ernest Newman that he had 'a nice sub-acid feeling when they come together'. If energy is a vital component of genius, there is surely no doubt in this Scherzo of the powerful current that takes one inexorably forward.

Ex. 1. Elgar: Symphony No. 1

Nor can there be any doubt as to his command of the most subtle processes of thematic metamorphosis or his mastery of the art of transition. The diversity and richness of material that unfolds in the Scherzo, and the magical way in which the transformation of its opening idea is celebrated at the opening of the *Adagio* (and the many other examples of subtlety in which this symphony abounds) mark Elgar out as a master of the first order. The depth of the slow movement and particularly the sighing phrase which he originally inscribed with Hamlet's last utterance ('The rest is silence') was never in doubt and was instinctively recognized. Hans Richter spoke of it as a *real Adagio*, and worthy of Beethoven while Nikisch hailed the symphony as Brahms' Fifth, perhaps prompted by the Finale's allusion to the Third Symphony.

Elgar's Second Symphony appeared at the very height of his success during the coronation year of King George V, and bears an inscription from Shelley, 'Rarely, rarely comest thou, Spirit of Delight'. The lines come from his 'Invocation', an essentially melancholy work in which the Spirit of Delight appears but fleetingly. The symphony's opening bars bear witness to the sheer opulence and majesty of Elgar's world: their exuberance and sense of onward movement have all the outward confidence of the age. The music surges forward in a way that has prompted the obvious parallel with the opening of Schumann's 'Rhenish' Symphony in the same key, but here the onward momentum is sustained over a larger time-scale:

Ex. 2. Elgar: Symphony No. 2

In sheer grandeur and spaciousness the opening of the Second Symphony surpasses its predecessor. Nor does it lag behind in its abundant diversity and beauty of invention. Indeed it encompasses an extraordinarily wide range of feeling, and the profusion of ideas that burgeon forth from this long opening paragraph is, if anything, richer than in the First Symphony. The ideas are also as intimately related and grow with the same apparent effortlessness and organic coherence. Moreover they convey that rare quality that the flow of inspiration is so powerful that it cannot be arrested. Yet the inner doubts that never lurked very far below the surface are now more apparent. There is a sense of mystery that pervades the second group (and, even more, the development), and an inward-looking quality that foreshadows the introspection of the slow movement. It is this *Larghetto* that seems to sound dark and prophetic depths, as if at some psychic level Elgar sensed what was to come. It is elegiac but, in Elgar's words 'has nothing to do with any funeral march' though its C minor opening seems to suggest the *Eroica* slow movement in Edwardian attire. Despite the dedication to the late King, there is a deeper current of grief than official public mourning. An epoch is passing and with it the consciousness that the Spirit of Delight will come ever more rarely. Even the delicacy of the Scherzo, whose opening is a *tour de force* of instrumentation, is interrupted by disturbing hints of phantasmagoric visions. And the confidence of the Finale, with its opulent, strongly hewn ideas, does not ring wholly true. In the symphony there are hints of the seed of change which overcame his music in the Cello Concerto and the Piano Quintet. However commanding a figure Elgar may have seemed before the 1914–18 war, and still is to English audiences, it is a regrettable fact that his symphonies are still relative rarities in the concert halls of Europe and the United States.

There is a general (and on the whole accurate) conception that, musically, England has always lagged behind the rest of Europe, and that when Europe sneezed it took quite some time before England caught cold. Why, one might ask, was nationalism of the kind we encounter in Slavonic and Scandinavian music so slow to surface in England? Why, when Balakirev, Borodin, Musorgsky, Grieg, Dvořák, Svendsen and Smetana were exploring their own national roots, were English composers content to follow the furrows ploughed by Mendelssohn and Brahms? Stanford and Parry may have been vice-presidents of the Folk Music Society, but it was not until the next generation that folksong became a decisive force. For **Ralph Vaughan Williams** (1872–1958) it was not merely the English heritage of folk melody and rhythm that helped fashion his musical speech (as it had that of his contemporary, Kodály, in Hungary), but the heritage of art music, and in particular the church music of the Tudors. Their modality is central to his tonal language. His celebrated 'Fantasia on a theme by Thomas Tallis' (1910, rev. 1923) and less well-known *Flos Campi* (1925) betoken a mysticism that has its roots in the Tudor legacy and also runs through the work of his great contemporary, **Gustav Holst** (1874–1934). Indeed Holst's sole contribution to the genre, the strangely neglected 'Choral Symphony' (1924) may be more song than symphony – which does not prevent it from being a work of striking quality. It is a setting of four Keats poems including, as its slow movement, the 'Ode on a Grecian Urn'. (It would be difficult to imagine a work more completely imbued with nature mysticism than Holst's *Egdon Heath*; nothing more completely conveys the dampness, mist and, one is tempted to add, the bleakness and discomfort of life in rural England in the early part of the century.)

Even at his most meditative and pastoral Vaughan Williams possessed a natural sense of symphonic movement. His symphonies bestride the best part of half a century from *A Sea Symphony* (1910) to the Symphony No. 9 in E minor (1958) – indeed longer if one recalls that the first sketches of the former go back as far as 1903. But if, despite its undoubted individuality and grandeur, *A Sea Symphony* is indebted to the tradition of Elgar and Parry, with its successor *A London Symphony* (1913, rev. 1920) Vaughan Williams is completely his own man. Here is an entirely new voice in the world of the English symphony, at last totally different from Elgar and Parry in accent and utterance. It is difficult to believe that only two years separate it and the Elgar Second Symphony.

In a sense *A Pastoral Symphony* (1922) is quintessential Vaughan Williams. To say that it could have been written by no other composer at that time or in no other place is to say nothing and everything. It can be said of many great works, but in the *Pastoral* we have a symphony that is almost as different from the music of its time as is the Sixth Symphony of Sibelius. The first sketches were made in wartime France in 1916, when (as Michael Kennedy has reminded us) evening after evening at Ecoivres he went with his ambulance wagon up a steep hill at the top of which he was entranced by the view of a Corot-like landscape in the sunset. In one sense the lessons Vaughan Williams took from Ravel bear their finest fruit here, for the harmonic refinement is balanced by extreme simplicity and clarity, and the orchestral textures have a similar transparency; but above all, this music could not be more totally at variance with any fashion or more true to itself. Its first movement has a unique sense of movement: the forward current is almost imperceptible yet inexorable. Modality and pentatonicism, the lifeblood of this symphony, are normally inimical to the dramatic cut-and-thrust of the symphonic argument; but, as Tovey put it, 'the listener cannot miss the power behind all this massive quietness'.*

Ex. 3. Vaughan Williams: *A Pastoral Symphony*

The opening of the slow movement with its two pentatonic melodies underpinned by a dark F minor chord may appear to have an almost remote detachment or an air of calm resignation but it is in its way no

* Sir Donald Tovey, *Essays in Musical Analysis – Vol. II*, London, 1936, p. 129.

less anguished than the slow movement of the Fourth. The slow, reflective Finale, with its otherworldly ending fading into nothingness, was, of course, to recur in later symphonies (Nos. 6 and 7). It is often forgotten that by the time he composed the Third Symphony, Vaughan Williams was already fifty; by the time of the Fourth he was in his early sixties (while No. 6 was the work of a master in his mid-seventies). At the same age Sibelius had the Seventh Symphony and *Tapiola* behind him, Roussel had composed his Third, and Nielsen had finished his life's work, save for the two concertos and *Commotio*.

After the quietism of *A Pastoral Symphony*, the volcanic force of the Symphony No. 4 in F minor (1934) took its first audiences by surprise and the musical world by storm. It was soon recorded, whereas the *Pastoral* had to wait until 1952, thirty years after its première. No one familiar with such earlier works as *Flos Campi* or *Job* (1930) would have been wholly unprepared for its higher norm of dissonance, angularity of line and bold, strident scoring. However, its dense concentration, pace and the wide range of feeling encompassed within its four movements was something new. There is an eruptive vigour, an awareness of brutality and an ugliness (particularly in the closing pages of the first movement) that inspire awe. The work derives much of its power from the tension generated by the semitonal clash between D flat and C at the very opening and a four-note rising motive of fourths stated at the outset:

Ex. 4. Vaughan Williams: Symphony No. 4

One could perhaps argue that after the Fourth, the symphonies of Vaughan Williams explored no new terrain; that his highly individual musical profile was completely defined, and that the later symphonies explore various facets of a personality that was already fully formed. Yet the Fifth Symphony must be regarded as adding a dimension to his symphonic art that is altogether special. For many (including the present author) it remains his greatest and most perfect single achievement; if nothing else survived from his pen, the essence of his musical personality is distilled in its pages. Its pastoral feel has led some to seek a link with the Third Symphony, but there are even stronger links with the quiet episode in the Finale of the Fourth Symphony and passages in *A London Symphony* and *The Shepherds of the Delectable Mountains*. Its gestation was long; it occupied him over a five-year period (1938–43) and shares some of its thematic substance with *The Pilgrim's*

Progress. The opening, with its haunting harmonic ambiguity (the quiet D major horn figure is undermined by the flattened leading-note pedal C) resonates long in the memory. In its very simplicity lies its genius. After a mercurial Scherzo, worthy of *A Midsummer Night's Dream*, comes a *Romanza* which recalls the 'massive quietness' and tranquillity of No. 3. Along with the *Larghetto* of Elgar's Second, it must be counted the greatest slow movement in English music, and the noble Passacaglia in which it culminates must likewise surely be the greatest Finale. Michael Kennedy speaks of the Fourth, Fifth and Sixth as 'at once the summit and the kernel of Vaughan Williams's art' and goes on to say 'the greatest of the three – perhaps of all his works – is, in my opinion, this Symphony of the Celestial City'.

Appearing as the Fifth Symphony did at the height of the war, it seemed to sing of the works of peace, while the Sixth (1944–47), with its teeming activity and turbulence, looked back to the violence of the Fourth. The important rôle of the minor third in its musical processes and its clash with the major emerge at the very outset and are echoed in its closing bars. This and the rôle of the tritone or augmented fourth have been analysed in detail by Deryck Cooke in his book, *The Language of Music*. The tritone, or *diabolus in musica*, which explodes at the Scherzo and permeates the Finale prompted all sorts of speculation about nuclear destruction at the time of its first performance – of which the composer was duly dismissive. This Epilogue looks back to the inner desolation portrayed at the end of the Fourth Symphony and in the music of Holst.

Even Vaughan Williams's most fervent admirers must concede that the *Sinfonia Antartica* (1952), powerfully evocative though many of its episodes are, represents a lowering of the symphonic sights. Drawing on the music he composed for the film, *Scott of the Antarctic* (1948), it registers more as a sequence of atmospheres than a cogent symphonic argument, and much of the invention is thin. But neither of its successors, the Symphony No. 8 in D minor (1956) and the Symphony No. 9 in E minor (1958) is negligible: indeed the Ninth is an amazing achievement for a composer in his late eighties. Like Roussel, Vaughan Williams is underrated by his countrymen, but his artistic rôle was to cut the the newly-found English symphonic voice loose from the German tradition, just as his French contemporary turned his back on the Franckist symphony as represented by Chausson, d'Indy and Magnard. There is 'a big nature behind every note'.

Like Joseph Holbrooke, composer of 'the English Ring', **Havergal Brian** (1876–1972) enjoyed success in the years before the 1914–18 war only to succumb to cruel neglect in its wake.* Brian was basically self-taught (which at times shows) and ploughed a solitary furrow in English music. While, for example, the Third Symphony (1936) of **Rutland Boughton** (1878–1960), is unashamedly Elgarian in utterance, the mature Brian is difficult to place.

* Reginald Nettel charts his extraordinary career up to the Sixth Symphony and *Prometheus Bound* in his book, *Ordeal by Music*, Oxford, 1945, but the resurgence of interest in his music belongs to the 1960s and 70s.

He is not obviously English, yet he could not be anything else; his music exhibits some qualities of imagination, genius even; moments such as the middle section of the Symphony No. 10 (1953) or the opening pages of the *Sinfonia tragica*, which are both original and visionary, yet there is little sense of (what the Germans call) *Meisterschaft*. He was a musician of wide culture and possessed a deep enquiring mind, and however you may react to it, his music is unlike anything else! The *Gothic Symphony* (1919–27), which Eugene Goossens, among others, planned to perform in the 1930s, remained neglected for over thirty years.

In the late 1950s a broadcast performance of the Symphony No. 8 in B flat minor (1949) proved a turning-point in his fortunes, and largely thanks to the efforts of Robert Simpson at the BBC, and other admirers*, his music began to come in from the cold. This upsurge in interest served to rekindle his creative fires and in his later years, when he was in his eighties, he embarked on a series of one-movement symphonies (Nos. 13–17) that consumed his energies during the last year or so of the 1950s and were followed by no fewer than fifteen others, the last in 1968 when he was ninety-two.

Why, then, given such tenacity of spirit, was his music cold-shouldered for so long? Of course, his temperamental inclination towards the grandiose in the *Gothic Symphony* or the rich post-Mahlerian-Straussian vocabulary one encounters in parts of the massive Symphony No. 3 in C sharp minor (1931–32), must have seemed out of tune with the spirit of the inter-war years. And what his admirers would proclaim as independence of vision must have equally struck his contemporaries as eccentricity.

The idea engendered by the *Gothic* that all Brian's symphonies are huge, gargantuan edifices dies hard, yet few outstay their welcome. The postwar Symphony No. 6 (*Sinfonia tragica*; 1948) offers a foretaste of the one-movement structures with which he was to experiment in the late 1950s, and with it we enter an entirely new and mysterious world. Its achievement is all the more remarkable when one thinks that it was written when he was in his early seventies and had still to hear any of his symphonies performed. By this time Brian had developed into a composer of real vision and concentration. The slow lyrical idea in the Symphony No. 8 (1949), a long line on the strings accompanied by harps and celeste, is dreamlike, one of the most beautiful moments in any postwar symphony, like an idealized Elgarian vision stripped of romantic opulence. The harmonic subtlety of the Symphony No. 11 almost calls to mind Busoni, whose *Doktor Faust* Brian revered, yet the work as a whole is handicapped (as is so much Brian) by too little variety of pace and too great a reliance on a limited repertory of rhythmic patterns. Faced by so vast an output, most music-lovers do not know where to begin, but Nos. 8, 9 and 10 remain peaks in his creativity and to their number should be added No. 16 among the one-movement symphonies.

* Most notably and persuasively Malcolm MacDonald, whose study *The Symphonies of Havergal Brian* Volumes I–III, London, 1982, argues his cause with coherence and balanced judgment.

Composers such as **Arnold Bax** (1883–1953) and **E. J. Moeran** (1894–1950) are strongly Celtic but both bring the landscape of these islands before our eyes. Sibelius was a potent influence in their music: the final movement of Moeran's Symphony in G minor (1934–37), a work of astonishing freshness and inspiration, is heavily indebted to *Tapiola* (and the Finnish master casts a heavy shadow over Walton's Symphony in B flat minor). The Moeran Symphony is not structurally unsound but its seams are all too visible; the transitions from one theme to another are all too clearly signposted and there is none of the mastery of the underlying process of symphonic thought and none of the concentration and coherence of the Walton Symphony in B flat minor which had not long preceded it. Yet the sheer quality of its invention is such that it carries all before it. It remains, as any good work of art must, more than the sum of its parts. What a marvellous idea the opening theme is! It is lyrical – almost too lyrical, one thinks, for its generative function, yet it has that surging onward sweep that a great symphony must have as well as a generosity of feeling that warms the spirit.

Ex. 5. Moeran: Symphony in G minor

The seven symphonies of Arnold Bax encompass less than two decades and differ far less one from the other than do those of Vaughan Williams. Much has been made of their rhapsodic character, the subtlety and profusion of the colours, the sheer richness of the imagination in evoking the landscapes of Ireland and Scotland. Yet there is an epic quality, a sense of mystery about it, and, above all, a vision that is undoubtedly symphonic. One is launched upon a journey even if time is taken to admire the view. Bax's pre-war admiration for Russia is reflected in his Symphony No. 1 (1922).* Its trenchant seminal opening motif or that of the Symphony No. 5 stand in strong apparent contrast with the Third, whose sinuous opening theme yet provides something of the same motivic power. For many music lovers it served as an entry point into Bax's symphonic landscape for it was the first (and for many years the only one) of his symphonies to be recorded.

Ex. 6. Bax: Symphony No. 3

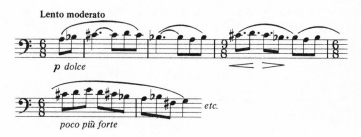

It engenders a fugal threnody of great harmonic resource and some emotional anguish, and is perhaps one of the most imaginative examples of its kind at a time when they were still in currency (as in the Walton B flat minor Symphony, the Fourth and Sixth symphonies of Vaughan Williams and the Third and Seventh of Edmund Rubbra). True, the underlying nature of the Third Symphony is more episodic than organic in conception but, one is tempted to say, what episodes! Yet it is probably in the Symphony No. 2 in E minor and C that his imagination is most prodigal; its profusion of ideas and luxuriance of texture render it the most rewarding of the seven. The Sixth Symphony was the last major work to find Bax in the fullness of his creative powers, its invention rich and full of resource. Formally the work is full of interest, its Finale (comprising an Introduction, Scherzo and Trio, and Epilogue) being particularly powerful. It seems to emerge naturally from the turbulence that preceded it. I am not always convinced by the rambunctious opening of the Finale but Bax's imaginative resources seems to me as richly stocked as in almost any other of his symphonies, save perhaps the Second. The Seventh, composed for the New York World Fair of 1939, shows a

* See Lewis Foreman, *Arnold Bax. A Composer and his Times*, Aldershot, 2nd edn, 1988.

flagging creative energy and its ideas lack the impetus and freshness of its immediate predecessors.

Whatever the structural weakness of the Bax Seventh Symphony, there can be no such qualifications about the Symphony No. 1 of **William Walton** (1902–83). In some ways – and not just in such obvious works as 'Crown Imperial' and the film scores to *Henry V* and *First of the Few* – he seems to inherit an Elgarian mantle. Yet he was outward-looking, responding strongly to the example of Prokofiev in the Viola Concerto and *Les Six* in *Façade*, while at the same time making every note sound very much his own. In the Symphony in B flat minor it is the example of Sibelius that looms largest. After the great success of the concerto and the oratorio *Belshazzar's Feast*, the hopes invested in the symphony ran so high that the public could not contain its impatience for its completion. Sir Hamilton Harty conducted its first three movements in 1934 and the complete work two years later. The allusion to the closing bars of Sibelius's Fifth Symphony, then still relatively new music, is an obvious gesture of tribute, but it is in its use of the pregnant melodic cell and command of the long-breathed line, and of the paragraph rather than the sentence, that Sibelius's influence best shows (Ex. 7):

Ex. 7. Walton: Symphony in B minor

Ex. 7. Walton: Symphony in B minor

The first movement teems with ideas that are all developed in their own time rather than fitted into a preconceived mould. Sibelius's celebrated remarks comparing the symphony with a river come to mind, for nowhere does the *flow* of the ideas dictate the course of the musical current more strongly. The explosive vehemence of the Scherzo suggests an energy that is more volcanic. The Second Symphony (1957–60) breaks no new ground but it is a far from negligible achievement. Its reliance on what are familiar elements in the composer's vocabulary, the anguished rising interval of a seventh, diminish its impact: the score, with its lush textures, is expertly laid out with Walton's customary expertise, but did not take the world by surprise as had its predecessor.

The preoccupation with nature that one finds in the generation of Vaughan Williams, Debussy, Sibelius and Delius soon gave way to other concerns. They were almost the last generation to respond keenly to nature even if it resurfaces from time to time in more recent works, such as the powerfully expressionistic First Symphony (1976) of **Peter Maxwell Davies** (b. 1934), which derives so much of its atmosphere from the wild landscape of the Orkneys. However, respect for tradition, which is so inherent in the English, remained. While Vaughan Williams had turned primarily to Tallis, Byrd and Gibbons, for **Benjamin Britten** (1913–76), Purcell was also a source of inspiration. It is a measure of the recognition accorded to his precocious talent that he was still only in his twenties when the Japanese government of the day commissioned his *Sinfonia da Requiem* (1940). But Britten's primary impulse was not symphonic; his sensibility was fired by verbal images more than by the awesome logic and severity of form of the Classical symphony.

If Britten's response to words and mood was acute, so, too, in a different way is that of **Michael Tippett** (b. 1905). His art is also fertilized by the past – Purcell, the Elizabethan madrigal (as for instance in his String Quartet No. 2) – and enriched by a lifelong admiration for Beethoven, to which the most recent of his piano sonatas bears witness. Works like *The Midsummer*

Marriage and the Piano Concerto have a visionary quality that has earned him an audience outside England, though there was a time when his music – and in particular the symphonies – made scant progress. In the 1970s *The Midsummer Marriage* became something of a vogue work and attention rather shifted away from his achievement in the symphonic field.

To tell the truth, the Third Symphony (1972) offered hostages to fortune and seemed at the time to surrender to ephemeral fashion. Its slow movement, like so much Tippett, has genuine poetry and spirituality, and makes a strong impression; the first movement, too, has music of commanding power and vitality. But the Finale, with its incongruous blues, is not wholly convincing and many find it difficult to be persuaded by the brief lurch into Beethoven's Ninth Symphony in the Scherzo. This bears to some extent at least the stamp of literary contrivance rather than the intuitive musical feeling Ian Kemp claims for it in his *Tippett, the Composer and His Music* (London, 1984).

The inspiration for the Second Symphony (1956), so the composer himself recalled, came from hearing a Vivaldi concerto while staying on the shores of Lake Lucerne. The pounding Cs with which it opened resonate in the first group of Tippett's symphony. Yet this is not 'music about music', nor is it music where the listener feels that the current on which he is borne proceeds on any lines other than those of that logic which the musical ideas themselves predicate. There is a lot of Stravinsky in it but the warmth of its lyricism is undeniable (Ex. 8).

Writing in the 1960s, Harold Truscott thought the First (1945) an even finer achievement* – and its relative neglect is puzzling. It was his most ambitious structure up to that point, and has an abundant contrapuntal and rhythmic vitality; its centre of gravity is a semi-palindromic *Adagio*, a series of variations on a chromatic ground bass. The Fourth Symphony marked a return to a purely orchestral medium, though, as David Matthews put it,† in its one-movement structure Tippett was more influenced by the Strauss symphonic poems and by Elgar's *Falstaff* than by other one-movement symphonies such as Sibelius's Seventh. Tippett described it as 'a birth-to-death piece' and extra-musical preoccupations rather than 'the profound logic' of the symphony seem to govern the course it takes.

By comparison, **Edmund Rubbra** (1901–86) has still to stake his claims. He belongs to the same generation as Walton and Tippett but has never enjoyed anywhere near the same measure of exposure. It has often been said that his music is not of our time but could not have been written in any other. Be that as it may, it is rooted in place: England, and more specifically her musical heritage, lies at its heart. All the same there is little

---

* In *The Symphony*, Vol. 2, London, pp. 187–8.
† David Matthews, *Michael Tippett – an Introductory Study*, London, 1979, p. 99.

Ex. 8. Tippett: Symphony No. 2

of the overtly pastoral in his music, though he revered Vaughan Williams and also possessed a keen sense of nature's power which you can feel in the opening pages of the Symphony No. 7 (1957). Yet his was a far from insular outlook: he set poetry ranging from the Chinese T'ang dynasty, Icelandic ballads, medieval Latin and French verse, and his interest in Eastern culture was lifelong. There is nothing in Rubbra for those who set store by exciting sounds rather than profound sense. Matter and not manner is of the essence.

Rubbra's early upbringing was far from upper-crust: like Alwyn he left school at fourteen, worked briefly as an errand boy and then a railway clerk. As a youngster he was much drawn to the music of Cyril Scott and Debussy. Eventually he came to take lessons with Scott, and later with Holst and R. O. Morris, who fostered his love of Tudor polyphony. He was in his mid-thirties by the time he wrote his Symphony No. 1 (1936), about which commentators have tended to be a bit apologetic. The trouble is that it demands enormous concentration of the listener and its orchestration is persistently thick and unrelieved.* Rubbra finished the Symphony No. 3 in 1939, the year in which the war clouds that had long been gathering finally burst. The Third has been called 'a reaction – a positive reaction' to much of the experience of the Second. The late Hugh Ottaway called it 'outwardly the most genial and relaxed' without any suggestion of the 'over-zealousness that mars No. 2'. The opening of the Fourth is one of the most beautiful things not just in Rubbra but in all the English music of our time. These pages are free from any kind of artifice, and their serenity and quietude resonate long in the memory (Ex. 9).

But this symphony, like the Third, is not so dense contrapuntally as the first two, and though practically every idea evolves in some way or another out of the opening figure, its first movement is a sonata design. Nothing could be further removed from those grim war years than this symphony.

In 1949 came the Fifth and most often played of the Rubbra symphonies, which enjoyed something of a vogue in the fifties. Boult premièred it, Barbirolli recorded it and Stokowski briefly included it in his repertoire. Rubbra possessed a deeply religious nature which shines through much of his music: the slow movement of the Sixth (1954), for example, has some essentially choral writing that is close to the two Masses he composed in the post-war years, and the Eighth (1968) is subtitled *Hommage à Teilhard*

---

* Harold Truscott has gone so far as to say it is not primarily an orchestral sound at all and you have to forget colour and concentrate on line development. They are difficult, though not in the way that some contemporary music is – for the musical language itself is quite straightforward. Wilfred Mellers, himself a composer, summed it up in the 1954 *Grove* by saying there is 'nothing abstruse about their tonality and harmony, which is basically diatonic', but they are difficult because 'the continuity of their melodic and polyphonic growth is logical and unremitting. The orchestration shows scarcely any concern for the possibilities of colour, nothing on which the senses can linger and the nerves relax. Second subjects are hardly ever contrasting ideas but rather evolutions from or transfigurations of the old.'

Ex. 9. Rubbra: Symphony No. 4

de Chardin. But the Ninth remains his most visionary utterance and its stature appears to have gone unrecognized so far. It tells the story of the Resurrection and with its soloists and chorus would closely resemble a Passion were it not for its symphonic cohesion. Like most of Rubbra's finest music, it unfolds with a seeming inevitability and naturalness and a powerful sense of purpose that justify its inclusion in the symphonic canon. It deserves a place in the repertoire alongside Elgar's *Dream of Gerontius* and Britten's *War Requiem*.

After the Seventh Symphony, Rubbra's music fell on hard times and enjoyed relatively little exposure, but he never lost this feeling for organic growth essential to the symphony: Nos. 10 (*Sinfonia da camera*, 1974) and 11 (1979) are highly concentrated one-movement affairs of much substance.

Perhaps to escape from a musical world dominated by Vaughan Williams, many composers sought the stimulus of study abroad, while the exodus of such talents as Matyás Seiber and Egon Wellesz from wartime Europe served as an enriching stimulus. **Lennox Berkeley** (1903–88) went to Nadia Boulanger in Paris, and although he is at his most effortlessly fluent in the beguiling *Divertimento in B flat* or the *Sinfonietta*, it is a pity that his coolly elegant, finely structured Symphony No. 1 (1940) has fallen from the repertoire. There is a pale luminous quality to the writing, as if the whole landscape is bathed in moonlight, but the sharp contours show his Classical sympathies and the musical ideas and their presentation betray the same distinctive lucidity that mark his work on a smaller scale. Neither the Second Symphony (1959) nor its two successors are quite as inspired or successful. **Arnold Cooke** (b. 1906) attracted attention immediately after the 1939–45 war with an excellently crafted Symphony in B flat (1949) that proclaimed a natural feeling for form and a fluent control of movement; three others followed and his Symphony No. 3 in D (1967) has been commercially recorded. However, he has never been able fully to cast off the mantle of Hindemith, with whom he studied in the late 1920s and early 1930s, and who formed his vocabulary.

Humphrey Searle (1915–82), on the other hand, studied with Webern, though his use of serial techniques was never doctrinaire. Like many composers at this period, such as Berkeley and Simpson, he spent some time on the BBC's music staff, and was a powerful force in the newly founded Third Programme. Speaking of the twelve-note series, he once remarked; 'One can use it or not use it, it depends on whether one gets anything out of it. I've written without it myself . . . but I feel happier with it.'* In his Symphony No. 1 (1952–53) he uses a series used by Webern in his String Quartet, Op. 28, based on the name BACH (B flat-A-C-B natural), the rest of the row being made up of other versions of that four-note cell (D sharp-E-C sharp-D), an inversion of it and a transposition (G flat-F-A

---

* For a longer exegesis, see Humphrey Searle and Robert Layton, *Twentieth Century Composers*, Vol. III Britain, Scandinavia and the Netherlands, London, 1972, p. 113.

flat-G), but this bald fact can give little idea of the powerful internal landscape it portrays. There is a particularly impressive sense of forward movement, an imaginative (at times almost Sibelian) use of *pianissimo* strings and a sense of menace that prompted one critic to hail it as 'a powerful, even terrifying symphony'. It is the only one of his five symphonies to make use of Classical forms, though the intermezzo between the slow movement and the Finale is a kind of free fugato. Later essays in the form derive their structure from the series itself.

The twelve-note technique, with its inevitable abandonment of the tension between key areas central to the Classical symphony, generally prompted composers to look away from the symphony as a form. **Egon Wellesz** (1885–1974), Schoenberg's first biographer and an authority on Byzantine and Eastern chant among other things, was in his sixties before he turned to the genre,* and his Symphony No. 1 (1945), No. 2 in E flat (1948) and their two immediate successors were clearly tonal in outlook. But after the Fifth he returned to serial methods. Wellesz was always a strong believer in contrapuntal rather than harmonic tensions, and mistrusted expressive dissonance because it is so transient in effect.†

Given the diversity and range of styles that have emerged in the 1950s and 1960s, it is virtually impossible to impose the kind of order beloved by historians, and in any event we are inevitably too close to the period to do so. Art is a report on inner experience, on a quintessentially private world, and these pages can serve only as the sketchiest of briefings for the listener to some of the symphonies that have appeared in the post-war years. Inevitably some work within the received framework of Classical sonata procedures, such as Alwyn, Fricker and Rawsthorne, while others have turned away from the sustained argument of the symphony to different kinds of musical thought.

William Alwyn (1905–85) was a composer who accepted the inheritance very much as he found it. A man of unusually wide accomplishments, a fine painter and no mean writer, he came, like Rubbra, from Northampton and

---

* 'I thought I would never write in my life symphony – because Mahler had said the last word about the symphony, therefore the form had come to an end – at least for half a century. And it was only when I came to England that I started writing, and then the first symphonies were really taking up the tradition of the Viennese school and very much the line which was left by Bruckner and Mahler. And from the Fifth Symphony, a completely new scheme arrived. I came back to a very strict twelve-note composition, together with symphonic technique . . . Then came the Sixth, Seventh and Eighth, in which I tried more and more to get free from all patterns of exposition'. In a conversation with the present author broadcast on BBC Radio 3, 26 January 1971.
† 'When I went to Schoenberg he had the score, the piano score of course, of *Salome* on his desk and said to me, 'Well, look, there are chords on this first page which perhaps in twenty years one will be able to analyse.' Three years afterwards he himself had surpassed the novelty of these chords. Therefore I think novelties in harmonic writing are the most dangerous things because they fade so soon, and part-writing is something that remains.' Ibid.

from an unprivileged background and like him left school at fourteen. His
early studies left him feeling ill equipped in terms of technical expertise and
it was not until his mid-forties that he embarked on his Symphony No. 1
(1950). 'Originality,' he once wrote, 'does not come by rejection of one's
heritage but through its acceptance; individuality or style is founded on the
past. And I believe with Turgenev that "it is possible to be original without
being eccentric".' No. 1 is very much in the received tradition of Walton
and Bax but it reveals the pace and breadth of a genuine symphonist. New
ideas evolve naturally from the germinal material; they are introduced in
such a way as to sustain that sense of momentum so vital in symphonic
writing. There is a good deal of Bax in the Third Symphony (1956), which
again has the measure of real symphonic argument. The first movement in
particular exhibits a genuine organic coherence – and what a master of the
orchestra he is!

William Wordsworth (1908–88) was a direct descendant of the poet's
brother Christopher. His Second and Third symphonies have the breadth
of a real symphonist, conceived in long paragraphs and carefully controlled
in pace. He wrote eight in all, the last in 1986, two years before his death.
The Third once enjoyed the advocacy of Barbirolli, but in the last two
decades his music has migrated to the uttermost fringes of the repertoire.
The Second has a real feeling of space; it is distinctly Nordic in feeling and
there is an unhurried sense of growth. It is serious, thoughtful music, both
well crafted and well laid out for the orchestra. At times it almost suggests
Sibelius or Walter Piston in the way it moves, though not in its accents, and
is both powerful and imaginative. The long first movement is particularly
impressively sustained.

Robert Simpson (b. 1921) was at first destined for medicine (he is
descended from Sir James Simpson [1811–70] who pioneered anaesthetics)
but was soon drawn to music. A pupil of Herbert Howells, he found nour-
ishment in the Scandinavian symphonic tradition, though his is primarily a
temperamental affinity. He has written perceptively and authoritatively about
Nielsen, Bruckner and Beethoven. His First Symphony (1951),* a doctoral
thesis at the University of Durham, has remarkable coherence and power; his
discovery of Nielsen emerges in its slow middle section as it does in the first of
his string quartets (1951–52) but its assimilation was rapid. His predilection
for the palindrome surfaces in the slow movement of his Second Symphony,
composed for Anthony Bernard's London Chamber Orchestra and scored
for the same forces as Beethoven's Seventh Symphony. It is a work of both
ingenuity and inspiration. (Most contemporary composers have difficulty
enough moving forwards, let alone moving backwards as well!)† Simpson
has followed his symphonic course with the same unflinching tenacity as

---

* He composed and destroyed four symphonies before publishing No. 1.
† See *The Symphonies of Robert Simpson*, ed. Robert Matthew-Walker, London,
1991, p. 73.

he has the string quartet. His is a mind with a natural symphonic bent. He shares Tippett's veneration for Beethoven, but has the stronger grasp of musical continuity and a stronger command of the organic processes that fertilize them. The tension between key centres that lies at the heart of the symphonic experience is exemplified in the two-movement Third Symphony (1962), in which the musical substance is pulled between B flat and C. The Fourth (1970–72) is the one that reveals the influence of Beethoven more strongly than any other. As Simpson himself put it, the significance of his music surpasses that of any other composer before or since, and its slow movement must be numbered among his most serene and inspired compositions. With the Fifth Symphony (1972), we encounter the first of the big one-movement edifices (Nos. 6 and 7, both 1977), which culminate in his monumental Ninth (1985–87). Here and in the equally massive Tenth (1988), the same masterly handling of a large canvas ('a mighty study of musical motion, comparable with those we find in Beethoven and Sibelius . . . a study of the power of a simple musical germ to generate enormous paragraphs of music'*. The debts to Beethoven, Nielsen and Bruckner are by now acknowledged and discharged. Its closing pages, which seem to evoke outer space, call to mind his cosmological preoccupations, as do such other works as the Seventh Quartet (1977). He is a keen amateur astronomer and a Fellow of the Royal Astronomical Society.

Simpson's immediate contemporary **Peter Racine Fricker** (1920–90) came to prominence in the 1950s with a wind quintet (1947) and his First Symphony, Op. 11 (1948), which won the Koussevitzky Award. (His middle name derives from a great-grandmother who was a descendant of the great French dramatist.) His outlook was profoundly influenced by Hindemith and to a lesser extent Bartók, as in the closing paragraphs of the *Andante* of the Second Symphony, Op. 14 (1951). He was a pupil of Matyás Seiber so that his music has the merit of impeccable craftsmanship and proportions. If his work has the breadth of a real symphonist, the melodic substance of the first two symphonies has a certain anonymity that militates against their wider acceptance. Of the later symphonies, the Fifth (1976) impresses by its uncompromising integrity and sense of scale.

But Fricker is not the only composer who has not had his due: the ten symphonies of **Daniel Jones** (b. 1912) are far from negligible and the six of **Alun Hoddinott** (b. 1929) are unfailingly imaginative. Daniel Jones is a born symphonist who can think in terms of long paragraphs, and whose musical thought is borne along by strong currents. He has a genuine sense of scale, though again the ideas themselves are not always sufficiently distinctive to establish him as the powerful voice his gifts would otherwise proclaim. His musical language at times turns one's thoughts to Rawsthorne or Hindemith. His is a serious and thoughtful talent,

* Op. cit., Lionel Pyke, p. 50.

though the imagination that emerges in the Hoddinott symphonies is more richly stocked and the variety of textures and the quality of the invention are more likely to ensure them an enduring audience. His melodic invention is often distinguished, the ideas are admirably sustained and there is a refined harmonic and orchestral palette. Moreover, at their best, in No. 3, Op. 61 (1965), and No. 6, Op. 116 (1983), they impress by their total integrity and absence of any attempt to play to the gallery.

So, for that matter, do those of **Bernard Stevens** (1916–83), who gained a sudden and short-lived celebrity when his 'Symphony of Liberation' won a 1945 competition mounted by a popular newspaper, the *Daily Express*. (Imagine that happening now!) His Symphony No. 2, Op. 35 (1964), like so much of his music, is expertly wrought and has a powerful Sibelian breadth but a distinctive, immediately recognizable sound world is slow to surface.

There are many such composers working in the received tradition – and writing with distinction – who come to mind. The symphony has attracted composers writing in a popular diatonic idiom, like **Malcolm Arnold** (b. 1921) and **George Lloyd** (b. 1913), whose work enjoys a wide following, while others as diverse in gifts as **Richard Arnell** (b. 1917), **Geoffrey Bush** (b. 1921), **John McCabe** (b. 1939) and **Robert Still** (1910–71) have enriched the genre. Their work is generally in the received tradition in which Classical forms are not extended. Some have not maintained their hold on the repertory, like the finely wrought but somewhat Baxian Symphony (1947) of **John Gardiner** (b. 1917). Malcolm Arnold enjoys enormous melodic facility and, though some of his ideas may at first seem to sit uneasily in a symphonic context, there is no doubt of his orchestral expertise or his popular touch.

With the 1960s the symphony, with its tensions between key centres and its closely integrated motivic relationships, held fewer attractions for a younger generation excited by serial and post-serial techniques, but the genre continued to remain a challenge for composers in their fifties. The eight symphonies of **Benjamin Frankel** (1906–73) enjoyed some exposure in the 1960s but have since lost their hold on the repertory. In his early career he earned a living in light music, playing in the Savoy Orpheans before developing into one of the most successful composers for the cinema, where his fine musicianship and distinctive individuality make him immediately recognizable. He composed some impressive quartets and a much admired Violin Concerto, coming to the symphony relatively late in life. His First, Op. 33 (1960), shows great skill in marrying serial principles without loss of tonality. The twelve notes of his series unfold, leaving in their wake a series of tonal suggestions:

Ex. 10. Frankel: Symphony No. 1

On one occasion Frankel spoke of Sibelius as 'the true post-Beethoven symphonist in the same way that Mahler is the true symphonist post-Wagner',* and his own symphonies evince a Mahlerian sensibility tempered by Sibelian instinct. Although some of the later symphonies (No. 6, for example) are not untouched by moments of routine, the finest of the symphonies – the First, Third and Fourth – are distinguished by sustained musical argument and depth of feeling.

In Frankel's music one recognizes a distinctive musical landscape, just as one does in the symphonies of **Alan Rawsthorne** (1905–71), another figure whose work flourished in the 1950s and early 1960s only to fall out of the repertoire in later years. If anything, Rawsthorne inhabits a more strongly defined sound world. He has never enjoyed anything like the celebrity of his exact contemporary Tippett, perhaps understandably so, though nothing he has composed falls below a high standard of accomplishment nor is his best music wanting in vision. He is an outward-looking eclectic who responded keenly to the examples of Hindemith, Roussel and Busoni (he studied for a time with Egon Petri), yet from these disparate influences he forged a wholly distinctive and original idiom – and one that is curiously English. He first

* Benjamin Frankel: 'Sibelius and his Critics'. The Listener, 29 June 1961.

came to international prominence with his Symphonic Studies (1938), which caused a stir at the Warsaw ISCM, and have the stuff of which symphonies are made – a powerful sense of momentum and firmness of purpose. This is strongly in evidence in his First Symphony (1950), a beautifully proportioned and vitally imaginative work. So immediately recognizable is the Rawsthorne idiom, so clear are its fingerprints, that one feels at times he is almost the prisoner of his own world. However, after the 'Pastoral' Symphony (1959) with its soprano solo, his music appears to escape from his dependence on certain harmonic sleights of hand and melodic formulae which had so dominated his musical language. The four-movement Third Symphony (1964) has a greater density of incident and darker colourings than either of its predecessors, and its emotional centrepiece is the second movement, a Sarabande, as finely sustained and imaginative a piece as any of his compositions.

Another outward-looking composer whose star was at its height in the 1960s was the Catalan-born **Roberto Gerhard** (1896–1970), who made his home in Cambridge after the Spanish Civil War. He was a man of vital intelligence and wide culture who was drawn towards serial techniques and studied with Schoenberg between 1923 and 1928. His best-known work, the ballet *Don Quixote*, shows his mastery of what one might call the post-nationalist style of *El retablo de Maese Pedro* or the Falla Harpsichord Concerto, and his Violin Concerto (1943) shows his command of a lush post-Romantic palette. But, like Wellesz and Searle, he retained a fascination for the twelve-note technique. The highly sophisticated aural imagination evident in his music from the 1940s stands him in good stead in the symphonies. Writing of his First Symphony (1952–53), Gerhard argued against the concept of a symphony generated purely by motivic forces.

> The appearance and recurrence of themes provide landmarks that help the listener to find his formal bearings . . . but it is possible to imagine an infinite variety of landmarks of an entirely different type that will orientate the listener equally well. Melody is not necessarily embodied in lines or tunes alone but can well up from within the music and suffuse even the most complex sound structures.

Yet, whether it is the serialism of the First or the extraordinary sound world he evokes in the Fourth (1967), one is conscious of a current on which musical ideas are borne. The Fourth is a score of great brilliance, particularly imaginative in its handling of sonorities and its almost explosive energy. There is little sense of traditional symphonic form in its vehement, athematic course, yet there is the feeling of a highly disciplined mind imposing order on a sound world of distinctive originality.

The future of the symphony as we know it is far from certain. After all, the epochs of Greek tragedy and Elizabethan drama can be measured in decades rather than centuries, and after evolving and flourishing for almost three centuries, there is no reason to imagine that the symphony might not follow the motet, the madrigal or the fugue into history. Moreover technological advances have altered our music life beyond recognition. The very means which make our symphonic inheritance so widely accessible also threatens its survival. When Constant Lambert spoke in *Music Ho!* of 'the appalling popularity of music', he could not have conceived of its accelerating dissemination in the intervening years. Composers in the Baroque era were able to relate to their immediate heritage, extending back in time no more than a century or two, and no further than a circumscribed geographical limit. Even as late as the beginning of the present century, Medieval and Renaissance music was the preserve of a handful of scholars. Now with the LP and CD explosion of the last two or three decades, a creative mind is less certain of the tradition to which he can relate. Vaughan Williams could turn to Elgar, Parry and to folk music and the tradition of Tallis and Byrd; a modern composer is confronted with a repertoire extending back to the Middle Ages and outwards to the whole of the western world. In addition, he is more aware than any generation before him of the music of India and the Orient, which stands at the opposite pole to the kind of musical dynamic of Western symphonic music, and to some extent explains the fascination of certain kinds of minimalism.

Although this enriched repertory may be a source of delight for listeners and music lovers, to the creative mind it poses greater challenges than ever before. The sheer volume of musical impulses is intimidating and inhibiting. Moreover, folk music can no longer be the source of inspiration it was for the generation of Vaughan Williams, Bartók and Kodály, for the wells have been polluted by the all-pervasive phenomenon of pop, with its impoverished (or indeed absence of) vocabulary – to the justified alarm of ethnomusicologists. In addition, with the phenomenon of muzak, a generation has been fostered to regard music as a background, to be disregarded, only its absence noted. This is hardly an environment in which a form as sophisticated as the symphony can be expected to flourish. Of course, composers of quality and imagination will battle against all these odds, and the fact remains that talents as vital and as varied in their expressive vocabularies as **Anthony Milner** (b. 1925), **Hugh Wood** (b. 1930), **Alexander Goehr** (b. 1932), **Richard Rodney Bennett** (b. 1936), **David Matthews** (b. 1943) and **Oliver Knussen** (b. 1952) have all responded to the symphonic call. Sibelius's prophecy that, 'as I see it, classicism is the way of the future', looks almost as unlikely a prospect now as it did in the 1960s; it seems more likely 'to embrace the world'. But history has a habit of confounding prediction, and while there are composers of imagination and ambition, they will surely want to rise to the symphony's intellectual and spiritual challenge.

Recommended Further Reading

Abraham, Gerald, *A Hundred Years of Music*, London, 1974
——*Studies in Russian Music*, London, 1935, r. 1969
——*The Tradition of Western Music*, Oxford, 1974
——*The Concise Oxford History of Music*, Oxford, 1979
——(with Brown, David, Lloyd Jones, David) *The New Grove Russian Masters – I* (incl. Borodin, Balakirev, Tchaikovsky), London, 1986
Abraham, Gerald (ed.), *New Oxford History of Music, Vol VIII – The Age of Beethoven, 1790–1830*, Oxford, 1982
——*New Oxford History of Music, Vol IX – Romanticism 1830–90*, Oxford, 1990
Arnold, Denis and Fortune, Nigel, *The Beethoven Companion*, London, 1971
Austin, William, *Music in the Twentieth Century*, New York, 1966
Barford, Philip, *Mahler Symphonies and Songs*, London, 1970
——*Bruckner Symphonies*, London, 1978
Benser, Caroline, *Egon Wellesz – Chronicle of a Twentieth-Century Musician*, New York, 1985
Blume, Friedrich, *Classic and Romantic Music, A Comprehensive Survey*, New York, 1970
Brook, Barry, *La symphonie française dans la seconde moitié du XVIIIe siècle*, Paris, 1962
Brown, David, *Tchaikovsky, Vols. I – The Early Years 1840–74; II – The Crisis Years 1874–78; III – The Years of Wandering 1878–85; IV – The Final Years 1885–93*, London 1978–91
Browne, Maurice J.E., *Schubert Symphonies*, London, 1970
——*The Genesis of the Great C major Symphony*, (in *Essays on Schubert*), London, 1966
Cairns, David, *Berlioz – Vol. 1*, London, 1989
Carse, Adam, *The Orchestra from Beethoven to Berlioz*, Cambridge, 1948
——*Eighteenth Century Symphonies, A Short History*, London, 1951
Carraud, Gaston, *La vie, l'oeuvre et la mort d'Albéric Magnard*, Paris, 1921
Chissell, Joan, *Schumann*, London, 1948, r. 1988

Cooke, Deryck, *Gustav Mahler: An introduction to his Music*, London, 1980
——*The New Grove Late Romantic Masters (Bruckner)*, London, 1985
Cooper, Martin, *French Music from the death of Berlioz to the death of Fauré*, London, 1951
Cooper, Martin (ed.), *New Oxford History of Music Vol X – The Modern Age 1890–1960*, London, 1974
Clapham, John, *Dvořák – Musician & Craftsman*, London, 1966
Cudworth, Charles, *The English Symphonies of the Eighteenth Century*, Proceedings of the RMA (1951–52), vol. 78
Cuyler, Louise, *The Symphony*, New York, 1973
Dahlhaus, Carl, *Ludwig van Beethoven – Approaches to his Music*, Oxford, 1991
Deane, Basil, *Albert Roussel*, London, 1961
——*Cherubini*, London, 1965
Einstein, Albert, *Music in the Romantic Era*, New York, 1947
Fanning, David J., *The Breath of the Symphonist: Shostakovich's Tenth*, London, 1988
Foreman, Lewis, *Arnold Bax – A Composer and his Times*, London, 1988
Garden, Edward, *Balakirev – A critical study of his life and music*, London, 1967
Griffiths, Paul, *A Concise History of Modern Music*, London, 1978
Halbreich, Harry, *Bohuslav Martinů: Werkverzeichnis: Dokumentation: Biographie*, Zurich, 1968
Harman, Alec, Mellers, Wilfred and Milner, Anthony, *Man and his Music*, London, 1962
Hartog, Howard (ed.), *European Music in the Twentieth Century*, London, 1961
Helm, Eugene, *C.P.E. Bach (in The New Grove Bach Family)*, London, 1983
Hitchcock, H. Wiley, *Music in the United States: A Historical Introduction*, New Jersey, 1969, r. 1974
——*Ives*, London, 1977
Vagn Holmboe, *Experiencing Music, A Composer's Notes*, London 1992
Horton, John, *Scandinavian Music – A Short History*, London, 1963
——*Brahms' Orchestral Music*, London, 1968
Kay, Norman, *Shostakovich*, London, 1971
Kerman, Joseph and Tyson, Alan, *The New Grove Beethoven*, London, 1983
Kemp, Ian, *Hindemith*, London, 1962
——*Tippett, The Composer and his Music*, London, 1984
Kennedy, Michael, *The Works of Ralph Vaughan Williams*, London, 1964
——*Portrait of Elgar*, Oxford, 1968, r. 1982
——*Elgar's Orchestral Music*, London, 1970
——*Mahler*, London, 1977

——(with Stewart Craggs) *The Music of William Walton*, London, 1990

Keys, Ivor, *Johannes Brahms*, London, 1989

Krebs, Stanley Dale, *Soviet Composers and the Development of Soviet Music*, London, 1970

Landon, H. C. Robbins, *The Symphonies of Joseph Haydn*, London, 1955

——*Haydn Symphonies*, London, 1966

——*Haydn, Chronicle & Works, Vols. I – The Early Years 1732–65; II – Haydn at Eszterháza 1766–90; III – Haydn in England 1791–95; IV The Years of 'The Creation' 1796–1800; V The Late Years 1801–09*, London, 1976–80

——(with Wyn Jones, David) *Haydn: His Life and Works*, London, 1984

——*Mozart: The Golden Years, 1781–91*, London, 1989

Láng, Paul Henry, *The Symphony in the Nineteenth Century*, New York, 1969

Láng, Paul Henry (ed.), *100 Years of Music in America*, New York, 1961

Larsen, Jens Peter, *The Symphonies* (in *The Mozart Companion*, ed. H.C. Robbins Landon and Donald Mitchell), London, 1956

——(with Feder, Georg) *The New Grove Haydn*, London, 1986

Layton, Robert, *Franz Berwald*, London, 1959

——*Sibelius*, London, 1965, r. 1992

——*Dvořák Symphonies and Concertos*, London, 1978

Macdonald, Hugh, *Berlioz' Orchestral Music*, London, 1969

——*Berlioz*, London, 1982

MacDonald, Malcolm, *The Symphonies of Havergal Brian – Volumes I–III*, London, 1982

——*Brahms*, London, 1990

Matthew-Walker, Robert (ed.) *The Symphonies of Robert Simpson*, London, 1991

Matthews, David, *Michael Tippett – an introductory study*, London, 1979

Matthews, Denis, *Beethoven*, London, 1985

McAllister, Rita, *Prokofiev* (in *The New Grove Russian Masters 2*), London, 1986

McDonald, Ian, *The New Shostakovich*, London, 1990

Mellers, Wilfred, *Studies in Contemporary Music*, London, 1947

——*Romanticism and the Twentieth Century*, London, 1957

——*The Sonata Principle from c1750* (*Vol III* of *Man and his Music*), London, 1957

——*Music in a New Found Land*, London, 1964

Mitchell, Donald, *Gustav Mahler – The Early Years*, London, 1958, r. 1980; *The Wunderhorn Years*, London, 1975

Myers, Rollo (ed.), *Twentieth-Century Music*, London, 1960, r. 1968

Nabokov, Nicholas and Anna Kallin (ed.), *Twentieth Century Composers.* 5 vols, London, 1972

Newbould, Brian, *Schubert and the Symphony*, London, 1992

Newlin, Dika, *Bruckner, Mahler, Schoenberg*, New York, 1947, r. 1979

Norris, Geoffrey, *Rakhmaninov*, London, 1976.

Northrop Moore, Jerrold, *Elgar – A Creative Life*, Oxford, 1984

Ottaway, Hugh, *Vaughan Williams Symphonies*, London, 1972

——*Shostakovich Symphonies*, London, 1978

Palmer, Christopher, *Szymanowski*, London, 1983

Parmet, Simon Pergament, *The Symphonies of Sibelius*, London, 1959

Piggott, Patrick, *Rahhmaninov Orchestral Music*, London, 1974

Pike, Lionel, *Beethoven, Sibelius and 'the profound logic'*, London, 1978

Radcliffe, Philip, *Mendelssohn*, London, 1954

Rapaport, Paul, *Opus Est* (Essays on Vagn Holmboe, Allan Pettersson, Havergal Brian, Mathijs Vermeulen, Fartein Valen etc), London, 1978

Redlich, Hans, *Bruckner and Mahler*, London, 1955, r. 1979

Reed, John, *Schubert, The Final Years*, London, 1972

——*Schubert*, London, 1987

Robertson, Alec, *Dvořák*, London, 1964

Robinson, Harlow, *Prokofiev*, London, 1987

Rosen, Charles, *The Classical Style*, New York, 1971

——*Sonata Forms*, New York, 1980

Sadie, Stanley, *The New Grove Mozart*, London, 1983

——*Mozart Symphonies*, London, 1986

Saint-Foix, Georges de, *Les Symphonies de Mozart*, Paris, 1932, Eng. tr., London, 1947

Samson, Jim, *The Music of Szymanowski*, New York, 1981

Samson, Jim (ed.), *The Late Romantic Era*, London, 1990

Schwarz, Boris, *Music and Musical Life in Soviet Russia*, London, 1972

——*French Instrumental Music between the Revolutions*, New York, 1982

——*Shostakovich* (in *The New Grove Russian Masters 2*), London, 1986

Simpson, Robert, *Beethoven Symphonies*, London, 1970

——*The Essence of Bruckner*, London, 1967, r. 1992

——*Carl Nielsen – Symphonist*, 1952, r. 1979

Simpson, Robert (ed.), *The Symphony – I. Haydn to Dvořák; II Elgar to the Present Day*, London, 1967

Skelton, Geoffrey, *Paul Hindemith: The Man behind the Music*, London, 1976

Slonimsky, Nicholas, *Music since 1900*, London, 1971

Stuckenschmidt, H.H., *Twentieth-Century Music*, London, 1969

Tawaststjerna, Erik, *Sibelius Vol. 1 (1865–1905)*, (Eng. tr.) London, 1976; *Vol. 2 (1904–1914)*, London, 1986; *Vol. 3 (1914–57)* in preparation

Terry, Charles Sanford, *John Christian Bach*, London, 1967

Tovey, Donald Francis, *Essays in Musical Analysis Vols. I & II*, London, 1935

——*Beethoven*, Oxford, 1944

Warrack, John, *Tchaikovsky Symphonies and Concertos*, London, 1969

——*Carl Maria von Weber*, London, 1976

Watson, Derek, *Bruckner*, London, 1975

Wellesz, Egon and Sternfeld, Frederick (ed.), *The New Oxford History of Music, Vol VII – The Age of Enlightenment 1745–90*, London, 1973

Whittall, Arnold, *The Music of Britten and Tippett*, Cambridge, 1982

Wyn Jones, David (with Landon, H.C. Robbins), *Haydn: His Life and Works*, London, 1984

Zaslaw, Neal, *Mozart's Symphonies – Context, Performance Practice, Reception*, Oxford, 1989

Zaslaw, Neal (ed.), *The Classical Era*, London, 1989

CD Checklist

Robert Layton

So extensive are the present-day CD and cassette catalogues and so ephemeral their contents, that any discography is out-of-date before it appears. However, I append a list of recordings that should afford a useful basis for futher listening. I have included some historical recordings of special interest, such as Elgar, Rakhmaninov and Vaughan Williams conducting their own symphonies, as well as other pioneering recordings that bring us close to the composer's intentions. For the most part I have included classic performances from the LP era alongside modern digital recordings, and although the list is of course selective and omits many performances of artistic and technical excellence, it should, I think, prove a useful starting-point for further exploration. Inevitably not all these recordings will be locally available, and I have not hesitated to include a number of currently deleted issues in the confident expectation that they will soon resurface on other labels. In any event they can easily be traced in well-stocked public or subscription libraries. Nearly all the composers discussed in the text are to be found here, and I have included a handful that are not, in the hope and belief that readers will be stimulated to explore further for themselves.

Abel, Carl Friedrich (1723–87)

Symphonies, Op. 7, Nos. 1–6
Chandos CHAN 8648 Cantilena, Shepherd

Agrell, Johan (1701–65)

Sinfonias, Op. 1, Nos. 1–6
Polar LS349 Stockholm National Museum CO, Claude Genetay

Aho, Kalevi (born 1949)

Symphony No. 1
BIS CD 396 Lahti SO, Osmo Vänskä

Alfvén, Hugo (1872–1960)

Symphony No. 1 in F minor, Op. 7
BIS CD 395 Stockholm PO, Järvi

Symphony No. 2 in D, Op. 11
BIS CD 385 Stockholm PO, Järvi

Symphony No. 4 in C minor, Op. 39 (Från Havsbandet)
BIS-CD 505 Christina Högman, Claes-Håkan Ahnsjö, Stockholm PO, Järvi

Alwyn, William (1905–85)

Symphonies Nos. 1 (1950) & 4 (1959)
Lyrita SRCDS86 LPO, Alwyn

Symphony No. 4 (1959)
Chandos CHAN 8902 LSO, Hickox

Arensky, Anton (1861–1906)

Symphonies Nos. 1 in B minor, Op. 4; 2 in A, Op. 22
Olympia OCD 167 USSR Academic SO, Svetlanov

Arne, Thomas (1710–78)

Symphonies Nos. 1 in C; 2 in F; 3 in E flat; 4 in C minor
Chandos 8403 Cantilena, Shepherd

Arnold, Malcolm (born 1921)

Symphony No. 2, Op. 40; (i) Symphony No. 5, Op. 74
EMI CDM7 63368–2 Bournemouth SO, Groves; (i) CBSO, Malcolm Arnold

Atterberg, Kurt (1887–1974)

Symphony No. 3 in D, Op. 10 (Västkustbilder)
Musica Sveciae CAP1250 Stockholm PO, Ehrling

Bach, Carl Philipp Emanuel (1714–88)

Six Hamburg Sinfonias, Wq. 182, Nos. 1–6
O-L 417 124–2 AAM, Hogwood
DG 415 300–2 English Concert, Pinnock

Hamburg Sinfonias, Wq. 183, Nos. 1–4; Sinfonias: in E minor, Wq. 177; in C, Wq. 182, No. 3
Philips 426 081–2 ECO, Leppard

Virgin VC7 90806–2 Age of Enlightenment, Leonhardt

Bach, Johann Christian (1735–82)

Six Sinfonias, Op. 3 (ed. Erik Smith)
Philips 422 498–2 ASMF, Marriner

Baden, Conrad (born 1908)

Symphony No. 6 (Sinfonia espressiva)
Norwegian Composers NC4900 Oslo PO, Karsten Andersen

Balakirev, Mily (1837–1910)

Symphony No. 1 in C
EMI CDM7 63375–2 RPO, Beecham
Hyperion CDA 66493 Philharmonia O, Svetlanov

Symphony No. 2 in D minor
Hyperion CDA 66586 Philharmonia O, Svetlanov

Barber, Samuel (1910–81)

Symphony No. 1 in one movement, Op. 9
RCA RD60732 St Louis SO, Slatkin
Chandos CHAN 8958 Detroit SO, Järvi

Symphony No. 2
Strad SCD8012 New Zealand SO, Schenck

Bax, Arnold (1883–1953)

Symphony No. 2
Lyrita SRCS 54 LPO, Myer Fredman
Chandos CHAN 8493 LPO, Bryden Thomson

Symphony No. 3
EMI CDH7 63910–2, Hallé Orchestra, Barbirolli (r. 1942)
Chandos CHAN 8454 LPO, Bryden Thomson

Symphony No. 5 in C sharp minor
Lyrita SRCS 58 LPO, Leppard

Chandos CHAN 8669 LPO, Bryden
Thomson

Symphony No. 6
Chandos CHAN 8586 LPO, Bryden
Thomson

Beach, Amy (1867–1944)

Symphony No. 1, Op. 32
Chandos CHAN 8958 Detroit
SO, Järvi

Beethoven, Ludwig van (1770–1827)

Symphonies 1–9
RCA mono GD 60324 (5) NBC SO,
Toscanini (r. 1951)
EMI mono CDH7 63033–2 Vienna
Philharmonic & Stockholm PO,
Furtwängler
DG429 036–2 (5) Berlin
Philharmonic, Karajan (r. 1963)
Philips 416 274–2 (6) Leipzig
Gewandhaus O, Masur
DG 423 481–2 (6) Vienna
Philharmonic, Bernstein
Teldec 2292 46452–2 (5) COE,
Harnoncourt

Symphony No. 1 in C, Op. 21
RCA GD60002 Chicago SO, Reiner
Sony CD45891 Marlboro Festival
O, Casals
Philips 416 329 Eighteenth-Century
O, Franz Brüggen

Symphony No. 2 in D, Op. 36
EMI CDM7 69811–2 RPO, Beecham
(r. 1957)
Sony CD44775 Columbia SO, Bruno
Walter
Sony CD46247 Marlboro Festival
O, Casals

Symphony No. 3 in E flat, Op. 55
Eroica
EMI CDM7 63855–2 Philharmonia
O, Klemperer (r. 1955)
EMI CDZ7 62623–3 Berlin
Philharmonic, Kempe

Supraphon 28C374 Czech
Philharmonic, von Matacic
RCA CVV5023 Chicago SO, Reiner
CBS 61902 New York Philharmonic,
Bernstein
DG 419 597–2 Vienna Philharmonic,
Abbado

Symphony No. 4 in B flat, Op. 60
DG 427 777–2 Berlin Philharmonic,
Furtwängler (r. 1943)
Sony CD46246 Marlboro Festival
O, Casals
Olympia OCD225 Leningrad PO,
Mravinsky
Sony CD42011 Columbia SO,
Bruno Walter

Symphony No. 5 in C minor, Op. 67
DG 415 861–2 Vienna Philharmonic,
Carlos Kleiber
DG 410 028–2 Los Angeles
PO, Giulini
RCA GD89288 Chicago SO, Reiner
Sony CD42011 Columbia SO,
Bruno Walter
Decca 417 367–2 Concertgebouw O,
Erich Kleiber (r. 1953)

Symphony No. 6 in F, Op. 68 ('Pastoral')
CBS MK42012 Columbia SO, Bruno
Walter (r. 1959)
RCA GD 60002 Chicago SO, Reiner
Decca 417 367–2 Concertgebouw O,
Erich Kleiber
Sony CD45983 Marlboro Festival
O, Casals
DG413 721–2 (2) Vienna
Philharmonic, Böhm
EMI CDC7 49746–2 London
Classical Players, Norrington

Symphony No. 7 in A, Op. 92
Pearl GEMMCDS 9793 New York
Philharmonic, Toscanini (r. 1936)
DG mono 427 775–2 Berlin
Philharmonic, Furtwängler (r. 1943)
CDM7 69183–2 Philharmonia O,
Klemperer (r. 1955)
RCA VICS 1523 Chicago SO, Fritz
Reiner (r. 1958)

Sony CD45983 Marlboro Festival
O, Casals
DG 415 862–2 Vienna Philharmonic,
Carlos Kleiber
EMI CDC7 49816–2 London
Classical Players, Norrington

Symphony No. 8 in F, Op. 93
EMI CDMD63 326 Vienna
Philharmonic, Karajan (r. 1947)
EMI CDC7 49746–2 London
Classical Players, Norrington
Sony CD45893 Marlboro Festival
O, Casals

Symphony No. 9 in D minor, Op. 125
(Choral)
EMI mono ED27 0123–1 Berger,
Pitzinger, Ludwig, Watzke,
Philharmonia Ch., Berlin
Philharmonic, Furtwängler (r. 1937)
EMI mono CDH7 61076–2
Schwarzkopf, Höngen, Patzak,
Hotter, Vienna Singverein & Vienna
Philharmonic, Karajan (r. 1947)
EMI CDM7 63359–2 Nordmo-
Lövberg, Ludwig, Kmentt, Hotter,
Philharmonia Ch. & O, Klemperer
EMI CDC7 49221–2 Kenny, Walker,
Power, Salomaa, L. Schutz Ch.,
London Classical Players, Norrington
Decca 417 800–2 Norman, Runkel,
Schunk, Sotin, Chicago Ch. &
SO, Solti
DG 427 655–2 Varady, van Ness,
Lewis, Estes, Ernst Senff Ch., Berlin
Philharmonic, Giulini

Berlioz, Hector (1803–69)

Symphonie fantastique, Op. 14
Philips 422 253–2 LSO, Colin Davis
Philips 411 425–2 Concertgebouw O,
Colin Davis
EMI CDM 764032–2 French Radio
O, Beecham (r. 1957)
Decca 414 203 Montreal SO,
Dutoit
EMI CSZ762739–2 Orchestre
National de France, Martinon

Harold in Italy
RCA RD85755 Cooley, NBC SO,
Toscanini (r. 1953)
Philips 416 431–2 Imai, LSO,
Colin Davis
EMI CDC7 542372 Caussé, O du
Capitole de Toulouse, Plasson

Roméo et Juliette, Op. 17
RCA GD 60681 (2) Roggero,
Chabay, Sze; Boston SO & Ch.,
Münch
Philips 416 962–2 Kern, Tear,
Shirley-Quirk, LSO & Ch.,
Colin Davis
Denon CO 73210/11 Nadine Denize,
Vinson Cole, Robert Lloyd, Frankfurt
RSO Ch. & O, Eliahu Inbal

Symphonie funèbre et triomphale, Op. 15
Philips 416 283–2 LSO, Colin Davis
Calliope CAL9859 Gardiens de la
Paix O, Dondeyne

Bernstein, Leonard (1918–90)

Symphony No. 1 'Jeremiah'
DG 431 028–2 Ludwig, Israel PO,
Bernstein

Symphony No. 2 'Age of Anxiety'
DG 431 028–2 Foss, Israel PO,
Bernstein
Virgin VC7 91433–2 Bournemouth
SO, Litton

Berwald, Franz (1796–1868)

Symphonies 1–4
DG 415 502–2 (2) Gothenburg
SO, Järvi

*Sinfonie singulière; Symphony No. 4
in E flat*
Bluebell ABCD037 LSO, Ehrling

Bizet, Georges (1838–75)

Symphony in C
DG 423 624–2 Orpheus Chamber
Orchestra

CDC7 47794–2 Orchestre National de la RTF, Beecham
Decca 417 734–2 ASMF, Marriner

Borodin, Alexander (1833–87)

Symphonies Nos. 1 in E flat; 2 in B minor; 3 in A minor
DG 435 757–2 Gothenburg SO, Järvi

Boughton, Rutland (1878–1960)

Symphony No. 3 in B minor (1937)
Hyperion CDA66343 RPO, Handley

Boyce, William (1710–79)

Eight Symphonies, Op. 2 (1760)
DG 419 631–2 English Concert, Pinnock

Brahms, Johannes (1833–97)

Symphonies Nos. 1–4
EMI mono CHS7 64256–2 (2) LSO, or LPO, Weingartner
RCA GD60325 (4) NBC SO, Toscanini
DG 429 644–2 (3) Berlin Philharmonic, Karajan
Sony SB3K 48398 Cleveland O, Szell

Symphony No. 1 in C minor, Op. 68
DG mono 427 402–2 Berlin Philharmonic, Furtwängler
EMI CDZ7 62604–2 LPO Jochum
CBS MYK 44827 Columbia SO, Bruno Walter
DG 427 804–2 Los Angeles PO, Giulini

Symphony No. 2 in D, Op. 73
EMI CDM7 69227–2 Philharmonia O, Karajan
CBS MYK 44870 Columbia SO, Bruno Walter
DG 427 643–2 Berlin Philharmonic, Abbado
EMI CDM7 69650–2 Philharmonia O, Klemperer
EMI CDM7 63221–2 RPO, Beecham

Symphonies Nos. 2–3
DG 429 153–2 Berlin Philharmonic, Karajan

Symphony No. 3 in F major, Op. 90
EMI CDH7 63085–2 Philharmonia O, Cantelli
Sony CD42022 Columbia SO, Bruno Walter

Symphonies Nos. 3–4
EMI CDM7 69649–2 Philharmonia O, Klemperer

Symphony No. 4 in E minor, Op. 98
EMI mono CDH7 69783–2 BBC SO, Toscanini (r. 1937)
DG 400 037–2 Vienna Philharmonic, Carlos Kleiber
EMI CDM7 69228–2 Philharmonia O, Karajan
CBS MYK 44776 Columbia SO, Bruno Walter
DG 410 084–2 Vienna Philharmonic, Bernstein

Brian, Havergal (1876–1972)

Symphony No. 3 in C sharp minor
Hyperion CDA 66334 BBC SO, Friend

Symphonies Nos. 7 in C; 31
EMI CDC7 49558–2 Royal Liverpool PO, Mackerras

Symphonies Nos. 8 in B flat minor; 9 in A minor
EMI CDM7 69890–2 Royal Liverpool PO, Groves

Britten, Benjamin (1913–76)

Simple Symphony (for strings), Op. 4
DG 423 624–2 Orpheus Chamber Orchestra

Sinfonia da requiem, Op. 20
Decca 425 100–2 LSO, Britten

Bruch, Max (1838–1920)

Symphonies Nos. 1 in E flat, Op. 28; 2 in F minor, Op. 36; 3 in E, Op. 51
Philips 420 932–2 (2) Leipzig Gewandhaus O, Masur

Bruckner, Anton (1824–96)

Symphonies Nos. 1–9
DG 429 648–2 (9) Berlin
Philharmonic, Karajan
DG 429 079–2 (9) Berlin
Philharmonic or Bavarian Radio SO,
Jochum
RCA GD 60075 (10) Cologne Radio
SO, Wand

Symphony No. 0 in D minor
Decca 421 593–2 Berlin Radio
SO, Chailly

Symphony No. 1 in C minor
DG 435 068–2 Chicago SO, Daniel
Barenboim

Symphony No. 2 in C minor (ed. Haas)
Teldec 2292 43718–2 Frankfurt Radio
SO, Inbal

*Symphony No. 3 in D minor (1873
version)*
Teldec 2292 42961–2 Frankfurt Radio
SO, Inbal

*Symphony No. 3 in D minor (1877
version)*
Philips 422 411–2 Vienna
Philharmonic, Haitink

*Symphony No. 3 in D minor (1888–9 ed.
Nowak)*
DG 421 362–2 Berlin Philharmonic,
Karajan

*Symphony No. 4 in E flat major
('Romantic') (original 1874 version)*
Teldec 2292 42960–2 Frankfurt Radio
SO, Inbal

*Symphony No. 4 in E flat major
('Romantic')*
DG 427 200–2 Berlin Philharmonic,
Jochum
CBS MYK 44871 Columbia SO,
Bruno Walter
Denon C37 7126 Staatskapelle
Dresden, Blomstedt
EMI CDM7 69006–2 Berlin
Philharmonic, Karajan

Philips 420 881–2 Concertgebouw O,
Haitink

Symphony No. 5 in B flat major
Philips 422 342–2 (2) Vienna
Philharmonic, Haitink

Symphony No. 6 in A major
EMI CDM7 63351–2 New
Philharmonia, Klemperer
DG 419 194–2 Berlin Philharmonic,
Karajan

Symphony No. 7 in E major
DG 429 226–2 Vienna Philharmonic,
Karajan
Philips 420 805–2 Concertgebouw O,
Haitink
Denon C37 7286 Staatskapelle
Dresden, Blomstedt
EMI CDM7 69923–2 Berlin
Philharmonic, Karajan

Symphony No. 8 in C minor
DG 427 611–2 Vienna Philharmonic,
Karajan
Philips 412 465–2 (2) Concertgebouw
O, Haitink
DG 415 124–2 (2) Vienna
Philharmonic, Giulini

Symphony No. 9 in D minor
CBS MYK 44825 Columbia SO,
Bruno Walter
DG 427 345–2 Vienna Philharmonic,
Giulini
Philips 410 039–2 Concertgebouw O,
Haitink

Chadwick, George (1854–1931)

Symphony No. 2 in B flat (1885)
New World NW339–2 Albany
SO, Heygi

Chausson, Ernest (1855–99)

Symphony in B flat, Op. 20
Erato 2292 45554–2 Basel SO,
Armin Jordan

RCA GD 60683 Boston SO, Münch
(r. 1962)

Chavez, Carlos (1899–1978)

Symphony No. 4 (Romantic)
ASV CDDCA653 RPO, Bátiz

Cherubini, Luigi (1760–1842)

Symphony in D
Euro 350221 Tuscany Radio TV O,
Renzetti

Copland, Aaron (1900–90)

Short Symphony
Sony CD47232 LSO, Copland

Symphony No. 3
Sony CD46550 New Philharmonia,
Copland
DG 419 170 NYPO, Bernstein

Corigliano, John (born 1938)

Symphony No. 1 (1990)
Erato 2292 45601–2 Chicago SO,
Barenboim

Cowell, Henry (1897–1965)

Symphony No. 5
Bay Cities BCD 1017 Vienna
SO, Dixon

Cowen, Frederick (1852–1935)

Symphony No. 3 (Scandinavian)
Marco Polo 8223273 Kosiče State
Philharmonic, Leaper

Creston, Paul (1906–85)

Symphony No. 2, Op. 35
Koch 37036–2 Cracow PO, Amos

Symphony No. 3 ('3 Mysteries'), Op. 48
Delos DEL 3114 Seattle SO, Gerard
Schwarz

Diamond, David (born 1915)

Symphonies Nos 2; 4
Delos D/CD 3093 Seattle SO, Gerard
Schwarz

Symphony No. 3
Delos DE 3103 Seattle SO, Gerard
Schwarz

**Dittersdorf, Carl Ditters von
(1739–99)**

*Six Symphonies after Ovid's
'Metamorphoses'*
Chandos CHAN8564–5 Cantilena,
Shepherd
Supraphon 110579–2 Prague CO,
Gregor

Dukas, Paul (1865–1935)

Symphony in C
EMI CDM7 63160–2 Orchestre
National de France, Martinon

Dutilleux, Henri (born 1916)

Symphony No. 1 (1950)
Harmonia Mundi HMC90 5159 Lyon
Nat. O, Baudo

Symphony No. 2 (1959) (Le double)
Mont TCE8730 Orchestre National
de la RTF, Münch

Dvořák, Antonin (1841–1904)

Symphonies Nos. 1–9
Decca 430 046–2 (6) LSO, Kertesz
DG 423 120–2 (6) Berlin
Philharmonic, Kubelik
Philips 432 602 LSO, Rowicki

Symphony No. 3 in E flat, Op. 10
Virgin VC 790797–2 Royal Liverpool
Philharmonic, Pesek

Symphony No. 4 in D minor, Op. 13
Chandos CHAN 8608 SNO, Järvi

Symphony No. 5 in F major, Op. 76
EMI CDC7 49995–2 Oslo PO,
Jansons
Chandos CHAN 8552 SNO, Järvi

Symphony No. 6 in D major, Op. 60
Chandos CHAN 8530 SNO, Järvi

Symphony No. 7 in D minor, Op. 70
Philips 429 890–2 Concertgebouw O,
Colin Davis
Chandos CHAN 8501 SNO, Järvi

Symphony No. 8 in G, Op. 88
CBS MYK 44872 Columbia SO,
Bruno Walter
Philips 429 890–2 Concertgebouw O,
Colin Davis
EMI mono CDM7 63399–2 RPO,
Beecham
Decca 417 744–2 Vienna
Philharmonic, Karajan

Symphony No. 9 in E minor ('From the New World'), Op. 95
Philips 420 349–2 Concertgebouw O,
Colin Davis
CfP CD-CFP 9006 LPO, Macal
Decca 400 047–2 Vienna
Philharmonic, Kondrashin
DG 429 676–2 Berlin Philharmonic,
Karajan
EMI CDM7 69005–2 Berlin
Philharmonic, Karajan
Decca 417 678–2, Vienna
Philharmonic, Kertesz
DG 423 384–2 Berlin Philharmonic,
Fricsay
EMI CDC7 49860–2 Oslo PO,
Jansons
Decca 417 724–2 LSO, Kertesz
EMI CDZ7 62514–2 Philharmonia
O, Giulini

Elgar, Edward (1857–1934)

Symphonies Nos. 1–2
EMI CDS7 54560–2 LSO, Elgar
(r. 1930)
EMI CMS7 63099–2 (3) LPO or
LSO, Boult

Symphony No. 1 in A flat, Op. 55
CfP CD-CFP 9018 LPO, Handley
Decca 421 387–2 LPO, Solti

Symphony No. 2 in E flat, Op. 63
CfP CD-CFP 9023 LPO, Handley
Decca 421 386–2 LPO, Solti
RCA RD 60072 LPO, Slatkin

Englund, Einar (born 1916)

Symphonies Nos. 1–2
Ondine ODE 751–2 Estonian SO,
Peeter Lilje

Symphonies Nos. 2; (i) 4 (for strings and percussion)
Finlandia FACD 017 Helsinki PO,
Berglund; (i) Pekkanen

Fibich, Zdeněk (1850–1900)

Symphonies Nos. 2 in E flat, Op. 38; (i) 3 in E minor, Op. 53
Brno State Philharmonic, Jírí
Waldhans; (i) Jírí Bělohlávek

Franck, César (1822–90)

Symphony in D minor
RCA GD86805 Chicago SO, Monteux
EMI CDM 7633962 Orchestre
National de la RTF, Beecham
Decca 430 278–2 Montreal
SO, Dutoit
EMI CDM7 69008–2 Orchestre de
Paris, Karajan
DG 4199 605 Berlin Philharmonic,
Giulini

Gade, Niels (1817–90)

Symphonies Nos. 3 in A minor, Op. 15; 4 in B flat, Op. 20
BIS CD-338 Stockholm Sinfonietta,
Järvi

Symphonies Nos. 5 in D minor, Op. 25(i); 6 in G minor, Op. 32
BIS CD-356 Stockholm Sinfonietta,
Järvi (i) Roland Pöntinen

Glazunov, Alexander (1865–1936)

Symphonies Nos. 1–8
Olympia OCD5001 (6) USSR
Ministry of Culture SO,
Rozhdestvensky

*Symphonies Nos. 1 in E flat, Op. 5; 5 in
B flat, Op. 55*
Orfeo 93101A Bamberg SO, Järvi

*Symphony No. 2 in F sharp minor, Op.
16*
Orfeo 14810A Bamberg SO, Järvi

Glière, Reinhold (1875–1956)

Symphony No. 3 in B minor Il'ya
Muromets
Chandos CHAN9041 BBC PO,
Downes

Gounod, Charles (1818–93)

*Symphonies Nos. 1 in D major; 2
in E flat*
EMI CDM 763 949–2 Orchestre du
Capitole de Toulouse, Plasson

Grieg, Edvard (1843–1907)

Symphony in C minor (1864)
DG 427 321–2 Gothenburg SO, Järvi

Hanson, Howard (1896–1981)

Symphony No. 4 ('Requiem'), Op. 34
Delos DE 3105 Seattle SO, Gerard
Schwarz

*Symphonies No. 5 (Sinfonia sacra) Op.
43; 7 (A Sea Symphony)*
Delos DE 3130 Seattle SO, Gerard
Schwarz

Harris, Roy (1898–1979)

Symphony (1933); Symphony No. 3
Pearl mono GEMMCD9492 Boston
SO, Koussevitzky

Symphony No. 3
DG 419 780–2 NYPO, Bernstein

Hartmann, Karl Amadeus (1905–1963)

*Symphonies Nos. (i) 1 (1936); (ii) 2
(1946); (iii) 3 (1948–49); (ii) 4 (for
strings) (1947); 5 (1950); 6 (1953); (iv)
7 (1958); (ii) 8 (1962)*
Wergo 60187 (4) Bavarian Radio SO,
(i) Riegger; (ii) Kubelik; (iii) Leitner;
(iv) Macal

Haydn, Franz Joseph (1732–1809)

*Symphonies Nos. 1–104; A (1762) &
B (1765)*
Decca 430 100–2 (32) Philharmonia
Hungarica, Dorati

Symphonies Nos. 1–5
Hyperion CDA66524 Hanover Band,
Goodman

*Symphonies Nos. 6 in D (Le matin); 7
in C (Le midi); 8 in G (Le soir)*
DG 423 098–2 English Concert,
Pinnock
Philips 411 441–2 ASMF, Marriner

*Symphonies Nos. 22 in E flat
('Philosopher'); 63 in C (La Roxelane);
80 in D minor*
DG 427 337–2 Orpheus Chamber
Orchestra

*Symphonies Nos. 26 in D minor
(Lamentatione); 52 in C minor; 53 in D
major (L'Impériale)*
Virgin VC 790743–2 La Petite Bande,
Sigiswald Kuijken

*Symphonies Nos. 44 in E minor
(Trauer); 77 in B flat*
DG 415 365–2 Orpheus Chamber
Orchestra

*Symphonies Nos. 45 in F sharp minor
('Farewell'); 81 in G*
DG 423 376–2 Orpheus Chamber
Orchestra

Symphonies Nos. 48 in C ('Maria Theresia'); 49 in F minor (La Passione)
DG 419 607–2 Orpheus Chamber Orchestra

Symphonies Nos. 59 in A ('Fire'); 100 in G ('Military'); 101 in D ('Clock')
Philips 420 866–2 ASMF, Marriner

Symphonies Nos. 78 in C minor; 102 in B flat
DG 429 218–2 Orpheus Chamber Orchestra

Symphonies Nos. 82 in C ('The Bear'); 83 in G minor ('The Hen'); 84 in E flat
Virgin VC7 90793–2 Age of Enlightenment, Kuijken
Hyperion CDA66527 Hanover Band, Goodman

Symphonies Nos. 85 in B flat (La Reine); *86 in D; 87 in A*
Virgin VC7 90844–2 Age of Enlightenment, Kuijken

Symphonies Nos. 88 in G; 89 in F; 92 in G ('Oxford')
DG 429 523–2 Vienna Philharmonic, Böhm

Symphony No. 88 in G
DG 427 404–2 Berlin Philharmonic, Furtwängler

Symphonies Nos. 88 in G; 92 in G ('Oxford')
DG 413 777–2 Vienna Philharmonic, Bernstein

Symphonies Nos. 91 in E flat; 92 in G ('Oxford')
Philips 410 390–2 Concertgebouw O, Colin Davis

Symphonies Nos. 93–104 (London symphonies)
Philips 432 286–2 (4) Concertgebouw O, Colin Davis

Symphonies Nos. 93–98 (London symphonies – I)
CMS 7643892 RPO, Beecham

Symphonies No. 94 in G; 101 in D ('Clock')
DG423 883–2 LPO, Jochum

Symphonies Nos. 99–104 (London symphonies – II)
CMS 7640662 RPO, Beecham

Haydn, Michael (1737–1806)

Symphonies in B flat, P28 (1788); B flat, P52 (1766); D major, P29 (1788); E flat, P26 (1788); D major, P42 (c1778)
Olympia OCD404 Oradea PO, Acél

Hindemith, Paul (1895–1963)

Mathis der Maler Symphony
DG427 407–2 Berlin PO, Hindemith (r. 1955)
Decca 421 523–2 San Francisco SO, Blomstedt
Telarc CD 80195 Atlanta SO, Yoel Levi

Symphony in E flat
Chandos CHAN 9060 BBC PO, Tortelier

Honegger, Arthur (1892–1955)

Symphonies Nos. 2 for strings with trumpet obbligato; 3 (Symphonie liturgique)
DG 423 242–2 Berlin Philharmonic, Karajan

Symphony No. 2 for strings with trumpet obbligato; Symphony No. 4 (Deliciae Basiliensis)
Virgin VC7 91486–2 Lausanne CO, López-Cobos

Symphonies Nos. 4 (Deliciae Basiliensis); 5 (Di tre re)
EMI CDM 7 64275–2 O du Capitole de Toulouse, Plasson

Symphonies Nos. 3 (Symphonie liturgique); 5 (Di tre re)
Supraphon 11 0667–2 Czech Philharmonic, Serge Baudo

d'Indy, Vincent (1851–1931)

Symphonie sur un chant montagnard
Decca 430 278–2 Jean-Yves
Thibaudet, Montreal SO, Dutoit
EMI CDM7 63952 Ciccolini,
Orchestre de Paris, Baudo
Sony CD46730 Casadesus,
Philadelphia O, Ormandy

Symphony No. 2 in B flat, Op. 57
EMI CDM7 63952 O du Capitole de
Toulouse, Plasson

Ives, Charles (1874–1954)

Symphony No. 1 in D minor.
Chandos CHAN 9053 Detroit
SO, Järvi

Symphonies Nos 2; 3 ('Camp Meeting')
Sony CD 46440 Concertgebouw O,
Tilson Thomas

Symphony No. 4
Sony CD 46939 Chicago SO, Tilson
Thomas

Kalinnikov, Vasily (1866–1901)

Symphony No. 1 in G minor
Chandos CHAN 8611 SNO, Järvi

Symphony No. 2 in A
Chandos CHAN 8505 SNO, Järvi

Kancheli, Giya (born 1935)

*Symphonies Nos. 4 ('In commemoration of
Michelangelo'); 5*
Olympia OCD 403 Georgia State O,
Kakhidze

Khachaturian, Aram (1903–78)

Symphony No. 2
Decca 425 619–2 Vienna
Philharmonic, Khachaturian
Chandos CHAN 8945 Royal Scottish
O, Järvi

Kokkonen, Joonas (born 1921)

Symphony No. 2
BIS CD 498 Lahti SO, Vänskä

Symphony No. 3
BIS CD 508 Lahti SO, Söderblom

Lajtha, László (1892–1963)

Symphonies Nos. 4 (Le Printemps), *Op.
52; 9, Op. 67*
Hungaroton HCD 31452 Hungarian
State O, Ferencsic

Lalo, Édouard (1823–92)

Symphony in G minor
EMI CDM 7633962 Orchestre
National de la RTF, Beecham

Landowski, Marcel (born 1915)

Symphonies Nos. 1 (Jean de la peur); *3*
(Des espaces); *4*
Erato 2292 45018–2 Orchestre
National de France, Prêtre

Larsson, Lars-Erik (1908–86)

Symphony No. 3 in C minor, Op. 34
BIS CD-96 Hälsingborg SO, Frykberg

Le Flem, Paul (1881–1984)

Symphony No. 4
Cybelia CY 866 Rhenish PO, James
Lockhart

Liszt, Franz (1811–86)

A Faust Symphony
EMI CDM7 63371–2 Alexander
Young, Beecham Ch. Soc., RPO,
Beecham
DG431 470–2 Kenneth Riegel,
Tanglewood Fest. Ch., Boston SO,
Bernstein

Lutosławski, Witold (born 1916)

Symphony No. 3
Philips 416 387–2 Berlin
Philharmonic, Lutosławski
CBS M2K 42271 Los Angeles PO,
Salonen

Madetoja, Leevi (1887–1947)

Symphony No. 3 in A, Op. 55
Chandos CHAN 9036 Iceland SO,
Petri Sakari

Magnard, Albéric (1865–1914)

*Symphonies Nos. 1 in C minor, Op. 4; 3
in B flat minor, Op. 11*
EMI CDC7 54015–2 O du Capitole
de Toulouse, Plasson

*Symphony No. 4 in C sharp minor, Op.
21*
EMI CDC7 47373–2 O du Capitole
de Toulouse, Plasson

Mahler, Gustav (1860–1911)

Symphonies 1–9 & 10 (Adagio)
DG 429 042–2 (10) Bavarian Radio
SO, Kubelik
DG 435 162 (13) Concertgebouw
O, NYPO, Vienna Philharmonic,
Bernstein

Symphony No. 1 in D (Titan)
DG 431 036–2 Concertgebouw O,
Bernstein
Decca 417 701–2 LSO, Solti
Philips 420 936–2 Berlin
Philharmonic, Haitink

Symphonies Nos. (i) 1; (ii) 2 in C minor
('Resurrection')
CBS M2YK 45674 (i) Columbia SO;
(ii) Cundari, Forrester, Westminster
College Ch., NYPO, Bruno Walter

Symphony No. 2 in C minor
('Resurrection')
EMI CDS7 47962–8 (2) Auger, J.
Baker, CBSO Ch., CBSO, Rattle

DG 427 262–2 (2) Neblett, Horne,
Chicago Symphony Ch. and O,
Abbado

Symphony No. 3 in D minor
DG 410 715–2 (2) J. Norman, Vienna
State Op. Ch., Vienna Boys' Ch.,
Vienna Philharmonic, Abbado
Philips 420 113–2 (2) Forrester,
Netherlands R. Ch., St Willibrod
Boys' Ch., Concertgebouw O, Haitink
Sony M2K 44553 (2) J. Baker, LSO
Ch., LSO, Tilson Thomas

Symphony No. 4 in G
Sony MK 47684 NYPO, Bruno
Walter
Sony MK 39072 Kathleen Battle,
Vienna Philharmonic, Maazel
Sony MYK 44713 Judith Raskin,
Cleveland O, Szell
DG 415 323–2 Edith Mathis, Berlin
Philharmonic, Karajan
EMI CDM7 69667–2 Schwarzkopf,
Philharmonic O, Klemperer

Symphony No. 5 in C sharp minor
Sony MK47683 NYPO, Bruno Walter
DG 415 096–2 (2) Berlin
Philharmonic, Karajan
EMI CDM7 69186–2 New
Philharmonia, Barbirolli
EMI CDC7 49888–2 LPO, Tennstedt
DG 431 037–2 Vienna Philharmonic,
Bernstein
Philips 416 469–2 Concertgebouw O,
Haitink
DG 427 254–2 Chicago SO,
Abbado

Symphony No. 6 in A minor
DG 415 099–2 (2) Berlin
Philharmonic, Karajan

Symphony No. 6 in A minor; (i)
Kindertotenlieder
DG 427 697–2 (2) (i) Thomas
Hampson; Vienna Philharmonic,
Bernstein
Philips 420 138–2 Concertgebouw O,
Haitink

Symphony No, 7 in E minor
DG 413 773–2 (2) Chicago SO,
Abbado
DG Dig. 419 211–2 (2) NYPO,
Bernstein
Philips 410 398–2 (2) Concertgebouw
O, Haitink

Symphony No. 8 in E flat
EMI CDS7 47625–8 (2) Connell,
Wiens, Lott, Schmidt, Denize,
Versalle, Hynninen, Sotin,
Tiffin School Boys' Ch., LPO Ch.,
LPO, Tennstedt
Decca 414 493–2 (2) Harper, Popp,
Auger, Minton, Watts, Kollo, Shirley-
Quirk, Talvela,
Vienna Boys' Ch., Vienna State Op.
Ch. & Singverein, Chicago SO, Solti

Symphony No. 9 in D
EMI mono CDH7 63029–2 Vienna
Philharmonic, Bruno Walter (r. 1937)
DG 410 726–2 (2) Berlin
Philharmonic, Karajan
EMI CDM7 63115–2 Berlin
Philharmonic, Barbirolli
Philips 416 466–2 (2) Concertgebouw
O, Haitink

Symphony No. 10 in F sharp
(performing version by Deryck Cooke
of Mahler's incomplete sketch)
EMI CDS7 54406–2 Bournemouth
SO, Rattle
Decca 421 182–2 Berlin RSO, Chailly
Sony MPK 45882 Philadelphia O,
Ormandy

Martinů, Bohuslav (1890–1959)

Symphonies Nos. 1 & 2
BIS CD 362 Bamberg SO, Järvi

Symphony No. 1
Chandos CHAN 8950 Czech
Philharmonic, Jírí Bělohlávek

Symphonies Nos. 1, 3 & 5
Multitone 310023 (2) Czech
Philharmonic, Ancerl

Symphonies Nos. 3 & 4
BIS CD 363 Bamberg SO, Järvi

Symphonies Nos. 5 & 6 (Fantaisies
symphoniques)
BIS CD 402 Bamberg SO, Järvi

Symphony No. 6 (Fantaisies
symphoniques)
Chandos CHAN 8897 Czech
Philharmonic, Jírí Bělohlávek

Martucci, Giuseppe (1856–1909)

Symphony No. 1 in D minor, Op. 75
ASV CDDCA 675 Philharmonia O,
D'Avalos

Méhul, Etienne-Nicolas (1763–1817)

*Symphonies Nos. 1 in G minor; 2 in D
(1908–09)*
Erato 2292 45026–2 Les Musiciens du
Louvre, Marc Minowski

*Symphonies Nos. 1 in G minor; 2 in D
(1908–09); 3 in C; 4 in E (1810)*
Nimbus NI5184 Lisbon Gulbenkian
O, Swierczewski

Mendelssohn, Felix (1809–47)

Symphonies Nos. 1–5
DG 429 664–2 (3) (with Mathis,
Rebman, Hollweg, German Op. Ch. in
Symphony No. 2) Berlin Philharmonic,
Karajan
DG 415 353–2 (4) (with Connell,
Mattila, Blochwitz and LSO Ch. in
Symphony No. 2) LSO, Abbado

*Symphonies Nos. 3 in A minor
('Scottish'); 4 in A ('Italian')*
Decca 417 731–2 Vienna
Philharmonic, Dohnányi
Decca 425 011–2 LSO, Abbado

*Symphony No. 4 in A ('Italian'), Op.
90*
DG 415 848–2 Berlin Philharmonic,
Karajan
EMI mono CDM7 63398–2 RPO,
Beecham

Pickwick PCD 824 Berne SO, Maag
Virgin VC 790725–2 Age of
Enlightenment, Mackerras

*Symphonies Nos. 4 in A ('Italian'); 5 in
D minor ('Reformation'), Op. 107*
Philips 422 470–2 New Philharmonia,
Sawallisch

Messiaen, Olivier (1908–92)

Turangalîla symphony
CBS M2K 42271 (2) Crossley,
Murail, Philharmonia O, Salonen
EMI CDS7 47463–8 (2) Donohoe,
Murail, CBSO, Rattle

Milhaud, Darius (1892–1974)

Symphonies Nos. 1–2
DG 435 437–2 O du Capitole de
Toulouse, Plasson

Moeran, Ernest J. (1894–1950)

Symphony in G minor
Chandos CHAN 8577 Ulster O,
Handley
EMI CDM7 69419–2 English
Sinfonia, Dilkes

**Mozart, Wolfgang Amadeus
(1756–91)**

*Symphonies Nos. 1, 4–6, 7a, 8–20,
42–7, 55; in C, K.208/102; in D, K.45,
111/120, 141a & 196/121*
Philips 416 471–2 (6) ASMF,
Marriner

Symphonies Nos. 21–41
Philips 415 954–2 (6) ASMF,
Marriner

Symphonies Nos. 21, 23, 24, 27
Erato 2292–45544–2 Amsterdam
Baroque, Ton Koopman

*Symphonies Nos. 25 in G minor; 28 in
C; 29 in A*
Telarc CD 80165 Prague CO,
Mackerras

*Symphonies Nos. 29 in A; 31 in D
('Paris'); 34 in C; 35 in D ('Haffner');
36 in C ('Linz'); 38 in D ('Prague');
39 in E flat; 40 in G minor; 41 in C
('Jupiter')*
CHS7 63698–2 (3) LPO, Beecham
(r. 1939–40)

*Symphonies Nos. 29 in A; 32 in G; 33
in B flat; 35 in D ('Haffner'); 36 in C
('Linz'); 38 in D ('Prague'); 39 in E flat;
40 in G minor; 41 in C ('Jupiter')*
DG 429 668–2 (3) Berlin
Philharmonic, Karajan

*Symphonies Nos. 29 in A; 33
in B flat*
Philips 412 736–2 English Baroque
Soloists, Gardiner

*Symphonies Nos. 31 in D ('Paris', 1st
version); 34 in C*
Philips 420 937–2 English Baroque
Soloists, Gardiner

*Symphonies Nos. 35 in D ('Haffner');
36 in C ('Linz'); 38 in D ('Prague');
39 in E flat; 40 in G minor; 41 in C
('Jupiter')*
CBS M2YK 45676 (2) Columbia SO,
Bruno Walter
DG 419 427–2 (3) Vienna
Philharmonic, Bernstein

*Symphonies Nos. 38 in D ('Prague'); 39
in E flat*
CBS MDK 44648 Bavarian Radio
SO, Rafael Kubelik
DG 429 802–2 Berlin Philharmonic,
Karajan

*Symphonies Nos. 40 in G minor; 41 in C
('Jupiter')*
EMI CDC7 47147–2 ECO, Jeffrey
Tate
CBS MDK 44649 Bavarian Radio
SO, Kubelik

Symphony No. 41 in C ('Jupiter')
EMI CDM7 69811–2 RPO,
Beecham

Myaskovsky, Nikolay (1881–1950)

Symphony No. 3 in A minor, Op. 15
Olympia OCD 177 USSR SO,
Svetlanov

Symphonies Nos. 5 in D, Op. 18; (ii) 11 in B flat, Op. 34
Olympia OCD 133 USSR SO, Ivanov;
(ii) Moscow SO, Dudarova

Symphony No. 7 in B minor, Op. 24
Olympia OCD 163 USSR RSO,
Ginsburg

Symphony No. 8 in A, Op. 26
Marco Polo 8223297 Slovak Radio SO
(Bratislava), Robert Stankovsky

Symphony No. 22 in B minor, Op. 54
Olympia OCD 134 USSR SO,
Svetlanov

Symphony No. 27 in C minor, Op. 85
Olympia OCD 168 USSR SO,
Svetlanov

Nielsen, Carl (1865–1931)

Symphonies Nos (i) 1, (ii) 2, (iii) 3, (ii) 4, 5, (i) 6
Sony 45989 (4) (i) Philadelphia O,
Ormandy; (ii) NYPO; (iii) Royal
Danish O, Bernstein

Symphonies Nos. 1 in G minor, Op. 7; 6 (Sinfonia semplice)
Decca 425 607–2 San Francisco SO,
Blomstedt

Symphony No. 1 in G minor, Op. 7
BIS CD 454 Gothenburg SO,
Myung-Whun Chung

Symphonies Nos. 2 in B minor ('The Four Temperaments'); (i) 3 (Sinfonia espansiva)
Decca 425 280–2 (i) Kromm,
McMillan; San Francisco SO,
Blomstedt

Symphony No. 2 in B minor ('The Four Temperaments')
BIS CD 247 Gothenburg SO,
Myung-Whun Chung

Symphony No. 3 (Sinfonia espansiva)
BIS CD 321 Pia Raanoja, Knut
Skram; Gothenburg SO, Myung-
Whun Chung

Symphonies Nos. 3 (Sinfonia espansiva); 6 (Sinfonia semplice)
RCA RD60427 Royal Danish O,
Berglund

Symphonies Nos. 4 ('Inextinguishable'); 5, Op. 50
Decca 421 524–2 San Francisco SO,
Blomstedt
Virgin VC7 91210 BBC SO, Andrew
Davis

Paine, John Knowles (1839–1906)

Symphony No. 2 in A, Op. 34
New World 350–2 NYPO, Mehta

Panufnik, Andrzej (1914–91)

Sinfonia rustica (1948); Sinfonia sacra (1963)
Unicorn UKCD2016 Monte Carlo
Op. O, Panufnik

Symphony No. 9 (Sinfonia della speranza)
Conifer CDFC 206 (i) Ewa Poblocka;
LSO, Panufnik

Parry, Hubert (1848–1918)

Symphonies Nos. 3 in C ('English'); 4 in E minor
Chandos CHAN 8896 LPO, Bamert

Symphony No. 5
Chandos CHAN 8955 LPO, Bamert

Persichetti, Vincent (1915–87)

Symphony No. 5 (Symphony for strings), Op. 61
New World NW370–2 Philadelphia
O, Muti

Symphony No. 8, Op. 106
Albany TROY 024–2 Louisville
O, Mester

Pettersson, Allan (1911–1980)

Symphony No. 5
BIS CD480 Malmö SO, Atzmon

Pfitzner, Hans (1869–1949)

Symphony in C, Op. 46 (1940)
Preiser 90029 Berlin Philharmonic,
Pfitzner

Piston, Walter (1894–1976)

Symphonies Nos. 2 (1943); 6 (1954)
Delos DE 3074 Seattle SO, Gerard
Schwarz

Symphony No. 2 (1943)
DG429 860–2 Boston SO, Tilson
Thomas

Symphony No. 4 (1950)
Delos DE 3106 Seattle SO, Gerard
Schwarz

Symphony No. 6 (1954)
RCA RD60798 St Louis SO, Slatkin

Prokofiev, Sergey (1891–1953)

Symphonies Nos. 1–7
Chandos CHAN 8931–4 SNO, Järvi
Decca 430 782–3 LPO or LSO,
Weller

*Symphonies Nos. 1 in D ('Classical'); 4
in C, Op. 112 (revised 1947 version)*
Chandos CHAN 8400 SNO, Jarvi

*Symphonies Nos. 1 in D ('Classical'), Op.
25; 5 in B flat, Op. 100*
DG 423 216–2 Berlin Philharmonic,
Karajan
Decca 421 813–2 Montreal
SO, Dutoit
Philips 420 172–2 Los Angeles
PO, Previn

*Symphonies Nos. 1 ('Classical'); 7 in C
sharp minor, Op. 131*
CfP CD-CFP 4523 Philharmonia
O, Malko

Symphony No. 2 in D minor, Op. 40
Chandos CHAN 8368 SNO, Järvi

*Symphonies Nos. 2 in D minor, Op. 40;
3 in C minor, Op. 44; 6 in E flat minor,
Op. 111*
VoxBox 5054 O National de l'ORTF,
Martinon

*Symphonies Nos. 3 in C minor, Op. 44;
4 in C, Op. 47 (original, 1930, version)*
Chandos CHAN 8401 SNO, Järvi

Symphony No. 5 in B flat, Op. 100
Chandos CHAN 8576 Leningrad PO,
Jansons

Symphony No. 5 in B flat, Op. 100
Decca 417 314–2 Concertgebouw O,
Ashkenazy

*Symphony No. 6 in E flat minor,
Op. 111*
Hunt CD783 Leningrad PO,
Mravinsky
Chandos CHAN 8359 SNO, Järvi

Raff, Joachim (1822–82)

*Symphony No. 1 in D An das
Vaterland), Op. 96*
Marco Polo 8.223165 Rhenish PO,
Friedman

Symphonies Nos. 3; 10
Marco Polo 8.223321 CSS PO,
Schneider

Rakhmaninov, Sergey (1873–1943)

Symphonies Nos. 1–3
Sony CD45678 Philadelphia O,
Ormandy
Chant du Monde LDC 278 836/7
Moscow PO, Dmitri Kitaenko

Symphonies Nos. 1–3; 'Youth' Symphony
Decca 421 065–2 (3) Concertgebouw
O, Ashkenazy

Symphony No. 2 in E minor, Op. 27
RCA VD 60132 Philadelphia O,
Ormandy

RCA VD 60791 LSO, Previn
Olympia OCD 237 Moscow SO,
Dmitri Kitaenko

Symphony No. 3 in A minor, Op. 44
Pearl GEMMCD9414 Philadelphia O,
Rakhmaninov
EMI CDM7 69564–2 LSO, Previn

Rautavaara, Einojuhani (born 1928)

Symphonies 1–3
Ondine ODE 740–2 Leipzig Radio
SO, Max Pommer

**Rimsky-Korsakov, Nikolay
(1844–1908)**

*Symphonies Nos. 1 in E minor, Op. 1; 2
('Antar'), Op. 9; 3 in C, Op. 32*
DG 423 604–2 (2) Gothenburg
SO, Järvi

Symphony No. 2 ('Antar'), Op. 9
Hyperion CDA 66399 Philharmonia
O, Svetlanov

Roman, Johan Helmich (1694–1758)

*Sinfonias in A, BeR I: 26; D, BeRI: 14;
F; BeR I: 17*
BIS CD 284 Orpheus Chamber
Ensemble, Nils-Erik Sparf

Ropartz, Joseph Guy (1864–1955)

Symphony No. 3 in E
EMI CDC7 447558–2 Pollet,
Stutsmann, Dran, Vassarm Orféon
Donostiarra, O du Capitole de
Toulouse, Plasson

Roussel, Albert (1869–1937)

*Symphonies Nos. 1 (Le Poème de la
forêt), Op. 7; 2 in B flat, Op. 23; 3 in
G minor, Op. 42; 4 in A, Op. 53*
Erato ECD88226 Orchestre National
de France, Dutoit

Symphony No. 3 in G minor, Op. 42
Chandos CHAN 8996 Detroit
SO, Järvi

Rubbra, Edmund (1901–86)

Symphonies Nos. 3 (1939); 4 (1942)
Lyrita SRCD202 Philharmonia O,
Del Mar

*Symphonies Nos. 6 (1954); 8 (Hommage
à Teilhard de Chardin) (1968)*
Lyrita SRCD234 Philharmonia O,
Del Mar

Rubinstein, Anton (1829–94)

Symphony No. 2 ('Ocean')
Marco Polo 8.223449 Slovak PO,
Gunzenhauser

Symphony No. 6
Marco Polo 8.220489 Philharmonia
Hungarica, Varga

Saeverud, Harald (1897–1992)

Symphony No. 9, Op. 45 (1966)
Norwegian Composers NCD4913
RPO, Per Dreier

Saint-Saëns, Camille (1835–1921)

*Symphonies in A (1850), in F (Urbs
Roma) (1856); Nos. 1 in E flat, Op.
2; 2 in A minor, Op. 55; 3 in C
minor, Op. 78*
EMI CSZ7 62643 Orchestre National
de la RTF, Martinon

Symphony No. 3 in C minor, Op. 78
Decca 439 729–2 Montreal
SO, Dutoit
RCA GD60817 Boston SO, Münch

Sallinen, Aulis (born 1935)

Symphonies Nos. 1 & 3
BIS CD 41 Helsinki PO, Kamu

Symphony No. 4
Finlandia FACD346 Helsinki
PO, Kamu

Schmidt, Franz (1874–1939)

Symphony No 3 in A (1927–28)
Chandos CHAN 9000 Chicago
SO, Järvi

Symphony No 4 (1933)
Decca 430 007–2 Vienna
Philharmonic, Mehta

Schnittke, Alfred (born 1934)

Symphony No. 3
BIS CD 477 Stockholm PO, Eri Klas

Symphony No. 4
BIS CD 497 Stockholm Sinfonietta,
Kamu

Symphony No. 5
BIS CD 427 Gothenburg SO, Järvi

Schoenberg, Arnold (1874–1951)

*Chamber Symphonies Nos. 1, Op. 9;
2, Op. 38*
DG 429 233–3 Orpheus Chamber
Orchestra

Schreker, Franz (1878–1934)

Chamber Symphony (1916)
Schwann 311078 Berlin Radio SO
Michael Gielen

Schubert, Franz (1797–1828)

*Symphonies Nos. 1–3; 4 ('Tragic');
5–7; 8 ('Unfinished'); 9 ('Great'); 10,
D.936a; Symphonic fragments in D,
D.615 and D.708a (completed and orch.
Newbould)*
Philips 412 176–2 (6) ASMF,
Marriner

*Symphonies Nos. 1–7; 8 ('Unfinished'); 9
('Great')*
DG 419 318–2 (4) Berlin
Philharmonic, Böhm
DG 423 651–2 (5) COE, Abbado

*Symphonies Nos. 3 in D, D.200; 5 in B
flat, D.485; 6 in C, D.589*
EMI CDM7 69750–2 RPO, Beecham

*Symphonies Nos. 3 in D, D.200; 8 in B
minor ('Unfinished'), D.759*
DG 415 601–2 Vienna Philharmonic,
Carlos Kleiber

*Symphony No. 8 in B minor
('Unfinished'), D.759*
EMI CDM7 69227–2 Philharmonia
O, Karajan

Symphony No. 9 in C ('Great'), D.944
Decca 400 082–2 Vienna
Philharmonic, Solti
EMI CDM7 69199–2 LPO, Boult
Virgin VC 790708–2 Age of
Enlightenment, Mackerras
CBS MYK 44828 Columbia SO,
Bruno Walter
DG mono 427 781–2 Berlin
Philharmonic, Furtwängler
RCA RD60978 North German
RSO, Wand

Schuman, William (1910–92)

Symphony No. 3 (1941)
DG 419 780–2 NYPO, Bernstein

Symphony No. 4 (1941)
Albany TROY027–2 Louisville
O, Mester

Symphony No. 5 for strings (1945)
Delos DE 3115 Seattle SO, Gerard
Schwarz

Schumann, Robert (1810–56)

Symphonies Nos. 1–4
DG 429 672–2 Berlin Philharmonic,
Karajan
EMI CDM7 69472–2 Staatskapelle
Dresden, Sawallisch

*Symphonies Nos. 1–4; Symphony in G
minor ('Zwickau')*
Philips 426 186–2 New Philharmonia,
Inbal

Symphony No. 2 in C, Op. 61
Sony SMK47297 Marlboro Festival
O, Casals

*Symphony No. 3 in E flat ('Rhenish'),
Op. 97*
DG 427 818–2 Los Angeles
PO, Giulini

Symphony No. 4 in D minor, Op. 120
DG 427 404–2 Berlin Philharmonic,
Furtwängler
EMI CDH763 085–2 Philharmonia O,
Cantelli

Sessions, Roger (1896–1985)

Symphonies Nos. 4 (1958); 5 (1964)
New World NW345–2 Columbus
SO, Badea

Shapero, Harold (born 1920)

Symphony for classical orchestra
New World NW373–2 Los Angeles
PO, Previn

Shostakovich, Dmitri (1906–75)

Symphonies Nos. 1–15
Chant du Monde 278 1001/10
Moscow PO Kondrashin

Symphony No. 1 in F minor, Op. 10
Decca 414 677–2 LPO, Haitink
DG427 632–2 Chicago SO, Bernstein

Symphony No. 4 (1936)
RCA RD60887 St Louis SO, Slatkin

Symphony No. 5 in D minor, Op. 47
Erato 2292 45752–2 Leningrad PO,
Mravinsky
RCA GD86801 LSO, Previn

Symphony No. 6, Op. 54
dell'Arte CDDA9023 Philadelphia O,
Stokowski (r. 1940)
EMI CDM7 54339–2 Oslo PO,
Jansons
EMI CDM7 69564–2 LSO, Previn

Symphony No. 7 ('Leningrad'), Op. 60
DG427 632–2 Chicago SO, Bernstein

Symphony No. 8 in C minor, Op. 65
Decca 411 616 Concertgebouw O,
Haitink
Philips 422 442 Leningrad PO,
Mravinsky

Symphony No. 9 in E flat, Op. 70
Sony CD45698 NYPO, Efrem Kurtz

EMI CDM7 54339–2 Oslo PO,
Jansons

Symphony No. 10 in E minor, Op. 93
Sony CD45698 NYPO, Mitropoulos
(r. 1955)
DG429 716–2 Berlin Philharmonic,
Karajan (r. 1966)
Erato 2292 45753–2 Leningrad PO,
Mravinsky

Symphony No. 11 in G minor, Op. 103
Delos DE3080 Helsinki PO, de Preist

*Symphony No. 12 in D minor ('The Year
1917'), Op. 112*
Erato 2292 45754–2 Leningrad PO,
Mravinsky

Symphony No. 15 in A, Op. 141
Olympia OCD5002 Leningrad PO,
Mravinsky
Olympia OCD179 USSR Ministry of
Culture SO, Rozhdestvensky

Sibelius, Jean (1865–1957)

Symphonies Nos. 1–7
Decca 421 069–2 Philharmonia O,
Ashkenazy
Philips 416 600–2 (4) Boston SO,
Colin Davis
Decca 430 778–2 (3) Vienna
Philharmonic, Maazel
EMI CMS7 64118–2 CBSO, Rattle
Vanguard 08 404373 Utah SO,
Abravanel

Symphonies Nos. 1, 2, 3, & 5
Finlandia FACD 81234 (3) LSO,
Kajanus (r. 1930–32)

Symphony No. 1 in E minor, Op. 39
EMI CMC 7542732 Oslo PO, Jansons
DG 435 351–2 Vienna Philharmonic,
Bernstein

Symphony No. 2 in D, Op. 43
EMI CDM7 69243–2 Berlin
Philharmonic, Karajan

*Symphonies Nos. 4 in A minor, Op. 63;
(i) 6 in D minor, Op. 104*
DG 415 108 Berlin Philharmonic,
Karajan

EMI mono CDM7 64027–2 LPO, (i)
RPO, Beecham (r. 1937 & 1948)

Symphony No. 5 in E flat, Op. 82
DG 415 107 Berlin Philharmonic,
Karajan

Symphony No. 7 in C, Op. 105
Pearl GEMMCDS 9408 BBC SO,
Koussevitzky (r. 1933)

Simpson, Robert (born 1921)

Symphony No. 3
Unicorn UKCD2020 LSO,
Horenstein

Symphony No. 9
Hyperion CDA 66299 Bournemouth
SO, Handley

Symphony No. 10
Hyperion CDA 66510 Royal Liverpool
PO, Handley

Skryabin, Alexander (1872–1915)

Symphonies Nos. 1–5
EMI CD7 54112–2 Philadelphia
O, Muti

*Symphonies Nos. 2 in C minor, Op. 29;
4 (Le poème de l'extase), Op. 54*
BIS CD 535 Stockholm PO,
Segerstam

*Symphony No. 3 (Le divin poème), Op.
43*
Chandos CHAN 8898 Danish Radio
SO, Järvi
Decca 430 843–2 Berlin Radio SO,
Ashkenazy

*Symphonies Nos. 4 (Le poème de
l'extase), Op. 54; (i) 5 ('Prometheus')*
Decca 417 252–2 Cleveland O, (i)
Ashkenazy, LPO, Maazel

Spohr, Ludwig (1784–1859)

*Symphonies Nos. 1 in E flat, Op. 20; 5
in C minor, Op. 102*
Marco Polo 8.223363 Slovak State
Philharmonic (Kosiče), Alfred Walter

**Stanford, Charles Villiers
(1852–1924)**

*Symphony No. 3 in F minor ('Irish'), Op.
28*
Chandos CHAN 8545 Ulster O,
Handley

Symphony No. 7 in D minor, Op. 124
Chandos CHAN 8861 Ulster O,
Handley

Stenhammar, Wilhelm (1871–1927)

Symphony No. 1 in F (1902–03)
BIS CD-219 Gothenburg SO, Järvi

Symphony No. 2 in G minor (1915)
Caprice CAP21151 Stockholm PO,
Westerberg
BIS CD-251 Gothenburg SO, Järvi

Stevens, Bernard (1916–83)

Symphony No. 2, Op. 35
Meridian CDE84174 BBC
Philharmonic, Downes

Stravinsky, Igor (1882–1971)

Symphony in E flat
Sony CD46290 Columbia SO,
Stravinsky

Symphony in C
Sony CD46290 Columbia SO,
Stravinsky
DG 423 252–2 Berlin Philharmonic,
Karajan

Symphony in three movements
Sony CD46290 Columbia SO,
Stravinsky

Symphony of Psalms
Sony CD46290 Columbia SO,
Stravinsky

Suk, Josef (1874–1935)

Asrael Symphony
Chandos CHAN 9042 Czech
Philharmonic, Jírí Bělohlávek

VC7 91 221–2 Royal Liverpool
Philharmonic, Pesek

**Svendsen, Johan Severin
(1840–1911)**

*Symphonies Nos. 1 in D, Op. 4; 2 in B
flat, Op. 15*
BIS CD-374 Gothenburg SO, Järvi

Szymanowski, Karol (1882–1937)

Symphony No. 2 in B flat, Op. 19
Decca 425 625–2 Detroit SO, Dorati
Polskie Nagranie PND062 Warsaw
National PO, Rowicki

*Symphony No. 3 ('Song of the
Nightingale'), Op. 27*
Polskie Nagranie PND063 Woytowicz,
Warsaw National PO, Rowicki
Decca 425 625–2 Karczykowski,
Detroit SO, Dorati

Taneyev, Sergey (1856–1915)

Symphony No. 4 in C minor, Op. 12
Chandos CHAN 8953 Philharmonia
O, Järvi

Tchaikovsky, Pyotr (1840–93)

Symphonies Nos. 1–6
DG 429 675–2 (4) Berlin
Philharmonic, Karajan
Decca 430 787 (4) Vienna
Philharmonic, Maazel
Philips 426 848 (4) LSO, Markevitch

*Symphonies Nos. 1–6; 'Manfred'
Symphony*
Chandos CHAN 8672/8 (7) Oslo PO,
Jansons

*Symphony No. 1 in G minor ('Winter
Daydreams')*
DG 431 606–2 Berlin Philharmonic,
Karajan

*Symphony No. 2 in C minor ('Little
Russian'), Op. 17 (original 1872 score)*
Chandos CHAN 8304 LSO, Simon

*Symphony No. 2 in C minor ('Little
Russian'), Op. 17; (i) No. 4 in F
minor, Op. 36*
DG 429 527–2 New Philharmonia; (i)
Vienna Philharmonic, Abbado

Symphony No. 3 in D ('Polish')
DG 431 605–2 Berlin Philharmonic,
Karajan

Symphonies Nos. 4–6
DG 419 745–2 (2) Leningrad PO,
Mravinsky (1961)

Symphony No. 4 in F minor, Op. 36
DG 415 348–2 Vienna Philharmonic,
Karajan
DG 419 872–2 Berlin Philharmonic,
Karajan

Symphony No. 5 in E minor, Op. 64
Olympia OCD221 Leningrad PO,
Mravinsky (1975)
DG 419 066–2 Berlin Philharmonic,
Karajan (1975)

*Symphony No. 6 in B minor
(Pathétique), Op. 74*
Virgin VC7 Russian National O,
Pletnev
EMI CDZ7 62603–2 Philharmonia
O, Giulini
DG 419 486–2 Berlin Philharmonic,
Karajan
EMI CDM7 69043–2 Berlin
Philharmonic, Karajan (1971)
DG 415 095–2 Vienna Philharmonic,
Karajan
DG 423 223–2 Berlin Philharmonic,
Karajan

'Manfred' Symphony, Op. 58
EMI CDC7 47412–2 Philharmonia
O, Muti

Thompson, Randall (1899–1984)

*Symphonies Nos. 2 in E minor; 3 in
A minor*
Koch 3–7074–2 New Zealand SO,
Andrew Schenck

Tippett, Michael (born 1905)

Symphonies Nos 1, 2, 3 & (i) 4
Decca 425 464–2 LSO, Colin Davis;
(i) Chicago SO, Solti

Tishchenko, Boris (born 1939)

Symphony No. 5
Olympia OCD213 USSR Ministry of
Culture SO, Rozhdestvensky

Tubin, Eduard (1905–82)

Symphony No 2 ('Legendary', 1937); No. 6 (1954)
BIS CD-304 Swedish Radio SO, Järvi

Symphonies No 4 (1943, rev. 1978); (i) No. 9 (1969)
BIS CD-227 Bergen SO; (i)
Gothenburg SO, Järvi

Symphony No. 5 in B minor (1946)
BIS CD-306 Bamberg SO, Järvi

Symphony No 8 (1966)
BIS CD-342 Swedish Radio SO, Järvi

Symphony No. 10 (1972)
BIS CD-297 Gothenburg SO, Järvi

Valen, Fartein (1887–1952)

Symphonies Nos. 1 (1939) & 4 (1948)
Norwegian Composers CDN31000
Bergen SO, Ceccato

Vanhal, Jan (1739–1813)

Symphonies in G minor (c1770); A; D
Supraphon 110756–2 Prague
CO, Vlcek

Vaughan Williams, Ralph (1872–1958)

Symphonies Nos. 1–9
Various soloists, LPO, Boult

A Sea Symphony
EMI CDC7 49911–2 Lott, Summers,
LPO Ch. & O, Haitink

Virgin VC 790843–2 Marshall,
Roberts, LSO Ch., Philharmonia
O, Hickox
Decca mono 425 658–2 Isobel Baillie,
Cameron, LPO Ch., LPO, Boult

Symphony No. 2 (A London Symphony)
CDM7 64197–2 Hallé Orchestra,
Barbirolli
RCA GD 90501 LSO, Previn
EMI CDC7 49394–2 LPO, Haitink
Chandos CHAN 8629 LSO, Bryden
Thomson

Symphony No. 3 (A Pastoral Symphony)
Decca mono 430 060–2 Ritchie, LPO,
Boult (r. 1952)
Chandos CHAN 8594 Yvonne Kenny,
LSO, Bryden Thomson

Symphony No. 4 in F minor
Koch Int. 37018 BBC SO, Vaughan
Williams (r. 1937)

Symphony No. 5 in D
EMI CD-EMX 9512 Royal Liverpool
PO, Handley
RCA GD 90506 LSO, Previn
Chandos CHAN 8554 LSO, Bryden
Thomson

Symphony No. 6 in E minor
EMI CDH7 63308 LSO, Boult
(including orig. scherzo)
Tel 9031-73127-2 BBC SO, Andrew
Davis
Chandos CHAN 8740 LSO, Bryden
Thomson

Symphonies Nos. 6 in E minor; 9 in E minor
RCA GD90508 LSO, Previn

Symphony No. 7 (Sinfonia Antartica)
EMI CDC7 47516–2 Sheila
Armstrong, LPO Ch., LPO, Haitink

Symphonies Nos. 7 (Sinfonia Antartica); 8 in D minor
RCA GD 90510 Heather Harper,
LSO Ch., LSO, Previn

Symphony No. 8 in D minor
EMI CDM7 64197–2 Hallé
Orchestra, Barbirolli
Chandos CHAN 8828 LSO, Bryden
Thomson

Symphony No. 9 in E minor
Chandos CHAN 8941 LSO, Bryden
Thomson

Walton, William (1902–83)

Symphony No. 1 in B flat minor
RCA GD 87830 LSO, Previn
Virgin VC 790715–2 LPO, Slatkin
EMI CDC7 49671–2 Bournemouth
SO, Handley

Symphony No. 2
Chandos CHAN 8772 LPO, Bryden
Thomson

Weber, Carl Maria von (1786–1826)

Symphonies Nos. 1 in C; 2 in C
ASV CDDCA 515 ASMF, Marriner
Orfeo C 091841A Bavarian Radio SO,
Sawallisch

Webern, Anton (1883–1945)

Symphony, Op. 21
DG 427 424–2 Berlin Philharmonic,
Karajan

Wirén, Dag (1905–86)

Symphony No. 4, Op. 27
Swedish Soc. SCD1035 Swedish
Radio SO, Ehrling

**Zemlinsky, Alexander von
(1871–1942)**

Symphony No. 1 in D minor
Marco Polo 8.223166 Czecho-Slovak
Radio SO (Bratislava), Ludovít Rajter

Lyric Symphony, Op. 18
Supraphon 11 0395–2 Armstrong,
Kusjner, Czech Philharmonic,
Bohumil Gregor

Zwilich, Ellen (born 1939)

Symphony No. 2
First Edition LCD 002 Louisville O,
Leighton Smith

Index

General subheadings are followed by symphonies/other works. Footnotes are indicated by n after the page number. Musical examples are indicated by numbers in *italics*.